Criminal Law in Uganda

Criminal Law in Uganda

Daniel David Ntanda Nsereko

This book was originally published as a monograph in the International Encyclopaedia of Laws/Criminal Law.

General Editors: Roger Blanpain, Frank Hendrickx
Volume Editors: Frank Verbruggen, Vanessa Franssen

Wolters Kluwer

Published by:
Kluwer Law International
PO Box 316
2400 AH Alphen aan den Rijn
The Netherlands
Website: www.kluwerlaw.com

Sold and distributed in North, Central and South America by:
Aspen Publishers, Inc.
7201 McKinney Circle
Frederick, MD 21704
United States of America
Email: customer.service@aspenpublishers.com

Sold and distributed in all other countries by:
Turpin Distribution Services Ltd.
Stratton Business Park
Pegasus Drive, Biggleswade
Bedfordshire SG18 8TQ
United Kingdom
Email: kluwerlaw@turpin-distribution.com

ISBN 978-90-411-6255-7

This title is available on www.kluwerlawonline.com

To my parents
Mr Obadiya Yese Busuulwa
Mrs Tolofaayina Ndagire Busuulwa

The Author

Judge Daniel David Ntanda Nsereko was born and raised in the Masaka District of Uganda. He attended Kabuwoko Boys' Primary School, Kako Junior Secondary School and King's College Budo. He holds an LLB degree from the University of East Africa, MJC degree in Comparative Jurisprudence from Howard University and LLM and JSD degrees from New York University. Judge Nsereko was appointed by the UN Secretary-General Appeals Judge of the Special Tribunal for Lebanon on 29 February 2012. Before his appointment, Judge Nsereko served as Judge of the International Criminal Court (ICC). He served as President of the Appeals Division from March 2009 to March 2010.

Before his election to the ICC, Judge Nsereko served as Professor of Law at the University of Botswana, where he headed the Law Department for eight years. He also previously served as the *Walter S. Owen Visiting Professor of Law* at the University of British Columbia Faculty of Law, Vancouver, Canada, Visiting Professor at Teramo University in Italy and as Senior Lecturer at Makerere University in Uganda. As a professor and scholar, Judge Nsereko specialized in the areas of Public International Law, International Criminal Law, International Human Rights Law, Criminal Law and Criminal Procedure and Constitutional Law. He has also published extensively in these areas. He is a member of the editorial boards of several international learned periodicals, including *Criminal Law Forum*, *Journal of Church and State* and the *University of Botswana Law Journal*.

Judge Nsereko also served on the Advisory Committee of the War Research Office of the American University Law School in Washington DC, provided expert legal opinions to various international adjudicatory bodies and served as a trial observer in several countries.

He is an advocate of the Supreme Court of Uganda and has practised law as a private practitioner.

The Author

Table of Contents

List of Abbreviations

AC	Appeal Cases (Law Reports)
All E.R.	All England Law Report
B.L.R.	Botswana Law Reports
C.A.Cr.App.	Court of Appeal Criminal Appeal
Ch.	Chancery Division Reports
Cox C.C.	Cox Criminal Cases
Cr.App.Rep.	Criminal Appeal Reports
DPP	Director of Public Prosecutions
DRC	Democratic Republic of the Congo
E.A.	East African Law Reports
E.A.C.A.	Reports of the Court of Appeal for Eastern Africa
H.Ct.Cr.App.	High Court Criminal Appeal
H.Ct.Cr.Session	High Court Criminal Session
H.Ct.Misc.Appl.	High Court Miscellaneous Application
H.Ct.Monthly Bulletin	High Court Monthly Bulletin
ICC	International Criminal Court
ICTR	International Criminal Tribunal for Rwanda
ICTY	International Criminal Tribunal for Yugoslavia
K.B.	Kings Bench Division Reports
K.L.R.	Kenya Law Reports
L.R.	English Law Reports
L.T.	Law Times Reports
NRA	National Resistance Army
N.Z.L.R.	New Zealand Law Reports
P.	Probate Reports (UK)
Q.B.	Queen's Bench Division Reports
Q.B.D.	Queen's Bench Division
R. & N.L.R.	Rhodesia & Nyasaland Law Reports
S.Ct.Cr.App.	Supreme Court Criminal Appeal
S.A.	South African Law Reports
S.C.R.	Supreme Court Reports (Canada)
T.L.R.	Tanganyika Law Reports
UBLJ	University of Botswana Law Reports
UGCA	Uganda Court of Appeal
UGCC	Uganda Constitutional Court
UGHC	Uganda High Court

List of Abbreviations

UGSC	Uganda Supreme Court
U.S.	United States Reports
U.L.R.	Uganda Law Reports
USh	Uganda Shilling
W.L.R.	Weekly Law Reports

Preface

Useful works on the law of criminal procedure in Uganda have appeared in print during the past decades. The last one was Francis Ayume's *Criminal Procedure and Law in Uganda* which was published in 1986. There is, however, no published treatise on the substantive criminal law to date. In interpreting the Penal Code and other criminal legislation students, scholars and practitioners have had to rely on foreign texts and on decisions of Uganda's superior courts. Until recently, most of the decisions were inaccessible, as the last law reports covering Uganda's court decisions appeared in 1975. For a legal system to which the doctrine of precedent is central, the absence of easily accessible court decisions is clearly untenable. However, some efforts to publish some of the decisions have recently been undertaken. They nevertheless remain infrequent and inadequate.

This book, in its third edition, remains the only attempt at a comprehensive treatment of the substantive criminal law of Uganda. It attempts to fill the void described above, albeit to a limited extent. A treatise cannot be a substitute for reported cases or easily accessible up-to-date legislation. It is nevertheless hoped that the book will prove valuable to students, scholars and practitioners alike.

Although English law is the fountainhead of Uganda's legal system, there are many instances where the two are divergent. Wherever appropriate, the book tries to pinpoint these divergences. It endeavours to illustrate the way Uganda's superior courts have interpreted the criminal legislation. In doing so, it draws on the experience of the courts of other English-speaking jurisdictions with similar legislation. It identifies areas of the criminal law that need reform to bring it in line with current social, political and economic realities. The classification of crimes as felonies or misdemeanours, for example, only serves to obfuscate the law; the differential treatment of spouses married under different marriage regimes perpetuates discrimination. The unequal treatment between men and women as exemplified by the cautionary rule works injustice to the womenfolk; the definition of rape is antiquated and needs to be brought in line with international human rights standards. Both the Constitutional Court and the Supreme Court have made significant contributions to the development of the law in some of these areas through interpretation. For instance, they have struck down as unconstitutional, provisions of the Penal Code that made the death penalty mandatory for certain offences or prescribed beating as punishment; they also invalidated the provisions on adultery and sedition and, in effect, abolished those offences. Parliament, too, has contributed to these developments by passing the International Criminal Court Act which, for the first time, made aggression, genocide, crimes against humanity and war crimes offences and triable by Ugandan courts; and by amending the Penal Code to redefine such offences as aggravated robbery and defilement. However, much remains to be done.

Lest it be forgotten, this book is about Criminal Law and Procedure in Uganda. However, for limitations of space and the fact that there already exist some works on procedure, more space has been devoted to the substantive law.

DANIEL DAVID NTANDA NSEREKO
The Hague
Netherlands
May 2013

General Introduction

§1. Characteristics of the Country

I. Geography and Population

1. Uganda is a landlocked African state lying astride the Equator. It is surrounded by Kenya on the East, Democratic Republic of the Congo (DRC) on the West, the Sudan on the North, and Rwanda and Tanzania on the South. It is approximately 241,139 square kilometres in size. Most of it is a high plateau, approximately 2,300–3,300 metres high with the high Rwenzori Mountain range in the West. It has ever-green vegetation watered by a number of lakes, the largest of which is Lake Victoria, the source of the Nile River and the world's largest freshwater lake.

2. Uganda has a population of approximately 34,000,000 people, almost all Africans. They fall under four major ethnic or language groups. The first, the Sudanic group, consists of the Lugbara, Madi and Kakwa in the Northwest. The second, the Nilotic group, consists of the Acholi, Lango, Alur, Padhola and Jonam in the North and some parts of the East. The third, the Nilo-Hamitic group, consists mainly of the Iteso, Kumam, Karamajong, Sebei, Pokot, Labwor and Tepeth in the Northeast. The fourth, the Bantu group, consists of all the nationalities in the Central, Western and most of the Eastern regions. They include the Banyoro, Batoro, Banyankore and Banyakigezi, Bakonjo, Bamba, Baganda, Basoga, Banyole, Basamia, Bagweri and Bagisu.

3. Until the onset of British colonization toward the end of the nineteenth century, the various peoples that constitute Uganda did not live under a single political authority. They existed side by side as independent entities, with various forms of political and social organization. Some such as the Banyankore, Banyoro, Batoro and Baganda, were kingdoms with centralized governments. The rest were in the main acephalus, the clan being the largest political unit.

4. The Kingdom of Buganda, from which the name Uganda is derived was the most prominent of the entities referred to above.[1] It was the most influential and most powerful – politically and militarily. It was with the king of Buganda, Kabaka Mutesa I, that the British made their initial contacts. It was Kabaka Mutesa I who, on the persuasion of British explorer H.M. Stanley, invited European missionaries

1. The British colonizers, under the influence of the Swahili language of the East African Coast, originally called Buganda *Uganda*, which is the Swahili version of *Buganda*. To distinguish Buganda from the rest of the Protectorate, the name *Uganda* was retained for the whole country.

to Buganda in 1876.[2] In response to this invitation, Church Missionary Society (Anglican) missionaries arrived in the country from Britain in 1877, followed by the White Fathers (Catholics) from France in 1879. Kabaka Mutesa I died in 1884. His heir, Kabaka Mwanga, who was inexperienced and was beset with problems arising out of European missionary rivalries and the Anglo-German competition for spheres of influence in the region, was forced to conclude a treaty with the Royal British East Africa Company. Under the treaty, Kabaka Mwanga surrendered sovereignty over Buganda to the Company. Similar treaties were subsequently made with the rulers of the Kingdoms of Ankore, Bunyoro and Toro.

II. Political System

5. The British Government formally declared a protectorate over the Kingdom of Buganda in 1884. With Buganda as its base and with the assistance of the Kabaka and his chiefs, the British Government proceeded to subjugate, and to extend the protectorate to the adjacent territories. By 1896, it had succeeded in establishing control over almost all of present-day Uganda. In 1900, it concluded a treaty, commonly known as the Uganda Agreement, with the Kingdom of Buganda. Under the Agreement, Buganda formally became a province of the Uganda Protectorate but retained some measure of internal self-government. Similar treaties were made with the Kingdoms of Toro in 1900, Ankore in 1901 and Bunyoro in 1933. The non-kingdom districts of the country were administered directly by the Protectorate Government. The Protectorate Government, for its part, was established in 1902 under the Uganda Order-in-Council, a legislative fiat of the British monarch. The Government was headed by a governor, assisted by Executive and Legislative Councils both of which were appointed by the selfsame governor. Thus, Uganda as it exists today is a creation of British colonization.

6. Uganda attained Independence from Britain on 9 October 1962. It adopted a Westminster-type of constitution. This constitution, commonly known as the Independence Constitution, established a parliamentary system of government. It set up a legislature and an executive, consisting of a titular Head-of-State and a cabinet, headed by a prime minister. It also provided for an independent judiciary, with power to review the acts of both the legislature and the executive. The Constitution also preserved the autonomy hithertofore enjoyed by the Kingdoms of Buganda, Bunyoro, Toro, Ankore and the Territory of Busoga, by granting them quasi-federal status. The non-kingdom districts retained a direct unitary relationship with the central government. Important, too, the Constitution embodied a justiciable bill of rights. Based on the European Convention for the Protection of Human Rights and Fundamental Freedoms, this bill set out individual rights and freedoms and established a mechanism for their enforcement at the instance of any aggrieved person.

7. The Independence Constitution was, however, short-lived. It was abrogated in a snap coup in 1966 by the then prime minister, Mr Milton Obote who proceeded

2. See D.A. Low, *The Mind of Buganda* 5 (Heinemann Educational Books Ltd. 1971).

to declare himself president with full executive powers. Obote abolished the kingdom states, annulled their quasi-federal status and declared a unitary system of government. Since then, Uganda has experienced six military *coups d'état*. The first was in 1971 when Idi Amin Dada, Obote's army chief of staff, overthrew him. The second was in 1979 when Tanzania invaded Uganda, drove out Amin and replaced him with a civilian administration under Professor Yusufu Lule. The third was in the same year, when a faction of the civilian government with the connivance of the Tanzanian occupying forces, toppled Lule and replaced him with Godfrey Binayisa. The fourth was in 1980, when a military commission, again with the blessing of the Tanzanian Government, overthrew Binayisa. The military commission organized an extremely flawed election that brought Obote back to power. The fifth coup was in 1985 when the Uganda Army once again overthrew Obote and replaced him with its commander, General Tito Okello Lutwa. The Lutwa regime was short-lived. It was toppled in 1986 by Mr Yoweri Kaguta Museveni and his National Resistance Army (NRA) which had been waging a guerilla war against Mr Obote in the preceding four years. During Museveni's tenure, a new constitution was drafted and promulgated in 1995.

III. Social and Cultural Values

8. The people of Uganda are culturally heterogeneous. They speak over twenty languages, some of which have no resemblance whatsoever with each other. In terms of social organization, sections of the population, such as the Baganda, Banyoro, Batoro, Banyankore and Basoga, are organized in closely knit clusters of clans with a paramount head of all the clans and is at the same time the political leader of the whole entity. Others are organized in loose kinship units.

9. Regarding indigenous occupations, the people around Lake Victoria and the other smaller lakes tend to be cultivators, owners of fixed homesteads. Plantains and tubers such as sweet potatoes, yams and cassava are their staple food. The people who live in places distant from the lakes tend to be nomadic pastoralists. Generally speaking, their staple foods are grains, such as maize, millet and sorghum.

10. It should, however, be pointed out that after more than a century of living together in one country, freely migrating from and to all the parts of the country, living together in urban centres, attending the same schools and marrying across the ethnic line, the people of Uganda have been forging a common culture. The lines of distinction between the people of the various ethnic origins are gradually but imperceptibly getting blurred. It is therefore risky to over-generalize about these distinctions.

11. With regard to cultural values, however, it can be asserted with confidence that there are certain traits which the people of Uganda share with each other by virtue of being Africans. For example, the extended family and the practice of communal living in varying degrees, continue to be pervasive phenomena among all the

Ugandan communities. Second, as a general rule, all the communities are patriarchal. By and large, the role of the woman continues to be that of a bearer and rearer of children and of performing household chores. Also as a general rule, marriages continue to be polygamous. In matters of religion, polytheism and animism continue to be the order of the day for many Ugandans. Western-type education, Western and Eastern religions, and the introduction of the cash economy have admittedly affected the social values, attitudes and practices of many people – particularly the educated and the urbanized. For example, these 'moderns' usually marry in church or mosque. They are more individualistic than their forebears. They are more conscious of their individual and democratic rights. They are more assertive. Nevertheless, to the bulk of the population, including – puzzling as it may seem – even those who profess the Western and Eastern religions, traditional values, attitudes and practices remain strong.

IV. Economic Orientation

12. Save for the brief flirtation with the 'turn to the left strategy' under Mr Obote prior to his overthrow in 1971, Uganda has for the most part pursued mixed economy policies. Privately owned economic enterprises operate alongside public enterprises without let or hindrance. Parastatal bodies, created under specific statutes, are the vehicles which the government uses to engage in business-type activities. They are, however, mainly concerned with the management of certain services or industries which the government considers to be crucial to the welfare of the public or to the economy in general. These services or industries include public utilities such as water, electricity, telephone and railway transport. Parastatals do not, as a general rule, engage in business or trade. However, this has not always been so. When Idi Amin Dada came to power in 1971, he expelled all Asian and other foreign nationals who at that time dominated most of the commercial and industrial life of the country. He created myriad parastatal bodies to operate the commercial and industrial concerns left behind by the expatriates. These concerns included farms, factories, retail and wholesale shops, as well as import and export trading.

13. With the coming to power by Yoweri Kaguta Museveni in 1986, many of these concerns were privatized. The government found that it had neither the financial resources nor the managerial expertise wherewithal to operate them efficiently or profitably.[3] Moreover, the government found that it needed outside assistance to resuscitate the economy which had been shattered by years of war and mismanagement. A condition set by foreign governments and by international financial bodies,

3. Justifying the government's decision to privatize the concerns, a government official said 'Over the years some of these companies have been existing simply by government assistance financially, drawing heavy loans which they were never able to repay and only operating on the treasury's vote for their survival. Administratively government has been bogged down in the running of these enterprises by providing Boards of Directors which sometimes ended up getting involved in their day to day running.' See *Foreigners Rush to Buy Uganda Parastatals* Weekly Topic (newspaper) 1 (21 Aug. 1992).

such as the World Bank and the International Monetary Fund, was that the government pursues market-oriented economic policies and also returns nationalized enterprises to their former owners. The government readily complied. It steered the economy more and more in the direction of the free enterprise system. This continues to be the trend today.

V. The Legal System

14. The Uganda Order-in-Council promulgated by the British monarch in 1902 established the High Court of Uganda and the subordinate courts. These courts were to exercise jurisdiction in accordance with local ordinances and, subject to such ordinances, in conformity with the Civil Procedure, Criminal Procedure and Penal Codes of India. The Order-in-Council was amended in 1911 to the effect that where the Indian Codes were inapplicable then the courts were to exercise jurisdiction 'in conformity with the substance of the common law, doctrines of equity and the statutes of general application in force in England on 11 August 1902 and with the powers vested in and according to the procedure and practice observed by and before courts of justice and justices of the peace in England according to their respective jurisdictions'. However, the common law, doctrines of equity and statutes of general application were to apply only so far as 'the circumstances of the Protectorate and its inhabitants and the High Court's jurisdiction permit and subject to such modifications as local circumstances render necessary'. Additionally, in matters to which Africans were parties the courts were to be guided by customary law, so far as such law was applicable and not 'repugnant to justice, morality and good conscience and not inconsistent with the Order-in-Council'. The courts were also required to decide cases according to substantive justice and without undue regard to technicalities or undue delay. At Independence, these provisions were re-enacted with slight modifications merely to take cognizance of the fact that it was now the Uganda Parliament, and not the British monarch, which was the sovereign law-making authority for Uganda.[4] These provisions imported into Uganda English law, and the English legal culture continue to form the basis of the country's legal system.

§2. Criminal Law, Criminal Justice and Criminal Science

I. Definition and Forms of Criminal Law

15. Criminal law is a branch of public law. It deals with wrongs against the general public. Under the pain of punishment, it proscribes certain conduct which is perceived to be harmful to the public weal.[5] Such conduct, be it doing a forbidden

4. See the Judicature Act, Cap. 13.
5. The Uganda Penal Code, Cap. 120, sec. 2 (s), defines an offence as 'an act, attempt or omission punishable by law'. The elements of prohibition and the accompanying punishment were underscored by Lord Atkin in the English case of *Proprietary Articles v. Attorney General for Canada* [1931] A.C.

act or omitting to perform a legally imposed duty, is often of such a nature as to tend to seriously disturb the peace, tranquillity and general welfare of the community. It is, in actuality, often directed at individual members of the community. Nevertheless, because of its potential to disturb the harmony, tranquillity and cherished values of the community at large it is considered to be an offence against the whole community.

16. Conduct which has been proscribed for being harmful to the community includes acts which undermine state institutions. Examples of these acts would include acts aimed at overthrowing by the force of arms a legally constituted government (treason). Other proscribed conduct includes acts of violence directed against individual members of the community and their property, such as murder, manslaughter, assault, rape, robbery, theft, forgery, arson and malicious injury to property. It also includes acts and omissions that endanger public safety, public health and public standards. This species of conduct encompasses the whole gamut of the so-called regulatory offences against codes of conduct that set standards of behaviour in almost all imaginable spheres of human endeavour.[6] Proscribed conduct also includes immoral acts or acts of a depraved nature, the so-called 'victimless' crimes, which are considered to be injurious to society's moral values and are a threat to its very existence. These acts include: homosexuality, sodomy, bestiality, prostitution, gambling and drug or substance abuse.

17. How, then, does the proscription of the above conduct by the criminal law protect society? First, the very act of forbidding harmful conduct helps to a large degree, to prevent such conduct. As Smith and Hogan have written, 'The fact that an act is known to be forbidden by the criminal law may, for many persons, be sufficient to ensure that they will not commit such an act … '[7] Second, conviction, which is an act of public condemnation of the perpetrator of the offensive conduct, also has preventive value. Self-respecting members of the community will not want to be condemned and ostracized, and will therefore desist from conduct that might result in such condemnation. Third, the sentence imposed on the convicted offender serves to deter him or her and other potential offenders from committing similar conduct. Fourth, where the punishment meted out is incarceration, the offender is incapacitated and, meantime and depending on the regimen of treatment he or she receives whilst in prison, he or she is assisted to reform and to become a responsible, useful, and law-abiding citizen.

18. This view of the purpose of the criminal law contrasts somewhat with the indigenous African view that prevailed in pre-colonial Uganda. The indigenous view focused more on the victim of the offensive conduct than on the protection of

---

318, 324, when he said: 'The criminal quality of an act cannot be discerned by intuition; nor can it be discovered by reference to any standard but one: is the act prohibited with penal consequences?'

6. See for example, the Traffic and Road Safety Act, Cap. 361; Public Health Act, Cap. 281; Food and Drugs Act, Cap. 278; Shop Hours Act, Cap. 99, and Weights and Measures Act, Cap. 103. These statutes set standards and impose penalties on those who transgress them.
7. J.C. Smith & Brian Hogan, *Criminal Law* 4 (6th ed., English Language Book Society/Butterworths. London 1988). Also see generally Tom R. Tyler, *Why People Obey the Law* (Yale U. Press 1990).

the nebulous 'public'. According to this view, the most important function of the criminal law was to vindicate the victim and his rights. The sanctions of the criminal law were more compensatory than punitive. They were intended to restore the victim to the same position as he might have been in had the offender not wronged him or her. To facilitate compensation, civil and criminal proceedings were often assimilated in one and the same action. The proceedings against the offender were often commenced by the victim himself and in his own names.

19. The modern view on the question of victim rights is that conviction and punishment of a criminal offender does not preclude his or her victim from instituting civil proceedings against him for compensation. Civil courts are available just for that purpose. Moreover, desirable as victim-compensation may be it does not always adequately protect the public as a whole. For example, some offences such as rape, armed robbery and arson are so serious that payment of compensation alone would not deter the offender and other would-be offenders from committing similar offences in the future. In respect of these offences, adequate protection of the members of the public may thus require that the offender be *punished*, by say, a term of imprisonment. Additionally, there are certain offences, such as substance abuse and trafficking, offences against the environment, offences against public morality such as prostitution and unnatural offences, which do no particular harm to anybody. With respect to such offences no one would be sufficiently interested as to institute legal proceedings against the perpetrators. But they are latently harmful to the general welfare and need to be repressed. It is for this reason, therefore, that the enforcement of the criminal law cannot be left to individual victims even when they exist. The state, acting on behalf of the whole community, thus assumes primary responsibility over its enforcement and for the prosecution of its violators. It is for this reason, too, that in Uganda criminal proceedings are instituted in the names and on behalf of the state. A charge sheet is thus usually headed as follows: *Uganda v. Gusula.*

20. It must, however, be pointed out that although the state thus has the primary responsibility to enforce the criminal law and to institute criminal proceedings against alleged offenders it does not always have to do so. It may, for overriding policy considerations, decline to institute the proceedings, even in the face of compelling evidence of commission of criminal conduct by known individuals. It cannot be forced to do so.

21. Where the state declines to institute criminal proceedings, an individual may do so, but in the names and on behalf of the state.[8] These are what are known as private prosecutions. The policy underlying private prosecutions is the recognition that every citizen has an interest in the repression of crime and in the enforcement of the criminal law. The other is the need to prevent individuals who might have been hurt as a result of the criminal conduct in question from taking the law in their own hands and avenging themselves against the suspected criminal. Nevertheless, because the state, through the Office of the Director of Public Prosecutions (DPP),

8. Section 42 of the Magistrates Courts Act.

has primacy in all criminal prosecutions throughout the country, it also has power to take over at any stage of the proceedings initiated by a private prosecutor or any other authority, so that they may be instituted or continued at public instance subject to certain limitations. These will be discussed in Chapter One of Part II of this book.

22. It is also apropos to point out here that in deference to the indigenous African notions of criminal justice, the law now permits a criminal court after passing sentence on an accused person to order him or her to pay compensation to the victim. A detailed discussion of victim-compensation will be delved into in subsequent chapters.

23. A popular conception of crime would restrict the appellation *crime* to conduct that is wrongful in itself, *crimes mala in se*. The wrongfulness of the conduct is said to stem from its being offensive to the moral sense of the people and not from any specific act of prohibition by the law maker. For example, witchcraft, murder, theft and other conduct involving moral turpitude or violence or dishonesty would easily qualify for reprobation as crimes and their perpetrators as criminals. However, conduct which does not involve moral turpitude, violence or dishonesty but is merely prohibited by the law, known as *crimes mala prohibita*, is not according to the popular conception considered criminal. For example, violators of much of the traffic code and of other regulatory legislation do not suffer as much social stigma as the perpetrators of *crimes mala in se*. Thus, a job seeker who has been convicted of a traffic offence will not encounter as much difficulty in finding employment as one who has been convicted of rape. Likewise, a lawyer who has been convicted of tax evasion will probably not incur as much wrath and censor of the disciplinary committee of the Law Society as a colleague who has been convicted of armed robbery. Nevertheless, at least for the purposes of definition, there is no distinction in law between the two types of crimes. Persons who are found guilty of either of them are all criminals. Whether a crime is grave in terms of the potential harm it can inflict or the degree of moral blameworthiness involved in its commission generally or in a particular case is a different issue. That issue is invariably addressed by the legislature in prescribing the penalty for that particular offence and by the courts in determining the condign sentence to impose in a particular case.

II. Overview of the Criminal Justice System

24. The principal components of the Uganda criminal justice system are the police, the courts and the prison service. These three components function as indispensable parts of the criminal justice machine whose sole purpose is to protect society by ensuring justice and tranquillity for everybody. Nevertheless, each of them serves a distinct role within the system.

A. The Police

25. The Uganda Police Force is centrally organized. There is one force, with local units in the districts, all under an Inspector-General of Police. The Inspector-General is in turn answerable to the Minister of Internal Affairs.[9] The major police functions in the system are:

(i) to protect the life, property, and other rights of the individual;
(ii) to enforce the laws of Uganda;
(iii) to maintain security within Uganda;
(iv) to ensure public safety and order; and
(v) to prevent and detect crime in the society.[10]

26. Protecting the life, property and other rights of the individual covers the whole range of police activities as is discussed below. It also includes the rendering of specialized services such as guarding particularly vulnerable members of the community, guarding public property and putting out fires.

27. Ensuring public safety and order and maintaining security are related. The two functions encompass the whole gamut of police efforts in the area of prevention of crime, reduction of the incidence of crime, arrest and detention of suspected criminals, controlling crowds at public functions, and quelling riots and other unlawful assemblies or processions.

28. Law enforcement includes securing suspected individuals for trial in the courts of law. Having investigated the crime, the police are responsible for initiating proceedings against suspected offenders and for collecting, preserving, marshaling and producing in court the evidence against them. They identify and secure the attendance of witnesses, including officers who witnessed or investigated the crime in question, to testify against the accused. Until recently, it was the police who actually conducted the bulk of the criminal prosecutions against criminal suspects on behalf of the state in the magistrates' courts. Today, however, that role has been taken over by prosecutors working under the direct authority and control of the DPP.

29. Also related to law enforcement is the regulation of non-criminal activities such as superintending the traffic code through inspections and the granting of permits, and authorizing such activities as public processions, demonstrations and public solicitations.

30. Crime prevention encompasses all police efforts aimed at eliminating causes of crime, reducing the incidence of crime, and educating members of the public on

9. For a general discussion of the impact of police organization on the effectiveness of the force, see Daniel D.D. Nsereko, *The Police, Human Rights, and the Constitution: An African Perspective*, 15 Hum. Rights Q. 465 (1993).
10. Police Act, Cap. 303, sec. 4.

how to avoid becoming victims of crime and on what to do should they become victims. Detection includes investigating crimes that have already been committed, and gathering information on the activities and movements of suspected criminals, and on situations that conduce to commission of crime. It also includes preparing and marshaling evidence in support of court proceedings against suspected offenders.

B. The Courts

31. The primary role of the courts in the criminal justice system is to determine whether, on the strength of the evidence adduced before them, the accused is guilty of the offence with which he or she is charged. If they find him or her guilty, they must also decide on the appropriate sentence to impose on him or her or on any other method of disposition. In determining the sentence or any other method of disposition, the courts are duty bound to take into account the nature of the crime committed, the offender and the need to protect the public. An equally important role of the courts is to ensure that the accused's rights have been or are observed by the various components of the justice system before, during and after the trial. If they have not been observed, the courts must then ensure that the accused obtains redress. In this respect, the courts play the role of watchdog over the rights of the accused.

32. The court system of Uganda consists of a hierarchy of courts of varying grades and powers. The central and most important of these courts is the High Court of Uganda. It is a superior court of record with unlimited original jurisdiction in both civil and criminal cases. As far as criminal cases are concerned, this means that it has power to try any case involving any offence which has been committed anywhere in Uganda however serious or petty. In practice, however, it tries only the most serious offences such as treason, murder, manslaughter, robbery and kidnapping with intent to murder. It also hears appeals from magistrates' courts presided over by Chief and Grade I magistrates. In its appellate capacity, the High Court has power to confirm, reverse or revise decisions or orders of the inferior courts. Additionally, the High Court exercises revisional jurisdiction over magistrates' courts.[11] It also has the power to confirm sentences passed by magistrates' courts under certain circumstances.[12]

33. Above the High Court is the Court of Appeal and the Supreme Court. The Court of Appeal's jurisdiction is limited to hearing and determining appeals from the High Court in exercise of its original, appellate and revisional jurisdiction. It also serves as the Constitutional court. In that capacity, it exercises original jurisdiction.[13]

Above the Court of Appeal is the Supreme Court. It is the final Court of Appeal. It hears appeals from decisions of the Court of Appeal as may be prescribed by law.

11. Criminal Procedure Code Act, Cap. 110, sec. 50. For a full discussion of this topic, see Ch. 4 of Part II of this book.
12. Magistrates Courts Act, sec. 173.
13. See Art. 137.

It also hears appeals from decisions of the Court of Appeal sitting as a Constitutional court. Such appeals lie as of right by any party to the proceedings.[14]

34. Below the High Court are the magistrates courts, presided over by magistrates of varying grades of seniority: Chief Magistrate, Magistrate Grade I and Magistrate Grade II. The Chief Magistrate may try any offences committed under any law other than an offence that carries the maximum penalty of death.[15] Provided he has jurisdiction to try the offence, a Chief Magistrate may impose the maximum penalty prescribed in respect of any offence. In other words, there are no restrictions on his or her sentencing powers. In addition to his or her original jurisdiction, a Chief Magistrate hears appeals from the decisions of Magistrates Grade II.[16] Additionally, he or she plays a supervisory role over all the magistrates within his or her magisterial area,[17] and has power to transfer cases from any magistrate to himself or herself or to another magistrate within the area.

35. Magistrates Grades I and II, however, have jurisdiction to try any offences created under any law with the exception of those that are specifically excluded from their jurisdiction.[18] Unlike the Chief Magistrates, the sentencing powers of Magistrates Grades I and II are circumscribed. Even when they have the jurisdiction to try a particular offence, they may not have the power to impose the maximum penalty prescribed by the law creating that offence. Thus, the sentencing powers of Magistrates Grade I are limited to ten years imprisonment and to a fine not exceeding Uganda Shilling (UGX) 4,800,000. Those of Magistrates Grade II are limited to three years imprisonment and to a fine not exceeding UGX 500,000.[19] However, where Magistrates Grades I and II form the view that a person they have convicted of a particular offence deserves a severer sentence than they have power to impose, they may commit or send the accused to the Chief Magistrate of their area for sentencing. In doing so, they must indicate on the court record the grounds for their views on the matter.[20]

36. The Chief Magistrate and Magistrate Grade I are lawyers who qualify to practise law in Uganda. Magistrates Grade II are lay people, comparable to the justices of the peace in Britain. They do, however, undergo some training in the rudiments of the law and procedure at the Law Development Centre. Salutary as the training may be, it is not adequate. Magistrates must be able to evaluate the evidence adduced before them as well as the arguments of counsel, and be able to decide on the issues raised thereby in accordance with the law applicable. These

14. See Art. 132.
15. Magistrates Courts Act, sec. 161.
16. *Ibid.*, sec. 204(1)(b).
17. *Ibid.*, sec. 221. Currently, the whole country is divided into about twenty magisterial areas each of which is headed by a Chief Magistrate.
18. Section 161 of the Magistrates Courts Act, lists the offences that are excluded from Grade I Magistrates Courts. Schedule I of the Magistrates Courts Act, lists the offences that are excluded from the jurisdiction of Magistrates' Grades II.
19. Magistrates Courts Act, sec. 162.
20. *Ibid.*, sec. 164.

qualities and skills can be attained only through thorough and rigorous training. Moreover, since lawyers are allowed to appear before them, there is a danger that the unscrupulous ones among them may mislead them as to the law and procedure, to the prejudice of the ends of justice.[21]

37. Two points remain to be pointed out regarding Uganda's judicial system.

38. The first is that, unlike many Western industrialized nations, there is no jury system in Uganda. The magistrate or judge is the sole trier of the facts. However, in the proceedings before the High Court at least two lay persons, known as assessors, are required to participate in the proceedings. At the close of the case for the defence but before the court's verdict, the presiding judge must give the assessors an opportunity to express their opinions as to the appropriate verdict he or she should return in the case. Their opinions are, however, not binding on the judge.[22] Nevertheless, where the judge disagrees with the majority of the assessors he or she must, in the course of his judgment, give reasons for his or her disagreement.

39. The second point is that under the Constitution of Uganda every person charged with a criminal offence is entitled to be represented by a lawyer of his or her own choice and at his or her own expense. In the majority of cases, however, the accused persons are unrepresented, because they are indigent. Unlike developed countries such as the United States of America where the Constitution obliges the state to provide free legal assistance to any person charged with a criminal offence and who is willing to avail himself or herself of it, there is no such provision in the Uganda Constitution. The state's obligation in this matter is limited to permitting the accused to be represented by a lawyer of his or her own choice.[23] There is as yet no legal aid scheme in place. It is only in capital offences that the state is now obliged to provide free legal assistance to defendants who are willing to accept it. To the majority of the defendants, the right to legal representation remains illusory.

C. *Prisons*

40. Like the police, the prisons service falls under the Ministry of Internal Affairs. The prisons in Uganda are also centrally organized and are under the overall charge of the Commissioner of Prisons. The Commissioner superintends the forty-six central government prisons and, indirectly, the local government detention centres. He or she is answerable to the minister.

41. The Central Government prisons fall under two broad categories: those for the unconvicted prisoners and others for the convicted prisoners. There is one type of prison under the first category. It is called a reception centre or district prison.

21. For example, see *Uganda v. Edirisa* [1974] E.A. 555.
22. Trial on Indictments Act, sec. 3 and sec. 81.
23. Failure to permit, it would vitiate the entire proceedings. See the cases of *Muyimba v. Uganda* [1969] E.A. 433, and *Ogola v. Republic* [1973] E.A. 277.

Reception centres are as a general rule situated in urban centres where there are courts. Prisoners on remand or awaiting trial, usually from upcountry areas, are kept here. In this respect, district prisons serve to facilitate court attendance by the prisoners. Convicts sentenced to short-term imprisonment also often serve their sentences in these prisons. Prisons for convicted prisoners tend to be specialist and currently fall under six classes, depending on the type of convicts kept there and the nature of treatment they need. The first type of prison under this category is called the *preventive detention* prison, designed for habitual offenders. The second type are the *prison farms*, for prisoners serving medium to long-term sentences. Prisoners in this type of prison are trained in agriculture and animal husbandry and in other useful vocations or industries. The third is the *maximum-security* prison for hard-core criminals, or criminals convicted of very serious offences such as murder and armed robbery. The fourth and fifth are the *reformatory schools* for juveniles and the *young persons'* prison. The sixth are the *women's prisons*, for women serving various types of sentences.

42. Prisons play an important role in the criminal justice system. They receive and securely confine persons awaiting trial or those already convicted of crimes and sentenced by the courts to terms of incarceration. For the unconvicted persons, prisons ensure that such persons are available to answer charges against them. For the convicted offenders prisons help to incapacitate such offenders from committing further crimes and from menacing innocent members of the public. Additionally, by isolating the offenders from their loved ones and by depriving them of their liberty and of their pastimes, prisons help to teach them a lesson as to the unpleasant consequences of engaging in crime. This deters them from engaging in further criminal activities.

43. Prisons also assist the prisoners to reform and to become responsible, productive and law-abiding members of the community. Nevertheless, the attainment of these *desiderata* depends, to a large degree, on the mode of treatment that the inmates receive whilst in prison. This will in turn depend on the availability of resources, such as trained manpower, facilities necessary for the training of prisoners in useful industrial skills, appropriate physical structures, provision of adequate diet, and health care, recreational and educational facilities. The lawlessness, political chaos, moral decadence and economic decay that have plagued Uganda since Independence have severely hampered the prisons authorities in attaining these goals. The woefully inadequate facilities referred to herein and the concomitant harsh conditions that have existed in Ugandan prisons during this period have tended to embolden rather than deter or sober up the inmates. This has in turn resulted in a cycle of violence and criminality.

§3. Historical Background

I. Historical Development of Criminal Law

A. *The Penal Code*

44. The criminal law of Uganda is contained in a code, the Uganda Penal Code.[24] The Code lays down general principles of criminal law, which are applicable to all criminal legislation. Exceptions to these principles, if there be any, are contained in separate statutes creating those exceptions. The code also defines specific offences of general application and permanent nature (as opposed to offences that are created by special statutes dealing with conduct in certain specialized fields).

45. The Penal Code came into force in 1938. It replaced the Indian Penal Code which was applied to Uganda by the Uganda Order-in-Council of 1902.[25] The Indian Penal Code was said to have been based on 'the law of England, stript of technicality and local peculiarities, shortened, simplified, made intelligible and precise'.[26] Nevertheless, the style of the old Indian Code did not impress the English-trained colonial law officers and magistrates who had to apply it on a day-to-day basis.[27] Therefore, the Indian Code was discarded and was replaced by the present code which was more faithful to the then current English criminal law and principle. This code, which was to be a model for other British dependencies in Eastern Africa and beyond,[28] was drafted by law officers at the Colonial Office. It was based on a code previously drafted and promulgated for Nigeria.[29][30] The Uganda Penal Code is, then, like the code on which it was based, a codification of the English criminal law as it was at the time of promulgation.

46. English criminal law, for its part, developed from decisions of the English judges. The judges, acting as *custos morum*, declared which conduct was to be considered criminal. In doing so, they drew on the common experience and attitudes of

24. Cap. 120.
25. See page para. 14, *supra*.
26. Whitley Stokes, *Anglo-Indian Codes*, vol. I, at 71. Cited by James S. Read, *Criminal Law in the Africa of Today and Tomorrow* J. African L. 5 (1963).
27. According to the Secretary of State for the Colonies, these 'Officers [found] it easier to apply a Code which employs the terms and principles with which they are familiar in England than one in which the terms and principles have been discarded for others of doubtful import.' Despatch No. 380, 10 May 1927. Cited by James S. Read, *ibid.*
28. This is true of the codes in Botswana, the Gambia, Kenya, Malawi, Seychelles, Tanganyika, Zambia, and Zanzibar. Similar codes are to be found in Cyprus and Fiji.
29. See H.F. Morris, *How Nigeria Got its Criminal Code,* J. African L. 37 (1975).
30. The Nigerian Code for its part owed its origins to the Queensland Criminal Code of 1892. The Queensland Code was, in turn, based on a draft prepared by James Fitzjames Stephen. It has been said of the Queensland Code that 'although comparatively young as a Code, [it] is in substance old as the Criminal Law of England itself'. See Martin L. Friedland, *Codification in the Commonwealth: Earlier Efforts,* 2 Crim. L. Forum 45 (1990).

the people. This was not a particularly difficult task, because, as we have noted earlier, some conduct was by the common consent of the people already considered to be inherently wrongful – the *mala in se* crimes.[31] Nevertheless, the bulk of the English criminal law is today found in statutes and in other legislative enactments. In interpreting these statutes or enactments, the judges follow rules and principles which they themselves have developed over the years, such as the rule that penal statutes must be interpreted restrictively.

47. To ensure that English criminal law remained the basis and point of reference for the criminal law of Uganda, the drafters of the Penal Code inserted in the Code a provision which requires the courts to interpret it according to English legal principles. Section 1 of the Code provides as follows:

> This Code shall be interpreted in accordance with the principles of legal interpretation obtaining in England, and expressions used in it shall be presumed, so far as is consistent with their context, and except as may be otherwise expressly provided, to be used with the meaning attaching to them in English criminal law and shall be construed in accordance therewith.

Thus, where the code is unclear, the courts are expected to have recourse to the decisions of the English superior courts and to English commentaries for guidance. This they do liberally. English cases and English practice books such *Archibold's Criminal Pleadings* are cited frequently and extensively before the Ugandan courts.

48. As is to be expected, the Penal Code has been amended from time to time in order to bring it in line with the changing social, political and economic conditions in the country. The latest major amendments were enacted in 2007. Among other things, they abolished corporal punishment. They made defilement gender neutral, imposed a total ban on sexual intercourse with or between persons below the age of 18 years and created a distinction between simple and aggravated defilement, making the latter punishable by death. The aim was to increase protection for persons of tender years, to curb casual sex by the youth and to contribute to the fight against the spread of the HIV/AIDS pandemic. With respect to aggravated robbery, the notion of 'deadly weapon' was redefined to include toy guns and the mere possession of the weapon was made sufficient for the commission of the offence. In addition, simple robbery was made punishable by life imprisonment while aggravated robbery is now punishable by death at the discretion of the court.[32] These amendments were meant to make conviction for armed robbery easier and thereby assist in stemming the tide of its incidence.

31. In this respect, note should be made of the apt observation by James Fitzjames Stephen that 'the criminal law may be considered with truth as an expansion of the second table of the Ten Commandments. The statement in the Catechism of the positive duties of man to man corresponds step by step with the prohibitions of a Criminal Code'. Parker, *James Fitzjames Stephen: Some of his correspondence*, 2 Now & Then 63, 85–86 (1982). Cited by J.W. Mohr, *Criminal Law: is there a Legal or Social Logic left for its Renewal?* in *Crime, Justice & Codification* 33 (Patrick Fitzgerald ed., Carswell. Toronto, Calgary & Vancouver 1986).
32. These changes were introduced by the Penal Code (Amendment) Act, 2007.

The Code has also over the years been supplemented by other statutes, whose contribution to the body of criminal law is discussed in subsequent paragraphs of this chapter.

B. Customary Law

49. Prior to British colonization, the criminal law in force in the various areas that today constitute Uganda was contained in the respective customs of the people living in those areas. From a legal stand point, a custom is a practice that has been followed for a considerable period of time and believed by the people concerned to be binding on them. Customs were by and large unwritten. They were nevertheless known to the people and particularly to the elders and to the chiefs whose duty it was to enforce them in appropriate cases. All conduct that was injurious to the common good or tended to disturb the social equilibrium was proscribed under the customs of the Ugandan communities.[33] Another common feature of the customary criminal justice systems of all indigenous African communities was the payment of compensation by the accused person to the complainant. Compensation was over and above the punishment meted out to the culprit for the purpose of atoning the community at large. The primary aim of compensation was to vindicate the victim and his rights and to do him justice as inexpensively and as expeditiously as possible.[34]

50. After the establishment of the Protectorate and the introduction of the English law, customary law continued to exist side by side with the English law. The local courts in the various areas of the country applied it in cases to which the accused were Africans.[35] However, an essential condition for the application of the customary law was that it was not repugnant to justice, morality or good conscience and was not in conflict with statutory law. It should also be noted that customary law did not remain entirely unwritten. For example, the Great Lukiiko of the Kingdom of Buganda had power to enact and did enact certain laws criminalizing certain conduct that it perceived to be contrary to the customs of the Baganda. These laws were, however, always subject to the consent of the Governor before they came into force.[36] The councils of the other kingdom and districts were also

33. Among the Baganda, for example, the proscribed conduct included treasonable manifestations against the authorities, homicides, rape, assault, theft, cheating and malicious damage to property, witchcraft and incendiarism.
34. See D.D. Ntanda Nsereko, *Victims of Crime and their Rights*, in *Criminology in Africa* (Mushanga ed., UN Intl. Crime & J. Research Inst. 1992).
35. These courts were initially known as 'native' courts and later on as 'African' courts. The courts in Buganda were governed by the Buganda Courts Ordinance, Cap. 39. The courts in the rest of the country were initially governed by the Native Courts Act, Cap. 40, and later on by the African Courts Ordinance, Cap. 38.
36. Examples of such laws include the following: Carrying of Knives Law, Adultery and Fornication Law, Cheating Law, Prostitution Law, Native Liquor Law, Incendiarism Law, Native Tabbulu Law and the Indecent Language Law. These laws are reproduced in the *Native Laws of Buganda*, 1957.

empowered, subject to the consent of the Governor, to pass bylaws relating to customary matters within their respective areas of jurisdiction.[37]

The customary law as administered by the courts was of course not static It was organic and dynamic. With time it came to assimilate a lot of the concepts of the received English law. Many, nay, most of the offences that the local courts tried under the label of 'customary offences' were also crimes under the received law.[38]

However, since 9 October 1964, with the sole exception of the crime of contempt of court, all unwritten penal laws were abolished. In accord with the principle *nullum crimen, nulla poena sine lege*, the Constitution provides that 'Except for contempt of court, no person shall be convicted of a criminal offence unless the offence is defined and the penalty for it prescribed by law.'[39] Consequently, 'criminal customary law' in the meaning of *unwritten* customary law no longer exists.[40] The rationale for the abolition of unwritten criminal law will be discussed later on in this book.

II. Historical Sketch of the Criminal Justice System

A. The Police

51. There is as yet no documentation of the development of the law enforcement machinery prior to colonization. It is, however, clear that in the kingdoms of Buganda, Bunyoro, Toro and Ankore, and in the territory of Busoga, some form of security forces were organized in the king's palace and at the courts of senior chiefs to guard the king or chief and their household and to maintain law and order.[41] Police forces, as we know them today, did not exist to patrol the villages. The maintenance of law and order was the collective responsibility of the villagers under the leadership of the village chief. In the case of a mishap or criminal incident in a village the chief sounded the *ggwangamujje* drum, summoning all adult males to go to the rescue of the victim and to apprehend the perpetrators of the outrage.[42]

37. This was provided for under the District Administrative (District Councils) Ordinance of 1955.
38. For an interesting discussion of the ability of customary law to assimilate new notions from foreign law, see H.F. Morris, *Jurisdiction of the Buganda Courts and the Scope of Customary Law in Uganda*, J. African L. 54 (1965). But in *Mathias Kitimbo alias Motyansi Ngobi v. Busoga* [1965] E.A. 162, the High Court held that the offence of obtaining by false pretences was not known to customary law.
39. Article 28(12) Constitution. Cf. Art. 24(9) of the Independence Constitution which provided: 'No person shall be convicted of a criminal offence unless that offence is defined and the penalty therefor is prescribed in a written law.'
40. To avoid confusion, the aforementioned laws and bylaws enacted by the Great Lukiiko and other kingdom or district councils are now referred to as 'enacted criminal laws of customary origin.' H.F. Morris & James S. Read, *Uganda: The Development of its Laws and Constitution* 290 (Steven & Sons 1966).
41. Among the Baganda, for example, this role was played by the *bambowa* and *bagalagala*.
42. In some communities such as the Baganda, it was an offence for anybody to fail without a valid excuse to answer the alarm.

52. In modern times, particularly after colonization, police forces were organized and assumed the primary responsibility for law enforcement and for the maintenance of law and order. However, with a population thinly interspersed throughout the country, it has not been possible to establish police stations and posts in all the population centres of the country. Police presence is virtually limited to urban and major trading centres. For this reason, chiefs continue to wield law enforcement powers in most parts of the country, particularly in the rural areas. Under the old Local Administrations Act, it was part of the chief's duties to: execute orders and warrants, collect and communicate intelligence affecting the public peace; prevent the commission of offences and public nuisance; to detect and bring offenders to justice; and apprehend all persons they were legally authorized to apprehend and for whose apprehension sufficient grounds existed.[43] The chiefs' powers have however, waned since the coming to power of the NRM Government. Today, it is the Local Committees that are entrusted with the duty of assisting in the maintenance of law, order and security in their respective localities.[44]

B. The Courts

53. Up until 1964, there existed a dual court system in the country: the central government or English-type courts, and the 'native' or African courts.

54. The central government courts administered the received English law as well as the local statutes. They consisted of the Judicial Committee of the Privy Council in Britain, the Court of Appeal for Eastern Africa, the High Court, and the subordinate or magistrates' courts. The Judicial Committee of the Privy Council was abolished as the court of last instance for Uganda in 1964, as being incompatible with the country's independent status.[45] The Court of Appeal for Eastern Africa was replaced by the Uganda Court of Appeal after the collapse of the East African Community in 1977. The Court of Appeal was subsequently renamed as the Supreme Court in 1987. The 1995 Constitution further changed the system by re-establishing the Court of Appeal and the Supreme Court above it.

55. The 'native' or African courts were established in various local administrative districts of the country. Under the general supervision of Central Government administrative or judicial officers, these courts exercised jurisdiction in both civil and criminal proceedings to which all the parties were African; hence the appellation 'native' and later on 'African'.[46] They administered the customary laws of their

43. Act No. 18 of 1967, sec. 40.
44. The National Resistance Movement (NRM) was the political umbrella for Museveni's National Resistance Army (NRA) that seized power in 1986. The NRM Government established 'ten-house' cells or 'Resistance Committees' in every village. The committees were later re-named 'Local Committees' that took over the functions of village chiefs. Every committee has an individual who oversees security issues in the village and, depending on the seriousness of an incident, refers it to the committee as a whole or to the police, for action.
45. See the Appellate Jurisdiction (Amendment) Act, Act 32 of 1964.
46. See *supra* n. 35.

respective areas of jurisdiction, both civil and criminal. With respect to criminal proceedings, however, they were forbidden to exercise jurisdiction in homicide cases and over offences created by specific statutes, unless they were so specifically authorized.[47] A characteristic feature of the African courts was the informality of their procedures. With time, however, the procedures became more and more assimilated to the procedures followed before the Central Government courts.[48] But lawyers were not allowed to appear before the African courts, principally because the judges who presided over them – usually chiefs – were not trained lawyers.

56. With the coming into force of the Magistrates Courts Act in 1964, the Central Government and the African courts were integrated into a single system. At the magisterial level a hierarchy of courts, ranging from the Chief Magistrate to Magistrates Grades I, II and III was created.[49] From then on, jurisdiction in these courts would no longer depend on the parties' race. Additionally, since criminal customary law was constitutionally abolished (*supra*), magistrates' courts now administered only written criminal law.

C. Prisons

57. Prior to colonization, prisons did not exist in Uganda, as elsewhere in Africa South of the Sahara. Death, corporal punishment, mutilation, stocks, fines and banishment were the commonest forms of punishment for convicted offenders.[50] As we have noted earlier there was the possibility of compensation for the victims of the crime (*supra*, paragraph 49).[51]

58. With the introduction of English criminal law and English penal principles came imprisonment as a form of punishment. Besides fines imprisonment is the commonest form of punishment in Uganda today. The first prison in the country, the *Njabule Prison*, was established by the Government of the Kingdom of Buganda in 1894. The Central government's first prison was established in 1903.

---

47. African Courts Ordinance, Cap. 38, sec. 8.
48. African courts, with the exception of the Buganda courts, were specifically required to be guided by the Criminal Procedure Code and by the Evidence Act when trying criminal cases.
49. The Act was introduced in Buganda after 1966, when Milton Obote abrogated the Independence Constitution and abolished the Buganda Government. Magistrate Grade III was abolished in 2007 under the Magistrates Courts (Amendment) Act.
50. Generally see *African Penal Systems* (Alan Milne ed., Routledge & Kegan Paul 1969). See also Jomo Kenyatta, *Facing Mount Kenya* 227 (Ecker & Warburg 1937). John Roscoe, *The Baganda. Their Customs and Beliefs* 258–270 (2d. ed., Franck Cass & Co. Ltd. 1965). John Roscoe, *The Banyankore* 20 (Cambridge U. Press 1924).
51. Even murders could be resolved by payment of compensation. This is what is known as 'blood money' or *dia.* See the Restitution of Cattle and Payment of Blood money (Procedure) Regulations, Statutory Instrument No. 101 of 1965. See also P. Cantini, *The evolution of blood-money for Homicide in Somalia,* J. African L. 7 (1971). R.C. Cook, *Blood-money and the law of homicide in the Sudan,* Sudan L.J. 170 (1962).

§4. Sources and Classification of Criminal Law

I. Sources

A. The Constitution

59. The Constitution is an important source of criminal law in Uganda in four respects. First, being the fundamental law of the land, the Constitution may be likened to Kelsen's *Grundnorm* which, as long as it lasts, may not be derogated from. It sets the tenor and the general framework into which all other laws must fit. Any law or custom that is out of step or inconsistent with the Constitution is null and void to the extent of the inconsistency.

60. Second, the Constitution embodies a chapter on human rights and fundamental freedoms of the individual. These rights and freedoms include the right to life, the right to personal liberty; the right to privacy; the right to own property; freedom from slavery and from forced labour; freedom from torture and other inhuman and degrading treatment or punishment; freedom of conscience; freedom of expression; freedom of association and peaceful assembly; freedom of movement; and freedom from discrimination on the grounds of race, ethnicity, religion or gender. Where, in the opinion of the courts, any provision of a criminal or penal statute derogates from any of these rights, the courts will declare them null and void, since the Constitution takes precedence over any other law; it is supreme. They have done so in respect of provisions of the Penal Code relating to the crimes of sedition[52] and adultery,[53] the death penalty[54] and to corporal punishment.[55] They have also done the same in respect of the Deportation Act.[56]

61. Third, the Constitution also has provisions that closely relate to criminal proceedings. These provisions spell out certain procedural guarantees that are universally acknowledged to be essential to a fair trial. These guarantees include the right to be tried in public by an independent and impartial court; the right to be informed of the offence with which one is charged in a language that one understands; the

52. *Mwenda & Anor v. Attorney General* Const. Petition Nos. 12 of 2005 and 3 of 2006 [2010] UGCC 5 (25 Aug. 2010).
53. *Law Advocacy for Women in Uganda v. Attorney General*, Const. Petition Nos. 13/05& 05/06 [2007] UGCC 1 (5 Apr. 2007). In this case, the Constitutional Court struck down the crime of adultery as defined in the Penal Code as being discriminatory against women. See paragraphs 372 to 375 of the second edition of this monograph.
54. *Attorney General v. Susan Kigula and 417 Others*, Const. App. No. 3 of 2006, [2009] UGSC 6, 21 Aug. 2009.
55. *Kyamanywa Simon v. Uganda*, Constitutional Reference No. 10 of 2000.
56. Cap. 308. The Act authorized the government to deport and restrict any person that it considered subversive to an area of the country distant from his home. See for example *Ibingira & Anor. v. The Attorney General* [1966] E.A. 306. In this case the plaintiffs, ministers who had been arrested whilst attending a cabinet meeting presided over by Mr Obote, were served with deportation orders, rusticating them to a remote part of the country. They successfully challenged the constitutionality of the orders. The High Court held the Deportation Act to be unconstitutional as it violated the plaintiffs' freedom of movement.

right to be afforded the opportunity and facilities to prepare one's defence, the right to confront prosecution witnesses and to call one's own witnesses to testify on one's behalf, the right to legal representation; and the right to an interpreter if one does not understand the language of the court. Again, any provision of any statute that unduly restricts any of these guarantees will be declared null and void.

62. The Constitution spells out the permissible limitations to the enjoyment of the rights enumerated above. The limitations must be solely for the protection of other people's rights and of the general public, since, as it often said, 'my rights stop where yours start'. For instance, while guaranteeing the right of every person to personal liberty, the Constitution at the same time permits the arrest and detention of any person that may be suspected, on reasonable grounds, to have committed, or who has been convicted of, a criminal offence. Furthermore, the Constitution guarantees the right of every individual to privacy of his person, home and mails, but at the same time permits searches, frisks and seizures for purposes of criminal investigations. The Constitution also guarantees the right of everyone to own property, and at the same time allows the state to seize or to freeze private property in the course of an investigation for use as evidence in subsequent criminal proceedings. Finally, while the Constitution guarantees the right of anyone not to be discriminated against, it might be justifiable in the public interest to require compulsory medical examination for individuals charged with defilement to determine their HIV/AIDS status. Perpetrators who are found positive are punished more harshly.

63. Lastly, the Constitution also sets forth other general principles which are of fundamental importance to criminal law. These principles include the principle of presumption of innocence, the principle of non-retroactivity of penal law, the *ne bis idem* principle or the rule against double jeopardy, the rule against self-incrimination, and the *nullum crimen sine lege* and *nulla poena sine lege* or the principle of legality. These principles will be discussed in detail in subsequent chapters.

B. Statutes

64. The most important statute in the area of criminal law is the Penal Code. The Code, as has been pointed out, lays down general rules and principles applicable to criminal legislation. It also defines specific offences of a general and permanent nature, such as murder, rape and theft. Other sources of criminal law are statutes that regulate certain activities or set standards in given areas of human endeavour. They forbid certain acts and impose certain duties. They also prescribe penalties for persons who commit the forbidden acts or fail to perform the duties they impose. Common among these statutes are the Traffic and Road Safety Act,[57] the Factories Act,[58] the Official Secrets Act[59] and the Shop Hours Act.[60] The Penal code explicitly

57. Act 38 of 1970.
58. Cap. 198.
59. Cap. 311.
60. Cap. 105.

recognizes these statutes as a source of criminal law.[61] Closely related to statutes, are rules, regulations, orders and bylaws, commonly known as subordinate or delegated legislation. Quite often Parliament, through a parent statute, empowers a minister or some other authority to make rules or regulations for the purpose of giving effect to the provisions of the statute. These rules or regulations, when made, usually include provisions which create offences and prescribe punishments for violations. Example of such regulations include the Traffic and Road Safety (Restriction of Vehicles Weights) Order of 1987[62] and the Speed of Motor Vehicles (Exemption No. 2) Order of 1990.[63] City or municipal councils and other urban or local authorities do also have power under relevant enabling statutes to pass bylaws on matters pertaining to the health, order and good government in their respective areas of jurisdiction. These matters usually include such things as markets, cemeteries and burial grounds, advertising, dangerous trades, nuisances, noise, and street collections.[64] To be valid, however, subordinate legislation must strictly confine itself within the limits of the parent statute, must not be unreasonable, must not violate general principles of justice, must be made in accordance with the procedures laid down by the parent statute and may have to be approved by a minister before they take effect.

C. *English Law*

65. English law is still a subsidiary source of Uganda's criminal law, first as an aid to interpretation and, second, as substantive criminal law. As has been noted above (*supra*, paragraph 47), the Penal Code provides that it must be interpreted in accord with the principles of interpretation obtaining in England, and the expressions used in it must be presumed to have the meaning attaching to them in English criminal law; unless, of course, the Code expressly provides otherwise.

66. An example of such principles of statutory interpretation ordains that penal statutes must be construed strictly, and that where there is doubt that doubt must inure to the benefit of the accused. Another is the principle of *stare decis*. According to this principle, decisions of superior courts are binding on the inferior courts seized with cases based on similar facts or involving identical issues. In a sense, therefore, authoritative or precedent-setting decisions of Uganda's superior courts, say on the construction of a particular statutory provision, are a source of law.

61. Section 3 of the Code specifically provides that:'Nothing in this code shall affect –

(a) the liability, trial or punishment of a person for an offence against any other written law in force in Uganda other than this Code.'

62. Statutory Instrument No. 76 of 1987.

63. Statutory Instrument No. 44 of 1990.

64. For example, see the Nebbi District Protection of Health Bylaws, 1990, Statutory Instrument No. 37 of 1990, and the Kampala City (Maintenance of Premises and Road Verges) Bylaws, 1989, Statutory Instrument No. 13 of 1987.

67. An example of an expression that has been presumed to have the meaning attaching to it in English criminal law is 'contempt'. Section 3 of the Penal Code provides that nothing in this Code shall affect:

> (c) the power of any court to punish a person for contempt of such court.

The Constitution similarly recognizes the inherent powers of any court to punish any person for contempt of itself notwithstanding that the act or omission constituting the contempt is not defined in a written law, and the penalty therefor is not so prescribed.[65] Neither the Penal Code nor the Constitution nor any other statute defines the offence of contempt or prescribes a penalty therefor. For guidance in this matter, the courts must have recourse to the English common law.[66] According to English common law, contempt is an 'act done or writing published calculated to bring a court or a judge into contempt or to lower his authority', or something 'calculated to obstruct or interfere with the due course of justice or the lawful process of the court'.[67]

68. Regarding substantive criminal law, the Penal Code provides for the direct importation of English law in at least two instances. In the first instance, it provides in section 15 that:

> Subject to any express provisions in this Code or any other law in force in Uganda, criminal responsibility –
>
> (a) for the use of force in defence of person and property;
> (b) in respect of rash, reckless or negligent acts, shall be determined according to the principles of English law.

It is not clear from the Code whether 'principles of English law' are limited to those that are found in the common law, or whether they extend to those found in English statutes as well. For example, in England today, use of force in defence of person is governed by the common law. However, use of force in defence of property is governed by provisions of the Criminal Damage Act.[68] Crimes involving rash, reckless or negligent acts are similarly governed by both the common law and by statute.[69]

69. The second instance of direct importation of substantive English law is in respect of the crime of piracy. The Code provides that 'Any person who is guilty of piracy or any crime connected with or relating or akin to piracy is liable to be tried

---

65. Article 28(12).
66. Dealing with a provision in the Seychelles Penal Code in *para materia* with section 3(c) of the Uganda Code, the former Court of Appeal for Eastern Africa said that 'the offence of contempt and power of the court for punishing it are the same as in England, not by virtue of the Penal Code … but by virtue of the common law of England.' *Robert Austin Mullery v. R.* [1957] E.A. 138, 140. For a Ugandan case dealing with contempt see *Kasturilal Laroya v. Mityana Staple Cotton Co. Ltd. & Anor.* [1958] E.A. 194.
67. *R. v. Gray* [1900] 2 Q.B. 36, 40; *Perera v. The King* [1951] A.C. 482, 488.
68. 12 *Statutes* 557, sec. 3.
69. For example, the Road Traffic Act, 1972.

and punished according to the law of England for the time being in force.' It is noteworthy that the provision does not provide a cut-off point at which the English law on piracy is deemed to apply. Therefore any statutory changes in the law made by the British Parliament would automatically apply to Uganda. This is an embarrassing compromise to the Uganda Parliament's legislative sovereignty!

D. International Law

70. The importance of international law for Uganda criminal law is twofold: it influences national criminal law and creates crimes that may be tried by national courts.

71. The influence of international law on national criminal law is visible in the area of jurisdiction. Because of the principle of territorial integrity and independence of states, Uganda's criminal jurisdiction is limited to crimes committed on Ugandan territory. Again, growing out of the principle of the sovereignty and independence of states, Uganda's courts cannot exercise their criminal jurisdiction over foreign heads of state or their duly accredited diplomats or implead their property without their consent. Moreover, international law, particularly as articulated in universal treaties or declarations of a norm-creating character, may be resorted to by our courts as an aid to the interpretation of our Constitution and other legislation. The Supreme Court extensively cited provisions of various international human rights instruments or treaties whilst interpreting provisions in the Constitution on the death penalty and on inhuman and degrading treatment or punishment.[70]

72. Substantive international law, including both customary and conventional international law, creates offences that national courts may assume jurisdiction over. Regarding customary international law, that law is part of the common law of Uganda unless national statutes provide otherwise. The basis for this proposition is the following dictum from the English case of *West Rand Central Gold Mining Co. Ltd. v. Rex*:

> It is quite true that whatever has received the common consent of civilized nations must have received the assent of our country, and that to which we have assented along with other nations in general may properly be called international law, and as such will be acknowledged and applied by our

70. *Attorney General v. Susan Kigula & 417 Ors.* Const. App. No. 3 of 2006, [2009] UGSC 6 (21 Jan. 2009). The Supreme Court cited the Universal Declaration of Human Rights, International Covenant on the Civil and Political Rights, Optional Protocol on the International Covenant on Civil and Political Rights, Convention Against Torture and other Cruel, Inhuman or Degrading Treatment or Punishment, Optional Protocol to the Convention Against Torture and other Cruel, Inhuman or Degrading Treatment or Punishment, and the African Charter on Human and People's Rights. It also cited the jurisprudence of the UN Committee on Human Rights.

municipal tribunals when legitimate occasion arises for those tribunals to decide questions to which doctrines of international law may be relevant.[71]

73. Customary international law creates offences billed as 'crimes against the law of nations', such as aggression, genocide, crimes against humanity, war crimes and piracy, which are considered to be crimes against the entire international community and their perpetrators as enemies of mankind, *hostis humanis juris*. Under the principle of *aut dedere aut judicare*, any country may either assume jurisdiction – universal jurisdiction – over these crimes, irrespective of the country where they were committed and irrespective of the nationality of the perpetrator or victim, or may surrender the perpetrators to any other country that may be ready and willing to assume jurisdiction. Nevertheless, under our Constitution customary international crimes would not be automatically amenable to the jurisdiction of our courts, because the Constitution bans non-statutory criminal law (*supra*, paragraph 50).[72] Our Parliament must enact a law specifically defining those crimes under our national law and prescribing penalties therefor. When enacted, such a law will have the same status, and be subject to amendment or repeal, as any other laws passed by Parliament.

74. Regarding conventional international law, certain treaties create crimes which states parties thereto are expected to repress by trying and punishing their perpetrators through national courts. However, according to the treaty practice obtaining in Uganda, our courts have no power to assume jurisdiction over treaty-based crimes, even those created by treaties to which our country is party, unless Parliament enacts an act domesticating those crimes and vesting in our courts power to try them. This is so because under our law treaties that our country enters into are not self-executing; they do not create enforceable rights or obligations for citizens unless they have been incorporated into the national body of laws by an Act of Parliament. Where such a statute has been enacted, then, it can be said that the treaty on which it is based is a source of criminal law. This is so in the case of the Rome Statute of the International Criminal Court (ICC). Under the International Criminal Court Act,[73] the ICC-based crimes of aggression, genocide, crimes against humanity and war crimes are now crimes under the laws of Uganda and the High Court now has power to try them, provided they are committed after 25 May 2010, the date on which the Act came into force.

II. Classification

75. The criminal law of Uganda can generally be classified as between civil and military criminal law, and as between felonies and misdemeanours.

---

71. [1905] 2 K.B. 391, 406, per Lord Alverstone. See also *Chung Chi Cheung v. The King* [1939] A.C. 160.
72. Article 28(12).
73. Act 11 of 2010, secs. 7, 8 and 9. Ugandan courts will have jurisdiction over the crime of aggression once Uganda ratifies the amendment to the Rome Statute defining the crime, in accordance with Article 121(5).

76. Civil criminal law is the general criminal law applicable to every person in the country, including members of the Armed Forces. It is the law which is contained in the Penal Code and in other specialized statutes. Military criminal law, on the other hand, specifically applies to members of the Armed Forces, and to certain categories of civilians who perform duties of a military nature or are connected with the military establishment. The Penal Code recognizes it as an independent regime. It provides, *inter alia*, that nothing in the Code shall affect, among other things, 'any of the written laws for the time being in force for the government of the Armed Forces of Uganda or any police force established in Uganda'.[74] Military criminal law is contained in the Uganda Peoples' Defence Forces Act and in the Code of Conduct which is a schedule to the Statute.[75] It aims at enforcing professionalism, efficiency and discipline among the members of the Armed Forces, whilst on or off duty. For instance, cowardice in action on the part of a commander, careless shooting, breach of concealment which results in loss of life and failure to protect war materials or misusing the same, are all capital offences under the Act.[76] Similarly, being drunk whether on duty or off duty, is also an offence punishable by up to seven years imprisonment.[77] Military criminal law is enforced by special military courts, whose composition and rules of procedure differ from those of the regular civil courts.[78]

77. Regarding the felony-misdemeanour classification, the Penal Code categorizes all criminal offences into two types: felonies and misdemeanours. It defines a felony as 'an offence which is declared to be a felony or, if not declared to be a misdemeanour, is punishable, without proof of previous conviction, with death, or with imprisonment for three years or more'.[79] It similarly defines a misdemeanour as 'any offence which is not a felony'.[80]

78. This classification is a carry-over from old English criminal law. Under that law, felonies were offences which the English judges considered to be particularly serious. They included murder, manslaughter, rape and arson. Misdemeanours, however, were the less serious ones. There were two practical consequences of characterizing an offence as either a felony or misdemeanour. The first was that an arrest could be effected without a warrant for felonies, but not for misdemeanours. The second was that it was an offence to conceal or to compound a felony. Not so with a misdemeanour. With time, however, the distinction between felonies and misdemeanours became blurred, and was ultimately abolished by the 1967 Criminal Law Act.[81]

74. Section 3(f).
75. Cap. 307.
76. See secs. 14 to 44 of the Act.
77. Section 28 of the Act.
78. They have a hierarchy ranging from the Unit Disciplinary Committee, Field Court Martial, Division Court Martial, General Court Martial, and Court Martial Appeal Court.
79. Section 2.
80. *Ibid.*
81. *12 Statute* 358.

79. It is submitted that the distinction between felony and misdemeanour does not serve any useful purpose in Uganda either. Its only practical effect is that it is an offence to compound or conceal a felony, but it is not so with a misdemeanour.[82] The distinction is not used as a criterion for conferring on the police power to arrest without a warrant, as used to be the case in Britain. The criterion used is that of 'a cognizable offence'.[83] Moreover, there seems to be no rhyme or reason for characterizing some offences as 'felonies' while not doing the same thing with respect to others which, in terms of the penalties prescribed for them, also qualify as felonies. For example, prostitution, which is a felony by definition (it is punishable by up to seven years imprisonment), is not specifically referred to in the Code as such.[84] However, conspiracy to defile a woman or girl, which is a lesser offence (it is punishable by three years imprisonment only), is specifically referred to by the Code as a felony.[85] Both offences are felonies. Why, then, is conspiracy specifically referred to as 'a felony', and prostitution which is the more serious of the two as merely 'an offence'? The classification thus only serves to obfuscate the law and principle and nothing else. Therefore, it would be preferable for Uganda to follow Britain's lead and abolish the distinction as well. It would suffice if all penal legislation referred to an 'offence', without classifying it into a felony or a misdemeanour. Concealing or compounding would be better defined if it was limited to offences punishable by a specified term of imprisonment and/or a specified amount of a fine.

82. See sec. 104 of the Penal Code.
83. According to sec. 23(a) of the Criminal Procedure Code Act, a 'cognizable offence' is one which is punishable by imprisonment for at least one year or a fine exceeding UGX 4,000.
84. Section 139 provides that 'Any person who practices or engages in prostitution is guilty of an offence and is liable to imprisonment for seven years.'
85. Section 140 provides that 'Any person who conspires with another to induce any woman or girl, by means of any false pretence … to permit any man to have unlawful carnal knowledge of her is guilty of a felony and is liable to imprisonment for three years.'

Part I. Substantive Criminal Law

Chapter 1. General Principles of Criminal Law

§1. THE PRINCIPLES OF LEGALITY

80. In a polity governed by the rule of law, one of the functions of the law is to shape the social order. It sets standards which all inhabitants of the country, regardless of their status, must respect when conducting their affairs. However, to be efficacious as a standard setter, the law must accord with the principle of legality. According to this principle, the law must be prospective; it must be certain or easily ascertainable and comprehensible; and it must be public or otherwise accessible.

I. Prospective Law

81. Prospective law is law that assigns legal consequences to conduct that is committed after the law has been passed or before it has entered into force. That law may either proscribe or legalize the conduct in question. By preceding the conduct that it proscribes or legalizes the law helps guide inhabitants in their conduct. In case of proscribed conduct, the law gives them warning of any prejudicial consequences of their intended or planned course of action. As one eminent British judge has said:

> The acceptance of the rule of law as a constitutional principle requires that a citizen, before committing himself to any course of action, should be able to know in advance what are the legal consequences that will flow from it.[86]

82. Retrospective law, however, is law that assigns legal consequences to conduct that has already taken place before the passing of the law or before it has entered into force. It is backdated to a prior period so as to proscribe or criminalize conduct that was lawful at the time of its commission or to legalize conduct that was unlawful or criminal at the time of its commission. Retrospective law is repugnant to the concept of the rule of law, because it cannot guide people in their conduct. For any law to be able to guide people's conduct, it should exist and be

86. *Black – Clawson Int. Ltd. v. Papierwerke Waldhof – Aschaffenburg A.G.* [1975] A.C. 591, 638 per Lord Diplock.

knowable at the time that the people are considering to conduct their affairs in a certain way. In the context of criminal law, it would be manifestly iniquitous to punish an individual for conduct that was lawful at the time it was committed. In this respect, another British judge has opined thus:

> Retrospective laws are no doubt, *prima facie*, of questionable policy, and contrary to the general principle that legislation by which the conduct of mankind is to be regulated ought, when introduced for the first time, to deal with future acts, and ought not to change the character of past transactions carried on upon the faith of the then existing law ... Accordingly the court will not ascribe retrospective force to new laws affecting rights, unless by express words or necessary implication it appears that such was the intention of the legislature.[87]

83. It is for this reason, therefore, that retrospective penal laws are universally condemned. This condemnation has found expression in the Latin maxims of *nullum crimen sine lege* (no crime without a law) and *nulla poena sine lege* (no punishment without previous legal authority).[88] In keeping with this condemnation, the Uganda Constitution also prohibits retrospective penal laws. Article 28(7) and (8) provides as follows:

> (7) No person shall be charged with or convicted of a criminal offence which is founded on an act or omission that did not at the time it took place constitute a criminal offence.
> (8) No penalty shall be imposed for a criminal offence that is severer in degree or description than the maximum penalty that could have been imposed for that offence at the time when it was committed.

84. For instance, in 1984 the Uganda Parliament passed the Penal Code (Amendment) Act (Act No. 9 of 1984) by which it vested the Uganda courts with jurisdiction over treasonable acts committed outside Uganda by Uganda citizens and other persons ordinarily resident in Uganda. The Act contained a provision giving it retrospective effect. In *Balaki Kirya & Anor. v. Uganda*,[89] two of the accused were charged with treasonable acts, meetings, which took place in Kenya. The state sought to apply the provisions of the Penal Code (Amendment) Act to these acts that took place prior to the passing of the Act, arguing that the Act was merely procedural and was therefore not affected by the constitutional ban on retrospective penal laws. While conceding that the presumption against retroactivity has no application to enactments which affect only the procedure and practice of the courts, the High Court held that the Penal Code (Amendment) Act was not merely procedural. Said Allen, J.:

---

87. *Phillips v. Eyre* (1870–1871) 6 L.R. Q.B. 1, 23, per Willes, J.
88. See Art. 11(2) of the Universal Declaration of Human Rights, Art. 15(1) of the International Covenant on Civil and Political Rights, Art. 7(2) of the African Charter on Human and People's Rights, Art. 9 of the American Convention on Human Rights, Art. 7(1) of the European Convention for the Protection of Human and Fundamental Freedoms.
89. H.Ct.Cr.Session No. 75 of 1984 (unreported).

> In my opinion the amended law cannot be regarded as being merely procedural for the following reasons:
>
> 1. The amendment is a part of the Penal Code Act which is a code of criminal offences. It does not contain procedural matter which is actually to be found in the Criminal Procedure Code, the Trial on Indictments Decree, 1971, the Magistrates' Courts Act, 1970, and the Evidence Act.
> 2. Jurisdiction is a matter of constitutional and substantive law concerning the power and authority of the courts and its limitation and extent. It cannot be said to be merely a matter of procedural law.
> 3. The effect of the amendment is to allow the courts to try offences and offenders which it could not do under the previous law because the particular acts did not then constitute actionable offences. Thus the amendment creates new classes of offences and offenders.
>
> As consequence I hold that Article 15(4) of the Constitution applies and these new offences cannot be applied retrospectively by charging persons like A.1 and A.2 who were not committing an existing criminal offence of this sort under the Penal Code at the time when the alleged offences took place in 1981 and 1982.

With respect to the severity of the penalty the Constitution means that, if after an offence has already been committed and the law relating to the offence is amended so as to increase the severity of the penalty therefor, the severer penalty should not be imposed. Only the penalty applicable at the time the offence was committed may be imposed.

85. It must, however, be emphasized that it is only *penal* retrospective laws that are condemned and, as far as Uganda is concerned, constitutionally outlawed. Moreover, it is implicit from the opinion of the British judge just cited above that although retrospective laws are undesirable they can still be passed. This position is reflected in the constitutions of many former British dependencies, including the 1967 Uganda Constitution.[90]

86. Retrospective laws, although exceptional, have been justified as a curative response to a breakdown in the legal order resulting from, say, an insurrection or successful overthrow of an existing regime.[91] Retrospective laws may be passed to indemnify persons who took up arms either to maintain the authority of the existing government or to overthrow it. The infinite actions, civil or criminal, that would otherwise arise out of such occurrences are thus killed in embryo. Successive Ugandan

90. Article 58(3) of the 1967 Constitution provided that: 'Without prejudice to the powers of Parliament to postpone the operation of any law or *to make laws with retrospective effect*, a bill shall not become law until it has been duly passed and assented to in accordance with this constitution.' This provision was omitted from the 1995 Constitution. See also Art. 81(4) of the Constitution of Belize, sec. 87(6) of the Constitution of Botswana, sec. 56(4) of the Constitution of Kenya, Art. 27(8) of the Constitution of Lesotho, Art. 35(8) of the Constitution of Malawi, Art. 53(5) of the Constitution of Sierra Leone, and Art. 79(8) of the Constitution of Zambia.
91. See the speech of Willes, J. in *Phillips v. Eyre*, [1870–1871] 6 L.R. Q.B. 1, 27.

regimes have in the past promulgated legislative fiats with retrospective effect prohibiting civil or criminal actions in respect of acts done in the course of either suppressing a revolt or successfully overthrowing a previous regime.[92] They have also been used to absolve security personnel of criminal and civil liability for their otherwise criminal, wrongful or tortious conduct.[93]

87. Retrospective laws may also be used to benefit a class of citizens that would otherwise be prejudiced for reasons for which they are not to blame.[94]

88. True, there is a difference between making an illegal act legal and making an innocent action criminal and punishing it as a crime. Nevertheless, it is submitted that the retrospective legalization of criminal conduct is also unjust, not only to the victims of such conduct but also to persons who might have committed such conduct and suffered prejudice without the benefit of the retrospective laws. It is because of this inherent inequity in retrospective laws that the English courts developed the rule of interpretation that presumes such laws to be illegal unless Parliament's intention to pass them is shown to be manifestly clear.[95]

---

92. For example, on assuming power on the 27 Jul. 1985, General Tito Okello Lutwa issued a Proclamation abrogating sections of the Constitution and legalizing his regime. He signed the Legal Notice on 2 Aug. 1985, but it was deemed to have come into force on 27 Jul. 1985. Section 11 of the Proclamation provided that 'No action or other legal proceedings whatsoever whether civil or criminal shall be instituted in any court for or on account of or in respect of any act, matter or thing done during the continuation upon or incidental to the said assumption of powers of the Government if done in good faith and done in the execution of his duty or for the defence of Uganda by a member of the Armed Forces.' See Legal Notice No. 4 of 1985.

   On toppling Okello's regime and seizing state power on 26 Jan. 1986, Yoweri Kaguta Museveni issued a similar Proclamation.
93. This was particularly the case during the Government of Idi Amin when security personnel were authorized to shoot at sight or shoot to kill any suspected 'robber' or *kondo*. See the Robbery Suspects Decree, Decree No. 7 of 1972 which was signed on 8 May 1972 but was deemed to have come in force on 1 Jun. 1971.
94. This point can be illustrated by an episode from Botswana. Prior to 1985, the University of Botswana had purported to validate examinations and to award certificates to nursing and midwifery students at the National Health Institute in Gaborone. This the University did without statutory authority. It was not until a student who had problems at the examinations challenged the validity of the examinations process that the University realized that it did not in fact have power to do what it had been doing, and that the certificates it had been awarding for some time were void. Something had to be done to ensure that the nurses and midwives who, for reasons for which they were not responsible, had received these 'void' certificates were not prejudiced. Parliament passed the Nurses and Midwives (Validation) Act appointing the University of Botswana 'the validating authority for the course of instruction, examinations and for the granting of examination certificates and other awards to nurses and midwives'. It also empowered the University to 'conduct examinations for nurses and midwives and to prescribe curricular, appoint examiners and grant certificates in relation thereto and to make awards to nurses and midwives'. The date of commencement for the Act was 29 Jul. 1988, but it was 'deemed to have come into operation on 20 Feb. 1985'. Act No. 12 of 1988 (Laws of Botswana).
95. See Judge Willes' statement *cited above*.

II. Certainty of the Law

89. Related to the virtues of prospective law is the need for the law to be certain or easily ascertainable. An individual contemplating a given course of action should know, with a reasonable degree of certainty, what the law provides and what the legal consequences of his or her action would be. With that knowledge, he or she should then be able to make an informed decision. It is submitted that this desideratum would be easiest to attain where the law was contained in an enactment, preferably a code or statute, which was accessible to all members of the public.

90. As indicated in the previous chapter, judges in England had power, acting as *custos morum*, to create offences. The shortcomings of judge-made laws are fourfold. First, the law-creating decision of the judge is retrospective. It declares the given conduct criminal after it has already been committed. Judges have to wait until conduct has already been committed, a complaint made and the perpetrator is brought before them, before they can pronounce themselves on his or her conduct. This species of law, as has been noted, defeats the purpose of law as a standard setter and as a guide for human conduct. Second, judge-made laws are not as easily accessible as they should be. They are scattered in cases throughout the law reports to which an ordinary member of the public has no easy access. Third, even when the cases can be located, their authority may depend on the level of the court within the hierarchy, the reasoning behind it and the reputation of the judge who decided it. Quite clearly, this state of affairs does not lend much certainty to judge-made laws. Fourth, judicial law-making may be objected to on the ground that it violates the principle of separation of powers. In a democratic polity, the power to make law should vest in the legislature which is the most representative of all the three branches of government. The legislature, because it represents and is accountable to the people, should be the one to decide which human conduct should be proscribed as criminal. The power of the courts should be to apply the law to given sets of fact-situations presented before them. In so doing, they may of course interpret and declare what the law is.

91. It is for these reasons that the Uganda Constitution, in line with those of other former British dependencies, insists that all penal laws, with only one exception, must be written. It provides as follows:

> Except for contempt of court, no person shall be convicted of a criminal offence unless the offence is defined and the penalty for it is prescribed in a written law.[96]

92. This provision denies the judges in Uganda power to create 'common law offences', as their forebears in England used to do.[97] It also abolishes unwritten

96. Article 28(12). See also sec. 10(8) of the Constitution of Botswana, sec. 77(8) of the Constitution of Kenya, and Art. 18(8) of the Constitution of Zambia.
97. English judges no longer have the power to create new offences since the decision of the House of Lords in *Director of Public Prosecutions v. Withers* [1975] A.C. 842, 860, 867.

customary criminal law.[98] Although the judges are thus not allowed to 'make law', we cannot gainsay their power to influence the development of the criminal law by extending it to new fact-situations,[99] and by interpretation. Indeed, it is often difficult to draw a distinction between interpretation and judicial law-making or creativity.[100] This observation is borne out by the fact that the rules that the courts use to interpret statutes were created by judges themselves – English judges.[101] Using these rules, they may put either an expansive or restrictive interpretation on a particular provision. Generally speaking, courts have traditionally interpreted penal provisions strictly or narrowly where this would benefit the accused person. This rule is predicated on the principle that any provision of the law that purports to impose criminal liability on an individual must be expressed in precise and unambiguous terms. Therefore where a provision is capable of more than one interpretation, the courts will adopt that interpretation which is the more favourable to the accused, in accord with the *in dubio pro reo* principle. Plowman, J. in the English case of *Re H.P.C. Productions Ltd* said as follows:

> In every case the question is simply what is the meaning of the words which the statute has used to describe the prohibited act or transaction? If these words have a natural meaning, that is their meaning, and such meaning is not to be extended by any reasoning based on the substance of the transaction. If the language of the statute is equivocal and there are two reasonable meanings of that language, the interpretation which will avoid the penalty is to be adopted.[102]

93. The rule of strict interpretation was more rigorously followed at a period when the criminal law in England was harsh and when the death penalty was more widely used than today. Of late it would appear to have been relaxed. Today the courts will not be so keen to apply the rule unless the doubt raised by the provision is a genuine, not a spurious or quibbling doubt. They are likely to construe the provision in order to uphold its substantive meaning and thus help suppress the mischief or conduct that was the legislature's manifest intention to proscribe. According to Professor Glanville Williams:

> Courts still pay lip-service to the ancient principle that in case of doubt a criminal statute is to be 'strictly interpreted' in favour of the defendant; but the principle is rarely applied in practice, if there are social reasons for convicting. Indeed, we may make bold and say that the looser the defendant's conduct, the more loosely the judges construe the statute designed to control him. When the defendant has acted immorally, nothing short of the most powerful reasoning

98. See discussion on this topic *supra* at paras. 49–50.
99. Or by new modes of committing an old crime.
100. For an excellent discussion of this subject see A.T.H. Smith, *Judicial Law Making in the Criminal Law*, 100 L. Q. Rev. 46 (1984).
101. Section 1 of the Penal Code obliges judges in Uganda to interpret the Code according to English principles of statutory interpretation.
102. [1962] Ch. 466, 485. See also *Tuck & Sons v. Priester* (1887) 19 Q.B.D. 629, 638.

based on the wording of the statute is likely to dissuade judges from holding that the statute applies to him.[103]

94. Furthermore, by applying the law to new fact-situations or to new modes of committing forbidden conduct which the legislature might not have contemplated at the time of the enactment, the courts are able to extend the law so as to cope with new developments in technology and in human behaviour. For example, theft can now be committed by means of computers, and murders can be committed by intentional HIV-AIDS virus transmission.

95. As noted earlier, contempt of court is an exception to the constitutional rule that requires crimes to be defined and penalties therefor to be in written form. It continues to be governed by the English common law. It should, however, be noted that precisely because of the uncertainty that is attendant to common law crimes Britain herself found it necessary to pass legislation governing criminal contempt. It is urged that Uganda do the same.

III. Accessibility of the Law

96. It is apposite, too, to note that Uganda subscribes to the principle that *ignorantia juris non excusat*, or, that ignorance of the law is no defence.[104] This, then, underscores the importance of the law being certain and accessible. It would be unfair for this principle to apply when the law in question was neither certain nor accessible. Admittedly, few, if any, wrongdoers ever stop to consult the text of the law before going on with their nefarious conduct. Nevertheless, law-abiding citizens involved in state-regulated activities might wish to conduct those activities in conformity with the law. They may want to consult the law before taking any course of action. It would be unfair to punish them for transgressing a law that was not certain or knowable in the sense that it was not accessible. It is for this reason, then, that the constitutions of some states provide that no law shall come into force before it has been published in the Government Gazette.[105] Publication in the Gazette informs members of the public that such a law exists and affords them an opportunity to consult it if they so wish.[106]

§2. The Rule against Double Jeopardy (NE BIS IN IDEM)

97. The Constitution of Uganda provides that:

> A person who shows that he or she has been tried by a competent court for a criminal offence and convicted or acquitted of that offence, shall not again be

103. Glanville Williams, *Textbook of Criminal Law* 12 (2d. ed., Stevens & Sons 1983).
104. See sec. 6 of the Penal Code.
105. For example, see sec. 87(6) of the Constitution of Botswana.
106. See Acts of Parliament Act, sec. 3. See also *Uganda v. Joseph Jwarira* [1972] U.L.R. 23.

tried for the offence or for any other criminal offence of which he or she could have been convicted at the trial for that offence, except upon the order of a superior court in the course of appeal or review proceedings relating to the conviction or acquittal.[107]

98. The provision embodies the rule against double jeopardy. This rule ordains that a person should not be brought into jeopardy of punishment more than once for the same offence. If the accused has been previously convicted of the same offence he or she is entitled to plead *autrefois convict* or if he or she has been acquitted he or she is entitled to plead *autrefois acquit* – which is a plea in bar or peremptory plea. The reason for the plea of *autrefois convict* has been succinctly stated by Professor Fitzgerald as follows:

> English criminal law is based on the idea that once a person has been convicted and sentenced and has undergone the punishment imposed upon him, he has paid the penalty. To allow the authorities to prosecute him again in order to seek the imposition of some further punishment would be oppressive. The law permits the accused, by serving the sentence, to wipe the slate clean and start again; and this he could not do if he were perpetually liable to further prosecutions for the same offence.[108]

99. Regarding the plea of *autrefois acquit* Professor Fitzgerald says:

> Once a man has been acquitted, it is felt that it would be too harsh to allow the prosecution further bites at the cherry. The defendant must be allowed to order his affairs with certainty. This means of course that occasionally the guilty slip through the net, and nothing can be done about it. This disadvantage is outweighed, however, by the gain in freedom from oppression, which the possibility of perpetual exposure to prosecution would entail.[109]

However, for these pleas to be valid, certain prerequisites need to be satisfied.

100. The first prerequisite is that there must have been a final verdict, either convicting or acquitting the accused. A plea of guilty which has been accepted by the court and not changed before sentencing is sufficient. A finding of not guilty may of course be changed to one of guilty by a higher court, and it is the higher court's verdict that will count for purposes of the plea of *autrefois convict*. For purposes of the *autrefois acquit* plea, the following will amount to acquittals: (i) a successful submission of no-case-to-answer; (ii) withdrawal of the charge after the accused has been called upon to make his defence;[110] (iii) dismissal of the charge for non-prosecution, for example, where leave to withdraw the charges has been denied, or

---

107. Article 28(9).
108. P.J. Fitzgerald, *Criminal Law and Punishment* 172 (Clarendon Press 1962).
109. *Ibid.*
110. See sec. 119(b) of the Magistrates Courts Act.

where the prosecution offers no further evidence,[111] or where the prosecutor does not appear to prosecute and the charge is dismissed; and (iv) a valid conviction which is quashed on appeal or review.[112] The following do not, however, amount to acquittals and do not entitle the accused to raise the plea of *autrefois acquit*: the withdrawal of the charges before the close of the prosecution case by the prosecutor with the leave of the court;[113] and the entering of a *nolle prosequi* by the DPP.[114]

101. Second, the tribunal that previously tried the accused must have had jurisdiction to do so.[115] Trial before a domestic tribunal for a disciplinary offence is probably not a trial by 'a competent court'. Thus where a member of a disciplined force, such as the army, police or prisons, is convicted of and punished for a disciplinary offence by a tribunal set up under the law governing the force, he or she may still be tried and punished by an ordinary court for a criminal offence arising out of the same conduct.[116] For sentencing purposes, however, it is only fair that the court should take into account any punishment imposed against an accused person in the prior disciplinary proceedings against him or her.

102. Third, the offence preferred in the second charge must be based on the same facts as in the previous charge. Thus where the accused is acquitted for lack of sufficient evidence, he or she cannot be subsequently tried for the same offence based on the same facts even though the prosecution may now be in a position to adduce the requisite evidence.[117]

103. Similarly, where the accused has been convicted, he or she cannot be charged again with the same offence in an aggravated or minor form, because, as the Constitution provides, that person 'shall not again be tried for the offence or *any other criminal offence of which he or she could have been convicted* at the trial for that offence'. For example, where a person has been convicted or acquitted of common assault he cannot later be charged with assault occasioning actual bodily harm or of unlawful wounding. To prove these aggravated offences you have to establish assault, which has already been tried. Yet, a person should not be put in jeopardy of punishment more than once for the same offence.

---

111. See *Uganda v. Milenge & Anor.* [1970] E.A. 269 (East African Court of Appeal). This case was distinguished in *Uganda v. Okot* E.A. 8 and in *Director of Public Prosecutions v. Sezi & Anor.* [1974] E.A. 287.
112. In the Kenya case of *Re An Application by Ajut Singh* [1959] E.A. 782, a magistrate dismissed a charge after the complainant failed to show up in court. Complainant reinstituted the proceedings. The accused successfully raised the plea of *autrefois acquit*. On appeal to the Supreme Court, Rudd, J. held, obiter, that the initial dismissal of the charge amounted to an acquittal and that, therefore, the plea of *autrefois acquit* could be raised as a bar to the reinstatement of the proceedings.
113. See sec. 119(a) of the Magistrates Courts Act.
114. Trial on Indictments Act, sec. 133.
115. For example, see the Swaziland case of *Simelane v. Regina* [1955] H.C.P.T.L. 57.
116. See the following English cases applying these principles. *Lewis v. Morgan* [1943] 2 All E.R. 272; and *R. v. Hogan* and *R. v. Tompkins* [1960] 3 All E.R. 149.
117. See *Uganda v. Yowasi Birungi* [1973] U.L.R. 47.

104. An exception to this rule is where a person has been convicted of a less serious offence at a time when the *aggravated* offence arising out of the same act or transaction was not yet complete. When the aggravated offence becomes complete, the person may be charged with it notwithstanding that he has already been convicted of the less serious offence, because at that time it was not possible to prefer the more serious offence.[118]

105. Where a person has been acquitted of a cognate offence, he or she cannot again be tried or convicted for that offence in a *minor* form, except upon the order of a superior court in the course of appeal. This is so because the cognate offence contains elements of the minor offence involving the same conduct and established by the same evidence. To avoid this happening, both the Trial on Indictment Act and the Magistrates Courts Act in identical terms provide as follows:

> When a person is charged with an offence and facts are proved which reduce it to a minor cognate offence, he or she may be convicted of the minor offence although he or she was not charged with it.[119]

The Acts then list pairs of other offences in respect to which courts may convict even though they were not charged. These include the substantive offence and attempt;[120] a principal offence and being an accessory after the fact to that offence;[121] murder and infanticide;[122] murder or manslaughter of a child and killing an unborn child;[123] killing an unborn child and procuring abortion;[124] infanticide and concealment of birth;[125] manslaughter and reckless or negligent driving under the Road Traffic Act;[126] rape and indecent assault, defilement, procurement of defilement, incest and common assault;[127] incest and defilement and defilement of idiots;[128] defilement and indecent assault and procuring;[129] burglary, housebreaking and similar offences and receiving stolen goods;[130] stealing and receiving;[131]

118. See sec. 198(1) of the Penal Code. For example, in a South African case, the accused was convicted of the attempted murder of his wife by stabbing her in the spinal column and was sentenced to four years imprisonment. Whilst the accused was serving his sentence, the wife died. He was then charged with murder. He pleaded *autrefois convict*. It was held that the plea did not avail to bar the charge of murder, because at the time the charge of attempted murder was preferred the offence of murder was not yet complete; it was now complete and the accused could be validly charged with it. In Uganda, though, for the murder charge to be valid the victim must die within a year and a day after the last act that caused the death (*infra*, para. 374).
119. Trial on Indictment Act, sec. 87 and Magistrates Courts Act, sec. 145.
120. Trial on Indictment Act, sec. 88; Magistrates Courts Act, sec. 146.
121. Trial on Indictment Act, sec. 89; Magistrates Courts Act, sec. 147.
122. Trial on Indictment Act, sec. 90; Magistrates Courts Act, sec. 148.
123. Trial on Indictment Act, sec. 90; Magistrates Courts Act, sec. 148
124. *Ibid.*
125. *Ibid.*
126. Magistrates Courts Act, sec. 149.
127. Magistrates Courts Act, sec. 150.
128. Magistrates Courts Act, sec. 151.
129. Magistrates Courts Act, sec. 152.
130. Magistrates Courts Ac, sec. 153.
131. Magistrates Courts Act, sec. 154.

stealing and obtaining by false pretences;[132] and obtaining by false pretences and stealing.[133] Where, in spite of this mandate to convict for a 'minor' offence, the accused is not so convicted, he cannot be subsequently tried and convicted of that offence. To do so would be to expose him to double jeopardy for the same or substantially the same conduct.

106. Lastly, for the pleas in bar to apply, it is not sufficient that the charges in the previous and subsequent trials are based on the same facts. The offences in both charges must also be the same. The accused must have been in peril of being convicted of the offence contained in the second charge. However, sameness of the offences does not mean that they must be identical. It is sufficient if they are *substantially the same*. Thus it is not the names by which the different offences charged in the two indictments are called that matters, but the substance. If it is the same act that is being charged under different names, then the court will hold that there is substantial identity and will uphold the pleas of *autrefois acquit* or *autrefois convict* to bar the subsequent charge.

But when are the charges 'substantially the same'? They are substantially the same where the evidence necessary to prove the second charge would have been sufficient to secure a conviction on the first charge. The English case of *Connelly v. DPP* is in point.[134] The appellant took part in an armed robbery in the course of which one of the robbers shot and killed a person. The appellant was charged along with others with the murder and aggravated robbery. For some technical reasons, the prosecution did not proceed with the charge of aggravated robbery. The appellant was convicted of the murder. However, the conviction was subsequently set aside on appeal because of a misdirection by the trial judge. Thereupon the Crown resurrected the aggravated robbery charge. The appellant pleaded *autrefois acquit.* The issue was whether the acquittal for murder barred the appellant's subsequent trial for aggravated robbery. The answer to this question also turned on whether the charge of aggravated robbery was substantially the same as the charge for murder. The House of Lords answered the last question in the negative. In doing so, it applied the test whether the evidence necessary to prove murder in the previous trial would have been sufficient to prove the charge of aggravated robbery.[135] It held that it was not.[136]

132. Magistrates Courts Act, sec. 155.
133. Magistrates Courts Act, sec. 155.
134. [1964] 2 All E R. 401.
135. See particularly the speech of Lord Morris of Borth-y-Gest in this case. The test used by the judge was 'whether the evidence which is necessary to support the second indictment, or whether the facts which constitute the second offence would have been sufficient to procure a legal conviction upon the first indictment either as to the offence charged or as to an offence of which, on the indictment, the accused could have been found guilty'.
136. Said Lord Morris: 'The crimes are distinct. There can be robbery without killing. There can be killing without robbery. Evidence of robbery does not prove murder or manslaughter. Conviction of robbery cannot involve conviction of murder or manslaughter. Nor does acquittal of murder or manslaughter necessarily involve an acquittal of robbery. Nor on a charge of murder or manslaughter could a man be convicted of robbery. The fact that the two trials have much in common is not a true test of the availability of the plea of *autrefois acquit.*' *Ibid.*, at 415.

107. Mention must also be made of continuing offences. Our courts have held that such offences are not the 'same offence' as in previous proceedings as to bar subsequent proceedings. The point is well illustrated by the case of *Tororo Town Council v. P.M. Luande.*[137] The respondent was acquitted in 1969 on two counts of using a building otherwise than in accordance with approved plans, contrary to Rule 21 of the Building Rules, and failing to provide separate latrine facilities for pupils of each sex over 7 years of age at his school, contrary to Rule 11(4) of the School Building Rules (made under the Public Health Act). He was charged again in 1970 on three counts, similar to the ones in 1969, save that they were more elaborate and were alleged to have been committed on different dates. The trial magistrate dismissed the charges on the grounds that the respondent was previously acquitted of the charges. On appeal by the Town Council, the High Court reinstated the charges. It held that for the doctrine of *autrefois acquit* to apply the accused must have been put in peril for the same offence, both in fact and law, as that with which he was previously charged. It could not be said that the offences the respondent was alleged to have committed in 1970 were the same offences as those committed in 1969 even though both sets of offences were in respect of the same premises. A continuous or continuing offence creates a new offence daily. Therefore the trial magistrate was wrong in applying the acquittal in respect of the 1969 offences to those committed in 1970.

108. Related to the issue of similarity of offences are acts which are punishable under different statutes or indeed under different provisions of the same statute. If a person is convicted and punished for that act under one statute he cannot again be charged, convicted and punished for the selfsame act under a different statute. The proviso to section 3 of the Penal Code specifically provides that: 'If a person does an act which is punishable under this Code and is also punishable under another written law … , he shall not be punished for that act both under that written law and also under this Code.' Section 18 similarly provides that 'A person shall not be punished twice either under this Code or under any other law for the same offence.' The case of *Henry Kato v. R.*[138] is in point. The appellant who had no driving permit drove a motor vehicle at excessive speed and caused a collision. Four persons were injured as a result. He was charged under the Traffic Ordinance with, among other offences, reckless driving. He pleaded guilty, was convicted and sentenced. Soon thereafter, he was also charged under the Penal Code for unlawfully doing grievous harm to the four persons who were injured as a result of the collision. He pleaded guilty to the charge. He was accordingly convicted and sentenced. On appeal, the High Court set aside the charges based on the Penal Code and quashed the convictions. Relying on the provisions of the Penal Code cited above, the Court said that the appellant had committed but one act which was punishable under both the Traffic Ordinance and the Penal Code. As he had already been punished for reckless driving, he could not be punished for the offence under the Penal Code.

137. H.Ct.Monthly Bulletin No. 357 of 1971.
138. [1960] E.A. 981.

109. The case of *Kassim Mpanga v. Uganda,* however, relates to cumulatively charging a person under different provisions of the same statute for offences based on the same conduct. The appellant was charged and convicted before a Magistrate's Court with, *inter alia*, the offences of causing financial loss, contrary to section 258(1) and abuse of office, contrary to section 83(1) of the Penal Code.[139] The transaction in both charges was identical. The particulars of offence for causing financial loss read as follows:

> Kassim Mpanga between November, 1989 and May, 1992 at Libyan Arab Uganda Bank, Masaka in Masaka District being employed as a Manager of Libyan Arab Uganda, Masaka branch while in due execution of his duties knowingly did an act or omission to wit he authorized without authority from the General Manager of the Bank the payment of overdrafts of Shs 150m/= thereby causing financial loss to the said Libyan Arab Uganda Bank.

The particulars of offence for abuse of office read as follows:

> Kassim Mpanga between November 1989 and May, 1992 at Libyan Arab Uganda Bank, Masaka Branch, in Masaka district, being employed in the said Libyan Arab Uganda as Manager did in abuse of the authority of his office, an arbitrary act prejudicial to the interests of his employer the said Libyan Arab Uganda bank to wit, by giving overdrafts totaling Shs. 150m/= without security thereby causing actual loss of the said amount to the Bank.

The elements of the two offences were slightly different and, *stricto sensu,* the appellant was not convicted of the 'same offence.' Nevertheless, the charges were based on exactly the same facts or transactions, i.e., the authorization of payment of overdrafts of UGX 150 as indicated in the particulars of offence above. In effect, the appellant was punished twice for exactly the same conduct. It appears that by convicting and punishing the appellant twice for the same conduct, the court violated the spirit of the Penal Code. It also violated the well-known English common law principle of *nemo debut bis puniri uno delicto*. Lord Cockburn summed it up well when he said that '[I]t is a fundamental rule of law that out of the same facts a series of charges shall not be preferred.'[140] It is against this principle, as was done in this case, to duplicate convictions out of conduct that is in essence one offence. The fact that the sentences on the two convictions were ordered to run concurrently does not excuse or mitigate the prejudice to the accused of the duplication of the charges and convictions. Such duplication unnecessarily magnifies the accused person's moral blameworthiness and his or her criminal record beyond what it actually is, complicates the defence and makes it more costly. So, in this case, the prosecution should have charged either the two offences in the alternative or only the one causing financial loss, which carries a heavier sentence.

---

139. Cr. App. No. 30 of 1994, [1995] UGSC 14 (13 Sep. 1995). See also *Namuddu Christine v. Uganda*, Cr. Appl. No. 3 of 1999, [2001] UGSC 2 (17 Jan. 2001) where the Supreme Court granted the applicant leave to appeal in a case of a similar nature.
140. *The Queen v. Elrington* 9 Cox C. C. 86 (1891), at 90.

110. It is noteworthy that the Constitution only refers to a person who has been tried by a competent court 'and either convicted' of a criminal offence as the beneficiary of the *ne bis in idem* protection. However, in *Attorney Genera v. Uganda Law Society,*[141] the Supreme Court extended the protection to cover persons who were being concurrently tried before different courts but for offences based on the same facts. It held that concurrent criminal proceedings in respect of the same facts entailed trial more than once. The facts of the case were that twenty-three persons were charged before the High Court with treason and, in the alternative, concealment of treason. They applied for and were granted bail, but while their release papers were being processed heavily armed security agents invaded the High Court and prevented their release, and they were instead returned to prison.[142] The next day they were taken to the General Court Martial and charged with terrorism and unlawful possession of firearms. These charges were based on the same facts as the charges before the High Court. In an appeal against the decision of the Constitutional Court condemning the concurrent proceedings before the High Court and the General Court Martial as a contravention of Article 28(9) of the Constitution, the Attorney General argued that the provision only applies to situations where a person has been convicted or acquitted and not, as here, where the accused persons had not been convicted or acquitted by any court. The Supreme Court rejected the arguments and dismissed the appeal on the ground, *inter alia,* that the concurrent proceedings before the two courts offended against the *ne ne bis in idem* rule. Mulenga JJ. S.C. said:

> I also agree with the majority of the Constitutional Court that the concurrent proceedings in the two courts were inconsistent with the principle underlying the provision in Article 28 (9) of the Constitution, which prohibits the trial of a person for an offence of which he or she has been convicted or acquitted. In effect that provision is an aspect of the protection of the right to fair hearing, namely the right not to be tried more than once on the same *actus reus.* The principle behind that right originates from an old English common law maxim that '*no man is to be brought in jeopardy of life or limb more than once for the same offence.*' I agree with the proposition invoked by Okello J.A (as he then was) that a constitutional provision which relates to a fundamental right must be given an interpretation that realises that full benefit of the guaranteed right. Article 28 (9) is such a provision that must be given such interpretation, and not the narrow interpretation urged by the appellant.

The Supreme Court also found the proceedings before the General Court Martial to be a nullity, because in the circumstance of the case that court had no jurisdiction to try persons who were not subject to military law; it also had no jurisdiction to try the accused for terrorism, because under the Anti-Terrorism Act only the High Court

141. Const. Appeal No. 1 of 2006 [2009] UGSC 2 (20 Jan. 2009).

142. The Constitutional Court held that the actions of the security personnel 'fostered fear and anxiety especially as the security went beyond their security intentioned limits and they entered the criminal registry and cells where it is alleged they interrupted the course of the court's normal processing bail for the accused persons'.

has power to try that offence. As we shall see in the subsequent sections of this book, the state's actions and charges not only constituted a flagrant violation of the accused persons' constitutional 'rights and of the independence of the judiciary,[143] but were also an unfortunate abuse of prosecutorial power and of the courts' processes.

111. Related to the issue of double jeopardy is the question of pardon. Article 28(10) of the Constitution provides that 'No person shall be tried for a criminal offence if the person shows that he or she has been pardoned in respect of that offence.' For this provision to operate, the accused person must prove to the court that he or she has actually been pardoned by exhibiting an instrument to that effect signed by the President. A mere general government declaration of amnesty is not sufficient to bar proceeding.[144]

143. The Constitutional Court held that 'the acts of the security agents at the High Court premises constituted acts of security interference that contravened Article 23(1), (6), 28(1) and violated the Judiciary's independence'.

144. *Brigadier Smith Opon Achak & Anor v. Uganda* Cr. App. No. 18 of 1992, [1993] UGSC 10 (5 Nov. 1993).

Chapter 2. Enforcement of Criminal Law

§1. Principles Concerning the Enforcement of Criminal Law in Relation to Time

112. Some countries impose time-limits within which criminal proceedings against an individual must be commenced.[145] Once the prescribed time lapses, any criminal proceedings commenced afterwards are time-barred.

113. Time-limits are more common in civil than in criminal proceedings. There are merits in imposing such limits in criminal proceedings as well. It is a fundamental constitutional principle that when a person is suspected of having committed a crime, he or she must be brought to justice within a reasonable time. As is often said, 'justice delayed is justice denied' and 'justice is sweetest when it is freshest'. Time-limits force the hand of an otherwise tardy prosecuting authority to expeditiously investigate crime and to prosecute suspected criminals in a timely manner.

114. Timely institution of criminal proceedings enables the affected individual to order his or her affairs with certainty. If he or she is found guilty, he or she pays the penalty and thereafter makes a fresh start in life. If he or she is found not guilty, his or her name is cleared and he or she is able to go about his or her affairs without psychological or other inhibitions. Barring the institution of stale cases also ensures that criminal proceedings are not used as an instrument of oppression by resurrecting matters that are long forgotten by the community. Moreover, delayed prosecutions prejudice the proper administration of justice. Witnesses to the alleged crime may have long died, left the jurisdiction for unknown destinations, or, because of the long lapse of time, forgotten what had actually transpired. The evidence, too, may have been damaged, destroyed or lost.

115. However, save for a few specific exceptions, Uganda does not impose time-limits within which criminal proceedings may be commenced. In this respect, Uganda is again following the English practice. According to an English constitutional principle, the Crown does no wrong, and the Crown's delay in instituting criminal proceedings cannot operate as a bar to any proceedings it may be minded to institute at any time. The indigenous view on the matter expressed in a Luganda adage is that *Omusango teguvunda* (i.e., to say, 'a case does not rot'). The case stays alive and can be taken up at any time.

116. The exceptions in which time-limits are imposed include the following offences: acts of treason, (with the exception of causing or attempting the death of the President, or wounding or pointing a gun of any description at the President); acts intended to annoy, alarm or ridicule the President; concealment of treason; and

145. See for example, the Botswana Criminal Procedure and Evidence Act, Cap. 08:02, sec. 26. It provides as follows: 'The right of prosecution for murder shall not be barred by any lapse of time; but the right of prosecution for any other offence, whether at public instance or at the instance of a private party, shall, unless some other period is expressly provided by law, be barred by the lapse of 20 years from the time when the offence was committed.'

promoting war on chiefs. Prosecution for these offences must be commenced within five years after the commission of the offence.[146] Additionally, according to the Magistrates Courts Act, the lapse of twelve months is a bar to the prosecution before the magistrates' courts of any offence which is punishable by imprisonment of up to six months or a fine of up to UGX 1,000.[147]

117. It is only a matter of conjecture why the above offences were singled out as exceptions to the general rule and subjected to time prescriptions. The reasons or the criteria used for the exceptions are not mentioned anywhere in official records. Treason is an offence against the political order and tranquility of the country. It excites political passion. With the lapse of five years, the threat it might have posed to the political order and to the calm and repose in the country might have ebbed and the political excitement it might have stirred will have died down. Prosecutions after five years might therefore be counter-productive. They might reopen old wounds and unnecessarily jeopardize the peace and calm that might otherwise be prevailing in the country. With minor offences whose adverse effect to the public weal is slight, it might not be worth the effort and expense to commence prosecutions after twelve months. Benefits that might accrue from belated prosecutions might be outweighed by a competing public interest: that persons suspected of having committed criminal offences be brought to justice within a reasonable time. The triviality or otherwise of an offence is a factor which is taken into account in determining what is reasonable time.

§2. Principles Concerning the Enforcement of Criminal Law in Relation to Place

I. Territorial Principle

118. According to a general principle of customary international law, a state's competence to exercise its sovereignty is limited to things, persons and events that take place on its territory. It exercises that sovereignty through its legislative, administrative and judicial organs. Absent a recognized exception to that principle or a treaty provision to the contrary, a state's actions, be they legislative, administrative or judicial, purporting to exercise sovereignty over persons, things and events beyond its borders infringe the sovereignty and territorial independence of other states. The states affected by such actions are entitled to remonstrate with the erring state and to demand reparations from it.

119. Accordingly, absent a recognized exception or a treaty provision, a state's competence to enforce its criminal law is limited to crimes committed within its borders. Needless to say, persons who violate a state's criminal law and escape to the territory of another state can be returned for trial, but only with the consent and

146. See sec. 28 of the Penal Code.

147. See sec. 155. Proceedings commenced after the lapse of the time-limits are a nullity. See the English case of *R. v. Lewis* [1979] 2 All E.R. 665.

assistance of that other state. As is often said, crime is territorial. In this sense, territory includes a country's land and territorial sea as well as the air space above its land and territorial sea. Additionally, ships carrying a flag of a country are regarded as an extension of the territory of the flag state. Likewise airplanes bearing the registration of a country are also regarded as extensions of that country's territory. Crimes committed aboard such ships or on airplanes are therefore triable by the courts of the states concerned.

120. In deference to the territorial principle, the Penal Code provides that 'The jurisdiction of the courts of Uganda for the purposes of this Code extends to every place *within* Uganda.'[148] Therefore, absent a recognized exception explicitly provided for by statute, the courts of Uganda do not have jurisdiction over crimes committed outside Uganda, not even by a Ugandan citizen.[149] Indeed, as a rule of interpretation, the courts presume that Parliament never intended to pass laws with extra-territorial effect unless that intention was expressly stated in the given statute. In deference to this rule, the High Court in *Balaki Kirya & Anor. v. Uganda*[150] refused to assume jurisdiction over alleged treasonable acts and meetings, which took place in Kenya. The fact that some people travelled from Uganda to Kenya to attend the meetings did not affect those accused who were always in Kenya. In an earlier case in 1933, the court held that it could not convict the accused who stood charged with possession of or conveying in Uganda property stolen in Kenya.[151] However, the Penal Code has since been amended to provide as follows:

> Any person who, without lawful excuse, knowing or having reason to believe the same to have been stolen or obtained in any way whatsoever under such circumstances that if the act had been committed in Uganda the person committing it would have been guilty of a felony or misdemeanour, receives or has in his possession any property so stolen or obtained outside Uganda, is guilty of an offence of the like degree (whether felony or misdemeanour) and is liable to imprisonment for seven years.[152]

121. It should be stressed, however, that it is not the act of stealing or unlawfully obtaining property outside Uganda that is being punished. That would be assuming jurisdiction over conduct that occurred outside Uganda. It is rather the *receiving or possessing in* Uganda of property which is known to have been criminally obtained from outside the country that is the focus of the provision. The provision teaches persons who engage in trans-border crime that crime does not pay by denying them the fruit of such crime. It also serves to discourage the crime and to contribute to the world-wide fight against crime generally.

148. Section 4(1). Emphasis added.
149. See *Uganda v. Atama Mustapha* [1975] H.Ct.Monthly Bulletin 254 wherein Manyindo, J. said that 'The courts of this country have no jurisdiction in a case like the present one, over a Uganda national for his acts committed wholly outside Uganda.'
150. H.Ct.Session No. 75 of 1984 (unreported).
151. *R. v. Onyango s/o Nanzalo* [1932–1935] 5 U.L.R. 69.
152. Section 317.

II. Objective Territorial Principle

122. Closely related to the territorial principle is the objective territorial principle. This principle, based on customary international law,[153] relates to acts or offences that are started in one jurisdiction and completed in another. The state where the acts start has jurisdiction over the perpetrator because he is on its territory when he commits the act. The state where the act ends also has jurisdiction over the perpetrator (if he comes to its territory), because that is where the impact of the act is felt. Thus, section 5 of the Penal Code provides that:

> When an act which, if wholly done within the jurisdiction of the court, would be an offence against this Code is done partly within and partly beyond the jurisdiction every person who within the jurisdiction does or makes any part of such act may be tried and punished under this Code in the same manner as if such act had been done wholly within the jurisdiction.

123. According to this provision, the courts do not have jurisdiction over all acts done partly within and partly outside Uganda. For the courts to have jurisdiction over such acts, the perpetrator must be '*within the jurisdiction* when he does or makes any such act'. They will thus not have jurisdiction to try a person standing on the Kenya side of the Uganda-Kenya border who fires a shot across the border and kills somebody on the Ugandan territory, because that person is not 'within the jurisdiction' of the courts. But they will have jurisdiction to try a person who while on Ugandan territory fires a shot and kills a person across the border. It does not matter that the victim is on Kenyan territory and is not a Ugandan citizen.

124. Another related activity with trans-national dimensions is conspiracy to commit crimes in other countries. Section 390 of the Penal Code provides that:

> Any person who conspires with another to commit any felony, or to do any act in any part of the world which if done in Uganda would be a felony and which is an offence under the laws in force in the place where it is proposed to be done, commits a felony.

125. Conspiracy involves agreement between two or more persons. Where all the co-conspirators consummate the agreement on Uganda territory, Ugandan courts would doubtless have jurisdiction over them. The problem arises where one or more of the co-conspirators are in Uganda and the other or others are outside. The provision does not, as say, the Botswana Penal Code,[154] restrict the Ugandan courts' jurisdiction to only the co-conspirators on Ugandan soil. The question, then, is whether under international law, it would be valid or legitimate for the Ugandan courts to assume jurisdiction over the co-conspirators outside Uganda. Be that as it

153. See the S.S. Lotus Case (*France v. Turkey*) 1227 P.C.I.J. (ser.A) No. 10 (Sep. 7).

154. Section 61 (1) of the Botswana Penal Code restricts the Botswana courts' jurisdiction to 'Any person who while in Botswana – (a) conspires with any other person to commit within a state or territory other than Botswana … any act of violence … '

may, however, this provision aims at stopping people from using Ugandan territory as a launching pad for criminal activities in other countries. It enables Uganda to cooperate with those countries in the fight against trans-national crime, particularly at a time of an ever escalating incidence of terrorism.

III. Exceptions to the Territorial Principle

126. The territorial principle is not absolute. There are several exceptions to the principle under which the courts of a country may assume extra-terrial jurisdiction. The exceptions are generally accepted under customary international law. They are however subject to the rule of statutory interpretation under which the Uganda courts presume that Parliament did not intend to give extra-territorial effect to any of its legislation unless it made that intention explicitly clear. Therefore in the absence of that explicit intention, the exceptions discussed below will not be given effect in Uganda.

127. The first exception is the universality principle. Under this principle, the courts of any country may exercise criminal jurisdiction over *any* person who commits acts that are recognized as international crimes, *irrespective of the place where they are committed and irrespective of the nationality of the perpetrator or of the victim.* International crimes are crimes that are reckoned to be committed against the entire international community. They threaten the very existence of the human race, violate internationally cherished values or interfere with normal intercourse between peoples and states, and imperil international travel, commerce and navigation. Perpetrators of such acts are regarded as *hostis humanis generis*, enemies of humankind. It is the duty of every state to repress these crimes. In doing so, states act as agents and on behalf of the international community as a whole.[155] However, to be able to do so they must, under the universality principle, vest their courts with jurisdiction to try the perpetrators. Moreover, under the principle of *aut dedere aut judicare* a state on whose territory a perpetrator of international crimes resides, has a duty either to prosecute or to surrender the perpetrator to any other state that may be able and willing to prosecute.

128. International crimes include aggression, genocide, crimes against humanity, war crimes, piracy *jus gentium* and airplane high jacking. Until the enactment of the ICC Act in 2010, Uganda had not yet legislated against any international crime, save for piracy.[156] The Act gives effect to the Rome Statute of the ICC to which Uganda is a party. The Statute, having stated in its preamble that ‘it is the duty of every state to exercise its criminal jurisdiction over those responsible for

155. It was under this principle that a Canadian court tried and convicted a Rwandan national, of genocide, crimes against humanity and war crimes committed in Rwanda in 1994. *Queen v. Desire Munanyeza* [2009] QCCS 2201 (Quebec Superior Court, 22 May 2009).
156. Section 55 of the Penal Code.

international crimes', goes on to provide in Article 1 that the Court 'shall be complementary to national criminal jurisdictions'. In compliance with Uganda's obligations under the Statute, the Act vests in the High Court jurisdiction to try any person who whether 'in Uganda or elsewhere' commits the crimes of genocide, crimes against humanity and war crimes.[157] By vesting in our courts jurisdiction over these crimes when committed outside the country, the Act ensures that Uganda is not a safe haven for the perpetrators of the crimes, thus contributing to the global effort against impunity. The Act also adopts wholesale the definitions of these crimes as contained in the Rome Statute.[158] It also lays down a legal framework for cooperation between Uganda and the ICC in the various matters provided for under the Rome Statute.

129. The second exception to the territorial principle is the nationality principle. The nationality principle is based on the bond of nationality under which an individual owes allegiance to the country of his or her country of nationality. One of the consequences of that allegiance is the individual's continued obligation to obey the country's laws. His or her absence from that country does not sever his allegiance to the country nor does it extinguish his or her obligation to obey its laws, particularly those that aim at protecting its national security and its economic well-being. Therefore, customary international law generally permits states to enforce their criminal laws against their nationals for acts which endanger their national security and their national economies that they commit whilst abroad. States are, however, careful not to extend unnecessarily the range of crimes committed by their citizens whilst abroad, for by so doing they will be purporting to regulate the conduct of persons on other states' territory, and this might amount to unwarranted interference in those states' internal affairs. In keeping with these principles, section 4 of the Penal Code empowers the Ugandan courts to try certain security-related offences committed 'outside Uganda by a Ugandan citizen or a person ordinarily resident in Uganda' as if they had been committed in Uganda. The offences are treason, acts intended to alarm, annoy or ridicule the President, concealment of treason, terrorism and promoting war on chiefs.[159] The only unsatisfactory feature of these provisions is the reference to 'a person ordinarily resident in Uganda'. Such a person is not defined anywhere in the Code.

130. Related to the nationality principle is the passive nationality principle exception. Under the passive nationality principle, a state may exercise jurisdiction over serious crimes involving life and limb committed against its nationals on foreign territory. The United States exercised such jurisdiction over persons that were suspected to have been responsible for the bombing of the US embassy in Nairobi,

157. With respect to war crimes it is noteworthy that the Geneva Conventions Act, which makes grave breaches of the Geneva Conventions an offence in Uganda, will continue to exist alongside the Act.
158. Sections 7, 8 and 9 of the Act.
159. Section 4(2) and (3). This provision was incorporated into the Code in 1984 by the Penal Code (Amendment) Act, Act No. 9 of 1984 and was given retrospective effect. However, *in Balaki Kirya & Anor. v. Uganda* H.Ct.Cr.Session No. 75 of 1984 (unreported), the High Court held that the provision did not apply to acts that were allegedly committed in 1981 and 1982.

Kenya and thereby killing or injuring US and other nationals. The principle grows out of every state's right to protect its citizens wheresoever they may be. However, to prevent abuse, particularly by powerful states over the weaker ones, the victim's state of nationality should not exercise jurisdiction unless the territorial state has proved to be unable or unwilling to do so. The territorial state should be given an opportunity to act first. To date there is no legislation giving our courts jurisdiction based on the passive nationality principle.

§3. Principles Concerning the Enforcement of Criminal Law in Relation to Persons

I. Infants

131. According to the Children's Act, 'the minimum age of responsibility shall be twelve years'.[160]

This means that a person below that age is not responsible or cannot, on account of his or her tender age, be blamed and justly punished for what he or she has done or omitted to do. He or she is said to be *doli incapax* (not capable of crime). However, for international crimes falling under the ICC Act, the age of responsibility is 18 years.[161]

132. Prior to 1996, the Penal Code made a distinction between persons 'under the apparent age of seven years' and persons 'under the apparent age of 12'.[162] The former were absolutely *doli incapax*. The latter were also presumed to be *doli incapax* 'unless it is proved that at the time of doing the act or making the omission, he had capacity to know that he ought not to do the act or make the omission'.[163] This meant that a child between 7 and 12 years of age could be convicted of a criminal offence if the prosecution proved that he had a 'mischievous intention' – knowledge that what he did or omitted to do was morally or legally wrong.

133. Thus in *Uganda v. Yowasi Birungi* the accused, a child of about 10 years of age, was convicted on his own plea of guilty of theft of a hen, and was sentenced to a two-year probation. On the matter being referred to the High Court, the conviction was quashed. The prosecution had apparently not led evidence or stated facts from the bar indicating that the accused had the requisite mischievous intention, and the accused was not asked whether he agreed with such evidence or facts.[164]

The prosecution could apparently rebut the presumption by showing that the child came from a good family and had good upbringing and should have known better. According to this view, a child from a bad family background with poor upbringing and who would probably derive more benefit from the criminal process fared

160. Section 88.
161. See Art. 26 of the Rome Statute which provides that 'The Court shall have no jurisdiction over any person who was under the age of 18 at the time of the alleged commission of a crime.'
162. Section 14(1).
163. Section 14(2).
164. [1973] U.L.R. 47.

better![165] All this is now history as the Children Act, by repealing section 14 of the Penal Code, also abolished the distinction between children below the age of 7 and those between 7 and 12 years of age. All children below 12 now enjoy immunity from criminal prosecution.

134. Are children who are *doli incapax*, then, at large to go on hurting members of the community with impunity? Does the law provide any protection against wayward children? It does. Such children may be dealt with civilly by a children's court, as children in need of care or protection or children beyond control. The children's court before which such children are brought can make an appropriate order for their care.[166]

135. In Britain, boys under the age of 14 are irrebuttably presumed to be incapable of having sexual intercourse.[167] In Botswana, the presumption attaches to boys under 12.[168] In these countries, a boy who has not attained the prescribed age cannot therefore be convicted of rape, attempted rape, defilement or any other offence involving sexual intercourse. There is no such provision in the Ugandan Penal Code or in any other statute. Children above the age of 12 years are thus legally capable of engaging in sexual relations and may be prosecuted and convicted of sex-related offences.

136. It is important to note that most people in Uganda do not have birth certificates or other written records regarding their date of birth. It is not therefore feasible to determine their ages with certainty. In determining the ages of the accused, the courts often rely on medical evidence, opinions of elderly people and on their own impressions of the appearances and demeanour of the accused.[169]

II. Corporations

A. General Rules on Corporate Criminal Liability

137. Corporations include companies registered under the Companies Act, cooperative societies registered under the Cooperative Societies Act, and parastatal bodies and other public institutions created under special statutes. In law, a corporation is a person. It has an existence which is independent of its members. It can

165. See Glanville Williams, *Textbook of Criminal Law*, 638, and Cross & Jones, *Introduction to Criminal Law*, 78.
166. See The Children Act, Cap. 59, sec. 58.
167. See Cross & Jones, *Introduction to Criminal Law* 79 (9th ed., Butterworths 1980).
168. Botswana Penal Code, Cap. 08:01, sec. 15(3).
169. In the Kenya case of *Republic v. Wamboi Kamau* [1965] E.A. 548, the accused, a girl below 10, was charged with the murder of a baby left temporarily in her care. The judge relied on views of a physician who had examined her and on his own impressions and those of the assessors and held that she had not, at the time of the alleged crime attained the statutory age of 8 and was therefore not criminally responsible. Section 108(2) of the Children Act provides that 'a certificate signed by a medical officer as to the age of a person under the age of eighteen years shall be evidence of that age'. It is moot whether such evidence is conclusive or may be rebutted.

sue and be sued in its own names. It can acquire property and incur debts in its own names and independently of its members. The members qua members have no title to such property and are not responsible for such debts (beyond their share holdings if it is a company limited by shares).

138. As a legal person, a corporation must obey the law regulating the type of activities it is engaged in. Failure to obey the law will invariably result in the corporation incurring sanctions. The irksome issue, however, is whether the corporation is capable of obeying the general criminal law of the land. Put differently, can a corporation commit criminal offences, particularly those that require a guilty mind or *mens rea*? As an artificial and impalpable being, a corporation has no soul or mind and is incapable of appreciating moral principles and duties. For this reason, courts in England did not hold corporations criminally responsible, save for statutory and strict liability offences.

139. However, under the principle of identification developed by the English courts since 1944, corporations can now be found criminally responsible even for offences that require *mens rea*. Under this principle, the acts and state of mind of the principal officers of the corporation are attributed to the corporation itself. The principle, which Professor Gower refers to as the organic theory, was crisply articulated by Lord Reid as follows:

> A living person has a mind which can have knowledge or intention or be negligent and he has hands to carry out his intentions. A corporation has none of these: it must act through living persons, though not always one and the same person. Then the person who acts is not speaking or acting for the company. He is acting as the company and his mind which directs his acts is the mind of the company. There is no question of the company being vicariously liable. He is not acting as a servant, representative, agent or delegate. He is an embodiment of the company, or, one could say, he hears and speaks through the *persona* of the company, within his appropriate sphere, and his mind is the mind of the company. If it is a guilty mind then that guilt is the guilt of the company.[170]

140. Before a corporate functionary's acts and state of mind can be attributed to the corporation that functionary must indeed be part of the brains or the prime movers of the corporation's policy and decision-making mechanism. Functionaries who meet these criteria include members of the board of directors, chief executive officers and others at the same or equivalent level. Thus in the *Tesco Supermarkets* case, the English court ruled that a shop assistant who, contrary to the manager's instructions, sold an item in the shop at a price higher than the advertised price and in contravention of the Trade Description Act 1968, was not a person senior enough to represent 'the directing mind and will of the of the company'. Moreover where there has been delegation of authority, such delegation must be total, and the delegate must not be subject to supervision or control of someone else. Importantly, too,

170. *Tesco Supermarkets Ltd. v. Nattrass* [1971] A.C. 153, 170.

before a functionary's actions can be ascribed to the company, such functionary must have acted managerially on matters that concern the corporation's affairs, and not in a private capacity. Whether a given individual satisfies these indicia is always a question of fact depending on the circumstances of each case.

141. Although under the doctrine of identification corporations are liable for a myriad of crimes, they cannot be liable for offences such as rape whose *actus reus* can only be committed by natural persons. Similarly, they cannot be liable for offences such as treason, murder, manslaughter or rape which are punishable only by physical sanctions, for example death or imprisonment. These punishments cannot be imposed on corporations, and courts of law do not act in vain. It is nevertheless within Parliament's Powers to amend the law and prescribe different punishments for corporations that commit these offences.

142. Generally speaking, since a corporation commits crimes only through its principal officers it would be fair to punish those officers as accessories to their *alter ego's* crimes. This is necessary for effective deterrence, which is a principal objective of the criminal law.[171] It is important to stress, though, that before such officers are punished they should also be charged alongside the company and tried. They should not be punished unless they have been given an opportunity to be heard according to the *audi altarem partem* principle.[172] Though desirable, the cited provision or its equivalent does not exist in the Uganda Penal Code or any other statute.

143. To facilitate the bringing of corporations to court, section 53 of the Magistrates Courts Act provides as follows:

(1) Appearances before a magistrate's court by a corporation in criminal proceedings shall be by an advocate or by an officer of the corporation.
(2) Notwithstanding anything contained in the articles of association, bylaws or other document governing the constitution of such corporation and notwithstanding anything in any other law contained, an officer appearing in court on behalf of a corporation shall be deemed so to appear with the full authority of such corporation, and to have full power to represent the corporation.

144. 'Officer' of the corporation means the secretary, local manager or other principal officer of the company. It is thus on the officers of the corporation that the court process such as summons are served. If an officer who has been duly served

171. Section 26 of the Botswana Penal Code is instructive to this effect. It provides as follows: 'Where an offence is committed by any company or other body corporate, or by any society, association or body of persons, every person charged with, or concerned or acting in the control or management of the affairs or activities of such company, body corporate, society, association or body of persons shall be guilty of that offence and liable to be punished accordingly, unless it is proved by such person that, through no act or omission on his part, he was not aware that the offence was being or was intended or was about to be committed, or that he took all reasonable steps to prevent its commission.'
172. See the Botswana case of *In re Wright* [1996] B.L.R. 689.

with the court processes fails, without cause, to appear he may be compelled to appear by way of a warrant of arrest.

145. Lastly, it is worth noting that when a company or corporation is wound up, liquidated, dissolved or otherwise struck off the register, it ceases to exist; it is dead in law. Criminal proceedings against it and against its erstwhile officers would be incompetent. In this connection, it is conceivable that in dissolving the company its management may be attempting to avoid the company's criminal prosecution for crimes it committed during their stewardship. In this respect, then, it is important that government departments concerned with company matters act with utmost caution before they deregister any company or corporation.

B. The Particular Case of Unlawful Societies

146. Section 57 of the Penal Code makes it an offence for any person to manage or assist in managing an unlawful society. Similarly section 58 makes it an offence to be a member or to hold oneself as a member or in other ways spelt out in the provision to support such society. Section 56 defines a society to be 'any combination of two or more persons whether the society is known by any name or not'. A society is unlawful if it is formed for any of the following purposes or if it encourages or supports any such purpose:

(i) levying war or encouraging or assisting any person to levy war on the Government or the inhabitants of any part of Uganda;
(ii) killing or injuring or inciting to the killing or injuring of any person;
(iii) destroying or injuring or inciting to the destruction or injuring of any property;
(iv) subverting or promoting the subversion of the Government or of its officials;
(v) committing or inciting to acts of violence or intimidation;
(vi) interfering with or resisting or inciting to interfering with or resistance to the administration of the law; or
(vii) disturbing or inciting to the disturbance of peace and order in any part of Uganda.

A society would also be an unlawful society where the Minister by statutory order declares it to be a dangerous society.

147. The societies covered under these provisions include loose combinations that are unregistered with the Registrar of companies. The combinations cannot as such commit any offence and consequently cannot be prosecuted for so doing. It is membership in or support for the societies that the law focuses on and makes criminal. Nonetheless, if an individual in addition to being a member of an unlawful association commits any of the listed offences, he or she may additionally be charged with the offence.

III. The President

148. Section 98(4) of the Constitution provides that 'while holding office, the President shall not be liable to proceedings in any court'. This rule is derived from English constitutional law under which the king or queen is immune from court proceedings. The archaic basis for the immunity was the notion that the king or queen did no wrong. As the sovereign and the law giver, he/she was not subject to the law of his/her realm. During today's democratic era, immunity can only be justified on the need to protect the dignity of the high office of the head-of-state.

149. However, immunity from court proceedings does not place the President above the law. It does not confer on him or her license to violate the law. On the contrary, the President when assuming office swears to uphold and defend the law and the Constitution. He or she is therefore under a duty to observe the law. Immunity is only from court proceedings, not from liability or from the operations of the law. Therefore, on ceasing to be President, he may be prosecuted or sued for all crimes committed or obligations incurred whilst in office. He or she cannot avoid conviction or liability by pleading presidential immunity. Immunity, it must be stressed, is conferred on an incumbent solely for purposes of preserving the dignity of the office of President and for ensuring that whilst he or she is discharging the onerous responsibilities of President, he or she is not embarrassed. Thus, the High Court held in *A. Bauman & Co. (V) Limited v. Sir Wilberforce Nadiope* that the defendant on being stripped of immunity as the Kyabazinga of Busoga by virtue of Act 9 of 1966 could be sued just like anybody else in respect of all obligations he incurred whilst in office as the Kyabazinga.[173]

150. Ordinarily, because of the principles of sovereign independence and the equality of states, *par in parem imperium non habet*, or an equal has no power over an equal, a state is not amenable to the jurisdiction of another sovereign without its consent. According to customary international law, a sovereign and his or her duly accredited representative, absent his or her consent, is not amenable to the jurisdiction of the courts of another sovereign.[174] By visiting the territory of another sovereign, he or she does not thereby subject himself or herself to that sovereign's jurisdiction, for that would be to compromise his or her independence. Consequently, a visiting Head-of-State or his duly accredited representative cannot be arrested or prosecuted in the courts of the host state. In contrast, the Rome Statute for the ICC does not recognize any immunity based on office or any other status. Article 27 provides as follows:

1. The Statute shall apply to all persons without distinction based on official capacity. In particular, official capacity as Head of State or Government, a

173. H.Ct.Monthly Bulletin 58 of 1968.
174. For instance in the case of the *Arrest Warrant of 11 April 2000 (Democratic Republic of the Congo v. Belgium), Judgment, I.C.J. Reports 2002*, p. 3, the International Court of Justice held that on the basis of customary international law, Mr Abdulaye Yerodia Ndombasi as Foreign Minister of the DRC enjoyed immunity from criminal jurisdiction and could therefore not be prosecuted in the courts of Belgian.

member of a Government or parliament, an elected representative or a government official shall in no case exempt a person from criminal responsibility under this Statute, nor shall it, in and of itself, constitute a ground for reduction of sentence.

2. Immunities or special procedural rules which may attach to the official capacity of a person, whether under national or international law, shall not bar the Court from exercising its jurisdiction over such person.

151. The import of these provisions is that, unlike the Ugandan constitutional provisions discussed above, the Court does not have to wait for an incumbent to cease to be President before it can prosecute him or her for crimes under the Statute he or she might have committed. If that was the case, the Court would fail in its mission of ensuring that 'the most serious crimes of concern to the international community as a whole must not go unpunished'. Its mandate to end impunity for these crimes would come to naught. Too many leaders in too many places around the globe stay in office virtually for life and in the course of their tenure commit untold crimes against their citizens with impunity, sheltering themselves under immunities conferred on them under national law or customary and conventional international law. The ICC was created to counterbalance this unfortunate situation. For that reason, the Rome Statute disregards all immunities under those laws and authorizes the Court to indict, try and, on conviction, punish anyone – including serving Heads of State – irrespective of status.[175] However, for these provisions to be efficacious States Parties to the Rome Statute must: (1) ensure that under their ICC implementing law, no one enjoys immunity from prosecution for ICC-type crimes; and (2) be ready and willing to cooperate with the Court, when requested, to arrest and to surrender to the Court all indicted individuals, including serving Heads of State, who come to their territory; this is an obligation that they assume under the Rome Statute.[176] They must not refuse to do so, as some have done, claiming to be constrained by Head-of-State immunity under national, or customary or conventional international law.[177] The mandatory provisions of the Rome Statute and, particularly in the case of Security Council referrals, Articles 24(1), 25 and 103 of the UN Charter, override those 'constraints'.

---

175. See *Prosecutor v. Al Bashir*, Decision on the Prosecutor's Application for a Warrant of Arrest against Omar Hassan Ahmad Al Bashir ICC-02/05-01/09 4 Mar. 2009; *Situation in the Libyan Arab Jamahiriya*, Decision on the 'Prosecutor's Application Pursuant to Art. 58 as to Muammar Mohammed Abu Minyar GADDAFI, Saif Al-Islam GADDAFI and Abdullah AL-SENUSSI.'

176. See Art. 89 of the statute.

177. See *Prosecutor v. Al Bashir*, Corrigendum to the Decision Pursuant to Art. 87(7) of the Rome Statute on the Failure by the Republic of Malawi to Comply with Cooperation Requests Issued by the Coyrt with Respect to the Arrest and Surrender of Omar Hassan Ahmad Al Bashir, ICC-02/05-01/09-139-Corr 13 Dec. 2011, where Pre-Trial Chamber I stated as follows: '[A]ll the States referenced above have ratified this Statute and/or entrusted this Court with exercising 'its jurisdiction over persons for the most serious crimes of international concern.' It is facially inconsistent for Malawi to entrust the Court with this mandate and then refuse to surrender a Head of State prosecuted for orchestrating genocide, war crimes and crimes against humanity. To interpret Art. 98(1) in such a way so as to justify not surrendering Omar Al Bashir on immunity grounds would disable the Court and international criminal justice in ways completely contrary to the purpose of the Statute Malawi has ratified.'

IV. Diplomats and Consuls

152. Diplomatic agents accredited to Uganda also enjoy absolute immunity from local criminal jurisdiction. This is so by virtue of the 1961 Vienna Convention on Diplomatic Relations. The Convention has been incorporated into the Uganda law by the Diplomatic Privileges Act of 1965.

153. According to Article 1 of the Convention, 'a diplomatic agent' is the head of the mission or a member of the diplomatic staff of the mission or a member of the diplomatic staff having diplomatic rank. However, though not necessarily diplomats, members of the family of a diplomatic agent forming part of his or her household also enjoy immunity from local jurisdiction to the same extent as the diplomatic agents, provided that they are not nationals of the receiving state.

154. As is the case with Head-of-State immunity, diplomatic immunity is also predicated on the principle of sovereign independence and equality of states. Duly accredited diplomatic agents personify the foreign sovereign who sent them. The receiving state must therefore treat them in the same manner as it would treat the sovereign who sent them and accord them all the privileges and immunities due to him, including immunity from court proceedings. When a diplomatic agent violates the law all that the receiving state can do is to request the sending state to recall him or her or to declare him or her *personam non grata*, for conduct incompatible with his or her status as a diplomat.

155. It should, however, be stressed that diplomatic immunity belongs to the sending state, not to the individual diplomatic agent. The sending state may waive it,[178] and the agent concerned will be amenable to the jurisdiction of the receiving state.[179] He or she should not be heard to say as an answer to the proceedings that at the time he committed the offences in question he was a diplomat. That may be true, but it was not a license for him to violate the laws of the receiving state. He or she was immune from court proceedings, not from liability.

156. Unlike diplomats, consuls or consular representatives do not enjoy immunity from prosecution in the receiving state save in respect of their official duties. This is so because consuls are not diplomats. Save in the erstwhile communist countries where the state was total, consuls generally do not engage in diplomatic activities or in the political relations between the sending and receiving states. Their function is generally limited to promoting trade and commerce and to facilitating travel between the two states.[180] Another reason why consuls are not granted immunity from prosecution is that they are often nationals of the receiving state. Nevertheless, under the 1963 Vienna Convention on Consular Relations, consuls enjoy

178. Article 32(1) of the Vienna Convention provides that 'The immunity from jurisdiction of diplomatic agents and of persons enjoying immunity under Art. 37 may be waived by the sending State.'

179. See *Dickson v. Del Solar* [1929] All E.R. 140.

180. Generally see Daniel D. Ntanda Nsereko, *The Consul as a Defendant. His Amenability to the Jurisdiction of the Receiving State*, 15 Indian J. Intl. L. 333–350 (1975).

some protections. For instance, according to Article 41, consuls must not be arrested or detained pending trial, except in the case of a grave crime and pursuant to a decision of a competent judicial authority; again, except in the case of a grave crime they must not be restricted in their personal freedom save in execution of a judicial decision of final effect. Lastly, where it is necessary to detain a consul charged with a grave crime the ensuing proceedings must be conducted with the minimum of delay. Generally, where a consul is charged with any offence, the case must be conducted in a manner that respects his official position as a representative of a foreign sovereign and, save in the case of a grave crime, which hampers the exercise of his official functions as little as possible.

Chapter 3. Criminal Responsibility

§1. General

157. To prove that the accused committed the offence charged the prosecution must establish two things: (i) the *actus reus* and (ii) the *mens rea* of the offence. The *actus reus* of an offence is the conduct, whether acts or omissions, or the occurrence of a state of affairs, that the law prohibits, commands, or otherwise seeks to repress. *Mens rea* of the offence, however, is the guilty mind that actuates the *actus reus*. According to the law, a mere act, omission or existence of a state of affairs per se does not make a person guilty of an offence. Such act, omission or state of affairs must co-exist with or be accompanied by a guilty mind or evil intention to commit, omit or bring about the outlawed state of affairs. As the Latin maxim puts it, *actus non facit reum nisi mens rea* (an act does not make a man guilty of a crime unless his mind be also guilty). *Actus reus* and *mens rea* go hand in hand. Failure by the prosecution to prove them may result in the accused being acquitted. Nevertheless, sometimes the two elements are so entwined that it is difficult to distinguish one from the other. For example, offences of possession include not only the physical act of possession but also knowledge, which is a mental element. The offence of obtaining by false pretences includes not only the physical act of obtaining but also 'with intent to defraud'. The offence of receiving or retaining also requires that the physical element be accompanied by knowledge that the thing received or retained was unlawfully obtained. Some offences, such as assault include the defence in the definition; the alleged assaulter must have done so unlawfully. The issue is whether these mental elements are part of the *actus reus* or of the *mens rea*. Is it really necessary to separate them and to confine them in water-tight compartments? Smith and Hogan opine that it is not. 'The only thing that really matters is whether they are elements in the crime. If they are, it is immaterial whether they are assigned to the *actus reus* or to the *mens rea*.'[181] For the convenience of analysis, we shall now consider them one by one.

§2. *Actus Reus (External Element)*

158. An evil-inclined mind, though a prelude to actual evil, is not per se criminal. According to the law, that state of mind must be accompanied by deeds that result in conduct that is forbidden under the law. These deeds variously referred to as the 'physical element' or 'external element of the offence' are the *actus reus*. Depending on the offence in question, they may be acts or omissions or a state of affairs. The consequences of those acts or omissions, and the time and place at which they take place, may also be essential to their completion. To ascertain what the *actus reus* of a particular crime is one must refer to the definition of that crime. For the *actus reus* to be complete, *all* the elements of the crime in question must be shown to exist. It must also be emphasized that while in some offences, such as

181. Smith & Hogan, *Criminal Law: Cases and Materials* 2 (3d ed., Butterworths 1986).

negligence or strict liability crimes, the guilty mind may be dispensed with, the *actus reus* cannot.

I. Act

159. Acts are the commonest forms of *actus reus*. In some cases, it is the act per se which constitutes the *actus reus*. This is so in offences such as malicious damage to property, wounding with a knife, perjury and rape. In these offences, 'you do not have to wait to see if anything happens as a result of what the defendant does'.[182] In other types of offences, it is the result brought about by those acts, and not the acts themselves, that constitutes the *actus reus*. In murder, for example, it is the resulting death by whatsoever means (be it assault, stabbing, shooting, strangulation, suffocation, poisoning, burning, drowning or denial of the essentials of life) that is the *actus reus*, not the means employed to cause the death.

160. However, for an act to constitute the *actus reus* of an offence, it must be the result of the free exercise of the will; the accused must have acted with volition or voluntarily. Section 8(1) of the Penal Code provides that 'Subject to the express provisions of this Code relating to negligent acts or omissions, *a person is not criminally responsible for an act or omission which occurs independently of the exercise of his or her will* or for an event which occurs by accident.' For example, where Akiiki pushes Amooti into Abwoli who, as a result, is injured, Amooti is not criminally responsible for the injuries; he did not fall on Abwoli voluntarily. Similarly bodily movements brought about by such diseases as epilepsy do not constitute an *actus reus* by the person with the disease; they do not result from the free exercise of his or her will.

II. Omission

161. Omission means failure to do something or to act in a given way. However, for an omission to constitute an *actus reus*, there must be a legal duty imposed on a particular person to do something or to act in a certain way. In the absence of such a duty the criminal law attaches no responsibility for any failure to act. For example, Amooti, a mere bystander, commits no offence for failing to render assistance to a victim of a road accident unless he has some legal connection with that victim which obliges him to assist. And, save in a few exceptional circumstances, he is not even obliged to report the accident to the police. He may be morally condemnable for his callous and unneighbourly indifference to his fellow citizen's plight. But in law he is blameless. However, a motorist commits an offence under the Traffic and Road Safety Act for failing to stop after a motor accident, or for failing to report the accident, failing to stop at traffic lights, or to wear a seat belt.[183] The law requires him or her to perform these duties or to observe the safety precautions. Similarly,

182. Glanville Williams, *The Problem of Reckless Attempts*, Crim. L. Rev. 366, 368 (1983).

183. See sec. 132. According to *Uganda v. Mayombwe* [1973] E.A. 566 failing to stop or to report an accident is not an offence when no one is injured and no property is damaged.

any inhabitant of Uganda, with the exception of one who lacks capacity, commits the offence of misprision of treason if:

> knowing that any person intends to commit treason does not give information thereof with all reasonable dispatch to the Minister, an administrative officer, a magistrate or an officer in charge of a police station, or use all reasonable endeavours to prevent the commission of the offence of treason.[184]

Likewise, a person in charge of the affairs of a company incorporated under the Companies Act commits an offence if he or she fails to hold an annual general meeting or to file certain returns at prescribed times.[185]

162. As noted above, the *actus reus* of murder and manslaughter is causing death by either an act or an omission. The act may be assault, shooting, drowning, burning, poisoning and strangling. The omission would be failure to perform a legal duty imposed either by contract, or by law or by special relationships. For example, by dint of the contract with his or her guests, a hotel keeper has a legal duty to take reasonable steps to ensure the safety of those guests. Institutional authorities such as schools, hospitals, prisons, police, as well as chiefs, also have a legal duty to ensure the safety of and to provide necessaries of life to persons under their charge. Parents or guardians as well as masters and mistresses also have a legal duty to provide necessaries of life to their children or wards or domestic employees or apprentices. Employers do likewise have a legal duty to provide their employees with safe conditions of work. The law presumes them responsible for the consequences which adversely affect the health or life of those people by reason of the omission to fulfil that duty.[186] The case of *Regina v. Mukasa & Anor.* is a good example. A Muluka chief was convicted of manslaughter for failing to stop villagers from beating an alleged thief whom he had tied to a tree all night long.[187]

163. As noted above, where a person is unable to control his or her conduct, be it an act or an omission, he or she is not responsible for the harm that may result from such conduct. Consequently, a person who is physically unable to act as required by the law must not be found guilty of omitting to act. He or she could not help it.

164. Another instance where an omission may constitute an *actus reus* is in respect of offences of 'permitting'. These offences may be committed by either giving words authorizing or by failing to prevent the forbidden conduct. For example, section 318(4) of the Penal Code provides as follows:

---

184. Penal Code, sec. 25.
185. See secs. 130–132. See also *Krementi Lyangombe Anor v. R.* [1959] E.A. 678.
186. See offences under Ch. XIX of the Penal Code on Duties Relating to the Preservation of Life and Health.
187. [1956–1958] 8 U.L.R. 321.

> An authorized officer *shall not permit* the exportation or importation of any goods in contravention of this section but shall in each case detain the goods until he or she is satisfied that the appropriate licence has been obtained or any condition of such licence has been obtained or fulfilled, and any officer who fails to comply with this subsection commits an offence.

Thus the authorized officer, who may be a customs officer, a police officer, a trade officer, a chief, or a member of a vigilante group, commits an offence if he (i) authorizes or (ii) fails to take reasonable steps to stop the exportation or importation of goods without a valid license. Similar provisions are to be found under the Traffic and Road Safety Act. Section 35(1) forbids any person to drive any class of motor vehicle without a valid driving permit. Section 35(3) forbids any person who owns or has charge of a motor vehicle to allow or permit any person to drive that vehicle unless he is the holder of a valid driving permit. In *Prince Kesi Kagoro v. R*,[188] the appellant's son had pleaded guilty to driving his father's motor vehicle without a valid driving permit. It was held that the mere fact, unsupported by evidence, that the driver of the car was his son did not mean that the son's driving of the vehicle was with the appellant's permission. In other words, there must be evidence of permitting as shown above.

165. Offences of 'possession or retention' of prohibited objects do also involve an element of omission in their *actus reus*. These offences are committed by either physically grasping or keeping under one's control the forbidden object, or by failing to get rid of the object once its true nature has become apparent to the possessor. Thus, section 320 of the Penal Code provides that:

> Any person who is found in possession of property or goods reasonably suspected to have been smuggled into Uganda or about to be smuggled from Uganda in contravention of Sections 318 and 319 shall be guilty of an offence.

166. A possessor of goods might have initially come by the goods innocently, not knowing that they are contraband. The possessor might also not know that he or she is in fact in the physical possession of the goods. Without his or her knowledge, they might have been planted on him or her, in which case he or she lacked knowledge or *animus possidendi*. If he or she fails or omits to get rid of the goods after becoming aware of the possession or discovering their true nature then the *actus reus* of the offence is complete.

III. State of Affairs

167. The accused's personal situation at the time he or she commits the offence may also be part of the *actus reus*. For example, to prove that the accused committed the offence of being a rogue and a vagabond, the prosecution must show that at the time of the alleged offence the accused was 'a suspected person or a reputed

188. H.Ct.Cr.App. No. 259 of 1958; H.Ct.Monthly Bulletin No. 65 of 1958.

thief' with no 'visible means of subsistence', and was unable to give 'a good account of himself'.[189] Another example is that of bigamy. For the offence to be committed, the accused must be party to a subsisting marriage at the time he or she goes through another ceremony of marriage.[190]

168. The place where the offence is committed may also be part of the *actus reus*. Failure to allege or prove that certain acts were committed at a particular place will vitiate the charge. For example, the *actus reus* of driving whilst under the influence of drinks is not complete unless the driving took place *on a road*.[191] Similarly, the *actus reus* for the offence of being found in a *building* at night with intent to commit a felony therein will not be satisfied by merely showing that the accused was found in an enclosed compound. The place must be a *building*.[192] Likewise, the *actus reus* for the offence of carrying a weapon in a public place will not be satisfied by merely showing that the accused was found with a knife on a *verandah of a shop*. The place must be *public* in the sense that members of the public have access to it as of right.[193]

169. Time, too, may be part of the *actus reus*. Thus for the offence of burglary to be proved it must be shown that: (i) *during the hours of the night*; (ii) the accused broke into or out of a building, tent, or vessel used as a human dwelling; (iii) with intent to commit or after having committed a felony therein.[194]

170. The personal situation of the victim may also form part of the *actus reus*. In rape cases, for example, it must be shown that the victim did not consent to the sexual intercourse with the accused.[195] In defilement cases, however, consent of the victim is immaterial. What is material is that the victim be *a person who is below the age of 18 years*.[196]

171. In connection with certain offences, the Penal Code provides that where certain factors exist then the maximum penalty imposable for those offences will be higher than where they do not exist. In such cases, these factors form part of the *actus reus* of the offences and must be alleged and proved. For instance, the maximum penalty for the offence of being found armed with intent to commit a felony is imprisonment for seven years.[197] However, the maximum penalty rises to ten years in case of a person who has been 'previously convicted of a felony relating to

189. Penal Code, sec. 168(c).
190. Penal Code, sec. 153.
191. Traffic and Road Safety Act, sec. 111. Section 2(1)(hhh) defines road as 'any highway or any other road to which the public have access and includes bridges over which a road passes'. See *Basi v. Reginam* [1956–1957] 8 U.L.R. 189.
192. See Penal Code, sec. 300(1)(f) and *Odeke s/o Taran v. R.* [1958] E.A. 690.
193. See *Kekinyumu v. Uganda* [1969] E.A. 333.
194. Penal Code, sec. 295(2).
195. Penal Code, sec. 123. See also *Upar v. Uganda* [1971] E.A. 98.
196. Penal Code, sec. 129.
197. Penal Code, sec. 300(1).

property'.[198] The *previous conviction* then becomes part of the *actus reus* of the graver offence. Lastly, forging any document is punishable by up to three years imprisonment.[199] However, forging special documents such as wills, title deeds, judicial records, powers of attorney, banknotes, bills of exchange, promissory notes or other negotiable instruments, insurance policies and cheques is punishable by up to life imprisonment.[200] To bring the offence under this severer penalty then, the nature of the document alleged to have been forged must be proved.

§3. *Mens Rea (Mental Element)*

172. Save for crimes of negligence and strict liability, to prove a person guilty of an offence it is not sufficient to show that he or she brought about the *actus reus* of the offence. It must also be shown that he or she was in a certain state of mind, variously referred to as guilty mind, fault or moral element: the *mens rea*. This *mens rea* must co-exist with the *actus reus*. Some provisions of the Penal Code and other statutes with penal aspects specifically spell out the *mens rea* of the offences they create. Many others do not. In that case, the courts invariably read the *mens rea* element into them, unless by explicit language they exclude it.

173. The kind of *mens rea* required for a person to be pronounced guilty differs from crime to crime. Generally speaking, however, there are three types of states of mind under which most crimes may be grouped: intention, ulterior intention and recklessness.

I. Intention

174. Intention may manifest itself in three ways. First, when the accused person desires to bring about the *actus reus* of the offence in question and proceeds to bring it about through his or her conduct, he or she is said to have intended to commit the offence. This is *direct intention* or *dolus directus*. Second, when the accused person consciously does the forbidden thing (although he does not desire it in itself) in order to achieve some other consequence which he or she desires he or she is also said to have intended to do the forbidden thing. For example, if he or she kills a prison guard as a means of escaping from lawful custody, he or she will be held to have intended to kill the guard. Third, if the accused does something knowing that the forbidden consequence will certainly result, or from the circumstances of the case it is reasonably foreseeable that it will result, he or she will again be said to have intended to do the forbidden thing (even though he or she does not desire it or is indifferent to its occurrence). This kind of intention is variously referred to as 'oblique intention', 'constructive or legal intention', or *dolus eventualis*.[201]

198. *Ibid.*, sec. 300(2).
199. *Ibid.*, sec. 347.
200. *Ibid.*, sec. 348.
201. Speaking in support of this species of intention Lord Diplock said: 'I agree with those of your Lordships who take the uncomplicated view that in crimes of this class no distinction is to be drawn in

175. Thus in the case of murder, the Penal Code provides that *mens rea* is established if the accused had either actual intention to kill or had knowledge that his act or omission causing death 'will probably cause the death of some person, whether such person is the person actually killed or not, although such knowledge is accompanied by indifference whether death is caused or not, or by a wish that it may not be caused'.[202] Similarly, in the case of causing malicious damage to property, the *mens rea* will be held to exist where the accused either intended to cause the damage or could reasonably foresee that his acts would result in the damage. However, in one case where two police constables broke down a door to obtain entry into the building where a suspect was thought to be hiding and purported to be exercising their power under section 3 of the Criminal Procedure Code, they were held not to have acted maliciously. According to the High Court, acting maliciously involved acting unlawfully and wilfully. It interpreted the word 'wilfully' to mean acting more than intentionally, with some degree of guilty intention. In the case before it, the policemen did not intend to do anything wrong. They thought they were acting within their powers and did not intend to go outside their duty but were merely 'over-zealous of their duty'.[203]

176. In addition to incorporating the *dolus eventualis* principle in the Ugandan criminal law, the provision cited above also imports into the law the notion of 'transferred malice'. As long as the accused intended to kill or to injure someone or to damage some property, it does not matter that the person he or she kills or injures is not the one he or she actually intended to kill or injure or that the property he or she damages is not the property he or she intended to damage. Provided that the accused acted intentionally or (as we shall see presently) recklessly, it does not matter that the actual object of his actions (whether person or property) was intended or unforeseen.

177. The notion of transferred malice is, however, not limited to murder alone. It applies to other crimes as well, since section 8(2) is of general application. Thus, if Musoke aims a blow at Kiwanuka but misses him and instead hits Ddungu, he is guilty of assaulting Ddungu. He had the intention of assaulting. According to the law, it is not material that he did not intend to assault Ddungu. He intended to assault *someone*.[204] Likewise, if Musoke puts poison in Kiwanuka's food with the intention of poisoning him to death, but Ddungu eats the food instead and dies, Musoke is guilty of intentionally causing Ddungu's death.

English law between the state of mind of one who does an act because he desires it to produce a particular evil consequence and the state of mind of one who does the act knowing full well that it is likely to produce that consequence although it may not be the object he was seeking to achieve by doing the act. What is common to both these states of mind is willingness to produce the particular evil consequence: and this, to my view is the *mens rea* needed to satisfy a requirement whether imposed by statute or existing at common law, that in order to constitute the offence with which the accused is charged he must have acted with "intent" to produce a particular evil consequence … ' *Hyam v. Director of Public Prosecutions* [1974] 2 All E.R. 7 5

202. *Ibid.*, sec. 191.

203. *Nikolas Ogulu & Anor. v. Uganda*, H.Ct.Cr.App. No. 396-7 of 1968; H.Ct.Monthly Bulletin No. 181 of 1968.

204. See the English case of *The Queen v. Latimer* (1886) 17 Q.B.D. 359.

178. However, a limitation to the doctrine of transferred malice is that the *mens rea* and *actus reus* of the crime intended, and that of the one that is actually committed must coincide. Thus where a person intending to hit another person misses his target and instead hits and damages property, he will not be held to have intended to damage the property. This is *substituted* but not *transferred* malice. Thus, in the English case of *R. v. Pembliton*, the accused, after fighting for some time with persons in a crowd in front of a pub moved away from them and crossed to the other side of the street. He picked up a stone and threw it at the persons he had been fighting with. The stone passed over their heads and struck and damaged the glass window of the pub. He was charged with and convicted of unlawfully and maliciously causing injury to the window. The conviction was quashed on appeal.[205]

179. According to section 8(2) of the Penal Code, 'Unless the intention to cause a particular result is expressly declared to be an element of the offence constituted, in whole or part, by an act or omission, the result intended to be caused by an act or omission is immaterial.' It results from this section that, in cases where 'the intention to cause a particular result is expressly declared to be an element of the offence', constructive intention or *dolus eventualis* does not apply. This is so in the case of the inchoate crime of attempt. According to section 386(1) of the Penal Code, attempt is committed only when 'a person, intending to commit an offence' manifests his intention 'by some over act'. The accused must have had a direct intention to commit a particular offence. As was explained in the English case of *Regina v. Mohan*, when used to describe the *mens rea* in attempt, *intention* means 'a decision to bring about, in so far as it lies within the accused's power, the commission of the offence which it is alleged the accused attempted to commit, no matter whether the accused desired that consequence of his act or not'.[206] Offences relating to insult to religion also fall under the exception under section 8(2) of the Code. For destruction, damage or defiling of any place of worship to amount to an offence, it must be done 'with the intention of thereby insulting the religion of any class of persons, or with the knowledge that any class of persons is likely to consider such destruction, damage or defilement as an insult to its religion'.[207]

180. Acting intentionally involves the exercise of mental faculties. It involves volition, consciousness and knowledge. An accused person must have acted knowingly, voluntarily and consciously before he can be said to have acted with the necessary *mens rea*. It is for this reason that section 8(1) of the Penal Code provides that 'a person is not criminally responsible for an act or omission which occurs independently of the exercise of his or her will or for an event that occurs by accident'. Where, therefore, a person acts unknowingly, inadvertently or unconsciously, he or she cannot be said to have acted intentionally or with the necessary *mens rea*. As Professor Fitzgerald has opined, 'the unintentional producer of harm is less of a

205. [1874–1880] AU E.R. 1163.
206. [1976] Q.B. 1, at 11, per James, L.J.; [1975] 2 All E.R. 193.
207. See sec. 118.

menace to the community than one who pursues his own ends to the disregard of the law and of the interests of others'.[208]

181. Offences whose *mens rea* is the mere intent to do the forbidden thing itself do not usually include the mental element in their definitions. This is true of such offences as doing grievous harm,[209] wounding,[210] common assault,[211] rape,[212] bigamy[213] and elopement.[214] The courts do nonetheless imply the requisite mental element in the offences. *Uganda v. Rukwandura & Anor.* is a case in point. The two accused, a man and a woman, were charged with elopement. The man's defence was that the woman was his wife, and that he married her after taking steps to ascertain that she was not married. The woman's defence was similar. She averred that she had divorced the complainant after being married to him for six months. After the 'divorce', she went to live with her elder sister who found another man – the first accused – for her to marry. In other words, she considered herself to be an unmarried woman at the time the first accused took her to live with him. As indicated above, the definition of elopement does not include knowledge of the marital status of the people involved in the alleged elopement. Section 127(1) of the Penal Code simply provides that 'Any person who elopes with a married woman or entices or causes a married woman to elope with him commits an offence ... ' Section 127(2) similarly provides that 'Any female who elopes with a married man or entices or causes a married man to elope, commits an offence ... ' Seid, J. read or implied knowledge into the definition of the offence. He said:

> It is now settled ... that *mens rea* is just as much an ingredient of the offence of elopement under Section 121(A) as it is of the offence of adultery under Section 150(A) of the Penal Code. This means that it is a defence to the offence of elopement if the offender genuinely believed on reasonable grounds that the person with whom he or she eloped is [*sic* not] married.[215]

The court cited with approval an earlier case of *Uganda v. Nikolla* in which Udo Udoma, C.J. held that:

> In my view it would be competent for an accused person charged with having committed adultery with a married woman to show by evidence that in fact at the time of the commission of the adultery he did not know that the woman was married to any person.[216]

208. *Criminal Law and Punishment* (Oxford University Press, Oxford, 1962) 116.
209. *Ibid.*, sec. 219.
210. *Ibid.*, sec. 222(a).
211. *Ibid.*, sec. 235.
212. *Ibid.*, sec. 123.
213. *Ibid.*, sec. 153.
214. *Ibid.*, sec. 127.
215. [1973] E.A. 345, 575.
216. [1966] E.A. 345.

182. There are obviously gradations of knowledge. Knowledge may be actual, and this may be ascertained from the circumstances surrounding the commission of the offence. It may also consist of *willful blindness*. Here the accused has the opportunity to inquire and to ascertain the actual state of affairs of the matter in issue. He or she deliberately or wilfully avoids doing so, probably not caring what his inquiry would reveal. The court in *Uganda v. Rukwandura & Anor.* (*supra*, paragraph 181) alluded to this fact and hinted that had the accused taken away the woman without bothering to inquire whether or not she was married he would have incurred the risk of being held guilty of eloping with a married woman. Luckily for him, he had taken reasonable steps to inquire into her marital status, and thus avoided the risk of the court imputing guilty knowledge on him. Lastly, knowledge may be constructive. Here the accused does not know, but ought to know. This knowledge is inferred from the circumstances surrounding the commission of the offence, and from the opportunity that the accused, as a reasonable and prudent person, has to know or to inquire and ascertain the true state of affairs. Constructive knowledge differs from willful blindness in that failure to inquire is not deliberate or willful.

183. This analysis of guilty knowledge also applies to offences whose definitions expressly include knowledge. This would include the offences of receiving stolen property,[217] doing acts likely to spread infectious diseases,[218] selling noxious food or drink,[219] selling adulterated drugs,[220] knowingly living on the earnings of prostitution[221] and supplying drugs to procure abortion.[222]

184. Some of the offences mentioned above include in their definitions the word 'unlawfully' doing the forbidden thing, for example assault or having sexual intercourse with a girl under 18. Does the unlawfulness relate to the *actus reus* or the *mens rea* element of the offence? This is one area where the two concepts tend to merge or to overlap. If a parent slaps his or her child as chastisement, he or she does not thereby 'assault' the child. So, there is no 'unlawful assault' and therefore no *actus reus*. Likewise, there is no *mens rea*, because the parent has no evil intent. He or she is entitled to reasonably chastise his child, aware of the biblical admonition that, 'He that spareth his rod hateth his son: but he that loveth him chasteneth him betimes.'[223] What, then is the import of 'unlawful' in these definitions? It is simply that the accused acted without justification, or that he has no defence for his conduct.

217. Penal Code, sec. 314.
218. *Ibid.*, sec. 171.
219. *Ibid.*, sec. 173.
220. *Ibid.*, sec. 175.
221. *Ibid.*, sec. 136.
222. *Ibid.*, sec. 143.
223. Proverbs 13:241 (Kings James Version).

II. Ulterior Intent

185. The definitions of offences that incorporate this type of mental state require a further intent in addition to the direct or basic intent to do the forbidden act. These offences are usually indicated by phrases such as 'with intent to', 'dishonestly' or 'fraudulently and without claim of right'. They include assault with intent to commit a felony or to resist arrest,[224] breaking and entering with intent to commit a felony,[225] making a false declaration for the purpose of procuring a passport,[226] theft,[227] concealing wills or deeds with intent to defraud[228] and obtaining by false pretences.[229] With respect to some of these offences, it would appear that the policy of the law is the desire to punish otherwise minor offences more severely if they are committed with some further intent or ulterior motive. For example, kidnapping a person from Uganda or from lawful guardianship is a felony punishable by a maximum sentence of ten years.[230] However, kidnapping or abducting a person with intent that such person may be murdered, or with knowledge that such person will probably be murdered, or with intent to secure a ransom or benefit for the liberation of such a person, is punishable by the ultimate sentence of death.[231]

III. Recklessness

186. A person may, by his acts or omissions, bring about consequences that he or she does not intend to bring about or may simply be indifferent to. He or she may be held criminally responsible for those consequences if his or her acts or omissions are reckless. They are reckless if by acting, or omitting to act, as he or she does, he or she takes an unjustifiable risk of producing those consequences. Justifying the law's acceptance of recklessness as culpable, Lord Bingham of the English House of Lords said:

> The most obviously culpable state of mind is no doubt an intention to cause the injurious result, but knowing disregard of an appreciated and unacceptable risk of causing an injurious result or deliberate closing of the mind to such risk would be readily accepted as culpable also. It is clearly blameworthy to take an obvious and significant risk of causing injury to another. But it is not clearly blameworthy to do something involving a risk of injury to another if… one genuinely does not perceive the risk. Such a person may be accused of stupidity or lack of imagination, but neither of those failings should expose him to conviction of serious crime or the risk of punishment.[232]

224. *Ibid.*, sec. 238.
225. *Ibid.*, sec. 295.
226. *Ibid.*, sec. 313.
227. *Ibid.*, sec. 245.
228. *Ibid.*, secs. 277 and 278.
229. *Ibid.*, sec. 305.
230. *Ibid.*, sec. 244.
231. *Ibid.*, sec. 243.
232. *R v. G & Anor* [2003] All E. R. 765 at 784.

187. The risk is unjustified where, given the circumstances surrounding his or her acts or omissions, the accused person knows the risk involved in his or her conduct but nevertheless consciously or deliberately goes on with such conduct knowing full well or foreseeing that it will probably result in the proscribed consequence. According to Smith and Hogan, 'Whether it is justifiable to take a risk depends on the social value of the activity involved relative to the probability and the gravity of the harm which might be caused.'[233] There is thus no hard and fast rule as to the degree of probability of the occurrence of the proscribed consequence. It all depends on the social utility of the conduct in question. For example, for a doctor performing an operation to be said to be reckless, the degree of probability of harm must be very high. However, in the case of 'playing games' with a loaded gun only a slight degree of probability of harm resulting from such activity will be sufficient to constitute recklessness.

188. What is described above is the so-called *subjective recklessness.* It is the *mens rea* required for crimes whose definition requires that they be committed 'maliciously'. To prove such a crime it is sufficient to show either: (i) that the accused actually intended to do the forbidden thing, or (ii) that he was reckless in the subjective sense – he knew of the existence of the risk or foresaw the likely consequences of his conduct, and all the same deliberately or consciously went ahead and took the risk. According to the Uganda Penal Code, it is only in respect of murder that the term 'malice' is used.[234]

189. The accused will also be held to have acted recklessly where no reasonable and prudent person similarly circumstanced as he was would do what he did or behave the way he behaved. He may not have actually considered the risk or foreseen the consequences, but as a reasonable and prudent person, he ought to have foreseen them. He took an unjustified risk. For this reason, the law holds him as blameworthy as one who intentionally did the outlawed thing. This is *objective recklessness.*

190. Section 228 of the Penal Code lists certain acts, which, when done 'in a manner so rash or negligent as to endanger human life or to cause harm to any person', can be considered reckless.[235] They include driving any vehicle or riding on any public way; navigating or taking part in the navigation or working of any vessel; doing any act with fire or any combustible matter or omitting to take precautions against any probable danger from any fire or combustible matter in one's possession; omitting to take any precaution against any probable danger from any animal in one's possession; giving medical or surgical treatment to any person whom one has undertaken to treat; dispensing, supplying, selling, administering or giving away any medicine or poisonous or dangerous matter; doing any act with

233. J.C. Smith & Brian Hogan, *Criminal Law* 61 (Butterworth & Co. Ltd. 1988).

234. Section 187. The side note to sec. 335 refers to the offences of injuries to property as 'malicious injuries', but the epithet is not used in the definition. The definitions refer to 'willfully and unlawfully'.

235. Section 228 falls under Ch. XXII of the Penal Code titled 'Criminal Recklessness and negligence'.

respect to, or omitting to take proper precautions against, any probable danger, from any machinery of which one is solely or partly in charge, or doing any act with respect to, or omitting to take proper precautions against any probable danger from, any explosive in one's possession.[236]

191. Recklessness may also be used in manslaughter cases under section 187 of the Penal Code to qualify as 'unlawful any act or omission that causes death'. Finally while section 228 of the Code appears to focus only on reckless conduct that endangers human life or causes harm to people, there appears to be no good reason why recklessness cannot be extended to similar conduct that causes damage to property. Here one has in mind arson and malicious injury to property.

IV. Motive

192. Motive, however altruistic, for doing a forbidden thing or omitting to perform a duty imposed by the law does not trump the *mens rea* of an offence if it otherwise exists. Section 8(3) of the Penal Code expressly provides that:

> Unless otherwise expressly declared, the motive by which a person is induced to do or omit to do an act, or to form an intention, is immaterial so far as regards criminal responsibility.

Therefore the killing or wounding of a criminal suspect through use of wanton force would not be excused merely because the police officer's motive was to arrest the suspect and to bring him or her to justice. Similarly, a doctor or a nurse will not escape criminal responsibility for killing a terminally sick patient with a view to relieving the patient from pain. Observance of religious scruples or conscientious principles, and opposition to bad laws will likewise not absolve the offender from criminal responsibility.

193. Though the prosecution need not prove motive for the commission of the alleged offence, presence of motive is a factor that the court may take into account

---

236. The Tanzanian case of *Seidi v. Republic* is a good example in relation to reckless driving. The appellant, at the request of a friend, was driving a land rover to Nzenga to buy petrol. In the land rover were twelve cases of empty bottles and eleven passengers. On the way the appellant picked up three more passengers. After the land rover had travelled some distance, a rear left side tyre burst. It was duly repaired. Some distance further on the tyre which replaced the earlier burst one also burst, causing the land rover to overturn. As a result of the mishap, three people died and twelve others were injured. The appellant was charged with and convicted of, among other offences, causing death by reckless or dangerous driving. Confirming the conviction, the Tanzanian High Court said: 'In the mainland of Tanzania, it is notorious that road surfaces are poor and repair facilities few. An experienced driver, who overloads a vehicle with passengers and empty bottles and persists in driving it despite knowledge of defective tyres, must be aware of the potentially dangerous situation he is creating. His decision to go on driving in such circumstances amounted to recklessness, since the appellant must, as a reasonable man, have foreseen the possibility of death resulting from an accident occurring which would involve the closely packed human bodies and the empty bottles carried in the vehicle. His conduct amounted to a breach of duty to take care required under Section 44(A)(1)(a) of Cap. 168.' [1969] E.A. 280, 286 per Seaton, J.

when determining the issue of *mens rea*.[237] For sentencing purposes good motive may also be taken into account as a mitigating factor. However, bad motive, such a desire for revenge, greed and ill-will, will also be taken into account as an aggravating factor.

V. Ignorance of the Law

194. Ignorance of the law forbidding certain conduct, or the belief on the part of the accused that what he or she did was morally correct, does not negate *mens rea* if it otherwise exists. As long as the accused knew the facts constituting the offence that he or she committed and had the requisite state of mind, he or she will be guilty; it does not matter that he or she may not have known that those facts amounted to a criminal offence. Section 6 of the Penal Code specifically provides that:

> Ignorance of the law does not afford any excuse for any act or omission which would otherwise constitute an offence unless knowledge of the law by the offender is expressly declared to be an element of the offence.

So, when a statute criminalizing certain conduct uses the word 'knowingly', the word merely refers to knowledge of the facts constituting the offence alleged to have been committed by the accused, and not to whether or not those facts constitute a crime under the law. The rationale for this age-long rule is that it is well-nigh impossible to disprove ignorance of the law. Additionally, if not knowing the law was a defence, then this would perforce encourage ignorance of the law. Moreover, in cases of crimes *mala in se* which reflect the general morality of the people, it may be assumed that all people who have reached the age of discretion ought to know the law. This assumption may, however, not be necessarily applicable to crimes *mala prohibita*, especially to the mass of regulatory offences that seem to constitute the bulk of the national *juris corpus*. Finding out and educating oneself about the existence and content of these offences may be a gargantuan task even to an educated and inquisitive member of the general public. However, to an ordinary person on the street who may be illiterate it would be an impossible task. Even if he or she were literate he or she would, more likely than not, not be proficient at English – more so legal English, in which the law is written. Indeed, less than 10% of the Ugandan population can read or understand English. Therefore a rigid application of the rule of *ignorantia juris non excusat* to the circumstances obtaining in Uganda is bound to lead to unjust results. There is thus a need for flexibility, particularly as far as regulatory offences are concerned, at least at the sentencing stage.

195. Where the definition of the offence in question does, expressly or by implication, make knowledge of the law a defence then ignorance of the law will negative the *mens rea*.

237. See *Regina v. Magata s/o Kachehakana* 8 U.L.R. 294 (1956–1957).

§4. Crimes of Negligence

196. Negligence is conduct that departs from the standard of behaviour of a reasonable or prudent person. According to Professor Glanville Williams, a reasonable or prudent person or man is 'the ideal man, the moral man, the conscientious man – not setting the standard so high that life becomes impossible in ordinary terms, but nevertheless requiring the most careful consideration to be given, so that harm is avoided and the law obeyed'.[238] The reasonable or prudent person is not a perfect person, but he or she is a person who sets the standard for all others involved in a particular activity to emulate. Who a reasonable person is, is a matter for the courts to determine, guided by the common human experience of a given era in a given society.

197. Ordinarily, negligent conduct would only attract civil or tortious liability. However, in a few instances, the law makes negligence the basis for criminal liability. The intendment of the law is apparently to influence people's behaviour in the socially desirable direction and to improve people's standards of care in certain critical areas of human conduct. It should nonetheless be emphasized that while negligence imports some element of fault, falling below an expected standard of conduct, it does not necessarily involve *mens rea* or evil intention. This point is underscored by section 8(1) of the Penal Code which, 'Subject to the express provisions of this Code relating to acts and omissions', makes a guilty mind an indispensable prerequisite for criminal responsibility. However, with negligence, mere inattentiveness, if it results in harm, may attract criminal liability and sanctions.

198. Topping the list of crimes of negligence is manslaughter,[239] followed by the crime of causing death 'by any rash or negligent act, not amounting to manslaughter'.[240] The degree of negligence required to prove manslaughter is *gross* or *culpable* negligence. The degree of negligence required for causing death by rash or negligent act is 'higher than that required to establish liability in a civil case but less than that required to establish a charge of manslaughter'.[241]

199. Examples of offences that arise out of 'rash and negligent' conduct have already been discussed above in relation to recklessness (*supra*, paragraph 190). Another species of offences of negligence is one in which omission 'to take reasonable care' is the essence of the offence.[242] Such offences include offences under the Traffic and Road Safety Act, such as dangerous driving and careless driving without due care and attention or without reasonable consideration for other road users. However, the degree of negligence for these offences varies from one to another

238. Glanville Williams, *Textbook of Criminal Law* 89 (Stevens & Sons 1983).

239. Penal Code, sec. 187.

240. Section 227.

241. *Musa Kakade v. R.* [1963] E.A. 36, 37 per Sir Ronald Sinclare, P.

242. For example, see sec. 234 of the Penal Code providing that 'Any person who, by doing any act, or by omitting to take reasonable care with any property in his possession or under his charge, causes danger, obstruction or injury to any person in any public way or public line of navigation, is liable to a fine.'

(albeit not spelled out in the statute). Nevertheless, in all these offences, the test used to determine liability is the standard of a reasonable or prudent person similarly circumstanced as the accused was. It is an objective test, similar to the one used to establish negligence in civil cases.[243]

§5. Offences of Strict Liability

200. It has been observed above that sometimes provisions of statutes defining offences are silent on the element of *mens rea*. They do not contain such *mens rea* words as 'intentionally', 'knowingly', 'recklessly', wilfully, 'without claim of right' or 'without reasonable excuse'. It has been noted that in such cases the courts read the *mens rea* element into those provisions. Not all the time, though. On those occasions, when they refrain from so doing they are applying the principle of strict liability to the offence in question (on the criteria guiding the courts in this decision, see *infra*, paragraphs 204–6). In such cases, then, once the *actus reus* of the offence is established, the accused may be found guilty even though he did not act intentionally, recklessly or even negligently. He may also not have known that the offence was being committed.

This last point is well illustrated by the case of *George Buwanika & Anor. v. R.*, involving the application of section 90(5) of the then Traffic Ordinance. The section provided that:

> If any motor omnibus carries more persons, baggage or goods than it is licensed to carry, the conductor and the owner of such vehicle shall be liable on conviction to a fine not exceeding shillings 1,000/=.

The conductor and owner (a company) of an omnibus were charged with and convicted of violating this provision. What happened was that when the bus left the Masaka Town depot, it was carrying the permitted maximum of forty-one passengers. However, when it was stopped by the police about sixteen miles away from Masaka, it was carrying seventy-two adult passengers. The issue on appeal was whether the owner of the omnibus was liable for the offence committed by the conductor without its knowledge or consent. Was *mens rea* not an ingredient of the offence? The High Court answered the question in the negative. Said Bennett, J.:

> In my judgment, Section 90(5) of the Ordinance imposes an absolute prohibition against the carrying of excess passengers or goods and there is no obligation upon the prosecution to prove anything into the nature of scienter or *mens rea* ... In the instant case all the prosecution had to prove was that the omnibus carried more passengers than it was licensed to carry and that the

243. In *R. v. Wallace* [1958] E.A. 582, 585, the Tanganyika High Court held, per Wallace, J., that 'A conviction for driving without due care and attention cannot be founded on the mere fact of a collision but must be based on a finding of fact that the driver charged with the offence was guilty of some act or omission which was negligent and which was a departure from the standard of driving expected of a reasonably prudent driver.' Followed in the Kenya case of *Jeseni v. Republic* [1969] E.A. 600.

> appellant company was the owner of the omnibus. Both these two facts were proved to the satisfaction of the learned magistrate, and the magistrate's findings of fact have not been attacked. The appeal is dismissed.[244]

201. Strict liability is often applied to provisions of public welfare legislation in such matters as sale of food and drugs; industrial safety, public houses, clubs and hotels; traffic and road safety; public transport; and protection of wildlife and the environment generally. The rationale for strict liability is that public safety and public welfare demand very high standards of care on the part of those who engage in the activities in question and that strict liability helps induce people and organizations to aim at higher and higher standards. It is believed that entertaining the plea of lack of *mens rea* would make the enforcement of these standards difficult. It would be well-nigh impossible to prove that the accused had the necessary *mens rea* or to disprove his claim that he had taken reasonable care. For example, proving that a motorist who does not observe the stop sign or who runs the traffic light does so intentionally or negligently is a difficult task indeed. It would also be costly and time-consuming.

202. It must be conceded, however, that convicting a person who was blameless, did not intend to commit the offence, was not negligent, or did not know that the offence was being committed is unfair. This point is well illustrated by the case of *Regina v. Toro Tea Company Limited.*[245] The respondent company was charged with failing to fence securely a certain dangerous part of machinery at its factory as was required under sections 23(1) and 75 of the Factories Ordinance. As a result of that failure, an employee was injured. The trial magistrate acquitted the company on the ground that at the time he was injured the employee was just playing with the machine. On appeal by the State, the High Court set aside the acquittal and convicted the company, holding that the magistrate erred in law by holding that playing with the machinery constituted a defence to a charge under the provisions of the Ordinance. It held that liability for failing to fence the machinery was absolute, and that the security provided by means of fencing extends not merely to protection against accidental occurrences, but also to protection against negligent, ill-advised or indolent conduct. The company had failed to take all reasonable steps to prevent the employee [a sweeper] wilfully and without reasonable cause endangering himself by failing to fence the machinery.

It is submitted that strict liability, as demonstrated by this case, does not encourage a blameless person to be more careful in the future (since he was not less careful). It may also bring the law in disrepute. How, then, may breaches of these requisite high standards be prevented? One solution is for the state to flood the public thoroughfares with traffic police. It might do the same with respect to industries and licensed places. The visibility of law enforcement agents will probably impel road users, industrialists and licensees generally to act with utmost care or else be detected and prosecuted. This is likely to result in a high degree of voluntary compliance. Be that as it may, however, flooding these places with law enforcement

244. [1957] E.A. 279.
245. [1956–1957] 8 U.L.R. 343.

agents is impracticable, even if the state had limitless resources. The cost-effective way out, then, is to randomly pick a few violators and to impose strict liability on them with the hope that this will act as a deterrent on others. It is the lesser of two evils.[246]

203. Nevertheless, it is important to emphasize that strict liability being a radical departure from the ordinary principles of criminal justice should not be lightly or indiscriminately applied. It should be applied only where its application will assist in enforcing the objects of the statute in question. This point was underscored by the Judicial Committee of the Privy Council when it stated that:

> But it is not enough in their Lordship's opinion merely to label the statute as one dealing with a grave social evil and from that to infer that strict liability was intended. It is pertinent also to inquire whether putting the defendant under strict liability will assist in the enforcement of the regulations. That means that there must be something he can do, directly or indirectly, by supervision or inspection, by improvement of his business methods or by exhorting those whom he may be expected to influence or control, which will promote the observance of the regulations. Unless this is so, there is no reason in penalizing him, and it cannot be inferred that the legislature imposed strict liability merely in order to find a luckless victim.[247]

204. What criteria, then, do the courts use in determining whether or not to apply strict liability to a statute? In the first place, they start from the presumption that

---

246. Dickson, J., of the Supreme Court of Canada, summed up the argument this way: 'In short, absolute liability, it is contended, is the most efficient and effective way of ensuring compliance with minor regulatory legislation and the social ends to be achieved are of such importance as to override the unfortunate by-products of punishing those who may be free of moral turpitude. In further justification, it is urged that slight penalties are usually imposed and that conviction for breach of a public welfare offence does not carry the stigma associated with conviction for a criminal offence.' *Regina v. City of Sault Ste. Marie*, 85 Dominion Law Rep. (3d) 161, 171 (1978).

247. *Lim Chin Aik v. R.* [1963] 1 All E.R. 223, 228, per Lord Evershed. The Privy Council was here dealing with Section 6(2) of the Singapore Immigration Ordinance which provided that: 'It shall not be lawful for any person other than a citizen of Singapore to enter Singapore from the Federation [of Malaya] or having entered Singapore from the Federation to remain in Singapore if – (b) such person has been prohibited by order made under Section 9 of this Ordinance from entering Singapore.' Subsection (2) of the same section provided that: 'Any person who contravenes the provisions of subsection (2) of this section shall be guilty of an offence against this Ordinance.' In the case at hand, a minister made an order prohibiting the appellant from entering or remaining in Singapore, but the order was not served on him or brought to his attention. The appellant's defence was that since he had no knowledge of the order he had no *mens rea*, and was not guilty. The Singapore courts rejected his defence, holding that the Immigration Ordinance created an offence of strict liability. The Judicial Committee of the Privy Court held strict liability not to be applicable. It said: 'Where it can be shown that the imposition of strict liability would result in the prosecution and conviction of a class of persons whose conduct could not in any way affect the observance of the law, their Lordships consider that, even where the statute is dealing with a grave social evil, strict liability is not likely to be intended.' In this case, it was not shown by the prosecution what the appellant could possibly have done so as to ensure that he complied with the order – an order that was never brought to his attention. This decision was followed in the Tanzania case of *Abdu & Anor v. Republic* [1971] E.A. 198.

the legislature did not intend to oust the *mens rea* requirement. In the oft-cited English case of *Sherras v. De Rutzen* Wright, J., said:

> The presumption is that *mens rea*, an evil intention, or knowledge of the wrongfulness of the act, is an essential ingredient in every offence; but that presumption is liable to be displaced either by the words of the statute creating the offence or by the subject-matter with which it deals, and both must be considered.[248]

To rebut the presumption of the *mens rea* requirement, then, either of the two tests mentioned in the decision may be employed. These are: (i) the words of the statute, and (ii) the subject-matter of the statute.

205. (i) The words used in a particular statute may be decisive. For example, section 5 of the Uganda Game Ordinance made it an offence for any person to be found in possession of hides or horns of wild game without permission. It was silent on the requirement of *mens rea.* The High Court had no problem in holding that no particular intent or *mens rea* was required to constitute the offence under the section.[249] However, the fact that other sections of a statute expressly require *mens rea* by using such words as 'knowingly' is not of itself sufficient to justify a decision that a section which is silent on *mens rea* creates an offence of strict liability. All relevant considerations must be taken into account.[250]

206. (ii) More often than not, however, the language of a statute gives no clue as to whether *mens rea* was intended to be ousted or not. If it purports to do so it may do so in a vague or ambivalent fashion. In such a case, the courts rely on the subject-matter test. In applying this test the courts exercise their own discretion. Here, again, the decision of the Judicial Committee of the Privy Council in *Lim Chin Aik v. R.* is instructive, and has been cited and followed by the courts in East Africa. The Committee said:

> Where the subject-matter of the statute is the regulation for the public welfare of a particular activity – statutes regulating the sale of food and drink are to be found among the earliest examples – it can be and frequently has been inferred that the legislature intended that such activities should be carried out under conditions of strict liability. The presumption is that the statute or statutory instrument can be effectively enforced only if those in charge of the relevant activities are made responsible for seeing that they are complied with. When such a presumption is to be inferred, it displaces the ordinary presumption of

248. [1895] All E.R. 1167, 1169.
249. See *Pimako Karemira v. R.* [1957] E.A. 582. By contrast, Section 34(e) of the Tanzanian Traffic Ordinance provided that no owner, driver or person in charge of a public service vehicle shall 'while in charge of a public service vehicle permit to be carried a greater number of passengers … than that which the vehicle is licensed to carry'. According to the Tanzanian High Court, the use of the word 'permit' indicates that there must be some element of *mens rea*, and the notion of strict liability did not apply. See *Alli s/o v. R.* [1960] E.A. 404.
250. See *Sherras v. De Rutzen*, *supra.*

mens rea. Thus, sellers of meat may be made responsible for seeing that meat is fit for human consumption and it is no answer for them to say that they were not aware that it was polluted. If that were a satisfactory answer, then as Kennedy, C.J., pointed out in *Hobbs v. Winchester Corpn.* [1910] 2 K.B. 471 at pp. 482–495, the distribution of meat (and its far-reaching consequences) would not be effectively prevented. So a publican may be made responsible for observing the condition of his customers, *Cundy v. Le Cocq* [1884] 13 Q.B.D. 207.[251]

207. In a more recent case, *Sweet v. Parsley*,[252] Lord Reid sought to restrict the subject-matter test as laid down in *Sherras* to statutes dealing with acts which 'are not criminal in any real sense, but are acts which in the public interest are prohibited under a penalty'. These acts he called 'quasi-criminal acts'. He was averse to applying strict liability to acts 'of a truly criminal character'. The reason for his aversion was that a person convicted of one of this class of offences suffers odium or stigma, and the graver the offence the greater the odium. He doubted whether public interest really requires that 'an innocent person should be prevented from proving his innocence in order that fewer guilty men escape'.[253]

208. Ugandan courts have shown an inclination to follow Lord Reid's approach and to disallow the ousting of the *mens rea* presumption in offences which are created by statutes but are silent on the *mens rea* requirement.

For instance, in *Uganda v. Ndyomugyenyi & Anor*., the first accused was charged with corruption under the Anti-Corruption Act.[254] It was alleged that being a programme manager of the Malaria Control Programme in the Ministry of Health, he neglected to ensure a proper management and requisition and distribution of anti-malaria drugs. Section 2(i) of the Act defines the offence charged as follows: 'A person commits the offence of corruption if he or she does any of the following acts … neglect of duty.' The court found that the accused failed to put in place controls for the requisition and distribution of the drugs that might have prevented abuse. It also opined that the accused might have been negligent in his stewardship. Citing but without analysis some of Lord Reid's pronouncements in *Sweet v. Parsley*, the court acquitted the accused, holding that there was no evidence that he had the intention to act corruptly. On the contrary, it found that the accused on learning of the abuses, expressed a desire that a new approach be followed. Although the definition of the offence was devoid of the *mens rea* words such as 'wilfully' or the like, the court held nevertheless that *mens rea* was essential and that the prosecution failed or omitted to prove it.

With due respect, it is arguable that in the circumstances of the *Ndyomugyenyi* case the court was correct on insisting on *mens rea*. Neglect of duty does not appear to fall in the category of offences, such as theft or embezzlement, which Lord Reid had in mind; it seems to be more an offence of negligence, which does not require

251. [1963] 1 All E.R. 223, 228.
252. [1969] 1 All E.R. 347.
253. *Ibid*., at 350.
254. Cr. Sc 003 of 2010, [2010] UGHC 49, 31 Aug. 2010.

mens rea. Once negligence was shown to exist as it was here, the offence was complete. This was probably a case in which the subject-matter test, as articulated in *Lim Chin Aik v. R.*, ought to have been applied. By making neglect of duty an offence of corruption, couched in language that does not include *mens rea* words, Parliament must have intended to require persons in positions of stewardship to perform their duties to an objectively reasonable and high standard of care so as to avoid loss or abuse; and that this duty be carried out under conditions of strict liability. Such liability would inure to the public good, particularly in stemming the high tide of corruption in the public service.

Chapter 4. General Defences

§1. Unsoundness of Mind

I. Affecting the Proceedings

209. The question may arise whether, due to unsoundness of mind, an accused person is capable of pleading or of making his defence. Is he or she of sufficient intellect to plead, to differentiate between a plea of guilty and not guilty, to instruct counsel, to understand the evidence or to cross-examine witnesses?[255] These questions may arise at any stage of the proceedings. They may be raised by the accused person himself or herself or through his or her counsel, or by the prosecution, or by the court itself *mero motu*. Where such questions arise, both the Magistrates Courts Act[256] and the Trial or Indictments Act[257] provide that the court must stop the proceedings and conduct an inquiry into the mental condition of the accused. For that purpose, the court may examine witnesses who can speak to the accused's mental condition. These witnesses should include a medical practitioner who has had an opportunity to examine the accused. Relying on such evidence and on its own observations the court then determines whether or not the accused is of sound mind.

210. Where the court adjudges the accused to be of sound mind, then the trial proceeds or resumes if it had already started. If, however, it finds that the accused is of unsound mind and, consequently, incapable of pleading or making his or her defence, it must postpone the trial or further proceedings of the trial. Failure to hold the inquiry or to postpone the proceedings after it is manifestly clear that the accused is of unsound mind is a grave irregularity.[258] In *Uganda v. Baziraneyiza s/o Kasiku*,[259] the accused appeared before a Magistrates' Court charged with assault with intent to cause grievous harm. When called upon to plead he said, 'I admit I wounded T. because of my madness. I have never had treatment for my madness.' This statement should have raised doubt in the mind of the magistrate about the accused's sanity and his fitness to plead or make his defence. The magistrate should have proceeded to make an inquiry as indicated above. He did not do so. After several adjournments the magistrate made the following ruling: 'The accused convicted on his own plea of guilty but insane at that time.' As may be expected, the High Court set aside the ruling.

211. If the offence with which an accused person of unsound mind is charged is a bailable offence, the court may consider releasing him or her on bail with the necessary security to appear again after recovery and with adequate safeguards for his or her own safety and that of the general public. Where bail is not granted, the court must commit the accused to some safe custody and in the meantime transmit the

255. See *R. v. Robertson* [1968] 3 All E.R. 557.
256. Section 113.
257. Section 45.
258. See *Cheung Singh v. R.* [1956] 23 E.A.C.A. 459.
259. H.Ct.Monthly Bulletin 191/69.

record of the proceedings to the Minister of Justice. It is the Minister who decides whether the accused should be committed to a mental institution as a criminal lunatic or to some other safe place of detention. On a certification by a duly qualified practitioner that the accused has recovered and is fit to plead or to make his defence, the trial may resume or start de novo at the instance of the DPP. Where the DPP does not wish to continue with the proceedings, then the court discharges the accused.

212. It should be stressed that the foregoing discussion relates to the accused's unsoundness of mind at the time of trial and not at the time of the commission of the offence. To be sure, an accused may have been of unsound mind at the time of the alleged offence, but of sound mind at the time of the trial. Conversely, he or she may have been of sound mind at the time of the offence, but in the intervening period became of unsound mind so that by the time of the trial he or she is, by reason of that unsoundness, incapable of pleading or making his or her defence. We now turn to the situation where it is alleged that the accused was of unsound mind at the time of the offence.

II. As a Defence

A. General

213. Unsoundness of mind makes a person incapable of committing a crime. He or she may commit the proscribed conduct, be it an act or an omission. In law, however, he or she is not criminally or culpably responsible for that conduct. Like an infant, he or she is said to lack capacity to form the requisite intent to commit any crime. He or she is therefore excused for what he or she does. Unsoundness of mind or insanity is thus a complete defence to any criminal charge. Section 11 of the Penal Code provides as follows:

> A person is not criminally responsible for an act or omission if at the time of doing the act or making the omission he or she is through any disease affecting his or her mind incapable of understanding what he or she is doing, or of knowing that he or she ought not to do the act or make the omission; but a person may be criminally responsible for an act or omission, although his or her mind is affected by disease, if such disease does not in fact produce upon his or her mind one or other of the effects aforesaid in reference to that act or omission.

According to this provision, three elements must be shown to exist for this defence to be established: (i) a disease affecting the accused's mind; and (ii) incapacity to understand what he or she is doing; or (iii) incapacity to know that it is legally wrong.

B. Disease Affecting the Mind

214. Central to this element is 'the mind'. Mind constitutes the mental faculties of awareness, cognition, reason, understanding and memory.[260] Concerning 'disease affecting the mind' it must be noted that the Code does not, like the formulation found in the English M'Naghten rules, talk of 'disease of the mind'. The Code talks of 'any disease' *affecting the mind.* It is not limited to diseases of the brain or originating from the brain. It encompasses both diseases of the mind as well as physical diseases. A 'disease affecting the mind' is therefore any disease, mental or physical, that results in a malfunctioning of the mind in such a way as to adversely affect a person's cognitive powers, reasoning, understanding or memory. The effect may be temporary, intermittent or permanent.[261]

215. Diseases that are generally agreed by psychiatrists to be mental diseases or diseases affecting the mind include melancholia, schizophrenia, paranoia, the various forms of psychoses, 'high-grade mental deficiency',[262] communicated insanity or *folie a deux,*[263] epileptic twilight state and alcoholic dementia, irresistible impulse and depression. Physical diseases that have been acknowledged by the courts as capable of affecting the mind include *arteriosclerosis* (hardening of the arteries leading to a congestion of blood in the brain and to consequent loss of consciousness);[264] *hypoglycaemia* (a condition brought about when there is more insulin in the bloodstream than the sugar to cope with it – resulting in unconsciousness);[265] cerebral tumours;[266] psychomotor epilepsy (makes the victim unconscious and violent);[267] and concussions. Automatism, which has been said to be 'action without any knowledge of acting or action with no consciousness of doing of what is being done',[268] is also a disease that may affect the mind.[269]

216. Our courts have also recognized the condition of 'running amok' as a disease that affects the mind of an accused. This was in a case where the accused speared to death a man with whom he was friendly. The accused, the deceased, and others were assisting a mutual friend to weed his garden at Omiya Anyima in Acholi. After work they had food and drink and were resting. All of a sudden the accused, his eyes staring and looking fierce, rushed out of a hut shouting. 'I am

260. See *R. v. Kemp* [1956] 3 All E.R. 249, per Devlin, J.
261. *Ibid.*
262. See *Tadeo Oyee s/o Duru v. R.* [1959] E.A. 407.
263. For example, see the English case of *R v. Windle* [1951] 2 All E. R. 1. This disease arises when a person is in constant attendance of unsound mind.
264. *Ibid.*
265. *R. v. Quick & Anor.* [1973] 3 All E.R. 347.
266. *R. v. Charlson* [1955] 1 All E.R. 859.
267. *Bratty v. Attorney-General for N. Ireland* [1961] 3 All E.R. 523; *R. v. Sullivan* [1983] 2 All E.R. 673; *Uganda v. Tito Kasajagenda* H.Ct.Monthly Bulletin No. 1 of 1965.
268. *Bratty v. Attorney-General for N. Ireland* [1961] 3 All E.R. 523, 532 per Denning, L.J.
269. The Botswana case of *Kaome v. State* illustrates the automatism condition. [1999] B.L.R. 187 (HC). The appellant was charged and convicted by a Magistrates' Court of causing death by reckless driving. He told the court that as he drove the vehicle he had a headache.

dying'. He then seized a spear and stabbed the deceased to death. A psychiatrist called by the court opined thus:

> The African gets an idea that people are against him, he acts in a very excited and frenzied way and then runs away. Sometimes they remember and sometimes not. There may be complete confusion or partial mental confusion. This is common here and in Malaya – it is called 'amok'.

The court accepted and acted on this opinion.[270]

217. The courts have also recognized 'acute brain syndrome' as another disease that affects the mind. In one case the accused beheaded a Roman Catholic priest at Virika Mission in Fort Portal. He was on his way to the police station with the head of the deceased when he was arrested. He said that on the day in question he saw 'images of twenty-four children who were burnt … coming to my head as a dream, and that the footprints of a man and that of a dog on the rock are not of Jesus but of our grandfather'. He said that when he went to complain to the priest about the children, the priest turned him away. He went on to say that:

> The father then went to his work. I remained standing to the same place where I stood. I went to the father at the time when images of the burnt children came to my mind. I then cut the father with a panga on the head. I cut his head off which I was bringing to the police. I brought this head for O.C. Police to see and to confirm that I was annoyed when he sent me away.

The Court found that the accused was suffering from 'acute brain syndrome' and did not understand what he was doing and was therefore legally insane.[271]

218. More problematic, however, was the decision of the court in another case, recognizing fear of witchcraft as 'a disease of the mind'.[272] The accused believed that his father had bewitched and killed his two sons, his first wife, his goats and cow. He also believed that the father bewitched him and made him impotent, and bewitched his second wife who was always sickly. On the day in question, the accused and his father went to a funeral of a child. They returned together, talking in a friendly manner. All of a sudden and without any quarrel or provocation whatsoever the accused hacked his father with a panga and killed him. He then went to a Gombolola chief and reported the killing. He said to the chief, 'I have killed him because he was Satan' (meaning that he was bewitching him). An assessor assisting the court opined that the accused's belief that the father was bewitching him affected his mind, and the nadir of this effect was attendance at a funeral of a child and then thinking of his own children whom he believed to have been bewitched by his father. According to the assessor, this made the accused lose his mind and to kill the deceased. Could it be said that he was acting under sudden provocation? Faced

270. *Regina v. Candukmon s/o Oyaru* [1956–1957] 8 U.L.R. 337.
271. *Uganda v. Aventore Ovu* [1972] U.L.R. 14.
272. *Regina v. Mageta s/o Kachehakana* [1956–1957] U.L.R. 294.

with the Court of Appeal for Eastern Africa decisions which required 'sudden provocation' in cases involving belief in witchcraft, the Court ruled out provocation as a defence.[273] Clearly, the basis of the killing was the accused's belief, unscientific though it might have been to moderns, that the deceased was bewitching him. Should it then send the accused to the gallows for the killing? Rather than do this, the Court decided to avail him of the defence of insanity. It said:

> This case is not free from difficulty. I have considered the words 'disease of the mind' in Section 12 of the Penal Code [now Section 11]. I am of the opinion that an African living far away in the bush may become so obsessed with the idea that he is being bewitched that the balance of his mind may be disturbed to such an extent that it may be described as disease of the mind. Here the killing is unexplained, and in my opinion inexplicable; except upon the basis that the accused did not know what he was doing.[274]

219. The problem with this case is that it was generalist and did not pinpoint the 'disease' that affected the mind. Belief in witchcraft per se has been rejected in other jurisdictions as a defence, unless it is a product of a diseased mind.[275] As the Court of Appeal for Eastern Africa curtly observed in a case originating from Kenya, belief in witchcraft 'is a belief sometimes held by entirely sane Africans'.[276] It is no wonder that for twenty years, the decision was not cited nor followed. It was revived only in 1978, when the Uganda Court of Appeal likened fear of witchcraft to 'insane delusions', which are clearly 'a disease of the mind'.[277]

C. Incapacity to Understand What He or She is Doing or That It Is Wrong

220. This element has two arms: (a) understanding what is being done – material capacity, and (b) understanding that it is legally wrong or ought not to be done – normative capacity.

221. The inability of the accused to understand what he or she is doing should stem from the disease affecting his mind. So if the accused committed an offence for reasons other than suffering from a disease that affected the mind, he or she is not entitled to the defence of insanity. For instance where the accused says that he or she committed the offence as a result of a mistake of fact, he or she may be entitled to the defence of mistake of fact, but not of insanity. Whether or not the accused understood what he or she was doing is a question of fact that the court must resolve. In doing so, the court may take into account the amount of violence with which the accused committed the offence, the relationship between the accused

273. See *Eria Galikuwa v. R.* [1951] 18 E.A.C.A. 175.
274. [1956–1957] 8 U.L.R. 294, 298.
275. For example, see *Solomon Hotema v. United States*, 186 U.S. 313 (1901); *Philip Muswi s/o Mosola v. R.* (1956) 23 E.A.C.A. 622.
276. *Ibid.*, at 625.
277. *Okello s/o Kamuleti v. Uganda Court of Appeals Crim. App. No. 29* 1978 (unreported).

and the victim, any apparent lack of motive and the conduct of the accused after committing the offence. The court may also take into account expert opinion or evidence of psychiatrists or other medical people with experience in dealing with mental diseases; as well as observations of lay persons who may be acquainted with the accused and with his or her conduct before and after the event in question.

222. Similarly, as to the normative incapacity, the incapacity to appreciate that what he or she is doing is legally wrong must also be caused by the disease affecting the mind. If it is caused by other reasons other than a disease affecting the mind, then, the accused will be found guilty, as ignorance of the law is no defence, and good motives are not a defence either.

223. It must therefore be emphasized that for the defence of insanity to avail an accused, it is not sufficient merely to prove that at the time such accused committed the offence he or she was suffering from a disease that affects the mind. It must simultaneously be proved that because of that disease the accused did not know what he or she was doing, or that it was forbidden in law. Thus any evidence tending to show that the accused knew that what he or she did was wrong in law would disentitle him or her to the defence of insanity. The case of *Rex v. Kabande w/o Kihigwe*[278] is in point. The accused struck a little boy on the head with a heavy hoe handle, killing him by fracturing his skull. Upon her arrest immediately after the killing she told the deceased's father, 'Your children killed my children so I've killed your children.' It transpired, though, that all her six children were alive and well. Additionally, a few days previous to the killing, the accused shouted accusations of witchcraft against the deceased's family. The accusations were baseless, because there was no shred of evidence to show, as is usual in cases of suspicions of witchcraft, that she had had any misfortune, such as death, illness or the like, in her family. The Court found that although the accused was 'strongly deluded' at the time of the killing and was not completely sane, she did not lose her material or normative power of cognition. The Court said:

> Upon the doctor's evidence to which I must give weight, this woman is not a witless creature incapable of reason. I have pointed out that she knew that she was killing a child, and a particular child. Her flight from the scene and her throwing away of the weapon indicate a realization of wrongdoing. Therefore, though this woman has been proved as a matter of probability to have crazy beliefs I do not think that it has been shown as a matter of probability that she neither knew what she was doing nor that she failed to realize that what she was doing was wrong. The rule of law on this topic may appear harsh enough, but it is certain enough and I must abide by it.

The Court therefore turned down the accused's plea of insanity, and its decision was upheld by the Court of Appeal for Eastern Africa.

278. [1948] 15 E.A.C.A. 135. For a similar decision, see *Nyige s/o Suwatu v. R.* [1948] 14 E.A.C.A. 135, 136.

D. Presumption of Sanity and Burden of Proof

224. Section 10 of the Penal Code provides that 'Every person is presumed to be of sound mind, and to have been of sound mind at any time which comes in question, until the contrary is proved.' If the accused wishes to rely on the insanity defence, he or she must raise the issue. It is, however, not enough simply to assert that he or she was of unsound mind. He or she bears the evidentiary burden to prove it, by testifying and by calling evidence on his or her behalf. He or she discharges that burden by showing that it is more than probable that he was of unsound mind. As the Court of Appeal for Eastern Africa put it:

> An accused must not merely raise a reasonable doubt; his burden, as in a civil case, is to prove insanity upon a balance of probability; that is to say he must show, on all the evidence, that insanity is more likely than sanity, though it may be ever so little more likely. Merely to raise a reasonable doubt might still leave the balance on the side of sanity.[279]

The burden then shifts on the prosecution to adduce evidence to negative unsoundness of mind and overall to prove beyond reasonable doubt that the accused is guilty of the offence charged.

225. Ordinarily, it should be the accused who should raise the question of unsoundness of mind and prove it. Nevertheless, in most cases, except those involving capital offences, the majority of the accused persons are unrepresented. They are also invariably ignorant of whether or not to raise the question. For that reason, therefore, a practice has developed for the prosecution or the court itself on sensing that the accused might have a defence of unsoundness of mind to take the initiative and to subject the accused to psychiatric examination and to call the psychiatrist to give evidence.[280] On this point, the Court of Appeal for Eastern Africa has once again counselled as follows:

> For the Crown to call such a witness, in order that he may give evidence relevant to a defence of insanity which it lies on an accused to establish, would no doubt be justified, in the accused's own interest, if the latter were unrepresented at the trial. But where … he is represented by counsel, then the proper procedure in all ordinary cases is for the defence to call him … No doubt, in the present case, the Crown called Dr. Margetts as their witness with the best of motives, in order to assist the defence, conceding as they did that the appellant's mental state, from a medical if not from a legal point of view, was at least questionable, and having in mind, perhaps, that from a practical point of view it is easier for the Crown to secure the attendance of a government physician at a trial than it is for the defence to do so. But if that be so, the proper course

279. *Nyinge s/o Suwatu v. R.* [1959] E.A. 974, 980, per Windham, J.P.
280. See *Regina v. Candukmon s/o Oyaru* [1956–1957] 8 U.L.R. 337. In this case, the court took the initiative to call for psychiatric evidence at the end of the prosecution's testimony although the accused was represented by counsel.

is for the Crown to offer him to the defence, who would no doubt avail themselves of the offer and call him as their witness.[281]

Assume that the accused is unrepresented and the prosecution or the court itself raises the issue of his state of mind to the extent of calling evidence. Who bears the burden of proof and to what standard or quantum of proof? The question of the burden does not probably arise, particularly where the issue is raised by the court itself. Regarding the standard, however, there must be sufficient evidence to establish the accused's unsoundness of mind on a balance of probabilities.[282]

III. Verdict

226. Where the Court upholds the defence of insanity, it must pass a special verdict to the effect that the accused is not guilty by reason of insanity. It must then report the case to the Minister of Justice who may order the accused to be confined in a mental hospital, in prison, or in any other suitable place as he or she may determine, for safe custody. The person in charge of the hospital, prison or any other place where the accused is ordered to be confined, must submit periodic reports to the Minister as to the condition of the accused. Acting on such reports, the Minister may either order that the prisoner be discharged or be otherwise dealt with as he or she may deem appropriate.[283]

§2. Diminished Responsibility

227. Diminished responsibility is not a general defence. It is limited to murder cases only. It is discussed here because it is closely related to insanity.

228. Section 194(1) of the Penal Code provides that:

> Where a person is found guilty of the murder or of being a party to the murder of another, and the court is satisfied that he or she was suffering from such abnormality of mind (whether arising from a condition of arrested or retarded development of mind, or any inherent causes or induced by disease or injury) as substantially impaired his or her mental responsibility for his or her acts and omissions in doing or being a party to the murder, the court shall make a special finding to the effect that the accused was guilty of murder but with diminished responsibility.

This provision was added to the Code in 1960. It was an adaptation of section 2 of the English Homicide Act of 1957. It created a new defence called diminished responsibility. Where the insanity defence is turned down and no other defences are

281. *Ibid.*, 980.
282. See *Mbeluke v. Republic* [1971] E.A. 479, 481.
283. See sec. 117(5) of the Magistrates Courts Act and sec. 48(5) of the Trial Indictments Act.

available to save the accused from being sentenced to death for the murder, diminished responsibility could be his or her only salvation. If successful he or she is treated in exactly the same way as one who is found not guilty by reason of insanity, he or she may then be subject to life-long confinement at the pleasure of the Minister of Justice. This is in sharp contrast with the way his or her counterpart in England is treated. Under the English Homicide Act, a person who successfully asserts the diminished responsibility defence is entitled to be convicted of manslaughter and sentenced to an appropriate term which may vary from life imprisonment to probation. He or she is not liable to be subjected to life-long confinement which a verdict of not guilty by reason of insanity invariably entails. Indeed, it is said that in England many a defendant would prefer to be convicted of manslaughter to being 'acquitted' of murder by reason of insanity.

229. However, as originally conceived in England, the defence of diminished responsibility was intended to mitigate the harshness of the M'Naghten Rules. The Rules relate solely to a person's intellectual ability to appreciate: (a) the physical act that he or she is doing, and (b) whether it is wrong. Therefore, if he or she had the requisite intellectual ability, his or her inability to control his physical acts by the exercise of his or her will-power was irrelevant. A person may not, strictly speaking, fit into the technical categorization of legal insanity. Yet he or she may be suffering from some mental abnormalities which impair mental responsibility for his or her acts and omissions. What, then, are the essentials of the defence?

230. There must be: (i) an abnormality of the mind, and (ii) a substantial impairment of mental responsibility.

231. The abnormality of the mind must stem from a condition of arrested or retarded development of mind, or from any inherent causes, induced by disease or injury. According to Professor Glanville Williams, the defence of diminished responsibility is confined to mental abnormalities caused by these factors alone. Abnormalities stemming from intoxication or from the three emotions of hatred, jealousy and rage are excluded.[284]

232. What, then, is the nature and scope of this 'abnormality of the mind', and how does it differ from 'diseases that affect the mind' that are required for legal insanity? The Ugandan Courts have not yet come up with an authoritative statement on the question. Once again, resort must be had to English decisions. According to Lord Parker:

> Abnormality of mind', which has to be contrasted with the time-honoured expression in the M'Naghten Rules 'defect of reason', means a state of mind so different from that of ordinary human beings that the reasonable man would term it abnormal. It appears to us to be wide enough to cover the mind's activities in all its aspects, not only the perception of physical acts and matters and the ability to form a rational judgment whether an act is right or wrong, but

284. Glanville Williams, *Textbook of Criminal Law* 691 (2d ed., Stevens & Sons 1983).

> also the ability to exercise will-power to control physical acts in accordance with that rational judgment.[285]

Abnormality of the mind is thus a wider concept than 'diseases that affect the mind'. According to the case in which the above statement is extracted, it covers irresistible impulse. In that case, the appellant was charged with the murder of a girl by strangling. After the killing, the appellant mutilated her body. The appellant pleaded diminished responsibility, that he was a sexual psychopath. According to the medical evidence adduced on behalf of the appellant, the appellant suffered from violent perverted sexual desires which he found difficult or impossible to control. He killed his victim whilst labouring under these impulses. Lord Parker stressed that provided the appellant's inability to exercise will-power to control his physical acts was due to an abnormality of mind from one of the causes specified above he would be and was entitled to the defence of diminished responsibility. Thus where a person knows what he is doing and knows that it is wrong (and therefore not legally insane), but is unable to resist from doing it because of the abnormality he would be able to invoke the defence. But the accused must prove that he was suffering from the abnormality by adducing medical evidence. This evidence may include previous episodes when he behaved in a similar fashion as in the incident in issue. *Uganda v. Arafairi Karegyera*[286] is a case in point. The accused, a Munyarwanda refugee living at the Lake Nakivale Settlement in Ankore, had a dispute with his nephew with whom he was staying. The dispute related to cattle. Using a panga, he inflicted several cut wounds on the nephew's one-year old daughter and killed her. Asked why he killed the child, the accused said that he had in fact intended to kill the father who was not available at the time and that he decided to kill the child so as to make the father feel the pain. The court ruled out insanity, partly because a psychiatrist who examined the accused opined that whatever the accused suffered from did not constitute 'a true mental disturbance' and partly because the accused killed with a motive – showing that he knew what he was doing. It did, however, rule that he was mentally abnormal at the time of the killing and found him guilty of murder but with diminished responsibility. It relied on the evidence of the father of the deceased child who said that 'for a long time the accused had been in the habit of getting attacks which would make him shake and lose control of himself in such a way that he would get very strong and would be in a frenzy'.

233. In addition to the evidence that he or she was suffering from mental abnormality, the accused must show that the extent to which he or she suffered was such as to substantially impair his or her mental responsibility for his or her acts. The extent of suffering and the degree of impairment of the accused's ability to exercise his or her will-power is a matter of fact to be determined by the court. Though the impairment need not be total, it should not be trivial or minimal.[287]

---

285. *R. v. Byrne* [1960] 3 All E.R. 1, 4.
286. [1972] U.L.R. 10.
287. See *R. v. Lloyd* [1966] 1 All E.R. 107. In directing the jury, the trial judge said 'Substantial does not mean total, that is to say, the mental responsibility need not be totally impaired, so to speak,

234. Lastly section 194(4) makes it clear that where one of the parties to a murder is declared guilty but with diminished responsibility the rest of his or her co-dependents who are otherwise guilty are not absolved from being sentenced to death.

235. The only practical effect of the diminished responsibility defence in Uganda is that it relaxes the insanity rules and allows the courts to treat the accused person with a mental abnormality as an insane person. It saves such accused person from having a criminal record which his or her counterpart in England gets when he or she is convicted of manslaughter. It at the same time enables the government to exercise social control over him for his or her own safety and for the safety of the public at large.

§3. Intoxication

236. To intoxicate a person means to excite or stupefy him or her, especially by alcoholic drinks, narcotic or psychotropic drugs, to such an extent that that person's physical or mental self-control is markedly diminished. In varying degrees, an intoxicated person's senses of sight, smell, feeling, taste and hearing may become impaired. His or her ability to use his or her limbs may be reduced. His or her powers of judgment and discernment may be lowered. His or her mental faculties – reasoning, understanding and remembering may also be adversely affected. His or her power of self-restraint and inhibitions normally exercised by him or her may also be reduced. An intoxicated person may become incontinent, garrulous, excitable, irascible, aggressive and even violent. The amount of alcohol, narcotics or drugs that are enough to intoxicate a person depends on the degree of their toxicity and on the person himself or herself – his or her physical constitution and psychological or mental mettle. So does the extent of its effect on such a person.

237. As a South African judge once observed, intoxication is one of humanity's age-old frailties. In 'seeking solace or pleasure in liquor [man] may easily overindulge and thereby do the things which sober he would not do'.[288] Ugandans are no exception to this human frailty. Under the influence of drink, many easily fall prey to violent passions and commit crimes which sober they probably would not have committed. Indeed many crimes tried by the courts in Uganda, and especially those involving violence, have a liquor connection. What, then, is the response of the law to crimes committed under the influence of drink or drugs?

238. Section 12(1) of the Penal Code provides that 'Except as provided in this section, intoxication shall not constitute a defence to any criminal charge.' Therefore, intoxication per se is no defence. The policy underlying this provision would seem to be that a person who knowingly and voluntarily consumes liquor, narcotics

destroyed altogether. At the other end of the scale substantial does not mean trivial or minimal. It is something in between … ' The Court of Criminal Appeal approved this direction.

288. *S. v. Ndhlovu* [1965] 4 South African Law Reports 692, 695, per Holmes, J.A.

or psychotropic drugs and thus renders himself or herself a handy instrument to conduct harmful to others is not faultless. He should not escape liability because of his 'voluntary contracted madness'.[289] This policy is in accord with the traditional attitude of a section of the Ugandan people, expressed in indigenous maxims and adages.[290]

239. There is, however, another contending principle that must be considered when dealing with intoxication. This is the cardinal rule of the criminal law as received in Uganda that a person should not be found guilty of a criminal offence unless he is at fault. A person who commits an act or omission while under the influence of liquor, narcotics or psychotropic drugs often lacks knowledge, intention or volition. He or she has no *mens rea.* He or she cannot be said to be at fault. Is it not just to convict and punish him or her. However, in response to this argument, Lord Russell of Killowen of the English House of Lords had the following to say:

> There is, at least superficially, logic in that approach: but logic in criminal law must not be allowed to run away with common sense, particularly when the preservation of the Queen's Peace is in question. The ordinary citizen who is badly beaten up would rightly think little of the criminal law as an effective protection if, because his attacker had deprived himself of ability to know what he was doing by getting himself drunk or going on a trip with drugs, the attacker is to be held innocent of any crime in the assault. *Mens rea* has many aspects. If asked to define it in such a case as the present I would say that the element of guilt or moral turpitude is supplied by the act of self-intoxication reckless of possible consequences.[291]

The Code does recognize three exceptions to this general proposition.

240. The first exception relates to involuntary intoxication where, for example, a person is forced or tricked into consuming alcohol or drugs, say, by lacing his drink or food with such alcohol or drugs. The second exception is a state of intoxication equivalent to insanity, when the accused is said to suffer from *delirium tremens*. In connection with these two exceptions, section 12(2) and (3) provides that:

> 2. Intoxication shall be a defence to any criminal charge if by reason thereof the person charged at the time of the act or omission complained of did not know that such act or omission was wrong or did not know what he was doing and –

---

289. Expression used in Hale's *Pleas of the Crown*, vol. I, p. 32 and cited by Birkenhead, L.C. in *Director of Public Prosecutions v. Beard* [1920] All E.R. 21, 25.

290. For example, the Baganda say that *Omutamiivu tabaaga mbwa* (i.e., to say, a drunken person would not slaughter a dog for meat to eat) and that *Ggambo bbi: Wamwenge alisanga ku mutima* (i.e., to say, a bad word which a drunken person utters was already on his mind before he started to drink).

291. *Director of Public Prosecutions v. Majewski* [1976] 2 All E.R. 142, 171.

(a) the state of intoxication was caused without his consent by the malicious or negligent act of another person; or
(b) the person charged was by reason of intoxication insane, temporarily or otherwise, at the time of such act or omission.
3. Where the defence under subsection (2) is established, then in a case falling under subsection 2(a) thereof the accused person shall be discharged; and in a case falling under subsection 2(b), the provisions of the Magistrates Courts Act, 1970, relating to insanity shall apply.

241. It is apropos to point out that involuntary intoxication per se will not absolve the accused from criminal liability for an act or omission 'unless' the degree of intoxication was such as to render the accused not to 'know that such act or omission was wrong or did not know what he was doing'. Likewise, the level of insanity caused by voluntary intoxication must also reach the same degree before it can avail the accused as a defence. It must amount to legal insanity.

242. The third exception relates to offences the definition of which include intention as an essential element.
Section 12(4) of the Penal Code provides as follows:

> Intoxication shall be taken into account for the purpose of determining whether the person charged had formed any intention, specific or otherwise, in the absence of which he would not be guilty of the offence.

243. It is implicit from this provision that offences of negligence, strict liability and others in which drunkenness or labouring under the influence of drink is a constituent element are not amenable to the defence of intoxication. This is so because intention is not an essential element in those offences. What is not clear, however, is the import of the language 'any intention, specific or otherwise'. Early in the twentieth century, Lord Birkenhead stated that:

> Where a specific intent is an essential element in the offence, evidence of a state of drunkenness rendering the accused incapable of forming such an intent should be taken into consideration in order to determine whether he had in fact formed the intent necessary to constitute the particular crime. If he was so drunk that he was incapable of forming the intent required, he could not be convicted of a crime which was only committed if the intent was proved. This does not mean that the drunkenness in itself is an excuse for the crime, but that the state of drunkenness may be incompatible with the actual crime charged, and may, therefore, negate the commission of the crime.[292]

From this statement, the courts in Britain, Canada and other Commonwealth countries drew a distinction between crimes of 'specific intent' and those of 'general or basic intent'. Crimes of specific intent are offences whose definitions include a particular *mens rea* or some ulterior motive or intent. Crimes of general or basic intent

292. *Director of Public Prosecutions v. Beard* [1920] All E.R. 21, 27–28.

however are those whose definitions do not involve such requirements. Under this dichotomy, crimes of specific intent are amenable to the defence of intoxication. These include murder, robbery, breaking and entering, theft, and acts with intent to cause grievous harm. Crimes of general or basic intent include manslaughter, assault, rape and assault causing actual bodily harm.[293] They do not attract the defence of intoxication.

244. By using the language 'any intention, specific or otherwise' does the Code recognize the distinction between specific and general intent? It is submitted that it does not. If this submission were not correct what, then, would be the significance of 'otherwise' in the provision? The few reported cases from the Ugandan courts and from the former Court of Appeal for Eastern Africa do not draw this distinction. It may therefore be concluded that in Uganda intoxication can be taken into account in determining whether the accused had the requisite intention irrespective of whether that intention is specific or general.[294] It is a defence to any criminal offence, save those of negligence, strict liability and those in which drunkenness or labouring under the influence of drugs is an element. To succeed, however, it is not sufficient to show that because of the intoxication the accused readily gave way to some violent passion or other criminal inclination. The evidence must establish that he or she was incapable of forming the intention. He or she must have been so stupid by drink (or drugs) that he or she did not know what he or she was doing.[295]

245. In *R. v. Wedeza*,[296] for example, the High Court turned down the defence of intoxication because it was not satisfied that the accused because of influence of drink was incapable of forming intention to kill. According to the evidence, the accused had been drinking at a beer party. He got involved in a fight between him and other people at the party. He left the party, went to his house (a ten minutes' walk), brought a panga and hacked the deceased (one of the people involved in the fight with him) to death. He then ran back to his father and reported to him that he had killed a man, and two days later he gave the police a detailed account of what had happened. On this evidence, the Court was not persuaded that the accused was incapable of forming the necessary intention to murder.

246. Lastly, the defence of intoxication would not avail a person who while sane and sober forms an intention to commit a crime and then gets himself or herself intoxicated to get 'Dutch courage' and then commits the offence. It does not matter what degree of intoxication he or she gets into. To let him or her go scott-free on the pretext of the intoxication would be to make a mockery of the law.[297]

---

293. See *Director of Public Prosecutions v. Majewski* [1976] 2 All E.R. 142, especially the speech of Lord Elwyn-Jones, L.C.
294. In *Rwamunda v. Uganda*, Cr. App. No. 6 of 1993, [1994] UGSC 10 (2 Jun. 1994), the Supreme Court specifically referred to the provision and agreed with trial judge's finding that in the drunken state of the appellant, he might not have been able to form the necessary intention to kill; the appellant was convicted of manslaughter instead of murder.
295. *Attorney-General for Northern Ireland v. Gallagher* [1961] 3 All E.R. 299, 313.
296. *R. v. Wedeza* [1956–1957] 8 U.L.R. 241.
297. See *Attorney-General of Northern Ireland v. Gallagher* [1961] 3 All E.R. 299.

247. Regarding the burden of proof in cases where intoxication is raised as a defence the following rules apply: (i) the accused bears the burden of adducing evidence to that effect where the intoxication is said to amount to insanity;[298] (ii) the prosecution bears the burden in all other cases to prove that the accused was capable of forming and did form the necessary intention. In an often quoted passage, the former Court of Appeal for Eastern Africa said:

> It is of course correct that if the accused seeks to set up a defence of insanity by reasons of intoxication, the burden of establishing that defence rests upon him in that he must at least demonstrate the probability of what he seeks to prove. But if the plea is merely that the accused was by reason of intoxication incapable of forming the specific intention required to constitute the offence charged, it is misdirection if the trial court lays the onus of establishing this upon the accused.[299]

248. The Uganda Court of Appeal made that blunder in *Kiyengo Zaverio v. Uganda.*[300] The prosecution evidence at the appellant's trial tended to show that he was drunk at the time he allegedly committed the offence. However the appellant and his counsel did not raise the defence of intoxication but, on the contrary, disowned it. During his first appeal before the Court of Appeal, appellant's counsel raised the defence. The court rejected it, saying that 'to do so would be tantamount to putting a defence into his mouth'. This was unfortunately a misdirection, because as the Supreme Court held, a court has a duty to avail an accused person every defence disclosed by the evidence before it; with the exception of insanity, the accused does not bear a burden to raise a defence. According to the Supreme Court, 'where … there is credible evidence establishing a defence, the court should not refrain from availing it to the accused for fear of "putting a defence in his mouth".'

§4. Mistake

249. While ignorance of the law is no defence, mistake as to facts constituting the offence charged is a defence. Section 9 of the Penal Code provides as follows:

(1) A person who does or omits to do an act under an honest and reasonable, but mistaken, belief in the existence of any state of things is not criminally responsible for the act or omission to any greater extent than if the real state of things had been as he or she believed to exist.
(2) The operation of this section may be excluded by the express or implied provisions of the law relating to the subject.

298. See *Kiyongo George v. Uganda*, Cr. App. No. 13 of 1998, [1998] UGSC 12 (8 Nov. 1998).
299. *Chemingwa v. R.* [1956] 23 E.A.C.A. 451. Followed in *Nyakite s/o Oyugi v. R.* [1959] E.A. 322, *Malungu s/o Kieti v. R.* [1959] E.A. 797, and in *Kongoro s/o Mrisho v. R.* [1956] 23 E.A.C.A. 532.
300. Cr. App. No 35 2003, [2005] UGSC 6 (13 Apr. 2005).

250. The defence of mistake of fact is an extension of the general rule that the prosecution must prove *mens rea* or guilty knowledge, or fault or intention where this has not been excluded. A person who labours under a genuine mistake as to some material facts constituting the offence lacks guilty knowledge and is not at fault. However, for the defence to be sustained: (i) the mistaken belief must relate to the existence of a state of things, (ii) it must be honest or genuine, (iii) it must be reasonable, and (iv) the accused would not have been guilty of a criminal offence if the state of things he or she believed were such as he or she believed to exist.

251. Section 9(1) does not explicitly state that the state of things to which the accused's mistaken belief must relate must be factual or legal. Nevertheless, the side-note to the section uses the words 'mistake of fact'; and the former Court of Appeal of Eastern Africa has held that side-notes may be referred to in order to determine the construction of a section to which they refer. Using this rule of interpretation, the Court held that 'state of things' as found in an identical section of the Tanzanian Penal Code means factual and not legal state of things. It accordingly rejected as invalid the plea by the appellants that they had been advised by one of them that the law had been changed to entitle them to kill suspected thieves, and that they believed this to be the law when they killed the deceased. Their mistake was one of law, not of fact; it was therefore not a valid defence.[301]

252. The belief in the existence of a state of things must be honest or genuine. It must not be feigned belief; otherwise it would not be a belief at all. If the facts on which the accused based his or her belief were known to him or her to be fake or non-existent, then, the belief is not honest or genuine. Whether or not this is true will depend on the evidence and on all the surrounding circumstances.

253. Not only must the belief be honest, it must also be reasonable. What is 'reasonable belief'? It is a belief that a reasonable person would hold. What is 'a reasonable person'? This the Penal Code does not say. Nor have the Ugandan courts pronounced themselves on this point. The courts in other jurisdictions have interpreted reasonable person to mean 'an ordinary person of the community to which the accused belongs'.[302] This approach has much to recommend itself to the Ugandan courts.

254. Lastly, for the defence of mistake to be successful, the accused should not have been guilty of an offence to a greater extent than if the state of things were such as he or she believed them to be. Thus, if M shoots and kills N, honestly believing that the person shot is K, his enemy, he would not be able to set up the defence of mistake. His killing of K would not have been lawful, and he would have been guilty of K's murder. Similarly, if B burgles into C's house, honestly, but erroneously believing that it is D's shop, the mistake would not avail. The burgling of D's shop would not have been lawful. Lastly, if a policeman shoots and kills W, honestly but erroneously believing that W is a thief, he would be guilty of murder. Our

301. *Musa & Anor. v. Republic* [1970] E.A. 42.
302. See for instance the Botswana case of *Manjesa v. State* [1991] B.L.R. 391 (CA).

law does not permit the police or anyone else to kill a non-resisting suspected thief. However, section 16 of the Penal Code permits law enforcement agents to use force that is reasonable in the circumstances to prevent the escape of suspected criminals.[303]

255. Finally, subsection (2) of section 9 of the Code specifically provides that 'The operation of this rule [mistake of fact] may be excluded by the express or implied provisions of the law relating to the subject.' The drafters of the Code included this provision to make it clear that the common law rule that extends the defence of mistake to offences of strict liability,[304] did not apply in Uganda. This tallies in well with the previous discussion on strict liability offences in which *mens rea* is not a required element.

§5. Claim of Right

256. The defence of claim of right applies to offences relating to property, such as theft, burglary, robbery, receiving by false pretences, possession, etc., as well as malicious damage to property. Section 7 of the Penal Code provides that:

> A person is not criminally responsible in respect of an offence relating to property, if the act done or omitted to be done by him with respect to the property was done in the exercise of an honest claim of right and without intention to defraud.

257. The essence of this defence is the accused person's honest but mistaken belief that he has a right in law to act or deal with respect to property that turns out not to be his or hers or over which he or she does not actually have the claimed right. Honesty is a question of fact, turning on the merits and circumstances of each given case. The claim of right may relate to actual ownership, or possession, or right to deal with the property in question. Thus if X takes Y's cow honestly believing that it is his cow, he will not be guilty of theft. His honest belief to ownership negatives absence of claim of right and an intention to defraud, which are essential elements of theft. *Sewava v. Uganda* is a case in point.[305] The appellant was charged

303. Cf. the Botswana case of *State v. Ntsima* [1991] B.L.R. 251(HC). The accused, a sentry on night duty guarding the President's residence or State House in Gaborone, saw a vehicle approach the gate and signalled it to stop. The vehicle did not, but instead reversed and sped off. After a while it came back and again failed to stop when the accused signalled it to do so. The accused became suspicious and, believing that the occupant might be a South African commando, fired warning shots in the air. When it did not stop, he fired a single shot at its tyres with a view to immobilizing it and in the process killed the occupant. The court acquitted him of murder and upheld his defence of mistake of fact, holding that the mistaken belief was honest and reasonable. The force he used was reasonable in the circumstances. As to whether he would have been entitled to act the way he did had the facts been correct (that the occupant of the vehicle was a commando up to sinister business), the court asked rhetorically: 'How does an armed man stop a get-away motor vehicle? The answer lies in the ordinary common sense: deflate the tyres.' (*Ibid.*, at 267).

304. See *Tolson's* case [1889] 23 Q.B.D. 168.

305. [1966] E.A. 487.

with stealing and selling iron sheets and wooden doors, the property of the complainant. The appellant asserted that the house, a dilapidated structure, from which the sheets and the doors were extracted, was his and that he was entitled to sell them. The trial magistrate convicted the appellant without directing his mind to the appellant's claims. On appeal, the High Court held that by not so doing the magistrate erred. It was probable that if the magistrate had directed his mind to the claim, his decision might have been different.

258. Similarly, where a person damages property which he or she believes to belong to him or her he or she cannot be convicted of willful damage to property. Again, where a person finds property and, honestly believing that the owner cannot be found, damages it for purposes of disposing of it, he or she would not be convicted of malicious damage. However, the old English case of *R. v. Clemans & Anor*[306] tends to suggest that there might be limitations to a person's right to damage property as a means of exercising his of her rights related to it. A company bought property at Newquay, a town in Cornwall, and as a prelude to erecting a hotel on the property, put up a wooden structure there. The accused, inhabitants of the town, tore down and completely demolished the structure and hauled it into the sea. In so doing, the accused were apparently asserting what they believed to be their rights – the right of access to the sea and of using the land for purposes of recreation. The trial court in directing the jury said that if the accused did more damage than they could reasonably have supposed to be necessary for the assertion or protection of that right then they ought to be found guilty of malicious damage to property. They were so found and the Court for Crown Cases Reserved upheld the conviction.

259. The claim of right need not be limited to proprietary rights in respect of the property in question. It also applies to cases where the accused honestly believes that he or she has a claim of right against another person and honestly believes that he or she can enforce that right against that person's property. *Oyat v. Uganda*[307] illustrates the point. The appellant was charged with stealing the complainant's ox. The ox in question was one of five that had strayed into the appellant's farm garden and destroyed his crops. The appellant seized the oxen by way of distress damage pheasant. The matter was reported to a clan chief. It was resolved that the complainant should pay to the appellant the sum of UGX 20 as compensation for the damaged crops. The payment was to be effected within one week. In obedience to this agreement, the appellant returned four of the five oxen he had seized, retaining one ox as a lien for the sum of UGX 20 due to him as compensation. The complainant did not pay in due time, saying that he had no money. Thereupon, in exercise of his lien, the appellant sold the ox for the sum of UGX 140. The complainant reported the matter to the police who arrested the appellant and charged him with theft. He was convicted and sentenced to two years imprisonment. On appeal, the High Court quashed the conviction and set aside the sentence. Udo Udoma, C.J., said:

306. [1898] 1 Q.B.D. 556.
307. [1967] E.A. 827, 830. For a similar case see *Katorogo v. Reginam* [1956–1957] U.L.R. 358.

> The right of seizure of domesticated animals destroying another's crops either in his garden or farm is an ancient one. A person is entitled both by custom and under common law to exercise the right of detaining and impounding any animal which destroys his crops until the owner of such animal has compensated him in respect of the crops destroyed.
> Therefore, it cannot be doubted that the appellant, quite independently of the decision of the chief, had a lien over the ox and was entitled to detain it until the compensation awarded him had been paid by Petero (the complainant).

The learned Chief Justice held that by selling the ox, the appellant did not commit the offence of theft, since he firmly believed that because of the sum of UGX 20 awarded to him, he had a claim of right over the ox.

260. The *Oyat* case illustrates the other point that the defence will be available even if the claim of right asserted was unfounded, either in fact or in law. According to the English authorities cited by the Chief Justice, a distrainor in the appellant's situation was not entitled to sell nor use the animals seized. If he or she does so, he or she commits a tort and may be sued by the owner. In criminal law, however, as long as the distrainor *honestly* believes that he or she can sell the animals to enforce his or her claim against the owner he commits no offence. This is one instance where ignorance or mistake of the civil law may be a defence to a criminal charge.

§6. Compulsion and Coercion

I. Compulsion

261. Section 14 of the Penal Code frames the defence of compulsion as follows:

> A person is not criminally responsible for an offence if it is committed by two or more offenders, and if the act is done or omitted only because during the whole of the time in which it is being done or omitted the person is compelled to do or omit to do the act by threats on the part of other offenders instantly to kill him or her or do him or her grievous bodily harm if he or she refuses; but threats of future injury do not excuse any offence.

262. Compulsion means to overbear another person's will under threats of death or grievous harm and thus to induce him or her to commit an act or make an omission, which, but for the compulsion, he or she would not otherwise commit or make. Where a person acts or fails to act under compulsion he or she is not guilty of an offence even if such acts or omissions constitute the *actus reus* of an offence. By declaring him not guilty, the law is not justifying his acts or omissions. It is not encouraging violation of the law by permitting people to be used as agents for criminal designs, with the full knowledge that they will get away with it under the defence of compulsion. No, the law only excuses from criminal liability people who are forced to choose between two evils: resisting the threats of criminals and being killed or inflicted with grievous bodily harm or yielding to the threats and thus commit crimes with the concomitant possibility of prosecution, conviction and punishment. The law excuses them if they commit the crime under compulsion because they did not do so willingly. They are not blameworthy. It will not be fair and it will not serve to advance the cause of law-abidingness to punish them. Self-preservation is a natural instinct. If a person submits to the threats of criminals in order to save his or her life or to preserve his or her health, he or she ought not to be condemned, but pitied, provided that he or she acts under real threats. As Lord Morris put it:

> If then someone is really threatened with death or serious injury unless he does what he is told to do is the law to pay no heed to the miserable agonizing plight of such a person? For the law to understand not only how the timid but also the stalwart may in a moment of crisis behave is not to make the law weak but to make it just. In the calm of the courtroom measures of fortitude or of heroic behaviour are surely not to be demanded when they could not in moments for decisions reasonably have been expected even of the resolute and well disposed.[308]

263. Be that as it may, however, a person who acts under compulsion does so consciously and intentionally, albeit unwillingly. His or her acts may thus endanger the lives of innocent people. There is therefore need for vigilance to ensure that the defence is not claimed spuriously. Section 14 of the Penal Code casts the defence in restrictive terms, although on the whole it is more liberal than the law in England or in Canada. Some salient points in respect of this provision will now be considered.

264. According to the provision, the defence of compulsion applies to all offences.[309] Additionally, it is immaterial that the accused was the perpetrator or secondary participant or accessory before or after the offence. However, it must be emphasized that for the defence to succeed the accused must have committed the offence 'only because of' the threats exerted on him or her by the other co-accused. If he or she was a member of a criminal organization and thus made himself or herself readily available or amenable to use as a handmaiden of criminal gangsters, the defence will not avail him or her. Lord Lowry put it cryptically when he said:

> If a person behaves immorally by, for example, committing himself to an unlawful conspiracy, he ought not to be able to take advantage of the pressure exercised on him by his fellow criminals in order to put on when it suits him the breastplate of righteousness. An even more rigorous view which … prevails in the United States … is that, if a person is culpably negligent or reckless in exposing himself to the risk of being subjected to coercive pressure, he too

308. *Lynch v. Director of Public Prosecutions for Northern Ireland* [1975] 1 All E.R. 193, 917.
309. This is in sharp contrast to jurisdictions such as Canada where it is excluded from such offences as treason, murder, piracy, attempted murder, sexual assault, forcible abduction, hostage taking, robbery, assault with a weapon or causing bodily harm, etc. In England, it is excluded from treason and murder, although the trend is to abolish the exceptions.

> loses the right to call himself innocent by reason of his succumbing to that pressure.
>
> A practical consideration is that, if some such limit on the defendant's duress does not exist, it would be only too easy for every member of an unlawful conspiracy and for every member of a gang except the leader to obtain immunity denied to ordinary citizens. Indeed, the better organized the conspiracy and the more brutal its internal discipline, the surer would be the defence of duress for its members. It can hardly be supposed that the common law tolerates such an absurdity.[310]

The threats exerted on the accused must be of such a serious nature as to neutralize his or her powers of fortitude or resistance. They must be such that a reasonable person of the accused's background, age and gender would not have acted differently if he were exposed to them. According to the drafters of the Penal Code, such threats are limited to *killing* or inflicting *grievous bodily harm* to the accused. The grievous harm must be such harm as 'amounts to a maim or dangerous harm, or seriously or permanently injures health or which is likely to injure health or which extends to permanent disfigurement, or to any permanent or serious injury to any external or internal organ, membrane or sense' of the accused.[311] However, threats to inflict mental or psychological injury would not seem to be covered under 'grievous bodily harm' and would not entitle the victim to the defence of compulsion. So would threats to damage his or her character or reputation, or his or her property or business or professional interests. The injury is thus limited to physical injury. It is also clear from the provision that the threatened injury is limited to the accused himself or herself, not to third parties, however dear or close they may be to the accused. Furthermore, the threats must persist 'during the whole time' of the accused's participation in the criminal episode. If, therefore, there is evidence tending to show that there was a time when the accused was not under such a threat or that he or she had reasonable opportunity to flee or to seek assistance he or she would not be entitled to the defence. Again, the threats to the accused must have immediate effect, 'instantly to kill him or her or do him or her grievous bodily harm'. As the Code emphasizes, 'threats of future injury do not excuse any offence'. The rationale for immediacy is that the accused should not be excused from liability unless he or she had to act on the spur of the moment, with no surcease or no opportunity to plan or devise some means of escape. Moreover, if the threats relate to the future, then, the accused should resist and seek immediate police protection before the terrorists have had opportunity to implement their threats.

265. Lastly, the accused has the evidential burden to raise the defence of compulsion. When he or she has done so or when there is evidence on the record tending to show compulsion, the state must rebut it by evidence beyond reasonable doubt.

---

310. *R. v. Fitzpatrick* [1977] NI 20 Court of Criminal Appeal in Northern Ireland. Reproduced in Smith & Hogan, *Criminal Law: Cases and Materials* 217 (3d ed., Butterworths 1986).
311. See sec. 2(f) of the Penal Code.

II. Coercion

266. Section 17 of the Penal Code provides that:

> A married woman is not free from criminal responsibility for doing or omitting to do an act merely because the act or omission takes place in the presence of her husband; but on a charge against a wife for any offence other than treason or murder, it shall be a good defence to prove that the offence was committed in the presence of, and under the coercion of the husband.

This is a reproduction of Section 47 of the English Criminal Justice Act of 1925. That section abolished the English common law presumption that whenever a wife committed certain offences in the presence of her husband, she did so under coercion by him. This presumption entitled her to a defence unless the Crown rebutted it. The presumption was predicated on the notion of subordination of a woman to her husband who was her lord and master, and on the belief that whatever she did she did so under his influence or commands. Now that that presumption is abolished it is up to a woman who intends to raise the defence of coercion (as it is commonly known when the compulsion is exerted by a husband on his wife) to affirmatively raise it.

267. The advantage of the defence of coercion at the behest of a wife is that it is wider in scope than compulsion. It is not limited to threats of death or infliction of grievous bodily harm. It would seem to embrace pressures of a mental, psychological, moral and spiritual nature.[312] However, its major disadvantages are that: (i) it does not extend to wives of polygamous marriages (the Code defines wife as 'wife of a monogamous marriage');[313] and (ii) that it may not be invoked in cases of treason or murder. Where a wife is charged with these offences and claims that she acted under pressure from her husband she has to fall back to the general defence of compulsion, she must prove that the husband threatened to kill her or to occasion her grievous bodily harm.

268. The defence of coercion seems to be anachronistic. It has sexist overtones which are out of tune with the kind of society that Ugandans aspire to. It is inconsistent with our Constitution's principle of equality between the parties to a marriage relationship.[314] It is anomalous, and it is no wonder that it is seldom, if ever, invoked.[315] Its abolition would be in order.

312. See Smith & Hogan, *Criminal Law* 224 (7th ed., Butterworths 1992).
313. See sec. 2(gg).
314. See Art. 31(1).
315. In Britain, there are to date only three reported cases in which it has been invoked. See Smith & Hogan, *supra.*

§7. Defence of Person and Property

269. The rights to life, to personal integrity and to own property are fundamental human rights guaranteed by the Constitution.[316] Naturally flowing from these rights is the right and indeed the duty to defend one's self, one's loved ones and one's property from unlawful attacks. We refer to this right as the right to self-defence. If a person were to injure or kill another in the process of asserting this right by using reasonable force, he or she would not be guilty of an offence. He or she would be protected under the Constitution. Thus the proviso to Article 9 of the 1967 Constitution provided that a person shall not be regarded as having been deprived of his or her right if he or she dies as a result of the use of force to such an extent as is reasonably justifiable in the circumstances of the case 'for the defence of any person from violence or for the defence of property'. This provision, though omitted from the 1995 Constitution, is in accord with the principles of English law. According to section 15 of the Penal Code, criminal responsibility for the use of force in the defence of person and property 'shall be determined according to the principles of English law'. It is not clear whether these principles include both common law and statutory law. However, the courts in other East and Central African countries with Penal Code provisions identical to Uganda's seem to have limited these principles to the common law.[317]

270. The English common law on this point has been succinctly stated as follows:

> The common law has always recognized … the right of a person to protect himself from attack and to act in the defence of others and if necessary to inflict violence on another in so doing. If no more force is used than is reasonable to repel the attack such force is not unlawful and no crime is committed. Furthermore a man about to be attacked does not have to wait for his assailant to strike the first blow or fire the first shot: circumstances may justify a pre-emptive strike.[318]

271. According to English common law as thus stated, the following persons are entitled to exercise the right of self-defence. First, any person who is the subject of an unlawful attack to his or her person or property is, and naturally so, entitled to defend himself or herself against such attack. Second, any person who, though not the subject of attack, has a moral duty to defend those who have been unlawfully attacked may also exercise the right. The extent of the circle of persons to whom an individual owes a moral duty of protection is not fixed. It nevertheless includes one's family or kin and kith, classmates, bosom friends, girlfriends or boyfriends, workmates and others to whom one is closely associated. It also includes neighbours

316. Articles 22, 23 and 25.
317. See, for example, the Kenyan case of *Marwa s/o Robi v. R.* [1959] E.A. 660, the Malawian case of *Jackson v. R.* [1962] Rhodesia & Nyasaland Reports 157, and the Zambian case of *People v. Mudewa* [1973] Zambia Law Reports 147.
318. *Beckford v. R.* [1987] 3 All E.R. 425, 431 per Lord Griffiths.

and village mates.[319] One may also dare include in this category of persons the biblical neighbour to whom the Good Samaritan rendered assistance – anyone we chance to meet and who is in need of protection. Third, any person who has a legal duty to protect others may also exercise the right of defence of person to protect other persons. Indeed such person may be guilty of an offence if he did not take steps to protect those individuals in case of unlawful attack.[320] This includes any person who has charge and care over others, such as parents, guardians, teachers, employers and all heads of institutions, as well as administrators. All in all, in whatever capacity any person exercises the right of defence of person and property, that person must observe the conditions imposed by the common law for the exercise of the right.

272. The first condition for the exercise of the right of self-defence is that there must have been an *unlawful* attack on either the person defending himself or herself or his or her property; or on those he or she is entitled to defend in case of attack on their person or property. If the attack is lawful, then, forceful resistance to it would not be valid self-defence. For instance, to resist lawful arrest or to otherwise attack a police officer in the due execution of his or her duties would be criminal. However, where the arrest or other activities by the police officer are unlawful, then the person affected would be entitled to exercise the right of self-defence.

273. Implicit in the statement that there must be an unlawful attack before the right to self-defence can be exercised is the idea that the person exercising the right must have actually been attacked; or that his or her property must have been damaged. If this were the case, then the exercise of the right might in some cases come too late; the person entitled to exercise the right might have died or been disabled before he or she could exercise it; or in the case of the defence of third parties or property, the injury or harm might have been already inflicted. Fortunately, the common law does not insist on the unlawful attack actually taking place before the right to self-defence can be exercised. It is sufficient that there is an imminent and present danger of such attack. In that case, the defender may take a pre-emptive strike to repel or avert the anticipated or imminent unlawful attack with its accompanying harm and injury to him or others before it actually takes place. As Lord Griffiths has stated, 'a man about to be attacked does not have to wait for his assailant to strike the first blow or fire the first shot: circumstances may justify a pre-emptive strike'.[321]

274. Whether an unlawful attack is imminent and whether it is of such a serious nature as to warrant the defender's response is a question of fact turning on the circumstances of each case. It is nevertheless possible that in making a pre-emptive strike a person may be mistaken about the imminence of an attack or its existence at all. Such person will still be entitled to the defence, provided that belief that an attack was imminent, was genuine and that the means he used and the degree of

319. According to the customary law of the Baganda, it was a customary offence for any neighbour or villager to not to go to the rescue of another who might have been attacked.
320. Penal Code, sec. 199.
321. *Beckford v. R* [1987] 3 All E.R. 425 at 431.

force he employed to ward it off were reasonable under the circumstances.[322] In this respect, a model direction widely used by the English courts with the approval of the Lord Chief Justice and the Judicial Committee of the Privy Council reads as follows:

> Whether the plea is self-defence or defence of another, if the defendant may have been labouring under a mistake as to facts, he must be judged according to his mistaken belief of the facts: that is so whether the mistake was, on an objective view, a reasonable mistake or not.[323]

275. Furthermore, the fact that the person being unlawfully attacked or about to be unlawfully attacked does not retreat to avoid the attack and to obviate the need to hit back does not deprive that person of the defence. Failure to retreat may be an element that may be used in determining whether the accused's conduct was reasonable in the circumstances.[324]

276. The second pre-condition to the exercise of the right of self-defence is that before using force the person using it must be sure that his or her life or limb or that of another person is in actual or imminent danger, and the purpose of the use of force is to stop or to ward off the danger. Where the unlawful attack, actual or anticipated, is over and the danger to the victim is no more, use of force against the attacker will not be self-defence; it will be retaliation. And, unless it was reasonably necessary for the arrest of the attacker, such force will be unlawful.[325]

277. Lastly, for the defence of self-defence to be sustained, the force used by the accused must be reasonable. It must not be more than what was reasonably necessary for stopping or warding off the unlawful attack. What is reasonable in a given case will, however, turn on the facts peculiar to that case. However, certain general

---

322. *Ibid.*
323. *Ibid.*
324. *Palmer v. Reginan* [1971] 1 All E.R. 1077, 1085; *Regina v. Bumbakali Kyewalabye* [1956–1958] U.L.R. 4, 8.
325. Cf. the Botswana case of *State v. Chibidu* [1988] B.L.R. 467 (HC). The accused and the deceased, after a drinking spree, got involved in an altercation over a packet of cigarettes. The deceased ran away from the scene but the accused chased him; the deceased fell to the ground and the accused stabbed him; the deceased got up and ran away again, and the accused caught up with him and stabbed him again. Rejecting the claim of self-defence, the court said: 'I have no doubt that the accused stabbed the deceased when the latter was running away. He did not stab him only once, but at least twice. He was not repelling an attack at that stage. He was not defending himself. The inference is irresistible that he was acting in revenge and in pure aggression. I unhesitatingly find as a fact that the accused was acting in revenge when he committed the acts of stabbing the deceased. In the circumstances I am satisfied beyond reasonable doubt that the accused was not acting in self-defence.' *Ibid.*, at 475. See also *State v. Mokgosana* [2001] 1 B.L.R. 291 (HC). Here in the course of a fight, the deceased struck the accused with a stick. The accused disarmed him and used the stick to repeatedly hit the deceased. The deceased fell on the ground, but the accused continued to hit him. When others intervened to stop him, he attacked them as well and scattered them. He then continued to beat and kick the deceased until he died. The court rejected the accused's plea of self-defence, holding that his actions were disproportionate and were motivated by a desire for revenge.

factors need to be considered in determining reasonableness of the force used by the accused. These include the weapon, if any, which the attacker used. While the accused may be entitled to match the weapon used by the attacker to neutralize the attack, he would in most instances not be justified to respond to a weak fist blow with a lethal weapon. As a general rule, the amount of force used in self-defence must be proportionate to the force used by the aggressor. The injury already received by the accused is another factor. For instance, in *Regina v. Bumbakali Kyewalabye*,[326] the deceased attacked the accused at his house and inflicted a superficial wound, a scratch one-inch long on the left side of the face and some other minor wounds and abrasions on the heel and finger. In retaliation, the accused pounded the deceased several heavy blows on the head, fracturing the skull and killing him. The Court held that the force used was excessive. It withheld the defence of self-defence from the accused.

278. The comparative physical strengths of the accused and the attacker is another factor. If the accused is physically weaker than the attacker, he or she may in some cases be justified to use a weapon, and a lethal one at that, even if the attacker did not employ one or used a less lethal one. The fact that the attackers are more than one is another factor. So also is the fact whether the attack took place during the day or during night time. This factor is relevant in assisting the court in determining whether or not the accused was able to see the attacker or attackers and to appreciate the full extent of the force that was arrayed against him or her and to respond appropriately. All in all, the judge must always bear in mind that the accused does not have time to reflect and to weigh this against other modes of defence. He or she acts on the spur of the moment and under considerable stress.

279. We must also make special mention regarding the right to defend one's dwelling premises against trespassers. This right is predicated on the notion that a person's home is his or her castle. Defence of one's property generally is based on the right of ownership recognized by the Constitution. The principles governing defence of person do also apply with equal force to defence of property. No more force than is reasonably necessary to stop trespass, or damage or the unlawful taking of one's property need be used. Where the trespasser, attacker or thief puts up forceful resistance to being evicted or stopped from attacking, damaging or stealing one's property, such resistance may be countered by using means appropriate to the occasion. The facts of *Zedekia Lukwago v. Reginam* are instructive in this respect.[327] The appellant was asleep in his house. At about 7:00 pm, he was awakened by an intruder who was pulling his bedclothes off his bed. The appellant tried to capture the intruder. The intruder attacked him in the process. Acting in self-defence the appellant inflicted six severe wounds including the complete amputation of the intruder's right hand. In the course of convicting the appellant of manslaughter, the trial judge remarked:

326. [1956–1958] U.L.R. 5.
327. [1953] 23 E.A.C.A. 507, 508. See also sec. 28 of the Criminal Procedure Code.

> One must use all means of escape. In this case there was nothing to prevent the accused from running out of the back door ... In any event it is clear that according to the accused the deceased was trying to escape and all he need have done was to allow him to escape.

The Court of Appeal for Eastern Africa held this to be misdirection. It said:

> We do not think that it is the law that a householder attacked in his own house by an intruder is required to use all means to escape. It is a mistake in such circumstances to draw a hard and fast distinction between the right of defence of property and the right of defence of the person. The householder is entitled either to seek the arrest or to expel the intruder and, should he be attacked in so doing, to use all necessary force to repel such attack and to effect the arrest or the expulsion.[328]

280. More recently, the Supreme Court held the above statement to be applicable to a situation where the attack took place, not inside a house, but within a court yard.[329] Generally, however, the force used to defend one's property must be reasonable. Thus in the *Zedekia Lukwago* case, although the Court of Appeal, notwithstanding the misdirection it found, upheld the appellant's conviction for manslaughter, holding that in the circumstances of the case the force that he used was excessive. Similarly, in *Kasto Budebo v. Uganda*, the appellant suspecting that there was an intruder in his house decided to go out; as he did, the intruder apparently came as if to attack or push him aside; thereupon the appellant cut the stranger twice. The Supreme Court held that while the appellant was entitled to defend himself or his property, he used excessive force, because he was going out any way, and the intruder was unarmed and had not even touched him. The court reduced the conviction from murder to manslaughter.[330]

281. As with the defence of person, in determining the means or the amount of force to use in defence of property, the court must take into account not only the amount of force or the type of weapons used by the intruder or thief, but also the gravity of the offence and the circumstances in which it was being committed by such person.[331]

282. Regarding the onus of proof, whenever there is evidence that tends to disclose a possible defence of self-defence (or defence of person or property) the onus

328. *Ibid.*
329. *Byabagambi Gabriel v. Uganda*, Cr. App. No. 16 of 2002, [2004] UGSC 5 (15 Aug. 2004).
330. Cr. App. No. 22 of 1993, [1994] UGSC 13 (7 Oct. 1994). See also the similar Kenyan case of *Marwa s/o Robi v. R.* [1959] E.A. 660. In *Jongo s/o Kego v. R.* [1960] E.A. 130, for example, a chief authorized the deceased to take a cow from the accused as compensation for one that the accused owed him but failed to return. On seeing him drive away the cow, the accused speared the deceased to death. It was held that the killing could not be justified as being an act in defence of property.
331. Section 16 of the Penal Code.

is on the prosecution to disprove it beyond reasonable doubt. If the evidence adduced by the prosecution does not contain any suggestions of such self-defence, then, the accused bears the evidential burden to raise it. Once he or she has raised it, the prosecution must prove beyond reasonable doubt that he or she did not act in self-defence.

Chapter 5. Incomplete Crimes: Attempt, Conspiracy and Incitement

§1. ATTEMPT

I. General

282.1. Attempt is an incomplete crime. The aim of the law of attempt is deterrence. It enables law enforcement authorities to intervene and to thwart criminal conduct before it matures into full bloom crimes. Such intervention is necessary to avert harm that would otherwise result if the offender were allowed to do all the things that are necessary for the crime to be consummated.[332] Additionally, by making attempt to commit a crime, albeit not committed, an offence with consequent punishment, the law aims at discouraging people from having criminal inclinations or from engaging in criminal activities.

283. Section 386 of the Penal Code defines 'attempt' as follows:

1. When a person, intending to commit an offence begins to put his or her intention into execution by means adapted to its fulfillment, and manifests his or her intention by some overt act, but does not fulfill his or her intention to such an extent as to commit the offence, he or she is deemed to attempt to commit the offence.
2. It is immaterial –
   (a) except so far as regards punishment, whether the offender does all that is necessary on his or her part for completing the commission of the offence, or whether the complete fulfillment of his or her intention is prevented by circumstances independent of his or her will, or whether he or she desists of his or her own motion from the further prosecution of his or her intention;
   (b) that by reason of circumstances not known to the offender it is impossible in fact to commit the offence.

II. *Mens Rea*

284. As the Penal Code so clearly indicates, there must be an intention to commit a particular or substantive offence. Absent that intention, there would be no *mens rea*, and there would be no offence of attempt. There can, for example, be no attempt to murder unless the accused intended to cause death.[333] Similarly, there can be no attempt to burgle unless the accused intends to commit a specific felony after

332. This point is buttressed by sec. 389 of the Penal Code which provides that 'Every person who, knowing that a person desires to commit or is committing a felony, fails to use all reasonable means to prevent the commission or *completion* thereof, is guilty of a misdemeanour.' Emphasis added.
333. For example, see *Rex v. Luseru Wandera s/o Wandera* [1948] 15 E.A.C.A. 105. See also sec. 204 of the Penal Code.

breaking into a dwelling house at night time.[334] It is true that some offences may be committed with a *mens rea* that falls short of an intention to commit the offence. For example, offences such as causing malicious damage to property or manslaughter by negligent or reckless acts may be committed with recklessness as the *mens rea*. Yet others, such as crimes of negligence and of strict liability do not need intention or, for that matter, *mens rea* at all. But not attempt. This therefore means that there cannot be an attempt to commit any of these offences, since a specific intent is essential for attempt.

285. Intention to commit an offence may be proved by showing that the accused had expressly declared such intention. Short of such express declaration, intention may be inferred from the acts or omissions of the accused in a given case. However, such acts or omissions must be of such a character as to be incompatible with any other reasonable explanation but intention to commit the offence in question.

286. For example in *Sabane Bbale & Anor. v. Uganda*,[335] the appellants were charged with attempted robbery. They were part of a gang of five people who tried to ambush a car in which the complainant, carrying a large sum of money, was travelling. They got out of their own car ready to attack the complainant, but were stopped by another oncoming car which knocked down the first appellant and dispersed the rest. The first appellant was injured and was found by the police lying on the road holding a panga in his hand. Earlier in the day, the selfsame appellant was seen hovering around the complainant's office. Holding that the appellant had the intention to rob, the court said:

> His previous knowledge of what was afoot and his descent, armed, from the car which ambushed Lwanga amounted to an overt act towards the commission of an attempted robbery ... What other intention could the first appellant have had when he jumped out of the car with a panga, but to rob Lwanga, whom he knew was carrying a large sum of money?

III. *Actus Reus*

287. The first requisite for the *actus reus* of attempt is that the accused must begin to put his or her intention into execution by means adapted to its fulfilment. The second is that there must be some overt acts which manifest the accused's intention to commit the offence in question, since mere intention to commit an offence without more does not amount to an offence. For example, in the case of attempting to steal from a car, the act of forcing open the door of the car is an overt

334. See sec. 295 of the Penal Code. See also *Mohamed Sirimenda v. R.* H.Ct.Cr.App. No. 639 of 1962; H.Ct.Monthly Bulletin No. 48 of 1963.
335. H.Ct.Cr.App. No. 576 of 1968; H.Ct.Monthly Bulletin No. 143 of 1968.

act that manifests the accused's intention to steal.[336] In the case of attempting to steal cattle, the stealth entering upon a farm during the hours of darkness without invitation are overt acts which manifest the intention to steal cattle.[337] The third requisite is that the overt acts must be close or proximate to the commission of the offence in question. Although the accused might have begun to put his or her intention into effect, for one reason or another, he or she 'does not fulfil his intention to such as extent as to commit the offence in question'. For these actions to amount to attempt, he or she must have gone close or almost to fulfilling his or her intentions. Acts that are not close to the consummation or commission of the offence do not constitute attempt. They are considered to be mere preparation. Preparation is the devising or arranging of the means wherewithal to commit the offence in question. They include the acquisition of weapons or implements of the crime and moving to the scene of the crime. As a general rule, preparation stops when the accused begins to actually put his or her intention into execution by overt acts adapted to its fulfilment. Whether or not the acts in question are proximately or remotely connected to the commission of the offence is a question of fact, and often calls for a common sense determination by the court as there are no hard and fast rules to guide them. Nevertheless, proximity, which is measured in terms of time, distance, speed, and the number of remaining acts, depends on the nature of the offence charged. Thus in the case involving attempt to steal from a car, the accused's efforts to force open the door of the car was considered to be proximate to the commission of theft. Similarly in the case involving the stealing of cattle, the entering upon the farm was held to be proximate to the offence. In one case of attempted rape, the act of the accused getting himself erect, getting into the victim's bed uninvited, and trying to remove her nickers was held to be acts immediately connected with rape.[338]

288. However, in the case of *Constante Mbuzehasi & Anor. v. Lukiiko*,[339] the appellants' acts were held not to be so proximately connected. According to the facts, the first appellant in the presence of the second appellant knocked down the complainant, and she fell down on her back. The Buganda Principal Court convicted the first appellant of attempted rape and the second appellant of conspiring and aiding the first appellant to rape – especially as he failed to 'take care' of [protect] the complainant. On appeal, the High Court quashed the convictions, saying that 'Merely knocking down a girl as a result of which she falls on her back is not an act in law sufficiently proximate to constitute an attempt to rape her.' As for the offence of conspiracy and aiding the attempted rape, the Court said that 'the mere failure to take care of a girl or woman would not in itself constitute in law the offence of conspiracy or aiding the attempt to have unlawful sexual intercourse'. Similar conclusions were reached in *Adamu Mulira v. Regina*[340] in which the appellant was charged with attempt to rape his master's wife, because the appellant's acts

336. See *Ismail Bin Farah v. R.* [1956] 29 K.L.R. 183; *Mwankikwa s/o Mutisya v. R.* [1959] E.A. 18; *Mussa s/o Saidi v. R.* [1962] E.A. 454.
337. See *Keteta v. Republic* [1972] E.A. 532.
338. It was so held in the Botswana case of *Rakala Mokhompha v. State* H.Ct.Cr.App. No. 68 of 1981 (unreported).
339. H.Ct.Cr.App. No. 233 of 1964, H.Ct.Monthly Bulletin No. 4 of 1965.
340. [1953] 20 E.A.C.A. 223.

were held not to be proximate to the commission of the offence. Here the appellant entered the woman's bedroom where he found her lying on her bed reading a book. He switched off the lights, put one hand over her mouth and with the other removed his shorts and lifted up her petticoat. The woman screamed for help and a boy who was in a nearby room on the same floor flashed a torch through the opened uncurtained window of the woman's bedroom and saw the accused bending over her. The accused ran out of the room as the torch light was flashed on him. The High Court convicted the accused of attempted rape. On appeal, the Court of Appeal for Eastern Africa quashed the conviction, holding that the accused's acts were not sufficiently proximate to the commission of the offence of rape. They were, if anything, merely preparatory.

289. According to section 386(2)(a) of the Penal Code, it is not material to the completion of the *actus reus* of attempt 'whether the offender does all that is necessary on his or her part for completing the commission of the offence'. This is in sharp contrast with English law which requires the accused to have done all the acts on his part which are necessary for the completion of the crime in question.[341] According to the Uganda Penal Code, it is enough that the accused has done an act which is a step towards the commission of the crime and is proximate to but falls short of its consummation.

290. According to the same provision, it is also not material to the completion of the *actus reus* of attempt that 'the complete fulfilment of his intention is prevented by circumstances independent of his will' or that 'he or she desists of his or her own motion from the further prosecution of his or her intention'. The *actus reus* is complete where, as in car theft cases cited above, the accused is interrupted by the owner or by the police before he can complete the offence. In the cattle theft case, the accused was interrupted by night watchmen, and this was held not to afford him any defence. Likewise a would-be rapist, who, in the process of trying to have sexual intercourse with a victim, is repulsed by the victim, would also be guilty of attempt.

291. Similarly, the fact that the accused on his or her own volition changes his or her mind and desists from any further acts toward completing his or her criminal intention affords him or her no defence. Provided that by overt acts, he or she has begun to put his or her intentions into effect, the *actus reus* of attempt is complete. For sentencing purposes, however, his or her change of heart is taken into account as a mitigating factor.

292. It may, however, be argued that convicting and punishing a person who has repented, desisted and has not done any harm to anyone does not advance any of the goals of the criminal law: deterrence, reformation or retribution. A person who changes heart and does not inflict any harm deserves commendation, not condemnation. That may be true. Nevertheless, the problem attendant to affording that person a defence is the court's inadequacy to probe his or her mind and to determine

341. See *R. v. Eagleton* (1855) Sears C.C. 515.

the reason for his or her desistance. He or she may be genuinely repentant and contrite. He or she may, however, have desisted because of frustration (through ineptitude, inefficiency or insufficiency of means), or because he or she feels he or she will not succeed, or because he or she fears that he or she will be detected. In the latter case, his or her 'change of heart' is not genuine. He or she is not contrite. He or she still needs to be corrected. Therefore, given the difficulty entailed in adjudging the genuineness of the accused's change of heart, the law disregards the reasons behind his desistence and seeks to punish his or her criminal intentions when they are accompanied by overt acts although they fall short of a complete offence.

293. Again, according to section 386(2)(b) of the Code, it is immaterial 'that by reason of circumstances not known to the offender it is impossible in fact to commit the offence'. So, in the case where the accused opened the unlocked car with intent to steal from it but found nothing in it capable of being stolen it was held that he was guilty of attempt.[342] This is equally true of a pick pocket that puts his hand in his or her victim's pocket which, unknown to him or her, turns out to be empty.[343] It was also held to be true in a Tanzanian case where the accused sold certain objects which he or she believed to be diamonds but were in fact worthless pieces of glass.[344] In cases of this kind, the courts focus on the accused's intention and on what he or she thought he or she was doing when he or she began to carry it out. It is this intention (which must be accompanied with some overt acts) which the law seeks to repress. The individual who manifests such intention is anti-social. He or she knows that it is wrong to do what he or she sets out to do (although factually it is impossible to accomplish it), but goes on all the same with his determination to do it.

IV. Attempt As a 'Minor Offence'

294. Ordinarily, a person who is alleged to have attempted to commit a crime should be specifically charged with that attempt. However, the law permits a court to convict a person charged with a substantive or completed offence with attempting to commit that offence instead, even though he or she was not originally charged with attempt.[345] The court may do so either at the close of the prosecution's case,[346] or at the conclusion of the whole case. The rationale for allowing the court to convict of attempt is the need to ensure that an accused person who has manifested an intention to commit an offence and has carried out some acts towards the realization of his intentions does not go scot-free merely because there is a gap in the prosecution's evidence and thus making it impossible for the court to convict him of the

342. *Mussa s/o Saidi v. R.* [1962] E.A. 454.
343. *Rex. v. Brown* 24 Q.B.D. 57; *Rex v. Ring* 17 Cox C.C. 497.
344. *Edward s/o Michael v. Rex* [1948] 1 T.L.R. 308.
345. Section 146 of the *Magistrates Courts Act.*
346. See the Kenyan case of *Keteta v. Republic* [1972] E.A. 532 where a magistrate after having found that there was no case to answer on a charge of stock theft, convicted the appellant of attempted stock theft. The High Court confirmed the conviction.

substantive offence. However, 'offence' here means the offence charged and detailed in the particulars of the offence, and not an offence based on other facts.[347]

295. Lastly, where the prosecution evidence fails to establish attempt but, instead, it establishes a minor offence, the court may also convict the accused of the minor offence.[348] The basis for this position of the law is, again, to ensure that an accused whose conduct discloses some criminal culpability does not go completely scot-free. Thus a person charged with attempted murder may be convicted of occasioning grievous harm; and one charged with attempted rape may be convicted of indecent assault.

V. Punishment for Attempt

296. Generally speaking, attempt attracts a less severe punishment than a completed crime. This is so because it results in much less, if any, harm than the completed crime. And it is a cardinal principle of sentencing that punishment must be proportionate to the seriousness of the offence in question or to the harm or damage occasioned by a particular crime. For that reason the Penal Code classifies attempt to commit either a felony or a misdemeanour as a misdemeanour punishable by up to two years imprisonment, unless a particular law states otherwise.[349] However, where the attempted offence is a felony punishable by death or by imprisonment for a term of fourteen years or upwards with or without other punishment, the attempt amounts to a felony, punishable by up to seven years imprisonment.[350] Additionally, the Penal Code prescribes special sentences for certain attempts. These include treason,[351] inciting mutiny or mutinous assembly or seducing members of the security forces from their allegiance to the Constitution,[352] rape,[353] attempt to procure abortion,[354] attempt to commit unnatural offences,[355] attempt to murder,[356] attempt to murder by a person serving a term in prison of at least three years,[357] attempt to commit suicide,[358] attempt to injure by explosives,[359] attempt to rob,[360] attempt to

347. This could be illustrated by a Kenyan case, *Muiruri v. Republic* [1967] E.A. 808. In this case, the appellant was found manipulating a coin-operated gaming machine with a piece of wire. He was arrested and subsequently charged with stealing a sum of money found in his socks. The magistrate acquitted him of the offence as charged, but proceeded to convict him of attempting to steal from the machine. The High Court quashed the conviction, holding that the offence of attempt was not based on the facts detailed in the particulars of offence but on a completely different set of facts.
348. Section 145 of the Magistrates Courts Act: 'When a person is charged with an offence, and facts are proved that reduce it to a minor cognate offence, he or she may be convicted of the minor offence although he or she was not charged with it.'
349. See sec. 387 as read with sec. 22. See also *Uganda v. Polasi Kasumba* [1971] U.L.R. 34.
350. Section 388.
351. Punishable by death, sec. 23(1).
352. Punishable by death, sec. 23(2).
353. Punishable by life imprisonment with or without corporal punishment, sec. 125.
354. Punishable by fourteen years imprisonment, sec. 141.
355. Punishable by seven years imprisonment, sec. 146.
356. Punishable by life imprisonment, sec. 204.
357. Punishable by life imprisonment with or without corporal punishment, sec. 205.
358. Punishable by two years imprisonment, sec. 210 as read with sec. 22.

smuggle,[361] attempt to commit arson,[362] attempt to set fire to crops,[363] attempt to cast away ships[364] and attempt to destroy property by explosives.[365]

§2. CONSPIRACY

297. The object of the law of conspiracy, like that of attempt, is deterrence. However, the law of conspiracy casts a wider net than that of attempt. For example, an individual with a criminal intent cannot be found guilty of the offence of attempt unless he or she has by overt acts begun to put that intention into effect. However, if, he or she were to be joined by a like-minded person or persons and both or all 'agreed', maybe some time in the future to do what he or she intended to do alone he or she (and the others) will be guilty of the offence of conspiracy. Under the law of conspiracy, there is no need for any overt act or acts remotely or proximately connected with the commission of the contemplated crime. The agreement to commit the crime, albeit in the future, is sufficient to constitute the offence. Thus, what would, under the law of attempt, be dismissed as mere preparation, would, under the law of conspiracy, be an offence. The rationale for this apparent stringency of the law is its recognition of the potential harm that criminal combinations or organizations can pose to society and the need to avert such harm by repressing such combinations.[366]

298. Section 390 of the Penal Code provides that:

> Any person who conspires with another to commit any felony, or to do any act in any part of the world which if done in Uganda would be a felony and which is an offence under the laws in force in the place where it is proposed to be done, is guilty of a felony.

Similarly, section 391 provides that:

> Any person who conspires with another to commit a misdemeanour, or to do any act in any part of the world which if done in Uganda would be a misdemeanour, and which is an offence under the laws in force in the place where it is proposed to be done, is guilty of a misdemeanour.

---

359. Punishable by fourteen years imprisonment, sec. 220.
360. Punishable by seven years imprisonment if convicted by a magistrate's court or life imprisonment if convicted by the High Court, sec. 287.
361. Punishable by imprisonment of fourteen years and a fine of UGX 5 million, sec. 221.
362. Punishable by fourteen years imprisonment, sec. 328.
363. Punishable by imprisonment for seven years, sec. 330.
364. Punishable by fourteen years imprisonment, sec. 333.
365. Punishable by fourteen years imprisonment, sec. 336.
366. See, Notes *The Conspiracy Dilemma; Prosecution of Group Crimes or Protection of Individual Defendants* 62 Harv. L. Rev. 276 (1948).

299. Although the Code uses the word 'conspire', it nowhere defines it. For the meaning of 'conspire' or 'conspiracy' therefore, one has to have resort to English criminal law. According to English criminal law, conspiracy is an agreement to do an unlawful act or a lawful act by unlawful means.[367] The major elements of conspiracy therefore are: (1) an agreement, (2) for an unlawful purpose or for a lawful purpose by unlawful means.

I. Agreement

300. Agreement is the essence of the crime of conspiracy. It is the *actus reus* of the offence. It signifies mutuality or the meeting of minds to further an unlawful act or lawful act by unlawful means. It is axiomatic therefore that there must be at least two or more persons to the conspiracy, for there can be no agreement between one person. This is borne out by the meaning of the word 'conspiracy' which derives from two Latin words '*con*' and '*spirare*', and means 'to breathe together'. The Luganda equivalents of conspiracy *kwekobana* or *okwetaba mu lukwe* or *kussa kimu* also signify mutuality or agreement between two or more people to do something, or to join in a plot.

301. To be valid, therefore, the charge sheet for the offence of conspiracy must allege existence of at least two or more co-conspirators. However, if only one conspirator is named, the rest need not be named. They may, indeed, not even be known although, from the circumstances of the case, their existence must be inferred. It is sufficient to allege that the accused 'with persons unknown' conspired to commit a named offence.

302. Where two persons are charged with conspiracy and one of them is acquitted, the charge falls away as regards the second. As was stated by Lord Forter in one English case, 'It is well-established law that if two persons are accused of conspiracy and one is acquitted the other must also escape condemnation. Two at least are required to commit the crime of conspiracy: one alone cannot do.'[368] Where, however, the charge sheet alleges a conspiracy between two named defendants and others to the prosecution unknown, the acquittal of one will not result in the other going scot-free. This was the case in *Ongodia and Erima v. Uganda.*[369] Ongodia and Erima were charged with conspiring 'together and with other persons unknown to effect an unlawful purpose, namely to set up a road block near Baitababiri and arrest the then Prime Minister, Dr A.M. Obote'. The Court Martial Appeal Court acquitted Erima, for lack of evidence connecting him to the conspiracy. The charge and conviction in respect of Ongodia remained good. Similarly, where one of the co-conspirators after pleading not guilty later on changes the plea to one of guilty, it would be wrong to take that change into account when considering the other

367. See *Mulcahy v. R.* (1868) L.R. 3 H.L. 306, 317.
368. *Dharmasena v. The King*, [1951] A.C. 1, 6.
369. [196] E.A. 137

co-conspirators' liability. As the Supreme Court opined, criminal responsibility is personal, even in the case of conspiracy.[370]

303. Husband and wife cannot be convicted as sole co-conspirators, because in law they are fictionally one person and possess one will.[371] This rule will, however, not apply to parties to a polygamous or potentially polygamous marriage. This is so because section 2 of the Penal Code specifically defines 'husband' as 'husband of a monogamous marriage' and 'wife' as 'wife of a monogamous marriage'.

304. Regarding corporate defendants, companies may be charged with and convicted of conspiracy. A company may be convicted of a conspiracy with another company or companies or with an individual or individuals. A one-man company cannot, however, be convicted of conspiracy solely with the person controlling it and vice versa. In such a situation, there is in reality only one and the same person and one and the same mind.[372]

305. One final word to be said about parties to conspiratorial agreements is that people may join or be recruited into such agreements at different times. They may not know the identity of all the co-conspirators and may not have communicated with all of them. They do nonetheless know or should know of their existence – at least some of them. This point is well illustrated by a statement in the *Ongodia and Erima* case reproduced below.

306. Before a court can convict an accused of being a conspirator, it must be satisfied that such accused either masterminded the scheme or design or that he or she was aware of its existence and 'agreed' to be party to it. In other words, the accused must have had the necessary *mens rea*, which is intent to be a party to an agreement to do an unlawful act. This intent may be proved by direct evidence implicating the accused. However, such direct evidence is not always easily available. For that reason therefore, intent or indeed the existence of the agreement itself is usually inferred from the conduct of the accused and from all the circumstances surrounding the case. As was stated in *R. v. Gokaldas & Anor.*:[373]

> Certainly there was no direct evidence of an agreement but how rarely is conspiracy proved by such evidence. As Mr Southworth pertinently observed conspirators do not normally meet together and execute a deed setting out the

370. *Arvind Patel v. Uganda*, Cr. App. No. 36 of 2002, [2003] UGSC 35 (27 Oct. 2003).
371. See *Laila Jhina Mawji v. The Queen* [1956] 23 E.A.C.A. 609.
372. See *R. v. McDonnell* [1966] 1 Q.B. 233. The court ruled that conspiracy charges against the accused could not be sustained 'upon the footing that in the particular circumstances here, where the sole responsible person in the company is the defendant himself, it would not be right to say that there were two persons or two minds. If it were otherwise, I feel that it would offend against the basic concept of a conspiracy, namely, an agreement of two or more to do an unlawful act, and I think it would be artificial to take the view that the company, although it is clearly a separate legal entity, can be regarded here as a separate person or a separate mind, in view of the admitted fact that this defendant acts alone so far as these companies are concerned'.
373. [1949] 16 E.A.C.A. 116, 120.

details of their common unlawful purpose. It is a commonplace to say that an agreement to conspire may be deduced from any acts which raise the presumption of a common plan.

307. In the *Ongodia and Erima* case, there was no direct evidence pointing to Ongodia combining with others to effectuate the unlawful plan. However, the court was able to make an inference of his complicity from the circumstances of the case. It stated:

> In our judgment, there was sufficient evidence to justify an inference that Ongodia had conspired with a person or persons unknown to arrange for a road block to be placed on the Kampala/Entebbe road with the object of arresting the Prime Minister. Both Anguram and Guweddeko testified that Ongodia had said to Anguram that reinforcements were on the way. How could Ongodia have known about reinforcements unless he was a party to some scheme to send them to Entebbe? Plainly, Ongodia must have been collaborating with those who were to send reinforcements. Ongodia's words seem to us to contain an implied invitation to Anguram to join a conspiracy which was already in existence and an implied promise that if he assisted by setting up a road block, he would be joined by other forces which were on the way.[374]

308. Mere presence at a meeting at which the agreement is hatched does not automatically make a person a party to the agreement. There must be evidence of his or her intention to be a party. There must be mutuality of wills or a meeting of the minds of the supposed co-conspirators to commit the offence in question. In the *Ongodia* case, for example, Erima was absolved from complicity although he came with Ongodia to talk to and recruit Anguram and occasionally nodded his head as Ongodia spoke. Since he did not utter a word throughout the meeting, the court was not satisfied that the nodding signified assent to what Ongodia was saying. A similar conclusion was reached in *Constante Mbuzehasi & Anor. v. Lukiiko*, *supra*, where the High Court held that mere presence and failure on the part of the second appellant to protect the complainant from being attacked by the first appellant did not amount to conspiracy to rape.

309. The offence of conspiracy is complete as soon as the agreement is concluded. Each and all co-conspirators become responsible for each other's acts done in furtherance of the conspiracy, before, during or after his or her or their adhesion to the conspiracy.[375] However, unlike attempt there need not be any overt acts for putting the agreement into operation. Indeed, it may be that the details for putting it into operation still remain to be worked out or to be refined at a future time. Prevention, it should be remembered, is the aim of the law of conspiracy. There is therefore no need for law enforcement authorities to wait for such details to be worked out or for some steps for putting the agreement into operation to be taken before they can move in and frustrate the design and prosecute those involved.

374. [1967] E.A. 137, 141.
375. See *Stanley Musinga & Anor. v. Rex* [1951] 18 E.A.C.A. 211.

Nevertheless, where the co-conspirators carry out overt acts in pursuance of the agreement, the court may infer from such acts existence of the agreement. Again, unlike attempt, it does not matter that such acts are remote and therefore merely preparatory. Conspiracy reaches further back into these preparatory activities to reach and to punish as many actors in a criminal enterprise as possible. This is one of the major advantages of the crime of conspiracy. It has been well articulated in the following passage:

> Except for the conspiracy device, society would be without protection until the criminal object is actually executed or at least sufficiently approached to become indictable as an attempt; and then, often only the actual perpetrator and perhaps, his immediate accessories could be reached. Through the conspiracy dragnet, all participants in gang operations, the cat's-paw and his principal, those who contribute from afar as well as the immediate actors can be punished, often before the evil design has fully matured into the criminal act.[376]

It is because of this potential to reach 'remote' but influential criminal actors that the law of genocide makes conspiracy a crime.

II. Purpose

310. The purpose of a conspiratorial agreement must be the commission of a criminal offence or the effectuation of certain non-criminal wrongs. These other wrongs are specified in section 392 of the Penal Code as follows:

(a) to prevent or defeat the execution or enforcement of any written law; or
(b) to cause any injury to the person or reputation of any person, or to depreciate the value of any property of any person; or
(c) to prevent or obstruct the free and lawful disposition of any property by the owner thereof for its fair value; or
(d) to injure any person in his trade or profession; or
(e) to prevent or obstruct, by means of any act or acts which if done by an individual person would constitute an offence on his part, the free and lawful exercise by any person of his trade, profession or occupation; or
(f) to effect any unlawful purpose; or
(g) to effect any lawful purpose by any unlawful means.

311. It is understandable that the law should seek to criminalize agreements to commit crimes. But why does it also criminalize agreements to commit acts that are not criminal? It is noteworthy that when a single individual attempts to commit these acts, he or she does no wrong. Yet when he or she combines with others and agrees to commit them he or she and his or her confederates commit an offence!

376. Notes, *The Conspiracy Dilemma: Prosecution of Group Crimes or Protection of Individual Defendants*, 276 Harv. L. Rev. 62 (1948).

The probable answer may be the recognition of the harm to societal interests by conspiratorial combinations and the need to prevent such harm.

312. The public has an interest in, say the due administration of justice or the enforcement of the law, and in the success of citizens in the running of their businesses or the practice of their professions. Any act aimed at frustrating the due administration of justice or the injuring of people in their trade, or in the practice of their professions does not conduce to the public welfare. This is the more so if the act is perpetrated by groups or combinations.[377]

313. Concerning conspiracy to commit crimes, it is worth noting that the law extends to crimes that are intended to be committed outside Uganda. Is this consonant with International Law which ordains that crime is local? Does it not purport to give Uganda's law of conspiracy extra-territorial effect? It may appear so, *ex facie*. However, when it is borne in mind that the law is only concerned with the agreement to commit crimes and that that agreement is made in Uganda, it becomes apparent that the law of conspiracy remains local and has no extra-territorial effect. Furthermore, Uganda has an interest to prevent or discourage people on its territory from hatching plots to commit crimes at all or to use its territory as a base for such plots, even if they are to be consummated abroad. For all you know, these plots may have a domino effect or may be infectious.

314. Concerning the question of charging, it is noteworthy that when the conspiratorial agreement to commit a crime is put into effect and the offence is committed, the co-conspirators become and are liable to be charged for the completed offence as principals under section 19 of the Penal Code. The question that arises from this is whether in addition to being charged with the completed offence, the co-conspirators can also be charged cumulatively with the crime of conspiracy. Courts in some jurisdictions, notably Britain, frown on this practice, pointing to its tendency to prolong and complicate the trial, to the prejudice of the accused.[378] Nevertheless, the practice has some advantages that might outweigh its disadvantages. One of the most important of these advantages is that the cumulative charging facilitates the prosecution of all participants in a gang operation. It ensures that none of them goes scot-free. This is particularly true in cases in which not all parties to a conspiratorial agreement participate in the execution of the objectives of the agreement and are therefore not included in the charge for the completed offences. Concerning the possibility of prejudice to the accused, it is apposite to point out that the facts that constitute the conspiracy charge do not merge with those constituting the substantive or completed offence. Therefore, the accused is not

377. See *Rex v. Mulji Jamnadas & Anor.* [1946] 13 E.A.C.A. 147 where the appellants were convicted of conspiring together to intimidate 'natives' to work for the Kakira Sugar Works.

378. See, e.g., *Verrier v. Director of Public prosecutions* [1967] 2 A.C. 195, at 223 where Lord Pearson said the following. 'Although … it could in a very exceptional case be right to charge conspiracy even when the substantive offence had been committed and was charged, it should undoubtedly remain the general rule that, when there is an effective and sufficient charge of a substantive offence, the addition of a charge for conspiracy is undesirable, because it will tend to prolong and complicate the trial.' See also *R v. Dawson* and *R v. Wenlock* [1960] 1 All E.R. 558, at 563.

prejudiced. He cannot, for example, complain of violation of the *nemo debet bis puniri uno delicto* (it is a fundamental rule of law that out of the same facts a series of charges shall not be preferred) or *nemo debet bis vexari pro una et edem causa* (nobody should be twice troubled or jeopardized for one and the same matter) principle.

315. The Penal Code spells out the punishments for conspiracy to commit certain offences. This is true of conspiracy to defeat justice and interference with witnesses,[379] conspiracy to defile,[380] conspiracy to murder[381] and conspiracy to defraud.[382] Where no specific punishment is provided for, then, the punishment will be imprisonment for up to seven years in case of conspiracy to commit felonies or where the greatest punishment to which a person convicted of the felony in question is less than imprisonment for seven years, then to such lesser punishment.[383] For conspiracy to commit misdemeanours, the punishment is imprisonment for up to five years.[384]

§3. INCITEMENT

316. Section 21(1) of the Penal Code provides that:

> When a person incites any other person to commit an offence ... whether or not any offence is committed in consequence of the incitement, ... he or she is liable to imprisonment.

The Code does not define what incitement is. However, in its common usage, the verb 'incite' means to urge, spur, stir up, animate or stimulate a person to do something. Therefore for purposes of the criminal law, the external element or *actus reus* of incitement is the active encouragement, persuasion, threats or other forms of pressure on another person to commit an offence. Acts of incitement may be explicit or implicit. They may be by the word of mouth, by the written word or by other conduct. They must also have a reasonable possibility of spurring the persons to whom they are addressed to commit the offence in question. In other words, they must be capable of operating on the mind or minds of another person. Whether or not they are capable of achieving the intended result will depend on the nature of the offence in question, the social, political or other relevant stature or influence of the alleged inciter and the targeted person, persons or audience. It is therefore important that acts of incitement must be received by the person or persons who is or are intended to be incited. If they are not, as say, where the letter conveying them does not reach the addressee, incitement is not complete. Nevertheless, it must be stressed that the acts of incitement need not be directed at a particular person. It is sufficient that they are directed at a general body of persons who can act on them.

379. Five years imprisonment, sec. 103.
380. Imprisonment for three years, sec. 140.
381. Imprisonment for fourteen years, sec. 208.
382. Imprisonment for three years, sec. 309.
383. Section 390.
384. Section 391.

Moreover, they need not be acted on by the person or persons to whom they are directed, since by its nature incitement is an incomplete or inchoate crime whose aim is prevention. While underscoring the importance of charging and, if convicted, punishing persons who incite others to commit crimes, albeit not committed, the International Tribunal for Rwanda said as follows:

> It should be noted ... that such offences are an exception, the rule being that in theory, an offence can only be punished in relation to the result envisaged by the law-maker. In the opinion of the Chamber, the fact that such acts [*infractions formelles* – or acts constituting an offence *per se* irrespective of their results] are in themselves particularly dangerous because of the high risk they carry for society, even if they fail to produce results, warrants that they be punished as an exceptional measure. The Chamber holds that genocide clearly falls within the category of crimes so serious that direct and public incitement to commit such a crime must be punished as such, even where such incitement failed to produce the result expected by the perpetrator.[385]

317. If, however, the acts of incitement are effective and the person or persons incited actually commit the offence, then, the inciter becomes a party to the substantive offence and may be charged along with the incited persons as a principal offender. Additionally, it is submitted, in addition to the substantive crime, it is desirable that the inciter should also be charged cumulatively with the crime of incitement. As the aim of the law on this subject is prevention, the cumulative charging of both offences would serve to deter him or her and others from engaging in this socially dangerous activity. This is particularly so in the case of political leaders, media practitioners and other powerful and influential persons who use such power and influence to incite others under their sway to commit particularly heinous crimes, such as genocide and crimes against humanity. Such persons should not complain of being 'twice troubled or jeopardized', since the elements constituting incitement and the substantive offence may be totally different. For sentencing purposes, however, the court may order the sentences on both offences to run concurrently, since they arise out of the same transaction.[386]

318. The *mens rea* of incitement is the intention on the part of the offender to encourage someone else to commit the crime in question coupled with a desire that the offence be committed. It also includes knowledge of the circumstances that make his actions criminal.

319. As is the case with other incomplete crimes, punishment for incitement depends on the nature and gravity of the substantive offence incited to be

385. *Prosecutor v. Jean-Paul Akayesu*, Case No. ICTR-96-4T, Judgment, 2 Sep. 1997, at para. 562.

386. See for instance *Prosecutor v. Georges Ruggiu*, Case No. ICTR-97-32-1, Judgment and Sentence, 1 Jun. 2000, in which the accused, after pleading guilty to the charges of direct and public incitement to commit genocide and crimes against humanity, was sentenced to twelve years imprisonment on each count – both to run concurrently.

committed. Specific punishments are prescribed for incitement to violence,[387] incitement to refuse or delay payment or taxes,[388] and incitement to violence against another person by reason of his race, place of origin, political opinions, colour, creed, sex or office.[389] In the case of offences for which no specific punishment is prescribed the punishment would be ten years imprisonment if the substantive offence is punishable by death,[390] and for other offences imprisonment for one-fourth of the term of imprisonment provided for the substantive offence or one-fourth of the fine as the case may be; but the ratio changes to one-half in case of an accused person who is a public servant whose duty is to prevent the commission of the offence incited.[391]

387. Punishable by three years imprisonment, sec. 51.
388. Punishable by three years imprisonment, sec. 52.
389. Punishable by fourteen years imprisonment, sec. 83.
390. Section 21(1).
391. Section 23(3).

Chapter 6. Participation in Crime

§1. General

320. Two or more people may participate in committing a crime. However, their participation may take place at different times: either before, at or after the commission of the crime. Their roles in the crime may also be different. One may instigate, another may assist before or at the time when the crime is committed, while another actually commits the crime. After the crime is committed yet another person may help all the accomplices to escape and to avoid capture or punishment. Nevertheless, even though these people get involved at different times and play different roles, they all contribute to the consummation of the crime. According to section 19 of the Penal Code, all participants are 'deemed to have taken part in committing the offence and to be guilty of the offence and may be charged with actually committing it'. Consequently, the distinctions between the various modes of participation in crime by the principals are of little practical importance. For that reason, it is often not necessary to state in the charge sheet or indictment the capacity in which any of the accused persons is charged or to state the role which he played in committing the crime. This is a matter of evidence that must be established later on at the trial. Additionally, on conviction all participants are liable to suffer the same penalty that may be prescribed by the law. If the offence they are convicted of is murder, they may all be sentenced to death, save for any one of them who might have been under the age of 18 years.[392] Nevertheless, as we shall see, it is a cardinal principle of sentencing that the punishment must fit the offender; and, as a general principle, the sentencing court has discretion to impose different sentences on the participants according to their antecedents and to the extent of their involvement and moral culpability.

321. Under the old English common law, the actual perpetrator of the crime was referred to as the principal in the first degree. The person who was present at and assisted in the commission of the crime was referred to as principal in the second degree. The one who assisted the perpetrator prior to the actual offence was called accessory before the fact. Lastly, the person who facilitated the others to escape and to avoid punishment was known as the accessory after the fact. The Uganda Penal Code dispenses with this terminology. Save for the accessory after the fact all persons who participate in committing a crime are referred to as 'principal offenders'.[393]

392. See *infra*, paragraphs 638–652.

393. See side note to sec. 19. This terminology is not altogether satisfactory, because there are no non-principals or minor offenders to contrast with the principal or principal offenders.

§2. Forms of Participation in Crime

I. Perpetrator (or Primary Offender)

322. The Penal Code (section 19(1)(a)) lists among the principal offenders 'every person who actually does the act or makes the omission which constitutes the offence'. This is the perpetrator. It is he who actually commits the *actus reus* or part of the *actus reus* of the offence. He must of course do so with the necessary state of mind where this is not dispensed with. In murder, he is the one who stabs, shoots, wounds, strikes, administers the poison or withholds the necessaries of life from the victim. In rape he is the one who ravishes the victim. In theft, he is the one who appropriates the property (asportation). In forgery, he is the one who writes the document in question. And so on and so forth.

323. Two or more people may be perpetrators of a crime if they act jointly. This is true of the thief-beating cases where many people strike the victim simultaneously. They may all be charged with and convicted of assault or wounding. Where the victim dies as a result of the beatings and it is established that they all acted with a common intention, then they may all be taken to have caused the death and charged and convicted accordingly. It would not matter which of the blows struck by the multiple accused persons was the fatal blow.[394] In a robbery case, each one of the perpetrators may perform distinct acts that constitute the *actus reus*. One may point the gun at the complainant while the other demands money from him, or one may order the complainant to lie down and guard him while another appropriates the property.[395] In a burglary, one may break open the door to the house while the other enters and takes the property.

324. Where a person who possesses the necessary mental element does not himself commit the *actus reus* but, by deceit and trickery, induces another to commit it and that other person is unaware of the inducer's intentions and has no *mens rea*, the inducer will be regarded as the perpetrator. The other person is a mere conduit pipe, an innocent agent. Thus in the old English case of *Regina v. Manley*,[396] the accused induced a 9-year-old son of the complainant to take some money from the complainant's till and to give it to him. In summing up to the jury, the judge said:

> Apart from the consideration of the guilt or innocence of the prisoner generally, if you believe the story of the child, you will have to determine whether that child was an innocent agent in this transaction – that is, whether he knew that he was doing wrong, or was acting altogether unconsciously of guilt, and entirely at the direction of the prisoner; for if you should be of the opinion that

394. See *Uganda v. Leo Nyendwoha* H.Ct.Cr.Session No. 253 of 1991 (unreported), *R. v. Mikairi Kyeyune & Anor.* [1941] 8 E.A.C.A. 84, *R. v. Tabulayenka* [1943] 10 E.A.C.A. 51.

395. See, for example, *Uganda v. Obedi Asumani & Anor.*, H.Ct.Cr.Session No. 78 of 1990 (unreported).

396. (1844) 1 Cox C.C. 104. The accused was found not guilty.

he was not an innocent agent, you cannot find the prisoner guilty under this indictment.

II. Secondary Participants (or Helpers)

A. Aider

325. The first among this category of participants is the aider. According to section 19(1)(b), an aider is 'every person who does or omits to do any act for the purpose of enabling or aiding another person to commit the offence'. In essence, the aider helps the perpetrator to commit the offence. Technically, he or she renders the help to the perpetrator before the commission of the offence. There are myriad ways of aiding, 'enabling or aiding' a person to commit a crime. It depends on the nature of the particular crime. These include facilitating the commission of the crime by, say, supplying the tools of the crime such as the weapon that is used in inflicting or threatening physical harm, or the poison used to poison the victim, or the housebreaking implements used for housebreaking, or lending, or letting an unqualified driver drive a vehicle. They also include instructing the perpetrator on how to commit a crime. To show a person how to do something knowing that that person intends to use that knowledge to commit a particular crime is to help him to commit the crime.It may also involve providing the perpetrator with transport to and away from the scene of the crime. It may also involve supplying information to the perpetrator on the whereabouts of the victim or actually luring the victim to the scene of the crime and encouraging the perpetrator to commit the offence.

B. Aider and Abettor

326. The second among the category of secondary participants is the aider and abettor. According to section 19(1)(c), aider and abettor is 'every person who aids and abets another person in committing the offence'. Unlike the aider, the 'aider and abettor' renders the assistance to the perpetrator at the very time of the perpetration of the offence. Aiding and abetting may also take various forms, depending on the nature of the crime in question. These include giving instructions or orders to the perpetrator in the course of committing the offence. In *Uganda v. Nelson Kamugisha*,[397] for example, the accused together with a group of six other military policemen went to the home of one Bebwa whom they alleged to be a guerilla. They tied him with a rope and took him away to an unknown destination from whence he was never to be seen again. Charged with kidnapping with intent to murder, the accused pleaded that his presence at the victim's home was merely to show the military policemen the home and to interpret for them (since they did not speak Lunyankore, the language spoken in the locality), and that he had nothing to do with

397. H.Ct.Cr.Session No. 27 of 1988 (unreported).

the kidnapping. The evidence, as believed by the Court, indicated the contrary. He was the officer in charge of the mission, and he is the one who ordered one of the policemen to bring a rope and to tie up the victim although he did not do it himself. He was convicted as charged, although the court did not specify whether as *the* perpetrator or as the aider and abettor.

327. Another mode of aiding and abetting is cooperating with the perpetrator. This cooperation may take different forms. It may involve physically assisting the perpetrator in the course of committing the crime, such as holding a woman down while the perpetrator rapes her. It may involve acting as a look-out for possible witnesses or the police whilst the perpetrator is committing the crime,[398] or illuminating the scene to enable the perpetrator to see what he is doing.[399]

The case of *Yusufu Ssebuguzi v. Uganda, supra*, involved several facets of aid and abetting. The appellant, together with two other persons, was charged with the murder of his father. The other two persons, Ssembatya and Mwasampijja, had a land dispute with the appellant's father. The appellant was also estranged from his father. It was agreed between all three that Ssembatya and Mwasampijja would attack the father whilst he was with the appellant in the garden where the appellant was expected to be doing some work. The two men paid the appellant some money and gave him accommodation as part of the deal. On their first visit to the garden, Ssembatya and Mwasampijja did not find the father there but the appellant was there. All the same, Ssembatya dug a hole at the place where the appellant was working. On the second visit, they hid in a nearby bush until the father appeared and started to talk to the appellant. They suddenly attacked the father, taking a hoe from the appellant and killing the father with it. The appellant did not resist surrendering the hoe. They then buried the father's body in the hole they had dug previously. For over three years, the father's other relatives did not know of his fate. Meantime, the appellant assumed control over his property, selling some of it to various people, including Ssembatya and Mwasampijja. Even assuming that the appellant was not aware of the exact time that Ssembatya and Mwasampijja would come, and that the attack was a surprise attack, the High Court had no hesitation in holding that the appellant intended to and did help in the murder of his father. Upholding the conviction, the Supreme Court said:

> The situation was that the Appellant knew that Ssembatya and Ali wanted to kill the deceased, and that they all thought that the deceased would probably visit the Appellant. … Moreover, he knew that they were relying upon him to assist and conceal their plan. In these circumstances he could not stand idly by, since the situation had gone further than a case of mere presence or merely

398. In *Matovu Musa Kassim v. Uganda, supra*, all that the appellant did was to keep watch. The Supreme Court upheld his convinction for murder and rape, saying: 'We agree with the learned trial judge when he observes that the appellant cannot be heard to say that for him he was left outside to keep a watch on whoever would be approaching and then warn those who were inside actively committing the offence. He is as guilty as if he was inside the house looting like the rest of them.'

399. For example, see *Opoya v. Uganda* [1967] E.A. 752. Here the first appellant shone a torch on the complainant while the second appellant was striking him. It was held that the first appellant aided and abetted the second appellant.

> doing nothing to prevent a crime. Allowing Ssembatya to take his hoe without any resistance or other action, was a very material assistance, since Ssembatya had no other weapon. Clearly the Appellant, if it is true that he thought the whole plan a joke at first, could not possibly have continued to think so, after the hole had been dug, his Father had been seized, and the hoe had been taken away from him. … To evade responsibility the Appellant had to take some step to indicate his unwillingness to be part of the crime. As the learned Judge pointed out, he raised no alarm, he never warned his father and he never escaped or refused to give Ssembatya the hoe. His inaction could only be construed as acquiescence in the offence committed.

Lastly, aiding and abetting may involve selling a forbidden article or selling at a forbidden price; the seller is the perpetrator while the willing or solicitous buyer is the aider and abettor, since there can be no selling without buying and no seller without a buyer.

328. Although aiding and abetting as a form of secondary participation applies to all offences, there are instances when the legislature makes it a substantive offence. For example, the Penal Code makes it an offence punishable by up to five years imprisonment for any person to aid or abet any non-commissioned officer or member of the Armed Forces to mutiny, or to desert the respective services.[400] The Code similarly makes it a capital offence for anyone who 'aids and abets another person in the commission' of treasonable acts under the Code 'becomes an accessory before or after the fact' to any of those acts.[401] In any of these cases, then, the accused must be charged either as perpetrator of the substantive offence or as aider and abettor. In one case, the appellant was charged with the substantive offence of treason but was convicted of aiding and abetting as a secondary participant.[402] The Supreme Court quashed the conviction, holding that since there existed a specific offence under section 25(1)(d) [now section 23(1)(d)] of the Code, the appellant should not have been convicted of aiding and abetting under section 19(1)(c). Additionally, the particulars of offence and the evidence led by the prosecution and the defence focused on the substantive offence. Therefore, it was not fair to convict him of an offence with which he was not charged.

C. A Crime Must Be Committed by a Perpetrator

328.1. The chapeau to section 19(1) of the Penal Code provides that '*When an offence is committed,* each of the following persons is deemed to have taken part in committing the offence and to be guilty of the offence … ' It is thus vital that before any person is charged or convicted for playing the role of secondary participant, i.e.,

400. Sections 29 and 30 respectively.
401. Section 23(1)(d).
402. *Hofni Topacho Ongiretho & Anor v. Uganda*, Cr. App. No. 1 of 1993, [1994] UGSC 9 (4 Mar. 1994).

as an aider or aider and abettor, an offence must have been committed by a perpetrator. In *R. v. P. Ruberangero & Anor.*,[403] for example, the first accused was charged with being the perpetrator of a murder and the second accused with being an aider and abettor (or helper). After some inquiry, the first accused was found to be unfit to plead or to defend himself because of insanity. It was not possible to establish whether he had also been insane at the time he allegedly committed the offence. The High Court held that as the alleged perpetrator was insane at the time of the offence, no person could be convicted as an aider and abettor for his act.

329. Where there are several persons alleged to have been involved in committing an offence as perpetrator and helper, it is desirable that they all be joined and tried together. Failure to join and try them together would not, however, necessarily vitiate the proceedings. For example, where the perpetrator has escaped or is dead, the helper may be tried by himself or herself. The perpetrator may likewise be tried by himself or herself where the helpers are unavailable. Where this is done and the perpetrator is acquitted, maybe on some technical grounds or insufficient identification or evidence, his acquittal does not necessarily preclude the trial and conviction of the helper.[404] This happened in the case of *Yusufu Ssebuguzi v. Uganda.*[405] The appellant had confessed to helping the co-defendants to murder his father. This confession was the only evidence against the co-defendants, but the Court found it to be unreliable as the basis for convicting the co-defendants. They were accordingly acquitted while the appellant was convicted as a helper. On appeal, the Supreme Court confirmed the conviction, holding that there was no inconsistency in acquitting the co-defendants as the perpetrators and convicting the appellant as a helper. It should also be pointed out that conviction of the perpetrator is no evidence against an alleged helper.

330. Lastly, it should also be pointed out that it is possible for a person to be convicted as a helper even though he or she could not commit the crime as the perpetrator. For example, a woman who helps a man (say her brother) to rape another woman is a helper and may be charged with, convicted of, and punished for, the rape. The English case of *R. v. Bourne* is also in point. Bourne was alleged to have sexually excited a dog and then compelled his wife to have sexual intercourse with it. He was charged with and convicted of aiding and abetting the offence of bestiality. In his defence, he argued that since his wife had acted against her will she was not a principal offender but a victim; *ergo* there was and could be no crime to aid and abet. His appeal against conviction was dismissed, the court holding that as long

403. H.Ct.Cr.Session No. 8921959; H.Ct.Monthly Bulletin No. 66 of 1959.
404. See, for example, *Matovu Musa Kassim v. Uganda*, Cr. App. 27 of 2002, [2005] UGSC 17 (18 Aug. 2005). In this case, the appellant was charged along with others of murder and rape. The court found that he played minor roles in the commission of the crimes. The main planners and principal participants in the two crimes were either not charged or were not successfully prosecuted because of lack of adequate investigation by the police. He was nevertheless convicted of the offences and sentenced to death.
405. S.Ct.Cr.App. No. 6 of 1984 (unreported).

as he caused his wife to have connection with a dog he was guilty 'whether you call him an aider and abettor or an accessory, as a principal in the second degree'.[406]

D. Helper or Victim?

331. It is apropos at this stage to mention cases of corruption or of demanding and receiving bribes. Is the person who pays a bribe to a public official in order to receive a favour an aider and abettor, or a helper to the official – a principal offender? This question often arises in the law of evidence when the testimony of such a person is impugned on the ground that he was an accomplice with the accused. The Ugandan courts seem to have answered the question by, first, inquiring into that person's attitude and conduct at the time of the crime. When they find him or her to have been an unwilling or reluctant 'participant' they treat him or her as a victim, and not an accomplice. Thus in *J.S. Wafula v. R.*,[407] the appellant, a police officer, was convicted of corruption in that he had received a bribe in the course of his official duties. His ground of appeal was that the person who paid him the money was an accomplice with him, and that his evidence should have been corroborated. The High Court thought otherwise. It held that the giver of the money was the victim of extortion, and that there was therefore no need for corroboration.

332. However, if the Court finds the second person guilty of some culpable collusion, it holds him to be an accomplice. This was the case in *Haji Moledina & Anor. v. R.*[408] The first appellant was a police officer who went to a state witness' factory to search for 'Bugisu coffee'. He found none. He nevertheless accused the witness of having got rid of the coffee. He then told the witness, 'If you don't want to get in trouble, pay me UGX 10,000 and I will close the case.' After considerable bargaining through an intermediary, the witness offered and the appellant accepted to take the sum of UGX 6,000. The appellant was charged with and convicted on two counts: demanding money with menaces, and corruption by a public officer. One of the appellant's grounds of appeal was that the witness was an accomplice with him; *ergo* his evidence should have been corroborated. The High Court held that the witness was not an accomplice as far as the demanding of money with menaces was concerned. The offence was complete when the appellant uttered the demand for UGX 10,000. Nothing up to that point had made, or could have made, the witness an accomplice. Regarding the offence of corruption, the Court held that the witness was an accomplice. It based its decision on the fact that he bargained with the appellant about how much should be paid, and it was this bargaining which led to the appellant's agreeing to permit his conduct to be influenced by a gift of UGX 6,000. Moreover, as was found by the trial court, he did not report to the

406. (1952) 35 Cr.App.R. 125, 129. See also *R. v. Cogan* [1976] Q.B. 217.
407. H.Ct.Cr.App. No. 272 of 1958; H.Ct.Monthly Bulletin No. 73 of 1958.
408. [1960] E.A. 678.

police or to other authorities what the appellants had done until after they were arrested in respect of other charges. However, a witness in a related count in the same case who had agreed to pay to the appellant but surreptitiously arranged with the police for him to pay the appellant in their concealed presence and with marked notes provided by them was held not to have been an accomplice.

E. Presence at the Scene of the Crime

333. Presence at the scene of a crime may be evidence of participation in crime. It may contribute solace and comfort to the perpetrator and thus encourage him in his criminal enterprise. This is more so if prior to the crime there was a relationship between the 'bystander' and the perpetrator. If the bystander is a *muleebeesi*[409] who accompanies the perpetrator to the scene of crime, he is liable as a helper even if he himself does nothing. Nevertheless, save for a *muleebeesi*, presence per se does not constitute help so as to render a person an accomplice in a crime. To do so, a person's presence at the place of crime must be 'for the purpose of' facilitating or assisting in the commission of the crime. It should not be accidental or merely fortuitous. Thus, in *Uganda v. Musana & Anor.*,[410] a driver who, at the bidding of the accused, drove the accused to a lake where the accused shot and killed their captive was absolved from complicity in the murder. The court said that although he drove the accused and his group and was present when they shot their captive, he did not culpably help them nor acquiesce in what they did. His failure to immediately report the incident to the authorities was due to fear and shock and to the then prevailing state of insecurity in the country. His presence at the scene of the crime may be said to have been involuntary. It would have been unjust to consider him a party to the crime. In contrast, the second appellant in *Constante Mbuzehasi & Anor. v. Lukiiko*, a case already discussed under the section on attempt, was voluntarily present at the scene of the 'attempted rape'. The High Court absolved him from involvement as an aider and abettor. Udo Udoma, C.J. said:

> Even if the offence had been committed, the mere presence of the second appellant would not have been sufficient to implicate him, unless it could be shown that he participated in the commission either directly or indirectly by word or deed.

With due respect, this statement is too sweeping and needs qualification. It is submitted that presence at the scene of a crime by a person who has a duty to act to prevent the commission of a crime but who does nothing and merely looks on while

409. The Luganda term *muleebeesi* was coined at a time when violent crimes by armed soldiers were commonplace. It means a civilian person who escorts armed soldiers around villages, pointing to them homes of people who might be 'enemies'. See *Sergeant Kelly Omuge & Anor. v. Uganda*, C.A.Cr.App. No. 3 of 1988 (unreported).

410. [1985] H.Ct.Monthly Bulletin 20. See also *Regina v. Sumba s/o Semafa & Anor.* [1956–1957] 8 U.L.R. 28.

the offence is being committed can be deemed to have helped the perpetrator. It is no excuse for him to say that he did nothing positive to assist the perpetrator. It is submitted that his silence, passivity and inaction when he should be doing something to stop the perpetrator amounts to encouragement. This view is borne out by section 19(1)(b) which refers to 'every person who does or *omits to do any act for the purpose of enabling ... another person to commit the offence*'. It was so held in the *Ssebuguzi* case (*supra*, paragraph 327, when Ssebuguzi failed to warn his father of his impending fate or to raise an alarm when Ssembatya and Mwasampijja attacked him. It was also held to be the case in *Etyeku & Anor. v. Regina.*[411] Here the appellants were policemen. They were charged with official corruption. They arrested one Pausitino Lemi for manufacturing waragi contrary to the Waragi Ordinance and took him to the Masindi Port police sub-station where the second appellant was the officer in charge. The second appellant demanded and received a bribe of UGX 200 in order to release Lemi. He did not release him, but tried to raise more money from him by threatening to charge Lemi's brother-in-law with *attempting to bribe him.* The second appellant was convicted as the perpetrator. Regarding the first appellant, the High Court said the following:

> The first appellant played a minor role throughout the transaction but he was with the second appellant from its inception when they went to arrest Lemi. Mere presence when a bribe is asked for might not connote complicity in the case of a layman but the same cannot be said of a uniformed policeman whose duty it is to see that the law is not infringed. Further, the first appellant was responsible for the delayed entry of the police diary and the reasons he gives for it are unconvincing.

The Court convicted him with the offence as a helper to the second appellant.

334. Lastly, in *Nanyonjo & Anor v. Uganda,*[412] the Supreme Court confirmed the first appellant's conviction for manslaughter together with the second appellant, his wife. The second appellant, in the presence of the first appellant, brutally chastised her two-and-half-year-old step son and made him eat his faeces for wetting and soiling his bed and clothes and thereby caused its death. Rejecting the second appellant's defence that he did not participate in the chastisement, the Supreme Court said:

> [L]earned counsel argues that there was not sufficient evidence to prove that the 2nd appellant participated in the assault, as no witness described precisely what he did. We also find no merit in this submission. While it is correct that PW3's testimony that he found the 2nd appellant torturing the deceased lacks particularity, we find that there is other ample evidence that he had common intention with the 1st appellant in the perpetration of the ill-fated chastisement. He witnessed the 1st appellant assaulting the deceased but did not disassociate

411. [1956–1957] 8 U.L.R. 96. For a similar case with different results, see *Haji Moledina & Anor. v. R.* [1960] E.A. 678.
412. Crim. App. No. 24 of 2004, [2007] UGSC 10, (5 Jul. 2007).

himself from the assault by stopping her or by otherwise protecting the deceased child. He was undoubtedly in a position to prevent the assault and indeed under duty to do so. In choosing to do nothing about the assault he associated himself with it.

335. It is submitted that the second appellant was not a joint perpetrator of the offence together with the first appellant, since the court did not find that he participated in 'actually committing' it. In this author's view, he was an aider in terms of section 19(1)(b) of the Penal Code. Be that as it may, however, according to the chapeau of section 19(1) of the Code, his mode of participation in the commission of the crime is of little or no legal import. Consequently, the High Court initially convicted him along with his wife of murder and sentenced them to death; the Court of Appeal confirmed both conviction and sentence. However, for reasons that we shall see later on in this book, the Supreme Court quashed the murder conviction and substituted it with manslaughter; in place of the death sentence, it sentenced both of them to seven years imprisonment.

F. Mens Rea *for Secondary Participation*

336. The *mens rea* required for secondary participation in the commission of crime, as either an aider, or aider and abettor is intention to help, enable or facilitate the commission of the crime. It is not enough that the accused helped the perpetrator to commit the crime. It must be proved that he did so consciously and intentionally. He must know all the facts or circumstances essential to the commission of the offence or offence intended or likely to be committed. He does not, however, need to know the details of the crime but should at least know some facts which are sufficient to indicate the type of offence intended and subsequently committed. Therefore, if Musoke intends to help Mande to commit a crime of a particular nature, but Mande commits one of a completely different nature, Musoke is not liable as a helper to Mande's crime. In *Regina v. Sumba s/o Semafa & Anor.*,[413] the three accused set out to burgle the house of the deceased. In the course of the burglary, one of them throttled the deceased to death. They were charged with murder as each other's accomplice or helper. The prosecution was not able to show which one of the three defendants killed the deceased, but relied on the fact that property belonging to the deceased was found in their possession. The Court found that none of them was armed when they set out for the house of the deceased, and there was no evidence that any of the accused knew that violence was going to be used against the occupants of the house. Was murder the type of crime that the accused intended to help each other commit? According to the High Court, it was not. Said Bennett, J.:

> Burglary is not an offence which necessarily involves violence to the person, and the mere fact that it is shown that an accused person is a party to a burglary

413. [1956] 8 U.L.R. 28, 30.

> does not make him liable for every act of a co-accused committed in the course of burglary.

However, a person will be liable as a helper even if he had not expressly or implicitly agreed to the commission of a different type of crime if it can be proved that in the circumstances he must have contemplated that his confederate in the principal crime would commit that offence. In the burglary case, for example, if one of the accused went to the house to be burgled armed and the others were aware of this fact and said or did nothing to distance themselves from him or her, it must be reasonably foreseeable that he or she might use the weapon to overcome resistance by the inhabitants of the house.[414]

337. Lastly, the fact that the perpetrator committed the crime in a way that is different from that contemplated by the helper does not absolve that helper from liability. Similarly, the fact that he or she did not desire or was indifferent to the perpetrator committing the offence will not avail him or her any defence. It is enough that he or she intended to help him or her. So a taxi driver will be liable as a helper if, knowing the criminal nature of his customers' mission, allows thieves to hire him to convey them to the scene of their crime. As Devlin, J. said in the English case of *National Coal Board v. Gamble*:

> An indifference to the result of the crime does not of itself negative abetting. If one man deliberately sells to another a gun to be used for murdering a third, he may be indifferent about whether the third lives or dies and interested only in the cash profit to be made out of the sale, but he can still be an aider and abettor. To hold otherwise would be to negative the rule that *mens rea* is a matter of intent only and does not depend on desire or motive.[415]

III. Procurer

338. Section 19(2) provides that:

> Any person who procures another person to do or omit to do any act of such a nature that, if he or she had done the act or made the omission, the act or omission would have constituted an offence on his or her part, is guilty of an offence of the same kind, and is liable to the same punishment, as if he or she had done the act or made the omission; and he or she may be charged with doing the act or making the omission.

414. See *Chan Wing-Siu & Anor. v. The Queen* [1985] A.C. 168, 175 and 177. See also *R. v. Hyde* [1990] 3 All E.R. 892.
415. [1959] 1 Q.B. 11, 23.

To procure means to produce the desired result by some positive effort. It includes hiring, ordering, instigating, counselling and actively or aggressively encouraging another to commit a crime. In the context of organized crime, the procurer is the offender behind the offenders. He or she does not participate in the actual perpetration of the crime and may not even be at the scene of the crime. He or she is nonetheless the moving force behind the activities of the perpetrator or of a criminal group. He or she is the architect and master planner of its activities. For example, in *Uganda v. Tigawalana Bakali Ikoba & Ors*, the Court of Appeal found that the killers of the deceased 'were being controlled by someone powerful who for some reason wanted [the deceased] dead'.[416] The court found that it was the first respondent who 'invited and plotted' the killing, and that 'it was done in his own way under his supervision and it was him who ordered the killers to travel up to his home to receive payment for a job accomplished'.[417] In *Teddy Sseezi Cheeye v. Uganda*, the appellant was charged with, among other offences, forgery in that he made false documents with intent to defraud. The trial court found that an accomplice prepared the false documents on the instructions of the appellant. The court held the appellant liable for the forgery as a procurer. In doing so, it stated:

> A procurer uses the hands and eyes of the person procured to commit a crime as his own. The actions of the person procured become the actions of the procurer. In fact the section [19 (2)] says not merely that a person who procurers another to commit an offence may be convicted of the offence but that 'he or she may be charged with doing the act or making the omission.[418]

While in the *Tigawalana* and *Cheeye* cases, the procurer was not present at the scene of the crime, in the Kenyan case of *Ondimu s/o Ondimu v. Rex*[419] he was. In this case, the appellants were brothers. They were convicted of murder. The evidence against the second appellant was that he instigated the first to stab the victim, saying, 'Do not whip him, stab him.' Confirming the conviction, the Court of Appeal for Eastern Africa said:

> We cannot say that, on the evidence which the judge accepted, he was legally wrong in convicting him, too, of murder, for on that evidence he verbally instigated the first appellant to stab the deceased. Under Section 22 of the Kenya Penal Code one who counsels another to commit an offence may himself be convicted as a principal offender. We add this *caveat*, however, that we think a trial judge should, before convicting on verbal incitement alone, be abundantly satisfied that the words used can bear only one implication. In this case ... there can be no doubt that the second appellant encouraged his brother to use a lethal weapon.

---

416. Cr. App. No. 21 of 2005, [2009] UGCA 51, 17 Dec. 2009.
417. *Ibid.*
418. Cr. App. No. 105 of 105, [2010] UGCA 41 (20 Oct. 2010). The Court of Appeal upheld the conviction.
419. [1951] 19 E.A.C.A. 239.

339. Where a procurer is not successful in inducing those that he instigates or orders to commit the crime he will be guilty of the incomplete crime of incitement which has been discussed in the previous chapter.[420] If he succeeds, then, as the cited provision provides, he may be prosecuted and, if convicted, punished as a principal offender, as happened in the *Tigawalana* and *Cheeye* cases.

340. The *mens rea* required for procuring is the same as that for the incomplete crime of incitement. It is the intention on the part of the procurer to induce or encourage someone else to commit the crime in question coupled with a desire that the offence be committed. It also includes knowledge of the circumstances that make his actions criminal. It must nevertheless be stressed that where the perpetrator commits an offence which is different from the one that the 'procurer' ordered or instigated him to do, the 'procurer' will not be liable. However, as is the case with helping, if the crime committed is incidental to the one that the 'procurer' wanted the perpetrator to commit and was reasonably within his or her foresight, he or she is liable.[421] The rationale for this proposition is that as it is the procurer who triggered the commission of the crime in question, set in motion a series of criminal activities that resulted in the crime that was actually committed. He or she must be held responsible for doing so. The protection he or she has is that the crime committed should have been reasonably foreseeable. It will also afford the procurer no defence to contend that the perpetrator carried out the crime in a different mode than that they had agreed. For example, if a person procures another to commit murder by witchcraft but that person commits it by physical means, the procurer will be guilty of the murder.[422]

IV. Joint Offenders in Prosecution of a Common Purpose

341. Suppose Wasswa, Kato and Kizza agree to participate in committing a particular crime, either as principal offenders or procurers. Suppose that in the course of doing so one or more of them commits a further or other offence. Are they all responsible for that *other* offence? The doctrine of common purpose addresses this question. It is crystallized in section 20 of the Penal Code, which reads as follows:

> When two or more persons form a common intention to prosecute an unlawful purpose in conjunction with one another, and in the prosecution of such purpose an offence is committed of such a nature that its commission was a probable consequence of the prosecution of such purpose, each of them is deemed to have committed the offence.

420. In *John Lwasa v. R.* H.Ct.Cr.App. No. 149 of 1960; H.Ct.Monthly Bulletin No. 33 of 1960 the appellant was charged with attempting to procure another person to fabricate evidence. The High Court substituted the conviction with incitement, holding that incitement was a minor offence in relation to attempt, and the offences of attempt and incitement are cognate.

421. But see the Tanzanian case of *Rex v. Biguli s/o Lwemera & Anor.* [1947] 14 E.A.C.A. 115.

422. For example, see the Zambian case of *Twelve & Anor. v. R.* [1957] R. & N.L.R. 265. See also *Choitram v. Reinem* [1952] 26 K.L.R. 93.

342. Under the scenario described by the cited provision, the person who actually commits the offence (if he can be identified) is primarily liable as the perpetrator. For his confederates to be liable as helpers, the following must be proved: (i) a common intention; (ii) the offence must be committed in the course of prosecuting a common unlawful purpose; (iii) the offence committed must be a probable consequence of the prosecution of the common purpose.

A. *Common Intention*

343. There must be a common intention or a shared intent to procure, or assist in bringing to fruition a common unlawful purpose. The common intention in this sense may be proved by establishing existence of a prior agreement between the parties concerned to prosecute an unlawful purpose. Alternatively, and usually, common intention may be inferred from the conduct of the parties and from all the circumstances surrounding the commission of the offence. The following are some of the factors that the courts have taken into account in deciding whether or not a common intention exists in a given case. Presence at the scene of the crime and failure to disassociate oneself from what the other party or parties do. Such presence may suggest being an associate with the others and having a shared common intention with them. *Y. Katalagala & Anor. v. R.*[423] is a case in point. A taxi driver conveyed burglars to the house that was burgled. There was evidence to indicate that he might not have been privy to the plot to burgle the house. Nevertheless, the court found him to be an approver and therefore *particeps criminis*, because he must have realized that he was conveying a gang of thieves to the scene of a felonious enterprise and did nothing to disassociate himself from the gang before they were arrested. Conduct of the party at the scene of crime may also indicate intent to adhere or not to adhere to a common unlawful purpose. In *Uganda v. Leo Nyendwoha*, where a father joined his son in chasing and beating the deceased a common intention was inferred from his conduct.[424] In *Rex v. Erunasani Sekoni s/o Eria & Anor.*,[425] the first and second appellants ran after the deceased; the first appellant carried a rifle; the second appellant called the deceased to come back to the place where he was immediately shot, probably by the first appellant. The court held that even if the second appellant did not actually shoot the deceased, he aided the one who did. It has also been held that where a number of people take part in beating a thief a common intention is to be inferred. In *Medadi Tindarwesire & Anor. v. Uganda*,[426] the appellants were part of a gang of people who looted, damaged property, and attacked and killed the deceased as a result of a land dispute. The Supreme Court held that:

---

423. H.Ct.Cr.App. No. 6-7-30 of 1959; H.Ct.Monthly Bulletin No. 28 of 1959. See also *Haji Muhamed & Senyomo Birikadde v. Uganda* H.Ct.Monthly Bulletin 6 (1986).
424. H.Ct.Cr.Session No. 253 of 1991 (unreported).
425. [1947] 14 E.A.C.A. 74.
426. S.Ct.Cr.App. No. 14 of 149 (unreported). See also *R. v. Mikaeri Kyeyune & Anor.* [1941] 8 E.A.C.A. 84, *R. v. Tabulayenka* [1943] 10 E.A.C.A. 51, *Rex v. Dominiko Onenyi s/o Obuko* [1943] 10 E.A.C.A. 81. In *Celestino Alango & Anor. v. Uganda* S.Ct.Cr.App. No. 2 of 1992 (unreported) the appellants were part of a group of rebels who attacked and killed four people at Pajule Village

> There could not have been a more classic example of a group of people having formed a common intention within the meaning of Section 20 [sic 22] of the Penal Code to prosecute an unlawful purpose in concert the consequence of which was the killing of the deceased. Consequently, it does not matter which of the injuries inflicted by the two appellants caused the death of the deceased. The medical evidence indicates that the deceased died from the cut wounds which the two of them inflicted during the course of the incident.

344. However, a common intention will not be inferred where sets of different people beat a person at different times albeit proximate to each other. *Okute s/o Kaliebi & Anor. v. R.*[427] is in point. The appellants were charged with murder. The first appellant together with other people forced the deceased to dig up meat of a cow that his sons were alleged to have stolen. When the deceased refused to do so, they beat him up until he agreed. They then forced him to carry the meat to a Muluka Chief. On the way to the Muluka Chief, the second appellant came carrying a heavy knobbed stick and assaulted the deceased. The second appellant's assault was the immediate cause of the deceased's death. The High Court convicted the second appellant of murder while it convicted the first one of manslaughter. It convicted the first appellant of manslaughter on the basis that he had formed a common intention with the second appellant to cause grievous bodily harm to the deceased. The Court of Appeal for Eastern Africa quashed the conviction, holding that there was no common intention between the first and the second appellants. The fact that they might have had similar intention does not necessarily mean that they had a common intention. The circumstances of the case showed that the appellants acted independently of each other. Wrote Sir Henry Webb, C.J.:

> Where several persons together beat another, then, though each may have a different reason, and though some may join in the beating later than others, it is plain that all have what the law calls, 'common intention', which does not necessarily connote any previous concerted agreement between them. But, where, as in the present case, first a party of four beat the victim, and then, after some interval and in a different place, another person comes up and beats him, then even though his reason may have been the same as theirs, it seems to us impossible to say on the evidence of such facts alone, that the first party, whose acts are finished, the purpose for which they were done accomplished, are necessarily to be deemed to have had a common intention with the newcomer so as to be guilty of murder if the combined result of the two beatings is to cause death of the victim. How, in such circumstances, can the first party be said to have had a common intention with a person whose intervention in the affair they (so far as the evidence in this case goes) can have had no reason to anticipate.

---

in Kitgum District. Upholding their conviction for murder the Supreme Court held that it was satisfied that they were some of the rebels who attacked and killed people.

427. [1941] 8 E.A.C.A. 78.

The Court found that the first appellant did not associate with nor approve of the actions of the second appellant. It also made the interesting point that no common intention could be inferred from the first appellant's presence when the second appellant beat the deceased; he was there merely for the purpose of taking the deceased to the Chief.[428]

345. It must be stressed that the common intention must be for prosecuting a common unlawful purpose or enterprise. If the enterprise is lawful it cannot be used as a basis for fixing liability on the parties thereto for subsequent crimes committed by their associates. This point is well illustrated by the case of *Bumbakali Lutwama & Anor. v. Uganda.*[429] The first appellant was the head of a ten house cell in his village. With the assistance of the other appellants he arrested the deceased for some criminal offences. He tied the deceased's hands behind his back but did not beat him. The deceased died of cut wounds at the hands of unknown people. The prosecution sought to make the appellants liable for the killing on the basis that there was a common intention between them and the unknown perpetrators of the murder. The trial court accepted the prosecution's view, but not so the Supreme Court. Said the Supreme Court:

> It appears that there was some valid cause for arresting the deceased, which was done without harming him. It was not an unlawful arrest. The first appellant was a junior official. He would be expected, therefore, to participate in arresting an alleged offender in his area even if he was not a complainant. In the circumstances, we think that the appellant did not have common intention of prosecuting an unlawful purpose, namely of harming the deceased or his house. His door was probably broken because he was apparently resisting arrest by refusing to open it. That would not make the conduct of the appellants of arresting the deceased any less lawful.

There being no nexus between the appellants and the people who killed the deceased the appellants could not be made party to the killing under section 20 of the Penal Code.

B. In the Course of Prosecuting the Common Unlawful Purpose

346. The new or further crime must be committed in the course and within the scope of prosecuting the common purpose. Cpl *Kasirye Hamuza & Anor. v. Uganda* is a good example.[430] The five appellants set out to rob a coffee factory at Jinja. The fourth appellant hired a vehicle for the purpose. For one reason or the other, the appellants found the robbery at Jinja impossible and they abandoned it. Instead, still using the car hired by the fourth appellant, they went to another town of Kamuli

428. For similar decisions see *Dracaku s/o Afia v. R.* [1963] E.A. 363, *Francis Sebanenya & Anor. v. Uganda* S.Ct.Cr.App. No. 17 of 1989 (unreported).
429. S.Ct.Cr.App. No. 38 of 1989 (unreported).
430. Cr. App. No. 44 of 2001, [2004] UGSC 36 (36 May 2004).

where they committed robberies and murder for which they were jointly charged. The fourth appellant stayed in Jinja and did not go with the rest of the group to Kamuli. The issue was whether he had common intention and therefore was liable together with the rest of the group for those offences. The Supreme Court upheld his conviction, holding that he had a common intention with the rest of the group that went to Kamuli with the vehicle hired by him, although he remained in Jinja. It held that the purpose of hiring the vehicle was to use it for robbery, and it was immaterial where that robbery was eventually committed. In other words, the crime eventually committed was within the scope of the original common purpose. However, suppose a taxi driver in the course of conveying a gang of thieves away from the scene of the crime knocks down and injures a pedestrian. Should the members of the gang be liable for the offence of reckless driving along with the driver? No, he should not, because this offence is not committed in the course of prosecuting the common purpose of stealing. It was merely fortuitous.

347. In *Uganda v. Angello Musese & Anor.*,[431] the accused set out together with another person who was armed with a gun to burgle a shop. The gunman fired shots in the air to frighten away people in the shop. The deceased, one of the people in the shop, cut the accused on the head with a panga. The accused ran out of the house followed by the deceased. As the deceased came out of the rear door, the gunman shot him in the stomach, killing him instantly. The gunman made off with a bicycle and a sum of money. The accused was charged with murder as a helper. The High Court held that the accused was not liable, because he was not present when the murder was committed. Additionally, the murder was not committed 'in the prosecution of the common purpose' – stealing. The Court pointedly held that the accused was out only to steal, and that the gunman was on his own when he shot the deceased. The decision is not altogether satisfactory. Might it not be argued that the shooting was intended to defend the accused that the deceased had hacked with a panga, and to facilitate their escape? If so, can it not be said that it was committed in the course and for the furtherance of the common purpose? Was it not a probable consequence of the prosecution of that purpose? Did the accused not contemplate that his partner in crime might use the gun the way he did?

C. Probable Consequences of the Prosecution of the Common Purpose

348. For an associate of the perpetrator to be liable for the further crime committed by the perpetrator, the crime must be of such a nature that he ought to have foreseen that it would probably be committed. The offence committed must be within the range of offences that must be within the contemplation of the associate as likely to be committed by the perpetrator in the course of prosecuting the common purpose. If the common purpose is to commit burglary then offences such as possession of implements of house breaking and malicious damage to property should be contemplated as likely to be committed in consequence of prosecuting the common purpose. If the common purpose is to commit robbery and the members of the group carry an assortment of weapons and in the course of the robbery one of

431. H.Ct.Cr.Session No. 22 of 1982; [1982] H.Ct.Bulletin 7 2 .

them commits a murder then, as was held in *Ezera Kyabanamaizi v. R.*[432] all members of the group will be guilty of the offence, since murder is an offence which they must have known to be likely to be committed in the prosecution of their common purpose. Similarly, when a gang of people set out to mercilessly beat another and that person dies, they are all responsible for his death – be it murder or manslaughter, for the causing of death is a probable consequence of their unlawful purpose.[433] Still, even if the plan is that only one member of the gang should carry a weapon, its use for purposes of overcoming resistance or facilitating escape is also a probable consequence of prosecuting the burglary. Even where the carrying of weapons was not discussed and, to the knowledge of one, the other was carrying a weapon, the party not carrying the weapon would be liable if the other uses it to commit a crime. However, where a group member was not aware that another was carrying a weapon he would most likely not be liable for the offence committed with the weapon. Similarly, members of a thieving gang or robbers would not to be liable for rape, defilement or kindred offences committed by a member of the gang, because these crimes are not of the same genre as burglary or robbery– the common purpose.[434] Their commission is not a probable consequence of carrying out a burglary or robbery.

349. Finally, it should be pointed out that under the common purpose doctrine, the actual perpetrator's culpability is judged by subjective standards: actual *mens rea* (where this is not excluded) to commit the further offence. The secondary participant or helper's liability, however, is judged by objective standards. He or she does not need to have intended to commit, procure or help in committing the offence. He or she may not even be aware that his confederates are committing it. It is enough if he or she contemplated or ought to have known that it would probably be committed.

V. Entrapment

350. Entrapment is a practice in which the police plant an agent to lure others, sometimes for a fee, to commit a crime, to advise them on how to do it or to participate in the commission of the crime; the police then use that agent as a witness against the others. Strictly speaking, such agent is an accomplice or participant, either as an aider, aider and abettor or counsellor or procurer, who should be treated as such. The practice is objectionable in the sense that it is morally wrong to tempt

432. [1962] E.A. 309.
433. See *Dafasi Magayi & Anor. v. Uganda* 1965 E.A. 667. See also the Tanzanian case of *Andrea Obonyo v. R.* [1962] E.A. 542. See also *Agastino Orete & Anor. v. Uganda* [1966] E.A. 430.
434. In *Muhwezi Alex & Anor. v. Uganda* Cr. App. No. 21 of 2005, [2010] UGSC 12 (13 Apr. 2010), in the course of a robbery by the appellants, the first appellant defiled the daughter of the complainant. It was only the first appellant that was charged with and convicted of defilement (and robbery), while his confederates were charged with and convicted of only robbery.

fellow human beings into wrong-doing.[435] As Justice Frankfurter of the United States Supreme Court insightfully observed, 'human nature is weak enough and sufficiently beset by temptations without government adding to them and generating crime'.[436]

351. Nevertheless, entrapment is defended as an effective investigative tool into crime. However, given its questionable nature, the issue is to what the extent is it legitimate to resort to it? Two tests have been used by the courts to determine the extent to which it may be legitimate to resort to it: (1) the nature of the crime in which it is employed and (2) the state of mind of the accused. These tests were articulated by the Court of Appeal for Eastern Africa in the Kenya case of *Wanjiko w/o Mukiri v. Regina*, in the following terms:

> The test is not, we think, the provision of the means to commit the offence; otherwise it would be wrong to furnish marked notes in order to prove corruption. The real questions are first, the nature of the offence: obviously it could never be right to allow a murder to be committed and then arrest the murderer: but if an offence is of such a type that it can be repeatedly committed, is difficult to prevent or detect, and may be completed on one arranged occasion without actual harm to the community being done, a trap may be not only legitimate, but the correct method of preventing future offences. The seriousness of the offence does not seem to affect the matter. The next question is, we think, the frame of mind of the accused. If his presumed intention is to commit that single crime and then desist, it may be better, in most cases, merely to prevent the commission of the offence. If that is done it may or may not be possible to charge an attempt. But if it may be presumed that the intention is to commit, whenever opportunity offers, a series of offences of the same kind which it would be difficult to detect or prove, the case is especially suitable for a trap, and we see no objection to it.[437]

352. Regarding the nature of the crime, mention may be made of crimes such as bribery and corruption, which are usually surreptitious, involve highly placed and powerful public officials who have the means to conceal the evidence of their participation. Another characteristic of these crimes is that they are 'victimless' in the sense that there may be no person who is directly hurt by them and thus willing to come forward and to report their occurrence to the police. *Misaki Choda v. Regina* is a good example.[438] The appellant was a Muluka Chief. He asked for a bribe. The person from whom he asked for the bribe informed the police. The police set up a trap. As in the *Haji Moledina* case, *supra*, they provided a marked UGX 20 note to the person from whom the bribe was asked. He in turn gave it to the appellant who was subsequently arrested, charged and convicted of corruption by a public official

435. D.D.N. Nsereko, *Police Informants and Agents Provocateurs: Accomplices or Handmaidens of the Law? Perspectives from the Courts of Eastern and Southern Africa* 9 Crim. L. Forum 151, 157 (1999)..
436. *Sherman v. United States*, 356 U.S. 369, at 384 (1958).
437. [1954] 21 E.A.C.A. 386, 387.
438. [1957] E.A. 495.

contrary to section 78(1) of the Penal Code. On appeal to the High Court, the appellant contended that by entrapping him the police lured him into committing the crime. According to him, the police were procurers and accomplices. Relying on the *Wanjiko* case, *supra*, the High Court dismissed the appeal, saying that the appellant was not persuaded by the police to commit the crime; 'he needed no persuasion since, as found by the learned magistrate, he had already solicited a gift of UGX 20 from J ... I cannot see the slightest reason to suppose that the appellant was wrongly convicted.'

353. Other types of 'victimless' crime are possession of and dealing in prohibited articles such psychotropic or narcotic drugs; crimes that involve sale of alcohol to young persons or selling certain articles above set prices; drinking at prohibited places or at prohibited hours; solicitation in public places; living off the earning of prostitution; and illegal practice of certain professions.

354. Concerning the test of the accused person's state of mind, the courts inquire to see whether the accused would have committed the crime anyway, with or without the assistance of a trap.[439] Where the accused would not have committed the offence if he were not lured or instigated by the trap, the courts might consider the trap an agent provocateur. He or she might be charged as a procurer under section 19(2) of the Penal Code and for the purposes of the law of evidence be treated as an accomplice. In *Capt. Mike Muwonge & Anor v. Uganda*,[440] the appellants were charged with and convicted of treason. Two of the prosecution witnesses were police officers who participated in meetings at which plots to overthrow the government were hatched. These officers in fact arranged the places where the meetings were held and persuaded the appellants to go there. The Supreme Court held that these officers were 'genuine spies' and not agents provocateur or accomplices whose evidence needed corroboration. It said:

> Treason lay in what was said at those meetings and not the meetings themselves. If the alleged treason was discussed by the appellants then PW1 and PW2 could not be guilty of any impropriety. The actors would have been the appellant.

The act of the two witnesses arranging the venues and persuading the appellants to go there tended to border on active participation and to qualify them as *crimen participe*. Nonetheless, given the facts, the Supreme Court was probably justified to conclude that the crime would have been committed with or without the assistance of the police officers and to accept the officers as genuine spies.

---

439. See for instance the Botswana case of *Molelekedi v. State* [1990] B.L.R. 630 (CA). The accused, a former soldier in the Botswana Defence Force, offered to sell some arms of war to a friend. The friend informed the police. The police, in turn, provided marked notes to some junior officers, who pretended to be South Africans arms buyers. As a result of this trap, the accused showed them the arms and was subsequently arrested and charged with and convicted of unlawful possession of arms of war. The High Court dismissed his appeal and also declined to grant him leave to appeal to the Court of Appeal. The Court of Appeal upheld the High Court's decision.
440. Cr. App. No. 6 of 1990 [UGSC 11 (19 Jul. 1993).

In the old case of *R. v. Muttra Prasad*, the police secured a conviction for selling liquor to 'natives' by sending 'a native' with marked coins to buy liquor from the accused. The High Court quashed the conviction, saying that 'The facts ... show clearly that the commission of the offence was procured by the police and their agents, and that they were liable to be punished as abettors.'[441] Given the tests in the *Wanjiko* tests, this decision is probably of doubtful authority today.

355. Although entrapment may be legitimately used to detect crime and to prosecute criminals, it may, like other human practices, be abused. To prevent such abuse, it is suggested that traps be conducted in as a fair a manner as possible and be closely supervised and monitored by senior officers within the police service. Where the courts detect abuse and unfairness, they should be willing to protect the accused by exercising their discretionary powers and exclude evidence that is unfairly obtained.[442]

§3. Accessory after the Fact

356. Section 393(1) of the Penal Code provides as follows:

> A person who receives or assists another who is, to his knowledge, guilty of an offence, in order to enable him to escape punishment, is said to become an accessory after the fact to that offence.

An accessory after the fact is not involved in committing the offence in question. His or her only role is that knowing that another person has committed an offence assists that other person to escape justice. By so acting, the accessory after the fact frustrates the wheel and aims of criminal justice. For so acting, he or she deserves punishment.

357. The *actus reus* for the offence of being an accessory after the fact is 'receiving' or 'assisting' a person who is 'guilty of an offence' to enable him or her to escape punishment. Receiving in this context means and includes giving sanctuary to the offender on one's premises and concealing him or her from law enforcement agents. Assisting includes giving the offender a lift on one's bicycle, motor vehicle, or boat or providing him with means of transport to evade arrest or capture by law enforcement agents. It also includes warning the offender that the police are looking for him or her. It also includes destroying the object or evidence of the crime, which would make the prosecution and conviction of the offender difficult. This was the case in *Rex v. Erunasani Sekoni s/o Eria & Anor*[443] where after killing the deceased the second appellant paid witnesses to carry away the body and to burn it

441. [1913] 2 U.L.R. 76.
442. See for instance *R v. Smurthwaite* [1994] 1 All E.R. 898. Generally see D.D.N. Nsereko, *Police Informants and Agents Provocateurs: Accomplices or Handmaidens of the Law? Perspectives from the Courts of Eastern and Southern Africa*, 9 Crim. L. Forum 151 (1999).
443. [1947] 14 E.A.C.A. 74.

to ashes – which they did. The witnesses were held to be accessories after the fact and accomplices for purposes of the law of evidence. In *Uganda v. Kalokole,*[444] a person was killed near the accused's house. The prosecution was unable to adduce satisfactory evidence identifying the killer. But there was evidence, including the accused's own admission, to show that the accused assisted in carrying the body and hiding it in a swamp where it would have been impossible to trace. The accused was acquitted of the murder but was convicted of being an accessory after the fact. His actions were tantamount to 'the hindrance of public justice by assisting the felon to escape the vengeance of the law'.

358. Can a person be an accessory after the fact by omission, say by failing to report the presence of a suspected offender in his neighbourhood or promptly reporting commission of a crime to the authorities to have the offender apprehended? The answer is no, unless that person has a legal duty to do any of these things. As the law now stands, an ordinary citizen does not have such a duty. The duty, if there be one, is purely a moral one.[445]

359. The *mens rea* of being an accessory after the fact is, first, knowledge that the person is 'guilty of an offence', and, second, intention 'to enable him to escape punishment'.

360. Concerning knowledge that the person who the accused assisted to escape was 'guilty of an offence', it is trite law that a person is not guilty until he or she is so proved and adjudged by a court of competent jurisdiction. Consequently, an accused person cannot be expected to know that another person alleged to have committed an offence is 'guilty' until there is a pronouncement to that effect by the court. It is therefore misleading to talk of the person being guilty before he is tried. Nevertheless, the essence of the offence of being accessory after the fact is knowledge that the person being assisted has committed an act, which the person giving assistance suspects or should suspect amounts to a crime. The question of guilt does not arise as yet, for all we know the person may be acquitted. This is the meaning that the courts attach to the section. However, this being a penal provision, it is urged that it be recast to make its import clear and unambiguous.[446]

361. Regarding the issue of enabling the criminal to escape, it is not sufficient that the accessory receives or does anything that enables the offender to escape

---

444. [1972] E.A. 313.

445. In the Tanzanian case of *Paskazia s/o Kabaikye v. R.* [1954] 21 E.A.C.A. 359, the Court of Appeal for Eastern Africa stressed that to prove the charge of being accessory after the fact there must be some act done to assist the felon. '*There must be some active steps taken with the object of hindering his apprehension, trial or punishment.*'

446. Section 23(1) of the Canadian Criminal Code has much to recommend itself for its clarity and precision. It provides that: '(1) An accessory after the fact to an offence is one who, knowing that a person has been a party to the offence, receives, comforts or assists him for the purpose of enabling him to escape; (2) No married person whose spouse has been a party to an offence is an accessory after the fact to that offence by receiving, comforting or assisting the spouse for the purpose of enabling the spouse to escape.'

justice. He or she must receive or assist him with that intention in mind. The accessory must act knowingly and for the purpose of enabling the offender to escape. The assistance must not be merely fortuitous.

362. In Uganda, as long as a person possesses the necessary *mens rea* (knowledge that a person has committed an offence *and* intention to enable him escape justice) and has taken active steps to assist the offender, he or she may be convicted even though no person has been convicted of the offence. This happened in *Uganda v. Kalokole*, *supra*. It also happened in *R. v. Sardi Nsubuga & Anor.*[447] In the latter case, the appellants were charged as accessories after the fact to murder and were tried together with the person who was alleged to have committed the crime. The person charged with the crime was acquitted. The appellants, who had assisted in concealing the body, were nevertheless convicted as accessories after the fact. As a matter of practice, it is advisable for the court intending to convict in these circumstances to have the charge sheet amended to strike out the name of the principal who has been acquitted and in instead add 'person or persons to the prosecution unknown'. This avoids an absurdity on the face of the record, showing that the accused has been convicted of receiving or assisting a person, knowing him to have committed an offence, when that person has in fact been held not to be guilty.[448] However, courts in other jurisdictions, such as Botswana, take the view that a person cannot be convicted as an accessory after the fact unless a principal has committed the offence and has been convicted for doing so. They take that view on the basis that a person cannot be an accessory after the fact to an offence which has not been committed, meaning, for whose commission none has been convicted. For that reason, the courts in those jurisdictions reserve the consideration of the liability of the person charged with being an accessory after the fact until after someone has been convicted of the principal offence.[449]

363. Concerning punishment, section 394 of the Penal Code provides that an accessory after the fact to a felony is guilty of a felony and, if no other punishment is provided, is liable to imprisonment for three years. Section 206 provides for one of those exceptions. It prescribes a term of seven years imprisonment for becoming an accessory after the fact to murder. Similarly section 395 provides that an accessory after the fact to a misdemeanour commits a misdemeanour and is liable to imprisonment for two years.[450]

---

447. [1941] 8 E.A.C.A. 81.

448. See *Nkabaremeheto s/o Masakura v. R.* [1959] E.A. 598.

449. See for instance *State v. Majeremane & Others* [1997]B.L.R. 630(HC). In this case, the third accused was charged with being an accessory after the fact to the murder of the deceased by two other accused persons. In the course of the trial, the prosecution withdrew the charge against one of the two men, and at the conclusion of the trial, the court acquitted the other. Consequently, the court acquitted the third accused of being an accessory after the fact.

450. Penal Code, sec. 395 as read with sec. 22.

364. Finally, section 393(2) reads as follows:

> A wife does not become an accessory after the fact to an offence of which her husband is guilty by receiving or assisting him in order to escape punishment; or by receiving or assisting, in her husband's presence and by his authority, another person who is guilty of an offence in the commission of which her husband has taken part, in order to enable that other person to escape punishment; nor does a husband become an accessory after the fact to an offence of which his wife is guilty by receiving or assisting her in order to escape punishment.

According to this provision, married persons cannot be found guilty of being accessories after the fact to crimes committed by their spouses. The exemption is, however, limited to spouses of monogamous marriages. As already noted, the Code's definition of a husband or of a wife is limited to a husband or to a wife of a monogamous marriage. People married under African customary law or under Mohamedan law may therefore be convicted of being accessories after the fact to crimes committed by their spouses.

365. This provision also extends the exemption to the wife in respect of other people who are accomplices with her husband. It is noteworthy though that the husband would not enjoy similar exemption if he received or assisted a person who was a party to his wife's crime. This differential and discriminatory treatment between spouses should no longer be countenanced in an era that stresses the equality of men and women.

366. As noted above, an accessory after the fact is not a party to the offence committed by the principal offenders. The exception is the person who is an accessory after the fact to treason. According to the Penal Code, such a person is treated at par with the principal offenders and is liable to the same punishment.[451]

§4. Framing of Charges

367. As noted above, all the participants in a crime, whatever be their roles, 'are deemed to have taken part in committing the offence and to be guilty of the offence' and 'and may be charged with actually commiting it'. It therefore is desirable that they all be joined together in the same charge sheet and tried together. This is convenient, expeditious and cost-effective. However, when the participants are so joined it is not necessary to spell out in the charge sheet their respective roles, that is, whether perpetrators or secondary participants.[452] It is indeed often very difficult, particularly in cases of gang or mob crime, to tell who was a perpetrator or a

451. Section 23(1)(d).

452. However, according to Glanville Williams 'it is customary and wise for the prosecution to charge the perpetrator and accessories in appropriate terms where the evidence is clear. The statement of the offence will give the name of the crime, but the particulars of the offence should, when possible, state that the defendant is charged with having aided, abetted, counseled or procured the crime, if such be the fact.' Glanville Williams, *Textbook on Criminal Law*, 333.

secondary participant. So, the practice of charging everybody as a principal, which is provided for under the law, serves to overcome this difficulty.[453] However, failure to join all of the participants in a crime does not necessarily vitiate the indictment. For example, where the perpetrator has escaped or is dead the secondary participant may be charged alone. The perpetrator may similarly be tried alone where the secondary participants are unavailable. However, where the secondary participant is charged alone, it is important, as indicated earlier, for the prosecution to prove that the offence was committed.

368. With respect to accessories after the fact, they too should be joined in the same charge sheet and be tried jointly with the principal offenders. They must, however, be charged in separate counts, unless they are charged with being an accessory after the fact to treason. The joining of the accessories after the fact in the charge sheet with the principals is also provided for under the law. Both the principal offence and being an accessory after the fact to that offence are offences committed in the course of the same transaction.[454]

453. Trial on Indictment Act, sec. 24(a) and sec. 87(1) of the Magistrates Courts Act provides for the joining in the same charge sheet 'persons accused of the same offence committed in the course of the same transaction'. See also *Attorney-General v. Onyango s/o Olude & Anor.* [1954] 2 E.A.C.A 238.

454. Trial on Indictments Act, sec. 24(d) and sec. 87(4) of the Magistrates Courts Act also provides for the joining of 'persons accused of different offences committed in the course of the same transaction'.

Chapter 7. Particular Crimes

§1. Crimes against the Person

I. Homicides

A. *Murder*

369. Besides treason, murder is the most serious crime on the criminal calendar. It constitutes the most flagrant violation of the most basic of all the rights of the human person – the right to life. If you take away a person's life you also extinguish all of his or her other rights. The aim of the law then is to protect this primordial right. This explains why murder attracts the ultimate sentence – death. Section 188 of the Penal Code defines murder thus:

> Any person who of malice aforethought causes the death of another person by an unlawful act or omission is guilty of murder.

Similarly, section 189 provides that 'Any person convicted of murder shall be liable to suffer death.'[455]

1. The *Actus Reus*

370. The *actus reus* of murder consists of the following three broad elements: (1) death of a person capable of being killed, (2) caused by an unlawful act or omission, (3) and the unlawful act or omission is attributable to the accused person.

Therefore before anyone can be convicted of murder, it must be shown that: (i) a human being (ii) died (iii) as a result of an unlawful act or omission (iv) attributable to the accused.

a. Death of a Person

371. As to when human life begins and thus becomes susceptible to being taken away, section 197 of the Penal Code provides as follows:

> A child becomes a person capable of being killed when it has completely proceeded in a living state from the body of its mother, whether it has breathed or not, and whether it has an independent circulation or not, and whether the naval-string is severed or not.

455. The provision originally provided that 'Any person convicted of murder shall ne sentenced to death.' The author has taken the liberty to rephrase the provision to reflect the Supreme Court's ruling abolishing the mandatory death sentence and making it discretionary.

Thus, destroying foetuses before they have been wholly expelled from their mother's womb is not murder. It may either be abortion[456] or 'preventing a child from being born alive'.[457]

372. Whether or not the person alleged to have been killed is dead is a question of fact. Normally a medical practitioner after examining the body should certify the person dead. Lay witnesses who saw and could identify the body as that of the deceased and witnessed its burial can also be relied on to prove that the person is dead. However, whether the proof is by a medical practitioner or by a lay witness, it is important that the witness swear to having seen the body and identified it as that of the person alleged to have been killed.[458] In *Rex v. Erusani Sekoni s/o Eria*, the body of the deceased was burned to ashes.[459] The Court accepted the evidence of three witnesses that a man known to them was slain, and his remains completely destroyed. Where such direct evidence is lacking and the prosecution relies on circumstantial evidence, Uganda courts follow the dictum of the Court of Appeal for Eastern Africa, in a case from Tanzania:

> While death may be proved by circumstantial evidence, without evidence as to the production of the body of the allegedly dead person and without any evidence of a person who saw the body of the dead person and without a confession by a person accused that he caused the death, yet where a court is asked to find in a murder charge that a person is dead in the circumstances which we have stated, the evidence on which the court is asked to infer the death must be such as to compel the inference of death and must be such as to be inconsistent with any reasonable theory of the alleged deceased being alive, with the result that taken as a whole the evidence leaves no doubt whatsoever that the person in question is dead.[460]

373. Before a person can be said to have caused the death of another, section 198(1) of the Code requires that the following prerequisites be satisfied:

(1) A person is not deemed to have killed another if the death of that person does not take place within a year and a day of the cause of death.
(2) Such period is reckoned inclusive of the day on which the last unlawful act contributing to the cause of death was done, and when the cause of death is an omission to observe or perform a duty, the period is reckoned inclusive of the day on which the omission ceased.
(3) When the cause of death is in part an unlawful act, and in part an omission to observe or perform a duty, the period is reckoned inclusive of the last on which the last unlawful act was done or the day on which the omission ceased, whichever is the later.

---

456. Section 142.
457. Section 212.
458. See *Bumbakali Lutwama & Anor. v. Uganda*, S.Ct.Cr.App. No. 38 of 1989 (unreported).
459. [1947] 14 E.A.C.A. 74.
460. *Kimweri v. Republic* [1968] E.A. 452, 453. The Supreme Court confirmed that this dictum expresses the law in Uganda. See *Bumbakali Lutwama & Anor. v. Uganda*, see *supra* n. 458.

374. The requirement that death takes place within a year and a day is predicated on two policy grounds. First, after the lapse of such a long interval as a year and a day, it becomes uncertain as to what the actual cause of death really is. Second, and probably the stronger ground, a person who has injured another should not remain indefinitely at risk for prosecution for murder. Thus, time is of the essence for the crime of murder, and the charge sheet must always allege the date on which the unlawful act or omission that caused the death occurred, and not the date of the death itself.[461] Why the period prescribed is a year and a day is inexplicable. Suffice it to say, however, that the rule was copied from old English law. England has long abandoned it as anachronistic. It is probably time Uganda abandoned it too.

b. Unlawful Act or Omission

375. That a person is dead is not sufficient to constitute the *actus reus* of murder. It must also be proved that that person died as a result of an unlawful act or omission. However, once death has been proved, the law presumes that it was unlawfully caused, unless it is shown that it was accidental or excusable.[462] Death will be accidental if the accused did not intend to kill or to inflict any harm at all. It will be excusable where the accused acted under an honest and reasonable mistake of fact; or where he or she was exercising the right of self-defence or defence of another person using reasonable force;[463] where he or she killed as an act of war; or whilst using reasonable force to effect an arrest or to prevent the escape of a prisoner from lawful custody.

c. The Accused's Unlawful Act or Omission Caused the Death

376. There must be a causal link between the accused and the unlawful act that caused the death, otherwise the *actus reus* is incomplete. The accused must have participated directly or indirectly (as actual perpetrator, aider, aider and abettor or procurer) in the unlawful act or omission that caused the death of the deceased. Such act or omission need not be the sole cause or the main cause of the death. It is sufficient that it significantly contributed to the death. Whether or not such act or omission is attributable or linked to the accused is a matter of fact which must be proved by evidence, whether direct or circumstantial.[464] Again, whether or not it was the

461. See, for example, *Regina v. Nasani Kibuka* H.Ct.Monthly Bulletin No. 207 of 1963; *R. v. Lujo Mgomba* [1946] 13 E.A.C.A. 156; *M'Liaro s/o Miyeka v. R.* [1951] 18 E.A.C.A. 169. See also the Kenyan case of *Kamau s/o Gikera & Anor. v. R.* [1955] E.A.C.A. 339.
462. See *Gusambizi a/o Wesonga v. R.* [1948] 15 E.A.C.A. 65.
463. As to which party has the onus to prove accident or self-defence, the Court of Appeal said in *Paulo Omale v. Uganda* Cr. App. No 6 of 1977 (unreported) that: 'It is for the prosecution to prove beyond reasonable doubt that the prisoner with malice aforethought killed the deceased. It is not for the prisoner to prove accident or self-defence and he is entitled to be acquitted even though the court is not satisfied that his story is true, so long as the court is of the view that his story might reasonably be true.'
464. In *Simoni Musoke v. R* [1958] E.A. 715 at 718, the former Eastern Court of Appeal stated that 'in a case depending exclusively on circumstantial evidence the judge must find before deciding on conviction that the inculpatory facts were incompatible with innocence of the accused, and incapable of explanation upon any other hypothesis than that of guilt.' See also *Mureeba Janet & Anor*

accused's unlawful act or omission which was *the cause of death* is a question of fact to be established by evidence. Ordinarily, a medical practitioner who carried out a *post mortem* examination should be called to give his or her opinion on what caused the death of the deceased.[465] Lay witnesses who saw the injuries on the deceased may also be able to testify as to the cause of death. Needless to say, the prosecution's failure to prove the cause of death will be fatal to its case.[466]

377. Where several persons, acting independently of each other, injure a person (say by beating) and cause his or her death and it is unclear as to whose blow was the fatal blow that caused the death, none of the persons taking part in the injuring can be convicted of murder or manslaughter. They may, instead, be convicted of occasioning actual bodily harm.[467] Where, however, it is established that in inflicting such injury the persons concerned acted with a common intention to prosecute a common purpose in conjunction with one another then they are all responsible for the resulting death, and it does not matter which one of them struck the fatal blow.[468]

d. Intervening Acts

378. Section 196 of the Penal Code carries elaborate provisions dealing with situations where the accused's act or omission is not the sole or immediate cause of death. They include medical treatment, neglect of the injured person himself or herself, the act of the deceased in trying to avoid violence, acts that hastened the death and accompanying acts of the deceased or other persons. We shall now deal with them one by one.

i. Medical Treatment

379. Where a person inflicts bodily injury on another as a result of which the injured person undergoes surgical or medical treatment which causes his or her death, the person who caused the injury is responsible for the death. His or her responsibility is predicated on the fact that the injuries are the operating cause of

---

v. Uganda Cr. App. No.13 of 2003 [2006] UGSC 7 (21 Jul. 2006) where the Supreme Court on confirming a conviction based on circumstantial evidence stated that 'Generally, in a criminal case, for circumstantial evidence to sustain a conviction, the circumstantial evidence must point irresistibly to the guilt of the accused.' In *Uganda v. Aggrey Kiyingi*, Cr. Session Case No. 30 of 2006 [2006] UGHC 52 (10 Dec. 2006) in which the prosecution case was based solely on circumstantial evidence, the High Court said 'The evidence on record merely leaves the accused as a high suspect in the death of his wife. But the law is very straight on that point, suspicion however high it may be can never be the basis for conviction … The circumstantial evidence against the accused did not point irresistibly at the accused unlike in the *Mureeba* case … the circumstantial evidence could not be tied around Dr Kiyingi … '

465. See for example *Jephlin Lubega & Anor. v. Uganda* S.Ct.Cr.App. No. 35 of 1992 (unreported).
466. For example, see *Regina v. Musisi* [1956–1957] 8 U.L.R. 17.
467. See *Francis Sebanenya & Anor. v. Uganda*, S.Ct.Cr.App. No. 17 of 1989 (unreported); *Okute s/o Kaliebi & Anor. v. R.* [1941] 8 E.A.C.A. 78; *Dracaku s/o Afia & Anor. v. R.* [1963] E.A. 363, *Uganda v. Leo Mubyazita* [1972] U.L.R. 3.
468. See *Dafasi Magayi & Anor. v. Uganda* [1965] E.A. 667; *Uganda v. Leo Nyendwoha*, H.Ct.Cr.Session No. 253 of 1991 (unreported); *R. v. Tabulayenka & Anor.* [1943] 10 E.A.C.A. 51.

the death and the surgical or medical treatment is the natural or foreseeable consequence of his or her conduct (inflicting injuries). Moreover, according to the Code, it does not matter that the treatment was proper or mistaken. As long as the treatment was conducted in good faith and with common knowledge and skill, the fact that it was not proper or was mistaken does not break the chain of causation. These are the risks that are inherent in the medical profession's attempts to save life.

ii. Neglect of Injured Person

380. If a person inflicts bodily injuries on another and the injuries would not have resulted in death had the victim submitted to proper surgical or medical treatment or had observed proper precautions as to his or her mode of living, that person would similarly be deemed to have caused the death of the victim. It is true that the lives of many victims of cut wounds or gunshots in Uganda today could be saved if such victims received prompt and proper medical treatment. As it happens, however, there are usually no hospitals nearby to which such victims can be taken. Where hospitals exist, they are not adequately equipped or stocked with the necessary appliances or drugs, or staffed with sufficient or properly trained staff. Lives would be saved if there were efficient means of transport to convey the victims to the hospitals in time. They would also be saved if power did not often go off in the middle of surgical operations. Therefore, even if the victim wanted to submit to proper medical care, that care is often not there. These are the risks that a person who inflicts injury on another assumes. They are the natural and foreseeable consequences of his or her unlawful conduct. He or she cannot escape responsibility for the death that results from them.[469]

iii. Act of the Deceased to Avoid Violence

381. A person causes the death of another if he or she unleashes or threatens to unleash violence on such other person and causes that other person to perform an act which causes his or her death, the act being a means of avoiding the violence and the act appears to that person to be the natural thing to do in the circumstances. Thus, in the English case of *Curley*[470] the appellant was charged with the murder of a woman who, in an attempt to avoid the appellant's violence, jumped out of a window and died. The appellant told the police, 'I ran at her to hit her. I didn't touch her. Out she jumped.' Confirming the appellant's conviction for manslaughter, the Court of Criminal Appeal said, 'On that statement a verdict of murder might well have been returned, but it was mercifully reduced to one of manslaughter. The jumping out of the window was contributed to by appellant's unlawful act.' Here, again, the causal link between the accused's conduct and the actual cause of death is apparent. If it were not for the accused's conduct, the deceased would not have done what

469. See *Tindigwihura Mbaha v. Uganda*, S.Ct.Cr.App. No. 9 of 1992 (unreported). The Court rejected appellant's contention that the deceased died due to the negligence of his relatives because they did not take him to the hospital for medical treatment as a result of the wounds inflicted on him by the appellant.

470. (1909) 2 Cr.App.Rep. 96, 109.

she did. Moreover, trying to save oneself from violence is natural and foreseeable conduct.

382. Whether the deceased's reaction was proper or reasonable in the circumstances is measured by subjective standards. According to the Code, the standard is what 'would appear natural to the person whose death is so caused'. If the person is the timid, hypersensitive type, his or her conduct has to be looked at that way. The accused should take the victim as he or she finds him or her.

iv. Hastening the Death

383. Here, too, a person causes the death of another if by his or her conduct he or she hastens the death of that other person who may already be suffering from any disease or injury which apart from such conduct would have caused death. According to the law, a person takes his victim as he or she finds him or her. It is no excuse for him or her to say that the victim did not have long to live anyway. In *Uganda v. L. Kakooza*,[471] the accused kicked the deceased in the abdomen and ruptured her spleen as a result of which she died. It was argued on the accused's behalf that the deceased's spleen was already weak, and that the deceased was a sickly person. The court curtly reminded him that this was no excuse and that he had to take the deceased as he found her. Another case in which the principle was invoked is that of *Okute s/o Kaliebi & Anor.*[472] Here the deceased had been subjected to severe beatings by other people and was already weak when the second accused, acting independently, struck him the fatal blow. The second appellant was convicted of the deceased's murder while those who had assaulted him earlier were convicted of mere assault causing bodily harm.

384. Taking the victim as he or she is, is not confined to physical conditions alone. It encompasses the victim's whole personality, including his or her psychological frame and beliefs. The English case of *R. v. Blaue* is in point.[473] The deceased was a Jehovah's Witness. The accused stabbed her with a knife which penetrated her lungs. As a result of the stabbing, the deceased lost considerable quantities of blood from the wound. Medical authorities told her that she needed a blood transfusion, and that she would die if she did not have one. She refused to have the transfusion administered because of her religious beliefs. She was adamant and died the following day. When charged with causing the deceased's death, the accused contended that the deceased's refusal to have a blood transfusion was unreasonable and had broken the chain of causation between the stabbing and her death. The trial court as well as the Court of Appeal rejected the contention. Said Lawton, L.J.:

> It has long been the policy of the law that those who use violence on other people must take their victims as they find them. This in our judgment means the whole man, not just the physical man. It does not lie in the mouth of the

471. H.Ct.Cr.Session No. 6 of 1991 (unreported).
472. [1941] 8 E.A.C.A. 78. See also *Regina v. Mukasa & Anor.* [1956–1957] 8 U.L.R. 314, 300.
473. [1975] 3 All E.R. 446.

assailant to say that his victim's religious beliefs which inhibited him from accepting certain kinds of treatment were unreasonable. The question for decision is what caused her death. The answer is the stab wound. The fact that the victim refused to stop this end coming about did not break the causal connection between the act and death.[474]

v. Accompanying Acts of Deceased or Other Persons

385. A person will be deemed to have caused the death of another if by his conduct he or she lays the trap which is triggered by the deceased's or some other person's acts or omissions. For example, the accused's act of laying a land mine does not per se cause death unless it is accompanied by the act of the deceased or some other person in stepping on the mine, causing it to detonate and to kill the deceased. A similar example is where a house servant laces a drink intended for his master and puts it away where the master will find it and drink it. The act of lacing per se does not cause death unless it is accompanied by the deceased's act of voluntarily drinking the laced drink.

386. The case of *Rex v. Nyansio Katunzi* is also in point.[475] The accused set fire to a grass-thatched hut in which one Zabalirwa, his son-in-law and four small children were sleeping. Zabalirwa helped his son-in-law to evacuate the children from the hut. However, labouring under the mistaken impression that one of the children was still in the hut, Zabalirwa re-entered it and sustained injuries from which he died. If Zabalirwa did not come out of the hut the first time and was burned to death there would be no doubt that the accused's act of setting fire to the hut was the direct cause of Zabalirwa's death. It ceased to be so when he came out apparently unscathed. Zabalirwa would not have died if he had not re-entered. Did the re-entering break the chain of causation so as to free the accused from responsibility? It did not. As the Court of Appeal for Eastern Africa stated:

> The setting fire to the hut did cause the death of Zabalirwa, one of the occupants. It is true that had Zabalirwa not returned into the hut in the mistaken impression that one of his children was still in the hut he would have escaped injury, but malice aforethought having been established the fact that the act of Zabalirwa in re-entering the hut intervened between the unlawful act of the accused and the fatal burning, the result of the unlawful act is in the circumstances no defence to the charge, as the trial Judge properly held. The appeal is dismissed.[476]

387. It is important to stress then that in all these situations once an accused person, with the requisite *mens rea,* does an unlawful act or makes an unlawful

474. *Ibid.*, at p. 450. See also the Uganda case of *R. v. Petrol Mangongo s/o Kalwa* [1944] 11 E.A.C.A. 100. With due respect, this case is no longer good law in Uganda.
475. [1946] 13 E.A.C.A. 154.
476. *Ibid.*, at 155.

omission vis-a-vis the victim, he or she will not escape responsibility for the victim's death simply because somebody else contributes to the causing of that death.

2. The *Mens Rea*: Malice Aforethought

388. The *mens rea* for murder is *malice aforethought*. The inclusion of the word 'malice' in the term does not necessarily mean that it is an essential ingredient of the definition of murder. One may cause the death of another without malice, for example, for altruistic motives, and still be guilty of murder.

Section 191 of the Penal Code defines 'malice aforethought' in the following terms:

> Malice aforethought shall be deemed to be established by evidence proving any of the following circumstances –
>
> a) an intention to cause the death of any person, whether such person is the person actually killed or not; or
> b) knowing that the act or omission causing death will probably cause the death of some person, whether such person is the person actually killed or not, although such knowledge is accompanied by indifference whether death is caused or not, or by a wish that it may not be caused.

a. Intention to Cause Death of a Person

389. Under this limb of malice aforethought, there must be direct intention to cause death of a person. Where the accused confessed to have shot at the tyres of a car with the intention of stopping it, it was held that this was not intention to cause death of its passengers.[477] Again, if all that the accused person intended to do was to inflict grievous bodily harm on the deceased, then he or she had no malice aforethought and he or she is not guilty of murder. This has been the law since the enactment of the Penal Code (Amendment) Act of 1970.[478]

390. Intention to cause death may be proved by showing that the accused actually expressed that intention by word of mouth or in written form. This is rarely done. Therefore the commonest way of proving intention is for the court to infer such intention from the conduct of the accused and from all the circumstances surrounding the killing. In making that inference, the courts take into account the following factors.

The nature of the weapon used to cause death. The use of a lethal weapon such as a gun, panga, sharp knife, spear or hoe tends to suggest an intention to kill. Use of a non-lethal weapon however, tends to suggest lack of such intention.[479] The part of the body on which the injuries are inflicted is another factor. Aiming at vulnerable

---

477. *Walusimbi & Anor. v. Uganda*, Cr. App. No. 28 of 1992, [1994] UGSC 6 (18 Mar. 1994).
478. Act 29 of 1970. See also *Bukenya & Anor v. Uganda* [1972] e.A. 549.
479. See *Yoweri Damulira v. R.* [1956] 23 E.A.C.A. 501.

parts of the body such as the head,[480] chest,[481] neck and cheeks,[482] and abdomen[483] tends to suggest an intention to kill. However, inflicting the injuries on less vulnerable parts of the body diminishes the presumption of the intention.[484] The nature of injuries and the amount of force used in inflicting them, whether they are multiple or one, and whether the accused aims one or more blows on the deceased is another. In one case, the accused speared the deceased in the chest. Prior to the killing, he had been imbibing liquor. Said the High Court:

> It is therefore my finding that the accused killed the deceased without malice aforethought and this may be supported by evidence of PW4 who saw him consuming enguli [a kind of liquor] that evening and may be corroborated by the doctor's report which showed that the deceased had only one wound on the chest if he had malice aforethought he would possibly have inflicted more injuries than one.[485]

391. In another case, the accused was walking away from his home armed with a panga and a bow with a bundle of arrows followed by a group of people. He shot one arrow into the group and killed the deceased. He said his aim was to scare them into not following him and not to interfere with his domestic affairs. Holding that the accused did not intend to kill, the Court said:

> It is my considered opinion that the intention of the accused was not to kill any of these people but to scare them away so that they could not continue bothering him with the private affair of his proposed love to his daughter-in-law. If the accused had in fact intended to kill any of these people he would have attacked them when he came out of the house with the arrows and the panga, he would also have used more than one arrow to shoot at them. The position would have been different if the accused had used a more deadly weapon like a bullet or a spear or if he had proceeded to beat the deceased after shooting him with the arrow.[486]

---

480. In *Sgt. Kelly Omige & Anor. v. Uganda*, C.A.Cr.App. No. 3 of 1986 (unreported) the first appellant shot the deceased with a pistol in the forehead. In *Uganda v. Musane & Anor.*, *supra*, the accused shot the deceased in the forehead and ribs which were vulnerable parts of the body with an SMG rifle (a deadly weapon). The Court considered these factors to be evidence of malice aforethought.
481. In *Uganda v. Josephat Byebandwa*, H.Ct.Cr.Session No. 25 of 1988 (unreported) the accused speared the deceased in the chest.
482. In *Uganda v. Bosco Obol*, H.Ct.Cr.Session No. 135 of 1991 (unreported) the accused inflicted deep cut wounds on the neck and head, resulting in the severance of carotid arteries on both cheeks.
483. In *Uganda v. Kakooza*, H.Ct.Cr.Session No. 69 of 1991 (unreported) the accused kicked the deceased and thereby ruptured her spleen. Nevertheless, the court was unable to say with certainty that the accused killed the deceased with the specific intention of killing her, or that he knew the probable result of such assaults would be death.
484. This does not always follow. See *Uganda v. Constantine Zake*, H.Ct.Cr.Session No. 20 of 1985; [1985] H.Ct.Bulletin 18. The accused inflicted a cut wound on the leg with a spear, resulting in the severance of all tibial blood vessels and causing deceased's death through excessive hemorrhage. He was found to have had malice aforethought.
485. *Uganda v. Byembandwa, supra.*
486. *Uganda v. Semeo Omulo*, H.Ct.Cr.Session No. 26 of 1986 (unreported). In *Uganda v. Poloneli Kasengaki & Anor.*, H.Ct.Cr.Session No. 111 of 1987 (unreported) the second accused struck the

392. Similarly in *Nanyonjo & Anor v. Uganda, supra*, the Supreme C reduced the murder conviction to manslaughter, because the first appellant hit deceased with one hand and the resulting injuries, as confirmed by a doctor, did suggest prolonged assault. For this reason, the court was unable to say that the d was a natural consequence of the assault inflicted.

The conduct of the accused before and immediately after the act or omis causing death is another factor that the courts take into account. Arming one before the killing is one good example of such conduct. This is illustrated by case of *Uganda v. Constantine Zake*.[487] The accused had a land dispute with deceased. A local chief summoned him and the deceased to a meeting with a v to settling the dispute. On his way to the meeting, the accused came armed wi spear, but concealed it so that no one could see it. When he saw the accused he towards him and thrust the spear on his leg, severing all the tibial blood ves causing excessive haemorrhage.

The Court held thus:

> In arming himself with a spear when he knew that the deceased was turnin for the settlement of the dispute, the intention was to kill the decea Although the spear landed on the leg which was not one of the vulnerable p of the body, nevertheless, in coming to the garden with a spear and hidin when he knew that the deceased would be turning up for settlement of t dispute glaringly showed that he had intention to kill. Further, picking the s from where he had kept it and running towards the deceased while armed it, when the deceased was not aware, showed nothing also but intention to him.

393. As to the conduct of the accused after the commission of the offence Supreme Court, in *Kyazike v. Uganda*, found the appellant's conduct after the causing death to have negatived the appellant's intention to cause death.[488] On day in question, the appellant found the deceased, her 10-year-old son, playing refusing to go to school, pretending that he was sick. The deceased's cond coupled with the fact that he had reportedly stolen money from neighbours ann her. Thereupon the appellant grabbed the deceased, tied him to a jackfruit tree. then tied dry banana leaves around his legs, arms and hands and set him ablaze. subsequently released the deceased who ran away to his father in the garden. W the deceased returned home with his father, the appellant took him to the hos where he died the following day of burns. In her confession statement to the po she admitted burning the deceased, but said: 'My intention to burn the deceased not to kill him, but to discipline him; unfortunately he died.' On convicting he murder, the High Court referred to the fact that she stood by the burning

---

deceased on the head with a short stick. The fact that the accused struck only one blow with a lethal weapon was taken into account to negative malice aforethought.

487. See *supra* n. 6.

488. Cr. Appeal No. 15 of 2009, [2010] UGSC 22 (25 Jan. 2010).

pushed him back deep into the fire whenever he struggled to break free; and her fury at his uncle and threats to also throw him into the fire when he attempted to save the boy. From all these facts the court concluded that the appellant 'wanted the deceased exterminated'. However, on a second appeal, the Supreme Court quashed the murder conviction and substituted it with manslaughter, holding that the appellant's subsequent conduct after the deceased got burnt was inconsistent with that of a person who intended to kill or who had knowledge that her action would probably cause death. The court said:

> [On] the basis of the evidence presented a reasonable doubt remains that her conduct, strange, cruel and outrageous as it was, was actuated by an intention to 'exterminate' the decease … The evidence that was accepted by, *sic,* that she herself cooled off the fire, allowed the deceased to get away from the scene, carried the deceased on a bicycle to the hospital and stayed with him until he died must be considered in her favour and consequently created doubt about her intention to cause the death of the deceased.

394. The Supreme Court correctly stated that intention to cause grievous bodily harm, which it found to exist in this case, could not be the basis for finding malice afore thought. It nonetheless discounted the possibility that the appellant had knowledge that her actions would 'probably cause death', but without engaging in any analysis of this issue. If it did, it would have probably come to a different conclusion. One explanation why it did not will be proffered in the following sections of this chapter.

The relationships and dealings between the deceased and the accused before the killing may also be a relevant factor. Conflict over women and tending to suggest motive for the killing is one example.[489] The fact that the deceased knew the accused to be probably involved in a robbery is a relevant factor – tending to suggest motive for the killing: so that the deceased may not report him to the authorities.[490] Motive per se is of course immaterial to criminal responsibility. Its presence does, however, tend to strengthen evidence of intention and has been so accepted in these two examples.[491]

Fleeing or disappearing from the village from where the killing takes place is another factor which may also be taken into account. For instance, in *Muzaya*

489. See *Kalisiti Sebugwawo v. Uganda*, C.A.Cr.App. No. 7 of 1987 (unreported). Here the accused was in love with the deceased's former wife, and the deceased alluded to this fact in his dying declaration naming the accused as his assailant.

490. See *Sgt. Kelly Omuge & Anor. v. Uganda*, C.A.Cr.App. No. 3 of 1986 (unreported).

491. See *Uganda v. Tigawalana Bakali Ikoba & Ors* Cr. App. No. 21 of 2005, [2009] 51, 17 Dec. 2009. The Court of Appeal found that the first respondent, an LCV Chairman, had a motive to eliminate the deceased who during 2002 elections had campaigned against him and subsequently filed a petition seeking to nullify his election. According to the Court, 'There is evidence on record showing that this worried the respondent so much. He would not have missed (sic) opportunity to eliminate Musitwa if he felt he had a chance to get away with it.'

Thomas & Anor. v. Uganda,[492] the Supreme Court inferred the second appellant's participation in the killing of the deceased from the fact that he inexplicably fled from the areas of both his workplace and residence; he also told lies about his whereabouts after the murder; and that these facts were corroborated by his confession. Fear and confusion in the accused's mind engendered by the belief that the deceased was bewitching him and his relatives has also been used to negative intention to kill.[493]

b. Knowledge that the Act or Omission Will Probably Cause Death

395. This leg of malice aforethought involves a conscious taking of risk. When a person, while not intending to kill, does an act or omits to do something knowing that death may probably result from such act or omission he or she has malice aforethought and is guilty of murder. That person may be indifferent whether death results from his or her act or omission. He or she may even entertain a wish that death does not result from such act or omission. All this is immaterial. What is material and morally reprehensible is that though fully aware that that act or omission will probably cause death he or she nonetheless consciously goes ahead and does it and causes death. The act or omission must, however, be unlawful, or else surgeons who perform high risk operations would be guilty of murder. Such acts as inflicting blows on vulnerable parts of the body, rape of girls of tender age, hurling a grenade at a crowd and arson, are unlawful acts which, in given circumstances, make it probable that death might result from them. Nevertheless, whether or not an act or omission will probably result in the death of someone is a matter that must be determined by means of an objective test. Would a reasonable person expect death to result from the act or omission in question? If the answer is in the affirmative, then, the accused will have acted with malice aforethought. If it is negative, then, he or she cannot be said to have had malice aforethought even though in the event death did result, as in the *Nanyonjo* case, *supra*. The courts have in this regard been insistent in pointing out that they are not bound to infer malice aforethought by reason only of the death being the natural or probable consequence of the accused person's actions or omissions. They have at times used subjective standards to determine whether in light of all the surrounding circumstances the accused intended to cause death or foresaw that death would result.

396. Few prosecutions or convictions have been based on this leg of malice aforethought. One possible reason for the nonuse of this provision is the objective element inherent in the probability standard and the courts' unwillingness to use

492. Cri. App. No. 3 of 2006, [2007] UGSC 1, 30 May 2007. The Supreme Court, which confirmed the charge of murder, did not specifically infer intention to cause death but generally the appellant's participation in the killing. The author nevertheless deduces from this inference another indirect inference of intention to cause death, because without it the conviction would not have been sustainable.

493. See *Uganda v. Gabriel Ojoba*, H.Ct.Cr.Session No. 260 of 1975 (unreported).

such a low standard in capital offences. It is just *probable*, not *highly* probable. One of the very few cases in which it was applied, albeit implicitly, was *Uganda v. John Kuka*.[494] Here the accused, after hearing the voice of his wife talking to a man he had long suspected to be her paramour, locked the house where they were and set it on fire. As it turned out the suspected paramour was not in the house. Instead, there were only his wife, his daughter and his daughter's friend. Because the accused had locked the house with a padlock the victims could not come out, and rescuers could not reach them. He was convicted of the murder of the three persons.

c. Transferred Malice Aforethought

397. The doctrine of transferred malice, discussed in Chapter 3, *supra*, applies to murder. Thus, in *Uganda v. John Kuka*, *supra*, the accused's intention was to kill his wife and her paramour. Unknown to him, his daughter and her friend were in the house together with his wife. He had no intention of killing his daughter and her friend and regretted it. He was nevertheless convicted of the murder of the girls as well, for the law conjoins the murderous intention with the event which then ensued.

B. Manslaughter

398. Manslaughter, though another serious form of homicide, is less morally reprehensible than murder, because it is not committed with malice aforethought. It does not attract the death penalty. Instead, it is punishable by up to life imprisonment. It may be committed in any of the four following ways: (1) unlawful act; (2) unlawful omission amounting to culpable negligence; (3) excess of justifiable force; and (4) provocation.

1. Unlawful Act

399. Section 187(1) of the Penal Code provides that:

> Any person who, by an unlawful act ... causes the death of another person is guilty of the felony termed manslaughter.

To secure a conviction under this provision it must, first and foremost, be shown that a person capable of being killed died within a year and a day. Second, it must be shown that it was the accused that caused the death; and, third that he or she did so by an unlawful act or omission. Here we are concerned with causing death by acts, *not* omissions. Causing death under this provision is commonly referred to as

494. H.Ct.Cr.Session No. 75 of 1990 (unreported).

'involuntary manslaughter', because the person causing the death does so unintentionally, as was the case in *Kyazike v. Uganda, (supra*, paragraph 393). Our courts have interpreted 'unlawful' to mean criminal acts. Civilly wrongful acts, such as those amounting to simple negligence, will not result in a conviction for manslaughter.[495] However, the courts have repeatedly held that causing a person's death is per se wrongful, unless the accused can show that it was either accidental or excusable (as in the case of self-defence). They have accordingly held such a person guilty of manslaughter where it was proved that he caused the death of another, and he was unable to show that it was accidental or excusable, and the prosecution could not prove malice aforethought.[496]

2. Unlawful Omission Amounting to Culpable Negligence

400. According to section 187(1) of the Penal Code:

> Any person who, by an unlawful … omission, causes the death of another person is guilty of the felony termed manslaughter.

According to section 187(2):

> An unlawful omission is an omission amounting to culpable negligence to discharge a duty tending to the preservation of life or health, whether such omission is or is not accompanied by an intention to cause death or bodily harm.

401. Manslaughter under this limb of the provision is also referred to as involuntary manslaughter, because the person causing death does not intend to kill. It involves failure to discharge a duty imposed by the Penal Code or some other law, relating to the preservation of life. Sections 199–203 of the Code spell out the duty that the law imposes on those who have charge of others, such as heads of families, masters, persons doing dangerous things, and those in charge of doing dangerous things, to protect the lives of others and deem them responsible for the consequences which may adversely affect those persons when such duty is not discharged. For example, section 203 which applies to motorists and others in charge of 'dangerous things' provides as follows:

> It is the duty of every person who has in his charge or under his control anything, whether living or inanimate, and whether moving or stationary, of such a nature that, in the absence of care or precaution in its use or management, the life, safety, or health of any person may be endangered, to use reasonable care and take reasonable precautions to avoid such danger; and shall be deemed to have caused any consequences which adversely affect the life or health of any person by reason of any omission to perform that duty.

495. See *R. v. Franklin* (1883) 15 Cox C.C. 163.
496. For example, see *R. v. Sharmpal Singh* [1962] E.A. 13.

However, to be convicted of manslaughter for failing to discharge this duty the accused must have been guilty of 'culpable negligence'. This species of negligence involves an extremely high degree of carelessness, higher than that required in civil cases. As was stated in the oft-quoted English case of *Rex v. Bateman*,[497] culpable negligence in the sense used in the Penal Code must go 'beyond mere matter of compensation and [shows] such disregard for life and safety of others as to amount to a crime against the State and conduct deserving punishment'. This negligence is also higher in degree than the negligence necessary to establish the offence of criminal recklessness or 'rash and negligent acts'.[498] The degree of negligence required for these offences is substantial and definitely higher than that required in ordinary cases of lack of due care, but not as high. Thus, in *Rex v. Edward Stanley Ross*[499] where the accused, an engineer, was charged with manslaughter resulting from his failure to take precautions to prevent injury to his men working in a pit he was constructing, was completely absolved of criminal responsibility because the prosecution did not prove beyond reasonable doubt that he was guilty of 'either of the very high degree of negligence laid down in the *Bateman* case, as being required to establish the felony of manslaughter, or of the lesser but still substantial degree of negligence, which … would be sufficient to the much less serious misdemeanours, created by sections 231 and 232 [now 227 and 228]'. In *Rex v. Yozefu Muinda*,[500] Edwards, C.J. said that 'if the manner in which and the circumstances in which the accused drove the car would appear to the ordinary person to show that the accused, when driving just before the accident, was *callously indifferent to human life*, then a conviction for manslaughter might ensue'. Using such a test, he convicted the accused of manslaughter.

402. Vehicular accidents, as the above case shows, are the most common source of prosecutions for manslaughter based on culpable negligence. But they are not the only source. *Regina v. Mukasa & Anor*[501] relates to a chief's duty to protect persons under his care. A chief's duty, like that of a warden and others in charge of institutions wherein inmates are kept, is covered by section 199 of the Penal Code which provides as follows:

> It is the duty of every person having charge of another who is unable by reason of age, sickness, unsoundness of mind, detention or any other cause to withdraw himself from such charge, and who is unable to provide himself with the necessaries of life, whether the charge is undertaken under a contract, or is imposed by law, or arises by reason of any act, whether lawful or unlawful, of the person who has such charge, to provide for that other person the necessaries of life, and he shall be deemed to have caused any consequences which adversely affect the life or health of the other person by reason of any omission to perform that duty.

497. (1925) 19 Cr.App.R. 8, 13.
498. See sec. 227 and sec. 228 of the Penal Code.
499. [1936–1951] 6 U.L.R. 37, 40.
500. [1936–1951] 6 U.L.R. 163, 164 (emphasis added).
501. [1956–1958] 8 U.L.R. 321.

The facts of the case were that the deceased, who was a stranger to the chief's village, was alleged to have assaulted a boy and made off with his bicycle. The boy raised an alarm. A group of villagers came to his rescue. They arrested the deceased, tied his hands behind his back, and marched him to a Mutongole chief, beating him along the way. The Mutongole chief in turn sent him to a Muluka chief. The Muluka chief ordered the deceased to be tied on to a tree in his compound while awaiting an escort to take him to the Gombolola Headquarters the next morning. While so tied a crowd of about twenty people beat him for some time, and eventually went away. The chief did not stop them; nor did he alleviate his suffering by untying him from the tree. Instead, he left him so tied throughout the night and exposed to the elements. As soon as he was untied the next morning, he collapsed and died. The chief, along with certain other villagers who participated in the beating, were charged with manslaughter. The villagers were convicted of assault only. But the chief was convicted of manslaughter. Citing *Andrews v. D.P.P.* [1937] A.C. 576 and stressing that a very high degree of negligence must be proved before an accused person can be convicted of manslaughter, Keating, J. said:

> It has been pleaded for A5 (the chief) that he had no facilities for looking after prisoners at his disposal. I cannot be impressed by this argument. I am convinced that A5 did nothing to exert his authority to help the deceased after the beating; he didn't even untie his bonds. In fact, he behaved in a most callous and inhuman manner towards the deceased. I find it difficult to imagine how A5 could be more neglectful in carrying out his duty. In my judgment A5's complete failure to carry out his duty in the circumstances amounted to culpable negligence. I find A5 guilty of manslaughter as charged contrary to Section 182 of the Penal Code.

403. In *R. v. Bisamuli s/o Kite*,[502] however, the Court of Appeal for Eastern Africa was not convinced that the accused, a prison warder, was negligent to the high degree required for manslaughter. The accused was a warder of a local prison. On the morning in question all the prisoners were evacuated from the cells and were not to be returned until the evening. The cells were fumigated with poison gas. One of the prisoners unfortunately fell sick and was allowed to return to the cell earlier. The windows to the cell remained closed and, as a result, the prisoner died of asphyxiation. The accused was convicted of manslaughter on his own plea of guilty, but the Court of Appeal quashed the conviction on the ground that the trial court had not explained to him fully the extent of his duty of care, and the fact that the degree of negligence required must be much more than the mere failure to take care which would be sufficient in ordinary compensation claims.

3. Excess of Justifiable Force

404. A person may be entitled to use reasonable force, for example, in exercising the right of self-defence, the right to defend person of others or property, in

502. [1943] 10 E.A.C.A. 42.

effecting a lawful arrest, or in resisting unlawful arrest. He or she will not be guilty of any offence if the person on whom he or she uses such force dies. He or she will, however, be guilty of manslaughter if the force he or she uses is adjudged to be excessive or unreasonable.[503] What is reasonable or unreasonable force is discussed under the section on self-defence and will not be repeated here.

4. Provocation

405. Provocation, when established, reduces the charge of murder to manslaughter. It is therefore a partial defence to a charge of murder. This defence is the law's acknowledgment of a human being's frailty and his or her proneness to lose self-control and to do things that he or she would not otherwise do when his or her passions are cool. Killing which takes place under provocation is often referred to by text writers as 'voluntary manslaughter' because the killer kills intentionally – albeit without malice aforethought.

406. Section 193 of the Penal Code provides that:

> When a person, who unlawfully kills under circumstances which, but for the provisions of this section, would constitute murder, does the act which causes death in the heat of passion caused by sudden provocation as hereinunder defined, and before there is time for his or her passion to cool, he is guilty of manslaughter only.

407. Section 188 defines 'provocation' as follows:

1. 'Provocation' means and includes, except as hereinafter stated, any wrongful act or insult of such a nature as to be likely –
   (a) when done or offered to an ordinary person; or
   (b) when done or offered in the presence of an ordinary person to another person –
      (i) who is under his immediate care; or
      (ii) to whom he stands in a conjugal, parental, filial or paternal relation, or in the relation of master and servant,

   to deprive him or her of the power of self-control and to induce him or her to commit an assault of the kind which the person charged committed upon the person by whom the act or insult is done or offered.

408. Although the provisions are unnecessarily repetitive, five key elements are discernible: sudden provocation, a wrongful act or insult, likely to deprive an ordinary person of self-control, no time for passion to cool off and nature of act committed. These elements will now be considered one by one.

503. See *Kasto Budebo v. Uganda*, Cr. App. No. 22 of 1993, [1994] UGSC 13 (7 Oct. 1994).

a. Sudden Provocation

409. The essence of provocation is that it is sudden, unanticipated and takes the affected person off guard. Rand, J. in the Canadian case of *Queen v. Tripodi* defined a provocative act as 'the wrongful act or insult upon a mind unprepared for it, that it must make an unexpected impact that takes the understanding by surprise and sets the passions aflame'.[504]

410. The Botswana case of *State v. Nyame* is instructive on this point.[505] The accused had been absent from home for a period of about two days. On entering his hut, he found his wife in bed with another man. He left the hut at once, seized a spear nearby, re-entered the hut, and speared the man to death. He was charged with murder. Convicting him of manslaughter instead of murder, Corduff, J. said:

> The realization on being confronted with the evidence of one's eyes can create its own shock. What the Accused says in this case described exactly such a situation. He had no conscious thought, only a confused feeling. He could go no further in his description of what he experienced. His reaction was immediate and spontaneous. Indeed it may well be that his recollection of events is blurred and that he remembers delivering only one thrust with the spear. To the provocation inherent in catching his wife in adultery must be added the grave insult by the Deceased of committing the adultery in the Accused's marital bed.
>
> It would be hard to envisage a greater provocation to any man of the Accused's class and background.

411. The Uganda se case of *R. v. Yafesi Nabende*,[506] also involved the killing of an adulterer. Here the appellant knew that his wife was having adulterous associations with the deceased. One night he went along with other people to a house where he thought that he would catch her with the deceased in the act of adultery. Sure enough he found them and killed the adulterer. It was nevertheless held that this discovery was not 'sudden provocation', and that the killing was premeditated murder. In contrast, in *Yolamu Arua v. R.*,[507] the husband did not have actual knowledge of adultery between his wife and the deceased, but suspected that they might have committed it. On the day in question, the husband allegedly found them in the act and he killed his wife's lover. It was held that since mere suspicion is not knowledge, the discovery amounted to 'sudden provocation'. It is thus unsafe to lay it down as a general rule that prior knowledge of adultery will always disentitle a man who catches his wife in the act of adultery to plead provocation. Each case must depend on its peculiar facts. The Court of Appeal for Eastern Africa which decided the above two cases was at pains to stress this point in the subsequent case of

504. [1955] Supreme Court of Canada Reports 438, 443.
505. H.Ct.Cr. Trial No. F8 of 1984 (unreported).
506. [1948] 15 E.A.C.A. 71.
507. [1960] E.A. 146.

Yokoyadi Lakora s/o Omeri v. R.[508] It there gave the example of a man who may have had prior knowledge of his wife's adultery and being assured by her that it will not recur. Yet in spite of this assurance she may repeat it and the husband may catch her in the act. This subsequent act of adultery may amount to sudden provocation.

b. Wrongful Act or Insult

412. As for 'act' there must be an overt physical wrongful act capable of derailing the accused's fortitude and power of self-control and to induce him or her to retaliate by killing the person who offers it. Assault is generally accepted as such an act.[509] Illicit sexual relations, as discussed above, is another activity that the courts recognize as 'wrongful act'. As Wrottestey, J. in the English case of *R. v. Leonard Holmes* said, 'it is indeed difficult to imagine circumstances more likely to deprive a reasonable man of his self-control'.[510] It is in this respect remarkable that the courts in East Africa and beyond have extended the provocation defence to relationships other than that of a man and a wife, to those of cohabitants and boyfriend and girlfriend. Declared the Court of Appeal for Eastern Africa:

> The mere fact that the parties are not married need not, in our view, prevent the seducer or the woman from committing a 'wrongful act or insult' within the meaning of Section 204 of the *Penal Code* [of Kenya] and there is no reason why it should not be found ... that the provocation was sufficient in fact.[511]

413. In the past, it was only the husband who was entitled to plead provocation if he killed either the wife or her paramour whom he found in the act.[512] This was so because in England, as in Uganda, a wife was considered the husband's property. In the changed environment of spousal equality, there seems to be no valid reason why a wife who kills her husband or his mistress caught in an act of adultery should not be allowed to plead provocation.

414. However, a spouse's refusal to have sexual intercourse with his or her partner does not, per se amount to provocation so as to reduce murder to manslaughter. Such refusal is a non-act, not covered under the Code.[513]

508. [1960] E.A. 322.
509. For example, see *Regina v. Wedeza s/o Fungo* [1856–1858] 8 U.L.R. 240; *Okeny Kamu s/o Okok v. R.* [1960] E.A. 178; *Rex v. Silvesteri Eleta s/o Egaru* [1936–1951] 6 U.L.R. 247.
510. [1946] 1 All E.R. 524.
511. *Kalume wa Tuku v. R.* [1954] 21 E.A.C. 201. This case was followed in *Olende Osajani v. Uganda* [1965] E.A. 627. See also the Botswana cases of *State v. Sibanda* [2002] 2 B.L.R. 386 (HC), and *State v. Nkatswe* [2002] 2 B.L.R. 441 (HC).
512. Parke, B. said in *R. v. Pearson* (1835) 2 Lew C.C. 216, 217 that 'If a man kills his wife, or the adulterer, in the act of adultery, it is manslaughter, provided the husband has ocular inspection of the act, and only then.'
513. See *Rex v. Zakayo Itima s/o Birigenda* [1948] 14 E.A.C.A. 154.

415. Mere threats to do harm in the future are not acts and do not qualify as provocation. The case of *Eria Galikuwa v. R.*[514] is a *cause celebre* on this point. The appellant sought the assistance of the deceased, a reputed witch doctor, to recover money stolen from him. It is not clear from the report whether the appellant did recover the money. What is clear is that the deceased demanded from the appellant remuneration for his services with such vigour that he told the appellant that if he did not pay him his [the deceased's] medicines would 'eat him up'. The appellant failed to raise the money. Fearing that the witch doctor's powers would kill him, he

514. [1951] 18 E.A.C.A. 175.

got a stick and struck the witch doctor five blows on the head and killed him. Charged with murder, he pleaded provocation. The plea was rejected, principally because there was no overt physical provocative act on the part of the deceased. There was merely a threat to cause injury in the future. Confirming the conviction the Court of Appeal for Eastern Africa said:

> It seems that a mere threat to cause injury to health or even death in the near future cannot be considered as a physical provocative act. In any case, the appellant's own evidence shows clearly (a) that he was motivated not by anger but by fear alone. He struck, not in the heat of passion, but in despair arising from the recognition of his inability to raise the money demanded and his hopeless fear of the consequences; and (b) that he was not suddenly deprived of his self-control but acted as he did deliberately and intentionally because of the impasse.

416. *R. v. Fabiano Kinene & Anor*[515] is one of the few cases in which an act of witchcraft was held to constitute legal provocation. The two accused persons had long suspected the deceased to have caused the deaths of their relatives by witchcraft. On the night in question, they found the deceased crawling naked in their compound. They seized him and killed him by forcibly inserting into his anus twenty unripe bananas. The Court of Appeal for Eastern Africa held that the deceased's act of crawling naked in the accused's compound at night amounted to 'sudden provocation'. Said Sir Joseph Sheridan, C.J.:

> We think that if the facts proved establish that the victim was performing in the actual presence of the accused some act which the accused did genuinely believe, and which an ordinary person of the community to which the accused belongs would genuinely believe, to be an act of witchcraft against him or another person under his immediate care [which act would be a criminal offence under the Criminal Law (Witchcraft) Ordinance of Uganda and similar legislation in the other East African Territories] he might be angered to such an extent as to be deprived of the power of self-control and induced to assault the person doing the act of witchcraft. And if this be the case a defence of grave and sudden provocation is open to him.

Threats of future harm by themselves, according to the *Eria Galikuwa* case, *supra*, are unacceptable as a foundation for the defence of provocation. However, according to more recent decisions 'a threat to kill taken with other existing circumstances could amount to legal provocation'.[516]

417. As for insults, words may also constitute sudden provocation. They do also have potential to inflame passions and to move persons to whom they are directed to react in a violent manner just as if they had been physically injured. However, to be accepted as provocative such words must amount to 'an insult'. An insult must

515. [1941] 8 E.A.C.A. 96.
516. See *Yovan v. Uganda* [1970] E.A. 405, 406 per Duffus, P.

be such as to amount to insolence or contempt. This will be the case if an insult injures one's dignity, modesty or self-respect. Whether the words in a particular case qualify as an insult is a matter of fact for the court to decide. In making the decision, the court must consider how a reasonable person in the community to which the accused belongs considers the words. For example, in *Rex v. Zakayo Itima s/o Birigenda*, *supra*, a wife who refused to have sexual intercourse with her husband, told him, 'You are no longer a man' – suggesting that he was impotent – whereupon he killed her. The Court of Appeal accepted these words to be sufficient to drive the man mad and therefore provocative. The court referred to an earlier case in which it held that to constitute legal provocation, an insult must be more than vulgar abuse.[517] It held that the words used in the instant case were more than vulgar abuse. Whether the words in question are provocative and not mere vulgar abuse is a matter that must again be resolved by the trial judge, according to his or her knowledge and the experience of the people of the community, to which the accused belongs, as well as his or her own wisdom and knowledge of life and the law.

418. The only exception to the rule that the words must be an insult is a wife's confession of adultery.[518] The reason for the exception is that a sudden confession is, according to the courts, equivalent to the discovery of the act itself.[519] However, mere suspicions of marital infidelity without 'an ocular inspection' of it will not amount to provocation. Suspicion has also often been the basis of the killing of so-called witches, and the courts have consistently rejected it as a valid basis for claiming the defence of provocation.

419. Somewhat troublesome, however, is the requirement that the provocative act or insult be wrongful. Wrongful in what sense: criminally or civilly? Assaults, acts of witchcraft and, until recently, adultery, usually held to be provocative acts, are criminal and pose no problem. What poses problems are acts such as seducing or having sexual relations with a person that the accused claims to be his or her concubine/paramour. This is neither a criminal nor a civil wrong. Yet the courts have held it to amount to legal provocation. In one case the deceased was alleged to have put a *yirizi* or talisman under a dead body, and the Uganda Supreme Court held that this 'physical abuse of a dead body' amounted to provocation of the relatives.[520] Is there such a wrong under our law? Additionally, what constitutes a 'wrongful insult'? Is an insult, which is not heard by a third party, wrongful – particularly as it does not amount to defamation? This unhappy state of the law, though not limited to Uganda,[521] needs to be straightened out.

517. *Rex v. Samson* [1939] 6 E.A.C.A. 154.
518. See the English case of *R. v. Rothwell* (1871–1874) 12 Cox C.C. 145, 147.
519. According to the Canadian Supreme Court, 'Whether the husband becomes aware of the fact of adultery by his own discovery, by his wife's confession, or by other information can make no difference from this standpoint. The "insult" is received upon discovery of the fact.' See *Queen v. Tripodi, supra*, at 446.
520. See *Francis Sebanenya & Anor. v. Uganda*, S.Ct.Cr.App. No. 17 of 1989 (unreported).
521. The problem is to be found in the Canadian Criminal Code as well. See Don Stuart, *Canadian Criminal Law* 450 (2d ed., Carswell Co. Ltd. 1987).

420. The definition of 'provocation' extends the defence to wrongful act or insult done or offered to not only the person of the accused but also to any other person: (i) who is under his or her immediate care or (ii) to whom he or she stands in a conjugal, parental, filial or fraternal relation, or (iii) in the relation of master and servant.[522] However, according to the former Eastern Court of Appeal for Eastern Africa, trespass to property can also amount to 'a wrongful act or insult ... done to ... a person'.[523] In the same vein, our Supreme Court held that physical abuse of a dead body amounted to provocation.[524]

421. Additionally, where the provocative act or insult is directed at a person other than the accused himself or herself, the act or insult must take place *in the presence* of the accused. This position was settled by the Court of Appeal for Eastern Africa in *Rex v. Emilio Lumu*.[525] A child belonging to the appellant's sister died after a short illness. It died in the appellant's hands. The appellant's sister told him that the deceased who happened to be his father-in-law and a reputed witch had administered some black powder, which she believed to be witchcraft medicine, to the child. The sister held the father-in-law to be responsible for the child's death. On hearing this allegation, the appellant went over to the father-in-law's house and stabbed him to death. The court was prepared to accept the alleged administration of the black powder as an act of witchcraft. However, since that act was performed several days before the stabbing and in the absence of the appellant, it could not amount to legal provocation. Additionally, even if it could be assumed that the deceased had killed the child by natural means [say by poisoning] rather than by witchcraft, the appellant would still not qualify for the defence of provocation. He did not satisfy the requirement of the Penal Code that the provocative act be done '*in the presence* of an ordinary person to another to whom he stands in conjugal, parental, filial or paternal relation'. The court emphasized that with the exception of provocation by adultery, in all cases the party alleged to have been provoked must see the act done.[526]

c. Ordinary Person

422. The fact that the accused was excited and lost control as a result of an act done or insult offered to him or her does not necessarily render that act or insult provocative in law. To amount to legal provocation, the act or insult must be one as would be sufficient to deprive an *ordinary person* of the power of self-control. The Code does not define who 'an ordinary person' is. The courts, relying on English common law, have done so. They have defined an ordinary person as the average

522. This was the view originally held by the Court of Appeal for Eastern Africa. See *Yusufu s/o Lesso v. R.* [1952] 18 E.A.C.A. 249.
523. See *Marwa s/o Robi v. R.* [1959] E.A. 660, and *Jogo s/o Kego v. R.* [1960] E.A. 130.
524. *Francis Sebanenya & Anor. v. Uganda*, S.Ct.Cr.App. No. 17 of 1989 (unreported).
525. [1946] 13 E.A.C.A. 144.
526. The decision of Oteng, J. in *Uganda v. Kwirimo Bua & Anor.* [1971] U.L.R. 24 seems to be at variance with this decision.

mber of the community to which the accused person belongs.[527] This is the pro-bial reasonable man of the accused's age, sex, race or ethnicity, or physical char-eristics. He or she is neither an unusually excitable or pugnacious person nor an ısually timid or placid person. The rationale for subjecting provocative acts or ults to the 'ordinary person' test – an objective test, has been stated to be 'to ›id the injustice' of a man or woman being entitled to rely on his or her 'excit-lity or pugnacity or ill-temper or on his drunkenness'.[528,529]

What kind of act or insult is likely or unlikely to deprive an ordinary person of power of self-control is a matter for the trial judge to determine. In so deter-ıing, the judge relies on his or her knowledge of the accused's community, its toms and attitudes, and on his or her own personal observations of human behav-r, and on his or her knowledge of the law. Again, whether or not a given act or ult which is sufficient to deprive an ordinary person of self-control did in fact ›rive the accused of such self-control is a separate issue which the trial judge st resolve using a subjective test. What must be emphasized for now is that the t that such an act or insult would be sufficient to strip an ordinary person of the ver of self-control does not necessarily follow that it had similar effect on the used. This is a matter of fact and evidence.

Before There is Time for the Passion to Cool

23. The essence of this element is that the accused must have acted on the sud- or on the spur of the moment when his or her anger, emotions or temper are aflame. Any act done after the passions have cooled is likely to be calculated or meditated self-help, which the law would not countenance.

24. What time is sufficient for passions to cool is a question of fact and varies n case to case. However, if a substantial period of time has elapsed between the vocative act or insult and the retaliation, it is likely that the courts will hold that e was sufficient time for the passions to cool. In *Regina v. Wedeza s/o Fungo*,[530] accused, the deceased and others fought at a beer party. The accused ran away to home and returned with a panga and hacked the deceased to death. The interval ween the running away and returning to the place of the beer party was estimated to

---

See *R. v. Fabiano Kinene, supra, Yovan v. Uganda* [1970] E.A. 405, and *Uganda v. Nabwengere s/o Rovumba, supra.*

R. v. Camplin [1978] A.C. 705, 726 per Lord Simon of Glainsdale.

Commenting on this rationale Chief Justice Dickson of the Supreme Court of Canada said:

'If there was no objective test to the defence of provocation anomalous results would occur. A well-tempered, reasonable person would not be entitled to benefit from the provocation defence and would be guilty of culpable homicide amounting to murder, while an ill-tempered or exceptionally excitable person would find his or her culpability mitigated by provocation and would be guilty only of manslaughter. It is society's concern that reasonable and nonviolent behaviour be encouraged that prompts the law to endorse the objective standard. The criminal law is concerned, among other things, with fixing standards for human behaviour. We seek to encourage conduct that complies with certain societal standards of reasonableness and responsibility. In doing this, the law quite logically employs the objective standard of the reasonable person.' *R. v. Hill* [1986] 1 S.C.R. 313, 324.

[1956–1957] 8 U.L.R. 240.

be ten minutes. The court held that this was not a long enough period for his passions to cool. In *Regina v. Wasikero s/o Watabe*,[531] the accused fought with the deceased inside a house. He went out of the house, picked up a stick, and re-entered the house and struck the deceased on the head. It was held that there was sufficient time for his passion to cool, and his assault on the deceased was an act of revenge.[532] Provocation was similarly denied in *Uganda v. John Kuka*, (*supra*, paragraph 397). This is the case where the accused set fire on the house in which his wife and children were sleeping, suspecting that the wife was committing adultery with another man. He did not, however, set the house on fire immediately on discovering the adultery. He went to his second home first and got a box of matches, padlock and key and when he arrived at the house he waited for some time before he lit the match. The judge concluded that 'The killing was therefore not done immediately on seeing his wife in the act of adultery. The killing was an act of punishment and was not done in the heat of passion. In my view the killing was premeditated.'

The conclusion that must be drawn from all these divergent decisions is that whether or not there was sufficient time for the passion to cool must depend on the facts of each case.

e. An Assault of the Kind Which the Person Charged Committed

425. According to the Code, the alleged provocation must induce the person to whom it is addressed to 'to commit an assault.' Therefore the first thing to note about this element is that the act of retaliation must be by way of an assault. Anything else, such as setting fire on the house where the victim is sleeping, or poisoning, will not qualify for the defence of provocation. This is so because the act of retaliation must be instantaneous. Second, it is apparently sufficient that the assault be 'of the kind which the person charged committed upon the person' who provoked him or her. The Code does not qualify the assault. For instance, it does not specifically require, as do the Codes of such countries as Botswana, Malawi and Zambia, that 'the act causing death bears a reasonable relationship to the provocation'. Nevertheless, one learned writer has opined that the concept of reasonable relationship must be read into the Code by the language 'assault of the kind which the person charged committed'.[533] This is the law in England,[534] and in determining whether the mode of retaliation bears a reasonable relationship to the provocation, English courts take into account the following factors: the nature of provocation, the instrument used to retaliate and the extent of the retaliatory acts. With regard to the instrument, it is pertinent to inquire whether the accused retaliated with a fist blow, a kick or a weapon – lethal or non-lethal.

426. However, with the exception of very few cases,[535] the courts in Uganda rarely discuss the issue of reasonable relationship. Killings that might otherwise be

531. [1956–1957] 8 U.L.R. 66.

532. The facts in *Uganda v. Quininto Etumu*, H.Ct.Cr.Session No. 110 of 1987 (unreported) were virtually similar to the above case, but the decision went in the opposite way.

533. See James S. Read, *Some Aspects of Manslaughter in East Africa* 1 E. Afr. L.J. 260 (1965).

534. See *Mancini v. Director of Public Prosecutions* [1942] A.C. 1.

535. For example, see *Orhuku s/o Orhede v. R.* [1955] 19 E.A.C.A. 220.

considered to bear no reasonable relationship to the provocation have been accorded the defence of provocation.[536] It is submitted that there is merit in our court's approach. Provided the accused retaliates whilst in the heat of passion when his power of reason is temporarily dethroned he or she should be entitled to invoke the defence, for that is what actually happens. He or she acts on the spur of the moment and does not have time to deliberate on the mode of retaliation and the instrument he or she uses. For this reason, he or she may retaliate to fist provocative act with a lethal weapon which happens to lie around.[537] Such things as the instrument used, the number of blows inflicted, the psychological frame of the accused's mind, his or her age, physical characteristics, as well as his or her conduct at the time of the crime should only be used to determine whether he or she was acting under sudden provocation whilst under the heat of passion.[538]

C. *Aiding Suicide and Suicide Pacts*

427. Suicide per se is not an offence in Uganda, because the suicide is gone and beyond the reach of the law. However, attempted suicide is an offence. It is a misdemeanour.[539] Its aim is to prevent suicides. More serious is the offence of procuring, counselling or aiding another person to kill himself or herself. It is a felony, punishable by life imprisonment.[540] Euthanasia or doctor-assisted death is not lawful. It is murder. The law does not recognize the so-called right to die. It does not allow a person to consent to his or her killing. Section 226 of the Penal Code specifically provides that 'consent by a person to the causing of his or her own death or his or her own maim does not affect the criminal responsibility of any person by whom such death or maim is caused'. The current pre-occupation of the law of Uganda is to preserve life, not to destroy it.

428. Suicide pacts are similarly viewed with disfavour by the law. A suicide pact is a common agreement between two or more persons having for its object the death of all of them, whether or not each is to take his or her own life. However, killing a person under a suicide pact is not visited with as severe a sanction as outright murder. It is instead treated as manslaughter only. For this dispensation to operate, however, it is up to the accused person to show that he or she killed under a suicide pact between him or her and the person he or she killed. He or she must further show that at the time of the killing, he or she was still under 'the settled intention of dying in pursuance of the pact'.[541]

---

536. See, for example, *Regina v. Wedeza s/o Fungo*, note 1 in para. 328, *supra*, and *Francis Sebenenya & Anor. v. Uganda*, note 1 in para. 323, *supra*.
537. For example, in *Rex v. Silvestri Eleto s/o Egeru* [1936–1951] 6 U.L.R. 247, the deceased punched the accused in the eye. So severe was the pain that the accused lost self-control and hit the deceased on the head with the hoe he was carrying and killed him. Although the accused's mode of resentment did not bear reasonable proportion to the provocation he was acquitted of murder and convicted of manslaughter only.
538. This is the Canadian approach. See *R. v. Hill* [1986] 1 S.C.R. 313.
539. Section 210.
540. Section 209.
541. Generally see sec. 195.

D. Child Destruction, Infanticide and Abortion

429. To kill a child while it is still in its mother's womb or in the process of being born is criminal. Section 212 of the Penal Code provides that:

> Any person who, when a woman is about to be delivered of a child, prevents the child from being born alive by any act or omission of such a nature that, if the child had been born alive and had then died, he or she would be deemed to have unlawfully killed the child, is guilty of a felony and is liable to imprisonment for life.

It would seem, however, that a doctor would not be guilty where in the process of trying to save the life of a woman with child, kills the unborn child. That killing would not be unlawful. However, to be exonerated, the doctor must act in good faith and with reasonable care and skill.[542]

430. Infanticide, however, is the killing by the mother of her own child after it is born and whilst still under the age of 12 months. This is an offence that is usually, though not exclusively, committed by young women who, after delivery, dump their children in pit latrines or abandon them in refuse dumps. Before any such woman can be convicted, it is vital that the prosecution prove that the woman bore the child alive and then 'by any willful act or omission' caused its death.[543] In the case of a child dumped in a latrine, the prosecution, in order to succeed, must show either: (i) that the woman knew that her hour was nigh and went into the latrine with intent to pass the child and leave it there, or (ii) that she did, after delivery, with homicide intent, abandon the child in the latrine knowing that she had given birth to it and that it was born alive.[544]

431. If it is established that the woman by willful act or omission caused the death of her child, she would ordinarily be guilty of murder. However, if it is shown that 'at the time of the act or omission the balance of her mind was disturbed by reason of her not having fully recovered from the effect of giving birth to the child or by reason of the effect of lactation consequent upon the birth of the child', she will be convicted of the lesser offence of infanticide and punished as if she had been guilty of manslaughter of the child. It is upon the prosecution to prove this element where the offence charged is infanticide instead of murder. However, if the original charge was murder, attempted murder or manslaughter and the accused wished it to be reduced to infanticide she would then have the evidential burden of establishing on a balance of probabilities that at the time of the offence her mind was disturbed by reason of her not having fully recovered from the effect of giving birth to the child or by reason of the effect of lactation consequent upon the birth of the child.

---

542. Section 224.
543. Section 213.
544. See *Yowanina Namayanja v. Reginam* [1953] 22 E.A.C.A. 204 and *Uganda v. Betrice Nanduga* H.Ct.Cr.Session No. 81 of 1990 (unreported).

The evidential burden on the accused is not onerous, because the condition of a 'disturbed mind' is a transient abnormality of the mind that is much less serious than insanity.

432. As for abortion, the Penal Code defines the offence as follows:

> Any woman who, being with child, with intent to procure her own miscarriage, unlawfully administers to herself any poison or other noxious thing, or uses any force of any kind, or uses any other means, or permits any such things or means to be administered to or used on her, commits a felony and is liable to imprisonment for seven years.[545]

The Code makes no exceptions to situations where the woman conceives as a result of rape, or incest, or where the foetus is congenitally and severely deformed or where if she went to full term with the pregnancy her health or life would be threatened. Abortion on demand that is permitted in some western countries on the basis of a woman's right of self-determination and of choice is not allowed in Uganda. The law intends to protect the foetus and its right to life at any cost. However, therapeutic abortion, carried out by a doctor for the purpose of saving the mother's life seems to be implicitly permitted under section 224 of the Penal Code. The English courts, dealing with a similar provision under English statutes, have interpreted 'saving life' to mean preserving the health of the mother – both physical and mental health.[546] With respect, this is a sound interpretation.

II. Assaults, Wounding and Grievous Harm

A. *Assault*

433. The law of assault and kindred offences aims at protecting the integrity, health and comfort of the individual. Section 235 of the Penal Code provides that 'Any person who unlawfully assaults another is guilty of a misdemeanour … ' It does not, however, define what 'assault' is. For the definition, we have to fall back to English common law.

434. English common law drew a distinction between assault or common assault and battery. Common assault is the intentional causing of apprehension in the mind of another person of the immediate unlawful application of force on his or her body. The essence of the offence is the *apprehension* of force. The force need not be applied.[547] Battery, however, is the intentional application of unlawful force on the body of another person. It does not matter how trivial such force is, provided that it is unlawful. It is likely to be unlawful where it is applied in an angry, insolent, hostile and rude manner.

545. Section 142.
546. For example, see *R. v. Bourne* [1939] 1 K.B. 887; [1938] 3 All E.R. 615.
547. See *Abubakali & Anor. v. Uganda* [1973] E.A. 230.

435. The Penal Code does not draw any such distinctions. It does not even mention battery at all, but the courts have assumed that battery is subsumed under the generic offence of assault. Therefore in Uganda, assault encompasses both common assault and battery. The *actus reus* of assault is either the causing of apprehension in the victim's mind about the immediate application of unlawful force on the body of the victim or the actual application of such force. The former is psychic assault while the latter is physical assault. It is relatively easy to establish the *actus reus* in the case of physical assault. The slightest degree of force, including a touch or even spitting, will suffice. It is not however as easy to establish the *actus reus* in cases of psychic assault where force is not applied but it is merely apprehended. Under what circumstances psychic assault may be said to have been committed? There must be such conduct on the part of the assaulter indicating an intention to immediately use violence against the victim and to cause apprehension in his or her mind. Such conduct may include menacingly shaking his fists or holding up a stick, drawing or brandishing a knife, or pointing a gun at the victim. However, where a person brandishing a stick says to another, 'If you come near me I will hit you' he or she is not guilty of assault since his or her threat is conditional.[548] Moreover, the circumstances must be such that the assaulter has present ability to unleash the violence. In this respect, the distance between the alleged assaulter and the victim may be crucial.[549]

436. In both types of assault, the force apprehended or actually inflicted must be unlawful, and the onus is on the prosecution to prove this. If the force is lawful, no offence is committed. The force will be lawful if the victim consented to it or it is justifiable or excusable. Consent may be express or implied. It is express in such situations as when a patient submits to medical or surgical treatment. It is also express where a person voluntarily participates in sporting activities such as boxing, wrestling, rugby, basketball and football, in which body contact or even force are the essence of the particular sport. Be that as it may, however, he or she consents only to such contact or force which is incidental to the sport. He or she cannot be said to consent to a touch, kick or a blow by another player which is in total disregard of the rules of the sport and is not incidental to the sport. Implied consent may also be deduced from ordinary social interactions with the rest of humanity: walking on crowded streets, riding on buses and trains, lining up at post offices, banks, ticket booths and theatres. Body contact or jostling with other people in these situations is inevitable. Nevertheless, whether or not a person has consented even to a social touch such as a handshake, hug or kiss is a matter of degree and, in turn, a question of fact which has to be established from all the circumstances surrounding each case.

437. Though an individual has a right to consent to some force being inflicted on him or her, yet this right is not without limits. As we have noted earlier on, he or she may not consent to be intentionally killed or maimed. Generally speaking, he

548. For example, see the Rhodesian case of *R. v. Meja* [1962] Rhodesia and Nyasaland Law Reports 45.
549. For example, see *Rex v. Mburugu* [1947] 22 K.L.R. 62.

or she cannot consent to excessive life-threatening force to be inflicted on him.[550] The Code in section 225 explicitly states that:

> Any person authorized by law *or by the consent of the person injured* by him or her to use force is criminally responsible for any excess, according to the nature and quality of the act which constitutes the excess.

Where the law allows use of force under certain circumstances then it does not amount to assault. Examples of this are chastising a child or pupil by a parent, guardian or teacher, and apprehending a criminal suspect or preventing the escape of a prisoner from lawful custody by law enforcement agents or private citizens. A person resisting an unlawful arrest, or exercising the right of self-defence or defence of the person or property is also allowed to use force. However, in all these situations, the force used must be reasonable. If it is not, then, section 225 of the Code will become operative, and the force will become unlawful and may amount to assault or even graver offences – depending on the injuries inflicted.

438. The *mens rea* of assault is the intention to cause apprehension in the mind of the victim of an imminent application of force, or the intention to apply unlawful force. It also includes recklessness as to whether the victim will be apprehended or whether force will be applied. Intention to injure is not necessary although it is evidence of the *mens rea.*

439. Since force need not be applied, and where it is applied it may be as trivial as simply touching another person's body or garment, the offence is considered a minor offence and triable by the lowest grade of magistrates. Indeed, it is an offence in respect of which magistrates are authorized to promote reconciliation between the parties.[551] In other countries it is punishable by lenient sanctions, the severe ones being reserved for the more aggravated forms of assault, 'assault occasioning actual bodily harm'.[552] As the name suggests, this form of assault involves infliction of harm as opposed to the mere body touch which is sufficient for common assault. Paradoxically, in Uganda both forms of assault are punishable by imprisonment by a term of not exceeding five years![553]

B. Unlawful Wounding

440. According to section 222 of the Penal Code, 'Any person who – (a) unlawfully wounds another … is guilty of a misdemeanour and is liable to imprisonment

550. See sec. 226 of the Code.
551. See the Magistrates Courts Act, sec. 160.
552. See sec. 236 of the Penal Code.
553. For example in Botswana common assault is punishable by imprisonment for a term not exceeding one year while assault occasioning actual bodily harm is punishable with imprisonment for up to five years. See Botswana Penal Code, sec. 246 and sec. 247.

for three years.' According to section 2 of the Code, *wound* means 'any incision or puncture which divides or pierces any exterior membrane of the body, and any membrane is exterior for the purpose of this definition which can be touched without dividing or piercing any other membrane'. In essence, a wound imports the breaking of the continuity of the outer skin of the body – the *dermis* as well as the *epidermis*.[554] Inclusion in the definition of the word 'incision' presupposes the use of a sharp instrument such as a knife and indicates something in the nature of a cut. In this sense therefore, a scratch is not a wound. Nor is an abrasion caused by a blow from a stick.[555] Internal ruptures are similarly excluded. This narrow construction of the term 'wound' stems from its restrictive definition by the Code which uses the word 'means' instead of 'includes', thus precluding the courts from giving it a wider common sense meaning.

441. Again to constitute a crime the wounding must be unlawful. It would be lawful and not criminal if it is the result of reasonable and justifiable force, as in the instances mentioned under assault. For example, in *Joseph Byarugaba v. Uganda*,[556] the appellant, a police officer, purporting to prevent the escape of two suspects in his custody shot at and inflicted wounds on them. The suspects were unarmed and were hand-cuffed. He was convicted of unlawful wounding, the court holding that in the circumstances the use of firearms constituted an unreasonable use of force.

442. The *mens rea* of unlawful wounding is the intention to inflict some unlawful bodily harm to another person or being reckless as whether such harm will occur.

C. Unlawful Grievous Harm

443. According to section 219 of the Penal Code 'Any person who unlawfully does grievous harm to another is guilty of a felony and is liable to imprisonment for seven years.' The first point to note is that to commit this offence there need not be an assault as is the case with 'occasioning actual bodily harm'. Unlawfully infecting another person, say with the HIV/AIDS disease, may amount to doing grievous harm. Again, to commit the offence the accused need not personally inflict the injuries. As was stated in one English case, 'Where one person creates in the mind of another person such an immediate sense of danger as causes such other person to escape, the person who created such a state of mind is responsible for any injuries which may result from his acts to the person endeavouring to escape.'[557]

554. See *Rahim Rajan v. R.* [1958] E.A. 448 where Sir Audley McKisack, C.J., held that the test whether an injury amounts to a wound is the same as under the English *Offences Against the Person Act*, 1861.
555. See *Attorney-General for Nyasaland v. Lojasi* [1962] R & N.L.R. 185 where it was held that a blow with a club taking out a large piece of flesh did not amount to a wound.
556. [1973] U.L.R. 4.
557. *R. v. Halliday* (1889) 61 L.T. 701.

444. Furthermore, it should be noted that not every bodily harm amounts to 'grievous harm'. According to section 2 of the Code:

> 'Grievous harm' means any harm which amounts to a maim or dangerous harm or seriously or permanently injures health or which is likely so to injure health, or which extends to permanent disfigurement, or to any permanent or serious injury to any external or internal organ, membrane or sense.

The section also defines *a maim* as 'the destruction or permanent disabling of any external or internal organ, membrane or sense. It also defines *dangerous harm* as 'harm endangering life'. Following these definitions the High Court has held injury to a thumb resulting in a deformity and contracture affecting its glass-holding position to be grievous harm',[558] and loss of a tooth not to be so.[559]

445. The last point to note is that to amount to an offence, the grievous harm must be unlawful. Where it is inflicted as a result of lawful or justifiable force as discussed above it will not amount to an offence. The *mens rea* is the same as in unlawful wounding.

III. Criminal Recklessness and Negligence

446. Offences of criminal recklessness and negligence fall within the category of crimes of negligence. Topping the list of these offences is the crime of causing death by a rash or negligent act not amounting to manslaughter. Section 228 of the Penal Code lists the specific offences of rash and negligent acts. Examples of these offences have already been cited under manslaughter. One may also add the case of *Hunter v. Regina*[560] in which the High Court held that driving a motor vehicle with a passenger on the bonnet is an inherently rash and negligent act.[561]

447. Similarly, in *James Philip v. Rex*,[562] the Court of Appeal for Eastern Africa upheld the conviction of the appellant for causing death by a rash and negligent act in that he had 'rashly and negligently authorized the switching on of electric current in a low voltage section of the electrical supply system in Kampala of which he was in charge without previously taking proper precaution against probable danger resulting from that act'.

448. If death results from any of any rash and negligent act, and the required degree of negligence is shown to exist, then the accused will be convicted and punished for causing death by a rash or negligent act. The punishment for that offence is imprisonment by a term not exceeding seven years and or a fine not exceeding

558. *Santa Aciro v. Uganda*, H.Ct.Cr. Revision No. 24 of 1991 (unreported).
559. *Peter Kilima v. Uganda*, H.Ct.Monthly Bulletin No. 148 of 1969.
560. [1956–1957] 8 U.L.R. 366.
561. See also *Musa Kakade v. R.* [1963] E.A. 36.
562. [1952] E.A.C.A. 231.

UGX 70,000. Where death does not result from the defendant's negligence, he or she is liable to imprisonment not exceeding two years. As noted earlier, the degree of negligence required for establishing the offences of criminal recklessness and negligence is lower than that required for manslaughter, but higher than that needed for ordinary civil negligence.[563]

IV. Kidnapping, Abduction and Wrongful Confinement

449. The object of the law of kidnapping and abduction is to uphold the personal liberty of the individual not to be taken anywhere without his or her consent, and to safeguard the right of parents or guardians to the custody of their children or wards.

450. The Penal Code seems to provide for four distinct types of kidnapping and abduction: (i) kidnapping from Uganda, (ii) kidnapping from lawful guardianship, (iii) kidnapping with intent to murder, (iv) kidnapping with intent to wrongfully confine.

451. Kidnapping from Uganda means to convey a person beyond the limits of Uganda without the consent of that person or of some other person legally authorized to consent on behalf of that person.[564] It is punishable by imprisonment for a term not exceeding ten years.[565] Kidnapping from lawful guardianship, however, involves taking or enticing any minor under the age of 14 years if a male, or under the age of 16 years if a female, or any person of unsound mind, out of the custody of the lawful guardian of such minor or person of unsound mind, without the consent of such guardian.[566] This type of kidnapping also makes the kidnapper liable to imprisonment for ten years.[567] Force may be and is invariably used in both of these two types of kidnapping, but it need not be. It is in abduction that force and fraud and deceitful means are central.[568] Abduction per se does not seem to be an offence. It is, however, a means by which the offences of 'kidnapping with intent to murder' or 'kidnapping or abducting with intent to confine' may be committed.

452. Kidnapping with intent to murder is currently the most common and most serious form of kidnapping. It addresses not only the issue of personal liberty but also the phenomenon of 'enforced disappearance' under which thousands of Ugandans have been seized, mostly by people connected with the army and other paramilitary secret security organizations, never to be seen or heard of again. Section 243 of the Code provides as follows:

563. Also see *Dabholkar v. King* [1948] A.C. 221.
564. Section 239.
565. Section 242.
566. Section 240.
567. *Ibid.*
568. See sec. 241 of the Penal Code which provides that 'Any person who by force compels, or by any deceitful means induces, any person to go from any place is said to abduct that person.'

(1) Any person who by force or fraud kidnaps, abducts, takes away or detains any person against his or her will:
   (a) with intent that such person may be murdered or may be disposed of as to be put in danger of being murdered; or
   (b) with knowledge that such person will probably be murdered; or
   (c) with intent to procure a ransom or benefit for the liberation of such a person from danger of being murdered, commits an offence and shall on conviction be liable to suffer death.

(2) Where a person so kidnapped is thereafter not seen or heard of within a period of six months or more the accused person shall be presumed to have had the intention and knowledge stipulated in paragraph (a) and (b) of subsection (1).

The inclusion of the words 'by force or fraud ... takes away or detains' in the definition of the offence is a mere surplusage, since these elements are inherent in the definition of 'kidnap' and 'abduct' which are already defined in sections 239 and 241.

453. The *actus reus* of this offence involves three elements: (i) seizing and taking a person away against his or her will or consent, (ii) by force or fraud, (iii) without legal justification.

454. The first element is satisfied by showing that the victim was physically seized or physically taken from one place to another without his or her consent or against his or her will. Force or fraud complements the non-consent element. Force includes physically dragging or carrying away of a person, or physical or verbal threats to make him or her move. It was held in *Uganda v. Nelson Kamugisha*[569] that tying the victim with ropes before he was led away amounted to force within the meaning of Section 243(1)(a) of the Code. Deception and trickery however will suffice to establish fraud. For example, in *Ibrahim Bilal v. Uganda*,[570] the victim, a police officer, was lured to leave his house on the pretext that he was required to repair a radio at the house of a senior police officer. He was subsequently dumped into the River Nile at the Karuma Bridge. It was held that he was taken away by fraud. Lastly, the taking must be without legal justification. Where, therefore, the taking amounts to a lawful arrest, no kidnap or abduction will have been committed. The case of *Uganda v. Hosia Rukagyaha & Anor*[571] is in point. The accused, a Muluka Chief and a village chief (*omukuru w'omugongo*) accompanied a group of soldiers who arrested the victim on suspicion of being 'a bandit'. They found army uniforms in his possession. They were however acquitted of the offence of kidnapping with intent to murder. Said Kato, J.:

> He [the victim] was not kidnapped but lawfully arrested; it is only unfortunate that after his arrest he has never been seen again. It is the law that the offence of kidnapping is completed the moment the victim is grabbed and carried away

569. H.Ct.Cr.Session No. 27 of 1988 (unreported).
570. C.A.Cr.App. No. 5 of 1983 (unreported).
571. H.C.Cr.Session No. 43 of 1986 (unreported).

> … In the present case the accused cannot be held liable for what happened after he had been lawfully arrested and taken away by the soldiers. According to the admitted evidence of Mikairi Magezi PWI Tofiro was in fact seen alive on 27 May 84 at Masindi Barracks.

Mens rea for the offence varies according to the paragraph under which the charge is framed. Under paragraphs (a) and (b), the *mens rea* is the intent that the victim be murdered or disposed of as to be put in danger of being murdered, or knowledge that he will *probably* be murdered. This offence was created because in cases of disappearance it is well-nigh impossible to prove murder: the actual perpetrator is usually unknown and the death of the victim itself virtually impossible to establish. Intent to murder would also be well-nigh impossible to prove, since the circumstances of the killing remain mysterious. For this reason by Act No. 9 of 1984 Parliament added subsection 2, under which kidnappers are presumed to have had the intention or knowledge if the person they kidnapped is not seen or heard of within a period of six months or more after the kidnap. In *Uganda v. Kamugisha*, *supra*, the victim had not been heard of by the time of the trial, which was five years and six months later. Intent to murder was therefore established. In *Uganda v. Hosia Rukagyaha*, *supra*, the victim was seen alive at an army barracks sometime after his seizure by the accused. This negatived the intent to murder. Similarly, in *Yunasani Balinda v. Uganda*[572] the victim, after being led away from the place of capture was taken to a trading centre where he was questioned 'for considerable time' by the accused and others. He was subsequently seen alive but unconscious by several passers-by at 6:00 pm at a road side, tied, his body swollen and full of blood and dust. On receiving the report his relatives went to the scene the following morning. He was not there and was never to be seen or heard of again. The Supreme Court held that since he was seen after the seizure, albeit momentarily and in a state of unconsciousness, the presumption of intent to murder did not apply! It would appear therefore that for the presumption to apply, the victim must disappear instantaneously after his capture. He must not be seen again by 'any other person', other than his captor. If, for example, an hour after his capture some wayfarers see him being taken to his slaughter and he is never seen again, the presumption of intention to murder is negatived! This construction is absurd. It defeats the very purpose of the law, which is protecting life by holding responsible those who unlawfully seize others and kill them secretly. Kidnapping should be considered a continuing offence and kidnappers and their accomplices should be held responsible for the fate of their victims who disappear at their hands.

455. Intent to procure a ransom must be specifically proved. So is intent to cause the victim to be secretly and wrongfully confined.[573]

---

572. S.Ct.Cr.App. No. 5 of 1989 (unreported).
573. Section 243(1)(i). See also *Haji Muhamed Senyomo Birikadde v. Uganda* [1986] H.Ct.Monthly Bulletin.

456. Wrongful confinement, a misdemeanour, is not defined by the Code.[574] Nevertheless, wrongful confinement is the equivalent of wrongful imprisonment under the English common law. The two have been held to be synonymous.[575] The essence of the offence is the wrongful restraint on a person's personal liberty, whether by detaining him or her against his or her will in a particular place or by constraining or compelling him or her to go to a particular place. It is not necessary that the victim be locked up in a prison, police cell or another place of detention – whether private or public. The mere handcuffing of a person would be enough to constitute wrongful confinement.[576] The confinement must, however, be wrongful. In other words, there must be no legal justification for it. There would be no offence if, for example, the confinement was a lawful exercise of arrest powers, either by a police officer, chief or private citizen. Additionally, the accused must have acted with the requisite *mens rea*: intentionally or recklessly.

V. Sexual Offences

A. *Rape*

457. The law of rape aims at protecting women against non-consensual sexual intercourse. Section 123 of the Penal Code provides that:

> Any person who has unlawful carnal knowledge of a woman or girl, without her consent, or with her consent, if the consent is obtained by force or by means of threats or intimidation of any kind, or by fear of bodily harm, or by means of false representations as to the nature of the act, or, in the case of a married woman, by personating her husband, is guilty of the felony termed rape.

Section 124 adds that 'Any person convicted of rape shall be liable to suffer death.'

458. The *actus reus* of rape consists of the following elements. First, there must be an unlawful 'carnal knowledge of a woman or girl'. This means that, unlike the case of defilement, only males can be perpetrators and only females can be victims of rape. 'Carnal knowledge' means sexual intercourse. Sexual intercourse in turn means penetration of the man's penis into the woman's vagina. Penetration into the anus is not, apparently, sexual intercourse and does not constitute the offence of rape.[577] For purposes of the criminal law the slightest degree of penetration is sufficient. The hymen need not be broken, but a recently broken hymen will be evidence of penetration. Penetration may be proven by the evidence of a doctor who

574. Section 248.
575. See the Tanzanian case of *Republic v. Sefu Said* [1964] E.A. 178.
576. *Ibid.*
577. For example, see *Gaston* [1981] 73 Cr.App.Rep. 164. It constitutes an 'unnatural offence' under s. 145 of the Penal Code.

examined the victim soon after the alleged sexual act showing presence of spermatozoa in the victim's vagina or injuries or bruises to her private parts. Likewise, it is not necessary that the act of intercourse be complete by, say, the emission of the male's seed. In England, a boy under 14 years is irrebuttably presumed to be incapable of having sexual intercourse.[578] There is, however, no such presumption under the Uganda Penal Code. Consequently, a male of the apparent age of 12 can be convicted of rape or any other sex-related offence, provided that it is proved that he had the necessary 'mischievous intention'.[579]

459. Second, the sexual intercourse must be without the consent of the victim. Whether or not there was consent will turn on who the court believes: the victim or the accused. However, in resolving this issue the courts consider the totality of the circumstances surrounding the commission of the offence. For instance, they take into account medical reports of injuries to the victim's private parts, thighs and other parts of the body as evidence of struggle as tending to show lack of consent. Evidence of the accused's efforts to gag the victim so that she may not scream or raise an alarm may also be accepted by the courts to establish her lack of consent to sexual intercourse. Evidence of the victim's torn underwear or dress may similarly be taken into account.

460. Third, the sexual intercourse must be 'unlawful'. In this context, 'unlawful' means extra-marital. A man cannot be found guilty of raping his wife, because on entering a marriage a woman is presumed to have irrevocably consented to sexual intercourse with her husband during the subsistence of the marriage. However, in case of judicial separation, or a *decree nisi* being issued but before it is made *absolute*, the consent is not presumed, and any sex without the wife's express consent may amount to rape. Where, during the subsistence of the marriage and outside the exceptional situations just mentioned, the husband acts unreasonably or in an oppressive manner and has sexual intercourse with his wife, he may be found guilty of assault, or occasioning actual bodily harm, because the wife cannot consent to all manner of harm on her person. But he cannot be found guilty of rape. Thus, while he may be punished for the unlawful means of getting sex, he cannot be punished for the sexual intercourse itself! This was also the law in England until 1991, when the English House of Lords decided to part with the past and to hold that a husband may be guilty of rape where he has sexual intercourse with his wife without her consent – after she has clearly withdrawn her supposed consent. The House quoted Hale in his *History of the Pleas of the Crown* in which Hale asserted that once married 'the wife hath given herself up in this kind unto her husband which she cannot retract'. It then stated:

> It may be taken that the proposition was generally regarded as an accurate statement of the common law of England. The common law is, however, capable of evolving in the light of changing social, economic and cultural developments. Hale's proposition reflected the state of affairs in these respects

578. See *Phillips* (1983) 8, p. 736.
579. See Ch. 2 under the sec. 'infants'.

> at the time it was enunciated. Since then the status of women, and particularly of married women, has changed out of all recognition in various ways … Apart from property matters and the availability of matrimonial remedies, one of the most important changes is that marriage is in modern times regarded as a partnership of equals, and no longer one in which the wife must be the subservient chattel of the husband. Hale's proposition involves that by marriage a wife gives her irrevocable consent to sexual intercourse with her husband under all circumstances and irrespective of the state of her health or how she appears to be feeling at the time. In modern times any reasonable person must regard that conception as quite unacceptable.[580]

This was clearly a radical rupture with the past, pointing the way that the Uganda law should move. Spousal equality aside, the onslaught of the current HIV/AIDS pandemic argues strongly in favour of protecting wives from unwelcome sexual advances from their husbands in the way the House of Lords has done.

461. Where the woman with whom the accused had sexual intercourse is not his wife, and she did not consent to the intercourse, that would be rape. The onus is on the prosecution to prove beyond reasonable doubt that the woman did not consent. Force or threats to injure the woman or some other person dear to her negatives consent. In this respect, a woman's submission for the sake of avoiding harm should not be interpreted as consent.[581] False representation as to the nature of the act also negatives consent. Personating the victim's husband, if the woman is married, also vitiates consent. It is submitted, however, that the person personated should not be limited to a husband, as the Penal Code tends to suggest. Inducing a woman to consent to sexual intercourse by any kind of deception, subterfuge or personation negatives the consent. Again, sexual intercourse with a person who is not in a position to give or withhold consent, such as a drunken, mentally confused or sleeping woman, is intercourse without that woman's consent.

462. The *mens rea* of rape is intention to have sexual intercourse with the victim, and knowledge that the victim has not given consent to the intercourse. What if the accused says that he honestly believed that the victim consented, particularly where they have in the past had consensual sexual relations? The answer to the question is that the belief must be reasonable. Second, where the woman has, by word or conduct, indicated that she is not consenting, this should be decisive. Consent is the unequivocal communication of voluntary agreement to the sexual act. Any sign of equivocation or involuntariness vitiates consent.

463. Generally speaking, before convicting an accused person of rape the courts require that the woman's testimony be corroborated in some material particular by

580. *R. v. R.* – (rape: marital exemption) [1991] 4 All E.R. 481, 483.

581. In *SGT Canbera Dickson v. Uganda*. Cr. App. No. 284 of 2003, [2010] UGCA 25 (6 Jun. 2010), the appellant who had killed his maternal uncle was wielding a gun and told the victim to choose between death and agreeing to have sexual intercourse with him. She chose life and had sexual intercourse with him. She later reported the rape as a result of which the accused was arrested and indicted.

independent evidence, tending to implicate the accused with the commission of the offence. Where there is no corroboration the trial court must, before convicting the accused, warn itself of the danger involved in such a conviction and proceed to show that in spite of non-corroboration, the woman's testimony is sufficiently credible and cogent to support a conviction. Evidence used to prove penetration as discussed above also serves to corroborate the victim's testimony. Courts also often accept as corroboration the complaint by the victim to third persons, usually parents, in-laws and other relatives, soon after the sexual attack.[582] However, a condition precedent for the admissibility of the complaint as corroborating evidence is that it must be made voluntarily and without prompting by the person to whom it is made; and it must be made within a reasonable time after the attack. What is reasonable time will usually turn on the circumstances of each case. When admitted, the complaint may also serve as proof of the identity of the assailant.[583]

Lastly, as the Penal Code provisions relating to defilement testify, trends in the world today show that there are other modes of performing the sexual act besides the penetration of a female's vagina by a male's penis. In the light of this trend, it is also possible for females to initiate a sexual act without the consent of the other party to the act. It is therefore urged that the law of rape be reformed to bring it in harmony with the provisions on defilement and in line with the modern trends. There is no rhyme or reason for the Penal Code to carry different definitions of a sexual act – one for rape and the other for defilement.

B. Elopement and Bigamy

464. The law of 'elopement' is intended to protect the marriage institution. It attains this goal by forbidding and punishing people who entice spouses away from their matrimonial homes. Section 127(1) of the Penal Code provides that, 'any man who elopes with a married woman or entices or causes a married woman to elope with him' commits an offence. In similar vein, section 127(2) provides that, 'any … female, who elopes with a married man or entices or causes a married man to elope, commits an offence'.

465. The *actus reus* of the offence is that the accused, be it man or woman, must entice or cause the other person to leave the matrimonial home or to run away with him or her. In *Uganda v. Olungu*,[584] four years after a wife left her husband, she went to stay with the accused. It was held that there was no elopement, because 'once she had permanently left the matrimonial abode the accused could not have committed the offence of elopement [with her]'. Similarly, in *Bernard Nyeko Nyeko & Anor. v. Uganda*,[585] a wife simply left her husband and went to live with the first accused. Since there was no evidence that she had been enticed to run away from

582. *SGT Canbera Dickson v. Uganda*. Cr. App. No. 284 of 2003, [2010] UGCA 25 (6 Jun. 2010).
583. *Kabegambire Wilber v. Uganda* Cr. App. No. 56 of 2006, [2010] UGCA 43 (24 Nov. 2010).
584. [1972] E.A. 136. See also *Uganda v. Ojok & Anor*. [1973] E.A. 489.
585. H.Ct.Misc.Cr.Rev. No. 8 of 1992 (unreported).

the husband's home, no elopement was committed. It is also important for the prosecution to prove that the person with whom the accused is alleged to have run away was a 'married man' or 'married woman'.[586]

466. The *mens rea* in elopement is that the accused must know that the person he or she is causing to run away with him or her is a married person. It is a good defence for the accused to show that he or she in fact did not know that his or her 'partner' was married.[587] However, as was pointed out in *Uganda v. Solomon*, 'this would be difficult if he knew her surname or the matrimonial abode or even if he didn't bother to inquire [into] her matrimonial status'.[588]

467. In addition to sentencing a convicted person to imprisonment or fine, the court 'shall order any such person on first conviction to pay the aggrieved party compensation of UGX 600, and on subsequent conviction compensation not exceeding UGX 1,200 – less than one US Dollar at current exchange rates! The Code does not define who 'the aggrieved party' is. However, the courts have limited 'aggrieved party' to the accused's spouse who must show that he or she has truly been aggrieved by the elopement.[589] For this reason, they have denied the father of the female accused the right to collect compensation from her seducer.[590] They have also denied the wife of a male seducer the right to receive compensation from the woman who eloped with her husband [the seducer].[591] Additionally, they have quashed decisions of magistrates' courts ordering an eloping wife to return to her husband, saying, 'The Court cannot force a wife to live with her husband.'[592]

468. The essence of 'bigamy', however, is the mere going through a ceremony of marriage with a person who is still legally married.[593] Here, again, it must be shown that the accused knew that his or her marriage or that of his or her partner was subsisting at the time they went through the ceremony. However, where seven years have passed and throughout that period a spouse to that other marriage has been continually missing from and unheard of by the 'surviving' spouse, then that marriage is deemed to have come to an end. The surviving spouse is then free to re-marry.

C. Indecent Assault, Defilement, Procuration and Unnatural Offences

468.1. According to section 128 of the Penal Code, it is a felony for any person to 'unlawfully and indecently' assault any woman or girl. If the girl so assaulted is

586. See *Uganda v. Wodada & Anor.* [1972] U.L.R. 25.
587. *Uganda v. Olunga, supra, Bernard Nyeko Nyeko & Anor. v. Uganda, supra* and *Uganda v. Rukwandura* [1973] E.A. 574.
588. [1971] E.A. 45, 48.
589. See *Uganda v. Akua & Anor.* [1973] E.A. 246.
590. See *Uganda v. Ojok & Anor.* [1973] E.A. 489.
591. *Uganda v. Olum Tanga*, H.Ct.Monthly Bulletin No. 33 of 1971.
592. *Uganda v. Akua & Anor., supra.*
593. Section 153.

under the age of 18 years it is no defence for the accused to say that the girl consented to the act of indecency.

469. The *actus reus* of the offence is unlawful assault on a female, as defined earlier, which is indecent. The Code does not define 'indecent'. However, according to English criminal law, indecency imports actions that right-minded persons would consider 'offensive to contemporary standards of modesty and privacy'.[594] Section 147 of the Code also makes it a criminal offence for any person to 'unlawfully and indecently' assault a boy under the age of 18. The assault may be committed by either a man or a woman. While a reasonable mistake as to the age of the victim is a defence where such victim is a girl, this is not so clearly stated where it is a boy.

470. As for the *mens rea*, it must be shown that the accused not only intended to assault the victim but also that he or she intended to commit an indecent assault – one that right-minded persons would think was indecent.[595]

471. 'Defilement', however, is gender neutral: it may be committed by a male or a female; the victim may also be a male or female. It falls under two categories: simple defilement and aggravated defilement. Simple defilement is the performance of a sexual act with another person, male or female, under the age of 18 years.[596] A person convicted of simple defilement is liable to life imprisonment. Aggravated defilement, however, is the performance of a sexual act with another person, male or female, under any of the following circumstances: [597] (i) the other person or victim is below the age of 14 years; (ii) the offender to his or her knowledge is infected with the Human Immunodeficiency Virus (HIV) or Acquired Immune Deficiency Syndrome (AIDS); (iii) the offender is a parent or guardian of or a person in authority over the victim; (iv) the victim is a person with a disability;[598] or (v) the offender is a serial offender.[599] A person convicted of aggravated defilement is liable to be sentenced to death. A person charged with defilement, simple or aggravated, must undergo a medical examination to determine his or her Human Immunodeficiency Virus (HIV) status.

472. Prior to the Penal Code (Amendment) Act, 2007, defilement was defined in terms of a man having 'unlawful sexual intercourse' with a girl under the age of 18 years. 'Unlawful' meant extra-marital sexual intercourse. It was and still is common in Uganda for girls to be married away before they attain the age of 18. This is especially so where they are married under Islamic law or under customary

594. See *R. v. Court* [1989] A.C. 28, 42.
595. *Ibid.*, at 45.
596. Penal Code sec. 29(1) as amended by the Penal Code (Amendment) Act, 2007.
597. *Ibid.*, sec. 129(3).
598. *Ibid.*, sec. 129(7) where 'disability' is defined as 'a substantial functional limitation of daily life activities caused by physical, mental or sensory impairment and environment barriers resulting in limited participation'.
599. *Ibid.*, sec. 129(7). 'Serial offender' is defined as 'a person who has a previous conviction for the offence of defilement or aggravated defilement'.

law.[600] Men who had intercourse with their wives who were under 18 years did not thereby commit defilement. However, as the law now stands, it appears that sexual intercourse with any person, who is under the age of 18, even if she is a wife, would be defilement and criminal. The effect of the new law, then, is to outlaw marriages by persons under the age of 18.

473. The *actus reus* of defilement consists of two elements. The first is the age of the victim, which must be shown to have been below 18 years at the time of the offence. It should be noted that mistake as to a girl's age (where a girl is the victim), however genuine, is ruled out as a defence under section 144 of the Penal Code. However, under the cautionary rule regarding the evidence of children of tender years, a complainant's evidence implicating the accused must be corroborated by independent evidence in some material particular. That corroboration is often found in the victims' complaints to third parties – usually parents and siblings, evidence of the rupture of the victim's hymen, bruises or injuries to her private parts, presence of spermatozoa in her vagina and from evidence of her distressed condition.[601] In the absence of such evidence, the courts would be wary in convicting anyone of defilement.[602] The second element is a sexual act. The Code defines 'sexual act' as 'penetration of the vagina, mouth, or anus, however slight, of any person by a sexual organ or the use of any object by a person on another person's sexual organ'.[603] In *Uganda v. Patrick Akol*,[604] penetration was proved by showing that the accused had ruptured the hymen of the vagina of the 6-year-old victim, and

600. See, for example, the Customary Marriages (Registration) Act, (Cap. 248). Under s. 10 of this Act, the minimum age for a woman to contract a valid marriage is 16 years while the minimum age for the man is 18 years.

601. In *Muhwezi Alex & Anor v. Uganda*, Cr. App. No. 21 of 2005, [2010] UGSC 12 (2010), the evidence of a mother who saw the appellant taking the victim to the sitting room where he ravished her was accepted as corroboration. In *Kabwiso Issa v. Uganda*, Cr. App. No. 7 of 2002, [2003] UGSC 36 (27 Oct. 2003), the court accepted a confession of the appellant to the father of the complainant as corroboration. In Silagi *Buroro Gordon v. Uganda* Cr. App. No. 122 of 2005, [2010] UGSC 42 (15 Nov. 2010), the court accepted as corroboration the victim's immediate report to her mother of what happened to her while pointing to her private parts. On examining her, the mother found semen in her vagina. This report was accepted as corroboration. In *Bukenya Joseph v. Uganda*, Cr. App. No. 222 of 2003, [2010] UGSC 32 (23 Jul. 2010), soon after being ravished by the appellant, the complainant told a 14-year-old boy what had happened to her; the boy told the court that at the time of the report to him the complainant was walking 'like a duck'. This report was accepted as corroboration. In *Christopher Kizito v. Uganda*, Cr. App. No. 18 of 1993, [1995] UGSC 12 (28 Jun. 1995), the appellant by his own unsworn statement put himself at the scene of the crime at the material time; the Supreme Court accepted this statement as corroboration of the 7-year-old complaint's unsworn evidence.

602. The courts interpret 'child of tender years' to mean any child of any age or apparent age of less than 14 years. Accordingly in *Nyondo Muhamed v. Uganda*, Cr. App. No. 198 of 2004, [2010] UGCA 24 (16 Jun. 2010), the Court of Appeal held that as at the time the complainant gave evidence she was 15 and no longer 'a child of tender years', her evidence needed no corroboration. Nevertheless, the court found corroboration in the evidence of another child who found the appellant on top of the victim, holding that evidence of a child can be given to corroborate evidence of another person given on oath.

603. Penal Code sec. 129(7).

604. H.Ct.Cr.Session No. 364 of 1991 (unreported).

seed was found in it. In *Constant Bagamuhunda v. Uganda*,[605] however, the girl's hymen was found to be still intact. So no penetration was held to have taken place. The charge of defilement was dismissed. Unlike rape where lack of consent on the part of the victim is an essential element of the *actus reus*, and consent is therefore a defence to the offence, this is not so with defilement. Therefore consent to the sexual act is no defence to the charge of defilement. This is so because the aim of the law is the need to protect persons of tender age against their immaturity, by imposing an absolute ban on knowing sexual acts with them. Another aim is to protect them from sexual abuse and from disease by making proof easy; hence, their consent is irrelevant. However, where the victim is a female and there is clear evidence of lack of consent, this would also amount to rape and the offender could be charged, in the alternative, with rape. As discussed earlier on rape involves 'unlawful carnal knowledge of a woman or girl without her consent'.[606] The age of the victim is irrelevant. As for the *mens rea*, it must be shown that the accused intended to perform a sexual act.[607]

474. While making defilement gender neutral is salutary in that it acknowledges that both males and females are capable of committing the offence, it at the same time creates knotty enforcement difficulties with respect to consensual sexual acts by teenagers. Suppose that John and Jane both aged 17 years engage in a consensual sexual act. Which one of them is the offender and which one is the victim? Culturally, it is assumed that it is the boy who makes the advances to the girl and is, in practice, often treated as the offender and routinely prosecuted on the complaint of the girl's parents. This practice is no longer legally tenable. Absent coercion, both the boy and the girl are offenders and should be treated alike. The assumption that it is the boy who takes the initiative is not always correct; because girls of similar age are often more mature than boys.

475. 'Procuration' is committed where a person induces or causes a woman under the age of 21 years to have unlawful sexual intercourse with any person, or to become a common prostitute or to leave Uganda or her usual place of abode to become an inmate of or to frequent brothels in Uganda or elsewhere.[608]

476. As for unnatural offences, section 145 of the Penal Code divides such offences into three categories. The first is one where any person has carnal knowledge of any other person 'against the order of nature'. This means having sexual intercourse between a man and a woman *per anum*, generally known as sodomy; or between a man and another man *per anum*, generally known as homosexuality. The second category consists of any person having carnal knowledge of an animal *per vaginam* or *per anum*, commonly known as bestiality. Bestiality may be committed by either a man or woman. The third category does not create a conceptually new

605. [1974] H.Ct.Bulletin 279. See also *Christopher Byamugisha v. Uganda* [1971] H.Ct.Bulletin 318.
606. See *Ochiti v. Uganda*, Cr. App. No. 15 of 1998, [1998] UGSC 2 (4 Dec. 1998).
607. See sec. 8(1) of the Penal Code.
608. Section 131.

offence. It merely refers to a man *permitting* 'a male person' to have carnal knowledge of him or her 'against the order of nature', that is *per anum*. This is really sodomy and the only difference with the first category is that here the accused permits a man to perform a sexual act with him or her against the order of nature. In all the three instances, penetration must be proved.[609] It is noteworthy, though, that sexual acts between females, known as lesbianism, are not covered by the provision. Lesbianism is therefore not an offence in Uganda.

477. All participants in unnatural offences are perpetrators, unless any of them is not a consenting party. The mental element needed for these offences is knowledge of what is being done coupled with the intention to do so. The consent of the 'complainant' or of both parties to the act is not relevant.[610] Nevertheless, before conviction there must be some corroboration: independent evidence which implicates the accused by tending to connect him or her to the crime and confirming in some material particular not only the evidence given by the complainant or accomplice that a crime has been committed, but also the evidence that he or she committed it.[611]

478. Acts that constitute unnatural offences, even between consenting adults, are generally viewed with revulsion in Uganda; they are traditionally regarded as an abomination – *ekivve*. They offend against the moral values of the people. It is against this cultural backdrop that Article 31(2a) of the Constitution provides that: 'Marriage between persons of the same sex is prohibited.' 'Unnatural' sexual acts, then, are likely to remain outlawed in Uganda for some time to come.

§2. Crimes against Property

I. Theft, Robbery and Extortion

A. *Theft*

479. The essence of theft is that the thief assumes or appropriates to himself or herself the rights of an owner of the property he or she takes or converts without the owner's consent. Owning property and enjoying the benefits that accrue from such ownership is a fundamental human right protected by the Constitution. The aim of the law of theft is to protect that right.

Section 254(1) of the Penal Code provides that:

> A person who fraudulently and without claim of right takes anything capable of being stolen, or fraudulently converts to the use of any person other than the general or special owner thereof anything capable of being stolen, is said to steal that thing.

609. See *Hoyle v. Reginam* [1956–1957] 8 U.L.R. 314.
610. *Ibid.*
611. *Ibid.*

1. *Actus Reus*

480. The *actus reus* of theft involves: (1) taking, or (2) converting to one's use, (3) anything capable of being stolen, and (4) belonging to some other person.

a. Taking

481. According to section 254(6) of the Penal Code, 'A person shall not be deemed to take a thing unless he or she moves the thing or causes it to move.' This is asportation. According to Kenny's *Outlines of Criminal Law*:

> The slightest removal will suffice; thus there is a sufficient asportation in taking a plate out of a chest and laying it on the floor; or in shifting a bale from the back of a cart to the front. The test seems to be: has every atom left the place in which that particular atom was before?[612]

482. In *Dim Kifuko v. Rex*,[613] for example, the duty of the appellant, a post office employee, was to collect local parcels for dispatch. Without authority, he removed an overseas parcel from the 'foreign parcels rack' and put it in a bag meant for local parcels. It was held that the appellant's action in removing the parcel from the foreign parcels rack amounted to taking and theft. It did not matter that the parcel never left the Post Office building or the van on which it was to be loaded. The court said: 'There is evidence that the clerk found that the parcel was missing from the rack. The parcel had been taken out of the control of the Post Office officials whose duty it was to look after parcels in the rack.'[614]

483. The essence of 'taking' or 'conversion' is that it is not, either expressly or by implication, authorized by the owner of the property in question, and it amounts to an adverse interference or usurpation of the owners' rights. There would therefore be no theft where the taking or conversion is authorized.

b. Conversion

484. Conversion, however, occurs when a person has come by property innocently or lawfully but later appropriates it or assumes a right to it by keeping it,

---

612. 5th ed., 1911, at 187.
613. [1936–1951] 6 U.L.R. 273.
614. The Kenya case of *Lerunyami v. Republic* ([1968] E.A. 107) is also in point. Napeikori had just bought a cow for Shillings 100/=. He put it in the cattle *boma* at the Baragoi Trading Centre and went to a nearby restaurant for a cup of tea. The appellant happened to be sitting outside the *boma*. A passerby came along and saw him there. He inquired from the appellant about the possibility of buying the cow. The appellant told him that it was his and offered to sell it to him for Shillings 40/= plus four goats. The passerby paid the Shillings 40/= to the accused. No sooner had he done so than Napeikori returned and stopped the transaction from going further. The appellant was charged with and convicted of theft of the cow. On appeal, the Kenya High Court quashed the conviction. It held that there was no 'taking' or 'conversion' of the cow. It said that for 'taking' or 'conversion' to take place there must at least be 'an act which results in a turning about, a change, in the control of a thing or in the possession of the thing'.

using it or dealing with it as if he or she were the owner or lawful possessor.[615] Conversion is most often committed by agents, servants or generally people entrusted with the custody of property on behalf of others. If they decide to use, sell or otherwise dispose of that property as their own or without authority or outside the mandate of the owner, they *convert* it. Examples of conversion include the following conduct: a chief executive officer of a company and the sole signatory to its bank account withdrawing money from the company's bank account entrusted to it by the Government to carry out HIV/AIDS, TB and Malaria activities on behalf of the Government and failing to account for its use;[616] paying a cheque received on behalf of someone else into one's own account;[617] taking a company's goods without instructions or permission and without signing a delivery book, selling them and not accounting for the proceeds;[618] an agent receiving money from his master's customers and not accounting for it;[619] an employee attempting to sell a motor boat of the employer;[620] a court clerk receiving money from a member of the public as court fees but filling in the duplicate of the receipt issued only half of the sum received and not accounting for the rest.[621] General deficiency in books of account for which an employee or agent is responsible as accounts clerk or storekeeper and inability to account for that deficiency may also amount to conversion.[622] The conduct in all these examples amounts to a usurpation of the rights of the true owner.

485. Regarding lost and found property, an ancient belief of the Baganda ordains that *kyerondera taba mubbi* (he or she who finds lost or abandoned property is not to be regarded as a thief). The received English law accords with this indigenous belief and provides that a person who finds property and decides to keep or use it is not deemed to have stolen it, if at the time of the conversion he or she does not know who the owner is 'and believes on reasonable grounds that the owner cannot be discovered'.[623] There is no duty on the part of a person who finds lost property to look for the owner or to notify the police. However, the finder is not allowed to convert things that he or she takes from other people's land or premises under the guise of 'finding'. As was stated by Lord Goddard in the English case of *Hibbert v.*

615. Section 254(4) of the Penal Code provides that 'When a thing stolen is converted, it is immaterial –
    (a) whether it is taken for the purpose of conversion or whether it is at the time of the conversion in the possession of the person who converts it;
    (b) that the person who converts the thing in question is the holder of a power of attorney for the disposition of it, or is otherwise authorised to dispose of it.'
616. *Teddy Sseezi Cheeye v. Uganda*, Cr. App. No. 105 of 2009, [2010] UGCA 41 (20 Oct. 2010). Section 105 of the Evidence Act provides that 'When a person is accused of any offence … the burden of proving any fact especially within the knowledge of that person is upon him or her, … ' Both the High Court and the Court of Appeal relied on this provision to hold the appellant liable for embezzlement, because he failed or refused to say 'where the money went', as the matter was especially within his knowledge.
617. *Hawkins v. R.* [1959] E.A. 47.
618. *R. v. Kantilal C. Raval & Anor.* [1960] E.A. 458.
619. *John Mubiru v. Uganda* [1971] U.L.R. 1.
620. *Christopher Kiwala v. Regina*, H.Ct.Monthly Bulletin No. 47 of 1962.
621. *Beigumamu v. Uganda* [1973] E.A. 26.
622. *Seni Longa v. Uganda* [1964] E.A. 512.
623. Section 254(5).

McKiernan, 'Every householder or occupier of land means or intends to exclude thieves and wrongdoers from the property occupied by him and this confers on him a special property in goods found on his land sufficient to support at indictment if the goods are taken therefrom, not under a claim of right, but with a felonious intent.'[624]

486. Related to taking or conversion is the doctrine of 'recent possession'. Possession of property recently stolen gives rise to a presumption of fact, not law, that the person in whose possession the property is found stole it or received it knowing the same to have been stolen. However, for the doctrine to apply, three conditions must be satisfied.

487. First, there must be possession of the stolen property. Unless the accused admits such possession, the prosecution must prove beyond reasonable doubt that he or she indeed was in possession of the property. However, as discussed elsewhere in this book, possession is not limited to personal possession; it also includes constructive possession. As section 2(v) of the Penal Code provides, 'to be in possession of' 'have possession' includes 'having anything in any place … for the use or benefit of oneself or any other person'. Related to possession, the property found in the possession of the accused must be produced in court as exhibits, and its identity strictly proved as the property allegedly stolen.[625] For example, in *Mabanga v. R.*,[626] the office of a cotton ginnery was broken into and a cash box containing UGX 830 in UGX 10 notes stolen. Shortly after the theft, the appellant was found in possession of UGX 10 notes. The appellant was convicted of the theft although there was no evidence to show that these were the notes stolen from the ginnery. The High Court quashed the conviction, saying that the doctrine of recent possession did not apply unless it was proved that the notes found on the appellant were either the very notes that were stolen from the ginnery or were the proceeds of the theft.

488. Second, possession of the property by the accused must not be innocent. Possession will not be innocent where the accused fails to give a credible explanation for being in possession of the property, or if he or she does so, the court does not believe it. According to the Supreme Court:

> The doctrine is applicable only where inculpatory facts, namely the possession of stolen goods, are incompatible with innocence and incapable of explanation upon any other reasonable hypothesis than of guilt. The court must also be sure that there are no other co-existing circumstances that weaken or destroy the inference of guilt.[627]

---

624. [1948] 2 K.B. 142, 149.
625. Mbazira Siraj *v.* Uganda Cr. App. No. 7 of 2004, [2007] UGSC 2 (20 Mar. 2007).
626. H.Ct.Monthly Bulletin No. 55 of 1959.
627. *Mbazira Siragi v. Uganda*, Cr. App. No. 7 of 2004, [2007] UGSC 2 (20 Mar. 2007). In *Mukwaya Manasse v. Uganda*, Cr. App. No. 7 of 1994 [2009] UGSC 12 (21 Dec. 2009), the appellant and another person were found driving a car at 'an awkward hour of the night' at Kakoba in Tanzania, five hours after it had been forcibly taken by two thugs who killed its driver at Buziga in Kampala Uganda. They did not go through the immigration and customs formalities at the Tanzania/Uganda

489. Lastly, the theft must be recent; the period between the theft and the possession must be relatively short, depending on the circumstances of the given case. The longer the interval between the theft and the possession, the weaker the inference that the person in whose possession the property was found stole them. In *Zus v. Uganda*,[628] for example, a bicycle was found with the accused seven months after it had been stolen from the complainant. It was held that this period could not be described as 'recent'. Additionally, in applying the doctrine the nature of the stolen property must be taken into account. For example, in *Ovuloo v. Regina*[629] one pillow, slip, and a child's frock, part of the stolen property, were found hidden in the appellant's kitchen seven days after the theft. Taking into account the fact that the two articles found were only a small part of the total articles stolen, the court held that the doctrine of recent possession did not apply. The lost articles were a type that might easily change hands several times within a period of seven days.

c. Anything Capable of Being Stolen

490. Section 253 of the Code lists the things capable of being stolen as follows:

(1) Every inanimate thing whatever which is the property of any person, and which is movable, is capable of being stolen.
(2) Every inanimate thing which is the property of any person, and which is capable of being made movable, is capable of being stolen as soon as it becomes movable, although it is made movable in order to steal it.
(3) Every tame animal, whether tame by nature or wild by nature and tamed, which is the property of any person, is capable of being stolen.
(4) Animals wild by nature, of a kind which is not ordinarily found in a condition of natural liberty in Uganda, which are the property of any person, and which are usually kept in a state of confinement, are capable of being stolen, whether they are actually in confinement or have escaped from confinement.
(5) Animals wild by nature, of a kind which is ordinarily found in a condition of natural liberty in Uganda, which are the property of any person, are capable of being stolen while they are in confinement and while they are being actually pursued after escaping from confinement, but not at any other time.
(6) An animal wild by nature is deemed to be in a state of confinement so long as it is in a den, cage, style, tank, or other small enclosure, or is otherwise so placed that it cannot escape and that its owner can take possession of it at pleasure.
(7) Wild animals in the enjoyment of their natural liberty are not capable of being stolen, but their dead bodies are capable of being stolen.
(8) Everything produced by or forming part of the body of an animal is capable of being stolen.

---

border; they did not have the requisite registration papers for the car; and were unable to explain their 'suspicious' presence in Tanzania, as a result of which they were arrested. The Supreme Court upheld his conviction for murder and aggravated robbery, holding that in the circumstances the inculpatory facts were incompatible with his innocence and incapable of explanation upon any other hypothesis than his guilt.

628. [1967] E.A. 420.
629. H.Ct.Monthly Bulletin No. 119 of 1957.

Excluded from this list are things like land and power such as electricity. Land and buildings thereon are not movable and are not capable of being stolen. The owner's rights, such as quiet enjoyment can, however, be protected by the crime of criminal trespass. Electricity is not a physical thing capable of being stolen. However, unauthorized use of electricity is punishable under section 283 of the Code which provides that:

> Any person who fraudulently *abstracts* or *diverts* to his or her own use or to the use of any other person any mechanical, illuminating or electrical power derived from any machine, apparatus or substance, the property of another person, is guilty of a felony and is liable to imprisonment for five years.

d. Belonging to Some Other Person

491. The property taken or converted must belong to someone other than the 'thief'. The person from whom it is taken may be the general owner or special owner. The general owner is the *real* owner of the property. Special owner, as indicated in section 254(2) 'includes any person who has any charge or lien upon the thing in question, or any right arising from or dependent upon holding possession of the thing in question'. A bailee, a repairman, a hirer and a mortgagee are all 'special owners' who are entitled to possession of property. Any person, including the general owner, who unlawfully interferes with their possessory rights, might be convicted of theft.[630]

492. Failure on the part of the prosecution to prove ownership of the property stolen does not affect the thief's guilt, except in cases where it is necessary to prove special ownership.[631] It is indeed usual for the prosecution to charge a person with stealing property belonging to 'a person to the prosecution unknown', and it is not necessary in drafting the charge sheet to name the owner of the property.[632] All that the prosecution has to prove is that the property fraudulently taken or converted 'did not belong to the accused'.

2. *Mens Rea*

493. The *mens rea* for theft consists of taking or converting something capable of being stolen *fraudulently* and *without claim of right.*

---

630. See sec. 259 of the Code.
631. See *Kamadi Kaibale v. Uganda*, H.Ct.Monthly Bulletin No. 2 of 1964.
632. See sec. 88(m) of the *Magistrates' Courts Act* and sec. 25(L) of the Trial on Indictments Act.

a. Fraudulently

494. Section 254(2) of the Penal Code provides that 'A person who takes or converts anything capable of being stolen is deemed to do so fraudulently if he or she does so with any of the following intents … ':

> i. 'an intent permanently to deprive the general or special owner of the thing of it'

This means that the person who takes or converts the property does so intentionally, not by mistake, and with the intention to permanently deprive the owner of the property in it, or with *animus furandi*. He or she need not actually deprive the owner of the property permanently. What is important is that at the time of the taking, he or she has that intention. Such intention, will invariably be deduced from his or her conduct.

> ii. 'an intent to use the thing as a pledge or security'

To use somebody else's property as a pledge or security without his or her consent is clearly to treat it as one's own regardless of the owner's interests. While it is so pledged or charged the owner cannot use it. Moreover, there is a risk of the property being lost to the owner, should the taker fail to fulfil his or her obligations under the pledge or charge agreement.

> iii 'an intent to part with it on a condition as to its return which the person taking or converting it may be unable to perform'

This clause is particularly applicable to agents or trustees who hold property on behalf of others. It will be to disregard the principal's/beneficiary's interests in the property for the agents or trustees to part with the property on conditions that they cannot fulfil and therefore risk permanent loss of the property.

> iv. 'an intent to deal with it in such a manner that it cannot be returned in the condition in which it was at the time of the taking or conversion'

This clause addresses situations of unauthorized borrowing or unauthorized taking with intent to return the property. If the property is to be returned in a changed state with all its goodness or value gone, then the taking or conversion is fraudulent. Thus, in the English case of *R. v. Beecham*[633] where the accused took tickets from a railway company, the judge directed the jury that if the accused took the tickets with intent to use them for his own purpose, whether to give to friends, or to sell them, or to travel by means of them, it would not be less larceny though they were to be ultimately returned to the company at the end of the journey.

633. (1851) 5 Cox C.C. 181.

v. 'in case of money, intent to use it at the will of the person who takes, or verts it, although he or she may intend afterwards to repay the amount tc owner'

This, again, concerns an agent or a person who is in a position of trust, includi treasurer and a cashier, who receives or holds money on behalf of some other son. If he or she uses that money without express or implied authority from the cipal or owner, he or she is guilty of theft. It is immaterial that he or she since intends to repay the money. Lawyers who receive money on behalf of their cli are required to promptly pay it over to the clients or, in the meantime, to depo in a bank on a trust account or 'client's account'. They are not allowed to withc it and to use it for their own purposes without the client's express or implied aut ity. The money is payable to the client on demand. If, therefore, a lawyer issu cheque to the client and the cheque is returned by the bank unpaid because of ir ficient funds, this means that the lawyer has fraudulently converted the cli money. He or she is guilty of theft. This is also true of a person who holds a pc of attorney and has power to dispose of funds entrusted in his or her care. He o can only dispose of the funds or property entrusted to him or her according tc or her express mandate or instructions or for the benefit of his or her principa

b. Claim of Right

494.1. It is debatable whether the appendage of 'claim of right' to 'fraudule adds any extra element to the *mens rea* for theft. Can a *fraudulent* taking or version ever be justified under the doctrine of 'claim of right'? What is sure, h ever, is that any genuine claim of right to the property taken, converted or dealt tends to negative the fraudulent state of mind. Indeed, claim of right is a defen respect of all offences relating to property generally This has already been fully cussed in chapter 4 and will not be repeated here.

3. Specialized thefts

495. For sentencing purposes, the Code classifies theft-related crimes accor to the offender, the property in question and the circumstances surrounding the t

496. For example, section 268 creates the offence of embezzlement: theft b employee, servant, or officer of the government or public body, or by a dire officer or employee of a company or corporation, or a clerk or servant employe any person, association or a religious or other organization. According to se 270, it is mandatory for the court which convicts a person of embezzlement to him or her 'to pay by way of compensation to the aggrieved party, such sum the opinion of the court is just, having regard to the loss suffered'. The order be executed as a civil decree, including attachment and sale.[634] Section 269 cr the offence of causing financial loss by an employee of the government, bank, c

634. See *Major John Kazoora v. Uganda*, H.Ct.Misc.Appl. No. 109 of 1991 (unreported).

tution, insurance company or public body. As is in the case of embezzlement, :onvict must be ordered to pay compensation to his victim, in addition to the ence. Sections 271 and 272 create offences of stealing by agents and stealing by nts or lodgers respectively.

)7. Offences which are defined according to the nature of the property stolen ide stealing of wills,[635] stealing postal matter,[636] stealing cattle[637] and stealing cles.[638]

)8. Offences defined according to the circumstances surrounding their com- ion or the place where they are committed include cattle rustling,[639] stealing the person of another, from a dwelling place, vessel or vehicle, from a railway a public office[640] or a locked room or other receptacle which the offender opens ieans of a key or other instrument.[641]

)9. The last point to note is that where a person is charged with stealing a num- of items, it is not fatal to the charge if the prosecution fails to prove theft of all tems mentioned in the charge sheet. It is sufficient if they prove theft of at least of the items. As it was stated in *R. v. Parker*,[642] 'it is clear law that if a person cused of stealing two articles, he can be convicted if it can be proved that he one only'. Similarly, the fact that the evidence shows that the accused stole items than those indicated in the charge sheet will not be a bar to a convic- For sentencing purposes, however, the Court must make it clear that it is pun- g the accused only for the items proved to have been stolen.

Robbery

0. Robbery is theft in an aggravated form. The aggravation is the use of vio- in the course of stealing. Section 285 of the Penal Code defines robbery as ws:

> Any person who steals anything, and, at or immediately before or immediately after the time of stealing it, uses or threatens to use actual violence to any per- son or property in order to obtain or retain the thing stolen or to prevent or to overcome resistance to its being stolen or retained, is guilty of a felony termed robbery.

Section 262.
Section 263.
Section 264.
Section 265.
Section 266.
t was held in *Tumuheire v. Uganda* [1967] E.A. 328 that a bank is not a public office, since a pub- c office is one which is maintained by public funds.
ection 267.
1969) 53 Cr.App.Rep. 289, 292.

1. *Actus Reus*

501. The *actus reus* of robbery has two key elements: (i) stealing and (ii) the use of violence. As for stealing, the definition of theft discussed in the previous sections of this book applies, with the exception that the offence must be committed by way of taking or asportation of the property in question, not conversion. The taking may be direct, as defined earlier on in this book,[643] or indirect according to the doctrine of recent possession. According to that doctrine, also discussed earlier on in this book, a person found in possession of property recently stolen may be convicted of robbery even if the victim did not recognize or identify him or her at the scene of crime, provided that he or she used violence in the course of the initial taking of the property.[644] The taking must be accompanied with the necessary *mens rea*. One aspect of this *mens rea* is *animus furandi*, the intention to permanently deprive the general or special owner of the property. Thus in one Botswana case, the accused tripped the complainant, and she fell to the ground. He wrenched her handbag from her, telling her that if she wanted it back, she should follow him in the nearby bush. He was acquitted of robbery on the ground that his intention in tripping the complainant and for taking her bag was to lure her into sex but not to permanently deprive her of that property.[645] Additionally, where a person uses violence to take something, reasonably believing that he or she has a claim of right to the thing, he or she does not steal the thing; he or she is therefore not guilty of robbery. Depending on the amount of violence the offender uses, he or she may be guilty of one of the offences against the person.

502. Regarding violence, the Code does not define what 'violence' is. According to the ordinary meaning of the word, violence involves exertion of physical force, or an intense, turbulent, or furious and often destructive force. In this sense then, mere body contact that suffices to constitute assault is not sufficient. Such body contact may facilitate a pickpocket taking the victim's property, but it is not sufficient to constitute robbery. For purposes of committing robbery, the violence must be of such a nature as to induce in the victim reasonable apprehension of danger and to lose his or her power to resist his or her property being taken against his or her will. Tying the victim or forcing him to lie down is sufficient.[646] It is however not necessary to prove actual infliction of personal harm or injury on the victim. Threats to use violence, by word or deed, will suffice. Thus threat to use a weapon

---

643. According to the principle enunciated in *Dim Kifuko v. Rex*, [1936-1951] U.L.R. 273, the slightest change of location of the property in question is sufficient to establish taking. As soon as the accused takes possession of the property, the offence of robbery is complete even if he or she later on abandons the property.

644. See *Yowana Sserunkuma v. Uganda*, S.Ct.Cr.App. No. 8 of 1989 (unreported) where robbers covered the complainant with a blanket, put a knife on her throat and threatened to kill her if she raised an alarm. See also *Mukwaya Manasse v. Uganda* Cr. App. No. 7 of 1994, [2009] UGSC 12 (21 Dec. 2009).

645. *Omar v. State* [1998] B.L.R. 237 (HC).

646. In *Haruna Tunyakira & Anor v. Uganda* Cr. App. 7 of 2009, [2011] UGSC 10 (5 Jul. 2011) the robbers tied several members of the household they robbed.

by saying to the victim that 'If you run away I will shoot you',[647] or 'choose between handing over the motor cycle or your life',[648] will satisfy the requirements of the law. Threat to use violence also includes brandishing or pointing a weapon, or an imitation thereof, at the victim to force him or her to submit to the robber's demands – to produce or surrender the article demanded or to open the door, to hand over the keys, to go somewhere, not to raise an alarm, to carry the booty[649] or to lie down.[650] It also includes shooting in the air to intimidate the victim into submission,[651] or to prevent neighbours from coming to the aid of the victim who might have raised an alarm.[652]

503. According to section 285 of the Penal Code, the use of violence may be against 'any person or property'. It is therefore not limited to the owner or person in possession of the property stolen. It could be used against a relative, a member of the household, a guard, gatekeeper, cashier or any person who happens to be around and who might constitute a hindrance to the robbery by, say, raising an alarm or assist the owner to prevent the robber's escape. The point to stress, however, is that the robber uses violence 'in order to obtain or retain the thing stolen or to prevent or overcome resistance to its being stolen'. In this respect, the charge sheet need not allege the specific purpose for which the violence was used. It is sufficient if it alleges that violence was used.[653] In *Kwezi v. Uganda*,[654] the High Court held, relying on authorities such as the English case of *R. v. Gnosil*,[655] that where the theft is carried out forcibly by a sudden taking or snatching away of a thing from a person unawares, it is not robbery.[656] The reasoning behind these authorities is that the violence used must have been intended to over-power the victim and to prevent his resistance; but not merely to get possession of the property snatched. It may be true that by suddenly snatching an article from an individual violence is not used against that individual. But the violence is undeniably used against the article. According to the definition of robbery, violence must be used to 'any person or property in order to obtain or retain the thing stolen'. It is therefore submitted that these decisions are of doubtful rectitude. They do not accurately interpret the Uganda Penal Code.[657]

504. Additionally, violence must be inflicted 'at or immediately before or immediately after the time of stealing'. It must be reasonably contemporaneous with the taking of the property. An interesting case in this regard is the Kenya case of

647. See *Wasaja v. Uganda* [1975] E.A. 181.
648. *Uganda v. Kagyenda Moses & Anor*, HCt. -05-Cr-Sc-0228 of 2003, [2007] UGHC 20 (23 May 2007).
649. *Uganda v. Abdalla Mukasa*, H.Ct.Cr.Session No. 139 of 1990 (unreported).
650. *Robert Sabiti v. Uganda*, S.Ct.Cr.App. No. 4 of 1989 (unreported); *Uganda v. Obedi Armeni & Anor.*, H.Ct.Cr.Session No. 78 of 1990 (unreported).
651. *Uganda v. Firimigiyo Kakooza* [1984] H.Ct.Bulletin 1.
652. *Robert Sabiti v. Uganda, supra* n. 3.
653. See *Kwezi v. Uganda* [1967] E.A. 298.
654. *Ibid.*
655. (1824) 171 E.R. 1206.
656. See also the earlier case of *Kiwanuka & Anor. v. R.*, H.Ct.Monthly Bulletin No. 50 of 1959.
657. The *Gnosil* case is no longer law in *England.* See *R. v. Clouden* [1987] Crim.L.R. 56.

Gathuri Njuguna v. Republic.[658] In this case, the complainant and neigbours tried to arrest and to stop the appellant from taking property that he was suspected to have removed from the complainant's house in the latter's absence. In resisting the arrest the appellant clubbed the complainant to death. The Kenya High Court held that the appellant's conduct did not qualify as robbery, because the violence was not 'immediate' or was not contemporaneous or concurrent with the theft.[659]

2. *Mens Rea*

505. As for the *mens rea* of robbery, two elements are needed: (i) the accused must have taken the property fraudulently and without any claim of right, as defined under the discussion on theft; and, (ii) he must have used the violence 'in order to obtain or retain' the property.

C. *Aggravated Robbery*

506. Ordinarily a person convicted of robbery by a Magistrates' Court is liable to imprisonment for a term of ten years imprisonment; and if convicted by the High Court to life imprisonment. That is 'simple robbery'. However, where, as discussed below, there exist aggravating circumstances surrounding the commission of the robbery then the offence becomes 'aggravated robbery', and the offender is liable to punishment by death. Prior to the Penal Code (Amendment) Act 2007, the death sentence was mandatory. However, today the sentence is discretionary.

507. Section 286(2) of the Penal Code, as amended by the Penal Code (Amendment) Act, 2007 provides:

> Notwithstanding subsection (1) (b), where at the time of, or immediately before or immediately after the time of the robbery, an offender *is in possession of* a deadly weapon, or causes death or grievous harm to any person, such

---

658. [1965] E.A. 583.

659. The concrete facts of the case were the following. The complainant returned from work one evening and met the appellant proceeding from the direction of his [the complainant's] house. The appellant was carrying a bundle. The complainant thought nothing of this. However, on reaching his house, he discovered that it had been broken into and that some property had been taken. He alerted his neighbours. The neighbours and the complainant pursued the appellant. They found him about 500 yards from the house and tried to arrest him or to stop him from taking the property. The appellant responded by killing the complainant with a club. He was charged and convicted of robbery. On appeal, the High Court of Kenya set aside the conviction, on the ground that the violence was not committed 'immediately after' the articles were stolen. The Court said:

> 'We think that the essence of the offence of robbery is an openly committed theft from or in the presence of someone or a theft where the offender is caught more or less in the act or immediately after the act. We do not think that it extends to a case such as this where the offence was committed clandestinely without the discovery or chase until after the offender had left the premises and had proceeded so far on his way as he had in this case without being discovered to be a thief.' *Ibid.*, at 584. See also *Gilbert v. Republic* [1972] E.A. 51.

> offender *or* any other person jointly concerned in committing the robbery shall, on conviction by the High Court, be *liable to suffer* death. [Emphasis supplied]

508. According to this provision, aggravated robbery may be committed in either of two ways: (i) the offender being in possession of 'a deadly weapon' or (ii) 'causes death or grievous harm to any person'.

509. As to the first mode of committing the offence, it is noteworthy that prior to the amendments, the Code required 'use' or 'threat to use' a deadly weapon. With the amendments, however, the robber only has to be 'in possession' of the deadly weapon. As long as he or she employs violence to steal, as discussed above, he or she need not actually use the weapon.

510. The weapon in possession of the robber must be 'a deadly weapon'. In this respect, section 286(3), also as amended by the Penal Code (Amendment) Act, 2007 provides:

> In subsection (2) 'deadly weapon' includes –
>
> (a)(i) an instrument made or adapted for shooting, stabbing or cutting, and *any imitation of such an instrument*;
>
> (ii) *any substance*, which, when used for offensive purposes, is *capable of causing* death or grievous harm or is capable of inducing fear in a person that it is likely to cause death or grievous bodily harm; and
>
> (b) *any substance intended to render the victim of the offence unconscious.* [Emphasis supplied]

According to this definition, 'deadly weapon' includes 'an instrument made or adapted to shooting, stabbing or cutting, and any imitation of such instruments'. Taking into account his or her common knowledge, a Ugandan judge would readily hold that guns, daggers, swords, spears, pangas, large knives, axes, hoes and picks are instruments that qualify as deadly weapons. With respect to guns, the court previously insisted that before a gun could be considered a deadly weapon, those asserting that it was had to prove that it was capable of being fired and had to be test-fired by an expert. For that reason, toy and dysfunctional guns did not qualify as deadly weapons, because they were not capable of causing death.[660] With the 2007 amendments, functionability is no longer necessary, because '*any* imitation' of the described instruments are now specifically included in the definition of 'deadly weapon'. It is noteworthy that the word 'imitation' is not defined in the Act. It is nevertheless submitted that *anything* that has the appearance of any of the defined instruments, irrespective of what it is made of, would qualify as an imitation of an instrument. The person must nevertheless be in possession of a thing; the thing possessed must be separate and distinct from the possessor. Mere pretence of

660. *Wasaja v. Uganda* [1975] E.A. 181, 182. See also *Shaban Birumba v. Uganda* S.Ct.Cr.App. No. 32 of 1989 (unreported).

possessing an instrument will not suffice.[661] Be that as it may, however, the emphasis of the law today is not so much the actual infliction of harm on the victim as the capacity to create in the mind of the victim of apprehension of the imminent infliction of such harm and to enforce compliance.

511. Additionally, 'any substance', though not inherently 'deadly', may become deadly when it is used for offensive purposes and is capable of causing death or grievous harm or depending on the way it is used 'capable of inducing fear in a person that it is likely to cause death or grievous bodily harm'. Thus a stone or a club, depending on the manner and circumstances in which they are used may qualify as deadly weapons.

512. Any substance intended to render the victim of the offence unconscious also qualifies as a 'deadly weapon'. The offender needs not use it; he or she is guilty of aggravated robbery if he or she has it in his or her possession when committing the offence.

513. The second mode of committing aggravated robbery is by causing death or grievous harm to any person. It does not matter what type of weapon the robber uses. It may be deadly or not. He or she may use a club, bare fists, or may simply kick the victim. The nature of the weapon or mode employed to cause death or grievous harm does not matter. What matters is its effect: death or grievous harm as defined under section 2 of the Penal Code. Grievous harm must, however, be strictly proved by medical evidence. If it is not proved and the weapon used to inflict the harm was not deadly, then the accused will be convicted of ordinary robbery only, either under section 286(1)(a) or (b).

Again, the death caused or the grievous harm inflicted is not limited to the owner or the person in possession of the property taken. It extends to any person that the robbers may kill or hurt in the course of the robbery.[662]

514. Regarding jurisdiction over robbery cases, the DPP may decide to charge an accused person under either subsection (1) or (2) of section 286 of the Penal Code. Where he or she decides to charge under subsection (2), he or she can only charge the accused before the High Court, for it alone has the power to pass a conviction and impose the sentence of death.[663] In subsection (1) cases, it is again within the discretion of the DPP to file the charges either before the Magistrates' Court or before the High Court. What criteria he or she uses is not indicated in the

---

661. In the English case of *R v. Bentham* [2005] UKHL 18, the appellant put his fingers in his jacket, causing a bulge that gave the impression that he had a gun. Even though the bulge was enough to frighten the victim of the robbery and to force him to surrender to the appellant money and jewellery, the House of Lords held that there was no possession of an imitation gun. It said that what is possessed must be a thing and that a person's hand and fingers is not a thing. One cannot possess something that is not separate and distinct from oneself. An unsevered hand or finger is part of oneself and therefore one cannot possess it.

662. See *Mukwaya Manasse v. Uganda* Cr. App. No. 7 of 1994, [2009] UGSC 12 (21 Dec. 2009) where in the course of stealing a Government car the appellant and his associate killed its driver.

663. See *Karamagi & Anor. v. Uganda*, H.Ct.Cr.App. No. 338-9 of 1969 (unreported).

Code. The DPP must doubtless take into account the seriousness of the injuries inflicted and the value of the property involved. Suppose, however, that the case is filed before a Magistrates' Court and in the course of the trial it transpires, according to the evidence adduced, that this is a subsection (2) case, what should be done? Should the magistrate stop the trial and refer the case to the High Court? Although the Code is silent, this seems to be the sensible thing to do.[664]

515. In all cases of robbery, whether tried by Magistrates' Courts or by the High Court, it is mandatory under section 286(4) that the court order convicted persons other than those sentenced to death to pay 'such sum by way of compensation to any person to the prejudice of whom the robbery was committed, as in the opinion of the court is just having regard to the injury or loss suffered by such person'.[665] The amount of compensation to be awarded must be carefully assessed, taking into account all the harm and damage suffered. It must not be arbitrary.[666]

D. Extortion and Demanding

516. In common parlance, extortion means to obtain something from a person by intimidation or undue or illegal power. Section 290 of the Penal Code provides that any person who, with intent to extort or gain anything from any person, and knowing the contents of the writing, causes any person to receive any writing demanding anything from any person without reasonable or probable cause, and containing threats of injury or detriment of any kind to be caused to any person, either by the offender or any other person, if the demand is not complied with, is guilty of a felony and is liable to imprisonment for fourteen years.

517. Section 291, billed as 'Attempts at extortion by threats', creates an offence akin to the English offence of blackmail. It provides that:

> Any person who, with intent to extort or gain anything from any person –
>
> (a) accuses or threatens to accuse any person of committing any felony or misdemeanour, or of offering or making any solicitation or threat to any person as an inducement to commit or permit the commission of any felony or misdemeanour; or

---

664. The magistrate may do so *mero motu* under sec. 162 of the *Magistrates' Courts Act* or an application of the DPP under sec. 163(2) of the same Act.
665. See *Sabani v. Uganda* [1974] E.A. 460.
666. See *Brian Mubiru Guweddeko v. Uganda*, S.Ct.C.App. No. 28 of 1991 (unreported). The trial court ordered the appellants to pay a sum of Shillings 300,000/= to the Ministry of Health pursuant to sec. 286(4) of the Penal Code. Setting aside the order, the Supreme Court remarked, 'Although the matter has not been raised we are of the view that there must be some evidence of the injury or loss suffered to enable the court to assess the sum payable. We do not think that the order for compensation is arbitrary. In this case the vehicle was recovered and it may well be that the compensation was in respect of such damage as was done to the vehicle related to the robbery. If this is correct the court should have said so.'

(b) threatens that any person shall be accused by any other person of any felony or misdemeanour, or of any such act; or
(c) knowing the contents of the writing, causes any person to receive any writing containing any such accusation or threat as aforesaid, commits a felony.

518. Section 293 creates the offence of 'demanding property with menaces'. It provides that 'Any person who, with intent to steal any valuable thing, demands it from any person with menaces or force is guilty of a felony and is liable to imprisonment for five years.' It is sufficient, according to *Haji Moiedina & Anor. v. R.*,[667] 'if the accused has intent to unsettle his victim's mind and the threat is of a nature to operate on a person of ordinarily firm mind'. So, when the appellant, a police officer, investigating a criminal case, told the victim that 'If you do not want to get in trouble, pay me UGX 10,000 and I will close the case' it was held that these words were sufficient to unsettle the victim's mind.

II. Burglary, Housebreaking and Criminal Trespass

A. *Burglary and Housebreaking*

519. According to section 294 of the Penal Code, any person who breaks and enters any building, tent or vessel used as a human dwelling with intent to commit a felony therein, or having entered any such place with felonious intent, or having committed a felony therein breaks out commits a felony termed housebreaking and is liable to imprisonment for seven years. If the offence is committed at night, the offence is called burglary, and it is punishable by imprisonment for ten years.

520. Breaking is the actual breaking of any part of the building, whether external or internal. It also includes opening by unlocking, pulling, pushing, lifting or any other means whatsoever, any door, window, shutter, cellar flap or other thing, intended to close or cover an opening in a building or an opening giving passage from one part of a building to another. From this definition, there would be no breaking where the door is left ajar thus enabling the thief to enter the building or room.

521. Entering is accomplished as soon as any part of a person's body or any instrument used by him is within the building. A person who might have already been in the building, say a house servant or guest, may be guilty of breaking and entering if say, he enters his host's bedroom or other part of the building. Breaking and entering may be constructive. It is constructive where the thief gains entry by threats or artifice or by collusion with a person already in the building. It is also constructive where the thief enters the house through a chimney or other aperture of the building which is left permanently open for some necessary purpose, a ventilator for example.

667. [1960] E.A. 678, 687.

522. The mental element for these offences is intent to commit a felony. Although theft is the most likely felony that the burglar would intend to commit whilst in the house, it need not be. It may be rape, homicide or damage to property. The intent must be present at the time of breaking and entering.

523. Entering a dwelling house without breaking but with intent to commit a felony is also an offence under section 296.

524. Breaking and entering other types of buildings such as schools, shops, warehouses, stores, offices, counting-houses, and places of worship accompanied by the commission of a felony is also an offence punishable by imprisonment of up to seven years under section 297. Where the breaking and entering is accompanied by an intent to commit a felony, the punishment is imprisonment for a term of up to five years.

B. Criminal Trespass

525. All the above offences focus on persons who gain ingress into or egress out of a building by breaking and whose purpose for so doing is the commission of felonies. What of people who enter or remain in buildings without breaking and whose intention is the commission of lesser offences? These persons are covered by the offence of criminal trespass. Section 302 of the Penal Code provides that:

> Any person who –
>
> (a) enters into or upon property in the possession of another with intent to commit an offence or to intimidate, insult or annoy any person; or
> (b) having lawfully entered into or upon such property, remains there with intent thereby to intimidate, insult or annoy any person or with intent to commit any offence
>
> is guilty of the misdemeanour termed criminal trespass and is liable to imprisonment for one year.

In *Kigorogolo v. Rushereka*,[668] the High Court interpreted the expression 'to intimidate' to mean 'to overawe, to put in fear by a show of force or threats to violence'. It interpreted the expression 'to insult' to mean 'to assail with scornful abuse or offensive disrespect'. It also interpreted the expression 'to annoy' as 'to molest'. It held that the respondent's refusal to vacate a piece of land belonging to the appellant after he had been so ordered by a court did not fall under any of these expressions and did not therefore amount to criminal trespass. The court said: 'The gist of the complaint was not more than that the respondent by his obstinacy in not complying with the order of civil court was keeping the appellant out of the possession of certain land.'[669]

668. [1969] E.A. 426.
669. *Ibid.*, at 429. See also *Norman Godinho v. Rex* [1936–1951] 6 U.L.R. 143.

III. Obtaining by False Pretences and Cheating

A. *Obtaining by False Pretences*

526. Section 305 of the Penal Code provides that:

> Any person who, by any false pretence, and with intent to defraud, obtains from any other person anything capable of being stolen, or induces any other person to deliver to any person anything capable of being stolen, is guilty of a felony and is liable to imprisonment for five years.

1. *Actus Reus*

527. The *actus reus* of this offence involves: (i) making false pretences, (ii) obtaining anything capable of being stolen, or (iii) inducing any person to deliver to any person things capable of being stolen.

a. False Pretence

528. Section 304 of the Code defines 'false pretence' as 'any representation made by words, writing or conduct of a matter of fact, either past or present, which representation is false in fact, and which the person making it knows to be false or does not believe to be true'. It will thus be false pretence for a person to tell others, by word of mouth or in writing, that he has lost a relative so as to induce them to give him or her money for *mabugo*, or funeral expenses. It would similarly be false pretence for an individual to tell another, as did the appellant in a Kenyan case that he possessed magical or supernatural powers, and that he could diagnose and cure the complainant's relative of his malady even without seeing her.[670] He knew that he did not possess those powers. He did not perform the services and yet refused to return the fat fee he was paid. It will also be false pretence by conduct for a person, knowing that his account at a bank was closed or that it has no sufficient funds in it, to write a cheque and to give it to somebody else as payment for goods or services received. By so doing, he or she represents to the person to whom he or she gives the cheque that the state of his account or his or her credit with the bank or his or her overdraft facilities are at the time he or she hands over the cheque such that the cheque will be honoured on presentment. It was also held to be false pretence for a man who had set fire to his house to file a claim to his insurers for indemnification, asserting in the claim form that the house 'had been burned down by accident'.[671]

529. However, it must be stressed that the representation must relate to some past or present fact. Promises to do something in the future and failure to live up to those promises do not amount to false pretence. For example, in *Henry Isiko*

670. *Athuman v. Republic* [1967] E.A. 401.
671. *Rasul & Anor. v. R.* [1954] 21 E.A.C.A. 229.

v. Uganda[672] the appellant, with intent to defraud the complainant, obtained a sum of UGX 1,500,000 from the complainant, promising to give the complainant the sum of US Dollars (USD) 50,000 which had allegedly been allocated to the appellant by the Bank of Uganda. The appellant did not honour his promise and was convicted of obtaining money by false pretences. On appeal, the High Court quashed the conviction on the ground that a breach of promise to do an act in the future is not an offence under section 305 of the Penal Code. It convicted him of theft instead, under section 155 of the Magistrates Courts Act.[673] However, where Tom represents to Lot that he is a car dealer and obtains money from Lot promising to deliver a car within a certain future time but fails to do so, that will be obtaining by false presences. The representation of being a car dealer relates to a present fact.[674]

b. Obtaining

530. The goods obtained must be capable of being stolen. A house or land, for example, is not capable of being stolen. Services are also not covered either. Obtaining apparently means gaining ownership, not mere possession or control,[675] but there is no rhyme or reason for this interpretation, since the essence of the offence is the fraud or deceit used to deprive a person of his proprietary rights. Be that as it may, however, the obtaining must be actually brought about as a result of a false pretence. The person who parts with the property must do so as a result of the false pretence made to him or her by the person who makes the representation.[676]

c. Inducing Any Other Person to Deliver Goods

531. It is not certain what additional element these words make to the provision. The only apparent addition they make is that they cover a situation where the accused by false pretences does not obtain the property for himself or herself but for a third party. For that purpose, he or she induces the complainant to deliver the goods to the third party.

2. *Mens Rea*

532. The *mens rea* of obtaining by false pretences is 'the intent to defraud'. Fraud has been defined as 'to deprive by deceit: it is deceit to induce a man to act to his injury'.[677] Deceit, however, means to induce a person to believe a thing is true which is false and which the person practising it knows or believes to be false. Whether or not there is intent to defraud is a matter of fact that is usually inferred

672. H.Ct.Cr.App. No. 7 of 1991 (unreported).
673. That section reads as follows: 'When a person is charged with obtaining anything capable of being stolen by false pretences with intent to defraud, and it is proved that he stole the thing he or she may be convicted of the offence of stealing although he or she was not charged with it.'
674. See the Botswana case of *Letsholo & Anor v. State* [1999] B.L.R. 278 (HC).
675. See the Tanzanian case of *Yusaf Omeri & Anor. v. Republic* [1964] E.A. 162.
676. See *Sarwano Mawanda v. R.* [1962] E.A. 119.
677. *Bennett & Newston* (1913) 9 Cr.App.R. 146, 154.

from all the surrounding circumstances. However, it has been stated that where goods are obtained by pretences that are false, there is prima facie intent to defraud.[678] Additionally, intent to defraud any particular person need not be alleged in the charge sheet; therefore failure to do so will not vitiate the charge.[679]

533. Two different but associated offences may also be mentioned here.

534. The first is obtaining execution of a security by false pretences. According to section 306 of the Penal Code, a person commits a misdemeanour if by any false pretence, and with intention to defraud, him or her induces any person to execute, make, accept, endorse, alter or destroy the whole or any part of any valuable security, or to write any name or impress or affix any seal upon or to any paper or parchment in order that it may be afterwards made or converted into or used or dealt with as a valuable security. The second one is obtaining credit by false pretences. Section 308 of the Code makes it a misdemeanour for any person: (a) in incurring any debt or liability, obtains credit by false pretence or by means of any other fraud; or (b) with intention to defraud his or her creditors or any of them makes or causes to be made any gift, or transfer of or any charge on his property; or (c) with intent to defraud his or her creditors or any of them sells or removes any part of his or her property since or within two months before the date of any unsatisfied judgment or order for payment of money obtained against him.

B. Cheating

535. Cheating, according to section 307 of the Code, is committed when a person by means of any fraudulent trick or device, obtains from any other person anything capable of being stolen or induces any other person to deliver to any person anything capable of being stolen or to pay or deliver to any person any money or goods or any greater sum of money or greater quantity of goods than he or she would have paid or delivered but for such a trick or device.

536. The key elements of the offence of cheating are: obtaining, inducing another person, and fraud. These elements have the same import as under the offence of obtaining by false pretences (*supra*, paragraphs 526–34). They are not therefore discussed again in detail. Four points must, however, be stressed.

537. The first is that the words 'fraudulent trick or device' appear to have a somewhat different connotation from the one under the offence of obtaining by false pretences. It connotes something in the nature of an artifice, contrivance and stratagem. For example, in a Tanzanian case, the accused obtained from the complainant a sum of money, falsely pretending that he knew and would show the complainant the site of the grave of a relative who had disappeared and was believed to have been murdered. The trial court convicted him of cheating, but the conviction was

---

678. See *Regina v. Ramzan Ahmed Jamal* [1955] 22 E.A.C.A. 504.
679. See *Chamba v. Republic* [1970] E.A. 280.

quashed on appeal on the ground that the accused's pretence did not amount to 'a fraudulent trick or device' as described above.[680] The conduct of the appellant in the Nyasaland (now Malawi) case of *Ali v. Regina*[681] did, however, amount to 'fraudulent trick and device'. The appellant went to the complainant's house and pretended that because of the magical powers he possessed, he could help the complainant increase her money. When she agreed, he dug a small hole inside her house. He put a bag in the hole. He then told her to put some money in the bag. She did. He then covered the hole with a plate and told her to go and get some ashes which he would mix with some of his medicine. While she was gone he removed the money from the hole and pocketed it. When the complainant returned with the ashes the appellant mixed the ashes with his medicine and poured the resulting concoction in the plate covering the hole. He then left, assuring the complainant that the following day she would find her money increased. He was convicted of cheating, and the High Court confirmed the conviction.

537.1. The second point is that, unlike in England, there is no need that the trick or device affect the general public, or that it should be of such a character that common prudence and caution are not sufficient security against the person being defrauded thereby.

537.2. The third point is that the accused must be shown to have obtained the thing *by means* of the fraudulent trick or device. In other words, the complainant must be made to believe in the existence of a certain state of affairs, be it the nature or quality of goods, or nature, quantity or value of some consideration, or the identity of the parties involved. In *Rex v. Ramazani Nswazalugudo*,[682] for example, the accused agreed with certain Barundi to convey them to Kyaka for the sum of forty cents each. On the way, he demanded more money from them before he could take them to their final destination. When they objected an altercation ensued. The accused struck one of them. He made them open their suitcases. He took their money as well as property. In the end, he refused to carry them any further. He was convicted of cheating. On revision, the conviction was quashed. The High Court found that the accused did not use any trick or device to take the Barundi's property. The Barundi were not misled into believing anything. They knew that the accused was demanding something to which he was not entitled. However, since the accused used violence to take the property, he was convicted of robbery.

537.3. Lastly, although cheating is loosely used by lay people to mean overcharging, it is not necessarily so. Therefore, the fact that a seller sells an article at a price which is higher than he ought to charge does not per se amount to cheating.

538. To amount to cheating, the act of over-charging must be accompanied by a fraudulent trick or device.[683]

680. *Masabi v. R.* [1921–1952] 1 T.L.R. 305.
681. [1959] Rhodesia and Nyasaland Law Reports 14.
682. [1932–1935] 5 U.L.R. 63.
683. See *Uganda v. Ndyanabo* [1974] E.A. 522.

IV. Receiving Stolen Goods and Related Offences

A. *Receiving and Retaining*

539. Section 314 of the Penal Code creates the offence of receiving or retaining property which has been 'feloniously stolen, taken, extorted, obtained, or disposed' or 'unlawfully taken, obtained, converted or disposed of in a manner which constitutes a misdemeanour'. When the offender receives or retains the property in question, he or she must know or have reason to believe that the property was taken criminally.

1. *Actus Reus*

540. The *actus reus* of the offence consists of: (i) receiving or retaining (ii) property which has been feloniously or unlawfully taken as indicated above.

a. Receiving or Retaining

541. Receiving or retaining means having in one's possession. Possession means to have the property under one's control, actually or constructively. It is actual possession when the possessor personally has the property under his or her physical custody. It is constructive if the property is under the custody of another person who is under the accused's authority and control, for example, an agent or servant. Mere physical or manual custody without control does not amount to legal possession.[684] It is conceivable that possession may reside with both the thief and the accused. However, if it appears that the thief retained exclusive control, then the accused does not have possession and will not be guilty of receiving or retaining. Thus, in *Karuna Bukenya v. R.*,[685] thieves hired the appellant, a transporter, to ferry eight boxes containing stolen nails. The appellant admitted in evidence that although the thieves told him that the nails were theirs, he did not believe them. The trial magistrate convicted him of theft as a principal along with the thieves. The High Court quashed the conviction and substituted a conviction for receiving stolen property. On further appeal, the Court of Appeal for Eastern Africa set aside the conviction, holding that the prosecution had not proved that the appellant had possession of the property. It said:

> Proof of some form of possession is essential to sustain an indictment for receiving stolen goods with guilty knowledge … and, even if there is proof of criminal intent to receive and a knowledge that the goods were stolen, if the exclusive possession still remains in the thief, a conviction for receiving cannot be sustained … There may, of course, be a guilty joint-possession with the

684. See *Said Kigozi v. R.* [1958] E.A. 1. In *Idi s/o Waziri v. R.* [1961] E.A. 146 bags of coffee were found 250–300 yards away from the appellant's house, hidden in a maize field. It was held that as long as the appellant had control over the coffee it was in his possession.
685. [1952] 19 E.A.C.A. 235.

> thieves, which is a question of fact. There is nothing, however, in the present case to indicate that the thieves ever intended to share or did in fact share their possession of the stolen goods with the appellant. He acquired no property or interest in them, and had no control over them nor any voice in disposing them. It is true that he controlled the vehicle in which they were being driven; but that is not the same thing as controlling the stolen property, in the sense in which that test of possession is used in, for example, *Wiles* case (1850) 4 Cox C.C. 414 or *Rex v. Berger* (1915) 11 Cr.A.R. 72. The goods were in fact never out of the manual possession of the thieves and the appellant was never in possession, either actual or constructive, of them.[686]

542. Lastly, for a person to be said to possess something he or she must have *animus possidendi*. That person must know that he or she is possessing and must intend to possess. If, therefore, unknown to the person and without his or her consent, third parties leave or plant property on him or her or on his or her premises, he or she does not legally possess that property.

543. While receiving is the initial assumption of possession over property, retaining is the continuation of possession after receiving information regarding the criminal manner in which the property was initially obtained by the person who passed it on to the receiver. Up to this moment, the possession may have been innocent or honest. From thence on up to the time when the property is recovered, the possession is wrongful. The fact that the retainer initially received the property or money in repayment of a debt is irrelevant. When he or she learns that it was criminally obtained, he or she must hand it over to the police or risk being charged with retaining.[687]

544. As a matter of practice, the former Court of Appeal for Eastern Africa has held that 'receiving and retaining' is one offence, and that it is open to the prosecution to frame the charge that way, leaving it to the trial court to decide, on the evidence adduced, which limb of the charge has been proved.[688] However, if the prosecutor decides to charge receiving only, then it must prove beyond reasonable doubt that the receiving was wrongful, that at the time of receiving the accused knew or had reason to believe that the property received was feloniously or unlawfully obtained property. However, according to section 154(2) of the Magistrates Counts Act, 'When a person is charged with receiving anything knowing the same to have been stolen, and it is proved that he retained the thing knowing the same to have been stolen, he may be convicted of the offence of retaining although he was not charged with it.' Similarly, where the prosecution charges the accused with only retaining and it is proved that the accused received the thing knowing the same to have been stolen, 'he or she may be convicted of the offence of receiving although he was not charged with it'.[689]

---

686. *Ibid.*, at 237.
687. See *Apulunari Butare v. Uganda*, H.Ct.Monthly Bulletin No. 19 of 1968.
688. *Jagat Singh v. Reginam* [1953] 22 E.A.C.A. 283.
689. Magistrates Courts Act, sec. 154(3).

545. Again, where a person is found in possession of stolen property and the evidence is as consistent with theft as with receiving or retaining, it is advisable that he should be charged with both stealing and, alternatively, receiving or retaining. It will then be up to the court to decide according to the evidence, which of the two offences is proved. If the person was charged with receiving or retaining only, he or she cannot be convicted of theft.[690] Additionally, although the doctrine of recent possession applies to theft and receiving, it does not apply to retaining.[691] The prosecution must therefore take care not to rely on it where they intend to charge the accused with retaining only.

b. Stolen Property

546. The property which the accused person receives or retains must have been 'feloniously stolen, taken, extorted, obtained or disposed of in a manner which constitutes a misdemeanour'. According to section 314(3) of the Penal Code:

> No person, except a person pleading guilty, shall be convicted of an offence under this section unless it shall first be proved that the property which is the subject matter of the charge has in fact been stolen or feloniously or unlawfully taken, extorted, obtained, converted or disposed of.

In *David Kasule v. Uganda*,[692] the property in question was not proved to have been stolen. Sixteen car armatures were missing from a store belonging to Cooper Motor Corporation in Kampala. Police found some armatures at the appellant's shop. Unfortunately, the Cooper Motor Corporation store manager who was called as a prosecution witness could not positively identify the armature produced in court as an exhibit as belonging to the Corporation or that it was one of those missing from its store. All he was able to say was that it resembled armatures that the Corporation dealt in. In spite of his finding that, 'It is not definitely proved that the armature (Ex. 1) is one of the fifteen armatures stolen from Cooper Motors on or before 16 or 17 March 1966' the magistrate convicted the appellant of receiving. On appeal, the conviction was quashed, because it did not comply with section 314(3) of the Penal Code.

2. *Mens Rea*

547. The *mens rea* for receiving or retaining is knowledge or having reason to believe that the property in question was property which was feloniously stolen,

690. Note that under sec. 154(1) of the Magistrates Courts Act, 'When a person is charged with stealing and (a) it is proved that he received or retained the thing knowing or having reason to believe the same to have been stolen, he may be convicted of receiving or retaining the thing, as the case may be, although he was not charged with it.' There is no provision for the converse situation. See also *Kantilal Jivraj & Anor. v. R.* [1961] E.A. 6.

691. See *Jagat Singh v. R., supra.*

692. [1966] E.A. 338.

taken, extorted, obtained, converted or disposed of or taken in a manner which constitutes a misdemeanour. In the case of receiving, the knowledge should exist at the time the accused received the property. In the case of retaining, the knowledge comes subsequent to receiving but before the recovery of the property. In either case, however, it is not necessary to prove that the accused knew or had reason to believe that the property was obtained under circumstances which amount to the specific felony or misdemeanour by which it was in fact obtained. It is sufficient if it is proved that the accused knew or had reason to believe that the property had been obtained under circumstances which in law amount to a felony or a misdemeanour.[693]

548. Whether or not the accused knew or had reason to believe that the property in question was stolen is a question of fact which may be inferred from all the surrounding circumstances. Generally speaking, false denial by the accused that the stolen goods were in his possession is evidence of guilty knowledge. Additionally, the court may infer guilty knowledge where the accused fails to give an explanation when an explanation might reasonably be expected. It may also draw the same inference where the explanation given is false.[694] In doing so, however, the court must exercise caution, bearing in mind that the onus to prove all elements of the offence rest on the prosecution and does not change. The way that the accused dealt with the property may also have a bearing on his knowledge. Hiding the property under a bed is one example.[695] Dismantling a bicycle and making up a new bicycle from some of those parts and parts from another source, coupled with removing the part that bears the serial number tends to suggest guilty knowledge.[696] Lastly, attempting to sell the property at a price much lower than its actual value is another factor that suggests that the seller had knowledge that the person he received it from acquired it illicitly.[697] However, mere suspicion that the property might have been stolen is neither knowledge nor reason to believe that it was stolen. Suspicion may not be based on reasonable grounds, while 'having reason to believe' means 'having reasonable grounds to believe'. Believing is thus a weightier concept than 'suspecting'.[698]

549. Subsection (4) of section 314 lays down other specific factors that may be taken into account in proving guilty knowledge. The subsection reads as follows:

> Whenever any person is being proceeded against under any of the provisions of this section for receiving or retaining any property, for the purpose of proving guilty knowledge, there may be given in evidence at any stage of the proceedings –

693. See *Director of Public Prosecutions v. Nieser* [1958] 3 All E.R. 662.
694. *Chhaganlal v. R.* [1956–1957] 8 U.L.R. 349.
695. *Mwangi Njoroge v. R., supra.*
696. *Said Kigozi v. R., supra.*
697. *Idi s/o Waziri v. R., supra.*
698. In the Tanzanian case of *Merali v. Regina* [1953–1957] 2 T.L.R. 100 a magistrate in convicting the appellant of receiving said, 'I am quite satisfied that this shows accused suspected the property to be stolen.' The conviction was quashed on appeal.

(a) the fact that other property stolen within the period of twelve months preceding the date of the offence charged was found or had been in his or her possession;

(b) the fact that within the five years preceding the date of the offence charged he or she was convicted of any offence involving fraud or dishonesty:

but this fact may not be proved unless –

(i) seven days' notice in writing has been given to the offender that proof of such previous conviction is intended to be given; and

(ii) evidence has been given that the property in respect of which the offender is being tried was found or had been in his or her possession; and

no evidence of the kind mentioned in this subsection may be given in any proceedings if there is included in the charge or indictment a count for any offence other than an offence under the provisions of this section.

This provision is an exception to the general rule of evidence that forbids use of the accused's character or past convictions as evidence that he or she committed the offence in question.

B. Having or Conveying Suspected Stolen Property

550. Section 7(1) of the Criminal Procedure Code Act empowers any police officer to stop, search or detain any vessel, boat, aircraft or vehicle in or upon which there shall be reason to suspect that anything stolen or unlawfully obtained may be found. It also empowers the police to stop and search any person who may be reasonably suspected of having in his or her possession or conveying in any manner anything stolen or unlawfully obtained. In both cases, the police may seize anything found as a result of the search. Subsection (2) in conjunction with section 71 of the Magistrates Courts Act also authorize the police effecting a search under a search warrant to seize anything which they reasonably suspect to have been stolen or unlawfully obtained, notwithstanding that the thing so seized is not the thing they were authorized to search for under the warrant.

551. Section 315 of the Penal Code provides that if the person in whose possession the seized thing is found fails to give a satisfactory account to the court of how he or she came by it, he or she shall be guilty of a misdemeanour. It is important, however, that before section 315 is brought into play, the criteria set out under the Criminal Procedure Code Act or the Magistrates Courts Act be satisfied.

552. First, the police officer's suspicions that the vessel, boat, aircraft or vehicle is conveying stolen or unlawfully obtained goods must be based on reasonable grounds. This is also true of the person whom the police officer suspects to be in possession or conveying such goods. The requirement for reasonable grounds is intended to prevent the police from acting arbitrarily and to protect the individual's right to liberty, privacy and property from unwarranted intrusion. 'Reasonable grounds' are, however, not defined in any of the statutes involved. They will doubtless depend on the facts of each case, considered against the background of the social and economic habits extant at the time. In *Kityo v. Uganda*,[699] for example, a police officer stopped a car driven by the appellant after it had been observed prowling around Kampala while the appellant looked at the left and then right sides of the road and driving the car very slowly. On inspection, the officer discovered that the car had a new engine and many other parts which did not correspond to the description of the car in the register at the Central Motor Registry. The officer also found that the appellant was carrying a large assortment of tools of all descriptions and sizes. It was held that under these circumstances the officer had reasonable grounds to suspect that some of the parts of the appellant's car were stolen or unlawfully obtained.

553. Second, it is not necessary that the police officer who stops and searches a vessel and the like or an individual should have in mind any precise suspicion about anything having been stolen or unlawfully obtained. As Udo Udoma, C.J., said:

> It is not necessary that at the time of the stopping and searching of the car a Police Officer must have in his mind a precise suspicion about anything stolen or unlawfully obtained as long as there is in all the circumstances of the case reason for such suspicion.[700]

The learned Chief Justice's views can be supported on the premise that the legislative intention in giving the police wide powers of stop and search was to enable them to deal indirectly with thieves or those in league with thieves in circumstances where it is impossible to prove theft. Suspicious possession and failure to give a satisfactory account is the *actus reus* of the offence under section 315. Were the law to insist that the police should have precise prior knowledge that the property in the possession of suspects were stolen or improperly obtained property then the type of mischief we are dealing with here could never be detected or punished. The antecedents of the property suspected to be stolen or unlawfully obtained are within the exclusive knowledge of the possessor. It is therefore reasonable to require him or her to give a satisfactory account of how he or she came by it so as to dispel the police officer's suspicion. It is his or her failure to give a satisfactory account that leads to the seizure of the property and to his or her arrest.

554. Third, before a suspect is required to give the account, he or she should be told the reasons for the police officer's suspicions. It is not enough for the police officer merely to say that he or she is suspicious. He or she must give reasons. In *Justine Ngozebwa v. R.*,[701] for example, the appellant was found riding a bicycle on a road at 8:30 am with a paper parcel on the carrier. A police officer stopped and

699. [1967] E.A. 23.
700. *Ibid.*, at 33.
701. H.Ct.Cr.App. No. 215 of 1954 (unreported). See also *Uganda v. John Mukasa* H.Ct.Cr.Rev. No. 715 of 1971 (unreported).

searched him and found 'M & B' tablets in the parcel. He took the appellant t police station where a syringe and needle were found on his person. The appell was subsequently convicted of failing to give a satisfactory account of how he ca about these articles. Quashing the conviction, Lewis, J., said:

> Before a person can be put to account for his possession under Section 315 circumstances set out under Section 7 of the Criminal Procedure Code must present. Before a police officer can act under Section 7 there must be a reas for suspicion. The police cannot stop and search anyone at any time unless th have reason to suspect that anything stolen or unlawfully obtained may found. A police officer must always give reasons for the suspicion wh prompted the arrest and if they are valid then and only then can the accused called upon to give an account.

555. Fourth, the police must act on their own initiative and not on the initiat of third parties.[702]

556. Fifth, the person stopped and searched must be 'having in his or her p session or conveying' suspected stolen property.

557. According to section 315(2) of the Penal Code, 'a thing is deemed to be the possession of a person' if:

(a) when found by a police officer acting under the provisions of section 7 of Criminal Procedure Code Act it is on the person of or being carried by such p son or is part of his or her goods or luggage on a vessel, boat, aircraft or vehi or
(b) when found by a police officer acting pursuant to a search warrant issued un section 70 of the Magistrates Courts Act, it is in a part of a building in wh such person resides, or which he or she occupies or is in a vessel, carriage, b receptacle or place under his or her control.

In *Semewa Kizza v. Regina*,[703] for example, the appellant was charged with be found in possession of motor spare parts which were suspected to be stolen unlawfully obtained. The spare parts were not found on the appellant when he stopped. They were found hidden in a bush. It was held that unless the per stopped is carrying something which excites the police officer's suspicion he or cannot be said to have committed an offence under section 315 of the Penal Co A similar holding was made in a Tanzanian case where the accused disposed of property in question before the intervention of the police.[704] However, in *R Anwali*,[705] where the accused dropped a bag containing bicycle spare parts after s ing the policeman approaching, it was held that the accused had possession of

702. For example, see *Uganda v. Dison Manyu & Anor.* H.Ct.Cr.Rev. No. 152 of 1968 (unreporte
703. H.Ct.Cr.App. No. 632 of 1962 (unreported).
704. *Kateba v. Republic* [1967] E.A. 215.
705. H.Ct.Monthly Bulletin No. 41 of 1958.

property. The fact that he had time to drop the bag before the police officer spoke to him could in no way alter the fact that it was found in his possession, since he had been seen carrying it.

558. Lastly, the accused must give an account, satisfactory to the court, of how he or she came by the property. Not every explanation will do.[706] It must be satisfactory. If the accused fails to do so, he or she must be convicted. In *Uganda v. Benedicto Karerengabo*,[707] two police officers stopped the appellant who was with another man at about midnight. The appellant appeared to have something hidden under his shirt. The officers searched him and found hidden under his shirt a lady's handbag which contained a torch and three screwdrivers. The other man ran away. The officers questioned the appellant about these articles. He could not give any satisfactory explanation on how he came by them. It was at the trial that he said that the handbag belonged to a girlfriend with whom he had been at a bar, and that he used the screwdrivers in his trade as a mechanic. Confirming his conviction under section 299, Saldanha, J., said:

> Assuming it is true that the appellant had been with his girlfriend in a bar, why should he have in his possession the handbag and why should he have been hiding it under his shirt? The burden was on the appellant to give a satisfactory account of how he came to be in possession of the handbag. It is a burden which can be discharged upon a balance of probabilities. But it can hardly be said that the appellant had discharged this burden by merely saying that he had been with his girlfriend in a bar and that it belonged to his girlfriend.

Knowledge that one might be punished for failing to give a satisfactory explanation of how one came into possession of the article in question, when there are reasonable grounds to suspect the innocence of the origin of that article, is the essence of this offence. It serves to deter people from handling stolen or unlawfully obtained property even though they themselves may not be thieves.

C. Smuggling

559. Smuggling is covered by sections 319 and 320 of the Penal Code. It includes the exportation or importation of any goods from or into Uganda without the requisite license from the minister responsible. It also includes exporting or importing goods in such a manner that the goods are concealed in any way, packed in any package (whether or not with other goods) in a manner calculated to deceive any authorized officer; or the goods may be contained in any package of which the entry or application for carriage out of or within Uganda does not correspond with such goods. Smuggling also includes importing or exporting goods in any manner

706. The High Court decision in *R. v. Ali Sokhair* [1932–1935] 5 U.L.R. 62 tends to hold this view. With respect, it is wrong.
707. [1971] U.L.R. 6.

by which the exporter or importer evades the control of customs over the exportation or importation as the case may be. Any person convicted of smuggling must be sentenced to a minimum sentence of imprisonment of not less than three years and not more than fourteen years and must be ordered to pay a fine of not more than UGX 5,000,000 or in default a further term of imprisonment of not more than two years. However, where in the course of committing the offence the offender uses or threatens to use a deadly weapon, causes death or grievous harm to any person or authorized officer he or she may, on conviction by the High Court, be liable to be sentenced to death.

560. Being found in possession of goods 'reasonably suspected' to have been smuggled into Uganda or about to be smuggled from Uganda is also an offence under section 320 of the Penal Code, punishable in the same way as actual smuggling.

D. Fraudulent False Accounting

561. Section 325 of the Penal Code provides as follows:

> Any person who, being a clerk or servant, or being employed or acting in the capacity of a clerk or servant, does any of the following acts with intent to defraud, that is to say –
>
> (a) destroys, alters, mutilates or falsifies any book, document, valuable security or account which belongs to or is in the possession of his or her employer, or has been received by him or her on account of his or her employer, or any entry in any such book, document or account, or is privy to any such act; or
> (b) makes, or is privy to making, any false entry in any such book, document or account; or
> (c) omits, or is privy to omitting, any material particular from any such book, document or account,
>
> is guilty of a felony and is liable to imprisonment for seven years.

The *actus reus* of this offence is the conscious or deliberate doing of any of the things listed in the provision. The *mens rea* is doing any of these things with 'intent to defraud'. 'To defraud' has been defined as 'to deprive by deceit' or 'by deceit to induce a man to act to his injury'.[708] Elaborating on this definition, the Court of Appeal for Eastern Africa said:

708. See *George Woodgate v. R.* [1959] E.A. 525, 529, adopting the definition in the English *locus classicus* on the point, *Re London and Globe Finance Corporation Ltd.* [1903] 1 Chs. 728, 732–733.

> To be defrauded, then, a person must either have been deprived, which has been held to mean deprived of something having some economic value (however small), or he must have been induced to act to his own injury, not necessarily an economic injury; and both from common sense and from the decided authorities it seems clear that, for this purpose, being induced to act would include being induced to remain inactive.[709]

Thus in that case the appellant, a manager of the Uganda Club, made false entries in the Club's bar account to show a higher bar profit than one actually made, was held not to have had the intent to defraud, because his conduct amounted to mere deceit. He was, however, held to have had the intent to defraud when he made other entries 'in order to cover up apparent shortages for the bar takings during those months'. In the latter case, the Court of Appeal held that 'to prevent the [management] committee from discovering a shortage and thereby from being given some opportunity of recovering it would … be to cause them to act to their own injury, since causing them to act must be deemed to include causing them to remain inactive'.

562. Sections 322, 323, 324 and 326 create offences of fraudulent disposal of trust property, frauds against company property by directors, fraudulent statements by company officials and false accounting by public officers, respectively. Constraint of space does not permit a discussion of those offences in this book.

V. Causing Injury to Property

A. *Arson*

563. Arson, which involves the setting of fire to a building, is one of the most serious offences of causing injury to property. Section 327 of the Penal Code defines it as follows:

> Any person who willfully and unlawfully sets fire to –
>
> (a) any building or structure whatever, whether completed or not; or
> (b) any vessel, whether completed or not; or
> (c) any stack of cultivated vegetable produce, or of mineral or vegetable fuel; or
> (d) a mine, or the working, fitting, or appliances of a mine, commits a felony and is liable to imprisonment for life.

The *actus reus* of the offence is the setting of fire to the building or any of the other objects listed in the section. Any amount of fire that results in the charring of the object and resulting in some damage to the object is sufficient. The *mens rea* is the setting fire to a building 'wilfully and unlawfully'. The Court of Appeal for Eastern

709. *Op. cit.*

Africa has interpreted 'wilfully and unlawfully' to mean 'in furtherance of an unlawful purpose'.[710] The act is unlawful where there is no legal justification for it. This will include the deliberate and unauthorized setting of fire to somebody else's house. It will also include, as it did in the *Rasul* case,[711] the appellant's setting fire to his own house in order to claim compensation from his insurer, which amounted to defrauding the insurer. It would also include setting fire to one's own house with the intention of injuring people in it or damaging somebody else's property in it.

B. Malicious Injury to Property

564. Section 335(1) of the Code defines the offence of malicious injury to property as 'wilfully and unlawfully' destroying or damaging any property. Destroying is the putting of the property out of existence. Damaging, however, is to cause physical harm or impairment as by breaking, tearing or rendering dysfunctional, property without necessarily putting it out of existence. The *mens rea* of the offence is 'wilfully and unlawfully' doing the forbidden act. This phrase must be interpreted in the same way as we have discussed it under arson. It means more than acting intentionally. Thus in *Nikolas Ogulu & Anor v. Uganda*,[712] the appellants, police officers, purporting to act in pursuance of their powers under section 16 of the Criminal Procedure Code, broke down a door to obtain entry into a building where a suspect was thought to be hiding. Setting aside their convictions for malicious injury to property, the High Court held that the appellants thought that they were acting within their powers. They did not intend to go outside their duty but were 'over-zealous of their duty'. They did not intend to do anything wrong. Although they might have committed a civil wrong, they were not guilty of malicious injury to property. As is the case with arson, there might be times when it is criminal to destroy or damage one's own property.

565. The punishment for malicious injury is governed by subsections (1)–(8) of section 335. It depends on the type of property damaged or destroyed, and varies from imprisonment for life to seven years.

VI. Forgery and Uttering

A. Forgery

566. Although forgery is a preliminary step toward the commission of another offence, the law retains it as a separate offence. This is probably so in order to expose its evil nature and to indicate the seriousness with which it is regarded. In a

710. *Rasul & Anor v. R.* [1954] 21 E.A.C.A. 229. Followed by the High Court in *R. v. Gabrieli Okulu* [1936–1951] 6 U.L.R. 17.
711. *Ibid.*
712. H.Ct.Monthly Bulletin No. 181 of 1968.

modern society, many transactions and dealings are based on all sorts of documents. These range from affidavits, cheques, notes, receipts, invoices, contracts, wills, title deeds, passports, marriage certificates and academic certificates and transcripts. It is important that these documents be genuine or authentic otherwise the integrity of myriad transactions and dealings based on them will be compromised. Those who tamper with such documents need to be punished in order to protect the sanctity and reliability of the documents. It is no wonder then that section 347 of the Penal Code provides that:

> Any person who forges any document is guilty of an offence which, unless otherwise stated, is a felony and is liable, unless owing to the circumstances of the forgery or the nature of the thing forged some other punishment, is provided to imprisonment for three years.

According to section 342 of the Code, 'Forgery is the making of a false document with intent to defraud or to deceive.'

1. *Actus Reus*

567. The *actus reus* of forgery offence is 'making a false document'. Save for providing in section 343 that 'document' does not include a trademark or any other sign used in connection with articles of commerce though they may be written or printed', the Code does not define what a document is. Fortunately, section 3 of the Evidence Act provides one. It states that '"document" means any matter expressed or described upon any substance by means of letters, figures or marks, or by more than one of these means intended to be used, or may be used, for the purpose of recording the matter'. The essence of a document, then, is that it conveys information-matter. The 'substance' upon which it may be expressed includes paper, parchment, cloth, skin, metal, wood[713] or any other material which is capable of being written on. The language of the document is irrelevant, as long as it has definite meaning to people who can decipher it. A bank note is not, however, a document within the meaning of section 351 of the Penal Code.[714] Section 345 lists instances of when a person is deemed to make a 'false document'.

a. 'Makes a Document Purporting To Be What in Fact It Is Not'

568. The document must tell a lie about itself. Thus where the person making the document does not have authority to make it or in making one he exceeds his authority then the document is false because it purports to be what it is not.[715] It would also appear that where a pay clerk prepares a requisition order and lists in it non-existent employees he makes a false document in the sense that the document

---

713. In *Gulamhusein Merali v. Rex* [1921–1952] 1 T.L.R. 358, a forgery was effected on a log of wood.
714. *Uganda v. Mbazira* [1973] E.A. 492.
715. See *R. v. Bateman* (1845) 1 Cox C.C. 184. Also see the Tanzanian case of *Ratensela v. Republic* [1969] E.A. 603.

purports to be a valid requisition made with authority.[716] In the *Cheeye* case, (*supra*, paragraph 484) the appellant, in an attempt to account for the way his company had used the money given to it for purposes of monitoring HIV/AIDS, TB, and malaria projects in the Rakai, Kabale, Mbarara and Ntungamo districts, instructed an accomplice to prepare 'receipts' showing how the money was used. Some of those 'receipts' showed that certain amounts of money were used on divers dates for paying for petrol at various petrol stations in respect of motor vehicles purportedly used to transport people in the course of the company's activities related to the HIV/AIDS, TB and malaria project. However it later transpired that one of these vehicles was a wheel loader caterpillar belonging to a construction company, which did not use petrol but diesel; another vehicle was an omnibus belonging to Mmengo Hospital which was never hired out to the appellant's company and did also use diesel and not petrol. The trial court held these documents to be false 'through and through', because they told lies about themselves; they purported to be what they were not. However, a document, otherwise authentic, is not a forgery merely because it contains falsehoods. Thus where a pay clerk in the course of his duties prepares salaries requisition order in which he includes inflated figures he does not thereby make a false document. The falsehood must be of the purport of the document, not its contents.[717]

b. 'Alters a Document without Authority in Such a Manner That if the Alteration Had Been Authorized it Would Have Altered the Effect of the Document'

569. The Kenyan case of *Chokwe v. Republic*[718] is in point here. The appellant was a station clerk at the Airways Corporation at Nairobi. He collected the sum of UGX 199 from a Rome-bound passenger as charges for excess baggage weighing 5 kilograms. He issued a receipt to the passenger. Thereafter the appellant made alterations on the retained carbon copies of the receipt as follows: he altered the name of the passenger from 'Goldsmith' to 'Goldsmithers'; he superimposed over the words ROM the words ENTEBBE; altered the excess baggage charge from UGX 39/80 to UGX 3/80, and altered the total payment received from UGX 199 to UGX 19. The appellant handed to his supervisor the duplicate receipts and the sum of UGX 19, while pocketing the balance. The High Court of Kenya confirmed his conviction for the forgeries.

c. 'Introduces in a Document without Authority Whilst It is Being Drawn Up Matter Which if It Had Been Authorized Would Have Altered the Effect of the Document'

570. This paragraph covers the scenario of a person who has authority to draw up a document but in the course of doing so introduces into it a certain matter without the authority of the person on whose behalf he purports to act. In so doing, he

716. See the Kenyan case of *Mbande v. Republic* [1971] E.A. 553 and the Tanzanian case of *Yeseya v. Republic* [1970] E.A. 667.
717. See *Baigumamu v. Uganda* [1973] E.A. 26.
718. [1969] E.A. 23.

changes the purport of the document. In this sense, this paragraph overlaps with paragraph (b).[719]

d. Signs a Document

(i) in the name of any person without his or her authority whether such name is or is not the same as that of the person signing;
(ii) in the name of any fictitious person alleged to exist, whether the fictitious person is or is not alleged to be of the same name as the person signing;
(iii) in the name represented as being the name of a different person from that of the person signing it and intended to be mistaken for the name of that person;
(iv) in the name of a person personated by the person signing the document, if the effect of the instrument depends upon the identity between the person signing the document and the person whom he or she professes to be.

571. One reported Ugandan case on this point is that of *Wombalugu v. Reginam.*[720] Here the appellant, a treasurer of a cooperative society, had to pay cash bonuses to members for cotton which they supplied to the society. The members acknowledged receipt of the bonuses by affixing their thumb marks on a document called a Multiple Payment Voucher. After a complaint over the appellant's conduct, it was discovered that thirteen thumb prints on the vouchers which purported to be those of different members of the society were in fact made by the appellant. The appellant was convicted of forgery. Another one is that of *Lukwago v. R.*[721] The appellant signed the name of a proposed guarantor on a Hire Purchase Agreement without that person's authority in order to secure a loan from a finance company. This was held to be making a false document.

2. *Mens Rea*

572. The *mens rea* for forgery is the intent to defraud or to deceive. The meaning of these terms has been discussed above. Suffice it to say that the prosecution may secure a conviction for forgery by proving either intent to deceive alone, as was the case in the *Wambalugu* case, *supra*, or intent to defraud. In the *Cheeye case, supra*, the court found that the documents in question were intended to deceive or to defraud the Programme Management Unit of the Ministry of Health; the appellant intended to induce the Unit to believe or accept them as true, though they were not. Proof of a general intent to defraud will be sufficient without having to prove intent to defraud a particular person. Note should also be made of section 346 of the Penal Code which provides as follows:

719. See *Mbande v. Republic, supra.*
720. [1956–1957] 8 U.L.R. 346.
721. H.Ct.Monthly Bulletin No. 34 of 1958.

> An intent to defraud is presumed to exist if it appears that at the time when the false document was made there was in existence a specific person ascertained or unascertained capable of being defrauded thereby, and this presumption is not rebutted by proof that the offender took or intended to take measures to prevent such person from being defrauded in fact, nor by the fact that he or she had or thought he or she had a right to the thing to be obtained by the false document.

Thus, in *Lukwago v. R.*, *supra*, the appellant sought to deny existence of intent to defraud by showing that he had paid some of the instalments due under the Hire Purchase Agreement. The High Court rejected his argument on two grounds. First, it was apparent from the evidence that the finance company would not have financed the transaction but for its belief that the purported guarantor had signed the Agreement as guarantor. The company was induced by the forged signature to act to its prejudice. Second, intent to defraud could exist without any intention to cause economic loss to the person defrauded.

B. Uttering

573. Section 351 of the Penal Code provides that 'Any person who knowingly utters a false document commits an offence of the same kind and is liable to the same punishment as if he had forged the thing in question.' Offence 'of the same kind' refers to the offence of forging a particular type of document mentioned in Chapter 34 of the Code.

574. Uttering is defined in section 2 of the Code to include 'using or dealing with and, attempting to induce any person to use, deal with or act upon the thing in question'. The essence of uttering is to use or to present to other people a false document and to induce them to act on it as if it were genuine. It is not necessary that the person to whom the document is presented is induced to act to his or her economic disadvantage. It is enough if an effort is made to induce him or her to act on it as if it were genuine. Thus presenting a false driving permit to the police and inducing them to forbear to prosecute the respondent was said to be uttering.[722]

575. It is also not relevant that the false document was forged outside the jurisdiction. Nor is it necessary that the person who utters it be physically within the jurisdiction.[723] What is important is that the people who are intended to be induced to act on the document are within the jurisdiction. The document uttered must, however, be false or a forgery in the sense discussed above.

576. The *mens rea* of the offence of uttering is using a false document 'knowingly and fraudulently'. To secure a conviction, therefore, the prosecution must prove that the accused knew that the document he or she was using or presenting

722. *Attorney-General of Uganda v. Ottii* [1957] E.A. 341.
723. See *Des Raj Sharma v. Reginam* [1953] 20 E.A.C.A. 310.

was false. It must also be shown that he or she intended to use or to present it to other people in order to induce them to act on it as if it were genuine.

§3. CRIMES AGAINST THE STATE AND PUBLIC ORDER

I. Crimes against the State

A. *Treason*

577. Treason is an offence aimed at the established political order. It is one of the most serious offences. It is punishable by death.

578. According to section 23 of the Penal Code, treason may be committed in any of the following ways:

(i) Levying war against the Republic of Uganda.
(ii) Unlawfully causing or attempting to cause the death of the President or, with intent to maim or disfigure or disable, unlawfully wounding or doing any harm to the person of the President or aiming at the person of the President any gun, offensive weapon, pistol or any description of firearms, whether the same contains any explosive or destructive substance or not.[724]
(iii) Contriving any plot, act or matter and expressing or declaring such act, plot or matter by any utterance or by any overt act in order, by force of arms, to overturn the Government as by law established. This has been the commonest form of treason that has been prosecuted in our courts. Although the Code talks of overturning 'the Government by law established', it does not thereby mean that the Government in question must have been established in accord with an existing constitution. Indeed, as it has been noted above, most Ugandan Governments have been established by force of arms. It is sufficient if that Government gained legitimacy by asserting effective control and authority over the population.[725] Regarding 'overt act', section 32 of the Code provides that 'every act in furtherance of the commission of the offence defined or every act of conspiracy with any person to effect that purpose and every act done in furtherance of the purpose by any of the persons conspiring, shall be deemed to be an overt act manifesting the intention'. More than one overt act may be alleged in the indictment, but it is not fatal to the indictment if only some and not all such acts are proved.[726]
(iv) Aiding or abetting another person in the commission of the above acts, or becoming an accessory before or after the fact to those acts, or concealing any of them. Under section 23(1)(d) of the Penal Code, aiding and abetting treason is a principal, and not a minor or cognate offence. In *Hofni Topacho Ongiretho & Anor v. Uganda*, the first appellant was charged under the old equivalent of

724. This is the equivalent of 'compassing the king's death' in Britain.
725. See *Uganda v. Commissioner of Prisons, Ex Parte Matovu* [1966] E.A. 514.
726. See *Uganda v. Yasin Amisi*, H.Ct.Cr.Session No. 4 of 1992 (unreported).

this provision with treason as a principal.[727] However, the trial judge fc that there was no evidence implicating him in any of the overt acts, but tha might have somehow facilitated in the plot. The judge therefore convicted of aiding and abetting under section 21(1)(c) instead. The Supreme C reversed, holding that the appellant should have been charged under the equivalent of section 23(1)(c). As he was not, the conviction could not st

(v) Forming an intention to compel by force or constrain the Government a law established to change its measures or counselling or intimidating or c awing the National Assembly, or instigating any person to invade Uganda armed force, and manifesting any such intention by an overt act or by uttering or by publishing any printing or writing.

(vi) Advisedly attempting to invite any person to commit an act of mutiny or treacherous or mutinous act, or inciting any such person to make or endea to make a mutinous assembly.

Who May Be Charged with Treason?

579. Any person, irrespective of nationality, who whilst on Ugandan terri commits any act of treason may be charged and, if convicted, punished by Uganda courts.[728] Any Uganda citizen or 'a person ordinarily resident in Uga who commits treasonable acts whilst outside Uganda and against Uganda may be charged and if convicted, punished by the Uganda courts.

B. Terrorism

580. The offence of terrorism was added to the Penal Code in 1984 as a resp by the Government of the day to the threat of guerrilla activities by various poli groups. Section 26(6) defines 'terrorism' to mean 'the use of violence or t thereof with intent to promote or achieve political ends in an unlawful manner includes the use of violence or threat thereof calculated to put the public in su fear as may cause discontent against the Government'. This is a bifurcated de tion, either of the two limbs having its own distinct constituent elements o offence.

Under the first limb, terrorism has an *actus reus* that involves use or threat of lence. Violence is not defined, but it might, in common parlance, involve us force by whatsoever means that results in personal injury and damage to prop The *mens rea* is the *dolus specialis* type. It is intent to promote political ends unlawful manner. Activities of rebel or liberation groups and other militant ac organizations with declared political goals will fall under this limb of the off

The *actus reus* of the second limb is also use or threat of violence as expla above but of a higher quantum and intensity. The *mens rea* is intention to pu public in fear or terror. This intent will usually be established by referring t degree and intensity of the violence unleashed or threatened. Such violence mu

727. *Hofni Topacho Ongiretho & Anor v. Uganda* Cr. App. No. 1 of 1993, [1994] UGSC 9 (4 1994).
728. See sec. 4(2) of the Penal Code.

both conspicuous and of widespread effect; otherwise, it will not be capable of occasioning public fear. This requirement will in turn often be established by referring to the means or type of weapons employed. Under this limb of terrorism, political motive is not necessary. Senseless violence by individuals or groups with no political agenda is an example of such violence. The matter is nevertheless complicated by the requirement that the fear engendered by the violence must be such 'as may cause discontent against the Government'. For example, a foreign terrorist may not care whether his or her actions result in discontent against the Government. Be that as it may, however, engaging in terrorist activities is criminal and is punishable by imprisonment up to life. Moreover, the Code empowers the minister responsible for internal security, with the prior approval of the cabinet, to declare any organization to be a terrorist organization. Membership or profession of membership and soliciting financial or other forms of support for such organizations is an offence punishable by up to ten years imprisonment.

II. Crimes against Public Order

A. *Unlawful Assembly and Riot*

581. Section 65(1) of the Penal Code provides that:

> When three or more persons assemble with intent to commit an offence, or being assembled with intent to carry out some common purpose, conduct themselves in such a manner as to cause persons in the neighbourhood reasonably to fear that the persons so assembled will commit a breach of the peace, or will by such assembly recklessly and without any reasonable occasion provoke other persons to commit a breach of the peace, they are an unlawful assembly.

It is immaterial that the original assembling was lawful if, being assembled, the people in the assembly conduct themselves with a common purpose in such a manner as aforesaid. An assembly or procession of three or more persons which neglects or refuses to disperse after the Inspector-General of police has outlawed it under the Police Act[729] is also an unlawful assembly. Section 66 of the Penal Code provides that, 'Any person who takes part in an unlawful assembly commits a misdemeanour and is liable to imprisonment for one year.'

582. As section 65(1) so clearly shows, there can be no offence unless the people assembled are at least three in number.[730] Second, they must be acting in concert. Mere presence at the place where other people have congregated does not necessarily import an assembly. The case of *Emmanuel Kayongo & Anor v. Regina*[731] is

729. Section 35.
730. In the Kenya Case of *R. v. Dishon Odinga* [1959] E.E. 12, four persons who by prior agreement went to the Nairobi railway station to exhibit placards to the view of visiting Sir Roy Welensky and others, were held to constitute a meeting.
731. H.Ct.Monthly Bulletin No. 3 of 1963.

in point. A police patrol car chased and stopped a car with twelve passengers in it and being driven by the first appellant. The first appellant was arrested and handcuffed. A crowd gathered and some people in the crowd assaulted the police party. The appellants were charged and convicted of taking part in a riot. The conviction was set aside on appeal, the High Court saying that:

> Here there was no evidence that the people assembled with intent to commit an offence or if they were assembled with intent to carry out some common purpose what that purpose was. The mere presence of the appellants at the scene did not mean that they were all animated by a common purpose within the meaning of Section 22 of the Penal Code in the assaults which were made on the police.

Furthermore, the persons assembled must have done so with the intention of committing an offence. In *Eryeza Munerya v. Uganda*,[732] for example, the appellant, a Muluka Chief, was engaged in arresting suspects in an assault case. He and his party forced their way into a house where the suspects were supposed to be. For reasons that are not apparent from the report, he was charged with and convicted of taking part in a riot. On appeal the conviction was set aside, as there was no evidence to show that the appellant assembled with intent to commit an offence but, instead, to arrest criminal suspects. Again, where persons are specifically charged with taking part in an unlawful assembly with intent to commit an offence, the charge sheet must specify the offence which they allegedly intended to commit. Failure to do so will vitiate the charge.[733]

583. If the purpose of the assembly is not to commit an offence but to carry out some common purpose, then there must be evidence to show that the people concerned conducted themselves in such a manner 'as to cause persons in the neighbourhood reasonably to fear that the persons so assembled will commit a breach of the peace, or will by such assembly recklessly and without any reasonable occasion provoke other persons to commit a breach of the peace'. It is pertinent to note that since the provision does not talk of conduct 'calculated to cause apprehension … ', there must be an actual causing of fear. Evidence that members of the assembly did in fact cause some members in the neighbourhood to apprehend a breach of the peace must be adduced.

Who are 'persons in the neighbourhood'? Must these people be living in or residents of the neighbourhood? Not necessarily. 'Persons in the neighbourhood' include any person who happens to be in the neighbourhood at the material time. This may include policemen or ordinary citizens.[734] Accepting policemen at the scene as persons in the neighbourhood thus enables the prosecution to use their apprehension as the basis for believing that a breach of the peace will be committed or that members of the neighbourhood will be provoked into doing so.

---

732. H.Ct.Monthly Bulletin No. 23 of 1966.
733. See *Chande & Anor. v. R.* [1961] E.A. 587. See also *Seleh Ahmed v. R.* [1961] E.A. 669.
734. See *Majawa v. Regina* [1959] R. & N.L.R. 52 dealing with an identical provision of the Nyasaland Penal Code.

584. An unlawful assembly degenerates into a riot when it begins to execute the purpose for which it assembled by committing acts that constitute a breach of the peace and 'to the terror of the public'. According to section 65(3), the persons so assembled are said to be 'riotously assembled' and are guilty of a misdemeanour and liable to imprisonment for one year.[735]

585. The expression 'to the terror of the public' has been interpreted by English courts to mean 'to alarm at least one person of reasonable firmness and courage'.[736] Evidence that someone has been alarmed or terrified must therefore be led to that effect. However, other authorities tend to suggest that it is not necessary to call a witness to say that 'I was terrified', but that it is sufficient to deduce from the evidence on record that the natural tendency of the conduct in question was to cause alarm to members of the public.[737] The Ugandan Courts seem to have followed the latter path, deducing terror from the general tenor of the conduct in question.[738]

586. Section 68 of the Penal Code empowers a magistrate or a police officer of or above the rank of inspector or any commissioned officer in the Uganda Armed Forces in whose view twelve or more persons are riotously assembled and who apprehends that such people are about to commit a riot, to make or cause to be made a Proclamation in the name of the President commanding those persons to disperse peacefully. If upon the expiration of a reasonable time they do not disperse, the person making the Proclamation is authorized to 'do all things necessary for dispersing the persons so continuing assembled, or for apprehending them or any of them'. If any of the rioters being apprehended resist, the person who made the Proclamation and those assisting him or her 'may use all such force as is reasonably necessary for overcoming such resistance, and shall not be liable in any criminal or civil proceeding for having, by the use of such force, caused harm or death to any person'.[739] It must be emphasized, however, that this provision does not license use of wanton force. Therefore where the force used is more than what was reasonably necessary, as was the case in the *Nakulabye Incident*, those responsible may be civilly or criminally responsible.[740]

587. To refuse to disperse after a Proclamation has been made is a felony, punishable by imprisonment for a term not exceeding five years.[741]

735. Section 66.
736. *Field & Anor. v. Receiver of Metropolitan Police* [1907] 2 K.B. 853.
737. *Regina v. Sharp* [1957] 2 W.L.R. 472. Here, Lord Goddard gives the example of the Trafalgar Square riots which took place towards the end of the nineteenth century, 'when most of the club windows in Pall Mall were smashed by an angry mob'. He goes on to say that, 'It would seem superfluous if someone had to go into the witness box and say that he or some passers-by felt or appeared afraid or apprehensive.'
738. See especially *Arafaeri Kirikarama & Anor. v. Uganda, supra.*
739. Section 69.
740. See *Muwonge v. Attorney-General of Uganda* [1967] E.A. 17.
741. Section 70.

B. Affray, Threatening Violence and Watching and Besetting, Etc.

588. Affray involves fighting in a public place. Section 79 of the Penal Code provides that, 'Any person who takes part in a fight in a public place commits a misdemeanour and is liable to imprisonment for one year.'

589. Fighting, the central element of the *actus reus* of the offence, means the unlawful display of force toward other people. If a person uses lawful force in his or her defence or defence of the person of someone else, or in lawfully effecting an arrest, he or she is not guilty of affray. Additionally, the use of force need not be jointly with another person, since the Code does not use language that requires taking part in 'a fight with another person'. A single individual may therefore be convicted of affray if he or she uses unlawful force against another, whether or not that other person fights back or submits. In one Kenya case, two persons were charged with 'jointly' fighting with each other. One pleaded guilty and was convicted. The other pleaded not guilty and was subsequently acquitted. On revision, the High Court quashed the first accused's conviction, since the acquittal of the second accused left no one with whom the first accused 'jointly' fought. The Court said:

> But for the wording of the particulars there would have been nothing inconsistent in the conviction of one accused and the acquittal of another on a charge of affray as it is not necessary to prove that each accused fought with each other. It is sufficient if each, or one of them, fought with a different person outside their number.[742]

590. The second important element of affray is that the fight must take place at a public place. Section 2 of the Code defines public place to include:

> any public way and any building, place or conveyance to which, for the time being, the public are entitled or permitted to have access either without any condition or upon condition of making any payment, and any building or place which is for the time being used for any public or religious meetings or assembly or as an open court.

In one case, the court held that the fact that a place was unfenced and abutted the highway was not enough to qualify it as public. To be considered public, a place must be one to which persons are in the habit of going without hindrance or interference.[743]

591. Threatening violence is covered by section 81 of the Penal Code. That section provides that:

> Any person who –

742. *Republic v. Mohamed* [1973] E.A. 238.
743. For example, see *Hassam v. R.* H.Ct.Monthly Bulletin No. 24 of 1959.

(a) with intent to intimidate or annoy any person, threatens to injure, assault, shoot or kill any person, or to burn, break or injure any property;
(b) with intent to alarm any person, discharges a firearm or commits any other breach of the peace, commits an offence and is liable to imprisonment for a period not exceeding four years.

In *Uganda v. Lochoro*,[744] the accused, a policeman at Iriri Police post, fired a rifle in the air within the police barracks. On being asked by the complainant, his superior, why he had fired the rifle, he told the complainant while pointing the gun at him, 'don't come near, I will kill you'. The complainant ultimately managed to wrest the rifle from the accused. It was held that the words used by the accused amounted to a threat within the meaning of section 81(a) of the Penal Code. It did not matter that the gun was unloaded at the time that the accused pointed it at the complainant, because the complainant did not know that it was unloaded. Moreover, it was debatable whether the accused himself knew that it was unloaded as he had just fired a shot from it. The court also held that the defence of intoxication was unavailable to the accused, because his conduct was incompatible with the conduct of a person who was insane from intoxication. It also indicated that he was able to form the intent of threatening the complainant.

592. Watching and besetting under section 82 of the Penal Code does not necessarily involve threats of violence. It entails keeping a vigil or keeping a person under close and constant observation as a way of harassing or bothering him or her. It is a form of picketing. Section 82(1) of the Penal Code provides that:

Any person who watches or besets –

(a) any premises or the approaches to such premises with a view to preventing any other person from doing any act which such other person has a legal right to do thereat; or
(b) the house or other place where any person resides or works or carries on business, or happens to be, or the approaches to such house or place, with a view of preventing such other person from doing or compelling him or her to do any act which such other person has a legal right to do or abstain from doing,

commits an offence and is liable to a fine not exceeding two thousand shillings or to imprisonment for a period not exceeding six months or to both such fine and imprisonment: except that the provisions of this section shall not apply to any watching or besetting which is lawful under the provisions of any law relating to trade unions or trade disputes.

Three points must be stressed. The first is that 'watching and besetting' is one offence and 'watching' and 'besetting' are different modes of committing it. The second is that as long as there has been some watching, it is not necessary that it be persistent or continuous for a considerable amount of time. For example, in *William*

744. [1982] H.Ct.Bulletin 80.

Sebugenyi v. R.,[745] the appellant stood on the road fronting the complainant's shop, telling the complainant's prospective customers not to buy goods from the shop. He stood there for about three minutes. It was held that as long as his conduct amounted to watching, its duration was irrelevant. The third point is that the *mens rea* of the offence is 'intent to preventing' the complainant from doing what he or she is legally entitled to do or not to do. To achieve this end, the accused need not talk to or threaten the complainant or any other person dealing with him or her. For example in *William Sebugenyi v. R.*, *supra*, the appellant did not talk to the complainant. Holding that his conduct amounted to watching or besetting, Bennet, Ag.C.J. said:

> A person who endeavours to persuade a shopkeeper's customers not to deal with him is endeavouring to prevent the shopkeeper from carrying on his business. That is precisely what the appellant did in the instant case and, in my view, the appellant's conduct came within the ambit of the section quite apart from any threats which he may have uttered to Odeke.[746]

593. Promoting sectarianism, which is covered by section 41, was added to the Code in 1988.[747] It prohibits the printing, publishing, making or uttering of any statement or doing any act which is likely to: (a) degrade, revile or expose to hatred or contempt; (b) create alienation or despondency; (c) raise discontent or disaffection; (d) promote, in any other way, feelings of ill-will or hostility among or against any group or body of persons on account of religion, tribe or ethnic or regional origin. The offence is punishable by imprisonment for a term not exceeding five years.

C. *Perjury*

594. The aim of the law of perjury is to enhance the quality of justice administered by the courts and other quasi-judicial bodies, by ensuring that the testimony given before such courts or bodies is truthful. The law punishes witnesses who deliberately tell lies before those courts or bodies. In so doing, it attempts to discourage lies and to deter liars. According to section 94(1) of the Penal Code:

> Any person who, in any judicial proceeding, or for the purpose of instituting any judicial proceeding, knowingly gives false testimony touching any matter which is material to any question then pending in that proceeding or intended to be raised in that proceeding, commits the misdemeanour termed perjury.

The proceedings at which perjury may be committed are not limited to court proceedings. Section 2 of the Penal Code defines 'judicial proceedings' to include 'any proceedings had or taken in or before any court, tribunal, commission of inquiry, or person, in which evidence may be taken on oath'. According to section 94(2), it is not necessary that the evidence be given on oath; it suffices if it is given under some

745. [1959] E.A. 411.
746. *Ibid.*, at 412.
747. See the Penal Code (Amendment) Statute, 1988.

other sanction authorized by law. This would cover evidence given on affirmation. Again, the evidence need not be given orally; it may be in writing in the form of, say, affidavits and depositions. The constitution of the court or tribunal or the place where it is held does not matter either, as long as it 'actually acts as a court or tribunal in which the testimony is given'.

595. To amount to perjury, the evidence given must not only be false, but the witness who gives it must also know that it is false at the time he or she gives it. This knowledge may be inferred from the evidence as a whole. The mere fact that a witness has on two different occasions made two contradictory statements on oath does not per se amount to perjury, 'For there are occasions upon which a person might honestly and conscientiously swear to a fact from the best of his recollection and belief, and, from other circumstances at a subsequent time, be convinced that he was wrong, and swear the reverse without meaning to swear falsely either time.'[748] Therefore, the fact that the accused in one case admits having made two contradictory statements at a trial was held does not mean that she thereby pleaded guilty to a charge of perjury.[749] However, section 95(1) [added to the Code by Act 1 of 1966 and Act 9 of 1984] now limits the application of this rule to 'person accused of an offence to which the proceedings relate'. Any other witness who makes contradictory statements 'with intent to deceive' may be guilty of an offence billed as 'making false statements'.

596. Where a person pleads not guilty to a charge of perjury it is important that the falsity of the statement in question be proved by the testimony of at least two witnesses who were present at the trial where the statement was made.[750] Those witnesses must testify orally, although they may be allowed to refresh their memory by referring to the record of the case.[751] Additionally, it must be proved that the alleged false statement was 'material to any question then pending in that proceeding'.[752] It must be one that might have affected the outcome of the case or matter that was being tried or investigated. False statements affecting a witness's credibility, though not germane to the substantive issues to be resolved, are material. As Lord Russell said, 'The defendant's answers would affect his credit as a witness, and all false statements, wilfully and corruptly made, as to matter which affect his credit, are material.'[753]

748. *Rex v. Jackson* 198 E.R. 1037. Cited with approval in *Rex v. Apili d/o Elok* [1932–1935] 5 U.L.R. 64.
749. *Rex v. Apili d/o Elok, ibid.*
750. See sec. 98 of the Penal Code.
751. *Rex v. Apili d/o Elok, supra.*
752. See *Manga Bhula v. Rex* [1936–1951] 6 U.L.R. 240.
753. *R. v. Baker* [1895] 1 Q.B. 797, 799.

III. Corruption

A. General

597. The aim of the law of corruption is to maintain integrity, honesty and uprightness in the public service, and to rid the service of graft and venality. It aims at ensuring that those in the service serve the public efficiently, fairly, and without showing favour to anyone. It forbids the offering or receiving of inducements or gratifications for what the public servant is supposed to do as part of his or her duties. Were the law to countenance such inducements or gratifications then members of the public that are unable to pay will not be served, or the quality of the service they receive will be poor. Corruption, particularly that which involves bribing the police, inspectors of buildings, hotels, factories, schools and other institutions that serve the public as well as of members of licensing authorities, lowers standards and endangers public safety. Corruption as currently practised in Uganda is no longer restricted to petty bribery. It involves massive theft and plunder of public resources at a grand scale by powerful politicians and public officials. It can have extreme consequences. In the *Cheeye* case, where the appellant converted to his personal uses UGX 120,000,000 meant for anti-HIV/AIDS, TB, and Malaria activities in four districts, Justice Katutsi described the appellant's conduct as follows:

> In siphoning funds meant to alleviate and ease the sufferings of the wretched of the earth, the victims of HIV/AIDS, TB, and Malaria into his own stomach, he is no better than a mass murderer, which in truth he is! Think of hundreds of thousands of the victims of HIV/AIDS, TB, and Malaria who include innocent children from whom he robbed the little opportunity to receive a bit of comfort, nay a new lease of life and you will know what beast he is.[754]

Additionally, grand corruption can scare away foreign and domestic investors into the economy and the withholding of vital foreign aid in government sectors that are vital to the welfare of the people and for the development of the country.[755] Ultimately, corruption results not only in inefficiency and erosion of confidence in the public service but also in gross social injustice, political decay and economic stagnation. It is the aim of the law to stem the tide of the plunder of national resources and to ensure social, economic and political well-being of citizens.

598. The law on corruption is contained in the Anti-Corruption Act, 2009.[756] This Act culls from the Penal Code all offences under chapter IX titled 'Corruption

754. *Uganda v. Teddy Sseezi Cheeye*, Cr. Case No. 1254 of 2008, [2009] UGHC 12 (8 Apr. 2009).
755. *Donors Slash government aid over corruption*, Daily Monitor, 16 Nov. 2011. The Dutch Government cut off aid to Uganda worth 50 billion Uganda Shillings designed to combat illiteracy in the country, citing corruption by Uganda Government officials in the use of the funds. The United Kingdom also suspended aid to Uganda in 2012 over allegations that it was being misused in the Prime Minister's Office. See www.theguardian.com/global-development/2012/nov/uk-suspends-aid-uganda-misuse.
756. Cap. 121.

and the Abuse of Office'[757] and property-related offences committed by public officials,[758] and combines them under one statute. Some of these offences have been dealt with in earlier sections of this book and will not be repeated. Only a few of the rest are highlighted here.

B. Corruption

599. Section 2 of the Anti-Corruption Act lists nine acts which it characterizes as 'corruption'. This discussion restricts itself to: a public official soliciting or accepting a gratification in exchange for an act or omission in the performance of his or her public functions; an outsider offering a public official a gratification in exchange for an act or omission in the performance of his or her public functions; offering a gratification to a person working in the private sector to induce that person to act or refrain from acting in breach of his or her duties; promising, in consideration of a reward to influence decisions in the public or private sector. This would include lobbyists influencing members of legislative bodies to pass or not to pass certain legislation; diverting public property a person receives on behalf of a public body for his or her personal use; and neglect of duty. Some of the key terms or expressions in this provision include 'gratification', 'public official' and, 'any other person or entity'.

600. In common parlance, the term 'gratification' means reward or something given to gain a favour; it is a bribe. Section 1 of the Anti-Corruption Act defines gratification as including money or any gift, loan, fee, reward, commission, valuable security, or other property or interest in property of any description, whether moveable or immoveable. It also includes any office, employment or contract, any payment, release, discharge or liquidation of any loan, obligation or other liability whatsoever, whether in whole or in part. It also includes any other service, favour or advantage of any description whatsoever, including protection from any penalty or disability incurred or apprehended or from any action or proceedings of a disciplinary or penal nature, whether or not instituted, and including the exercise or the forbearance from the exercise of any right or any official power or duty. An offer, undertaking, or promise of gratification also falls within the ambits of the term.

601. The person who solicits, accepts or is offered the gratification must be 'a public official', an employee of 'a public body'. The Anti-Corruption Act also defines the expression 'public body' in the broadest possible terms. It includes the Government and all departments, services or undertakings of the Government, the East African Community and all its institutions and corporations, the Cabinet, Parliament, any court, any district council and any committee thereof, any

757. The offences include: abuse of office, officers charged with administration of property of a special character, unauthorized administration of oaths, false assumption of authority, personating public officers and threat of injury to persons employed in public service.

758. These offences include embezzlement, causing financial loss, fraudulent disposal of trust property, false accounting by public officer, fraudulent false accounting, false claims by officials and false certificates by public officers.

corporation, committee, board, commission or similar body whether corporate or incorporate established by an Act of Parliament for the purposes of any written law relating to the public health or public undertaking of public utility, education, or for promotion of sports, literature, science, arts or any other purpose for the benefit of the public or any section of the public to administer funds or properly belonging to or granted by the Government, its institutions or its corporations or money raised by public subscription, rates, taxes, cess, or charges in pursuance of any written law. It also includes political parties, trade unions, societies registered under the Cooperative Societies Act, the Societies Act, any council, board, committee or society established by an Act of Parliament for the benefit, regulation and control of any profession and non-governmental organizations.

602. Section 2 of the Anti-Corruption Act also provides that the gratification may be paid to or received by the recipient for himself or herself or 'for any other person'. The Court of Appeal for Eastern Africa has interpreted this expression to mean any other person 'in whom the accused is interested such as, for example, a relative, friend, or superior, so that the gratification to the third party may itself be a gratification to the accused'.[759] Therefore, where a person obtains a benefit on behalf of another, in which he is entirely disinterested he does not do so corruptly.

603. For a public official to accept a reward for doing what he or she is already employed and remunerated to do or to forbear to do, is not only theft and unjust enrichment but also disloyalty to the employer. The official would be influenced by the person paying the gratification to do what is right or just or to forbear to do what is right and just. As the Holy Scriptures admonish, 'Do not accept a bribe, for a bribe blinds those who see and twists the words of the righteous.'[760] When received by judges, magistrates and others employed in the administration of justice, bribes pervert the course of justice, eviscerate the courts and their decisions of authority and legitimacy, erode public respect for and confidence in the justice system and ultimately may tempt aggrieved members of the public to take self-help measures to vindicate their rights – with catastrophic consequences. Corruption is thus a threat to public order and to national security.

C. Corrupt Transactions with Agents

604. Section 3 of the Anti-Corruption Act provides as follows:

> If,
>
> (a) any agent corruptly accepts or obtains, or agrees to accept or attempts to obtain, from any person, for himself or herself or for any other person, any gratification as an inducement or reward for doing or forbearing to do, or for having done or forborne to do, any act in relation to his or her principal's affairs or business, or for showing or forbearing to show favour

759. *Attorney-General v. Shemba Ali Kajembo* [1958] E.A. 505.
760. Exodus 23: 8 (NIV).

or disfavour to any person in relation to his or her principal's affairs or business; or

(b) any person corruptly gives or agrees to give or offers any gratification to any agent as an inducement or reward for doing or forbearing to do, or for having done or forborne to do any act in relation to his or her principal's affairs ... ; or

(c) any person knowingly gives to an agent, or if an agent knowingly uses, with intent to deceive his or her principal, any receipt, account or other document in respect of which the principal is interested, and which contains any statement which is false or erroneous or defective in any material particular, and which to his or her knowledge is intended to mislead the principal, he or she commits an offence.

The offence created under this section may be committed by any agent, whether of a private employer or of a public body. Its purpose is to promote fidelity among agents or persons in positions of trust. The term 'agent' is defined under section 1 of the Act to mean:

> any person employed by or acting for another, and includes a trustee, administrator and executor, and a person employed in the public service or under any corporation or public body ... and includes a sub-contractor or any person employed by or acting for sub-contractor.'

'Principal' is similarly defined to include 'an employer, a beneficiary under a trust, and a trust estate as though it were a person and any person beneficially interested in the estate of a deceased person and ... Government or public body.

605. It is worth noting that 'principal's affairs or business' is not necessarily limited to 'lawful' activities. An agent who corruptly accepts a gratification for doing any act in relation to his or her principal's affairs may be convicted although those affairs were not strictly lawful. As the Court of Appeal for Eastern Africa remarked in a case originating from Tanzania, 'Illegal acts by the principal do not negative the illegality of the acts of the agents', particularly where the acts were, as far as the agent was aware, perfectly lawful and proper.[761] Again, a person who accepts a gratification in relation to his or her principal's affairs or business which is beyond the scope of his or her employment will not escape liability for corruption. This point is illustrated by the case of *Haji Moledina & Anor. v. R.*[762] where a police officer offered to drop a prosecution even though he had no power to do so, and it was not lawful for him to do so.[763]

606. In addition to titling the offence we are discussing here as 'Corrupt Transanctions with Agents', section 3 of the Anti-Corruption Act repeatedly uses the

761. *The Attorney-General v. Jerome Silvester Chisonga* [1961] E.A. 312.
762. [1960] E.A. 678.
763. See also the Kenya case of *Ouko v. Republic* [1966] E.A. 286 where a police officer corruptly received money from a man whose son had been sentenced to a term in prison, promising that he would get the son released.

term 'corruptly' to qualify the forbidden actions of the agents and other persons. This is the *mens rea* or mental element that must accompany the conduct that the Act forbids – receiving, agree to receive, or attempt to obtain, accept, give, agree to give, offer, etc. The Act does not define the term. The Court of Appeal for Eastern Africa did so in cases originating from Tanzania and Kenya. In the Tanzanian case of *Rex v. Akbarali K. Jetha*,[764] the Court stated:

> The essence of the offence of official corruption is the motive which animates the giver; if he gives either on account of some past act or omission in his favour, or with the hope and expectation that his gift may influence the donee that something may thereafter be done or omitted in his favour the offence is complete. It is not necessary that there should be a corrupt and express bargain between the giver and the donee.[765]

This dictum was followed in the Kenyan case of *Sewa Singh Mandia v. Republic*.[766] The appellant was a magistrate. On the day in question, he was a fee-paying passenger in a certain vehicle. That vehicle was stopped by a policeman who noted certain defects on it. The policeman solicited a bribe in order to forbear from pressing charges. The driver told him that he did not have change. The appellant volunteered to pay and did pay UGX 15 to the policeman who, as a result, tore up the piece of paper on which he had noted the defects of the vehicle. The appellant subsequently summoned the policeman to his chambers and reprimanded him for taking the bribe. He also recovered his money from the policeman. The appellant later reported the matter to senior police officers. Surprisingly, the police subsequently charged him with corruption; he was convicted. At his trial, he told the court that he had paid the policeman because, 'I had heard of these things and I wanted to know if it was real.' On a second appeal, the Court of Appeal for Eastern Africa, relying on the above *Jetha* case and others, set aside the conviction, holding that the appellant did not act corruptly. The Court cited the following passage from the English case of *Bradford Election Petition* (No. 2):[767]

> Now what is the meaning of that word 'corruptly'? It is difficult to tell; but I am satisfied that it means a thing done with an evil mind or an evil intention; and except there be an evil mind or an evil intention accompanying the act it is not corruptly done.

The Court found that the appellant had no 'evil mind' or 'evil intention.' It based its finding on the appellant's conduct in reporting the incident to the senior police officers.[768]

---

764. [1947] 14 E.A.C.A. 122.
765. *Ibid.*, at 123.
766. [1966] E.A. 315.
767. (1869) 19 L.T. 723, 728.
768. In *R. v. Carr* [1957] 1 W.L.R. 165, 166, a case cited in the *Mandia* case, *supra*, Goddard, C.J., said: 'Of course, if a person takes a bribe and goes straight off to someone in authority and says, "here is the bribe he has given me", that may show he was not acting corruptly.'

D. Corruptly Procuring Tenders

607. Section 4 of the Anti-Corruption Act deals with this matter and provides as follows:

> A person,
>
> (1) (a) who, with intent to obtain from any public body a contract for performing any work, providing any service, material or substance, offers any gratification to any person who has made a tender for such contract, as an inducement or a reward for his or her withdrawing such a tender; or
>
> (b) who solicits or accepts any gratification as an inducement or reward for his or her withdrawing a tender made by him or her for such contract, commits an offence.
>
> (2) A public official, who provides any information relating to a tender for –
>
> (a) performing any works;
>
> (b) providing any service; or
>
> (c) supplying any article, material or substance to enable a person obtain the tender from the public body, to the prejudice of another person interested in the tender, commits an offence.

It is noteworthy that though section 4 of the Anti-Corruption Act titles this crime as 'Corruptly Procuring Tenders', it does not at all use the term 'corruptly', as does section 3 dealing with 'Corrupt Transactions with Agents'. Subsection (1) employs the words 'with intent' to describe the requisite mental element that must accompany the offering of the gratification. However, subsection (2) dealing with supplying information to a person's competitor does not use any words to indicate the requisite mens rea that must accompany the accused person's actions. It is therefore suggested that the courts should read the word 'corruptly', as discussed above, when they are dealing with this crime. That appears to have been the intention of the legislature.

E. Bribery of Public Officers

608. Section 5 of the Anti-Corruption Act defines the offence as follows:

> A person who,
>
> (a) directly or indirectly by himself or herself or through any other person offers, gives or agrees to offer any gratification to any member of a public body an inducement or reward so that the member -
>
> (i) votes or abstains from voting at any meeting of such public body in favour of or against any measure, resolution or question submitted to such public body;

(ii) performs, or abstains from performing his or her duty in procuring, expediting, delaying, hindering or preventing the performance of any official act; or

(iii) aids in procuring or preventing the passing of any vote or the granting of any contract or advantage in favour of any person; or

(b) being a member as is referred to in paragraph (a) directly or indirectly solicits or accepts any gratification for himself or herself, or through any other person, as an inducement or reward for any act or any abstaining from performing any act, referred to in sub-paragraphs (i), (ii) and (iii) of paragraph (a),

commits an offence.

The offence of 'bribery of public officials', as defined above, focuses on members of legislative or deliberative bodies, including Members of Parliament. It is not limited to their activities inside their legislative chambers; it extends to anything they do in and outside the chambers as people's representatives, including interceding or making representations on behalf of their constituents with government departments.[769] The law aims at ensuring that members of these bodies perform their duties selflessly, honestly, impartially, for public interest or the interest of sections of the public that fall under their mandate. Payment to or acceptance of gratifications by members of legislative bodies does clearly sway and deflect them from achieving this desideratum. Members of Parliament, in particular, are elected to assist Parliament to execute its awesome function of enacting laws 'for the peace, order development, and good governance of Uganda' (Article 79(1) of the Constitution). Payment to or acceptance of bribes is not only despicable but also results in the MPs acting in the interest of their bribers and not in the interest of the public. It is the briber who acts and not the MPs. This practice eviscerates the legitimacy of the laws that the MPs enact and other decisions that they make. It seriously erodes public confidence in Parliament and is, ultimately, an affront to representative government and to democracy in general.

F. Abuse of Office

609. Section 11 of the Anti-Corruption Act defines the offence of abuse of office. It has four essential elements: (1) the alleged perpetrator must be an employee of a public body, or of a company in which the Government has shares; (2) the perpetrator must do an arbitrary act; (3) the act must be prejudicial to the interests of the employer or of any other person; and (4) the act must be in abuse of the perpetrator's authority of his or her office.

Uganda v. Chemisto A. Mashandich & Anor. is a case in point.[770] The first accused was Town Clerk and the second accused the Town Treasurer of Kapchorwa Town Council. They were charged with and convicted on several counts of abuse of

769. See *Attorney General of Ceylone v. Livera & Anor.* [1963] A.C. 331.

770. Cr. Case No 2 of 2010, [2010] UGHC 50 (13 Sep. 2010).

office in respect of the manner in which they authorized payments for services rendered or goods supplied to the Council. The regular procedure was that before any payment was authorized a contract had to be awarded first. When the person awarded the contract performed the contract or part of it, that person made a claim for payment. In case of road works or the like, the Town Engineer inspected the work done and then issued a payment certificate in respect of the completed work. A payment voucher was then prepared; both the Town Clerk and Town Treasurer had to sign the voucher and the cheque where payment was by cheque. On several occasions, however, the first and second accused approved payments to various people without a claim or certificate of payment for completed work. On other occasions, they approved payments for work that was never performed or for goods that were never supplied or received by the Town Council. Clearly, to approve payments in such circumstances the accused acted arbitrarily; their conduct was a perverse use of their authority – an abuse of office; their actions were prejudicial, or detrimental and damaging to the interests of the Town Council in that its money was given out for services that were not rendered or goods not supplied.

The conduct of the appellant in *Kassim Mpanga v. Uganda* was just as prejudicial.[771] He was employed as a branch manager of the Libyan Arab Uganda Bank, a company in which the Government held shares. Without authorization from the General Manager and contrary to the bank's policy he granted almost twenty-six overdrafts without security. Confirming his conviction for abuse of office, the Supreme Court said that 'there could not have been a more arbitrary act and flagrant abuse of authority of the appellant's office'. On prejudice, the court said:

> [If] money was lent without approval and without security as the appellant did in the instant case, it meant that the interests of the Bank were put at great risk. The Bank stood the risk of not only losing the principal sums but also the interests thereon. This was prejudicial to the Bank's interests. Indeed, as evidence proved, the money so lent by the appellant was unrecoverable although all possible efforts to that end were made, but without success.

For abuse of office, it is not necessary to prove actual loss. However, because the prosecution used the same transactions to allege causing financial loss, they showed the loss that the bank incurred.

G. *Causing Financial Loss*

610. According to section 20 of the Anti-Corruption Act, the offence of causing financial loss is committed where: (1) an employee of a public body, financial institution or insurance company; (2) does an act or makes an omission; (3) in the course of his or her duties; (4) knowing or having reason to believe; (5) that such act or omission will cause financial loss to his or her employer. Unlike abuse of office, the offence of causing of financial loss requires that loss be proved.

---

771. Cr. App. No. 30 of 1994, [1995] UGSC 14 (13 Sep. 1995).

In the *Mpanga* case (*supra*, paragraph 609), the Supreme Court said that 'loss' was a concept that could not be cast in hard and fast terms, but was broad enough to include 'damage', 'deprivation', 'detriment' and 'privation'. It also stated that a thing could be said to be lost after reasonable time has passed to allow for a diligent search for and recovery of the thing but the search turns out to be fruitless. Thus in that case the court held that the appellant's act of paying out overdrafts without security and without authority had caused financial loss to the bank. This was so because the bank's efforts to recover the overdrafts proved fruitless in at least twenty-nine overdrafts, and there was no hope of success. As to whether the appellant knew or had reason to know that his acts would result in financial loss, the court held that he did. First, he acted in complete disregard of authority. Second, he acted deliberately in that in his defence he said that he gave out overdrafts without security because it was integrity and not security that was important. Third, he hid ledger cards of the accounts in question and destroyed others of overdrawn accounts – all evidence of guilt knowledge.

In the *Mashandich* case (*supra*, paragraph 609), the first and second accused persons were also charged with several counts of causing financial loss. They approved and paid out various amounts of money to companies with which the Town Council had no contracts and for work that the companies did not perform, thus causing financial loss to the Council. They were convicted. When passing sentence for both offences of abuse of office and causing financial loss, the court remarked:

> There is no doubt the people of Kapchorwa Town Council and Uganda at large looked up to the three gentlemen in the dock as stewards who would appropriately work towards the improvement of their living conditions. Instead the supposed stewards chose to fleece their flock by betraying the trust bestowed in them. They became sleaze bags. They must be held accountable.

In addition to imposing prison terms, the court ordered the accused to pay various sums as compensation to the Town Council for the losses it incurred as a result of their crimes.

Chapter 8. Punishment

§1. Concept and Aims of Punishment

I. Concept of Punishment

611. Punishment is the infliction of suffering by a duly authorized person on another person who has been duly convicted of an offence and on account of that offence.

612. In essence, punishment is unpleasant or supposed to be unpleasant to the person who receives it. It may involve infliction of bodily pain, such as corporal punishment or the ultimate penalty – death. It may also involve deprivation of something of value to the recipient such as personal liberty, property, disqualification from certain activities such as driving an automobile, practising a profession or carrying on a particular trade. The unpleasantness of the punishment is believed to meet the ends of criminal law: deterrence and retributive justice. Were a duly convicted criminal allowed to go scot-free or get away with what he or she has done, this may appear as a reward to him. This treatment may not only embolden the offender in his or her criminal ways, but may also encourage others to emulate his or her example. It would, in a way, also amount to an injustice to the law-abiding members of the community.

613. Judging by its severity in the past, punishment was indeed unpleasant. It included death which was inflicted in the cruelest way imaginable. It also included maiming, castration, mutilation, blinding, torture, public humiliation and ridicule, banishment, exile or deportation to foreign countries. These forms of punishment were practised by our forebears, not only here in Uganda but also elsewhere in the world. For example, it is reported that in Britain by 1800, over two hundred offences were punishable by death. Professor Fitzgerald writes:

> In some cases the carrying out of the sentence was accompanied by savage tortures, the victim being dragged to the scaffold, mutilated, and disemboweled. Even young children were not exempt from barbarous penalties of this nature.[772]

With the spread of civilization and the refining of human sentiments, these forms of punishment became less and less acceptable. They are today prohibited by International Human Rights law as cruel, inhuman and degrading. This prohibition is reflected in our Constitution and penal laws.

614. Punishment can only be prescribed by one who is authorized to do so by the law. It must also be sanctioned by one who has authority over the person being punished. The state and its duly authorized subdivisions or units have authority over

772. See P.J. Fitzgerald, *Criminal Law and Punishment* 208 (Oxford U. Press 1962).

inhabitants residing in their respective areas of jurisdiction. Because they have the primary duty of maintaining law and order, protecting the liberty and property of the inhabitants, they have the right and duty to proscribe anti-social conduct and to prescribe and impose punishment on the errant and disruptive members in their communities. Individuals, outside the legitimate and circumscribed bounds of self-defence, have no right to inflict suffering on others on account of what those people have done to them. Self-help and personal revenge are antithetical to a well-ordered civil society and cannot be countenanced. As Professor Fitzgerald has observed, 'A society which allowed blood feuds, vendettas, self-help, and private measures of justice, would find itself overrun by anarchy.'[773]

615. Lastly, it must be emphasized that the person being punished must have committed, and been tried and convicted of an offence. Needless to say, the offence must exist in law. It is only then that he deserves to be punished for the good of society and of himself or herself. In this connection, it should also be pointed out that punishment is personal and cannot be passed on to another person. It must be inflicted only on the person who committed and was convicted of the offence in question. He or she is the one who is at odds with society and needs to be deterred and reformed.

II. Aims of Punishment

616. The primary goal of punishment today is prevention of crime and, ultimately, the protection of society. This goal is attained through deterrence, incapacitation, reformation and rehabilitation, and denunciation. The other goals are retribution and atonement.

617. Deterrence. By deterrence, we mean the inhibition of criminal behaviour by fear of punishment. By subjecting the offender to unpleasant treatment, the law expects to evoke in the offender a determination to go straight and to not commit further offences lest he or she be punished again. This determination is most likely to be made by a person who acknowledges that he or she has been dealt with justly at all stages of the criminal justice system, and that he or she has nobody to blame but himself or herself. From this standpoint, then, it is important that the criminal justice system be as fair as possible and also appear to be so. The resolve not to revert to crime is also most likely to be made by first offenders to whom punishment is a shock. In this respect, too, it is important that such offenders continue to have an abhorrence of punishment and a desire to be relieved from it. They must not, because of the nature or duration of the punishment, get anaesthetized to it and thus become indifferent to it. Short and sharp sentences, where this is possible, are thus the most efficacious for deterrence purposes.

773. P.J. Fitzgerald, *Criminal Law and Punishment* 200 (Oxford U. Press 1962).

618. Punishing an offender also makes him an example to the public as to what the consequences of committing crime may be. This helps to deter would-be offenders, and is important for preventing crime.

619. Incapacitation. Certain forms of punishment, particularly the death penalty and imprisonment, by putting the offender out of circulation, ensure that he or she is incapacitated and not at large to continue with his criminal activities. The offender's incapacitation affords the public protection from the offender for the time he or she is away.[774] By the time he or she returns to the community, where the punishment is not death, it is hoped that he or she would have reformed. However, reformation largely depends on how the offender is treated while he or she remains incapacitated. Sadly treatment, when it is improper, may have the undesirable effect of turning the offender into an incorrigible criminal.

620. Reformation and Rehabilitation. These are also goals of punishment. The idea behind them is that punishment helps the offender to mend his or her ways and to become a responsible, useful and law-abiding citizen. The attainment of this goal depends largely on the form of punishment imposed and the way it is carried out.

621. Retribution and atonement. By committing a crime, the criminal makes himself or herself an outcast or an outlaw from society. By killing or injuring a citizen, he or she robs or deprives society of the company and services of that citizen. By taking, damaging, or destroying property, private or public, he or she deprives society of its use. By disturbing the peace, he or she interferes with the general quiet and peaceful life in the community. In a word, by committing crime, the criminal injures society. He or she owes it 'a debt'. Punishment thus serves as the expiation for this wrong and the means wherewithal the criminal is reconciled back to society. To achieve this goal, the courts endeavour to impose sentences that the offender deserves; their severity must be proportionate to the seriousness of the offence committed and to the degree of harm occasioned by the offender's conduct. In the past retribution and atonement imported notions of revenge. However, today penal theory puts more emphasis on just deserts rather than on revenge. Revenge does not necessarily protect society from crime, it does not heal wounds caused by crime; it seems to be out of step with modern standards of civilisation.

---

774. In *SGT Canbera Dickson v. Uganda*, Cr. App. No. 284 of 2003, [2010] UGCA 25 (6 Jun. 2010), the appellant was a thirty-year army sergeant. He killed his maternal uncle and went on to rape the complainant at gun point. The Court of Appeal upheld his conviction for rape. It also enhanced his sentence from ten to twenty-five years imprisonment. In doing so, the court said:' [T]he appellant was entrusted with the gun which was bought by the people of Uganda to guard them. Instead he abused with impunity the trust put in him. *If the death penalty was intended to terminate a dangerous person from society, then where the court is reluctant to impose it to a young offender like the appellant, it must however impose such an appropriate custodial sentence so as to ensure that society will be in peace for a reasonably long period of time.* In the circumstances of this case, a sentence of 15 years was very much on the lower side … We enhance the sentence from 15 years to 25 years.' [Emphasis added]

622. *Denunciation.* By prohibiting certain conduct, by prescribing a punishment for its perpetration, and by imposing it on the offender, the law reminds the offender that the prohibition was not an empty threat. By the sentence that it imposes, the court expresses the public revulsion to and condemnation of the crime that the offender committed. Again, through the sentence, the court endeavours to educate the offender and prospective offenders alike that crime does not pay. It also demonstrates to them the authorities' determination to enforce the law. As the International Criminal Tribunal for the former Yugoslavia (ICTY) so aptly stated:

> The purpose [of punishment] is to deter the specific accused as well as others, which means not only the citizens of Bosnia and Herzegovina but persons worldwide from committing crimes in similar circumstances against international humanitarian law.[775] The Trial Chamber is further of the view that another relevant sentencing purpose is to show the people of not only the former Yugoslavia, but of the world in general, that there is no impunity for these types of crimes. This should be done in order to strengthen the resolve of all involved not to allow crimes against international humanitarian law to be committed as well as to create trust in and respect for the developing system of international criminal justice.[776]

623. Ugandan courts have echoed similar sentiments. Thus in *Mugasa Joseph v. Uganda* while enhancing a sentence in a case involving defilement, the Court of Appeal said the following:

> After hearing both parties on this matter, we are totally dismayed that despite the fact that this offence of defilement attracts a death sentence, some people continue to defile babies with impunity. We think that it is high time courts raised (sic) [rose] up with Parliament and society as a whole to deal with this continuing menace. We feel that it is high time that the courts passed sentences that will send a message to society that enough is enough and that violating the rights of child females must stop.
>
> We find that the sentence of 17 years was on the lenient side where the appellant was a church official and a relative of the child who should have protected her. Though the state did not appeal, the court has powers to enhance the sentence as already stated.

775. *Prosecutor v. Anto Furundžija,* Case No. IT-95-17/1, Judgement, 10 Dec. 1998, para. 288. In discussing its sentencing policy, the Trial Chamber went on to state: 'It is the mandate and the duty of the International Tribunal, in contributing to reconciliation, to deter such crimes and to combat impunity. It is not only right that *punitur quia peccatur* (the individual must be punished because he broke the law) but also *punitur ne peccatur* (he must be punished so that he and others will no longer break the law). The Trial Chamber accepts that two important functions of the punishment are retribution and deterrence.'

776. *Prosecutor v. Zoran Kupreškić, Mirjan Kupreškić, Vlatko Kupreškić, Drago Josipović, and Dragan Papić,* Case No. IT-95-16-T, Trial Chamber Judgement, 14 Jan. 2000, para. 848.

> We accordingly set aside the sentence of 17 years ans substitute it with a sentence of 25 years imprisonment.[777]

As the statements from both the ICTY and from our Court of Appeal reveal, the aims of sentencing are inter-related and can be achieved in one and the same sentence. It is however important that the sentencing judge bears them in mind as he or she considers the sentencing options in any particular case.

§2. The Sentencing Process

I. General Principles

624. In accord with the principle of legality, *nulla poena sine lege*, all offence-creating statutes prescribe punishments for the offences that they create. This enables any person who might be planning any course of criminal conduct to know in advance the consequences of such conduct. The Penal Code does also provide for punishments for every offence it creates. It does so by either specifying the punishment or by simply classifying the particular offence as a felony or a misdemeanour. As it has been noted in the general introductory part of this book (*supra*, paragraph 77), felonies and misdemeanours are defined in terms of the type of punishment they are visited with.[778]

625. In a few cases, the law prescribes either fixed or minimum sentences which the courts must impose. For example, until recently in such cases as treason, murder, aggravated robbery and smuggling involving use of deadly weapons, death was the mandatory sentence. In cases of embezzlement, causing financial loss, or smuggling without violence, imprisonment for certain minimum terms and, in case of smuggling, a fine, must be imposed. In all these cases, the courts' discretion is restricted: they cannot go below the prescribed minimum. They must impose the prescribed minimum sentences irrespective of the circumstances of the offender. These cases are, however, an exception to the general rule. The general rule is that the legislature prescribes the maximum, leaving the courts with considerable discretion to impose a sentence within the prescribed limits that appear to them to be the most appropriate in the circumstances of each case. This is a salutary rule indeed, because, as we shall see presently, not all offenders deserve to be treated in the same way merely because they have committed the same offence. Their

777. Cr. App. No. 241 of 2003, [2010] UGCA 15 (15 Apr. 2010). In *Magezi Robert v. Uganda* Cr. Case No. 71 of 2006, [2010] UGCA 46 (11 Nov. 2010) where the appellant, aged 25 years, was convicted of defiling a 3-year child, the same court confirmed the eighteen-year sentence, saying that 'All in all, we hold that offences against children have become a menace in this country and this court must send the correct signal to the community that it will not be tolerated. The sentence of 18 years must stand.'

778. According to sec. 2, a felony is punishable either by death or by imprisonment for three years or more. According to sec. 22, 'When in this Code no punishment is specially provided for any misdemeanour, it shall be punishable with imprisonment for a period not exceeding two years.'

circumstances may be markedly different, calling for different considerations. How, then, does the sentencing court approach its sentencing task?

626. As a rule, the court must be guided by the statute that creates the offence in question. It must take care not to impose a sentence that is severer than that prescribed by that statute. Such a sentence would be *ultra vires* and illegal.[779] It must also ensure that it has jurisdiction to try the offence or to impose a particular *sentence.*[780] Trying an offence which is beyond its jurisdiction or imposing a sentence that is beyond its sentencing powers would also be *ultra vires* and a nullity. If, as we have seen in the general introductory part of this book, a court presided over by a magistrate forms the opinion that a convicted person merits greater punishment than it has power to impose it may commit such person to a Chief Magistrate's Court or to the High Court, as the case may be, for sentencing.[781]

627. Sentencing is a matter within the exclusive preserve of the trial court, or in the case of committal for sentence, the court to which the convict is committed.[782] In spite of the ambivalent meaning of Section 98 of the Trial on Indictments Act and section 133(2) of the Magistrates Courts Act, it is submitted that, the prosecutor is not entitled to suggest the type of sentence the court should impose or to demand a deterrent sentence. He or she must not try to influence the court in the exercise of its sentencing powers. As it is often said, 'The prosecutor is a minister of justice, and not an avenging angel.' Furthermore, the victim of the crime has no role to play in the sentencing process. The practice obtaining in other jurisdictions of allowing victims to make 'victim impact statements' to the court as an aid to the sentencing process has not yet found its way to Uganda.

628. Before passing sentence, the court must make an inquiry into the character and the antecedents of the accused, including his or her criminal record, if any, as well as his or her family background, education, employment and health. Further useful information may be obtained from the police on whether the accused cooperated with them in their investigations, and from prison authorities, if he or she attended the trial from prison, on his or her general behaviour, whilst on remand. Much of this information could also be obtained from the Probation Department. Unfortunately, probation services in Uganda are not as fully developed as they should be and are therefore not always available to the courts. So, in this respect, the courts have to rely on the prosecution for their information. As emphasized earlier, the prosecutor's role must be limited to supplying information and no more. Needless to say, the accused must always be given an opportunity to controvert any information that is either inaccurate or unfavourable to him or her.[783]

779. See *R. v. Hussein Bin Habib* [1960] E.A. 182.
780. The High Court's jurisdiction is unlimited. The jurisdiction of Chief Magistrates and Magistrates Grades I, and II are limited and regulated by sec. 161 of the Magistrates Courts Act.
781. Magistrates Courts Act, sec. 164.
782. *Ibid.*, sec. 165.
783. See sec. 80 of the Trial on Indictments Act and sec. 133(2) (a) of the Magistrates Courts Act.

629. Also important is the accused's right to make a plea in mitigation. Under this plea, the accused is afforded an opportunity to say everything he or she wants that tend to mitigate the offence he committed and to persuade the court to pass a more lenient sentence than it might otherwise impose. For this purpose, the accused is allowed to lead evidence and to tender exhibits as he or she deems fit. At this stage, strict rules of evidence need not be adhered to. All evidence, including hearsay, that tends to lessen the moral blameworthiness of the accused is relevant and may be admitted. If the accused adduces evidence, it is only fair that the prosecution be allowed to cross-examine him or her and his or her witnesses and to call rebutting evidence.

630. The right to a plea in mitigation does not appear to be provided for in the statutes. It is nevertheless a right which the courts invariably accord the accused before they sentence him or her. To deny him or her that right or to tell him or her that the court will not consider what he or she says is a gross irregularity that would vitiate the sentence.

631. The accused's plea, together with the information supplied by the prosecution and the Probation Department, assist the court to make an informed decision as to the most condign sentence to impose. Such sentence must not only fit the offence but must also fit the offender. For this reason, therefore the court may, in some cases, pass different sentences on people who have been jointly charged, tried and convicted of the same offence. Factors such as the offenders' age, the role they played in committing the offence, their antecedents, presence or absence of penitence, and their economic ability (in cases where the court is considering a fine) may influence the court in imposing different sentences. Where the court decides to impose different sentences on joint offenders, it must explain to them why it has done so, lest it be accused of favouritism. This explanation also serves to satisfy the cardinal principle that justice must not only be done but must also appear to be done.

This point is well illustrated by the case of *Uganda v. Muhanguzi & Anor.*[784] The three accused, soldiers in the National Resistance Army, were jointly charged with the murder of a man with whom they picked a quarrel over a woman at a bar. They pleaded guilty to manslaughter, and they were so convicted. They were sentenced to varying terms of imprisonment, the highest being seven years and the lowest being three years. Okalebo, J., justified the sentences as follows:

> The three convicts acted in a high handed manner and were irresponsible in their attitude in that they left work, to go and drink. As if that was not enough, they picked a quarrel with a simple civilian who was not even armed. A1 and A2 being military men had no reason to fear the deceased so that they had to send for A3 who had a gun. There was no question of the deceased becoming more hostile to A3, a man with a gun. Worse still, when the deceased ran away, A1 told A3 to arrest him but for no offence committed by him (deceased). A1 did not tell A3 to shoot as means of arrest but A3 shot three (3) bullets one of which killed the deceased.

784. H.Ct.Cr.Session No. 290 of 1991 (unreported).

> The act of the accused was but to show their power as men with a gun and there was no justification whatsoever in using it in the way they did.
> The accused are people charged with the public duty of protecting the lives of the people and their property but here they were destroying innocent life of the civilian citizen for no just cause. Drink is no licence to misbehave. They are first offenders as such who have pleaded guilty but still deserve severe sentences since the offence committed is of a very serious charge. A1, the in-charge of the group, could have controlled the situation by himself assisted by A2 or they could have gone away leaving the deceased alone. Death would not have occurred if they had done this. Instead A1 sends A2 to call A3 because he has a gun. At least A2 might have done the quarrelling and he was so sent to call A3. His role in the matter is not so significant. Had A1 not sent for A3, the killing might not have happened. So the blame of A1 is higher than that of A2. Then by A3 firing the three bullets, which was not the method of arresting the deceased as he might have been directed by A1, he took an independent decision to shoot and it is the shooting which killed the deceased. I rank his action worst of all and takes the lead in the blame in this matter.
> Sentence:A1 is sentenced to five (5) years imprisonment.
> A2 is sentenced to three (3) years imprisonment.
> A3 is sentenced to seven (7) years imprisonment.

632. Where an accused person is charged on several counts in a charge sheet, the court must pronounce a separate verdict for each count. If the court convicts him or her on more than one count, it must similarly pass a separate sentence for each count. In the case of capital offences, where the court convicts the offender on several counts and is minded to impose death sentences, it must pass the sentences, but suspend them save for one count only.[785] All in all, the courts must not pass blanket or omnibus sentences.[786] The reason for this requirement is that if the parties appeal the convictions and some of those convictions are confirmed and others quashed, those that are confirmed will have their respective sentences left intact. This desirable goal would be impossible where a blanket sentence had been passed for all the counts.

633. Again, where custodial sentences are passed on several counts, those sentences may be ordered to run concurrently or consecutively. Both the Trial on Indictments Act[787] and the Magistrates Courts Act[788] provide that where the sentences are custodial they are deemed to commence 'the one after the expiration of the other' unless the court specifically directs that they shall run concurrently. It is a well-established rule of practice, almost a rule of law, that the sentences must be ordered to run concurrently if the offences of which the accused is convicted constitute one

785. *Binuge & Anor. v. Uganda*, Cr. App. No. 23 of 1989, [1991] 5 (31 May 1991).
786. See *R. v. Dio Riri*, H.Ct.Monthly Bulletin No. 64 of 1959.
787. Section 122.
788. Section 175.

transaction or form part of a series of offences of a similar or associated nature.[789] For example, where an accused is convicted on counts of stealing a cheque leaf, forging the owner's signature on it, uttering the forged cheque, and obtaining by false pretences, the sentences passed on these counts may be ordered to run concurrently. Where the offences of which the accused is convicted do not form part of a series of offences of a similar associated nature, the sentences must be ordered to run consecutively. For example, where in the course of a burglary the accused rapes the householder the sentences for the offences need not be ordered to run concurrently. Although they were committed at the same time and formed part of a series of offences, they were not of a similar or associated nature.[790]

634. Lastly, it is important to note that the aggregate of sentences that a court imposes on any person convicted on several counts at a single trial is considered to be a single sentence.[791] A court must therefore not exceed the maximum sentence that it is permitted to impose. Where it considers that the aggregate of the sentences that the accused deserves to receive would exceed its sentencing powers, it must commit him or her to a Chief Magistrate's Court or to the High Court, as the case may be, for sentencing.[792]

635. Where a superior court in exercise of its appellate, revisional or confirmation powers deems it necessary to enhance a sentence imposed by a lower court it must, before doing so, give the accused an opportunity to show cause against such enhancement. Enhancing a sentence without hearing the accused would render the enhanced sentence a nullity. It is a breach of the rules of natural justice.[793]

---

789. See *R. v. Sawedi Mukasa s/o Abdulla Aligawesa* [1946] 13 E.A.C.A. 97; *J. Wasswa & Anor. v. R.* H.Ct.Monthly Bulletin No. 20 of 1961.
790. *Ibid.*
791. But see *Joseph Mogola s/o Pudha v. Regina* [1963] 20 E.A.C.A. 171 a Kenya case, where the contrary was held.
792. Section 175(2) and (3) of the Magistrates Courts Act reads as follows:

> '1. In the case of consecutive sentences *it shall not be necessary for the court*, by reason only of the aggregate punishment for the several offences being in excess of the punishment which it is competent to impose on conviction of a single offence, *to send the offender for trial before a higher court.*
> 2. For the purpose of appeal or confirmation the aggregate of consecutive sentences imposed under this section in case of convictions for several offences at one trial shall be deemed to be a single sentence.' [emphasis added]

The use of the italicized words conveys the meaning that the court need not consider itself incompetent to try the case merely because the aggregate punishment for the several offences is in excess of its jurisdiction. It need not send the offender to a higher court *for trial.* This however is not to say that it may impose sentences the aggregate of which exceeds its sentencing powers! In that case, it must send the offender to a higher court for sentencing. If Parliament intended to allow magistrates to pass sentences, the aggregate of which exceeded their sentencing powers then it should have said that '*it shall not be necessary ... to send the offender for sentencing before a higher court.*'

If the interpretation put on subsection (2) is correct, then subsection (3) would appear to be superfluous.

793. See *Amratlal v. Uganda* [1970] E.A. 401.

636. In cases where the law does not prescribe a minimum sentence, the court must exercise discretion as to the most appropriate sentence within the set limits to impose. It must exercise this discretion judicially. It has no mathematical scales or sentencing guidelines to follow. It must therefore tread the sentencing path with caution. It must be wary not to be swayed by factors that are extrinsic or irrelevant to the sentencing process. It must not, for example, allow its revulsion or oddity of the crime to sway it from the path of doing justice to the criminal. It may hate the crime, but must, if not love but at least not show hatred to the criminal. Although it may dispassionately comment on the heinousness of the crime, it must not vent out its anger on the accused by use of emotive or insulting language. Such language has a tendency to convey to the accused the message that he or she is being punished not for what he she did but because the judge hates him or her.

637. Above all, the court must give reasons for the sentences it imposes.[794] Reasons assist in minimizing arbitrariness in sentencing, and in enabling appellate courts to determine whether the sentence in question was based on sound principles.

638. The court in exercising its discretion must follow generally accepted sentencing principles. These principles have been developed by judges in the common law world over the years. Pre-eminent among them is the need to consider *the triad of sentencing: the offence, the offender and the community*. In the sentence that it imposes, the court must endeavour to strike an even balance between these three competing interests. The sentence must be proportionate to the gravity of the offence, as indicated by the maximum sentence prescribed by the legislature. Imposing woefully lenient sentences on people who have committed serious offences such as rape or defilement may serve to undermine legislative policy, bring the law into contempt and work to reduce public confidence in the law. However, imposing unwarrantably harsh sentences for minor offences which have occasioned minimal or no harm may serve only to create a public image of the law as an instrument of tyranny. Not to be lost sight of, at the same time, is the offender. He or she may have committed a serious crime, but there might exist extenuating circumstances that lessen the moral blameworthiness of his or her offence to warrant a lenient sentence. Such circumstances may include his or her youth, state of health, being penitent and the like.[795] However, the offender may have committed a minor offence, but there might exist aggravating circumstances warranting a severe sentence These circumstances may include the harm occasioned by the offence, the fact that because of his age, status and station in life he ought to have known better, the fact that he committed the offence for gain or that he has a string of previous convictions. The need to protect the community is an important element in the triad that must always

---

794. Trial on Indictment Act, sec. 86(4), Magistrates Courts Act, sec. 136(5),

795. For example in *Uganda v. Benjamin Bwambale & Anor.* H.Ct.Cr.Session No. 304 of 1991 (unreported) the accused, members of a local Resistance Council, were charged with the manslaughter of a man that they had tied to a *kandooya* and caned him for having stolen the sum of Shillings. 200/=. They pleaded guilty, thus 'saving the court's time'. They were first offenders. They had been on remand for four years. One had tuberculosis, another typhoid fever and the other leprosy. They were sentenced to a term of imprisonment 'to last up to the rising of this Court today and they then be set free'.

be borne in mind. For example, the fact that the offender is young should not automatically result in his being sentenced to a lenient sentence, particularly where he committed a serious crime and is likely to continue to do so if he is let loose. Additionally, the fact that the offender is a first offender should not automatically entitle him to a lenient sentence, especially where he was in a position of trust, was not penitent, or committed a serious or prevalent offence which, if unchecked, threatens sensitive or vital aspects of community life. The case of *Cheeye, (supra,* paragraph 484) is one in point. When confirming the sentences imposed on the appellant for embezzlement and forgery, the Court of Appeal said:

> We think the offences committed by the appellant were very serious indeed. The appellant may have been a first offender, but given that he was a public officer, holding a very high responsibility as Director for Economic Monitoring in the Office of the President, being entrusted with the duty, among other things, to fight corruption, he should have been the very last person to engage into the type of criminal activities he was convicted of. He should have led by example. We think the sentences of 10 years and 3 years were on the lower side.[796]

However, a young person who has committed a serious and prevalent crime should not, in the name of protecting the community, be sentenced to a shockingly harsh penalty. That leaves him with no chance for reformation. Less severe forms of punishment conducive to his reformation and social rehabilitation may therefore have to be devised.

II. Factors to Be Taken into Account

639. In an attempt to balance the three elements of the triad, the courts usually take into consideration some of the following factors. Plea of guilty by the accused is a factor that is usually used in his or her favour. The plea must, however, be accompanied by some evidence of genuine remorse and a determination to turn a new leaf. Where such remorse is lacking no leniency should be shown to the accused merely because he or she pleads guilty. It is apposite to point out in this respect that there is a tendency on the part of some judicial officers to be lenient to an accused who pleads guilty, because he or she 'has saved the court's time'. This is wrong in principle. Mercy goes to the contrite and to the penitent, not to the hard-hearted and the incorrigible.

796. Cr. App. No. 105 of 2009, [2010] UGCA 41 (20 Oct. 2010). See also in *Mugasa Joseph v. Uganda*, Cr. App. No. 241 of 2003, [2010] UGCA 15 (15 Apr. 2010), the appellant was a catechist, considered to be 'a custodian of morals in society', was convicted of defiling the complainant who was the daughter of his cousin. The Court of Appeal enhanced his sentence from seventeen to twenty-five years imprisonment in order to 'send a message to society that enough is enough and violating the rights of child females must stop'. In *Bukenya Joseph v. Uganda* Cr. App. No. 222 of 2003, [2010] UGCA 32 (23 Jul. 2010), the same court confirmed a life sentence for a 70-year old man who was convicted of defiling a six-year old girl as 'a deserving deterrent.'

640. Failure to plead guilty must not, however, be used against the accused to punish him or her more severely than he or she deserves. After all, he or she is presumed innocent until proved guilty beyond reasonable doubt. By pleading not guilty, which he or she is entitled to do, he or she is merely requiring his or her accusers to discharge the burden imposed on them by the law. The *Cheeye* case, *supra*, is also relevant here. In the course of sentencing the appellant, the trial judge remarked as follows:

> The number of cases that are reaching our court seem to suggest, unfortunately that this type of crime 'pays.' What is more alarming is that this type of crime is being committed with impunity! How do we explain the mentality of a man, whom in order to account for the money received, states that he transported people on a caterpillar wheel loader! That a caterpillar wheel loader that uses diesel this time was using petrol! Is this stupidity or impunity? Again how do we explain the mentality of a man against whom there is evidence that he received money, and that in a bid to account for the money received used forged documents and who beats his chest and says: *'there is no case against me. Do what you can, I will say nothing!'* If this is not impunity, then what else can it be?

Later on in the same remarks, the trial judge referred to the appellant as 'a beast'. Nevertheless, the appellant did not complain against the tone of the language used by the judge. If he did he probably might have had a point. In this author's view, the language tended to border on the emotive and emotive language, as indicated earlier on in this book, is improper. However, the appellant's complainant was that the trial judge should not have commented on the exercise of his right to remain silent, and that the comment in effect influenced the judge to convict the appellant. The Court of Appeal did not agree. First, the trial judge made the comment after the conviction stage. Second, the right to remain silent is not absolute, particularly in the light of section 105 of the Evidence Act which provides that 'When a person is accused of any offence … the burden of proving any fact especially within the knowledge of that person is upon him or her … ' According to the Court of Appeal, what happened to the money that the appellant withdrew from his company's account he alone knew; and that the trial judge was entitled to comment adversely on the appellant's failure to discharge that burden.

641. While the courts invariably take into account the seriousness and prevalence of a particular crime, they do also usually consider being a first offender to be favourable to the accused. Previous convictions, however, tend to suggest that the accused, a recidivist, deserves a stiff sentence that will serve to impress on him or her the evil of his or her criminal ways and to induce him or her to cease and desist from such ways. However, no account must be taken of offences of which he or she has not yet been convicted, 'unless the accused person specifically agrees that such offences shall be taken into consideration and note of such request shall have been recorded in the proceedings'.[797] Where the accused consents and other offences are taken into account it would be grotesquely wrong for the prosecution to subsequently initiate fresh proceedings in respect of those offences. It would be to punish him or her twice. Nevertheless, such proceedings would be proper if the sentence were to be set aside on appeal. In this respect, both the Magistrates Courts Act and the Trial on Indictments Act specifically provide that:

> If for any reason the sentence passed by the court is set aside, the accused person shall not be entitled to plead *autrefois convict* in respect of any offence taken into consideration in assessing the sentence that was set aside.[798]

642. The two statutes are silent about the kind of offences that the court may agree to take into account. It would appear that, as in England, the court should take into account only those offences that are of the same character as the one of which the accused was convicted.[799] The court must not, however, take into account offences which it has no power to try.[800]

643. It is convenient here to deal with the problem of *habitual offenders* and the issue of preventive detention which is provided for under the Habitual Criminals (Preventive Detention) Act.[801] This Act allows a court which considers an offender to be 'an habitual criminal' to impose on him or her a sentence of preventive detention *in addition* to or in lieu of the substantive sentence, if it considers this course of action 'expedient for the protection of the public'.[802] In this respect, it should be noted that Magistrates Grade II are not authorized to pass a sentence of preventive detention. Magistrates Grade I are so authorized but the total term of preventive detention and any additional sentence of imprisonment they may impose must not exceed ten years.[803] However, such sentence does not come into operation until it is confirmed by the High Court.[804] The relevant provisions are set out in full as follows:

> 1. When a person who in the opinion of the court is not less than thirty years of age –

---

797. Trial on Indictments Act, sec. 98(c) and Magistrates Courts Act, sec. 133(2)(c).
798. *Ibid.*
799. In *Joseph Ananda & Anor. v. Rex* [1936–1951] 6 U.L.R. 198, a magistrate took into account offences similar to the one that the accused was convicted of. The High Court set aside the sentence principally because at that time the Uganda law did not authorize the practice. For an English authority, see *R. v. McLean* [1911] 1 K.B. 332. See also *Uganda v. Thomas Baguma* [1970] E.A. 169.
800. See *R. v. Wern* (1936–1938) 25 Cr.App.R. 115.
801. Cap. 118.
802. Where a Magistrates' Court considers this course of action appropriate in the matter but has no jurisdiction to impose the additional preventive detention, it must refer the case to a higher court for sentencing. It must not impose the substantive sentence and then send the case to the higher court for the imposition of the preventive detention. This will be a nullity. See *Mahuku v. Uganda* [1970] E.A. 495.
803. Magistrates Courts Act, sec. 163.
804. *Ibid.*, sec. 173(2)(b).

a) is convicted of an offence punishable with imprisonment for a term of two years or more; and
b) has been convicted on at least three previous occasions since reaching, in the opinion of the court, the age of sixteen years, of offences punishable with such a sentence, and was on at least two of those occasions sentenced to imprisonment,

then, if the court is satisfied that it is expedient for the protection of the public that he should be detained in custody for a substantial time the court may pass on him or her, in addition to or in lieu of any other sentence, a sentence of preventive detention for such term of not less than five nor more than fourteen years as the court may determine: Provided that where a sentence of preventive detention is passed in addition to any other sentence the total term of preventive detention and imprisonment shall not exceed fourteen years.

2. No person shall be sentenced to preventive detention unless –
   a) the Director of Public Prosecutions either in person or in writing asks that such a sentence be imposed:
   Provided that no such request shall be deemed to fetter the discretion of the court as to whether or not such a sentence should be imposed; and
   b) at least three days' notice in writing has been given to the offender that it is intended to prove his or her previous convictions.
3. Without prejudice to any right of the offender to tender evidence as to his or her character and repute, evidence of character and repute may, if the court thinks fit, be admitted as evidence on the question whether it is expedient for the protection of the public that he or she should be detained in custody for a substantial time.

644. Preventive detention is a drastic measure indeed, particularly where it is imposed *in addition* to the substantive sentence meted out in the latest conviction. It is no wonder, then, that the courts have required strict compliance with the above provisions before they can impose it. For example, they insist that the age of the accused must be strictly proved. In *Yokana Mato v. Uganda*,[805] for instance, the appellant was convicted of shop-breaking and was sentenced to seven years imprisonment and in addition to five years preventive detention. No evidence was called in proof of the accused's age. The preventive detention was declared illegal by the appellate court on the ground that it had not been proved that the appellant was 'not less than 35 years'. The point about the age limit is that it is feared that if the preventive detention, which must not be less than five years, is imposed on a person who is relatively young he or she may become institutionalized and thus become hard to rehabilitate. The previous convictions, which must not be less than three, must also be proved. The requisite notice under subsection (2)(b) must have been served on the accused to enable him or her to oppose the application by the prosecution to treat him or her as 'an habitual criminal'. A copy of the notice duly signed by the accused must be filed in the record as evidence of service on him or

805. H.Ct.Monthly Bulletin No. 60 of 1965.

her.[806] The period between the last conviction and the one at which it is sought to treat the accused a habitual criminal must not be long. For example, in *Yakobo Abuni v. R.*,[807] the appellant was convicted of burglary and sentenced to two years imprisonment. He was *additionally* sentenced to five years preventive detention. On five occasions between 1939 and 1955, the appellant was convicted of offences punishable by imprisonment for more than three years. However, the last of those convictions happened seven years prior to the burglary conviction. On appeal, the High Court set aside the preventive detention, saying that:

> It must be assumed, that prior to his conviction for burglary, the appellant endeavoured to lead a law-abiding life for a considerable period. In the circumstances it was inappropriate to impose upon him a sentence of preventive detention.

645. In *Ojok v. Uganda*,[808] the appellant had gone straight for a period of twenty-two months before he was convicted of the offence in respect of which a preventive detention was ordered. The High Court held that given the length of this period and the fact that he was convicted of theft of only UGX 100 without violence, the preventive detention ought not to have been imposed.

646. Lastly, drastic as preventive detention is it should be imposed only as a last resort, where there are absolutely no alternatives for protecting the public. In cases of serious crimes, it might be advisable for the courts to impose a sentence of sufficient length which would be adequate to protect the public and to punish the offender.[809]

647. The fact that the accused was, at the time he committed the crime, 'relatively young' – usually in his or her 20s – is a factor that calls for leniency. The basis for this view is that young people tend to be impulsive and naturally lacking in self-control; they are also not yet settled in criminal ways and are easier to correct than older people. For example, in *Paulino Olarkar v. Uganda*,[810] the accused was convicted of defiling a girl aged about $9^1/_2$ years and was sentenced to eight years imprisonment and twelve strokes of the cane. He was aged about twenty years and was of previous good character. The High Court considered eight years imprisonment excessive in the accused's circumstances. It said that, 'If he was made to serve the term he would probably be turned into a hardened criminal.' It reduced the sentence to four years imprisonment, leaving the corporal punishment component undisturbed.

648. However, the relative youth of the accused must be balanced against the need to protect society against dangerous criminals, or the need to repress serious

806. See *Mustafa Huseni v. Uganda* H.Ct.Monthly Bulletin No. 182 of 1968.
807. H.Ct.Monthly Bulletin No. 55 of 1963.
808. [1970] E.A. 575.
809. See *Stefano Ochaya v. Uganda*, H.Ct.Monthly Bulletin No. 115 of 1964.
810. H.Ct.Monthly Bulletin No. 27 of 1971.

or prevalent crimes. Thus, in *Uganda v. Dominiko Musoke*,[811] the High Court enhanced from nine months to three years imprisonment the sentence of a youth, aged between 18 and 19 years convicted of burglary, saying that the accused, 'not only committed one of the most serious offences on the calendar, but it was an offence which was endemic in Uganda, and the opinion of the legislature on the sentence to be passed had been reflected in the maximum penalty prescribed by law, viz, ten years'. Similarly, in *Bwambale Muchunguzi v. Uganda*, the Court of Appeal confirmed the sentence of sixteen years imprisonment for the appellant, an 18-year old youth convicted of defilement, a capital offence, It stated that:

> It is true that the appellant was a young man of 18 years but we cannot accept that by that age, he had any justification whatsoever to venture into assaulting female children of any age. To hold so would be to give license to adolescents to assault the children with impunity.[812]

649. Prevalence of a particular crime is thus a factor that usually calls for deterrent sentences. The case of *E. Kayongo v. R.* is also in point.[813] The appellant was convicted of threatening to burn down a house with intent to intimidate, contrary to section 76(a) of the Penal Code. He was sentenced to four years imprisonment, the maximum sentence prescribed for the offence. Dismissing his appeal, McKisack, C.J., said:

> In the present state of lawlessness caused by the boycott of non-African traders a severe sentence is undoubtedly called for … The trial magistrate has given cogent reasons for regarding this as a case for imposing the maximum sentence which include what he terms 'the renewed reign of terror in this part of Buganda.' Its existence is well known to everybody here, and I do not regard that description as exaggerated. It is notorious that threats to burn or destroy property have in many cases been carried out. A person subjected to a threat of the kind uttered by the appellant must go about in fear for his property – and perhaps for his own life and the lives of his family – so long as the present lawlessness persists; and it shows little sign of abating. The evilly-disposed persons who utter such threats must, in these circumstances expect to be severely dealt with, even if they have been hitherto been of good character.

650. Imposing a deterrent sentence necessarily involves punishing the accused more than he or she deserves for the sake of sounding a warning to others who might be minded to behave as he or she did. There is an element of unfairness in this. For this reason, superior courts have been heard to say that the accused should not be made a scapegoat for other people who have committed similar offences but have not been caught, tried or convicted. How the sentencing court avoids doing so is not easy to say. All that the present writer can say is that the court must not be so

811. H.Ct.Monthly Bulletin No. 14 of 1968.
812. Cri. App. No. 96 of 2006, [2010] UGCA 44 (8 Nov. 2010).
813. H.Ct.Monthly Bulletin No. 24 of 1960.

preoccupied with protecting the public as to be oblivious to the other elements of the triad.

651. The *seriousness or triviality of the offence*, the harm done as a result of the offence, public attitude to the offence,[814] attitude and conduct of the offender since committing the offence [for example, assisting the police investigations, and willingness to pay compensation] are also pertinent factors. As to the seriousness of the offence, the court must ensure that the sentence it imposes is proportionate to the gravity of the offence and to the harm occasioned by its commission by the accused. This approach serves the ends of retributive justice and of deterrence.

652. Finally, it should be noted that an appellate court will generally not interfere with a sentence imposed by a trial court, unless in imposing that sentence the trial court proceeded along wrong principles, or the sentence was so harsh as to create a sense of shock. An appellate court is definitely not allowed to set aside a sentence imposed by a trial court merely because if it had tried the case, it would have imposed a different sentence. That would be to usurp the sentencing court's discretion. Additionally, the appellate court should not disturb a sentence, as happened in one case merely because 'it was not in keeping with the decisions and sentences imposed by the High Court of Uganda in similar cases'.[815] It is submitted that for sentencing purposes no two cases are similar. Each offence is committed under different circumstances by individuals who are peculiarly circumstanced. It is in this respect wrong to cite and rely on past decisions as the basis for the quantum of a sentence in a subsequent case. Sentences must be tailored to fit a particular offender as well as the offence. As long as the sentencing court is not arbitrary and does not transgress accepted sentencing principles, it need not be overly concerned about uniformity as a sentencing goal.[816]

§3. Forms of Punishment

I. The Death Penalty

653. Putting people to death as a form of punishment is universal and is as old as the human race itself. As we have seen earlier, as many as 200 crimes used to be punishable by death in Britain. Among the various nationalities of Uganda, death

---

814. See *Hoyle v. Reginam* [1956–1957] 8 U.L.R. 314. A magistrate convicted the appellant, an assistant hospital superintendent, of having carnal knowledge of a Karimajong peasant who was his patient against the order of nature. Calling the offence that the accused had committed as disgusting, the magistrate sentenced the accused to two years imprisonment with hard labour. On appeal, the High Court considered the sentence excessive in light of the changing attitude toward the offence of homosexuality. It therefore reduced the sentence to a fine of GBP 30 or in default two months imprisonment.

815. This was done in *Yunusu Musungu & Anor. v. Uganda*, H.Ct.Cr.App. No. MM3 of 1989 (unreported).

816. For an instructive opinion on this point, see the Botswana case of *Mudangule v. State*, [1986] B.L.R. 265. (CA).

was a common form of punishment for all sorts of crimes, especially crimes against the established authority. Today death is reserved for the most serious offences. Until the 2009 Supreme Court decision in *Attorney General v. Susan Kigula and 417 Others* (*infra*),[817] the death penalty was mandatory for offenders convicted of treason,[818] murder,[819] aggravated robbery[820] and smuggling involving use of deadly weapons.[821] In these cases, the Penal Code used the words 'shall be sentenced to death'.[822] In other cases, such as rape,[823] defilement[824] and kidnapping with intent to murder,[825] the penalty was already discretionary, as the Penal Code uses the words 'is liable to suffer death' or similar language.

654. In the *Kigula* case, the respondents, who had at various times been sentenced to death for various offences, challenged the constitutionality of the penalty and, in the alternative, its mandatory nature as well the mode of carrying it out.

Upholding the decision of the Court of Appeal, the Supreme Court ruled the penalty *constitutional* and not cruel, inhuman or degrading punishment as per articles 24 and 44 of the Constitution. In this author's view, the court could not have ruled otherwise, because the Constitution, in clear and unambiguous terms, provides for the death penalty as an exception to the right to life.[826] Under our constitutional scheme, the court does not have power to amend or to nullify any provision of the Constitution. Only the legislature can. It was probably for this reason that the court urged the legislature to consider amending the Constitution to abolish the penalty altogether. It did so after noting that for many years the Executive did not execute anyone sentenced to death by the civil courts and, as a result, many convicts remained on death row for long periods of time. The court interpreted this hesitation or reluctance by the Executive as a desire to do away with the penalty.

Concerning the *mandatory nature* of the penalty, the court held it to be inconsistent with Articles 24, 26, 44(a) and 44(c) of the Constitution. It held that laws that deny persons to whom the sentence applied an opportunity to make a plea in mitigation before sentence, which is available to all other persons convicted of any crime, violate the Constitution in the following respects: (1) they are discriminatory and contrary to the constitutional provisions that guarantee everyone the right to

817. Const. App. No. 3 of 2006, [2009] UGSC 6, 21 Aug. 2009.
818. The Penal Code, sec. 23.
819. *Ibid.*, sec. 189.
820. *Ibid.*, sec. 286(2).
821. *Ibid.*, sec. 319(2).
822. See *Opoya v. Uganda* [1967] E.A. 752.
823. *Ibid.*, sec. 124.
824. *Ibid.*, sec. 129.
825. *Ibid.*, sec. 243.
826. Article 22(1) provides that 'No person shall be deprived of life intentionally except in execution of a sentence passed in a fair trial by a court of competent jurisdiction in respect of a criminal offence under the laws of Uganda and the conviction and sentence have been confirmed by the highest appellate court.' See also Art. 28(3), which provides that 'No person shall be deprived of life intentionally except in execution of a sentence passed in a fair trial by a court of competent jurisdiction in respect of a criminal offence under the laws of Uganda and the conviction and sentence have been confirmed by the highest appellate court.'

equality before the law;[827] (2) they contravene the convicts' right to a fair trial – and trial includes sentencing; and (3) they deprive the courts of their power to determine the appropriate sentence to pass, and they give them to the Executive branch of government, thereby nullifying the constitutional principle of separation of powers. According to the court, 'Any law passed by Parliament which has the effect of tying the hands of the judiciary in executing its function to administer justice is inconsistent with the Constitution.' Consequently, any mandatory sentence passed could only be regarded as the maximum, the courts having discretion to impose the death penalty or a less severe one, depending on the antecedents of the accused. In doing so, however, the courts must afford the accused the opportunity to make a plea in mitigation.

This author suggests that the courts should allow the accused to say and they should take into account, all factors that tend to lessen the moral blameworthiness of the offence, as well as all aggravating circumstances. As South Africa's Justice Schreiner counselled in an oft-cited statement, a court should not rule out of consideration and 'factor, not too remote or too faintly or indirectly related to the commission of the crime, which bears upon the accused's blameworthiness in committing it'.[828] Finally, even though the court's decision was limited to mandatory death sentences, its broad and sweeping conceptual pronouncements would appear to apply with equal force to the mandatory sentences in respect of other offences under the Penal Code and other statutes. It is only a question of time before the Supreme Court might pronounce itself generally on the concept of mandatory sentences generally.[829]

655. As for the execution of the death penalty, various methods of execution have been used by different societies at different stages of their development. For example, the ancient Romans used crucifixion for some of the most heinous crimes on their criminal calendar. For other crimes they fed the convicts to hungry and ferocious animals at the coliseums. Other societies used drowning, burning at the stake, starving, disemboweling, beheading, beating, stabbing and asphyxiation in gas chambers. The burning to death at Namugongo of the palace pages who, contrary to Kabaka Mwanga's orders, embraced foreign religions is a *cause célèbre* in which the death penalty was used by our forebears. Otherwise spearing was the most common form of execution in pre-colonial Uganda. Today hanging, shooting by firing

827. Commenting on sec. 95 of the Trial on Indictments Act providing for pleas in mitigation, the court said: 'First it provides in essence that a person accused of stealing a chicken may not only be heard in mitigation, but may actually request the court to inquire into his character and antecedents for purposes of assessing appropriate sentence for him, while on the other hand, a person accused of murder and whose very life is at stake, may not do likewise. We think this is inconsistent with the principle of equality before and under the law. Not all murders are committed in the same circumstances, and all murderers are not necessarily of the same character. One may be a first offender, and the murder may have been committed in circumstances that the accused person deeply regrets and is very remorseful. We see no reason why these factors should not be put before the court before it passes the ultimate sentence.'

828. *R v. Fundakubi* [1948] 3 S. Afr. 810, 818 (AD). Generally see also Daniel D. Ntanda Nsereko, *Extenuating Circumstances in Capital Offences in Botswana*, 2 Crim. L. Forum 235–268 (1991).

829. Generally see Nsereko, Daniel D. Ntanda, *Minimum Sentences and Their Effect on Judicial Discretion* 31 Crime, L. & Soc. Change: Intl. J. 363–384 (1999).

squad, electrocution and the lethal injection are the commonest modes of execution. In Uganda, firing squads are used under the military code while hanging is used under the civilian law. Regarding the latter, the Trial on Indictments Act specifically provides that 'Sentence of death shall be carried out by hanging in accordance with the provisions of the Prisons Act.'[830] Subsection (2) also provides that 'When any person is sentenced to death the sentence shall direct that he or she shall suffer death in the manner authorized by law.'

In the *Kigula* case, the respondents had also sought to have hanging declared cruel, inhuman and degrading and contrary to Articles 24 and 44 of the Constitution because of the excruciating pain that accompanies it. The court declined to do so. It held that those provisions implement Article 22 of the Constitution. In so holding, it was aware of the UN standards for acceptable methods of execution, those that involve 'the least possible physical and mental suffering'. However, the court was unable to identify methods that inflict 'the least possible suffering', since all methods of execution to date inflict both physical and mental suffering on the convict. Having upheld the constitutionality of the death penalty the court could not say that hanging, which has been in use in Uganda since 1938, inflicted more suffering than any other methods of execution or that it was unconstitutional. It did nonetheless urge the legislature to continue to study existing methods of execution that accord with the UN standards and with evolving standards of decency. However, with respect to the timing of executions, the court found that some convicts had been on the death row for as long as twenty years. It said that the mental suffering resulting from such delays, coupled with the demeaning physical conditions in which death row inmates are kept, violates their constitutional rights. Consequently, it held that any delay beyond three years to carry out the sentence after it has been confirmed by the highest appellate court is inordinate delay, which makes the sentence cruel, inhuman and degrading punishment, contrary to the above provisions of the Constitution. Beyond three years, any death sentence that has not been carried out shall be deemed to have been commuted without remission.

656. There are other restrictions relating to the death penalty which the court imposing it and the Executive which has to carry it out must observe. The first restriction is that the sentence must not be passed on a pregnant woman; a sentence of imprisonment for life may be passed instead.[831] The rationale for this restriction would appear to be the need to spare the innocent foetus and to ensure that when it is born the mother is available, albeit in prison, to rear it. Whether or not the woman is pregnant is a matter that must be proved affirmatively to the satisfaction of the court. The woman may appeal a negative finding by the court to the Supreme Court.[832]

657. The second restriction forbids the court to impose the death penalty on a person convicted of an offence 'if it appears to the court that at the time when the

830. Section 99(1).
831. Trial on Indictments Act, sec. 103.
832. *Ibid.*, sec. 104.

offence was committed he or she was under the age of eighteen years'.[833] It must, instead, order that the person be committed in custody, pending a decision of the minister. It is within the discretion of the minister, after studying the case record to order that the person be detained in such prison or other place of custody and for such length of time as he or she may specify in his or her order. Again, the rationale for this lenient predisposition towards people below the age of 18 is their youth and the need to give them a second chance.

658. The last restriction is that the death penalty must not be carried out without the President's consent. Soon after pronouncing the sentence or at the conclusion of the last appeal proceedings where it is confirmed, the court must submit a written report together with any other information derived from the case file or from elsewhere to the Advisory Committee on the Prerogative of Mercy. The report and the information assist the Committee to provide informed advice to the President as to whether there are any mitigating circumstances that warrant the President to exercise the prerogative of mercy in favour of the convict. This procedure ensures that the President exercises his or her powers in council. Where the President does not exercise his or her prerogative powers of mercy, he or she issues a death warrant 'under his or her hand and the public seal'.[834] However, if he or she decides to exercise mercy and to commute the sentence, he or she issues an order again under his or her hand and the public seal, specifying the alternative punishment, if any, and the conditions of that punishment. Whatever the President's decision in a particular case may be, it is important that it be made expeditiously. As the Supreme Court held in the *Kigula case* (*supra*), keeping a condemned prisoner on death row beyond three years, amounts to inhuman or degrading punishment or treatment and contrary to the Constitution.[835]

659. The death penalty, being the ultimate penalty, is a contentious and often emotional subject. Proponents of the penalty contend that it constitutes the most emphatic public denunciation of particularly reprehensible crimes such as murder. Death is the only fitting punishment for such crimes. They also say that death is the most effective deterrent to the convicted murderer and to would be murderers. Opponents of the penalty, however, point out that execution is an act of violence, and that violence tends to beget violence. They assert that execution tends to brutalize those involved in imposing the penalty and in carrying it out. They say that the death penalty is inherently inhuman and degrading, and that there is no 'humane' way of killing a person. They also point to the absence of empirical evidence tending to prove that death is any more deterrent than, say, a long jail term. The use of the penalty does not have any bearing on the incidence of murder, aggravated robbery, and other crimes of violence which, to any casual observer, are ever on the increase in Uganda. Last, opponents of the penalty point out that death, an irrevocable penalty, may be imposed on the innocent. As Professor Charles L.

833. *Ibid.*, sec. 105.
834. *Ibid.*, sec. 102.
835. See also *Pratt & Anor. v. Attorney General for Jamaica & Anor.* [1993] 4 All E.R. 769, [1993] 3 W.L.R. 995.

Black, Jr., has argued, 'the penalty of death cannot be imposed, given the limitations of our minds and institutions, without considerable measures of arbitrariness and of mistake'.[836]

660. Although the movement for the abolition of the death penalty has been growing over the years, it has not yet gained sufficient support to raise abolition to the level of a rule of international law.[837] Many countries of the world retain and use the death penalty. Nevertheless, since the publication of the last edition of this book there has been a steady movement toward abolition. Thus, as of December 2014, ninety-eight countries had abolished it for all offences, while seven had abolished it for all but exceptional offences such as crimes under military law or crimes committed in exceptional circumstances; thirty-five countries had abolished it de facto or in practice – that is, retained it on the statute books but did not carry out any executions in the past ten years. Only fifty-eight countries retained and used the death penalty.[838] As far as Uganda is concerned, there is to date no evidence of popular public support for the abolition of the penalty. Abolition nonetheless remains a desirable goal, at least as far as the United Nations is concerned.[839]

II. Corporal Punishment

661. Until recently, corporal punishment was another form of punishment that has been practised in Uganda and elsewhere from time immemorial. The Penal Code made it mandatory for the offences of robbery and attempted robbery. It was *additional* to the sentence of imprisonment that could be imposed for these offences.[840] It was, however, discretionary in cases of attempted rape,[841] indecent assault[842] and attempted defilement.[843]

662. Corporal punishment involved the beating of the convicted person on the buttocks, using a cane. Parents at home and teachers at school use it to chastise children or pupils in order to correct them. Some believe that it works. However, opponents of beating as a form of punishing adult offenders point out that when used in the home or the school corporal punishment is administered summarily,

836. C.L. Black, Jr., *Capital Punishment* 22 (2d ed., enl. 1981).

837. In this respect, the Supreme Court was correct when it opined that 'the retention of capital punishment by itself is not illegal or unlawful or a violation of international law'.

838. See Amnesty International, https://www.amnesty.org/en/what-we-do/death.penalty/.

839. This assertion is borne out by G.A. Res. 2857, 26 U.N. GAOR Supp. (No. 29) at 94, U.N. Doc. A/8429 (1972), calling for the progressive restriction of the number of offences for which the death penalty may be imposed. The International Covenant on Civil and Political Rights, Art. 6(6), G.A. Res. 2200 (XXI) B., 21 U.N. GAOR Supp. (No. 16) at 176, U.N. Doc. A/6316 (1966), echoes a similar desire when it provides that '[n]othing in this article shall be invoked to delay or to prevent the abolition of capital punishment by any State Party to the present Covenant'.

840. Penal Code, sec. 288.

841. *Ibid.*, sec. 125.

842. *Ibid.*, sec. 128.

843. *Ibid.*, sec. 129(2).

soon after the child or pupil has committed a wrong and when the feeling of guilt is still fresh in his mind. Those who administer it have affection toward the child or pupil and have a personal interest in his or her reformation. This is not so with court-sanctioned corporal punishment. It is imposed months after the offence was committed, and administered by people who have no affection toward the recipient. It can also not be ruled out that some officials who administer it may even derive sadistic satisfaction out of it. Furthermore, it is said, it is a demeaning and degrading punishment, particularly when it is administered on adults. It tends to brutalize the recipient and the person who administers it. Like the death penalty, there is again no hard evidence that it has significant deterrent effects. For this reason attempts have been made at the international level to outlaw it as a cruel, inhuman and degrading punishment.[844] With the passing of the Penal Code (Amendment) Act, 2007 corporal punishment was abolished for all offences under the Penal Code.[845] In this author's view, it served no useful purpose other than perpetuating official violence.

III. Imprisonment

663. Imprisonment is the imposition of restraints on a person's liberty within a place of detention. This form of punishment was not known in Uganda until the onset of British colonization. The only form of restraint that was practised was the placing of the offender in stocks – *envuba*. As we have noted earlier, the first prison in the country, Njabule, was established by the Government of the Kingdom of Buganda in 1894. Today there are prisons in all the districts of the country, and imprisonment is the commonest form of punishment. Virtually all offences created by the Penal Code are punishable by imprisonment. When other forms of punishment, such as fines and other non-custodial penalties fail, imprisonment is the ultimate sanction. Civil creditors do also from time to time resort to it to force contumacious judgment debtors to pay their debts. Save for those offences which carry mandatory or minimum sentences, the law that prescribes imprisonment as the punishment for an offence does also set the maximum term that a convicted offender may be sentenced to, leaving it to the court to impose a term that it deems appropriate in a particular case. It is here appropriate to mention the issue of life sentences. The Penal Code provides that persons convicted of certain offences are

844. For example, Art. 31 of the U.N. Standard Minimum Rules for the Treatment of Prisoners [ECOSOC Resolution No. 663 C (XXIV) of 31 Jul. 1957] provides that, '*Corporal punishment*, punishment by placing in a dark cell, and all cruel, inhuman or degrading punishments shall be completely prohibited as punishments for disciplinary offences.' [emphasis added]

845. The prohibition was a sequel to a decision in *Kyamanywa Simon v. Uganda*, Constitutional Reference No. 10 of 2000, in which the Court of Appeal ruled that a 'the sentence of six strokes of the cane is inconsistent with article 24 of the Constitution'. The decision does not declare corporal punishment *per se* to be unconstitutional. It is therefore arguable that Parliament or other bodies with law-making powers could lawfully create offences punishable by, among other sanctions, corporal punishment of less than six strokes of the cane.

'liable to imprisonment for life'.[846] Because section 47(6) of the Prisons Act provides that for the purpose of calculating remission, a sentence of life imprisonment shall be deemed to be twenty years imprisonment, Ugandan courts developed a practice where on passing a life sentence would say 'life imprisonment (twenty years) – thus qualifying the sentence by limiting it to a specific term'.[847] Yet in many cases, the courts have imposed specific terms of imprisonment beyond twenty years. The Supreme Court found it to be absurd that those terms of imprisonment were more severe than a term of life imprisonment. For that reason, it disapproved of the practice referred to above and held life imprisonment to mean 'imprisonment for the natural life term of a convict, though the actual period of imprisonment may stand reduced on account of remissions earned'.[848]

664. While the High Court has jurisdiction to impose any term of imprisonment within the limits set by the law, the magistrates' courts' powers are limited, and this depends on their level of seniority.[849] Nevertheless, where a Magistrates' Court presided over by a magistrate other than a Chief Magistrate imposes a sentence of imprisonment for a period of two years or over such a sentence is subject to confirmation by the High Court.[850] When a court pronounces a sentence of imprisonment, that sentence is deemed to commence from and to include the whole of the day on which it is pronounced. This is also true of sentences which are subject to confirmation, unless the accused is released on bail. Importantly, the Constitution requires that when a court is pronouncing the sentence, it must also take into account the period that the convict has already spent in custody before the completion of the trial.[851] Lastly, the sentence must be served in a prison administered by the Central Government or by a District Administration.[852] These prisons are gazetted under the Prisons Act,[853] and their administrators are accountable for the safety and welfare of the prisoners. Secret detention centres, which are currently

846. These offences include attempt to murder, sec. 204, aiding suicide, sec. 209, killing unborn child, sec. 212, disabling, sec. 214, stupefying, sec. 215, acts intended to cause grievous harm, sec. 216, preventing escape from shipwreck, sec. 217, endangering safety of person travelling by railway, sec. 218, manslaughter, sec. 190, and simple robbery, sec. 286(1)(b).
847. See for example *Tigo Stephen v. Uganda* SC Cr. App. No. 8 of 2009, [2009] UGSC 7, 10 May 2011.
848. *Ibid.*
849. The Chief Magistrates' powers are unlimited. The powers of Magistrate Grade I are limited to ten years, those of Magistrate Grade II to three years, Magistrate Grade III to one year. Magistrates Courts Act, sec. 162(1).
850. Magistrates Courts Act, sec. 173.
851. Article 23(8). In *Kabwiso Issa v. Uganda* Cr. App. No. 7 of 2002, [2003] UGSC 36 (27 Oct. 2003), the Supreme Court gave the following guidelines to all trial courts on what to say when pronouncing a sentence of imprisonment: 'Taking into account the period of … years [months or weeks whichever is applicable] which the accused has already spent in remand, I now sentence the accused to a term of … years [months or weeks, as the case may be.']
852. *Ibid.*, sec. 177(1). Also see the Trial on Indictments Act, sec. 107(1).
853. Cap. 304.

euphemistically referred to as 'safe houses', are illegal and abhorrent.[854] They are repugnant to internationally accepted standards for the treatment of prisoners.[855]

665. Like most other forms of punishment, the purpose of imprisonment is to protect society by incapacitating the offender, deterring him and others, helping him to reform, and preparing him for reintegration into society. In this respect, the International Covenant on Civil and Political Rights declares that 'The penitentiary systems shall comprise treatment of prisoners the essential aim of which shall be their reformation and social rehabilitation.'[856] Imprisonment does, however, often have adverse effects on the prisoner, his or her family and the community generally. Where the prisoner is a first young offender it may turn him or her into a hardened criminal, especially if he or she is mingled with other seasoned criminals. If he or she has a family and is the sole breadwinner, family members will be deprived of support. If he or she is employed in a vital industry or public service, that industry or service will suffer. Therefore, unless the protection of society demands it, and his or her character and antecedents otherwise dictate, it is desirable that the sentencing court exhaust all available non-custodial alternatives before resorting to imprisonment.

666. In the case of young first offenders, the nature of whose transgression requires some term in prison, it may be desirable to suspend a portion of that term for a period of time on certain conditions that the court may deem appropriate. These conditions may include not committing offences of a similar nature during the time when the sentence is suspended, and paying compensation to the victim. Breach of these conditions may result in the full sentence being reactivated. To be effective, the period that the offender serves in prison should be much shorter than the suspended one. The aim is to give him or her a short sharp shock of prison life and to release him or her before he or she gets used to it. This short stay in prison may create in him or her distaste for prison life and to make him or her resolve not to want to return there. Suspended sentences would, of course, be improper in cases involving aggravated circumstances and in which the need to protect the public should be paramount.[857] Be that as it may, however, this desirable practice was deleted from the Uganda statutes. The reasons for this action are hard to come by.

667. With respect to persons under the apparent age of 18 years, the Children Court Act specifically forbids magistrates' courts to pass sentences of imprisonment on them. They must, instead, consider other non-custodial options for dealing with them. If, however, they find that there are no other appropriate options for dealing with them, they must order them to be detained in safe custody, pending an order of the minister. They must give reasons why they consider other measures inappropriate. Meantime, they must transmit the reasons to the minister who must direct that

854. See Frank Nyakairu *Horror Stories from Kololo Safe house*, Sunday Monitor (2–8 Apr. 2006) at p. 10, http://www.monitor.co.ug/sunday/news04023.php
855. See Principle 12 of the Body of Principles for the Protection of All Persons under Any Form of Detention or Imprisonment. General Assembly Resolution 43/173 of 9 Dec. 1988.
856. Article 10(3).
857. See *Uganda v. Baguma* [1970] E.A. 169.

the person in question be detained in such prison or other place of custody which he specifies in the order. Young offenders should not be detained in prison unless, in the opinion of the minister, no other place of custody is suitable for a particular offender. The minister also has the power to specify the period during which the offender may remain incarcerated, provided that the period must not exceed the maximum term prescribed for the offence which the offender committed. Meantime, the order of detention may be reviewed and revised from time to time as the minister sees fit. Where the offender is ordered to be detained in a place of custody other than a prison, and, in the opinion of the person in charge of such place, he or she proves to be beyond control, then, the person in charge of the place may apply to court to have the offender detained in a regular prison. If the court is satisfied that the offender is indeed beyond control, it may order that he or she is detained in a prison that the court specifies. The court may thus vary the minister's order.[858]

668. The reason for avoiding prison in the case of young offenders is that it might stigmatize them and make their reformation and social rehabilitation difficult. It might inhibit their education and preparation for a useful adult life. Lastly, it might turn them into hardened criminals, given the congested conditions in the prisons and the mingling with older, seasoned criminals.

669. Other places of custody to which young offenders might be sent include approved schools and reformatory schools. The latter is intended for offenders who need long periods of training and strong discipline.

IV. Fines

670. Fines as a form of punishment were known to the indigenous criminal justice systems of pre-colonial Uganda. Known as *mutango* in the Luganda language, fines were paid in kind by the convicted offender to the authorities. Livestock was the commonest form of fines. With the introduction of the cash economy, fines are today paid in money form.

671. The statute creating an offence may prescribe a fine as the punishment or one of the punishments for the offence. The fine may be the sole punishment with imprisonment as an alternative in case of default.[859] It may be an alternative to imprisonment at the discretion of the court. For example, section 82 of the Penal Code provides that anybody convicted of the offence of watching and besetting shall be 'liable to a fine not exceeding UGX 2,000 or to imprisonment for a period not exceeding six months or to both such fine and imprisonment'. In all cases where a penalty provision is couched in language similar to this, it must be presumed that the legislature intended that the accused should be given the first option of a fine, unless the protection of the public requires that he be imprisoned. A fine may also

858. Children Act, Cap. 59.
859. For example, see Penal Code, sec. 107(2).

be the second alternative to imprisonment.[860] It may also be combined with imprisonment, at the discretion of the court. For example, section 95 of the Penal Code makes the making of false statements punishable by 'a fine not exceeding UGX 10,000 or to imprisonment for a term not exceeding twelve months or to both such fine and imprisonment'. Lastly, the fine may be mandatorily payable *in addition* to imprisonment. This combination of sentence is usually reserved for very serious offences, such as smuggling,[861] in which the accused might have retained the proceeds of the crime.

672. May a court impose a fine for an offence when the statute creating the offence does not specifically prescribe it? According to current practice, the answer seems to be yes. The basis for the answer is section 180(2) of the Magistrates Courts Act which is identical to section 110(2) of the Trial on Indictments Act and provides that, 'A person liable to imprisonment may be sentenced to pay a fine in addition to or instead of imprisonment.' This is a confusing, if not controversial, provision. Take, for example, provisions of the Penal Code which declare certain conduct to be misdemeanours but prescribe no penalty for their transgression.[862] In this case, the court has to resort to section 22 which provides that, 'When in this Code no punishment is specially provided for any misdemeanour, it shall be punishable with imprisonment for a period not exceeding two years.' Unlike similar provisions in the Codes of other countries,[863] fines are omitted from this section. Is it appropriate to impose a fine in such cases? Again, consider section 384(1) of the Code which provides that, 'Any person who, for the purpose of obtaining any employment, utters any document of the nature of a testimonial of character given to another person, is guilty of a misdemeanour *and is liable to imprisonment* for one year.' Given the specificity of the provision is it appropriate to impose a fine *in addition* to the imprisonment? It is submitted, not. These are penal provisions and must be construed strictly. The provisions of the Magistrates Courts Act and the Trial on Indictments Act, which are merely procedural, must not be construed as authorizing imposition of fines where the substantive law did not prescribe them. They must be understood as clarifying for the courts their power to impose fines in addition to or in lieu of imprisonment where the substantive law permits them.

673. The amount of fines that may be imposed by the courts of various grades is also regulated by statute. The High Court may impose the maximum fine prescribed by the law for a particular offence. Where no limit is set, the Court may impose any amount, provided that it is not excessive.[864] A Chief Magistrate may also impose any fine within the limits set by the law, provided it is not excessive. A Magistrate Grade I may impose a fine up to UGX 4,800,000 and a Magistrate

860. For example, see sec. 385(1).
861. Penal Code, sec. 319(1).
862. For example, obtaining credit by false pretences under sec. 308, pretending to tell fortunes under sec. 311, false declaration for a passport under sec. 313.
863. For example, see sec. 33 of the Botswana Penal Code which provides that, 'When in this Code no punishment is specially provided for any offence, it shall be punishable with imprisonment for a term not exceeding two years or with a fine, or with both.'
864. Trial on Indictments Act, sec. 110(4).

Grade II, up to UGX 500,000.[865] In determining the appropriate amount to impose in a given case, the court must take into account the gravity of the offence charged, the value of the property involved (in offences involving property) and the accused's means and ability to pay.[866] Imposing a fine that is beyond the accused's ability to pay may be counter-productive. The offender may be forced to commit further crimes in order to get the money with which to pay the fine. To avoid this possibility, therefore, the court must conduct a careful inquiry into the accused's means before deciding on whether to impose a fine at all, or the amount. While it is wrong to impose a fine that the accused cannot pay because of lack of means, it is also unjust to impose an otherwise excessive fine merely because the accused is a person of means. The court must never lose sight of the fact that the sentence must fit not only the offender, but the offence as well.

674. Where the court has decided to impose a fine, it may also provide an alternative term of imprisonment in case of default of payment. This imprisonment is in addition to any other imprisonment to which the accused may have been sentenced. Both the Magistrates Courts Act and the Trial on Indictments Act provide a scale to guide the courts in determining the additional term of imprisonment in case of default. Section 180 of the Magistrates Courts Act provides as follows:

(d) the period of imprisonment ordered by a court in respect of the nonpayment of any sum of money adjudged to be paid by a conviction or in respect of the default of a sufficient distress to satisfy any such sum shall be such term as in the opinion of the court will satisfy the justice of the case, but shall not exceed in any case the maximum fixed by the following scale,

Amount	*Maximum period*
Not exceeding Shs. 2,000:	7 days
Exceeding Shs. 2000 but not exceeding Shs. 10,000:	1 month
Exceeding Shs. 10,000 but not exceeding Shs. 40,000:	6 weeks
Exceeding Shs. 40,000 but not exceeding Shs. 100,000:	3 months
Exceeding Shs. 100,000:	12 months

(e) the imprisonment which is imposed in default of payment of a fine shall terminate whenever the fine is either paid or levied by process of law.[867]

The court should give the accused thirty days within which to pay the fine before sending him or her to prison for defaulting.[868] However, where it appears to the court that the accused has sufficient means to pay the fine forthwith, or when he or she is asked by the court whether he or she wishes to have time to pay but he or she

865. Magistrates Courts Act, sec. 162(1).
866. *Ibid.*, sec. 180, and Trial on Indictments Act, sec. 110.
867. In *Emilio Guma v. Uganda*, H.Ct.Cr.Revision No. 103 of 1991 (unreported), the accused was convicted of occasioning actual bodily harm contrary to sec. 236 of the Penal Code and was sentenced to a fine of UGX 8,000 or in default of payment to six months imprisonment. On revision, the High Court set aside the default sentence as illegal. It reduced it to one month.
868. Trial on Indictments Act, sec. 111(1); Magistrates' Courts Act, sec. 180(1).

does not ask for such time, or he or she fails to satisfy the court that he or she has a fixed place of abode, or there are special circumstances relating to the gravity of the offence and the character of the accused warranting immediate committal, the court may commit him or her to prison. In the committal warrant, the court must state the reasons for not giving the accused time to pay.[869] The court also has power to allow the accused to pay the fine by instalments, or where he or she is employed, to attach the monthly salary. However, only half of the salary may be attached for this purpose.[870] Finally, the court may enforce payment of a fine by the attachment and sale of the accused's movable and immovable property.[871] An unpaid fine is a debt owed to the state and may thus be enforced like any other civil debt. For that reason, the fine does not become extinguished with the death of the accused. It may be enforced against his or her estate.[872]

V. Forfeiture

675. Forfeiture is provided for under section 202 of the Magistrates Courts Act and under section 131 of the Trial on Indictments Act.

676. In the course or at the conclusion of a criminal trial, the court may order any property produced before it forfeited, confiscated, destroyed or delivered to any person as it deems appropriate. This is property which might have been used to commit or facilitate a crime. It may be a weapon or a vehicle. It may also be proceeds of crime such as money obtained from sale of prohibited substances or stolen property. The idea behind these measures is to deprive the accused of the means wherewithal to commit further crimes or to prevent him or her from benefiting from crime. It is for this reason that the Penal Code provides for the forfeiture of any die, plate, instrument or other thing 'found in possession of a person convicted of possessing articles for making counterfeit stamps',[873] or 'all chattel, articles or instruments' to which a counterfeit trademark has been applied.[874]

677. Where the court orders forfeiture or confiscation of the property without having it destroyed, it may order it kept or sold. The proceeds of the sale go to the general revenues of the state in the Consolidated Fund, unless within six months after the date of forfeiture some person establishes to the satisfaction of the court that he or she was entitled to the property. In this respect, where the original owner of the property is known, he or she should be given an opportunity to be heard and to prove his bona fides before the court orders forfeiture or confiscation of his property. It may so happen that the property, say a weapon or vehicle, was taken from him or her without his or her consent. It would be unfair to penalize him or her, too, when he or she was not

869. *Ibid.*, sec. 180(6) and sec. 111(2) respectively.
870. *Ibid.*, sec. 180(3) and sec. 111(3) respectively.
871. *Ibid.*, sec. 181(3) and sec. 111(2) respectively.
872. See the English case of *Treasury v. Harris* [1957] 2 All E.R. 455.
873. Section 375.
874. Section 380.

party to the crime or was not in any way negligent or culpable.[875] However, there are instances where Parliament deliberately requires the confiscation of property used in connection with crime, irrespective of who the owner is and whether or not he has been negligent or culpable. An example of such a requirement is section 7(3) of the Coffee (Export Duty) Act which provides as follows:

> If any person is convicted of an offence under the provisions of this section, any coffee which is the subject of the offence and the vehicle on which such coffee was carried shall be ordered by the court to be confiscated.

In *Joseph Bukenya v. Uganda*,[876] the owner of a lorry which was used to carry coffee in contravention of the Act sought to impugn an order confiscating his lorry. He contended that he had neither given authority to his driver to use the vehicle for the purpose of smuggling coffee, nor had any knowledge that it was being used for that purpose. He also argued that he was not given an opportunity to be heard before the confiscation order was made. It was held that the owner of the vehicle had no right to be heard, since the order was mandatory. Said Goudie, J.:

> It might be argued that it is somewhat unfair that an innocent owner of a vehicle which has been used for an unlawful purpose without his knowledge or consent should automatically have his vehicle confiscated. However, I think this is intentionally a very stringent provision, the effect of which is to throw a burden on the owners of vehicles to see that such vehicles are not used for illegal purposes. It is also obvious that if any owner were to deny knowledge of an illegal use by his driver it might be extremely difficult to disprove the denial whether or not there was guilty knowledge.

It must nevertheless be emphasized that, with the exception of cases of this kind, the power to order forfeiture or confiscation of property is discretionary. It must therefore be exercised judicially.

678. An order for forfeiture or confiscation of the property may be appealed to a higher court. When such an appeal is lodged, the order must not be carried out until the final disposal of the appeal. The exception to this rule is in respect of livestock or other property which is subject to speedy and natural decay.

VI. Other Measures

A. Reconciliation and Discharge

679. Section 160 of the Magistrates Courts Act provides that:

> In criminal cases, a Magistrates' Court may promote reconciliation, and encourage and facilitate the settlement in an amicable way, of proceedings for

875. See *Rex v. Mbugeramula* [1951] 18 E.A.C.A. 207.
876. [1971] U.L.R. 50.

> assault, or for any other offence of a personal or private nature, not amounting to felony and not aggravated in degree, in terms of payment of compensation or other terms approved by such court, and may thereupon, order the proceedings to be stayed.

The aim of the provision is to provide for an avenue for diversion; to normalize relations between the accused and his or her victim by removing the additional scar that criminal proceedings may leave; to expedite the criminal justice process; and to clear the court's docket.

680. Words such as 'encourage and facilitate' settlement connote an active role on the part of the court. The court must not simply sit back and wait for the parties to say to it that they want to reconcile. It can and should take the initiative in appropriate cases and suggest reconciliation to the parties. It may call the parties to chambers to suggest terms of settlement to them or to enable them to talk to each other. It may also adjourn or stay the proceedings to enable the accused to fulfil his or her part of the settlement. The settlement may be payment of compensation. In case of stolen or damaged property, it may be the return or repair of such property. It may also be just an apology by the accused to the victim. Where reconciliation is accepted and the terms of settlement agreed on and approved by the court, the court must record such terms before staying the proceedings.[877] The stay must be for a sufficient length of time to enable the accused to carry out the terms of the settlement. Where the terms of the settlement are fully carried out to the satisfaction of the victim and the court, the court must discharge the accused and close the case. If the accused fails to carry out the terms of the settlement within the time allowed, the court must reopen the case and proceed to trial in the normal way.

681. Lastly, it must be noted that reconciliation is permitted only in proceedings for 'assault or for any other offence of a personal or private nature, not amounting to felony and not aggravated in degree'. In *Uganda v. Odura*,[878] the magistrate purported to promote reconciliation in proceedings in which the accused was charged with threatening violence, which is a felony. The High Court set aside the reconciliation proceedings and ordered the case to proceed in the normal way unless the charges were withdrawn. In *Uganda v. Zaberi Bakenge*,[879] the complainant applied for and the trial magistrate accepted reconciliation and discharged the accused who was charged with theft from the person – again a felony. The discharge was also declared a nullity. These cases present no problems because felonies are clearly defined by the Penal Code. What presents problems are cases of 'a personal nature' and those 'aggravated in degree'. These terms are not defined in the Code. Cases involving personal injuries would clearly be of a personal nature. They would, however, be aggravated in degree if the injuries are extensive or have been inflicted with a show of brutality. Would thefts or damage to property also be of a personal nature? Yes, provided the value of the property is small or the damage to the property not

877. See *Uganda v. Odura* [1974] E.A. 553.
878. *Ibid.*
879. [1971] U.L.R. 48.

extensive. In *Uganda v. Zadoki Olowo*,[880] the accused was charged with careless driving. The court discharged him on the ground that the prosecution had agreed to reconciliation with him. The High Court set aside the order of discharge, saying that a charge for careless driving was not of a personal or private nature. It was, on the contrary, an offence that affected the public at large and could constitute a danger to the public in general.

682. What should be done in cases where the parties desire reconciliation but because of technicalities the court cannot grant it? One way out is for the prosecution to withdraw the charges. The other alternative, which was recommended to the magistrate in the *Bakenge case, supra*, is to discharge the accused under section 190 of the Magistrates Courts Act. That section, which is identical in terms to section 119 of the Trial on Indictments Act, reads as follows:

> 1. Where, in any trial before a Magistrates' Court, the court thinks that the charge against the accused person is proved, but is of the opinion that, having regard to the character, antecedents, age, health, or mental condition of the accused, or to the trivial nature of the offence, or to the extenuating circumstances in which the offence was committed, it is inexpedient to inflict any punishment, the court may,
>   (a) without proceedings to conviction, make an order dismissing the charge, or
>   (b) convict the accused person and caution him or her.
> 2. When an order is made by a court under this section dismissing a charge, such an order shall be deemed to be a conviction for the purposes of Subsection (1) of Section 195, Section 197 and Section 201 of this Act.[881]

B. Compensation

683. Compensation, known as *engassi* in the Luganda language, is the payment of money or other valuable assets by the convicted offender to the victim. Payment of compensation serves to restore the victim, as much as money can do, to the same position as he or she would have been had the offender not inflicted the injuries or loss on him or her. Payment of compensation in the course of criminal proceedings is expeditious. It obviates the need to institute fresh or separate civil proceedings for the same thing. It is in accord with the indigenous conception of criminal justice that made little distinction between civil and criminal proceedings and considered compensation as a primary aim of the proceedings.[882] According to a Luganda maxim, *Kantanyi kaggweerawo: kafumitabagenge w'akufumitira w'omweggiramu* – that is to say, an offence is settled swiftly: you pull out the spiky seeds of a plant called *kafumitabagenge* at the very spot where they sting you – you do not have to

880. H.Ct.Monthly Bulletin No. 745 of 1969.
881. It was held in *Uganda v. Hadi Jamal* [1964] E.A. 294 that a caution under sec. 190(1)(b) is a sentence, since it is made in consequence of a conviction.
882. See Katende, J.W., *Why Were Punishments in Pre-Colonial Africa Mainly Compensatory Rather than Punitive?* J. Denning L. Soc. 2 (1967).

wait. Thus in deference to this conception, the law permits the courts to award compensation to a victim of crime against the convicted criminal. Section 197 of the Magistrates Courts Act and section 126 of the Trial on Indictments Act provide for compensation against a person convicted of a crime. Compensation may be awarded to any person 'whether or not he is the prosecutor or a witness in the case' who 'has suffered material loss or personal injury in consequence of the crime committed'.

684. The first issue, then, is who is entitled to compensation? The direct victim of the crime – an individual natural person, or a body corporate, which includes government departments and local administration bodies, that has suffered actual bodily harm, or one whose property was stolen, damaged or lost, and one who suffered material loss in consequence of the crime committed is entitled to it. Compensation thus covers economic loss as a reasonably foreseeable consequence of the crime. It also covers personal injury, physical or mental, as a result of the crime. In cases of defilement the Penal Code specifically extends the injury to 'physical, sexual and psychological harm'.[883] Would third parties also be entitled to recover compensation? For instance, would dependents of a victim who has either been killed or disabled from supporting his or her family be entitled to compensation? Have the dependents suffered 'in consequence of the crime'? Yes, they have and, it is submitted, should in principle be entitled to compensation from the criminal. There are, however, no Ugandan precedents on the issue. But the High Court in neighbouring Tanzania in interpreting a statute *in pari materia* with ours held that people other than direct victims were not eligible for compensation. For that reason, it held that the Government was not entitled to recover compensation from the accused who had injured a policeman as a result of careless driving and thus deprived the Government of his services for the period he was unable to work. The court said that 'compensation ... should be awarded to persons who have directly suffered natural loss or personal injury in consequence of the offence committed and not third parties against whom the accused may have a defence in a civil suit for damages'.[884] The only third parties who are explicitly allowed to recover compensation are bona fide purchasers of any property in relation to which offences under Chapter XXVI to XXXI of the Penal Code were committed for the loss of the property which might have been returned to their rightful owners.[885] The UN Declaration of Basic Principles of Justice for Victims of Crime and Abuse of Power is instructive on this point.[886] Article 2 thereof provides that 'the term "victim" also includes, where appropriate, the immediate family or dependents of the direct victim and persons who have suffered harm in intervening to assist victims in distress or to prevent victimization'. It is urged that our courts interpret the relevant provisions of the law liberally and in accordance with the UN Declaration to permit dependents and others covered by the Declaration to recover compensation in the course of the criminal proceedings.

883. Penal Code, sec. 129.
884. *Republic v. Anael* [1967] E.A. 378.
885. Trial on Indictments Act, sec. 126(2) and Magistrates' Courts Act, sec. 197(2).
886. UN General Assembly Resolution 40/34, 29 Nov. 1985.

685. The second question is whether the victim himself must apply for the compensation as a condition precedent to its being awarded to him. Ordinarily, he or she should apply for it. There is, however, nothing in the statutes to preclude the court from broaching the issue *mero muto* or for the prosecutor from suggesting it. Given the fact that victims are not represented at criminal proceedings and are invariably ignorant of their rights, it is only fair that the court should advise the victim to apply for compensation. However, in the case of robbery and corruption-related offences such as embezzlement and causing financial loss, the court is obliged to award compensation to the 'aggrieved party' whether or not such party has applied for it.[887] However, they must require the parties to strictly prove their claims as they would in a civil case and seek assistance of counsel if they want. Needless to say, the court must also give the accused ample opportunity to be heard on the matter.[888]

686. The next question relates to the quantum of compensation that the victim may recover for his or her injury, loss or damage. In cases tried before the High Court, the victim would be able to recover to the full extent of his or her damage as adjudged by the court to be 'fair and reasonable'.[889] As long as he or she can prove it, he or she should be able to recover compensation for all the loss or damage flowing directly and foreseeably from the crime. In cases tried before magistrates' courts, recovery is severely limited. In the first place, it will not be granted unless 'substantial compensation is, in the opinion of the court, recoverable' by the victim by civil suit.[890] If only small amounts would be recoverable in a civil suit then the court will not award any compensation. It is submitted that there is no rhyme or reason for this restriction. The *raison d'être* for awarding compensation in criminal proceedings is to obviate the need for instituting separate civil proceedings and thus do justice to victims expeditiously. Civil proceedings are complex, time-consuming and expensive. Many victims cannot invoke them. They should therefore not be used as the yardstick for granting compensation in criminal proceedings. Furthermore, to deny compensation to a victim merely because it is not substantial is to do him or her an injustice. As the Baganda and Banyankore people say, '*N'ow'emu akoomera*' (i.e., to say, a person with only one cow has the right to take care of that cow just like the one with many; he or she is entitled to the same degree of protection). The absurdity of the 'substantial compensation' requirement is demonstrated by the case of *Uganda v. Karaso*.[891] The accused pleaded guilty and was convicted of stealing trees from the Ministry of Works. He was cautioned and ordered to pay the sum of UGX 42, the value of the trees to the Ministry. On revision, however, the High Court declared the compensation order 'misconceived' and set it aside. Apparently, the order did not meet the 'substantial compensation' requirement. The court interpreted 'substantial compensation' to mean 'a relatively large sum of money' and held that the sum of UGX 42, was not substantial. Thus the accused was left to go scot-free without being given the opportunity to atone for

887. See secs. 170 and 286 of the Penal Code.
888. See *Kyagoga v. Uganda* [1973] E.A. 486.
889. Trial on Indictments Act, sec. 126(1).
890. Magistrates Courts Act, sec. 197(1).
891. [1974] E.A. 458.

his wrong. The owner of the trees [body of tax payers] was also denied the right to recover the value of the trees which the accused admitted to have stolen and was probably able and willing to pay!

687. It should also be noted that magistrates' courts cannot award sums exceeding their subject-matter jurisdiction. For full compensation for the loss or harm suffered, the complainant must file a civil suit against the accused. The court hearing the civil suit must take into account the sum already recovered in the criminal proceedings.[892] It should, however, be noted that in cases of embezzlement,[893] causing financial loss,[894] and robbery[895] the court is duty bound to award full compensation against the convicted offender. The amount it may award is unlimited.[896] But in cases of elopement,[897] in which compensation is also mandatory, the Penal Code fixes the amount at UGX 600 only.

688. With the exception of the few cases noted above, award of compensation, whether by the magistrates' courts or the High Court, is a discretionary matter. In exercising that discretion, the Courts usually take into account three factors: the accused's means, the complexity of the case and the amount involved. They generally refrain from making compensation orders against defendants whom they consider to have no means wherewithal to satisfy such orders. They are also usually reluctant to make the orders save 'in simple straight forward cases where no substantial amount is involved'.[898]

689. Section 199 of the Magistrates Courts Act and section 128 of the Trial on Indictments Act also authorize courts on imposing a fine or a sentence of which a fine forms part to order the whole or any part of the fine recovered to be applied:

(a) in defraying expenses properly incurred in the prosecution; and
(b) in the payment to any person of compensation for any loss or injury caused by the offence when substantial compensation is, in the opinion of the court, recoverable by civil suit.

These provisions are too narrow in scope. They serve no purpose. In the first place, they are of no use to victims of such offences as rape, which are not punishable by fines. Second, if in a given case, the trial court considers it inappropriate to impose a fine there would be no compensation. Compensation can only be paid out of a fine. Third, in determining the appropriate amount of the fine to impose, the courts are

892. *Ibid.*, sec. 197(4).
893. Penal Code, sec. 268.
894. *Ibid.*, secs. 269, 270. See also *Major John Kazoora v. Uganda*, H.Ct.Misc.Cr.Appl. No. 109F of 1991 (unreported).
895. *Ibid.*, sec. 286(4).
896. See *Sabani v. Uganda* [1974] E.A. 460.
897. Section 127(1).
898. See *Uganda v. Alozio Kibombo* 9 H.Ct.Monthly Bulletin 153 (1971). For an extensive discussion of the criteria used in various jurisdictions, see Nsereko, *Victims of Crime and their Rights*, in *Criminology in Africa* (Mushanga, T.M. ed., U.N. Intl. Crime & J. Research Inst. 1992).

guided solely by the nature of the offence committed and by the financial situation of the accused and his ability to pay the fine. This being the case, then, the fines imposed may be woefully inadequate to compensate the victim for the damage, loss or injury suffered as a result of the crime. In one case, for example, the accused pleaded guilty to ten counts of forgery and to ten counts of obtaining by false pretences. On each of the ten counts of forgery, he was sentenced to two years imprisonment, all sentences to run concurrently. On each of the counts of obtaining by false pretences, he was sentenced to a fine of UGX 1,400, a total of UGX 14,000. It would appear that, in imposing these fines, the trial magistrate was influenced by the desire to create a sufficiently large fund from which compensation could be paid to the victims of the fraud. On appeal, the High Court set aside the sentences of fines, saying that they were based on wrong principles. It then laid down the following rules for the future guidance of the inferior courts:

(1) A criminal court never imposes a fine except as punishment.
(2) Regardless of any loss suffered by a victim of the crime, a criminal court must first make up its mind how much that fine should be.
(3) When the court has decided on the amount of the fine, the court may order part or even the whole of the fine to be paid to the victim.
(4) The criminal court must not be made the means of helping people to recover debts.[899]

Lastly, compensation can only be paid if, in the opinion of the court, substantial compensation would be recoverable by civil suit. As we have noted above, this restriction is unfair.

C. Restitution

690. Section 201 of the Magistrates Courts Act and section 130 of the Trial on Indictments Act deal with restitution. Restitution is the return of property, the subject of criminal proceedings, to its rightful owner. The criminal must not be allowed to retain any benefits of crime.

691. Both sections authorize the court which convicts a person of property-related offences covered by Chapters XXVI and XXI of the Penal Code to return to the owner of such property or proceeds thereof as is still available. In cases of stolen property which is recovered from a person who bought it from the thief, the court is empowered to order return to such purchaser the amount he or she had paid to the thief, provided that: (i) he or she had no knowledge that the property was stolen and (ii) the money from the sale has been recovered from the thief on his or her arrest. Unless the court orders the contrary, restitution orders do not come into operation until the lapse of time allowed for appeal and, where an appeal has been filed, it has been finally disposed of.

899. *Behar Singh v. R.* [1936–1951] 6 U.L.R. 265.

692. Restitution is forbidden in case of goods, as defined by the Sale of Goods Act, which were obtained by fraud or other wrongful means not amounting to theft. It is also forbidden in respect of a negotiable instrument which has been received for value and in good faith and without reasonable cause to suspect that it was stolen. The same applies to valuable security which has in good faith been paid or discharged by some person who is liable to the payment thereof.

D. Probation

693. Probation is the release to freedom of a convicted offender without sentencing him or her, on condition that: (i) he or she behaves himself or herself and (ii) is subject to supervision of a probation officer. Probation avoids unnecessary imprisonment with all the attendant undesirable effects on the offender, his or her family and the public at large. It also facilitates the offender's reintegration into society while at the same time helping him or her to turn from his or her criminal ways. The element of supervision ensures public protection in case the offender relapses or is tempted to relapse into his or her criminal ways.

Section 2 of the Probation Act provides as follows:

(1) Where a court by or before which a person is convicted of an offence (not being an offence the sentence for which is fixed by law) is of opinion after due inquiry has been made that having regard to the circumstances, including the nature of the offence and the character of the offender, it is expedient to do so, the court may, instead of sentencing him or her, make a probation order.
(2) Before making a probation order, the court shall explain to the offender in ordinary language the effect of the order and that, if he or she fails in any respect to comply therewith or commits another offence, he or she will be liable to be sentenced for the original offence; and if the offender is not less than 14 years of age, the court shall not make a probation order unless the offender expresses his or her willingness to comply with the requirements of the order.

According to this provision, a probation order must not be made where the offender is convicted of an offence for which a minimum sentence is prescribed and the court is in duty bound to impose it.[900] Again, before the order is made, the court must make an inquiry into the offender's background and antecedents, and the circumstances under which he committed the offence. The court must ask itself the question whether, given the nature and gravity of the offence and the character of the offender, it would be safe to release the offender back to the community. In this respect, a probation officer's report on the accused would be extremely useful to the court in enabling it to make an informed decision. Additionally, the success of the probation exercise depends to a large extent, on the offender himself or herself. He or she must be willing to comply with the conditions of the judicial order. He or she must be willing to cooperate with his or her supervisor, the probation officer. It is

900. *Uganda v. Kayondo* [1973] E.A. 269; [1972] U.L.R. 41.

for this reason that the provision requires the court to explain to him or her 'in ordinary language' the full implications of the order and to insist on his or her express willingness to comply as a *sine qua non* to the order. The provision does, however, exempt offenders who are below 14 years of age from the requirement of consent.

694. The duration of a probation order must be specified in the order itself, but must not be less than one year nor more than three years from the date of the order. During the subsistence of the order, the offender or probationer must submit to the supervision of a probation officer appointed or assigned for the district in which the probationer will reside. In the case of a female offender, the supervisor must wherever possible be a woman.[901] The order must contain requirements which the court considers necessary for securing the supervision of the offender. It may, for example, put restrictions on where he or she may reside. It must not, however, contain a requirement for compensation.[902] Where the offender is required to stay in an institution, such institution must be under the control of or be subject to the inspection of the Government or be approved for the purpose by the Government.[903]

695. Where the offender violates any of the requirements under the probation order, he or she may either be fined a sum which does not exceed UGX 200 or be dealt with for the offence in respect of which the probation order remains in force. If the offender is dealt with for the original offence, this means that he or she is sentenced. If the sentence is a fine, the probation order continues in force with any modifications that the court may deem appropriate. If the sentence is imprisonment, the probation order ceases to have effect.[904] Whichever option the court adopts, the alleged violations of the probation order must be strictly proved, and the offender must be heard and allowed to controvert those allegations.

E. Police Supervision

696. Police supervision applies to persons who are sentenced to imprisonment for terms of less than life imprisonment. It comes in operation after their discharge from prison. It is mandatory for persons convicted of robbery and of any other offences which the Minister may by a statutory order declare to be offences to which police supervision applies.[905] The Minister has to date made no such orders. Therefore, police supervision applies to robbery convicts only.

A police supervision order must not exceed five years from the expiration of the offender's term of imprisonment. It requires the offender on his or her discharge from prison to be issued by the police with an identity card in prescribed form and to report himself or herself personally at such intervals of time and at such places and to such persons as are endorsed on the card. The offender must also notify his

901. Section 13(2).
902. Section 3(1).
903. Section 3(2).
904. Section 10(2).
905. Trial on Indictments Act, sec. 124 and Magistrates' Courts Act, sec. 194.

or her police supervisor of the place of his or her residence and of any changes in such residence. Failure or neglect to comply with these requirements constitutes an offence punishable by imprisonment for a term not exceeding two years. It is, however, a defence, if the offender can satisfy the court that 'he or she did his best to act in conformity with the law'.[906]

906. *Ibid.*

Part II. Criminal Procedure

Chapter 1. Introduction

697. Substantive criminal law defines the conduct that the law forbids under the pain of punishment. The law of criminal procedure lays down the procedure that must be followed in dealing with persons suspected of having committed such conduct. It sets out the rules that all actors involved in the criminal justice system must follow. These actors include the complainant, the police, judges and magistrates, court personnel, probation officers, prisons officers and ministers. The law of criminal procedure also establishes certain checks and standards that serve to guard against improper police conduct, unjustified prosecution, unfair trial and unjust punishment.

698. As noted earlier, the 1902 Uganda Order-in-Council which set up the High Court and the subordinate courts, introduced the Indian Penal and Criminal Procedure Codes Act into Uganda. When the Indian Codes were discontinued, a Ugandan Penal Code as well as a Criminal Procedure Code Act was promulgated in 1930. The Criminal Procedure Code Act was amended from time to time until 1950 when it was re-enacted and consolidated. It governed the procedure in both the High Court and the subordinate courts. When, in later years, it was considered desirable to have separate sets of rules regulating the procedure in the High Court and in the subordinate courts, the Magistrates Courts Act was passed in 1970, to be followed by the Trial on Indictments Act in 1971. The Magistrates Courts Act regulated the proceedings in the magistrates' courts while the Trial on Indictments Act regulated those in the High Court. The Criminal Procedure Code Act was repealed save for the provisions relating to interpretation, arrest, escape and retaking, police preventive action, appeals, and revisions. Though the bulk of the law on criminal procedure is thus found in the Magistrates Courts Act, Trial on Indictments Act, and the residue of the Criminal Procedure Code Act, there are other statutes that complement them. These statutes include the Judicature Act, Police Act, Prisons Act, Probation Act, Habitual Criminals (Preventive) Act, Children Act and the Constitution.

As was noted in the introductory part of this book, the Constitution is the most important source of the law of criminal procedure in Uganda. It sets forth minimum standards that are universally considered to be indispensable to a free and fair trial. In a way, the law of criminal procedure may be viewed as an extension of constitutional law: the protection of individual liberties.

Chapter 2. Criminal Prosecutions

§1. Prosecuting Authorities

I. Public Prosecutions

699. The state bears the primary responsibility of enforcing the criminal law and of bringing offenders to justice. This responsibility arises out of its inherent duty to protect the public. Crimes, it should be noted, are offences that are notionally committed against the general public. Although a private citizen may also take the initiative to ensure that the criminal law is enforced and criminals brought to justice, the state retains overall primacy in the institution of criminal proceedings. Decisions of its agents in these matters take precedence over those of private citizens.

700. The Constitution vests in the DPP, the power to institute criminal proceedings against any person in all courts of Uganda with the exception of the courts martial. The office of DPP is a public office. Its holder is appointed by the President acting on the recommendation of the Public Service Commission.[907] To qualify for appointment, a person must be qualified to be appointed as a judge of the High Court.[908] That means that he or she must have practised law before courts with unlimited civil and criminal jurisdiction for a period of not less than seven years, and must be a person of high moral integrity. The requirement that the DPP should possess such qualifications ensures that, like a judge, he or she is a person with sufficient professional experience and personal character; and he or she is fit to competently exercise the discretionary powers vested in the Director. It also ensures that he or she is a person who can be entrusted with the onerous responsibility of making decisions that affect the safety of the public in general and the liberty of the individual in particular. Lastly, to ensure his or her high professional status and level of conduct, Article 120(7) of the Constitution provides that the DPP 'shall have the same terms and conditions of service as those of a High Court judge'.

701. Article 120(3) of the Constitution sets out the functions of the DPP to be:

(a) to direct the police to investigate any information of a criminal nature and to report to him or her expeditiously;
(b) to institute criminal proceedings against any person or authority in any court with competent jurisdiction other than a court martial;
(c) to take over and continue any criminal proceedings instituted by any other person or authority;
(d) to discontinue at any stage before judgment is delivered any criminal proceedings to which this article relates, instituted by himself or herself or any other person or authority; except that the DPP shall not discontinue any proceedings commenced by another person or authority except with the consent of the court.

907. The Constitution, Art. 120(1).
908. The Constitution, Art. 120(2).

702. The decision to prosecute or not to prosecute or to exercise any of the powers vested in the DPP is within the Director's exclusive discretion. In making the decision, he or she 'shall not be subject to the direction or control of any person or authority'.[909] Neither the President nor any of his ministers or officials can order the DPP to institute criminal proceedings against anybody or to refrain from doing so. Nor can the courts, *proprio motu* or at the instance of any other person or authority order him or her to do so.[910]

A. The Decision to Prosecute

703. What considerations, then, does the DPP take into account in the exercise of his or her discretion to prosecute? The Constitution neatly articulates three major considerations. It provides that:

> In exercising his or her powers ... , the Director of Public Prosecutions shall have regard to the public interest, the interest of the administration of justice and the need to prevent abuse of legal process.[911]

Public interest must thus be a primary consideration behind every decision to prosecute or not to prosecute. Since the resources available to the Director are not infinite, they must not be used to pursue prosecutions that are not in public interest.

704. In deciding whether public interest requires that a prosecution be pursued, a variety of factors must be considered. Pre-eminent among these factors is the likelihood of the prosecution resulting in a conviction. It is submitted that public interest would not be served by prosecutions that are clearly unlikely to result in a conviction. Such prosecutions will serve only to squander available meagre resources and to abuse the legal process. Therefore, before instituting a prosecution, the DPP must make a dispassionate assessment of all available evidence and determine whether it discloses a prima facie case. In doing so, he or she must consider the cogency of the evidence, its admissibility and the credibility as well as the availability and consistency of prospective prosecution witnesses.

705. Other factors which the Director may consider in determining whether public interest is served in pursuing a prosecution include: the seriousness or, conversely, the triviality of the offence in question; the prevalence of the offence and the need for deterrence, both personal and general; the staleness of the offence; public concern or lack of concern over the offence; the attitude of the victim of the offence over the prosecution; the youth, age, physical or mental health of the accused; the antecedents of the accused; the willingness of the accused to cooperate with the law enforcement agencies in the prosecution of others; the likely length and

909. The Constitution, Art. 120(6).
910. For example, see the English case of *Gouriet & Anor. v. Attorney General & Anor.* [1978] A.C. 435.
911. Article 120(5).

expense of the trial; the obsolescence or obscurity of the law; and the effect of the prosecution on Uganda's relations with other countries.

706. The other considerations articulated in the Constitution [the interest of the administration of justice, and the need to prevent abuse of the legal process] are subsumed under the above discussion. Clearly, where there is sufficient admissible and credible evidence to warrant a prosecution and it is not against public interest to prosecute, the DPP should prosecute all alleged offenders with zeal and vigour. Again, where there is no sufficient admissible and credible evidence that is likely to found a conviction, the Director should not commence any prosecution just for the sake of harassing the accused. Such prosecution constitutes an abuse of the legal process and turns the DPP into an office of public persecution.

707. In instituting criminal proceedings against an offender, the DPP does so in the name and on behalf of Uganda. He or she does so personally or through officers authorized by him or her generally or on special instructions. With respect to proceedings before the magistrates' courts, section 223 of the Magistrates Courts Act provides as follows:

1. The Director of Public Prosecutions may appoint generally or in any case or for any specified class of cases, in any local area, one or more persons to be called public prosecutors.
2. The Director of Public Prosecutions by writing under his or her hand may appoint any advocate or any person employed in the public service to be a public prosecutor for the purpose of any case or cases.
3. Every public prosecutor shall be subject to the express directions of the Director of Public Prosecutions.

Regarding the proceedings before the High Court, section 136 of the Trial on Indictments Act provides as follows:

1. All prosecutions before the High Court shall be conducted by a member of the Attorney General's Chambers or by such other person as the Director of Public Prosecutions may, by writing under his or her hand, appoint.
2. An appointment under the provisions of subsection (1) of this section may be for a particular case or for a specified class or series of cases and every person so appointed shall be under the express direction of the Director of Public Prosecutions.

B. Consent of the DPP

708. Some statutes require the specific written consent of the DPP in respect of certain offences before any prosecution can be instituted.[912] The personal consent of the DPP appears to be based on the need to ensure that prosecutions of certain offences that might involve public policy considerations or might affect Uganda's relations with other countries are not undertaken without his or her approval. There is however no logical consistency in the type of offences that are listed as requiring the Director's consent. Be that as it may, however, prosecution without the requisite consent is void *ab initio.*[913] However, proceedings are not vitiated by the mere fact that the accused is arrested, charged at the police station and released on bail pending trial before a written consent is sought and obtained. It is sufficient that at the time that the trial commences the consent has been sought and obtained.[914] The police are thus not precluded from taking the initial steps to bring a suspected offender to justice, including arresting, charging, and bringing him to court for mention or remand in custody pending the procurement of the written consent from the DPP.

C. Nolle Prosequi

709. As noted earlier, the Constitution authorizes the DPP 'to discontinue at any stage before judgment is delivered, any criminal proceedings instituted by himself or herself or any other authority'.[915] When the DPP exercises these powers, he or she is said to have entered a *nolle prosequi.* The DPP exercises the powers personally either in writing or by physically appearing before the court and informing the court that he or she is withdrawing the proceedings. In withdrawing the proceedings instituted by himself or herself, the DPP does not need the leave of the court. Nor does he or she have to furnish it with any reasons, because this is a matter within his or her absolute discretion. Similarly, once he or she has withdrawn the proceedings, he or she cannot be compelled to continue with them.[916] Nevertheless, in exercising these powers the Director must ever bear in mind that his or hers is an office of trust, and that he or she must exercise his or her powers in a way that best

912. For example, see the following sections of the Penal Code: 49(5) – inducing a boycott; 52 – incitement to non-payment of taxes; 57, 61(1) – managing unlawful societies; 82(2) – watching and besetting; 85, 87 – offences by officers charged with administration of property of special kind; 87 – abuse of office; 95 – false statements in judicial proceedings, 149, 150 – incest; 180 – publications of defamatory matter concerning a dead person. See also sec. 49 of the Anti-Corruption Act in respect of all the offences under the Act; and sec. 17 of the International Criminal Court Act – offences under secs. 7 to 16 of the Act.

913. See *Uganda v. Walusekhe* H.Ct.Monthly Bulletin No. 52 of 1964. The accused was charged and convicted on his own plea of guilty of an offence relating to an unlawful society, under sec. 56 of the Penal code. The consent of the director of Public Prosecutions to the prosecution was not obtained. The High Court declared the proceedings a nullity and quashed the conviction.

914. See *A.K. Mayanja v. R.* H.Ct.Monthly Bulletin No. 26 of 1960.

915. Article 120(3)(d). See also the Magistrates' Courts Act, sec. 121, and Trial on Indictments Act, sec. 134.

916. *Raymond v. Attorney-General* [1982] Q.B. 839.

serves public interest. That is the reason why he or she must exercise the discretion personally; he or she is not allowed to delegate it to his or her subordinates.[917]

710. Prior to the 1995 Constitution, the powers of the DPP to enter a *nolle prosequi* applied equally to prosecutions initiated by his or her Office and to those initiated by private persons or other authorities. With respect to the latter he did not have to seek the views, let alone the consent, of the private prosecutor or authority. This is well illustrated by the *Eriabu Lwebuga* Case. Eriabu Lwebuga was the leader of the *Abawejjere* (Common Men) Party. On 21 January 1963, he appeared before the Buganda Principal Court at Mmengo charged with sedition and with inciting the public against H.H. the Kabaka's Government which was then led by Katikkiro Michael Kintu. The then DPP ordered the Principal Court to drop the charges against Lwebuga and to release him forthwith. The Principal Court ignored the order. Thereupon Lwebuga's wife applied to the High Court for a writ of habeas corpus, seeking his release. For the Principal Court and the Kabaka's Government, it was contended that the DPP had not exercised his discretion properly; he had not, for example, given reasons for the order; moreover, he had not even taken the elementary steps of calling for and perusing the police docket to inform or satisfy himself whether or not there were merits in the case against Lwebuga. To the Kabaka's Government, the DPP appeared to have been influenced by the Central Government which was at the time wooing Lwebuga to join the ruling party. Rejecting the Kabaka's Government's contentions, the High Court held that it was not open to any one, not even the courts, to question the way the DPP exercised his or her discretion. It accordingly ordered that Lwebuga be released forthwith.[918] It was probably in reaction to cases such as this that the drafters of the 1995 Constitution stipulated that the DPP 'shall not discontinue any proceedings commenced by another person or authority except with the consent of the court'.[919] Here, then, the Director must furnish the court with reasons for his or her decision to discontinue the proceedings. If the court finds the reasons flimsy and unreasonable, it will withhold its leave and the proceedings will have to go on. This is a salutary check, albeit partial, on the Director's exercise of his or her wide discretion. It guards against abuse.

711. What, then, is the effect of a *nolle prosequi*? The answer depends on whether the accused is tried before a Magistrates' Court or before the High Court. Where the accused is tried before a Magistrates' Court the effect will, again, vary according to the stage at which the *nolle prosequi* is entered. Where it is entered *before* the accused is called upon to make his or her defence, he or she is merely discharged. This means that he or she may subsequently be charged for the same offence on account of the same facts. However, if the *nolle prosequi* is entered *after* the accused has been called upon to make his or her defence he or she must be

917. See Trial on Indictments Act, sec. 135.

918. See *in the matter of Habeas Corpus and in the matter of an Application by Joyce Lwebuga wife of Eriabu Lwebuga an Unconvicted Prisoner at Njabule Prison.* H.Ct.Misc. Cause No. 11 of 1963 (unreported).

919. Section 120(3)(d).

acquitted, and he or she cannot be charged again with the same offence in respect of the same facts.[920] However, where the accused is tried before the High Court and the DPP enters a *nolle prosequi*, the result will be that the accused is merely discharged. He or she may be subsequently charged for the same offence in respect of the same facts. It does not matter at what stage of the proceedings the *nolle prosequi* is entered, whether before or after the accused is called upon to make his defence.[921] There seems to be no rhyme or reason for these double standards. Suffice it to say, however, that where a *nolle prosequi* is entered either at a Magistrates Court or at the High Court, the accused is set at liberty if he or she was in prison. If he or she was remanded on bail his or her recognisance must be discharged.

II. Private Prosecutions

712. The rationale for private prosecutions has been discussed in the introductory part to this book. Suffice to point out here, however, that the power of private citizens to initiate 'private' prosecutions is limited to offences triable by magistrates courts only.[922] According to section 42 of the Magistrates Courts Act:

> 3. Any person, other than a public prosecutor or a police officer, who has reasonable and probable cause to believe that an offence has been committed by any person, may make a complaint thereof to a magistrate who has jurisdiction to try or inquire into the alleged offence, or within the local limits of whose jurisdiction the accused person is alleged to reside or be. Every such complaint may be made orally or in writing signed by the complainant, but if made orally shall be reduced into writing by the magistrate and when so reduced shall be signed by the complainant.
> 4. (a) Upon receiving a complaint under subsection (3) of this section, the magistrate shall consult the local chief of the area in which the complaint arose and put on record the gist of such consultation.
> Provided that where the complaint is supported by a letter from the local chief the magistrate may dispense with the consultation and thereafter put such letter on record.
> (b) After satisfying himself or herself that prima facie the commission of an offence has been disclosed and that such complaint is not frivolous or vexatious, the magistrate shall draw and shall sign a formal charge containing a statement of the offence or offences alleged to have been committed by the accused.

713. Worthy of note is the fact that the private prosecutor need not have been injured as a result of the alleged offence. It is enough if he or she has 'reasonable

920. Magistrates Courts Act, sec. 121.
921. Trial on Indictments Act, sec. 134(1).
922. Section 136(1) of the Trial on Indictments Act provides that 'All prosecutions before the High Court shall be conducted by a member of the Attorney-General's Chamber or by such other person as the Director of Public Prosecutions may, by writing under his hand, appoint.' This provision rules out the possibility of a private citizen initiating criminal proceedings in the High Court.

and probable cause to believe that an offence has been committed by any person'.[923] Additionally, the facts as alleged by the intending private prosecutor must disclose a prima facie case. They must also not be 'frivolous and vexatious'.[924] If, for some reason the magistrate allows the prosecution to go on and at the end of the trial comes to the conclusion that it was frivolous and vexatious, he or she may order the private prosecutor to pay the accused costs as well as compensation 'for the trouble and expense to which such person may have been put by reason of such charge'.[925] Ideally, where a private citizen is allowed to institute a private prosecution, he or she does so for and in the names of Uganda.[926] He or she may conduct the prosecution personally or through a lawyer and at his or her own expense.[927]

714. Needless to say, private prosecutions are also subject to the DPP's powers. The Director may take them over and continue them.[928] Again, if the purpose of his intervention is to discontinue the proceedings, he or she must also obtain the consent of the court. Can the Director intervene in a private prosecution at the appellate stage? There appears to be no reason why he or she cannot, since an appeal is also subsumed under the term 'criminal proceedings'. Where he or she takes over and continues the proceedings, whether at the trial or appellate stage, the Director is entitled to 'all reasonable information and assistance' from the private prosecutor. He or she is also entitled to receive from the private prosecutor 'any documents or other matters and things in his possession or under his control'.[929]

III. Abuse of Process

715. As noted earlier on under this chapter (*supra*, paragraph 702), whilst exercising his or her powers, the DPP is not subject to the direction or control of any person or authority – not even the courts. Nonetheless, where the DPP in the exercise of such powers acts *mala fide* or transgresses the Constitution, his or her decision may be challenged in the courts under the abuse of process doctrine or it may be subjected to constitutional review at the behest of the aggrieved individual; and the purported proceedings may be permanently stayed. Under either of the two types

923. For a case where a magistrate allowed a private prosecution by persons who were not connected to the case, see *Kupuliano Okello & Anor. v. Uganda* H.Ct.Monthly Bulletin No. 91 of 1967.
924. As to what is 'frivolous and vexatious' see *Kyagonga v. Uganda* [1973] E.A. 486, and *Amisi Magala & Anor. v. Uganda* [1971] U.L.R. 14.
925. Magistrates Courts Act, sec. 196. In contrast, a public prosecutor cannot be ordered to pay costs or compensation. See *Director of Public Prosecutions v. Edirisa Vazanye* H.Ct.Monthly Bulletin No. 43 of 1965.
926. However, there have been cases in the past when private prosecutors have prosecuted in their own names. For example, see *L.G. Mukasa v. A. Luzinda* H.Ct.Monthly Bulletin No. 4 of 1960.
927. See *L.G. Mukasa v. A. Luzinda* H.Ct.Monthly Bulletin No. 4 of 1960. It was held in this case that before engaging an advocate to conduct a private prosecution, the private prosecutor does not need the consent of the Attorney General.
928. Magistrates Courts Act, sec. 43.
929. *Ibid.*, sec. 43(1)(c).

of proceedings, the aggrieved party may be able to demonstrate that the proceedings constitute an abuse of legal process in breach of 120(5) of the Constitution or that they violate his or her constitutionally protected rights, such as the right to trial within a reasonable time.

716. Aside from the Constitution itself, the bases for the courts' powers to undertake such an exercise are: the inherent powers of the courts to supervise the executive branch of government; and their inherent powers to regulate their proceedings and to prevent a perversion of their processes. In articulating these powers, Lord Griffiths of the English House of Lords declared that courts must 'accept a responsibility for the maintenance of the rule of law that embraces a willingness *to oversee executive action* and to refuse to countenance behaviour that threatens either basic human rights or the rule of law'.[930] Lord Griffiths also asserted that in the same way as the courts have power to review executive action in administrative law, '[so] also should it be in the field of criminal law and if it comes to the attention of the court that there has been a serious abuse of power it should ... express its disapproval by refusing to act upon it'.[931] Concerning the courts' powers to permanently stay the proceedings, Lord Lowry also in the same case said:

> I consider that a court has a discretion to stay any criminal proceedings on the ground that to try those proceedings will amount to an abuse of its process either (1) because it will be impossible (usually by reason of delay) to give the accused a fair trial or (2) because it offends the court's sense of justice and propriety to be asked to try the accused in the circumstances of a particular case.[932]

717. Lord Lowrry refers to unfairness to the accused. While such unfairness is a factor that the courts take into consideration when considering whether or not to apply the abuse of process doctrine it is not the controlling factor. A New Zealand court put the matter this way:

> The yardstick is not simply fairness to a particular accused. It is not whether the initiation and continuation of the particular process seems in circumstances to be unfair to him. That may be an important consideration. But the focus is on the misuse of the court's process by those responsible for law enforcement. It is whether the continuation of the prosecution is inconsistent with the recognized purposes of the administration of criminal justice and so constitutes an abuse of process of the court.[933]

---

930. *R v. Horseferry magistrates' Court: Experte Bennett* [1994] 1 A.C 42, at 62. Emphasis added.
931. *Ibid.*
932. R v. Horsefery Magistrates' Court, Ex Parte Bennett [1994] 1 A.C. 42 at 74.
933. *Moevao v. Department of Labour* [1981] NZLR 464 at p. 482

718. The case of *Musoke v. Uganda*[934] is an example of an abuse of legal process on the part of the prosecuting authorities. The accused appeared before a magistrate on 16 June 1971 charged with simple robbery. He was remanded in custody until 10 August 1971 when he applied for release on bail. As the prosecutor did not object, he was released and warned to appear in court on 27 August. When he appeared on that date the prosecutor tendered an amended charge, charging the accused with aggravated robbery, which carried the death sentence. Given the seriousness of the new charge, the prosecutor asked the court to cancel the bail. The magistrate conceded, taking the view that he had no choice in the matter. He cancelled the bail and remanded the accused in custody till 10 September 1971. On that date, the magistrate further remanded the accused to 24 September 1971. On 24 September, the magistrate further remanded the accused to 8 October 1971 and on that day to 22 October 1971. Feeling aggrieved by these incessant adjournments, the accused applied to the High Court for release on bail. On 10 November 1971, when he appeared before the High Court to prosecute the application, the application was adjourned to 17 November at the request of the prosecution. There was reportedly a practice in Uganda at the time where, after prisoners were released on bail, the police amended the charges with the sole motive of putting the cases beyond the powers of the magistrates' courts and then asking for the cancellation of the accused's bail. The High Court suspected this to be the motive in this case. The suspicion was based on the fact that the only difference between the old and new charge sheet was the insertion of the phrase 'a deadly weapon to wit a panga'. Kiwanuka, Ag. C.J. commented on the amended charge sheet and said:

> Following what Mr. Ghelani [Counsel for the accused] said I began to doubt the sincerity of the police in this case. Who now told them that the accused used a panga? If, indeed, he used one he must have used it on the complainant, Mr. Isake Kaberuka. But Mr. Isake Kaberuka must have made a statement to the police a long time ago, at least long before the case was fixed for hearing. And if any such violence was used on him he must have told the police so. Now the question is: Did he? If he did why was the applicant charged with a lesser offence in the first place? If he did not, then is it not an afterthought? Can we allow a citizen's liberty to be juggled with in this form?
> I do not deny that the Director of Public Prosecutions has every right to alter charges as he sees fit. But as a judge of this court I am bound to come to the rescue of our citizens where *I detect an attempt on the part of those who have power to prosecute others to abuse the powers in their hands*. This, in my view is one of those cases.[935]

Another irregularity in the charge sheet that the High Court found was that the accused was alleged to have robbed the complainant of 'household properties' – an uncertain and vague and undefined term that did not give the accused reasonable information as to what property he was alleged to have taken. This irregularity,

934. [1972] E.A. 137.
935. *Ibid.*, at 139. [Emphasis added]

coupled with the fact that after amending the charge sheet the prosecuting authorities shelved it for several months with no attempt to complete their investigation and to bring the accused to trial within a reasonable time, led the Court to order the release of the accused on bail.

719. The Tanzania case of *Director of Public Prosecutions v. Mehboob Akbar Haji & Another*[936] is another example of *mala fide* conduct amounting to an abuse of process. The two accused appeared before the District Court at Illala on 25 October 1991 charged with possession of dangerous drugs, cannabis and sativa. On 8 November 1991, they applied for bail. The prosecutor objected. The magistrate adjourned the case to 20 November 1991, when he would deliver his ruling on the application. On that date, just when the magistrate was about to read his ruling, the prosecutor produced a certificate from the DPP under section 35(2) of the Tanzania Organized Crime Act objecting to the grant of bail. Under that provision, the DPP had power to issue the certificate informing the court that if the accused was admitted to bail there was likelihood that the safety or interests of the Republic would be prejudiced. According to an earlier decision of the High Court, the issue of the certificate was conclusive and was a bar to the grant of bail. So in this case it would appear that the object of producing the certificate was to forestall the grant of the bail application. But the defence objected to the filing of the certificate. The magistrate upheld the objection and proceeded to admit the accused to bail. Six days later, the DPP entered a *nolle prosequi*, and as a result the court discharged the accused. However, soon thereafter, the police re-arrested the accused and arraigned them again before another court, the Kivukoni District Court, on the same charges. The Director also filed a fresh certificate under section 35(2) of the Organized Crime Control Act objecting to the release of the accused on bail. The District Court admitted the certificate and remanded the accused in custody. Undaunted counsel for the accused filed an application before the Tanzania High Court challenging the Director's actions. He contended that they were aimed at defeating the previous District Magistrate's order releasing the accused on bail. The High Court concurred with counsel, granted the application and quashed the Kivukoni District Court's proceedings, including the *nolle prosequi*, the admission of the certificate as to non-admission to bail and the order remanding the accused to custody. In so doing, the High Court said that 'there was impropriety in the exercise by the DPP of his powers under the law. *The impropriety amounted to an abuse of the process of the Court*'.[937]

720. Dissatisfied with the High Court's ruling, the DPP appealed to the Tanzania Court of Appeal, contending that his powers were absolute and could not be challenged in court even when they were exercised *mala fide*. To this contention, the Court of Appeal responded thus:

> We are surprised because we did not think anyone in our country could be vested with such absolute and total powers. It would be terrible to think that

936. Cr. App. No. 28 of 1992 (unreported) - Tanzania.
937. *Ibid.* [Emphasis added]

> any individual or group of individuals could be empowered by law to act even *mala fide*. As it turned out to our great relief the exercise of the powers by the DPP under the Criminal Procedure Act is limited by the Act. Although the powers of the DPP appear to be wide, the exercise is limited by three considerations. That wherever he exercises the wide powers he must do so only in the public interest, in the interest of justice and in the need to prevent abuse of the legal process.[938]

721. The Court dismissed the appeal, holding that, 'The DPP acted *mala fides* and not in public interest, not in the interest of justice but in abuse of the legal process which he was required to prevent.'[939] This case particularly delineates the importance of the courts remaining vigilant to ensure that prosecuting authorities do not abuse their powers either to the detriment of the accused or to the integrity of the proceedings. The courts must insist that those who come to them, including the agents of the state, must come with clean hands. They must, in appropriate cases, also be ready and willing to permanently stay the proceedings to prevent the abuse of their processes.[940]

938. *Ibid.*
939. *Ibid.*
940. For a similar case originating from Jamaica, see *Bell v. DPP of Jamaica* [1985] 2 All E R 585, (PC). In this case, the appellant was arrested on 17 Apr. 1977 and charged with the illegal possession of firearms, aggravated robbery, shooting with intent and burglary. He was convicted as charged on 20 Oct. 1977. On appeal, the conviction was quashed on 7 Mar. 1979 and a retrial was ordered. On 10 Nov. 1981, the Crown withdrew the charges because of the unavailability of witnesses. The appellant was accordingly discharged. But he was re-arrested on 12 Feb. 1982 and charged again. The Privy Council held that the thirty-two-month delay, operative from the date when a retrial was ordered was unreasonable and violated his constitutional rights. It permanently stayed the proceeding, holding that to allow them to continue would be oppressive and abuse of process of the court. See also the Zimbabwean case of *In re Mlambo* [1992] 4 SA 144. Generally see Daniel D. Ntanda Nsereko, *The Abuse of Process Doctrine in the Administration of Criminal Justice before National Courts and International Tribunals*, 7 U. Bots. L.J. 29 (2008).

Chapter 3. Initiation of Proceedings

§1. Police Investigations

722. The focus of this chapter is on the initial steps taken by law enforcement agencies toward taking suspected offenders to court. As indicated earlier on in this book, the primary function of the police is to enforce the law, to maintain public safety and order, and to prevent and detect crime. It is therefore the police who invariably initiate criminal proceedings against suspected offenders. They often act on reports from victims, friends or relatives of victims, responsible citizens who may have witnessed the commission of the crime, or on reports from chiefs. They also often act on their own initiative, especially where the crime is committed in their presence. This is particularly true in the case of traffic offences.

723. On receiving any report of commission of a crime, the police investigate those reports and, if the reports are well-founded, take action against the persons suspected to be involved in the alleged crime. The investigations take the form of questioning of witnesses, victims, and the suspects, and in conducting searches and seizures.

I. Questioning Suspects

724. The police do have power under the Evidence (Statements to Police Officers) Rules of 1961, to question any person, suspect or not, from whom they believe they may obtain useful information relating to the commission of an alleged offence.[941] When the person to be questioned is a suspect already in police custody, they must observe the following precautions: (i) they must charge the person with an offence or at least inform him or her of the nature of the offence which they are likely to prefer against him or her or the acts he or she is alleged to have committed and in respect of which proceedings are contemplated; (ii) any officer who was involved in the investigation of the case must not record the statement and must not be present;[942] (iii) the person being questioned must be warned or cautioned that he or she is free to speak or not to speak, but that whatever he or she says may be used later or in evidence against him or her;[943] (iv) the police must record the person's statement in the language in which he or she makes it; (v) they must record the statement as nearly as possible the way the suspects says it; (vi) they must not torture or in any way offer inducements or coerce the person to talk or to incriminate himself or herself; (vii) where the person informs them that he or she wants his or her lawyer to be present, the police must ensure that this demand is honoured before the

941. Rule 1.
942. *Israel Kamukolse v. R* [1956] 23 E.A.C.A 521; *Walusimbi & Anor. v. Uganda*, Cr. App. of 1992, [1994] UGSC 6 (18 Mar. 1994).
943. Rule 5.

questioning begins or continues. Failure to observe these precautions often results in the prosecution not being able to use the suspects' statements at subsequent trials.

II. Identification Parades

725. Where the police are in doubt about the identity of the perpetrator of a crime, they are allowed to hold an identification parade or line-up to ascertain that identity. An identification parade is the placing of a person suspected to have committed the crime in question amongst other people of similar appearance and age to establish whether or not witnesses to the crime are capable of identifying him or her. The parade enables the witnesses to confirm that the person they identify at the parade is the selfsame person they saw committing the crime. The Court of Appeal for Eastern Africa approved a set of rules, later supplemented by the Police Standing Orders, which the police must follow when conducting identification parades. They are:

(1) That the accused person is always informed that he may have an advocate or friend present when the parade takes place.
(2) That the officer in charge of the case, although he may be present, does not carry out the identification.
(3) That the witnesses do not see the accused before the parade.
(4) That the accused is placed among at least eight persons, as far as possible of similar age, height, general appearance and class of life as himself or herself.
(5) That the accused is allowed to take any position he chooses, and that he is allowed to change his position after each identifying witness has left, if he so desires.
(6) Care to be exercised that the witnesses are not allowed to communicate with each other after they have been to the parade.
(7) Exclude every person who has no business there.
(8) Make a careful note after each witness leaves the parade, recording whether the witness identifies or other circumstances.
(9) If the witness desires to see the accused walk, hear him speak, see him with a hat on or off, see that this is done. As a precautionary measure, it is suggested that the whole parade be asked to do this.
(10) See that the witness touches the person he identifies.
(11) At the termination of the parade or during the parade ask the accused if he is satisfied that the parade is being conducted in a fair manner and make a note of his reply.
(12) In introducing a witness, tell him that he will see a group of people who may or may not contain the suspected person. Do not say, 'Pick out somebody', or influence him in any way whatsoever.

(13) Act with scrupulous fairness, otherwise the value of the identification as evidence will depreciate considerably.[944]

III. Search and Seizure

A. Meaning and Significance

726. Traditionally 'search' connotes the opening of something closed (e.g., a house, motor vehicle, a box or a pocket) and 'seizure', an assumption of complete control over a person or thing. The power to search and seize is often vital to the discovery of the evidence necessary to establish the commission of an offence. The evidence discovered may be the fruit or the means of committing of the offence. For example, possession of contraband may be evidence of theft; firearms evidence of possessing unlicensed firearms; *nguli* and the apparatus for brewing the same the evidence of unlicensed manufacture of *nguli*, a local spirit. However, the material discovered may only be incidental evidence of the crime. For example, the discovery of a blood-stained shirt may suggest connection with a recent homicide. Since it is their duty to investigate crime and to produce before the court all material evidence that may help secure the conviction and punishment of criminals, the police are given the powers of search and seizure.

B. Search Warrant

727. As in the case of arrest, the Magistrates Courts Act and the Police Act prescribe rules and regulations which govern search and seizure. These rules require a police officer intending to carry out a search to obtain a search warrant from a magistrate.

Section 70 of the Magistrates Courts Act provides as follows:

> Where it is proved on oath to a court that in fact or according to reasonable suspicion anything upon, by or in respect of which an offence has been committed or anything which is necessary to the conduct of an investigation into any offence is in any building, vessel, carriage, box, receptacle or place, the court may by warrant (called search warrant) authorise the person to whom the warrant is directed to search the building, vessel, carriage, box, receptacle or place (which shall be named or described in the warrant) for any such thing and, if anything searched for be found, to seize it and carry it before the court issuing the warrant or some other court to be dealt with according to law.

944. *R. v. Mwango s/o Manaa* [1939] 3 E.A.C.A. 28.

C. Execution of Search Warrants

728. At the request of the occupier or owner of any premises to be searched, the police officer must show such occupier the search warrant or warrant card[945] or else such person is not obliged to allow the officer free ingress into the premises. The requirement that the police produce the search warrant or warrant card is based on the traditional common law principle which regards a person's house as his or her castle. This principle in turn requires that prior to entry, the police officer must announce his authority and the purpose for seeking an entry, and thus afford the householder an opportunity to submit to the search peaceably before the officer can resort to force.

D. Property to be Seized

729. The searching officer's authority is limited to seizing things which are specified in the search warrant. If he or she seizes any other thing which is not so specified, he or she will be protected only if he or she reasonably believes it to be included.

730. A less obvious situation is the one where a searching officer acting under the authority of a search warrant seizes not only the things named in the warrant but also other things which, though not so named, he or she reasonably believes to be evidence of a crime. Section 7(2) of the Criminal Procedure Code covers this situation. It provides that:

> Any police officer searching any building, vessel, carriage, box, receptacle or place under Section 70 of the Magistrates Courts Act who finds in any such building, vessel, carriage, box, receptacle or place anything which he or she reasonably suspects to have been stolen or unlawfully obtained may seize such thing, notwithstanding that the said thing is not anything for which he or she is searching by virtue of the warrant.

This provision has much to commend itself: it takes into account society's interest in fighting crime while at the same time it accommodates the individual's rights by requiring the police officer to act reasonably. Surely, were the searching officer who, in the course of a search, stumbles upon other evidence of crime, required to go to a magistrate and to obtain a fresh search warrant in respect of that evidence, would by the time he or she obtains the warrant find the evidence gone. This would not only be frustrating to law enforcement, but would also be inimical to public interest.

945. Magistrates Courts Act, sec. 72(1); Police Act, sec. 27(8).

E. Search Without Warrant

731. As in the case of arrest, the police do have power under certain circumscribed circumstances to effect searches without warrant. They may carry out a search contemporaneously with a valid arrest.[946] The arrested person's clothing and the insides of his or her pockets may be examined and any weapons found on his or her body seized, lest he or she uses them against the arresting officer. His or her house or place of business or his or her immediate surroundings may also be searched. Any property which is material evidence of an offence for which the arrest has been made may be seized. If this were not permitted the suspect, his or her friends, or relatives might destroy or conceal the evidence and this would make the arrest itself an exercise in futility.

732. The Police Act provides that whenever a police officer, not being lower in rank than a sergeant, has reasonable grounds to believe that anything necessary for the purpose of an investigation into an offence which he or she is authorized to investigate may be found in any place and that such thing cannot in his or her opinion be otherwise obtained without undue delay, he or she may search or cause a search to be made for such thing.[947] The officer who invokes these powers is required to record in writing the grounds for believing that it is necessary for him or her to act 'without undue delay'. After the search, the officer must send copies of this record to the magistrate competent to take cognizance of the case and, on request, send a copy to the owner or occupier of the premises searched.[948] This requirement underscores the importance of the police officer having 'reasonable grounds'. It serves, at least in theory, as a check on police arbitrariness in the exercise of their powers.

733. Various statutes authorize what may be called regulatory searches and inspections. The object of these searches is to ensure that individuals carrying on given activities comply with the regulations imposed by the statutes. The Food and Drugs Act,[949] for example, empowers an authorized officer to enter any premises for the purpose of ascertaining whether there is or has been, on or in connection with the premises any contravention of the Act. The authorized officer must, however, produce a certificate showing his or her authority if it is requested by the occupier of the premises. Should such occupier refuse him or her entry, his or her only recourse is to obtain a search warrant from a magistrate. Forcible entry without such a warrant would be illegal.

946. Magistrates Courts Act, sec. 69.
947. Section 27(1).
948. Section 27(5).
949. Cap. 278, sec. 24.

§2. Laying of Charges

734. Once the police have established that an offence has been committed and have ascertained the identity of the offender, the next step is for them to bring that offender to court to be dealt with by the court. One way of bringing the offender to court is for a public prosecutor or police officer to lay a charge against the offender before a magistrate and to request the magistrate to issue or cause to issue a summons.[950] The summons is a formal document by which a person named in it is required to appear before the court at a set time and place to answer the charge against him or her. The summons must contain a brief statement of the offence charged and must be in duplicate, signed and sealed by the magistrate or any authorized officer.[951]

735. A police officer or any other authorized officer of the court serves the summons on the accused personally by tendering to him or her a duplicate copy of the summons and requiring him or her to sign a receipt therefor on the back of the original.[952] Where the accused cannot be served personally, he or she may be served by leaving the duplicate with an adult member of his or her family,[953] or by affixing it to some conspicuous part of the house or homestead where he or she ordinarily resides.[954] Where the accused person is a civil servant, he or she may be served by sending the summons to the head of his or her department.[955] Corporations may be served by serving the summons on the corporate secretary, local manager, or any other principal officer of the corporation or by registered letter addressed to its chief officer at its registered office.[956] If the accused does not obey the summons the court may, on being satisfied that he or she was duly served, issue a warrant of arrest to compel him or her to appear before it to answer the charges against him.

736. Instituting proceedings by the laying of charges is usually employed in connection with minor offences, particularly traffic offences. It gives the accused an opportunity to cooperate with the prosecuting authorities and obviates the need to resort to arrest.

§3. Arrest and Detention

737. In the case of serious offences, however, the commonest method of commencing criminal proceedings is by charging the suspect at the police station. This method involves the arrest of the suspect, with or without a warrant. The sequence of events is as follows: The police arrest the suspect [with or without warrant], take

950. Magistrates Courts Act, sec. 42(1)(b).
951. *Ibid.*, sec. 44.
952. *Ibid.*, sec. 45.
953. *Ibid.*, sec. 46.
954. *Ibid.*, sec. 47.
955. *Ibid.*, sec. 48.
956. *Ibid.*, sec. 49.

him or her to the police station, interrogate him or her, and, if they determine that they have sufficient evidence to warrant prosecution, they charge him or her.

738. Arrest is the 'physical restraint, conduct or word of mouth that indicates to that individual that he is not free to leave'.[957] To that end, the criminal Procedure Code Act provides that 'In making an arrest the peace officer or other person authorized to arrest shall actually touch or confine the body of the person to be arrested unless there is submission to the custody by word or action.'[958] The purpose of arrest is to secure the presence of the accused person in court to answer the charges against him or her. The other is to ensure that he or she does not impede or interfere with the on-going investigation, endanger witnesses or commit other crimes. After the arrest the prisoner is taken to the police station, where he or she is questioned, as discussed earlier on. When the police determine that there is sufficient evidence to establish commission of any crime, they then charge the suspect appropriately; thereafter they may release him or her and require him or her to execute a bond to appear before a named Magistrates Court on a stated date, or keep him or her in custody pending taking him or her to court. Where they do not release him or her on bond, they must produce him or her in court without delay and in any case not later than forty-eight hours after the arrest.[959] He or she is thereafter dealt with by the court. The police are forbidden to keep the prisoner in their custody beyond forty-eight hours purportedly for the purpose of 'assisting the police in their investigations'.

A. Arrest with Warrant

739. A warrant is the formal written document authorizing the police to arrest and detain the person named therein. According to section 56 of the Magistrates Courts Act, a warrant of arrest 'shall order the person or persons to whom it is directed to apprehend the person against whom it is issued and bring him or her before the court issuing the warrant or before some court having jurisdiction in the case, to answer to the charge mentioned in it and to be further dealt with according to the law'.[960] Any judicial officer in whose area of jurisdiction the offence was committed may issue the warrant on the application of the police or any representative of the DPP. A warrant of arrest may be executed at any place in Uganda; and it remains in force until it is either executed or cancelled by the court that issued it.[961]

740. In effecting the arrest on the basis of a warrant of arrest, the police officer doing so is required to 'notify the substance of the warrant to the person to be

957. *Murray v. Minister of Defence* [1988] W.L.R. 692.
958. Section 2(1).
959. Article 23(4)(b) of the Constitution, Trial on Indictments Act, sec. 10; Police Act, sec. 25; Criminal Procedure Code Act, sec. 14; and Magistrates Courts Act, sec. 42(1)(b).
960. Magistrates Courts Act, sec. 56. See also sec. 6 of the Trial on Indictments Act.
961. Magistrates Courts Act, sec. 56(3) and sec. 62(6). See also secs. 6 and 11 of the Trial on Indictments Act.

arrested, and, if so required shall show him or her the warrant'.[962] To be able to fulfil these requirements it is vital that at the time of the arrest the officer have in his or her possession the warrant. Possession of the warrant is important because it constitutes the authority on the basis of which the officer arrests the prisoner. It is also on the strength of that authority that the prisoner submits to the arrest. Without disclosure of that authority, the prisoner is entitled to treat the arrest as illegal and an unwarranted or unauthorized invasion of his or her personal liberty and, using reasonable force, to resist the arrest.[963]

741. In case the person to be arrested resists or attempts to evade the arrest, the Criminal Procedure Code Act authorizes the arresting officer to use 'all means necessary to effect the arrest'.[964] However, the Act hastens to add that 'Nothing contained in this section shall be deemed to justify the use of greater force than was reasonable in the particular circumstances in which it was employed or was necessary for the apprehension of the offender.'[965] The force used must therefore be reasonable. It must be proportionate to the force used by the offender. Where the offender submits to the custody, there would even be no need to handcuff him or her or to use other instruments of restraint. To this end, the Criminal Procedure Code Act admonishes that 'The person arrested shall not be subjected to more restraint than is necessary to prevent his or her escape.' The police do nonetheless have discretion to do so where they consider that not to do so might result in the prisoner escaping or injuring them or other people. In the exercise of this discretion, they take into account the prisoner's physical conditions, temperament, past criminal record and the nature of the offence for which the prisoner is arrested. Regarding the use of lethal weapons, section 28 of the Police Act authorizes the police to use firearms: (a) against a person charged or convicted of a felony who escapes from lawful custody; (b) against a person who through force, rescues another person from lawful custody; and (c) against a person who, through force, prevents the lawful arrest of himself or herself or any other person. The Act also imposes certain restrictions to guard against use of wanton force. Even then the police officer should not use lethal force unless he or she has reasonable grounds to believe that he or she cannot prevent the above conduct or otherwise effect the arrest and he or she has issued a warning of his or her intention to use the firearms, and the prisoner does

962. *Ibid.*, sec. 61.
963. In the English case of *Galliard v. Laxton* (1862) 2 B.F.S. 363; 5 L.J. 835; 121 E.R. 1109, a police constable who had been issued with a warrant for the arrest of the appellant did not have it with him when he effected the arrest. He left it with his superior officer at the police station. Although the appellant did not ask the constable to show him the warrant when he arrested him, it was all the same held that the arrest was illegal. The important point here is that if requested the constable was bound to produce the warrant; the keeping of the arrested person in custody after such a request was made and failure to comply with the request would render the arrest illegal. For a similar holding see *R v. Chapman* (1871) 12 Cox C.C. 4.
964. Section 2(2).
965. Section 2(3).

not heed the warning. The Police may also use firearms where he or she has reasonable grounds to believe that he or she or any other person is in danger of grievous bodily harm.[966] Even then 'only such force as is reasonable in the circumstances may be used'. Use of wanton or excessive force not only exposes the person who uses it to criminal prosecution for murder or manslaughter,[967] but also to civil suits by the victim.[968]

742. The Trial on Indictments Act and the Magistrates Courts Act do not indicate how a warrant of arrest is applied for. The practice seems to be for the police or public prosecutor to fill out a standardized form which they take to a judge or magistrate. The judge or magistrate invariably signs the warrant as a matter of course. Unlike a private citizen seeking an arrest warrant or summons, neither the police nor the public prosecutor is required to show that he or she has 'reasonable and probable cause to believe that an offence has been committed by any person'.[969] Nor does the judge or magistrate have to be satisfied that the police or public prosecutor's allegations disclose a prima facie case or that they are not frivolous or vexatious.[970] It is indeed debatable whether the judge or magistrate may refuse to sign a warrant of arrest. It is urged that in appropriate cases they should, if the courts' role as watchdog over executive exercise of arrest powers is to be effective.

743. A warrant of arrest may be issued for the arrest of a person who is already under illegal custody. The fact of the prior illegal arrest does not affect the validity of the warrant, provided it is properly executed. In *Re E. S. Lumu and Four Others* the applicants, then cabinet ministers in the Obote I Government, were illegally arrested whilst attending a cabinet meeting. On the day following the arrest, a warrant of arrest was applied for under the Deportation Ordinance and was duly executed. In subsequent proceedings for writ of habeas corpus, the applicants contended that because of the way they were initially arrested they were under illegal detention. The High Court rejected their contention, holding that the arrest was validated by the issuance of the warrant of arrest. A related point is that irregularity or defect in the warrant or illegality of an arrest does not vitiate the subsequent criminal proceedings.[971] This assertion is in accord with the *mala captus bene detentus* principle, which literally means badly captured well detained.[972] However, the defects of the warrant or illegality of the arrest may be relevant to the issue whether

966. A commentary to Art. 3 of the UN Code of Conduct for Law Enforcement Officials reads as follows: 'The use of firearms is considered an extreme measure. Every effort should be made to exclude the use of firearms, especially against children. In general, firearms should not be used except when a suspected offender offers armed resistance or otherwise jeopardizes the lives of others and less extreme measures are not sufficient to restrain or apprehend the suspected offender. In every instance in which a firearm is discharged, a report should be made promptly to the competent authorities.'
967. Penal Code, sec. 16.
968. Article 23(7) of the Constitution.
969. Magistrates Courts Act, sec. 42(3).
970. *Ibid.*
971. See Trial on Indictments Act, sec. 12 and Magistrates Courts Act, sec. 64.
972. But see *R v. Horseferry Magistrates' Court: Experte Bennett* [1994] 1 A.C. 42, at 62.

an individual was justified to resist an arrest. It may also give rise to civil proceedings for damages for wrongful arrest or to false imprisonment and malicious prosecution.

B. Arrest without Warrant

744. Section 10 of the Criminal Procedure Code Act authorizes a police officer to arrest without warrant any person in any of the following situations: any person whom he or she suspects on reasonable grounds to have committed a 'cognizable offence';[973] any person whom he or she suspects on reasonable grounds to have committed any offence under any of the provisions of Chapter XVI of the Penal Code – offences relating to nuisances and offences against health and convenience; any person whom he or she suspects on reasonable grounds to have committed any offence for which under any law provision is made for arrest without warrant;[974] any person who commits any breach of the peace in his or her presence; any person who obstructs a police officer in the execution of his or her duty, or who has escaped or attempts to escape from lawful custody; any person whom he or she finds in any highway, yard or other place during the night and whom he or she suspects upon reasonable grounds of having committed or being about to commit a felony; any person whom he or she suspects upon reasonable grounds of having been concerned in any act committed at any place out of Uganda which, if committed in Uganda, would have been punishable as an offence, and for which he or she is, under the provisions of any written law, liable to be apprehended and detained in Uganda; any person having in his or her possession without lawful excuse, the burden of proving which excuse shall be on that person, any implement of housebreaking; any person for whom he or she has reasonable cause to believe a warrant of arrest has been issued; and any person in whose possession anything is found which may reasonably be suspected to be stolen or who may reasonably be suspected of having committed an offence with reference to that thing. The Act also permits the police, under certain conditions, to arrest without warrant vagabonds and habitual robbers.[975]

745. The Act also authorizes a private person to arrest without warrant any person who in his or her view commits a 'cognisable offence', or whom he or she reasonably suspects of having committed a felony.[976] An owner of property or his or her servant or persons authorized by him or her is also authorized to arrest without warrant any person found committing any offence involving injury to such property.[977] A private person who carries out an arrest without a warrant is required

973. Section 1 defines a 'cognisable offence' as one which is punishable by imprisonment for one year or more or by a fine exceeding four thousand shillings.
974. Examples of statutes that specifically authorize the police to arrest without warrant include the Immigration (Control Act), Mining Act, Trout Protection Act, Official Secrets Act and Traffic and Road Safety Act.
975. Section 11.
976. Section 15.
977. *Ibid.*

'without unnecessary delay', to hand over the prisoner to a police officer, or ir absence of a police officer take the prisoner to the nearest police station. If the pc determine that there is no sufficient ground to believe that the prisoner comm any offence, they must release him or her 'at once'.[978] These provisions delir every citizen's role in enforcing the law and his or her moral obligation to com ment the police in fighting crime.

746. The rationale for permitting arrest without warrant in these situatio urgency and expediency. Were a warrant to be insisted on under all circumstar then, by the time it were sought and obtained from the court the suspected crim would have disappeared from the scene. Such a result would be against the int of the public to ensure that suspected criminals are brought to justice. It would undermine public confidence in the criminal justice system. Nevertheless, in mitting arrest without warrant in these circumstances, the law insists on certain ditions being satisfied as a safeguard against possible abuse of the procedure.

747. The first safeguard is the requirement that the offence for which arrest out warrant is permitted should be sufficiently serious as judged by the maxi penalty that it attracts. Not every offence on the criminal calendar calls for a without warrant. Only 'serious' offences should. The second safeguard is tha person who effects the arrest must have 'reasonable grounds' to suspect that the son to be arrested has committed or is about to commit one of those offences. requirement minimizes arbitrariness, impulse and overzealousness in matters involve the liberty of other people. Connected with this safeguard is the req ment under Article 23(3) of the Constitution that the person being arrested 'sha informed immediately, in a language that the person understands, of the reason the arrest, restriction or detention and of his or her right to a lawyer of his o choice'. The rationale for this requirement was well articulated by Viscount Si of the English House of Lords as follows:

> The requirement that he should be so informed does not mean that tech language need be used. The matter is a matter of substance, and turns o elementary proposition that in this country a person is, prima facie, entitl his freedom and is only required to submit to restraint on his freedom knows in substance the reason why it is claimed that this restraint shou imposed.[979]

748. Where the person carrying out the arrest fails to so inform the prisoner would be a serious violation of the prisoner's constitutional rights, and the pris would be entitled to treat the arrest as illegal and to put up resistance with re able force. Nevertheless, where the prisoner himself or herself creates a situ either by resisting or putting up a fight, as to make it impracticable for the pe carrying out the arrest to inform him or her of the reasons for the arrest, the prisoner will have himself or herself to blame. Again, as Viscount Simon sta

978. Section 16.
979. *Christie v. Lechinsky* [1947] 1 All E.R. 567 at 572–573.

The person arrested cannot complain if he has not been supplied with the above information as and when he should be if he himself produces a situation which makes it particularly impossible to inform him, e.g. by immediate counter-attack or by running away.[980]

749. The third safeguard is that, generally speaking, arrests are made by members of the police, who are specialists in law enforcement. For the safeguard to be efficacious, however, it is important that the police are thoroughly trained not only in the arrest tactics but also in human rights. Save for arrests in respect of property offences, a private person may arrest without warrant only those persons who commit cognisable offence 'in his or her view'. This condition guards against mere busybodies interfering with other people's affairs.

750. The fourth safeguard is that the person who makes the arrest must take the prisoner to the police station immediately after the arrest. The police must, in turn, charge the prisoner with some definite offence and, without any due delay take him to court to be dealt with by the court. As indicated earlier, the law, and no less the Constitution, limits the period during which the prisoner is kept in police custody to forty-eight hours. Custody at the police station may be necessary to enable the police to carry out some preliminary investigation and to determine whether the prisoner has actually committed any offence and, if so, to charge him with the offence.[981] If they do not charge and take him to court within that time, they must release him forthwith.

---

980. *Ibid.*

981. See, e.g., the English case of *Dallison v. Caffery* [1965] 1 Q.B. 348, at 367, in which Lord Denning stated as follows: 'When a constable has taken into custody a person reasonably suspected of a felony, he can do what is reasonable to investigate the matter, and to see whether the suspicions are supported or not by further evidence. He can, for instance, take the person suspected to his own house to see whether any of the stolen property is there; else it may be removed and valuable evidence lost. He can take the person suspected to the place where he says he was working, for there he may find persons to confirm or refute his alibi. The constable can put him up on an identification parade to see if he is picked by the witnesses. So long as such measures are taken reasonably, they are an important adjunct to the administration of justice. ... The measures must, however, be reasonable.'

Chapter 4. Pre-trial Proceedings

§1. Committal Proceedings

751. Section 1 of the Trial on Indictments Act provides that 'no case shall be brought under the cognizance of the High Court for trial unless the accused person has been committed for trial to the High Court in accordance with the provisions of Part XV of the Magistrates Courts Act, 1970'. Until 1967, all cases triable before the High Court were subject to a filtering process, then called preliminary inquiry, by which a magistrate determined whether or not there was sufficient evidence to warrant committing the accused to the High Court for trial. The prosecution adduced evidence before the magistrate. On the basis of that evidence, the magistrate determined whether or not there was a prima facie case. Prosecutions that were misconceived or unmeritorious were thus eliminated at an early stage and the High Courts' time and resources saved. Preliminary inquiries were however abolished by the Criminal Procedure (Summary of Evidence) Act of 1967 and replaced with a new procedure known as committal proceedings. Under this procedure, the DPP was required to draw up an indictment, prepare a list of prosecution witnesses and a summary of the evidence that each witness would be expected to give at the trial. The Director also had to indicate the exhibits that the prosecution intended to tender. In contrast with the preliminary inquiries, the Director did not have to call the witnesses. But the accused could make a sworn or unsworn statement and call witnesses if he or she so wished. At the conclusion of the proceedings, the magistrate committed the accused to the High Court for trial without exercising any discretion in the matter. As with the preliminary inquiries, committal proceedings were considered to be cumbersome and costly, and unnecessarily exposed state witnesses to risks of physical harm.[982] Their only usefulness was the disclosure to the accused of the prosecution's case and the opportunity such disclosure afforded him or her to prepare his or her defence.

752. In an attempt to simplify the proceedings and to make them less costly, the 1990 Magistrates Courts (Amendment) Statute dispensed with the summary of evidence of each prosecution witness and any reference to any exhibits that the state intended to tender in evidence. Indeed no evidence of any kind is now required to be presented before the magistrate at this stage. Section 168 of the Magistrates Act provides that:

> 1. When a person is charged in a Magistrate's Court with an offence to be tried by the High Court, the Director of Public Prosecutions shall file in the Magistrate's Court an indictment and a summary of the case. ...
> 2. The summary of the case referred to in subsection (1) shall contain such particulars as are necessary to give the accused reasonable information as to the nature of the offence with which he is charged.

982. There has, however, been no empirical evidence showing that state witnesses were ever threatened. See Benjamin J. Odoki, *Reducing Delay in the Administration of Justice: The Case of Uganda*, 5 Crim. L. Forum 57 (1994).

When the accused appears before the magistrate, the magistrate is required to give him or her copy of the indictment and the summary of the case. The magistrate then reads and explains the nature of the charge to him or her. Without calling upon him to plead or to make any statement, the magistrate commits him or her to the High Court for trial. Meantime, the magistrate remands him or her in custody pending his or her trial.

753. It is debatable whether committal proceedings in their present form serve any useful purpose. Unlike the preliminary proceedings, they do not help to filter meritorious from unmeritorious or unwarranted prosecutions. Unlike the proceedings under the Criminal Procedure (Summary of Evidence) Act, they do not give the accused advance notice of the prosecution's case and thus help him or her to prepare his or her defence. Nor do they facilitate the desirable admission of uncontested evidence by the parties which advance disclosure of the prosecution case made possible. If anything, they are an unnecessary stricture in the criminal justice process and a cause of delay in bringing the accused to trial.

§2. Release on Bail

I. Pre-Trial Custody

754. When the hearing of a criminal case before a court is adjourned or postponed, the accused person is remanded [sent away] for the time being. He or she is required to appear before the court again on a day and time set for the hearing of the case. This is true at both the trial and appellate stages. The accused may be remanded in custody or out of custody. When he or she is remanded in custody, this is what is referred to as pre-trial custody. Where he or she is remanded out of custody, he or she is said to be released on bail.

755. Until the accused has been convicted of the alleged offence, he or she is presumed to be innocent. To deprive him or her of his or her liberty by remanding him or her in custody is, *ex facie*, unjust: he or she is punished before he or she has been convicted and sentenced. However, overriding public interest considerations justify the accused's detention before conviction and sentence. These considerations include the need: (i) to ensure that the accused is available for his or her trial; (ii) to ensure that he or she does not impede on-going police investigations into the case by either intimidating or otherwise influencing prosecution witnesses; (iii) to ensure that he or she does not tamper with material evidence; (iv) to protect the accused from possible harm by his or her victims or their relatives and friends or by himself or herself by way of committing suicide; and (v) to protect the public against further criminal activities by the accused.

II. Bail Pending Trial

756. Nevertheless, to mitigate the injustice inherent in pre-trial custody and the prejudice it occasions to the accused, the law gives the court discretion to release the accused on bail. Article 23(6) of the Constitution provides that:

> Where a person is arrested in respect of a criminal offence –
>
> (a) the person is entitled to apply to the court to be released on bail and the court may grant that person bail on such conditions as the court considers reasonable;
> (b) in the case of an offence which is triable by the High Court as well as by a subordinate court, the person shall be released on bail on such conditions as the court considers reasonable, if that person has been remanded in custody in respect of the offence before trial for one hundred and twenty days;
> (c) in the case of an offence triable only by the High Court, the person shall be released on bail on such conditions as the court considers reasonable, if the person has been remanded in custody for three hundred and sixty days before the case is committed to the High Court.

In interpreting this provision, the Supreme Court held that irrespective of the class of criminal offence a person may be charged with – whether civil or military – he or she is entitled to apply for release on bail; and that the court before whom he or she is charged has the discretion to grant or not to grant the application. It accordingly ruled that this right extends to people charged before courts martial.[983]

757. Regarding the proceedings before the High Court, section 14(1) of the Trial on Indictments Act provides that:

> The High Court may at any stage in the proceedings release the accused person on bail, that is to say, on taking from him a recognisance consisting of a bond, with or without sureties for such an amount as is reasonable in the circumstance of the case, to appear before the court on such a date and at such a time as is named in the bond.

758. The magistrates' courts are given similar powers, with the exception of cases where the accused is charged with offences triable only by the High Court or offences under the Penal Code relating to acts of terrorism punishable by more than ten years imprisonment or cattle rustling, and offences under the Firearms Act punishable by more than ten years imprisonment, as well as rape and aggravated defilement.[984] However, whether the release is granted by the High Court or by a Magistrates' Court, it must be conditional. The accused and his sureties, if any, must undertake to the court that the accused will appear in court on the stated day and

983. *Attorney General v. Joseph Tumushabe Const.* Appl. No 3 of 2008. [2008] UGSC 9 (9 Jul. 2008).
984. Magistrates Courts Act, sec. 75, as amended by the Magistrates (Amendment) Act 2007.

time or else suffer penalty, such as paying the sum of money under the bond or forfeiting it if it was deposited in court.[985]

759. Commendably, section 77(1) of the Magistrates Courts Act requires a magistrate before whom an accused person charged with a bailable offence appears to advise the accused of his or her right to apply for release on bail.[986] Section 77(3) also requires a Magistrates' Court which has not granted bail to an accused person, either in the exercise of its discretion or for lack of power to do so, to advise him or her of his or her right to appeal to a Chief Magistrate or (in cases where it was the Chief Magistrate who turned down the application) to re-apply to the High Court. Where it is the High Court that has turned down an application for release on bail, there is apparently no right of appeal against that refusal to the Court of Appeal.[987] Nevertheless, the Court should advise the accused to renew his or her application at a later stage when his or her circumstances change. This is allowed, since bail is ambulatory. Though not required by any specific provision in the Trial on Indictments Act, it is suggested that the judges of the High Court should also inform the accused of his or her right to apply for bail, particularly when he or she is unrepresented.

760. In considering an application for bail, the court engages in a balancing exercise of the rights of the accused on the one hand and those of the prosecution and the public on the other. In so doing, it must act judicially and in accordance with statutory guidelines and other generally accepted principles governing bail. Both section 15(4) of the Trial on Indictment Act and section 77 of the Magistrates Courts Act lay down some of the factors that the court should take into account. These factors are no more than a codification of generally accepted principles of bail. They include the nature of the accusation, the gravity of the offence and the severity of the sentence, the antecedents of the accused, whether accused has fixed abode within the jurisdiction, and prejudice to the state if bail is granted.

A. Nature of the Accusation

761. Nature of the accusation means the quality and quantity of the evidence that the prosecution has so far collected and intends to use to substantiate the allegations against the accused. If such evidence is flimsy or utterly insubstantial and remotely incapable of proving the allegations, then, the court may decide to release the accused on bail. For this reason, it is important that the prosecution place some material before the court to enable it to properly exercise its discretion.

---

985. Section 21 of the Trial on Indictments Act and, sec. 83 of the Magistrates' Courts Act.
986. H.Ct.Monthly Bulletin No. 140 of 1968.
987. See *Uganda v. Zubairi & Anor.* [1973] E.A. 470.

B. Gravity of the Offence

762. The gravity of the offence is defined by its inherent heinous nature and the severity of the penalty prescribed for those convicted of committing it. This factor is important in two important respects. The first is the need to protect the public. Where the offence committed is a particularly serious one and one that has already caused serious harm, releasing the accused back into the community may cause fear and panic in the minds of the members of the community and may result in the members of the community taking self-help measures against the accused. Release may also cause further danger to the community in that the accused may commit further crimes of a serious nature. The second is the likelihood of the accused absconding to avoid trial and punishment. The graver the offence and the severer the attendant sentence on conviction the greater is the temptation on the part of the accused to abscond. It is for this reason that as a rule of practice amounting to a rule of law, the courts do not release on bail persons charged with capital offences unless exceptional circumstances are shown to exist. Section 15 of the Trial on Indictment Act now codifies this rule and spells out offences in respect of which the High Court may decline to grant bail if the accused person does not prove to its satisfaction that 'exceptional circumstances exist justifying his or her release'.[988] It also defines 'exceptional circumstances' as: grave illness as certified by a medical officer of the prison or other institution where the accused may be detained as being incapable of adequate treatment whilst the accused is in custody; or infancy,[989] or advanced age.[990] In both these circumstances, the DPP must issue a certificate of no objection before the court can act on them. It also places on the accused the onus to prove that exceptional circumstances do indeed exist. Nevertheless, the fact that these narrowly defined circumstances do not exist in a particular case does not justify the prosecuting authorities to dilly dally, sit back and keep the accused person on indefinite remand. It must be appreciated that the accused person has a right to be tried within a reasonable time, a right to liberty and a right to be presumed innocent.[991] To this end, the Act makes it mandatory for the High Court to release on bail any

---

988. The offences are: offences triable only by the High Court, acts of terrorism, cattle rustling, offences under the Firearms Act punishable by a term of imprisonment not exceeding ten years, abuse of office, rape, defilement, rape, defilement, embezzlement, causing financial loss, corruption, bribery of members of a public body and any other offence in respect of which a Magistrates' Court has no jurisdiction to grant bail.

989. In *Uganda v. Peter Wampamba* H.Ct. Misc. Cr. Appl. No. 76 of 10 of 1993, the High Court refused to release the accused, a boy aged between 17 and 18 years charged with defilement, holding that he was not an infant for purposes of bail; it also held that the fact that he was a Senior Six student and was about to sit his university entrance examinations was not an exceptional circumstance.

990. In *Uganda v. Hillary Yiga* H. Ct. Misc. Appl. No. 76 of 1993, the High Court considered seventy-four years as 'advanced age' to justify admitting the accused to bail.

991. Prior to the enactment of these provisions Kiwanuka, CJ said the following in *Musoke v. Uganda* [1972] E.A. 137: 'Exceptional grounds' have not been defined and many circumstances may become 'exceptional' because of the manner in which they occur. Inordinate delay in presenting the prisoner for trial on the part of the prosecution, or lack of interest in the prosecution of the accused do in my judgment, constitute exceptional grounds to justify the granting of bail in cases of this kind.'

person accused with a capital offence who has been in pre-trial custody for a continuous period of 480 days. It similarly requires the court to release any person charged with any other offence who has been in pre-trial custody for a continuous period of 240 days.[992] The exception to this mandatory release is where the court is satisfied that the accused person should not be released from custody 'for the protection of the public'. It is submitted that it would be only in extreme cases that the court would be justified to sanction continued detention of a person that has been incarcerated without trial for that long.

C. *Antecedents of the Accused*

763. The personal history of the accused constitutes his or her antecedents. They assist the court in determining whether or not the accused will abscond if released on bail. They include the accused person's education, employment record, family situation, status in society and whether or not he or she has property within the jurisdiction of the court. They also include past convictions, if any; it is believed that a recidivist is more likely to abscond than one who is not. They also include whether on previous occasions the accused failed to comply with bail conditions, and whether there are other charges pending against him or her.

D. *Fixed Place of Abode within the Jurisdiction*

764. A fixed place of abode within the jurisdiction of the court is a vital factor that the courts must consider along with other factors when determining whether a particular person is likely to answer his or her bail if released. A person who has a fixed place of abode within the jurisdiction is less likely to flee and abandon his or her home when released than a casual visitor with no such place. It is also easier for the police to monitor the movements of a person with a fixed place of abode within the jurisdiction and to ensure that he or she observes the conditions of release than those of a person who has none.

E. *Prejudice to the State*

765. Under this factor, the courts consider whether the accused, if released on bail, is likely to obstruct or interfere with ongoing investigations in his or her case. The courts consider whether he or she might bribe, intimidate or otherwise influence prospective prosecution witnesses. They are also concerned with whether the accused might hide, destroy or otherwise tamper with material evidence not yet in the possession of the police. In determining whether the accused is likely to do any of these things, the courts take into account his or her social status, his or her influence and wealth. A cultural leader, politician or prominent businessman, for

992. Section 16. For similar provisions see sec. 76 of the Magistrates Courts Act.

example, is more likely to influence witnesses than a social nobody. Thus in *Uganda v. Wilberforce Nadiope & Anor*, the first accused was a former Minister of Internal Affairs, Vice-President and Kyabazinga of Busoga. He was denied bail on the ground that 'the more prominent a person is the greater was his fear of conviction and the greater the temptation to use his influence to interfere with witnesses'.[993] Generally, however, before acting on allegations of obstruction of investigations or tampering with evidence, a court should insist on some substantiation or proof of such allegations. It should not act on unsubstantiated generalizations or mere speculation.[994]

III. Bail Pending Appeal

766. Section 205 of the Magistrates Courts Act specifically provides that:

> An appellant may, at any time before the determination of his or her appeal, apply for bail to the appellate court, and the appellate court may grant the bail.

Section 132(4) of the Trial on Indictments Act also provides that:

> Save in a case where the appellant has been sentenced to death, a judge of the High Court, or the Court of Appeal may, in his or her discretion, in any case in which an appeal to the Court of Appeal is lodged under this section, grant bail, pending the hearing and determination of such appeal.

Similarly, rule 5(2)(a) of the Supreme Court Rules provides, *inter alia*, that:

> Subject to sub rule (1) the institution of an appeal shall not operate to suspend any sentence or to stay execution, but the Court may –
> (i) in any criminal proceedings, where notice of appeal has been given in accordance with rule 55 and 56, order that the appellant be released on bail pending the determination of the appeal.

767. A condition precedent to release on bail pending appeal is that the accused must, at the time of the application for release, have lodged the appeal before the appellate court. As a practice amounting to a rule of law, however, a convicted person will not be released pending appeal unless exceptional circumstances are shown to exist. The reason for this rule is that the accused has already been convicted after a trial and his or her presumption of innocence is not operative anymore.[995] The fact that by the time the appeal is heard the accused will have finished serving his or her sentence is an exceptional circumstance which may justify releasing the appellant

993. H.Ct. Monthly Bulletin No. 153 of 1969.
994. See for example *Panju v. Republic* [1973] E.A. 282; *Jaffer v. Republic* [1973] E.A. 39.
995. See *Raghbir Singh Lamba v. R.* [1958] E.A. 337.

on bail pending the determination of his appeal.[996] The court must nonetheless be satisfied that there is no risk of the appellant failing to turn up to prosecute his appeal. Thus in one case, the Supreme Court granted bail to the applicant pending a third appeal on the grounds that although he was convicted of conspiracy to murder – a charge that did not involve the applicant personally harming the complainant; he was a first offender; did not abscond when he was released on bail by the three courts below; had a permanent place of abode in the jurisdiction; and had substantial sureties.[997] Lastly, before an appellate court releases an appellant on bail, it must be satisfied that there exist reasonable prospects of the appeal succeeding. Where prospects of success do not exist the court should not grant the bail. Apposite, however, is the question of what 'reasonable prospects of success' means. For instance, in *Jayesh Thakker v. Uganda*, the High Court turned down the appellant's application for release on bail pending appeal on the ground that he had not shown that 'there was overwhelming probability that the appeal will succeed'.[998] With due respect, this approach was wrong. It is unlikely that a judicial officer who initially considers the application for release on bail pending appeal and whose decision the appellant challenges on appeal will easily acknowledge that there is 'overwhelming probability that the appeal will succeed', i.e., that the decision was wrong. It is therefore suggested that when determining whether there are reasonable prospects of the appeal succeeding the court should simply ask whether there is a reasonably arguable case. This approach avoids putting the judicial officer in the invidious position of having to pass judgment on his or her own decision.

§3. Charges and Indictments

I. Definition

768. A charge is the formal written accusation against the accused person. It contains the allegations that form the basis of his trial. It states the offence he or she is alleged to have committed. It cites the provisions of the law defining or punishing the offence. It also briefly recites the facts on which the accusation is based. *Charge* is a generic term that covers indictments as well. An *Indictment* however is the term used to refer to a charge in proceedings before the High Court after the accused is committed for trial. In all other respects, charges and indictments are one and the same thing and are governed by substantially the same rules and principles. Charge, charge sheet and indictment are thus used interchangeably in this book.

769. It is the duty of the public prosecutor or the court, in the case of complaints made by private persons under section 42(1) of the Magistrates Courts Act, to draw and sign the charge sheet. All in all, the court bears the responsibility of carefully

996. In *Girdhar Dhanji Masrani v. Uganda* [1960] E.A. 320, the High Court relying on English precedents refused to release the appellant on bail, saying that 'It is unfortunate that some delay must occur before this appeal is heard but that, in itself, is not a good ground for granting bail at this stage.' But now see *R. v. Walton* (1979) 68 Cr.App.Rep. 292.
997. *Arvind Patel v. Uganda*, Cr. Appl. No. 1 of 2003, [2003] UGSC 25 (17 Jun. 2003).
998. Cr. Session Case No. 84 of 2007 [2007] UGHC 36 (5 Dec. 2007).

perusing the charge sheet and, in conjunction with the prosecutor in open court, to effect such amendments as are necessary, subject to affording the accused person ample opportunity to study it before he is asked to plead to it.

II. Joinder of Offences

770. Joinder of offences means joining more than one offence in the same charge sheet. The rationale for joining offences in the same charge sheet is convenience and expedition. It is desirable that offences that are connected should be tried and disposed of at the same time, since they often involve the same defendants, based on the same evidence which is often given by the same witnesses. It should, in this respect be noted in passing that offences that are charged in separate charge sheets cannot be tried together; hence the need to carefully consider joinder whenever it is permissible. Nevertheless, before joining several offences in one charge sheet, painstaking care must be taken to ensure that they qualify for joinder. An improper joinder (misjoinder) may vitiate the entire charge sheet.

771. More than one offence may be joined in one charge sheet where such offences are *founded on the same facts* or form or are a part of a series of *offences of the same or a similar character.*[999] For offences to be founded on the same facts, they should arise out of the same incident and should, in terms of the time when and place where they are committed, be proximate to each other. For example in the case of *R. v. Dalip Singh,*[1000] the appellant and another person were jointly charged with stealing certain property belonging to the Kenya and Uganda Railways. The appellant was also charged with giving a bribe to a police officer in order to procure his release from arrest and not to prosecute him for the theft. The Court of Appeal for Eastern Africa held that the two offences were properly joined. They were founded on the same facts, since the evidence showed that the bribe was offered within a very short time after the arrest of the appellant and his co-accused and while they were on their way to the police station.[1001]

772. However, it is submitted that proximity of the offences should not be an absolute prerequisite to the proof that such offences are 'founded on the same facts'. If two offences are separated in time but the latter one would not have happened without the prior occurrence of the first, it is fair to say that both are founded on the same facts.[1002]

773. For two or more offences to form or be part of a series of offences of the same or a similar character they must be connected. The connection is established

999. Trial on Indictments Act, sec. 23(1); Magistrates Courts Act, sec. 86(1).
1000. [1943] 10 E.A.C.A. 121.
1001. The same Court arrived at a different conclusion in the Tanzanian case of *Joseph s/o Odoro v. R.* [1954] 21 E.A.C.A. 311.
1002. See *R. v. Barrell & Anor.* [1979] 69 Cr.App.Rep. 250.

if the evidence of one offence would be admissible on the trial of the others. Thus where Mubi steals a cheque leaf, forges the owner's signature on it, and cashes it at a bank, he may be charged in the same charge sheet with: (i) theft, (ii) forgery, (iii) uttering and (iv) obtaining by false pretences. These wrongs form one chain of offences. They do therefore constitute a series of offences of the same or similar character – dishonesty. However, if on his way from the bank where he encashed the cheque Mubi drove his vehicle recklessly, the offence of reckless driving could not be properly joined with the others. It is not the 'same or of similar character' with theft, forgery, uttering and obtaining by false pretences. For the offences to be similar, the law creating them must be similar; so also must the facts on which they are based.

774. According to a rule of practice amounting to a rule of law, no other offence may be joined with murder or manslaughter. This is so even when all the offences are founded on the same facts. The rationale for the rule is that a trial on a charge of murder or manslaughter is so serious and complicated that the defence ought not to be embarrassed by the necessity of dealing at the same time with other matters.[1003] The exception to this rule is where the additional offence is based on precisely the same facts as the murder or manslaughter offence. In *Yowana Sebuzukira v. Uganda*,[1004] for example, the appellant was charged in one indictment with murder and arson. The two offences were held to be founded on the same facts, since the murder resulted from the arson. Dismissing the objection to the joinder, the Court of Appeal for Eastern Africa said:

> In this case the two offences charged were founded on the same facts, as the murder charged in count one resulted from the arson charged in count two ... We can see no objection to a departure from the established rule of practice that no other count should be joined to a count of murder or manslaughter, in a case such as the one under consideration, although it is not ordinarily desirable that the trial of such grave offences be complicated by the introduction into the proceedings of additional matter to which consideration must be necessarily given by the judge and assessors, and which might distract attention from the main issue. In this case all the evidence to support the charge of arson was relevant on the murder charge, and no possible prejudice could result from the charges being joined. The joinder of the arson charge did not involve the addition of any new matter, and we consider that in the circumstances of this particular case the charges of murder and arson were properly joined.[1005]

The same rule forbids the joining of more than one murder or manslaughter in one indictment. Departure from the rule will be accepted only where the overt act in each case is the same and the facts establish a single transaction with no interval of

1003. See *Valezi Kashizha s/o Madogede v. R.* [1954] 21 E.A.C.A. 389; *Aikaeli s/o Alifayo v. R.* [1954] 21 E.A.C.A. 371.
1004. [1965] E.A. 684.
1005. *Ibid.*, at 685.

time or space. An example is where the accused by a single shot or blow causes more than one death at the same time and place.[1006]

775. Where two or more offences are charged in one charge sheet, a description of each offence so charged must be set out in a separate paragraph of the charge sheet called a count and numbered consecutively.[1007] Charging two or more offences in one count, either cumulatively or in the alternative, renders the charge double or duplex and may be fatal. The rationale for the rule against duplicity is that they tend to mislead or confuse the accused and make it difficult for him or her to defend himself or herself. Additionally, the law requires the court to pass a clear and unambiguous verdict on each count, either acquitting or convicting the accused. A double charge renders the fulfilment of this requirement difficult; and the accused will not know with precision with what offence he or she is convicted or acquitted and may thus be prevented on a future occasion from pleading *autrefois convict*. Two cases will be cited as examples.

776. In *Wakigona v. Reginam*,[1008] the appellant was charged with fraudulent false accounting. The particulars of the offence alleged that while he was employed in the capacity of cashier for Buloki Cooperative Society, with intent to defraud, he altered one receipt No. 18 and destroyed certain pages of a cash book – all coming into his possession on account of his employer. It was held that the charge alleged two offences which should have been set out in two counts.

777. In *Owoo s/o Okot v. Reginam*,[1009] the appellant was charged with 'receiving and retaining' four motor tyres, knowing or having reason to believe that they had been feloniously stolen, taken or obtained. It was held that the charge was bad for duplicity, as receiving and retaining stolen property were two distinct offences. Receiving involves knowledge at the time the goods are received. Retaining however involves innocent receipt of the goods, the retainer acquiring knowledge or belief that they were stolen at a later stage. The judge said that it would have been proper if the prosecution joined the offences in one count as alternatives (receiving *or* retaining), but not cumulatively (receiving *and* retaining), as the two are mutually exclusive. Generally speaking, where the prosecution charges 'receiving or retaining', it remains the duty of the court to decide, on the evidence adduced, which limb of the charge (receiving or retaining) has been proved.[1010] The point to emphasize here is that 'receiving or retaining' is one offence which may be committed in two different modes.

778. An exception to the rule against duplicity is in cases where the accused is charged with embezzlement, causing financial loss or stealing by agent of specific

1006. But see *Mfaune v. Republic* [1973] E.A. 563.
1007. Trial on Indictments Act, sec. 23(2); Magistrates Courts Act, sec. 86(2).
1008. [1956–1957] 8 U.L.R. 160.
1009. [1956–1957] 8 U.L.R. 225.
1010. See *Harji Kuverji Patel v. R.* [1955] 22 E.A.C.A. 536. This case was followed in *Uganda v. E. Mutagobwa & Anor.* H.Ct.Monthly Bulletin No. 120 of 1969. See also *Uganda v. Amisi* [1970] E.A. 291.

sums of money or number of articles taken or lost over a period of time under sections 268, 269, 270 and 271 of the Penal Code. In these cases, it is sufficient to specify the gross amount of money or property involved and the dates between which the offence is alleged to have been committed without particularizing specific sums or items or specifying exact dates.[1011] The prosecution does nonetheless have discretion not to combine all the gross in one count, but to divide it into portions and make each portion the subject of a separate count. In the Kenyan case of *Attorney-General v. Onyango s/o Oludhe & Anor*,[1012] the respondents were charged with theft by clerks and servants of certain sums of money between the first day of January 1951 and the thirtieth day of December 1953. Instead of charging the respondents with one offence of theft of one grand gross sum of money within the period of three years, the prosecution charged them of three counts, each count covering the gross amount stolen in each of the three years. The Court of Appeal held this to be proper, holding that it was a matter of discretion provided that the accused was not prejudiced.

779. Offences charged in one charge sheet are ordinarily tried together. The court nevertheless has discretion to direct separate trials for any one or more offences charged in a charge sheet if it thinks that the accused person 'may be embarrassed in his or her defence by reason of being charged with more than one offence in the same charge'.[1013]

III. Joinder of Offenders

780. Again for convenience and expedition, certain categories of accused persons may be charged in the same charge sheet and tried together.[1014] The first category includes persons who are accused of the *same offence* committed in the course of the same transaction. This applies to the perpetrators or persons who actually do the act or make the omission which constitutes the offence. It also applies to their helpers, accomplices or accessories, i.e., those who aid, aid and abet, and counsel or procure the commission of the offence. This assertion is borne out by section 19 of the Penal Code which refers to all helpers as principal offenders who are 'deemed to have taken part in committing the offence and to be guilty of the offence and may be charged with actually committing it'.[1015] All these persons must be joined in the *same count* for *each offence* to which they are party.

781. The second category includes persons accused of an offence and persons accused of an attempt to commit such offence.[1016] These, too, may be joined in one count for each offence to which they are party.

1011. Trial on Indictments Act, sec. 25(k); Magistrates Courts Act, sec. 88(l).
1012. [1954] 21 E.A.C.A. 230.
1013. Trial on Indictments Act, sec. 52; Magistrates Courts Act, sec. 86(3). Also see *Sebuzukira v. Uganda* [1965] E.A. 684, 685.
1014. Trial on Indictments Act, sec. 24(a); Magistrates Courts Act, sec. 87(a).
1015. See *Attorney-General v. Onyango s/o Oludhe & Anor.* [1954] 21 E.A.C.A. 238.
1016. Trial on Indictments Act, sec. 24(b); Magistrates Courts Act, sec. 87(b).

782. Persons accused of more offences than one of the same kind (i.e., to say, offences punishable with the same amount of punishment under the same section of the Penal Code or of any other written law) committed by them jointly within a period of twelve months may also be charged and tried together. However, each of the offences involved must be charged in a separate count, but the co-accused persons may be joined in each of these counts.[1017]

783. Persons accused of different offences committed in the course of the same transaction may also be charged and tried together.[1018] It must, however, be emphasized that since they are not being charged with committing the same offence, each one must be charged in a separate count. For different offences to constitute one transaction, they must be 'so connected together by proximity of time, community of criminal intent, continuity of action and purpose or the relation of cause and effect as to constitute … one transaction'.[1019] In *Yakobo Uma & Anor. v. R.*,[1020] two men were charged in the same charge sheet with committing two separate offences of doing an act intended to cause grievous harm contrary to section 209(2) of the Penal Code. They committed the offences on the same village and against the same complainant, but on different dates. The first man committed the first offence on 14 April 1962 while the second man committed the second offence on 2 January 1963. Both men pleaded guilty and were convicted. On appeal the convictions were quashed, because the charge was demonstrably bad in law. The men committed two separate and distinct offences and on different occasions; they did not commit them in the course of the same transaction; nor did they commit them jointly.

784. Persons accused of theft and kindred offences as well as robbery, burglary and obtaining by false pretences under Chapter XXVI to XXX of the Penal Code, may also be charged and tried together with people accused of receiving or retaining property where possession of such property is alleged to have been transferred by the offence committed by the accused persons in the first category.[1021] Thus where X steals some property which he transfers to Y, both X and Y may be joined in one charge sheet, X charged with theft and Y with receiving or retaining.[1022]

IV. Framing Charges

785. The overriding principle that must be observed in framing a charge is that the charge must give the accused reasonable information as to the nature of the offence he or she is alleged to have committed. For this reason, both the Trial on Indictments Act and the Magistrates Courts Act lay down rules whose observance help attain this desideratum.

1017. Trial on Indictments Act, sec. 24(c); the Magistrates Courts Act, sec. 87(c).
1018. Trial on Indictments Act, sec. 24(d); the Magistrates Court Acts, sec. 87(d).
1019. *Saidi Nsubuga v. R.* [1941] 8 E.A.C.A. 81. See also *Akber Rashid Mathani v. Republic* [1965] E.A. 777.
1020. [1963] E.A. 542.
1021. Trial on Indictments Act, sec. 24(e); Magistrates Courts Act, sec. 87(e).
1022. See *Saidere v. Republic* [1973] E.R. 98.

786. The first rule is that each count in a charge sheet must contain a statement of the offence charged, together with a reference to the section of the enactment creating the offence.[1023] The statement of offence describes the offence by the name it is ordinarily known, for example common assault. The name of the offence is usually, though not always, indicated in the marginal notes of the statute. The section of the enactment to be cited is that one which creates or defines the offence. Where, however, the section defining the offence is different from the one prescribing the punishment, it is advisable to refer to the definition section, and add 'punishable under section … '[1024] Reference to these sections not only alerts the accused as to the law he or she is alleged to have contravened but also helps the court to know whether it has power to try the offences charged. Referring to the wrong section of the enactment will however not be fatal to the charge,[1025] unless the cited provisions have already been repealed and not re-enacted.

787. Next, the count must set out the particulars of offence in which the use of technical terms are avoided. Though not the evidence, the particulars must allege facts which are sufficient to give the accused 'reasonable information as to the nature of the offence charged'. They must disclose all the essential ingredients of the offence charged, as defined by the section of the enactment referred to in the statement of the offence. For example, in a charge for rape the particulars of offence must allege that the accused had sexual intercourse with a woman without her consent. In a charge for arson, the particulars must allege that the accused set fire to a building unlawfully or wilfully.[1026] In a case where the accused was charged under a Traffic Regulation prohibiting use of spotlights on a vehicle, the particulars alleged that he had permitted use of his vehicle without rear reflectors. The charge sheet was held to be incurably defective.[1027]

788. Additionally, the particulars must be certain as to the date of the offence. They must allege the date and place of the offence with reasonable clearness so as to enable the accused to know the case he or she has to meet. However, it is not essential to allege a specific date when the alleged crime took place. Language such as 'on or about' is acceptable. Nevertheless, the particulars must allege some reasonably ascertainable period of time during which the offence occurred. If this is not done the accused may be prejudiced and embarrassed in his or her defence, particularly where he or she has an alibi. For example, it is not sufficient simply to say 'during 1994 at an exact date unknown'[1028] or 'on various dates in 1994'.[1029] The only exception to this rule is the one contained in section 88(l) of the Magistrates Courts Act which states that:

1023. Trial on Indictments Act, sec. 25(a); Magistrates Courst Act, sec. 87(a).
1024. See *Cosma s/o Nyadago v. Reginam* [1955] 22 E.A.C.A. 450.
1025. See *Abdurasul G. Sabur v. R.* [1958] E.A. 126; *Pool v. R.* [1958] E.A. 688; and *Avone v. Uganda* [1969] E.A. 129.
1026. See *Sisipeter Opale s/o Idiawo v. R.* [1962] E.A. 661.
1027. *Uganda v. Hadi Jamal* [1964] E.A. 294.
1028. See the Botswana case of *Thomas Machola v. Regina* [1964–1967] B.L.R 143.
1029. See the Kenya case of *Wilson v. Reginam* [1955] 22 E.A.C.A. 372.

> When a person is charged with any offence under Sections 268, 269, 271 and 272 of the Penal Code, it shall be sufficient to specify the gross amount of property in respect of which the offence is alleged to have been committed and the dates between which offence is alleged to have been committed *without specifying particular items or exact dates.*[1030]

Similarly, a charge will not be fatally defective for want of a statement of time unless time is an essential element of the offence. Burglary and being found in a building by night with intent to commit a felony are examples of offences where time is an essential element and must be alleged in the particulars.

789. Where the charge involves property, the property must be described with reasonable clearness so as to be identifiable. A misdescription of the ownership of the property will not vitiate a charge, unless it is shown that such misdescription occasioned a miscarriage of justice.[1031] If the offence charged is against the person, the victim should be identified. If he or she is a victim of a particular kind, say girl below 18 years as in the case of defilement, this fact must be alleged. But where the identity of the victim is not an element of the offence, it may sometimes be sufficient simply to say 'a person to the prosecution unknown'.[1032]

V. Amending the Charge

790. Section 50(2) of the Trial on Indictments Act provides that:

> Where before a trial upon indictment or at any stage of such trial it is made to appear to the High Court that the indictment is defective or otherwise requires amendment, the court may make such order for the alteration of the indictment (by way of its amendment or by substitution or addition of a new count) as the court thinks necessary to meet the circumstances of the case, unless having regard to the merits of the case the required alteration cannot be made without injustice.

Though worded differently, section 132(1) of the Magistrates Courts Act is substantially the same as the above provision. It enumerates the instances when charges may be amended. They include the following:

(a) Where the evidence discloses an offence other than the offence charged. This means that a completely new count may be substituted for or added to the existing count or counts.[1033]

1030. Emphasis added. See also sec. 24(k) of the Trial on Indictments Act.
1031. See for example, *Festo Magambo v. R.* [1959] E.A. 258.
1032. Trial on Indictments Act, sec. 25(l); Magistrates Courts Act, sec. 88(m).
1033. For example in *William Sebugenyi v. R.* [1959] E.A. 411 where the charge originally alleged 'besetting' the magistrate amended it to 'watching and besetting'.

(b) Where the charge is defective in a material particular. In this case words may be added to or deleted from the charge to remedy the defect.[1034]
(c) Where the accused desires to plead guilty to an offence other than the offence with which he or she is charged. In this case, a new charge may be substituted for the original.

791. Where a charge is amended, the law requires that the accused be called upon to plead to the amended charge. Additionally, the accused has a right to demand that any of the prosecution witnesses be recalled for cross-examination. He or she is also entitled to give or to call such further evidence on his or her behalf as he or she may wish. He or she also has a right to apply for an adjournment to enable him or her to prepare his or her defence against the amended charge. The court must advise him or her that he or she has these rights.[1035] Failure to do so may amount to a fatal irregularity.[1036]

792. The court may allow the charge to be amended at any stage of the trial. It may do so at the close of the prosecution's case or at the close of the defence, provided that to do so does not prejudice the accused.[1037] By the nature of things, however, amendments should not be allowed during or after judgment. Were it to be allowed, the accused would not be able to enjoy the protection accorded to him or her by law, such as pleading again or calling or recalling witnesses.

1034. For example in *Regina v. Nyamitare s/o Kachumita* [1956–1957] 8 U.L.R. 292 on a charge of murder the particulars of offence gave the name of a victim following the date and place of the offence. It did not allege any act on the part of the accused. The Court amended the charge by inserting the word 'murdered' before the name of the victim.
1035. Trial on Indictments Act, sec. 51(3); Magistrates Courst Act, sec. 132(5).
1036. See *Musoke v. R.* [1956–1957] 8 U.L.R. 108. In this case, the trial magistrate refused to adjourn the proceedings to allow the accused to be represented by Counsel. He also omitted to advise him of his right to have prosecution witnesses recalled. This was held to have occasioned injustice to the accused. In contrast see *William Sebugenyi v. R.* [1959] E.A. 411 where the magistrate complied with the above requirements. It was held that no injustice was caused to the accused. See also *Hunter v. Reginam* [1956–1957] 8 U.L.R. 366.
1037. See *Uganda v. Mushraf Akhtar* [1964] E.A. 89.

Chapter 5. The Trial

§1. Rights of the Accused

793. Successive Uganda constitutions have embodied a bill of rights, with a section devoted to the rights of an accused person.[1038] The section, based on Article 6 of the European Convention for the Protection of Human Rights and Fundamental Freedoms, sets out the accused's rights. These rights are in turn embodied in various sections of the Trial on Indictments Act, the Magistrates Courts Act and the Criminal Procedure Code Act. Observance of the accused's rights is considered to be indispensable to a fair trial. Their non-observance usually results in a mistrial or in the vitiation of the entire proceedings.

I. Trial Within a Reasonable Time

794. Article 28(1) of the Constitution refers to a 'fair, speedy and public hearing before an independent and impartial court'. Article 126(2)(b) also proclaims that 'justice shall not be delayed'. As is often said, 'justice delayed is justice denied', and 'justice is sweetest when it is freshest'. Where it is alleged that a person committed an offence, it is vital that he or she be brought to trial as soon as possible so that if he or she is found guilty he or she pays the penalty and makes a new start in life. If he or she is found not guilty, he or she is set free, allowed to resume a normal life and freed from the stigma that allegations of criminal conduct engender.

795. Delay to bring the accused to trial works untold injustice to him or her. It inflicts mental suffering on him or her. It interferes with his or her freedom of movement, employment opportunities, as well as his or her social life.

796. Delay, per se, does not vitiate criminal proceedings. It is unreasonable or undue delay that is objectionable. What is unreasonable or undue delay varies from case to case depending on the nature, seriousness and complexity of the case, the circumstances under which it was committed, as well as the attitude and conduct of the criminal justice actors.[1039]

797. Courts of justice must always remain alive to the right of the accused to trial within a reasonable time. When they sense unreasonable delays, they must put prosecuting authorities to task by setting deadlines within which certain tasks must be performed or proceedings must commence. They must not accede to repeated and unreasonable applications for adjournments. They must, instead, proceed on the available evidence and if none is available dismiss the charge for there being no-case-to-answer.[1040] Additionally, they should ever bear in mind that the *raison*

1038. For example: see sec. 28 of the 1995 Constitution billed as 'Right to a fair hearing'.
1039. See *Musoke v. Uganda* [1972] E.A. 137.
1040. See Trial on Indictments Act, secs. 53(2) and 73(2). See also *Uganda v. Ibrahim Seguya* S.Ct. Cr.App. No. 3 of 1987 (unreported).

d'être for bail is the amelioration of the hardship caused by delay in bringing the accused to trial. They should therefore be ready and willing to release the accused in appropriate cases and, in extreme cases, permanently stay the proceedings for abuse of process. Lastly, they should, while passing sentence on a convict, take into account the suffering he or she has undergone as a result of unreasonable delay to bring him or her to trial.

798. Other actors in the criminal justice system do also have a duty to so act as not to cause unnecessary delays. The police must speedily and efficiently conduct their investigations and, as far as humanly possible, avoid the usual sing-song of 'investigations are not ready'. Prosecuting authorities must, in turn, manage cases referred to them by the police diligently and with due regard to the right of the accused to trial within a reasonable time. Defence counsel, too, must avoid causing delays by asking for too many adjournments, or by failing to turn up in court or, turning up late to defend their clients, or by indulging in dilatory tactics.

II. An Independent and Impartial Tribunal

799. Trial by an independent and impartial court is another element of a fair trial. Judicial independence is relational; it imports institutional autonomy and freedom from pressure, dictation or influence from outsiders, particularly from the executive branch of government. Impartiality, however, is attitudinal; it requires a fair and open mind, being even-handed, unbiased and not pre-judging the issues that fall for decision.

For the courts to be independent, they must be institutionally and functionally separate and autonomous from the executive or legislative branches of the government. As Montesquieu observed, 'There is no liberty yet if power to judge is not separated from legislative and executive power.' Autonomy of the courts entails the courts being responsible for their internal administration, organization of work and financial matters. They must have their own accounting officer. Their staff, both professional and administrative, should not perform executive or legislative functions, in the same way as the executive and the legislature or executive should not perform judicial functions. The courts must be directly answerable to the head of the judiciary – the Chief Justice – and subject to an independent disciplinary regime. The courts must not be mere mouthpieces of the legislature or the executive. They must decide cases according to the evidence and the law, without undue deference to those other branches of government. The executive, in particular, must also desist from interfering with the courts' independence by, say, creating a coercive environment for the courts or intimidating the judges or magistrates, or purporting to order them as to how they should decide cases. To do so would be to violate Article 128 of the Constitution, which provides, *inter alia*, that:

(1) In the exercise of judicial power, the courts shall be independent and shall not be subject to the control or direction of any person or authority.
(2) No person or authority shall interfere with the courts or judicial officers in the exercise of their judicial functions.

(3) All organs and agencies of the State shall accord to the courts such assistance as may be required to ensure the effectiveness of the courts.

800. Nevertheless, where the executive appears to be invading their independence, as it has unfortunately done in the past, the courts should resist such invasion by, say, remonstrating with the executive and, in extreme cases, refusing to exercise jurisdiction by permanently halting the proceedings. The Constitutional Court did so in *Dr Kizza Besigye & Others v. Attorney General.*[1041/1042] The petitioners were arrested and charged at different times and before different courts with treason, unlawful possession of firearms, terrorism, rape and murder. The petitioners sought to be released on bail. However, in a bid to prevent their release state agencies did on two occasions carry out an armed siege of the High Court premises with tanks and re-arrested them; they charged them with the selfsame offences based on the same facts before the General Court Martial even though that court did not have jurisdiction to try them for some of those offences; they kept them in continued detention despite several courts' orders that they be released; and they disregarded production warrants issued by the courts requiring some of them to be produced in court to seek judicial reliefs in respect of their detention. The Constitutional Court condemned the armed siege of the High Court premises as a gross interference with the exercise of judicial power and as 'an outrageous affront to the Constitution, constitutionalism and the rule of law'. It declared the simultaneous proceedings against the petitioners before different courts as unconstitutional. It characterized any continued trials as 'a waste of time and an abuse of process'. Finally, it ordered a permanent stay of all the proceedings against the petitioners, saying:

> We cannot stand by and watch prosecutions mounted and conducted in the midst of such flagrant, egregious and mala fide violations of the Constitution and must act to protect the constitutional rights of the petitioners in particular and the citizens of Uganda in general as well as the Rule of Law in Uganda by ordering all the tainted proceedings against the petitioners to stop forthwith and directing the respective courts to discharge the petitioners.

This was a bold and salutary statement in defence of judicial independence. Other mechanisms embodied in our Constitution for securing judicial independence include the doctrine of separation of powers; the methods used to appoint judges and magistrates;[1042.1] as well as their security of tenure, adequate remuneration and fair disciplinary procedures.

801. To be impartial, judges and magistrates must decide cases before them without fear, favour, affection or ill-will towards any of the parties before them.

1041/1042. Const. Petition No. 7 of 2007 [2010] UGCC 6 (12 Oct. 2010).
1042.1. See *Karuhanga v. Attorney-General* [2014] UGCA 14 (4 August 2014).

ey must not be biased or appear to be biased toward or against any of them. ven bias or appearance of bias will vitiate the proceedings. Appearance of bias sts where there are any factor which tends to indicate to any reasonable person officious bystander a likelihood of bias. There will be an appearance of bias ere a judge has any pecuniary interest, however slight, in the subject-matter of proceedings. There will be appearance of bias where a judge has close blood ations with the accused, the complainant, the prosecutor or the defence counsel. ere will also be appearance of bias where the judge or magistrate has in the past ibited friendly or hostile relations with any of the parties to the case as to impair impartiality. The same will be true where he or she has previously been asso-ed with the case in a way that affects his or her impartiality. In all these cases judge should, as a matter of conscience, voluntarily rescue himself or herself n the case. The need for recusal is premised on the maxim *Nemo judex in causa* or that nobody should judge in his or her own cause. The indigenous Ugandan ivalent is expressed in the Luganda maxim *Enkima tesala gwa kibira*, or that a nkey should not judge in the affairs of the forest; it is likely to be biased. The secutor or the accused may also ask the judge to recuse himself or herself if they e cause to believe that he or she is biased. The cause must, however, be well-nded and not flimsy.[1043] Where the judge refuses to recuse himself or herself, the rieved party may appeal to a higher court against the judge's decision not to use himself or herself, or may abide the conclusion of the trial and use the deci-n as a ground of appeal. Thus in *Isaac Newton Ojok v. Uganda*,[1044] the appellant o was charged with treason asked Mrs Justice C.K. Byamugisha to recuse her-, alleging that she was 'a blood sister of Hon. Eriya Kategaya, First Deputy ne Minister, and National Political Commissar of the National Resistance Move-nt' and that 'since I was indicted for allegedly fighting the NRM Government of ch the said Eriya Kategaya is a pillar-stone, it would be better if I were tried by ther judge'. The judge refused to recuse herself and proceeded to try and con-the appellant. On appeal, the Supreme Court quashed the conviction on the und of appearance of bias, saying that 'If all these facts were known to a rea-able person in court, we are sure that that person would have thought that the ge was probably biased in favour of the National Resistance Movement, con-usly or unconsciously.'

02. Lastly, in conducting the trial, the judge must be fair to both parties and to r witnesses. He or she must, in particular, avoid asking questions or ask them at a frequency or in such a tone or manner as to give the impression that he or she already taken sides. Ours being an adversary system, the judge must remain an

In *Ali Fadhul v. State* H.Ct.Misc.Appl. No. MMB 8 of 1992 (unreported) the applicant, charged with murder, asked Judge Karokora to recuse himself on the grounds that the victim of the murder lived on the same village with the judge, that the victim was a prominent personality in Mbarara, that the fact that all advocates in Mbarara refused to represent him indicated that he would not get justice if that particular judge presided over the case, since he also originated from Mbarara. The judge refused to recuse himself, denying that he knew the deceased.

S.Ct.Cr.App. No. 33 of 1991 (unreported).

impartial and detached arbiter.[1045] Save in the case of an undefended accused person, whom he or she should assist, he or she must keep his or her questions to a minimum: to clear up ambiguities or to clarify points that were over-looked or left obscure, and to ensure that he or she records the accused's or witness' testimony accurately.

III. Trial in Public

803. The accused must be tried in an open court. Members of the public, particularly the press, must have free access to the place where the trial is taking place.[1046] To fulfil this requirement, it is important that all court houses should be gazetted so that members of the public know their location and be able to access them. Public trial ensures that justice is not only done but also that it appears to be done. As the judges judge, they should also be judged by the members of the public. As Lord Diplock has observed:

> If the way that Courts behave cannot be hidden from the public ear and eye this provides a safeguard against judicial arbitrariness or idiosyncrasy and maintains the public confidence in the administration of justice.[1047]

804. However, the Constitution allows for two exceptions to open trial.[1048] The first exception relates to the need to protect interests of morality. This is particularly so in the case of offences of a sexual nature and those involving persons under the age of 18 years; it is important that in all cases involving these persons the trial be held in camera; such trials serve to protect the victims from further public shame or from stigmatization. The second exception concerns the need to protect public order or national security. This situation might arise in cases in which a public trial might result in information relating to the country's national security or public safety leaking out to the enemy or to criminals and being used against the country or the public. In all these situations, the trial may be held in camera, and members of the general public, save the parties to the case and their legal representatives, excluded from the proceedings or part of them.

IV. Presence of the Accused

805. The accused person has a right to be present at all stages of his trial,[1049] including the visit to the *locus in quo*[1050] and sentencing. Only when he or she is present can he or she know fully the case against him or her and be able to defend

1045. See for instance for instance *Yuill v. Yuill* [1945] P. 15 at p. 20.
1046. Article 28(2) of the Constitution.
1047. *Attorney-General v. Leveller Magazine & Anor.* [1979] A.C. 440, 450.
1048. See sec. 28(2) of the Constitution.
1049. Trial on Indictments Act, sec. 54(1); Magistrates Courts Act, sec. 137.
1050. In *Hoafeau v. R.* [1962] E.A. 809. A magistrate, together with the prosecutor visited the *locus in quo* in the absence of the accused or his counsel. The trial was declared a nullity.

himself or herself. Save with the consent of the accused person and in a few exceptional cases that we shall indicate presently, *in absentia* trials are not allowed in Uganda.[1051] Where the accused is unable to be present, say, due to illness, the trial must be postponed to a date when he or she is fit to attend. He or she cannot appear by his advocate.[1052] Again, if the accused is outside the jurisdiction the trial cannot start or proceed until he or she is physically before the court. For this purpose, the state may request the country where he or she happens to be to extradite him or her. However, that country may decline to comply with the request unless there exists an extradition treaty between the country and Uganda. It is for this reason that Uganda has entered into extradition treaties with a number of countries that impose reciprocal obligations on the parties to extradite, on request, fugitive offenders within their respective borders. A cardinal rule in all these treaties is that a state is not obliged to extradite any fugitive offender who is sought for an offence of a political character.[1053]

806. As indicated above, the presence of the accused person may sometimes be dispensed with where 'the person so conducts himself or herself as to render the continuance of the proceedings in the presence of that person impracticable'.[1054] In that case, the court may order the accused to be removed and the trial to proceed in his or her absence. The court must nevertheless make sufficient arrangements to have the accused apprised with what transpired at the trial to enable him or her to make his or her defence.[1055] The presence of the accused may also be dispensed with in petty offences, especially under the Traffic Code and any other law which the Minister, after consulting the Chief Justice, may designate. The sentence passed in such cases must not exceed a fine of UGX 100. However, even here a conviction passed *in absentia* may be set aside if the accused satisfies the court that his or her absence was from causes over which he or she had no control, and that he or she has a probable defence on the merits.[1056] The presence of the accused who is charged with a misdemeanour may also be dispensed with if he or she fails to appear on the day and time to which a hearing was adjourned. This is however not allowed where the accused is charged with a felony.[1057] In that case, a warrant of arrest must be issued to apprehend and to bring the accused before the court. Once again if the court convicts the accused in his or her absence, it may set aside the conviction upon being satisfied that his or her absence was from causes beyond his or her control, and that he or she has a probable defence on the merits.[1058]

1051. The Constitution, Art. 28(5).
1052. *Vithlani v. Reginam* [1956–1957] 8 U.L.R. 151.
1053. For a definition of an offence of political character see *Re Castioni* [1886] All E.R. 640.
1054. The Constitution, Art. 28(5).
1055. Trial on Indictments Act, sec. 54(2); Magistrates Courts Act, sec. 137.
1056. Magistrates Courts Act, sec. 123(2).
1057. See Magistrates Courts Act, sec. 123(1). See also *Vithlani v. Reginam* [1956–1957] 8 U.L.R. 155.
1058. Magistrates Courts Act, sec. 123(2).

V. Legal Representation

807. Article 28(2)(d) of the Constitution provides that 'Every person who is charged with a criminal offence shall be permitted to appear before the court in person or, at that person's own expense, by a lawyer of his or her own choice.'[1059] Lord Denning has underscored the importance of an accused person being represented by a lawyer in the following statement:

> It is not every man who has the ability to defend himself on his own. He cannot bring out the points in his own favour or the weakness in the other side. He may be tongue-tied, nervous, confused or wanting in intelligence. He cannot examine or cross-examine witnesses. We see it every day. A magistrate says to a man: 'You can ask any questions you like'; whereupon the man immediately starts to make a speech. If justice is to be done, he ought to have the help of someone to speak for him; and who better than a lawyer who has been trained for the task?[1060]

808. It is for this reason that our law recognizes it as a fundamental right for every accused person to be defended by a lawyer of his or her own choice but at his own expense. Save in capital cases, the state is not obliged to provide the accused with a lawyer.[1061] Its only obligation is to permit or facilitate the accused being defended by the lawyer he or she has hired and not to unreasonably prevent him or her from being represented by that lawyer. In practice, this means that the court must advise the accused of his or her right. It must give him or her reasonable time to engage the lawyer of choice at any stage of the proceedings. For this purpose, it must adjourn or postpone the trial to enable him or her to engage a lawyer and to enable the lawyer to be prepared for or to be present at the trial.[1062] Where the lawyer engaged by the accused is absent from the court on the day and time set for the trial and does not notify the court in advance of his or her absence, he or she may be guilty of professional misconduct and of discourtesy toward the court. Nonetheless, the court should still be indulging to the accused and should not visit the lawyer's sins on him or her. It should be willing to adjourn the case to enable him or her to contact the lawyer or to instruct a new one. The court will of course be justified to refuse to adjourn a trial where it is patently clear that the accused is acting unreasonably, is engaging in delaying tactics or that he or she is culpably responsible for the lawyer's absence.[1063]

809. Once engaged, the lawyer is entitled to be present and to participate at every stage of the proceedings: from the committal proceedings, arraignment, trial, visit to the *locus in quo*, through to sentencing. It is important that lawyers must

1059. See also Trial on Indictments Act, sec. 55; Magistrates Courts Act, sec. 158.
1060. *Pett v. Greyhound Racing Association* (No. 1) [1968] 2 All E.R. 545, 549.
1061. In the case of capital offences, Art. 28(3)(e) of the 1995 Constitution provides that every person who is charged with a criminal offence shall 'in any offence which carries a death penalty, be entitled to legal representation at the expense of the state'.
1062. *Muyimba & Anor. v. Uganda* [1969] E.A. 433; *Musoke v. R.* [1956–1957] 8 U.L.R. 108.
1063. See *Y. Gitta v. R.* [1959] E.A. 211.

also be allowed to be present when the police interrogate the accused at the police station, because this is a vital stage of the proceedings when the fate of the entire case may be determined.[1064] However, to be of value to the accused legal representation at all the stages of the proceedings must be effective, the lawyer must act competently and zealously. Ineffective representation is no representation and may therefore vitiate the proceedings.

VI. Cross-Examining Prosecution Witnesses

810. The accused person must be afforded facilities to examine in person or by his or her legal representative the witnesses called by the prosecution before the court.[1065] This is the right to cross-examine or to confront the opponent's witnesses. When properly exercised, the right of cross-examination enables the cross-examiner to test the opponent's case and to put the defence case to the opponent's witnesses and to give them an opportunity to comment on it. Cross-examination is important because, according to our law, if what a witness says during examination-in-chief is admissible in evidence and is otherwise credible it is assumed to be true. A party who fails to cross-examine his or her opponent's witnesses is presumed to have accepted what they said as true. Cross-examination also enables the court to test the witnesses' veracity, to ascertain whether under an 'unfriendly' examiner they will be consistent and remain unshaken.

811. Where the accused is unrepresented, the court must inform him or her of his or her right to cross-examine prosecution witnesses. It must also explain to him or her the consequences of failing to cross-examine them.[1066] Where it is apparent that the accused cannot conduct the cross-examination by himself or herself or, if he or she does, he or she does so inadequately, the court should assist him or her to do so. It must, especially, ensure that the accused's defence or version of the events is properly put to the prosecution witnesses. In cases of joint trials, the court must ensure that co-defendants give evidence in each other's presence and hearing and that they are advised of their right to cross-examine each other as well as their respective witnesses.[1067] Failure to do any of these things may result in a mistrial and vitiate the entire proceedings.

812. Additionally, where the accused engages the services of a lawyer after some or all of the prosecution witnesses have given evidence, the court must, if requested, recall the witnesses to be cross-examined by the lawyer. For this purpose, it must also allow the lawyer to peruse the court proceedings to date to inform himself or herself of what the witnesses said. Again, the court should be willing to

1064. See D.D. Ntanda Nsereko, *The Poisoned Tree: Responses to Involuntary Confessions in Criminal Proceedings in Botswana, Uganda and Zambia*, 5 Afr. J. Intl. & Comp. L. 606 (1993).
1065. Trial on Indictments Act, sec. 75; Magistrates Courts Act, sec. 128(2).
1066. Trial on Indictments Act, sec. 72; Magistrates Courts Act, sec. 126(3).
1067. *R. v. Suke d/o Samwe & Anor.* [1947] 14 E.A.C.A. 134.

adjourn the proceedings to enable the lawyer to peruse the court record. Failure to comply with these requests may also result in a mistrial.[1068]

VII. Giving Evidence and Calling Witnesses

813. Besides cross-examining prosecution witnesses, the accused also has a right to give evidence or make an unsworn statement on his or her own behalf.[1069] The right to be heard, *audi altarem partem*, is well understood under Ugandan indigenous jurisprudence. It is expressed in the Luganda maxim: *tosala gwa kawala nga tonnawulira gwa kalenzi*, [do not pass judgment based on only what the wife says until you have heard the husband as well; hear both parties]. The court has an obligation to inform the accused of his or her right to give evidence on his or her own behalf. Failure to do so may also result in a mistrial.[1070]

814. As part of his right to defend himself or herself, the accused also has a right to call witnesses to testify on his behalf. According to Article 28(3)(g) of the Constitution, the accused must 'be afforded facilities to examine witnesses and to obtain the attendance of other witnesses before the court'. To attain this requirement, the court must advise the accused of this right even when he or she is represented by a lawyer.[1071] To ensure that the court carries out this duty, the judge must always make a note on the record of the proceedings that he or she has so advised the accused and also note the accused person's reply. Where the accused person or his or her lawyer indicates that he or she wishes to call witnesses and requests the court to adjourn the proceedings to enable him or her to do so, the court should ordinarily grant the request. It should do so even without the request, if the interests of justice so demand. In one case, the appellants indicated that they wished to call a witness B who was sick. The magistrate, without asking the appellants whether they wanted an adjournment so that B's evidence could be heard, said that it was unnecessary, since it was to the same effect as that of two other witnesses whose evidence in support of the alibi he had already heard and rejected. On appeal, it was held that since the magistrate did not believe the evidence of the two witnesses who supported the alibi, it was all the more necessary that he should have given the appellants an opportunity to call B whose evidence might have convinced the magistrate. Ordering a retrial, the High Court said that:

> In a criminal trial, the accused has a right to have summoned any person who can give evidence relevant to the charge under enquiry and whose whereabouts are known, if that person is in Uganda. If an accused is deprived of that right, it cannot be said that he has had a fair trial.[1072]

1068. See for example: *James Sawoabiri & Anor. v. Uganda*, Cr.App. No. 5 of 1990, [1991] UGSC 1 (4 Jun. 1991).
1069. Trial on Indictments Act, sec. 75(2); Magistrates Courts Act, secs 106 and 128.
1070. See *Jada v. Reginam* [1956–1957] 8 U.L.R. 71.
1071. Trial on Indictments Act, sec. 75(2); Magistrates Courst Act, sec. 128.
1072. *Augustino Mbonye & Anor. v. Uganda.* H.Ct.Monthly Bulletin No. 33 of 1964.

815. Where the accused is unable by himself or herself to secure the attendance of witnesses, the court, as required by the Constitution and as indicated in the case cited above, must subpoena and compel the witnesses to attend court at state expense.[1073]

816. Witnesses, whether called by the defence or by the prosecution, must be allowed to testify freely without threats or harassment by the parties or by the court itself. Where it is established that witnesses were prevented to testify freely as a result of threats by the parties or the court, this may be a ground for vitiating the proceedings. The court does, however, have the right to warn refractory witnesses,[1074] or even to commit them to prison unless they sooner consent to do what is required of them.[1075] According to Jones, J. 'a convenient way of dealing with an obdurate witness is to commit him until such time as he changes his mind. I have found that even the threat of such an eventuality has a most salutary effect'.[1076]

VIII. Trial in a Language Understood by the Accused

817. Where the accused does not understand the language used at the trial, a competent interpreter must be provided at state expense to interpret the proceedings to him or her in a language that he or she understands.[1077] Before allowing any person to act as interpreter, the court must satisfy itself that that person is competent to interpret in the languages being used. It is only when the accused and his or her counsel understand what is going on in the court that they will be able to put up a defence. As a general rule, police officers, particularly those who participated in the arrest or investigations in the case, should not be used as interpreters. Their connection with the prosecution disqualifies them, and justice will not be seen to be done if they are used as interpreters.

818. In the case of an accused person who is a deaf-mute, the court should in the first place establish whether or not he or she is sane. When it is satisfied that he or she is sane, it must then decide after diligent inquiries from his or her relatives and friends whether sufficient contact can be made with him or her by sign language or otherwise for him or her to understand the charge and to defend himself or herself. If he or she understands and can be communicated with through sign language, then an expert in sign language must be employed to interpret the proceedings to him. If, however, he or she cannot be made to understand the proceedings, the judge must proceed to hear all the evidence available both for the prosecution

1073. See also the Trial on Indictments Act, secs. 33 and 75; Magistrates Courts Act, secs. 94 and 128(2).
1074. See *John Reuben Asia v. R.* H.Ct.Monthly Bulletin No. 722 of 1962.
1075. Trial on Indictments Act, sec. 41(1); Magistrates Courts Act, sec. 102(1).
1076. *Uganda v. Absolom Kagwisaye* H.Ct.Monthly Bulletin No. 6 of 1969.
1077. The Constitution, Art. 28(2)(f); Trial on Indictments Act, secs. 56 and 57; Magistrates Courts Act, secs. 139 and 140.

and for the defence. If the court is satisfied that the accused is guilty, it so dec pending an order by the Minister of Justice. As Ainley, J. said:

> The 'trial' which follows is, so it seems to me, called a trial for want of a ter word. It is in fact not a trial in the normally accepted sense of the wor is a recording of the evidence of the prosecution to which the accused make no answer. A so-called conviction may follow, it is true, but it is my sidered opinion that the Magistrate at any rate can pass no sentence ha recorded the conviction.[1078]

These procedures are provided for under both the Trial on Indictments Act[1079] the Magistrates Courts Act.[1080]

§2. Pleas

I. Arraignment

819. Arraignment is the process by which the court assumes jurisdiction ove accused. It involves three stages: calling the accused person to the bar by na reading and (if he or she does not understand the language of the court) interpre and explaining the nature of the charge to him or her; and asking him or her whe he or she pleads guilty or not guilty: 'How say you, are you guilty or guilty?'[1081] Unless the accused is insane, a deaf-mute or refuses to plead, he or must plead personally to the arraignment. A plea cannot be made by counsel or other person on behalf of the accused. If the accused person refuses to plead court must enter a plea of not guilty for him or her.[1082] If the charge sheet con several counts, each one of them must be read, interpreted and explained to accused separately. The accused must be asked to plead to each of them separa The exception to this rule is where the counts are charged in the alternative. I accused pleads guilty to the first pair of the counts, he or she need not be ask plead to the second one. Again, where several accused persons are charged tog in one charge sheet, each one must be arraigned separately.

820. A magistrate or judge who arraigns an accused for a given offence have jurisdiction to try him or her for that offence, because to arraign is to as jurisdiction. Therefore arraignment by a magistrate of a grade that does not jurisdiction over the subject matter of the charge is a nullity. However, whe accused person is arraigned by one magistrate or judge competent to arraign hi her, he or she may subsequently be tried by another magistrate or judge with

1078. *R. v. Katete s/o Muruli & Anor.* [1936–1951] 6 U.L.R. 200, 201.
1079. Section 49.
1080. Section 118.
1081. Trial on Indictments Act, sec. 60; Magistrates Courts Act, sec. 124(1).
1082. *Ibid.* Trial on Indictments Act, sec. 62; Magistrates Courts Act, sec. 124(4).

fresh arraignment. In *Saja s/o Mabako v. Reginam*,[1083] one judge arraigned the accused, entered a plea of not guilty and then adjourned the case. The case was subsequently called before another judge who, without further arraigning the accused, proceeded to try him. The issue on appeal was whether the second judge's omission to arraign the accused afresh was an irregularity. The Court of Appeal for Eastern Africa answered the question in the negative. It said:

> It appeared to us that the failure of the learned trial judge to arraign the accused might have the effect of making the trial a nullity. However, the authorities have satisfied us that, arraignment not forming part of the trial, there can be no objection to an accused being arraigned before one judge and tried by another judge without the latter taking any further steps in regard to arraignment. *We think however, that the better practice in such circumstances is for the second judge to arraign the accused afresh, or at least to remind him of the substance of the charge and of his former plea.*[1084]

821. A related matter is one where one magistrate or judge starts a trial and takes evidence from witnesses but for one reason or another cannot complete the trial and is replaced by another. Is it competent for the new magistrate or judge to continue with the trial from where the first stopped or must he or she start the trial *de novo*? In this author's view, fairness of the trial would require that the same magistrate of judge conduct the trial from beginning to end. This continuity is necessary; it enables the magistrate or judge to observe the demeanour of all the witnesses in the case. A magistrate or judge who joins the trial midstream is denied that opportunity, which might be crucial, and this might prejudice the fairness of the trial. Nevertheless, basing itself on the section 142(1) of the Magistrates Courts Act, the Supreme Court has held that a trial may be continued, not only by another magistrate or, by analogy judge, but also by any number of magistrates, or by analogy, judges as necessary. 'What matters is to ensure that the accused person is not thereby prejudiced by applying the proviso where appropriate.'[1085] The proviso entitles the accused to demand that any of the witnesses that previously appeared in the case be summoned and reheard by the new magistrate or magistrates.

822. Where the court omits to arraign the accused and proceeds to try him or her on the basis of a plea of not guilty, it may rectify the error by taking the plea before judgment. Suppose, however, it does not rectify the error and proceeds to convict the accused. Is the error fatal to the entire proceedings? It is submitted that it is not, unless such error occasioned injustice to the accused.[1086]

823. The accused may plead guilty, or not guilty to the charge. He or she may also object to the charge, by raising the special pleas in bar. These are the pleas of

1083. [1956–1957] 8 U.L.R. 56.
1084. *Ibid.*, emphasis added.
1085. *Arvind Patel v. Uganda* Cr. App. No. 36 of 2002, [2003] UGSC 35 (27 Oct. 2003). In this case, three magistrates were involved in the trial.
1086. See *R. v. Williams* (Roy) [1977] 1 All E.R. 874.

autrefois acquit, autrefois convict or presidential pardon. These pleas have already been considered under Chapter one of Part I. They will not be repeated here. Where the accused pleads not guilty or such a plea is entered for him or her, he or she is deemed to have put himself or herself upon his or her country for trial. The prosecution assumes the burden of proving all the elements of the offence charged. Where he or she pleads guilty and the plea is accepted by the court, he or she may be convicted and sentenced. He or she may also plead guilty to an offence other than the one charged. If both the prosecutor and the court accept the plea, the accused may be convicted of that offence in place of the one originally charged.[1087]

II. Plea of Guilty

824. Where the accused pleads guilty, admitting the accusations against him or her, he or she thereby renders proof of those accusations unnecessary. A plea of guilty has serious consequences for the accused, because from that plea the court can now proceed to convict and sentence him or her without any evidence being called by the prosecution. Indeed, in serious offences such as murder, pleas of guilty are rarely accepted by the courts, in which case they are a nullity. Special care needs therefore to be taken to protect the accused from prejudicing himself or herself through error, misunderstanding, or ignorance. The overall concern of the law is that the accused's plea of guilty be clear and unequivocal, and that it be made freely and in full knowledge and understanding of its implications.

825. To ensure that the above requirements are satisfied, the courts have developed the following rules of practice. When an accused person pleads guilty, the court must require the prosecution to read out to the accused a summary of the facts constituting the offence. It is not enough for the prosecutor simply to say 'facts as per particulars of offence'. These facts must be sufficiently detailed to disclose all the ingredients of the offence charged. The court must then put each ingredient of the offence to the accused and ask him or her whether he or she admits it. The accused's answer must be recorded in as nearly the same language as the accused says it.[1088] It must be unequivocal. It must not have double meaning. It must clearly admit all the ingredients of the offence. Said Jones, J.:

> If [the accused] does not accept [the facts as read to him], or if there is anything in the facts, or anything that the accused says in answer, which casts any doubt in the mind of the magistrate about the original plea, he should proceed to enter a plea of not guilty in spite of what might appear to be, on the face of it, an unequivocal plea.[1089]

826. Thus on a charge of possession of a home-made gun without a license, it was held to be no admission of the offence for a housewife to say 'It is correct. It

1087. Trial on Indictments Act, sec. 63 as read with secs. 87–90; Magistrates Courts Act, secs. 145–155.
1088. *Nakafunga v. Reginam* [1956–1957] 8 U.L.R. 151.
1089. *Uganda v. Christopher Lugaya* H.Ct.Monthly Bulletin No. 154 of 1971, per Jones, J.

was found in my house. I admit it.' This statement did not admit legal possession with the requisite *animus possidendi*. It did not even suggest that the housewife had no license.[1090] In another case, the accused was charged with murder. He was allowed to plead guilty to the lesser offence of manslaughter. He said: 'It is true I hit him with a hoe, but did not intend to kill him. I was feeling dizzy on that day (*sic*) I only realized I killed somebody after the victim had died.'[1091] It is submitted that his statement should not have been accepted as an admission of the offence of manslaughter. It tends to suggest that the accused, because of the dizziness, did not know what he was doing at the time. He therefore lacked cognitive powers at the time of the act and did not have the necessary *mens rea*. His statement amounted to a denial of liability.

827. Again, on a charge of attempted murder, it is not enough for the accused simply to say, 'I admit the offence.' The plea must contain words showing that the accused had a positive intention unlawfully to cause death.[1092]

III. Change of Plea

828. An accused person who pleads not guilty may in the course of the trial change his or her plea to that of guilty. Before accepting it, the court must satisfy itself that the plea is freely and voluntarily made and that it is unequivocal. Similarly, the accused may change the plea of guilty to one of not guilty. Change of plea can, however, only be accepted before and not after the trial is over. A trial is over after sentencing. After sentencing, the judge or magistrate cannot alter anything he or she has done in the case. He or she is said to be *functus officio*.[1093]

829. Whether or not an accused should be allowed to change his or her plea is a matter of discretion for the trial court. Said Lord Goddard in the English case of *Rex v. McNally*:

> We take this opportunity of stating firmly what is the position with regard to a prisoner who desires to change his plea. If he has pleaded circumstances from which the court can see that there is no question of mistake, the court is not bound to allow him to withdraw his plea. … If the Court came to the conclusion that there was a question of mistake or misunderstanding, or that it would be desirable on any ground that the prisoner should be allowed to join issue, no doubt, the court would allow him to do it.[1094]

1090. *Ibid.*
1091. *Uganda v. Gabriel Habaesi* H.Ct.Cr.Session No. 41 of 1992 (unreported).
1092. See *Uganda v. Manuel Obbo* H.Ct.Monthly Bulletin No. 32 of 1964.
1093. See *David Kamundi Gatihi v. Republic* [1973] E.A. 540; and *Richard Oneka v. Uganda* H.Ct.Rev. Order No. 107 of 1991 (unreported).
1094. [1954] 2 All E.R. 372. This case was followed in *Uganda v. Yonaseni Kirya* H.Ct.Monthly Bulletin No. 63 of 1969.

830. It is submitted that if, say, in the course of the plea in mitigation the accused says anything that tends to suggest that he or she has a defence or wishes to change the plea from one of guilty to that of not guilty, the court should be willing to cancel the guilty plea and enter the one of not guilty instead.[1095] The court should be ready to do so, particularly in cases where the accused is unrepresented.[1096] In case of joint trials, if one accused person pleads guilty and his or her co-accused pleads not guilty, it is desirable that the one who pleads guilty be convicted and sentenced before the court proceeds with the trial of his or her co-accused and the prosecution calling him or her as a witness. To call him or her as a prosecution witness whilst the spectre of the unpronounced sentence hangs around his or her neck may prejudice his or her co-accused. He or she may be induced to give untrue evidence against the co-accused, with the hope that in doing so he or she may earn the sympathy of the court when it sentences him or her.[1097]

§3. Order of Proceedings

I. Preliminary Hearing

831. In proceedings before the High Court and in which the accused pleads not guilty and is represented, section 66 of the Trial on Indictments Act requires the holding of a preliminary hearing. Such hearing must be held 'as soon as possible' and in open court in the presence of the accused, his advocate and the prosecutor. The purpose of the hearing is to consider such matters as will promote a fair and expeditious trial. In practice, the hearing affords the prosecution and the defence an opportunity to confer and agree on issues that are not in dispute. These facts may include extra-curial statements, mode of arrest, formal and non-contentious documents such as expert-witness reports. Regarding post mortem reports, the Supreme Court has held that they should not, as a general rule, be admitted.[1098] Instead, the doctor who carried out the post mortem should be called as a witness and be subject to cross-examination.[1099]

832. When there is agreement on certain matters, the prosecutor or defence counsel informs the judge of those matters. The judge in turn prepares a memorandum of the agreed matters. He or she reads and explains it to the accused in a language that he or she understands. The judge then requires the accused and his or her lawyer as well as the prosecutor to sign it. He or she files it away, and it forms part of the case record. All facts or documents admitted in the memorandum are deemed to have been duly proved. Nevertheless, the court has discretion, in the interests of justice, to require any such facts or documents to be formally proved at the trial.[1100] In this respect, the Supreme Court has said that:

1095. *Uganda v. Kalimalwa s/o Digarire* H.Ct.Monthly Bulletin No. 189 of 1969.
1096. *Allekisi Mukasa v. Rex* [1936–1951] 6 U.L.R. 162.
1097. See *Karuna Bukenya v. Reginam* [1952] 19 E.A.C.A. 235.
1098. See *Aramanani Kampayani v. Uganda* S.Ct.Cr.App. No. 5 of 1987 (unreported).
1099. *Ndege v. Uganda* [1979] H.Ct.Bulletin 162, 165.
1100. Trial on Indictments Act, sec. 66(3).

> Whether an admitted or agreed evidence under Section 64 should be proved depends on the evidence or document and the case in question. Normally, the section should be applied only to formal or non-contentious evidence or documents ... But where witnesses are considered controversial or vital, they should give evidence to enable their evidence to be testified (*sic*) in cross-examination.[1101]

ges should therefore be ready to call witnesses to ensure that verdicts are not ed on mere paper trials, and that the prosecution case is tested by the cross-mination of prosecution witnesses.[1102]

Assessors

33. Another feature of criminal proceedings before the High Court is the par-ation of assessors. Assessors are lay people akin to jurors in the United States in the United Kingdom. The institution of assessors was established during the nial times to assist judges of the High Court, staffed exclusively by expatriate ges, in matters of African customs, norms and behaviour.[1103] The assessor also ed to bridge the cultural gap between those judges and the predominantly Afri- accused persons who appeared before them. Their presence plausibly ensured the accused and witnesses before the court were not judged by the expatriate ges' yardstick or standards of behaviour that were not applicable to them. ough the High Court and, indeed, the entire judiciary have since been fully lized, the institution of assessors has been retained. At least two of them must icipate in the proceedings before the High Court.[1104] They are empanelled from t that is prepared by the Chief Magistrate of the area where the High Court may olding a session and kept by the Chief Registrar. Before assuming office, each ssor must take an oath undertaking to impartially advise the court on the issues re it to the best of his or her knowledge, skill and ability.[1105] However, both the ised and the prosecutor are entitled to object to any of the assessors participat-in the trial on certain grounds listed in the Act.[1106] If the objection is sustained, person objected to must be dropped from the case and another one empan-l.[1107] At the close of the case both for the prosecution and for the defence, the iding judge is required to sum up the law and the evidence to the assessors; he he must then ask each one of them to state his or her opinion, whether the

---

Isaya Bikumu v. Uganda, C.A.Cr.App. No. 24 of 1989 (unreported).

Abasi Kanyika v. Uganda, S.Ct.Cr.App. No. 5 of 1989 (unreported).

In cases where the parties were Africans, the High Court was enjoined to be guided by African customary law, provided that that law was not repugnant to morality and natural justice.

Trial on Indictments Act, sec. 3.

Ibid., sec. 67.

Section 68. These grounds include: presumed or actual partiality; personal cause such as infancy, old age, deafness, blindness or infirmity; his character, in that he has been convicted of an offence which, in the opinion of the judge, renders him unfit to serve as an assessor and his inability adequately to understand the language of the court.

Ibid., sec. 68.

accused should be acquitted or convicted. Failure to sum up is a fatal error that vitiates the entire proceedings.[1108] The views of the assessors are, however, not binding on the presiding judge. Nevertheless, where the judge disagrees with the assessors, he or she must state his reasons in the judgment. Interests of fairness and transparency dictate that he or she does so.

III. The Prosecution Case

834. In both the High Court and the magistrates' courts, the prosecution opens its case by leading evidence.[1109] It does this by calling and examining witnesses and tendering exhibits. At the conclusion of the testimony of each prosecution witness, the accused or his or her lawyer is entitled to cross-examine him or her. The prosecutor may in turn re-examine him or her, but the questions are restricted to what the witness said during cross-examination. When the last prosecution witness has been called, examined, cross-examined and re-examined, the prosecution is said to have closed or rested its case. Thereafter, it is not allowed to call witnesses, either to patch up or to bolster its case by leading fresh or additional evidence. However, the court has inherent power 'at any stage of any trial' to recall and re-examine any person already examined and to summon or call any person as a witness or examine any person in attendance though not summoned as a witness 'if his evidence appears to be essential to the just decision of the case'.[1110] A witness called at the instance of the court is liable to be cross-examined by both the accused and the prosecutor. The court may adjourn the case to enable either party to prepare for such cross-examination.[1111]

835. Courts exercise the power to call or recall witnesses *mero motu*, and not at the instance of either party to the proceedings. Even then, they do so solely for the purpose of remedying defects in the formal evidence, clarifying evidence already given, or resolving a conflict of evidence where this can be done without prejudice to either party. Nevertheless, given the adversarial nature of the criminal proceedings, courts exercise these powers only in exceptional circumstances, when a matter has arisen *ex-improviso*, and which no human ingenuity could foresee.

836. Similar to the tenor of section 73(1) of the Trial on Indictments Act, is section 127 of the Magistrates Courts Act which provides that:

> If at the close of the evidence in support of the charge it appears to the court that a case is not made out against the accused person sufficiently to require him or her to make a defence the court shall dismiss the case and shall forthwith acquit him or her.

1108. *Sam Ekolu v. Uganda*, Cr. App. No. 15 of 1994, [1995] UGSC 7 (5 May 1995).
1109. Trial on Indictments Act, sec. 71; Magistrates Courts Act, sec. 126(1).
1110. Trial on Indictments Act, sec. 39; Magistrates Courts Act, sec. 100. See also *R. v. Mohamed Ali* [1947] 14 E.A.C.A. 126; *Boniface Mohindi v. R.* [1957] E.A. 565.
1111. *Ibid.*

The prosecution must therefore make out a case for the accused to answer, in keeping with the principle that he who alleges must prove. It must establish a prima facie case against him or her. A prima facie case is established where the evidence adduced by the prosecution is such that if it be uncontradicted a reasonable tribunal properly directing its mind to the law and to the evidence would convict on it.[1112] However, a prima facie case is not established if:

(1) the evidence adduced does not link the accused to the offence or offences with which he or she is charged;
(2) the evidence does not prove all the ingredients of that offence;
(3) the evidence is so fragmentary and unreliable that no reasonable tribunal can believe it or safely convict on it; and
(4) key prosecution witnesses have been so discredited during cross-examination and their credibility so shaken that their testimony cannot be believed.

837. Ordinarily, submissions that a prima facie case has not been established [the no-case-to-answer submission] are made by the accused when he or she is represented by counsel. It is rare that an unrepresented accused person will be able to make such a submission. Nonetheless, it is the bounden duty of the court before it calls on the accused to answer the charge to make a determination whether he or she has a case to answer. Said the High Court:

> [A] judge or magistrate has not got to wait for a submission of 'no case.' It is the court's duty to consider and decide whether there is sufficient evidence that the accused committed the offence before calling for his defence.[1113]

The duty to make a ruling subsists even where the accused is represented, and counsel informs the court that he or she does not intend to make any submissions. The court must always rule one way or the other whether the accused has a case to answer, irrespective of whether counsel has made any submission or not. It is the court's duty, and not counsel's, to make the ruling.[1114] Where the court rules that there is no case to answer it is important that the trial court gives detailed reasons for the ruling,[1115] because this ruling in a way concludes the case. And it might be appealed against.

838. A ruling that there is no case to answer thus prematurely ends the prosecution case. However, the Supreme Court has held that there is no right of appeal against the ruling, because it is not 'a final judgment.'[1116] The prosecution may appeal against the ruling only with leave of the court. *A fortiori*, a ruling that there

1112. See *Ramantal T. Bhatt v. R.* [1957] E.A. 332.
1113. *Esparito Wasswa v. Uganda* [1977] E.A. 299.
1114. *Hofni Topacho Ongiretho & Anor v. Uganda*, Cr. App. No. 1 of 1993, [1994] UGSC 9 (4 Mar. 1994).
1115. See *Commissioner of Customs and Excise v. Justo Otya* H.Ct.Monthly Bulletin No. 4 of 1968.
1116. *Twagira v. Uganda*, Cr. App. No. 27 of 2003, [2005] UGSC 14 (3 Aug. 2005).

is a case to answer is similarly not 'a final judgment', and the accused has no automatic right of appeal against it. Be that as it may, however, such an appeal, interlocutory as it is, tends to offend against the principle *interest reipublicae ut sit finis litium* [it concerns the state that there be an end of lawsuits] in that it interrupts the trial which should proceed as continuously as possible. Therefore, an accused person dissatisfied with a ruling that there is a case to answer must abide the conclusion of the trial and, if convicted, appeal against both the original ruling and the final verdict.

IV. The Defence Case

839. Where the court determines that the accused has a case to answer, it must proceed to advise him or her of the options open to him or her. These options are that the accused: (1) may remain silent, or; (2) may give evidence on his or her behalf under oath from the witness stand, in which case he or she will be liable to cross-examination, or; (3) may make an unsworn statement from the dock, in which case he or she will not be liable to cross-examination; and (4) may call and examine witnesses in his or her defence even where he himself or herself chooses to remain silent or to make an unsworn statement. The judge or magistrate must note on the case record the fact that he or she has so advised the accused; he or she must also record the accused's response. In the proceedings before the High Court when the accused is represented, his or her counsel may respond to the questions.[1117]

840. In the case of the accused remaining silent or not adducing any evidence in his or her defence, the courts in some jurisdictions do, within certain parameters, draw adverse inferences to suggest that the accused is probably guilty.[1118] Courts in other jurisdictions do not draw such inferences, for to do so would be to render nugatory the accused's constitutional right to remain silent.[1119] The courts in Uganda, as evidenced by the *Cheeye* case, *supra*, would appear to be leaning on the side of allowing adverse inferences, albeit with caution.[1120]

841. Where the accused elects to give evidence and to call witnesses, it is desirable that he or she should give his or her evidence first. To allow his or her witnesses to give evidence before him or her would be to give the accused license to trim his or her evidence so as to accord with that of the witnesses. It will also be contrary to the rule of practice that, all witnesses as to fact must remain outside the courtroom until they are called in to testify.

1117. In *Capt. Mike Muwonge & Anor v. Uganda* Cr. App. No. 6 of [1990] UGSC 11 (Jul. 1993), the trial judge did not record the fact that he had advised the accused, who were represented, of their rights. The Supreme Court held that in the circumstances of that case the omission was curable and did not occasion a miscarriage of justice.

1118. For example: see *Waugh v. R.* [1950] A.C. 203 (P.C.); *Veseau v. R.* [1977] 2 S.C.R. 277 (Canada 1976); *S. v. Mehlap* [1963] 2 S.A 29, *Attorney General v. Moagi* [1981] B.L.R 1.

1119. This is so in the United States under the Fifth Amendment to the Constitution. See *Griffin v. California* 380 U.S. 609 (1965).

1120. See *Lugobo & Anor v. Uganda* [1967] E.A. 440.

2. In the case of joint trials, if any one of the co-accused elects to give evi-e on oath or to call witnesses in his or her defence, the other or others must be ved to hear all the evidence and to cross-examine both the co-accused and his r witnesses.[1121] It is no reason to deny an accused person the right to cross-ine a fellow co-accused or his or her witnesses merely because they did not pate him or her. The co-accused is entitled to cross-examine them to elicit from facts which may be favourable to him or her.

3. When the accused elects to make an unsworn statement, he or she must do assisted. He or she must narrate his or her story in his or her own words. The may ask him or her a few questions to clarify what he or she says so that it be recorded accurately. In doing so, however, the court must proceed with st caution and must avoid overstepping the bounds of seeking clarification into ealm of cross-examining the accused.

4. When the defence rests its case, no further evidence may be called either e prosecution or the defence. Only the court may call or recall witnesses *proviso* as noted above. The other instance when the court may allow the pros-on to call further evidence is where the accused in his evidence introduces new r 'which the prosecutor could not by the exercise of reasonable diligence have een' – in which case the prosecutor may, exceptionally, be allowed to adduce nce in reply or to contradict the new matter.[1122] Such evidence may be called out matters such as alibis or the accused's alleged good character.

inal Addresses

5. When the prosecution and the defence have closed their cases, they are both ed to address the court before the court gives its judgment. The purpose of the ss is to sum up the evidence, to highlight those salient points of fact and the at favour the party making the address and, to persuade the court to believe rty's case.

. The accused or his or her counsel addresses the court first, followed by the cutor. Where the accused does not call witnesses other than himself or herself, she is entitled to reply to the prosecutor's address. As a general rule, however, ver a party exercising the right of reply raises an issue of law the opposing may, at the discretion of the court, be allowed to address the court on the issue sed.[1123]

ee *R. v. Suke d/o Seriwe & Anor.* [1947] 14 E.A.C.A. 134.
rial on Indictments Act, sec. 76; Magistrates Courts Act, sec. 130.
Magistrates Courts Act, sec. 131.

§4. JUDGMENT, APPEALS AND REVISION

I. Judgment

847. At the close of the parties' cases and their final addresses and replies, if any, the judge in cases tried by the High Court sums up the law and evidence to the assessors. He or she then requires them to give their opinion on whether the accused is guilty or not guilty. The judge is not bound to accept their opinions. But where he rejects their opinions, particularly of the majority, he or she must give reasons in his judgment for so doing.[1124] From then on, the procedure is the same in both the High Court and in the magistrates' courts. The judge or magistrate, as the case may be, is required to pronounce his or her judgment in the case. He or she must pronounce it in the presence of the accused, unless his or her presence was dispensed with as indicated above. In the proceedings before the High Court, the judge must pronounce the judgment either immediately after the opinions of the assessors or at a subsequent date. In the case of the magistrates' courts, the magistrate must pronounce the judgment either immediately after the last speech by either of the parties or at a subsequent date.[1125] He or she must nevertheless not sit on the judgment for too long. Otherwise his or her ability to recall evidence and to assess its weight will be diminished and his or her impressions of the demeanour and credibility of the witnesses may be dimmed by the passage of time. Such delay may prejudice the accused and result in a mistrial.[1126] When pronouncing the judgment, the judge has the option of doing so only in summary form, merely explaining its essentials to the parties. However, he or she must subsequently read out the full judgment if any of the parties requests it.[1127]

848. Every judgment must be in writing and, currently, in the English language. It must be dated and signed by the judge or magistrate on the date on which it is pronounced. It must contain the point or points for determination, the decision reached and the reasons for the decision.

849. It is submitted that the point or points for determination must of necessity include the elements of the offence charged as defined by law and whether the evidence adduced establishes those elements to the degree of proof required by law. Similarly, where the accused sets up certain defences the issue may be whether he or she has discharged his or her evidentiary burden and the prosecution disproved it beyond reasonable doubt. The judgment should also mention the issues that are admitted and those that are in dispute and call for proof by way of evidence.

850. As to the decision or decisions, the judgment should indicate the specific determinations on each issue in dispute and the elements of the offence that have or

1124. Trial on Indictments Act, sec. 81(3).
1125. Trial on Indictments Act, sec. 85; Magistrates Courts Act, sec. 135.
1126. *Mulji Lalji Kotecha v. Uganda* H.Ct.Monthly Bulletin No. 1 of 1963; *Ediyamu v. Mengo Lukiiko* H.Ct.Monthly Bulletin No. 25 of 1958.
1127. *Ibid.*

have not been proved. Ultimately, the judgment must hand down a verdict on the whole case: whether guilty or not guilty. In case of a verdict of guilty, the court then proceeds to pass sentence. In case of a verdict of not guilty, the court must forthwith acquit and discharge the accused, unless he or she be acquitted on grounds of insanity.[1128]

851. Regarding the giving of reasons for the decisions reached, the Judicial Committee of the English Privy Council said:

> The need for a judge to state the reasons for his decision is no mere technicality, nor does it depend mainly on the rules of Court. It is an important part of the judge's duty in every case, when he gives final judgment at the end of a trial, to state the grounds of his decision, unless there are some special reasons, such as urgency, for not doing so. … The parties are entitled to know the judge's reasons; so are any appellate courts in the event of an appeal.[1129]

852. A reasoned judgment calls for an analysis of the evidence adduced and an evaluation of its credibility and cogency. Where there is conflicting evidence on an issue, the judgment must indicate how the judge has resolved the conflict, which version of the episode he or she believed and which one he or she rejected and why. Where in resolving the conflict the judge relied on the credibility of the witnesses, he or she must indicate which witnesses he or she believed or disbelieved and why. Where there exist conflicting legal authorities pertinent to the issues before him or her, the judge must also indicate which one he or she followed, and why. All in all, the judgment should reveal the working of the judge's mind on all the major issues involved in a case.

II. Appeals

853. Article 14(5) of the International Covenant on Civil and Political Rights provides that 'everyone convicted of a crime shall have the right to his conviction and sentence being reviewed by a higher tribunal according to law'.[1130] The right to appeal against an unfavourable decision is vital to a fair administration of justice, particularly criminal justice. It enables a party to court proceedings who may be dissatisfied with a decision of a lower court or tribunal to have that decision reviewed and, where justified, corrected by a higher court. The review serves to ensure that the court or tribunal below correctly applies the law, respects the parties' guaranteed rights, follows the right procedure and generally does substantive justice to the parties. In accord with the international standards cited above, Ugandan law respects the parties' right of appeal. In discussing appeals, we shall deal with the matter from two standpoints: first from the standpoint of the accused and, second, from that of the state.

1128. Trial on Indictments Act, sec. 86; Magistrates Courts Act, sec. 136.
1129. *Lai Wee Lian v. Singapore Bus Service* (1978) *Limited* [1984] A.C. 729, 734.
1130. See also Art. 7(1) of the African Charter on Human and People's Rights.

1. First Appeal by the Accused

854. Every accused person who is dissatisfied with or aggrieved by a decision of a trial court has a right of appeal to the next appellate court within the courts' hierarchy: from Magistrates' Courts Grade II to the Chief Magistrates Courts; from Magistrates' Court Grade I and Chief Magistrates' Court to the High Court, and; from the High Court to the Court of Appeal.[1131] The appeal may be on a matter of fact or law or mixed fact or law.[1132] However, an accused person who pleads guilty and is convicted on such a plea is not allowed to appeal except as to the legality of the plea or to the extent or legality of the sentence imposed on him or her.[1133] Similarly, an accused person is not allowed to appeal in cases where a court presided over by a Chief Magistrate or a Magistrate Grade I passes a sentence of imprisonment not exceeding one month only, or a fine not exceeding UGX 100 only.[1134]

855. Another restriction imposed on the right to appeal against decisions of the High Court relates to sentences. An appeal will not lie against sentence save with leave of the Court of Appeal. But leave will not be granted where the sentence is fixed by law.[1135]

2. Second Appeal by the Accused

856. An accused person who is not satisfied with the decision of the first appellate court, may appeal further to a higher court. He or she however does encounter some restrictions at this stage. He or she may appeal against the decision of a Chief Magistrate's Court in its appellate jurisdiction to the High Court, but only on points of law. He or she may not appeal against a decision relating to a point of fact or severity of sentence.[1136] Similarly an accused person who is aggrieved by a decision of the High Court in exercise of its appellate or revisional jurisdiction may also appeal against that decision to the Court of Appeal, but on points of law only, excluding severity of sentence or points of facts mixed with law.[1137] As to the meaning of 'point of law', the Court of Appeal for Eastern Africa has said:

> A criminal appeal lies to this court from an appellate judgment only on points of law (Criminal Procedure Code, Section 337), and accordingly it is not open to us to interfere with any finding of fact by the trial court or the High Court unless there was no evidence to support it, in which case the point becomes one of law.[1138]

1131. Trial on Indictments Act, sec. 132; Magistrates Courts Act, sec. 204.
1132. *Ibid.*
1133. *Ibid.*, sec. 132(3) and sec. 204(3) respectively.
1134. Magistrates Courts Act, sec. 204(4).
1135. Trial on Indictments Act, sec. 132(1)(b).
1136. Magistrates Courts Act, sec. 204(6).
1137. Criminal Procedure Code Act, sec. 45.
1138. *George Woodgate v. R.* [19591 E.A. 524, 526.

The effect of this statement is that a finding of fact by the High Court which is not supported by evidence becomes a point of law and may be appealed against before the Court of Appeal.

3. First Appeal by the State

857. The state's right to appeal against a decision of the court acquitting the accused is even more circumscribed. The state may appeal against such a decision, if made by a Magistrate Grade II to the Chief Magistrate, and if made by Magistrate Grade I or Chief Magistrate to the High Court, but on the sole ground that the acquittal was 'erroneous in law'.[1139]

858. Until 1985, the state did not have a right of appeal against a decision of the High Court acquitting the accused.[1140] The position was changed in 1985 by inserting section 132A in the Trial on Indictments Act. Under this section, the state may now appeal against an acquittal, but only on the ground that 'the appeal involves a point of law of public importance'. The Act does not define what 'a point of law of public importance' is. The Supreme Court defined it to be 'whether the point decided would bind other persons or bodies'. Using this definition, it held that a decision that resulted in the acquittal of a person charged with a serious offence, without being tried, involved a point of law of public importance. Such decision might affect decisions of other courts in many other cases.[1141]

859. On hearing the appeal by the state against a decision of the High Court acquitting the accused and finding that it was erroneous, the Court of Appeal issues a declaratory judgment. The judgment does not operate to reverse the acquittal. It only serves as a precedent binding the inferior courts in future cases with similar fact-situations.

4. Second Appeal by the State

860. The state has a right of second appeal to the High Court from a decision of a Chief Magistrate in his or her appellate jurisdiction on the ground that it was erroneous in law.[1142] It has a similar right of appeal against a decision of the High Court in its appellate or revisional jurisdiction to the Court of Appeal, again on 'a matter of law, not including severity of sentence, but not on a matter of fact or of mixed fact and law'.[1143]

1139. Magistrates Courts Act, sec. 204(5).
1140. See *Hitila v. Uganda* [19691 E.A. 219.
1141. See *Uganda v. Ibrahim Seguya* S.Ct.Cr.App. No. 3 of 1987 (unreported).
1142. Magistrates Courts Act, sec. 204(7).
1143. Criminal Procedure Code Act, sec. 45.

5. Third Appeal by Either the Accused or the State

861. After both the accused and the state have exercised their first and second rights of appeal, it is safe to say that the ends of justice have been met. The original decision has been checked and rechecked. Any error or injustice, if any, would have been spotted and corrected. Nevertheless, Uganda law in its generosity provides the possibility of a third appeal. The Criminal Procedure Code Act provides as follows:

> Where an appeal emanates from a judgment of a Magistrate Grade II, and either the accused person or the Director of Public Prosecutions has appealed to the Chief Magistrate, and from there to the High Court, either the accused or the Director of Public Prosecutions may lodge a third and *final* appeal to the Court of Appeal with the certificate of the High Court that the matter raises a *question of law of great public or general importance* or if the Court of Appeal in its overall duty to see that justice is done, considers that the appeal should be heard; except that in such a third appeal by the Director of Public Prosecutions, the Court of Appeal shall only give a declaratory judgment.[1144]

862. Similarly, section 5(5) of the Judicature Act provides as follows:

> Where the appeal emanates from a judgment of the chief magistrate or a magistrate grade I in the exercise of his or her original jurisdiction, and either the accused or the Director of Public Prosecutions has appealed to the High Court and the Court of Appeal, the accused or the Director of Public Prosecutions may lodge a third appeal to the Supreme Court, with the certificate of the Court of Appeal that the matter raises a question of law of great public or general importance *or if the Supreme Court, in its overall duty to see that justice is done*, considers that the appeal should be heard, except that in such a third appeal by the Director of Public Prosecutions, the Supreme Court shall only give a declaratory judgment. (Emphasis added)

Three salient points are worth noting in respect of these provisions. The first is that the decision of the Court of Appeal in the matter is final and may not be appealed further to the Supreme Court. Second, for a certificate to be issued by the High Court or, as the case may be, by the Court of Appeal, it must be shown that the intended appeal raises 'a question of law of great public or general importance', or in the view of the appellate court it would be in the interest of justice that the appeal is heard. Third, when considering an application for a certificate granting leave to lodge a third appeal to the Supreme Court, the appellate court is restricted to the consideration whether the intended appeal raises a question or questions of law of great public importance. However, where the application for leave is filed before the Supreme Court, the court is not shackled by the restrictions imposed on the Court of Appeal. It may grant leave if it considers that 'in its overall duty to see justice done' the appeal should be heard. As it stated in one case, 'Anything relevant to doing justice will be considered including questions of law of general or public

1144. See sec. 46. Emphasis supplied.

importance.' Unlike the Court of Appeal, the Supreme Court is also not restricted to only questions of law. For instance, in *Namuddu v. Uganda*,[1145] the applicant was charged with and convicted of two offences of causing financial loss and abuse of office. The two offences were based on the same facts or one transaction, in that she had signed Bank of Uganda cheques amounting to Uganda UGX 89,036,431. The issue was whether it was proper to convict and sentence the applicant for the two offences arising out of the same facts. Allowing the application for leave to appeal for a third time, the Supreme Court held that in light of section 20 [now18] of the Penal Code and section 39 of the Interpretation Act, which prohibit a person being punished twice for the same act, it was proper in order to do justice that the impugned decision be reviewed by the Supreme Court. Lastly, while on an appeal by the accused the decision of the Court of Appeal or, as the case may be, the Supreme Court may result in the acquittal of the accused or the lessening of his sentence, on an appeal by the state the Court can only issue a declaratory judgment for the guidance of the courts in the future in similar future cases.

863. Generally speaking, the appellate court may confirm, quash, or modify the decision or order appealed against. It may order a retrial. It may also order what the lower court had power to order. However, in matters involving the exercise of discretion, the appellate court will not disturb the decision of the lower court, unless that court did not exercise its discretion judicially or in so doing it did not comply with the law or generally accepted principles. Again, the appellate court will not set aside a decision of a lower court merely because there was an irregularity in the procedure followed. It will set it aside only if the irregularity was such as to occasion a miscarriage of justice.[1146]

III. Revision

864. Revision is the power of the High Court to revise or modify decisions of inferior courts. It affords the High Court an opportunity to review the work of those courts and to satisfy itself as to the 'correctness, legality or propriety of any finding, sentence or order recorded or passed, and as to the regularity of any proceedings of any Magistrates' Court'.[1147]

865. The process of revision may be initiated by the High Court itself, by calling for and examining the record of any criminal proceedings before any Magistrates' Court.[1148] It may also be initiated by a Chief Magistrate in respect of 'any criminal proceedings before a Magistrates' Court inferior to the court which he or she is empowered to hold'.[1149] The Chief Magistrate, like the High Court, can call

1145. Cr. Appl. No. 3 of 1999, [2001] UGSC 2 (17 Jan. 2001).
1146. Criminal Procedure Code Act, sec. 45.
1147. Criminal Procedure Code Act, sec. 48.
1148. *Ibid.*
1149. Magistrates Courts Act, sec. 221.

for and examine the inferior court's proceedings. If, on examination, he or she co siders that a finding, sentence or order of the inferior magistrate is illegal, impro or that the proceedings are irregular, he or she forwards the record to the High Co with such remarks as he or she considers appropriate.[1150] Lastly, any pers aggrieved by any finding, sentence or order made or imposed by any Magistrat Court may also petition the High Court to exercise its powers of revision.[1151] Ho ever, the High Court is precluded from entertaining petitions of people who co have appealed against such findings, orders or sentence, but did not appeal.[115 should, however, be stressed that though an aggrieved individual may be disqu fied from petitioning the High Court on the ground that he or she could ha appealed against the magistrate's decision in time, the Chief Magistrate is not p cluded from referring the matter to the High Court if he or she deems it appropri in the interests of justice.

866. Before making any decision in the matter, the High Court must seek opinion of the DPP.[1153] Current practice indicates that the Director or his or her r resentatives need not physically appear before the Court to be heard. It is suffici if he or she communicates his or her opinion to the court in writing. Additiona the High Court is forbidden to make an order to the prejudice of an accused pers unless it has given him or her an opportunity to be heard.[1154]

867. Where, after examining the record the High Court discovers an error wh is material to the merits of the case, it may revise the decision or order of the m istrate as it would do if the case came to it on appeal, including enhancement sentence.[1155] It may not, however, revise an acquittal so as to convert it into a c viction.[1156] Nevertheless, where a Magistrates' Court acquitted a person of offence with which he or she was charged but convicted him or her of anot offence, whether charged with such other offence or not, the High Court may, i reverses the conviction, itself convert the original acquittal into a conviction.[11

868. Most of the cases that come to the High Court for revision are referred to it Chief magistrates. Most of them would be appealable but for the ignorance or lack means on the part of the accused persons. The revisionary process thus enables High Court to right wrongs, correct mistakes, and ensure justice to the ignorant poor, and to guide magistrates as to how to proceed in the future. It is a salut process in our system of administration of justice. To be effectual, however, it must invoked speedily before the faulted magistrates' decisions have run their course.

1150. *Ibid.* Also see Criminal Procedure Code Act, sec. 49.
1151. Criminal Procedure Code Act, sec. 50(5).
1152. *Ibid.*, sec. 50(5).
1153. *Ibid.*, sec. 50(2).
1154. *Ibid.*
1155. *Ibid.*, sec. 50(1).
1156. *Ibid.*, sec. 50(4).
1157. *Ibid.*, sec. 50(4).

Part III. Execution and Extinction of Sanctions: The Prison System

Chapter 1. Introduction

869. As indicated in earlier chapters, imprisonment is the commonest form of punishment in Uganda today. Again, as noted earlier, the aim of imprisonment is protection of society by putting the offender out of circulation for a while, deterring him and others, and assisting him to reform. Whether or not these goals are achieved will largely depend on the way the prison system is organized, the way prisons are run and the way prisoners are treated. If proper care is not taken in these three areas, the prison system may become an instrument of tyranny, prisons may become centres of death and state crime, and breeding grounds for more crime.

870. An important element in the Uganda prisons system is that it is under a public officer, the Commissioner of Prisons, who is subject to the general control of a minister. The minister himself is politically accountable to Parliament.[1158]

871. The other element is that any 'building, enclosure or place', to qualify as a prison, it must be so declared by the minister by a statutory instrument published in the official gazette.[1159] This requirement enables members of the public to know the places where citizens are detained, to visit them and to check on their welfare. There is unfortunately no law specifically prohibiting the incarceration of alleged wrongdoers or suspects in secret detention centres, 'safe houses' or in military barracks – places to which members of the public have no access. Additionally, these centres are not built in accord with internationally acceptable standards, and are not managed along principles that govern the administration of penal institutions and inmates are not treated in accord with the UN minimum standards for the treatment of prisoners. Moreover, their keepers are not accountable to the courts. It is no wonder, then, that thousands of citizens have died or disappeared from these centres in the recent past.

872. Another important element is the requirement that every prison must be under an officer designated as 'the officer in charge'. This requirement ensures that

1158. Prisons Act, sec. 4.
1159. *Ibid.*, sec. 23(1).

there is always a responsible person who must be held accountable for the way inmates are treated.

873. These elements, together with the prison regimen that the Prisons Act and the Prisons Rules prescribe, are aimed at preserving the prisons system as a humane system and at guarding against abuse of power and the mistreatment of prisoners.

Chapter 2. Admission, Control and Discharge of Prisoners

874. The attainment of the aims of imprisonment requires the placing of convicts in prisons that suit them and meet their particular needs. It is for this reason that different types of prisons are established to admit different categories or classes of prisoners. These categories of prisons are discussed in the introductory section of this book (*supra*, paragraph 41). Suffice it to emphasize it here that the mere division of prisons into different categories will not serve any useful purpose unless each category of prisons is staffed by specially trained officers and fully equipped with the facilities suited to the type of prisoners admitted to them. For example, young offenders' prisons must be staffed by officers who are fully conversant with the problems of juveniles, and must be equipped with educational and recreational facilities that meet the social, moral and physical needs of the inmates and conduce to their reformation and social rehabilitation. Prisons in which long-term prisoners are kept must have industries and workshops to train inmates in trades and to provide them with useful work.

875. While completely separate prisons for each category of prisoners are ideal, the economic conditions of the country make it impossible to attain. Prisoners of all categories may therefore have to be kept at one institution. Efforts must, however, be made to keep them separate as much as possible. For this reason, Rule 5 of the Prisons Rules provides as follows:

> With a view to facilitating the training of prisoners and of minimizing the danger of contaminating, prisoners shall be classified having regard to their age, character and previous history in the following classes:
>
> (a) Young Prisoner Class, which shall consist of convicted criminal prisoners under the apparent age of seventeen years, or young convicted criminal prisoners of whatever age who in the opinion of the officer in charge should not, having regard to their age and character, be classed with adult prisoners;
> (b) Star Class, which shall consist of convicted criminal prisoners not being in the Young Prisoner Class who are first offenders or well behaved prisoners who the officer in charge is satisfied have no vicious tendencies or habits;
> (c) Ordinary Class, which shall consist of all convicted criminal prisoners who are in the Young Prisoner Class or Star Class;
> (d) Unconvicted Class, which shall consist of all debtors, persons on remand or awaiting trial, vagrants, or persons detained for safe custody or for want of sureties, who have not been convicted.

876. According to the Prisons Act, the officer in charge of a prison must admit to his or her prison only those persons in respect of whom 'a warrant of commitment' has been issued by a court or other competent authority.[1160] The warrant must

1160. Prisons Act, sec. 30.

be produced before the officer in charge. The officer in charge then detains the person according to the terms of the warrant and must cause him or her to be delivered to the court or competent authority, or must discharge him or her at the time named in and according to the terms of the warrant. The officer in charge has no authority to admit any person for whom no warrant is produced, save a 'person arrested in pursuance of any warrant or order of any court or other competent authority, if such court is not sitting'.[1161] Where the officer in charge admits such a person, he or she must cause such person to be brought before the court or other competent authority at its next sitting.[1162] The importance of a warrant of commitment is that it helps to ensure that decisions to deprive citizens of their liberty are made by the courts or other legally competent authorities, and not by every Tom, Jack and Harry. It also serves to protect the officer in charge of a prison from possible civil suits for wrongful imprisonment.[1163]

877. Upon a prisoner becoming entitled to *release*, he or she must be released by the officer in charge of the prison where he or she is detained. The prisoner must be released before noon on the date on which he or she is entitled to release, but should that date fall on a Sunday or any public holiday, he or she must be released before noon on the day preceding the Sunday or public holiday.[1164] A prisoner still undergoing treatment by the prison medical officer for the prison may not be released unless he or she so requests or until the medical officer certifies that the prisoner can be released without danger to his or her health.[1165]

878. A prisoner becomes entitled to release upon serving his or her sentence as indicated in the warrant of commitment. He or she may also become entitled to early release by earning a remission, usually one-third of the remaining period of his or her sentence or sentences.[1166] Any prisoner serving a cumulative sentence exceeding one month may earn remission. He or she earns it though 'industry and good conduct'. He or she is automatically entitled to it, unless by his or her bad conduct he or she forfeits it. According to section 47 of the Act:

> (3) A prisoner may lose remission as a result of its forfeiture as a punishment for an offence against prison discipline and shall not earn any remission in respect of any period –
>
> (a) spent in hospital through his or her own fault or while malingering; or
> (b) while undergoing confinement as a punishment in a separate cell.

1161. *Ibid.*, sec. 31.
1162. *Ibid.*
1163. Section 14(1) of the Prisons Act provides that 'Where the defence to any suit instituted against a prison officer is that the act complained of was done in obedience to a warrant purporting to be issued by a court or other competent authority, the court shall, upon production of the warrant and upon proof that the act complained of was done in obedience to such warrant, enter judgment in favour of such prison officer.'
1164. Prisons Act, sec. 46.
1165. *Ibid.*
1166. *Ibid.*, sec. 47(1).

879. Remission is a desirable inducement for the prisoner to behave well. It is for this reason that Rule 97 of the Prisons Rules requires prison authorities to explain the remission system to all prisoners on admission and on what grounds remission may be forfeited. Remission is so firmly entrenched as part of the prisons regime that no court has the power to pass a sentence of imprisonment 'without remission'.[1167]

880. Generally speaking, a prisoner who has earned remission must be released unconditionally. Not so with 'habitual criminals'.[1168] A habitual criminal must be released on license. The release is conditional, and the conditions are set out in the release.[1169] The released prisoner is liable to be recalled if he or she violates any of those conditions. On top of that, he or she may also be sentenced to imprisonment for a term not exceeding three months, since breach of the conditions of a sentence is a criminal offence.[1170]

881. A prisoner may also be entitled to release if he or she is pardoned by the President in exercise of the President's prerogative powers of mercy. The President exercises these prerogative powers on the advice of the minister. The minister bases his or her advice on a recommendation of the Commissioner of Prisons.[1171]

882. Lastly, a prisoner may be *temporarily released from prison* under the following circumstances: (i) he or she is serving a sentence of imprisonment for a period of four years or more, (ii) the release takes place within three months of the date he or she is due for release, (iii) the period during which he or she is absent from prison does not exceed fourteen days; and (iv) the conditions and reasons for the release must be approved by the Commissioner.[1172] Release of this kind is called *release on parole*. It is the release of a prisoner for a stated period on condition that he or she returns to the prison. It enables the prisoner to make arrangements for his or her final release. It enables him or her to seek accommodation, to look for employment and to re-establish social contacts prior to his or her final release. That way the release facilitates the prisoner's smooth reintegration into society. That is the reason why it is granted towards the end of his or her term. In the long run, release on parole also helps to reduce the prison population and to alleviate somewhat the effects of long periods of incarceration. The Commissioner of Prisons or officer in charge of the prison does however have power to recall a prisoner released

---

1167. In *Uganda v. Janesi Osinya & Anor.* H.Ct. Monthly Bulletin No. 168 of 1969 a magistrate sentenced the accused to six months imprisonment 'without remission'. The High Court set aside the sentence, holding that there was no power for a court to order that a sentence should be served 'without remission'. Such an order was contrary to section 49 of the Prisons Act.

1168. According to section 50(11) of the Prisons Act, 'habitual criminal' means 'a person who has been sentenced on four separate occasions to imprisonment for any offence contained in Chapters XXVI to XXXIX of the Penal Code … or for any attempt or conspiracy to commit any such offence'.

1169. For the enumeration of these conditions, see Rule 101 of the Prisons Rules.

1170. Prisons Act, sec. 48(2)–(5). Also see *Uganda v. Joseph Lubega.* H. Ct. Monthly Bulletin No. 37 of 1968.

1171. Prisons Act, sec. 47(4).

1172. *Ibid.*, sec. 50.

on parole.[1173] Additionally, if the prisoner fails to return to prison on the completion of his or her period of parole or when he or she is recalled, he or she commits an offence and may be arrested without warrant. On conviction, he or she may be punished to the same extent as if he or she had escaped from prison.[1174] Similarly, a prisoner who contravenes the conditions of parole commits an offence and is, on conviction, liable to imprisonment for a period not exceeding six months.[1175]

883. The parole system as currently conceived may be flawed on the following grounds. By vesting in the Commissioner the power to determine who should or should not be released, the system usurps the courts' prerogative of determining the magnitude of sentence. Additionally, it does not appear that in determining parole matters the Commissioner is required or does indeed abide by the principles of due process. For example, does the Commissioner give the prisoner a hearing in considering whether or not to release him or her on parole? Does he or she make known to the prisoner who might wish to apply for parole the criteria he or she uses in his or her determinations? Can the prisoner employ a lawyer to present his or her case? Most likely not. Lastly, release for only fourteen days does not appear to serve much useful purpose. The period is too short. The parolee cannot accomplish much, if anything, within such short a time.

884. The last noteworthy point about release is section 38(2) of the Prison Act. It provides that 'Prisoners shall, if practicable, be released from a prison situated in the area to which the prisoner belongs'. No doubt this provision is aimed at facilitating easy contact between the prisoner and the community to which he or she is about to return. It is submitted that this goal could be better attained if the prisoner served his sentence at a prison located in the area where he or she belongs. This will make it easy and convenient for relatives and friends to visit him or her and to keep him or her posted with the occurrences in his or her family and in the community. It makes it easier for social workers, lawyers and members of organizations working on behalf of prisoners to visit and counsel him or her. It makes it easier for the prisoner to arrange his or her affairs, and seek employment and housing and maintain relations with the community whilst he or she is in prison. Assuming that the prison's staff do also belong to and talk the language spoken in the community where the prison is situated and serve prisoners the diet of the community, this keeps the prisoner close to his community. Ultimately, all in all, it makes his social reintegration easier than when he or she is kept at a prison which is distant from his or her home area.

1173. Prisons Act, sec. 50(2).
1174. *Ibid.*, sec. 50(3).
1175. *Ibid.*, sec. 50(4).

Chapter 3. The Prisons Regime

885. The Prisons Rules, made under the Prisons Act, lay down in great detail the way prisons must be administered and prisoners must be treated. Patterned on the United Nations Standard Minimum Rules for the Treatment of Prisoners, the Prisons Rules do articulate the principles that permeate the entire prisons regime in Uganda. According to Rule 3:

> These rules shall be applied, due allowance being made for difference in character and respect for discipline of various types of prisoners, in accordance with the following principles –
>
> a) discipline and order shall be maintained with fairness but firmness, and with no more restriction than is required for safe custody and to ensure a well-ordered community life;
> b) in the control of prisoners, prison officers should seek to influence them, through their own example and leadership, so as to enlist their willing co-operation; and
> c) at all times the treatment of convicted prisoners shall be such as to encourage their self-respect and sense of personal responsibility, so as to rebuild their morale, to inculcate in them the habit of good citizenship and hard work, to encourage them to lead a good and useful life on discharge and to fit them to do so.

886. Observance of these principles is vital to the attainment of the aims of incarceration: protection of society, deterrence, reformation and social reintegration of the prisoner. The living conditions in the prison, the physical and mental health of prisoners, the general treatment of prisoners, and the prison's disciplinary code do have a bearing on the success or failure of the prison system in attaining these goals.

887. The Rules provide that prisoners shall sleep in communal wards or in separate cells as the officer in charge shall direct in respect of each prison.[1176] They also provide for the absolute separation of women from male prisoners. Female prisoners must, in all cases, be looked after by female prison officers. Male officers are not allowed to enter a prison or part of a prison where female prisoners are except whilst on duty and in the company of female officers.[1177] Prisoners appearing to be under the age of 17 years, whether male or female, must also as far as practicable, be confined in separate buildings or separate parts of the prison.[1178] The aim is to prevent physical abuse of the young by old prisoners, to protect the young from moral contamination by hardened adult prisoners and to ensure that they are treated

1176. Rule 33(1).
1177. Rule 33(2).
1178. Rule 33(3).

in a way that befits their age. Lastly a medical officer must certify the number of prisoners that may sleep in one ward or cell.[1179]

888. The Rules do not, unfortunately, say anything about the architectural design of prison facilities or their general physical condition. Without going into minute details some general statement on these matters should have found their way into the Rules, because they have a direct bearing on the health of the inmates. The United Nations Standard Minimum Rules on these issues are instructive and are quoted here *in extenso*:

> 10. All accommodation provided for the use of prisoners and in particular all sleeping accommodation shall meet all requirements of health, due regard being paid to climatic conditions and particularly to the cubic content of air, minimum floor space, lighting, heating and ventilation.
>
> 11. In all places where prisoners are required to live or work,
>
> a) The windows shall be large enough to enable the prisoners to read or work by natural light, and shall be so constructed that they can allow the entrance of fresh air whether or not there is artificial ventilation.
> b) Artificial light shall be provided sufficient for the prisoners to read or work without injury to eyesight.
>
> 12. The sanitary installations shall be adequate to enable every prisoner to comply with the needs of nature when necessary and in a clean and decent manner.
>
> 13. Adequate bathing and shower installations shall be provided so that every prisoner may be enabled and required to have a bath or shower, at a temperature suitable to the climate, as frequently as necessary for general hygiene according to season and geographical region for at least once a week in a temperate climate.

889. Regarding health, the Rules require every prison to employ a full time medical officer to regularly attend to the health needs of the prisoners.[1180] The medical officer is required to examine prisoners on the following occasions:

(a) on the prisoner's admission to prison;
(b) prior to the prisoner being required to undergo any class of labour of a more strenuous nature than labour that he has been certified fit to undertake, and shall certify whether the prisoner is to undergo the labour;
(c) prior to the prisoner undergoing corporal punishment or any other punishment likely to affect his health and shall certify whether the prisoner is fit to undergo the punishment;
(d) prior to discharge of the prisoner from prison; and
(e) prior to transfer of the prisoner to another prison.

1179. Rule 33(4).
1180. Rule 25.

890. Additionally, the medical officer is required to see every prisoner every week, no doubt to satisfy himself or herself of the prisoner's physical well-being and to receive complaints from the prisoner. The medical officer must also 'from time to time inspect prisoners at work to satisfy himself or herself that the place of work is safe and the work itself is not a health hazard'. Finally, he or she must at least once every month inspect the whole prison, paying particular attention to the cooking and sanitary equipment in the prison. As a result of the examination and inspections, the medical officer may make a report to the officer in charge, recommending modifications in labour, diet or punishment either generally or in relation to a class of prisoners or in relation to a particular prisoner.[1181] Regarding diet, it is submitted that the medical officer should not be concerned with merely the cooking equipment. He or she must also be concerned with the quantity, quality, preparation and service of the food for the prisoners.[1182] He or she should also be concerned that prisoners have access to clean and safe drinking water all the time. Additionally, he or she must be concerned with the general sanitation, heating, lighting and ventilation of the prison, as well as the suitability and cleanliness of the prisoners' clothing and bedding.[1183] Too often, prisoners go about in rags which are full of lice and fleas, and either sleep on the bare floor or in bedding replete with bed bugs. The food they are given is scarce, coarse, unhygienic and often not fit for human consumption. As a result, many prisoners die in prison because of the squalid prison conditions, poor diet and sheer neglect.[1184] The medical officer should vigilantly monitor these conditions and make constant recommendations to the authorities on how to remedy them.

1181. Rule 27.

1182. See Rule 26 of the United Nations Standard Minimum Rules.

1183. *Ibid.*

1184. See *Semayo Otika v. Acholi District Administration.* H.Ct. Civil Suit No. 206 of 1966 (unreported).

Chapter 4. Treatment

891. There exists a perception that prisoners go to prison to be punished. According to this perception, prisoners must be treated as harshly as possible. They must also be deprived of as many of their rights and of personal dignity as possible. In countries where this perception prevails, prisons are indeed places of horror. Prisoners are often yelled at, incessantly insulted and constantly assaulted for no reason. They are awakened up early in the morning and 'given tea', meaning being assaulted. This practice has been common to Uganda, particularly at police and army detention centres. Such brutal treatment brutalizes not only the prisoners but also the officers who mete it out. It strips prisoners of self-respect. It makes them lose all confidence in the criminal justice system. It creates in them a feeling of resentment against the system and against society as a whole. It breeds in them a desire to avenge themselves against other citizens for the injustice and suffering wrought unto them whilst in prison. It ultimately emboldens them in their criminal ways and turns them violent and dangerous to the communities to which they go after release. Brutal and inhumane treatment negates the legitimate goals of imprisonment: protecting society and assisting the prisoner to become a self-respecting, useful and law-abiding citizen.

Sight must never be lost of the fact that though temporarily deprived of their personal freedom and the attendant rights, prisoners remain human beings. They are entitled to their inherent *human dignity*. They are entitled to human rights. To this end, the Uganda Prisons Rules forbid prison officers to strike prisoners or to use force except where this is absolutely necessary. Rule 46 provides as follows:

> (1) No prison officer dealing with prisoners shall strike or use force unnecessarily and, when the application of force is necessary, no more force than necessary shall be used.
> (2) No prison officer shall punish any prisoner unless authorized to do so under the provisions of the Act and these Rules.
> (1) No prison officer shall deliberately act in a manner calculated to provoke a prisoner.
> (2) If a prison officer strikes or uses force against a prisoner he shall have the prisoner examined as soon as possible by the medical officer and shall immediately report the incident to the officer in charge.

892. On a more positive note, the Rules prescribe a mode of treatment that is conducive to the prisoners' reformation and rehabilitation. They provide for regular physical exercise except for prisoners in close confinement.[1185] They provide for intellectual self-improvement through education, particular attention being paid to the illiterate.[1186] They also provide for the practice of religion and observance of religious holidays within the prison and for visitations by ministers of religion of

1185. Rule 53.
1186. Rule 64.

the denomination to which a prisoner belongs.[1187] Practice of religion and visitations by ministers of religion are vital for the spiritual well-being and moral regeneration of prisoners.

Also important are visits and receiving letters from relatives, reputable friends, social welfare officers and representatives of non-governmental organizations working for the welfare of prisoners.[1188] Such visits enable prisoners to receive counselling. They also help to keep them in touch with the outside world, particularly with their families, and facilitate the conducting of their personal and business affairs and their reintegration into the community on their release.

893. Related to the right to receiving visitors and letters is *the right to communicate with the prisoner's lawyer*. Lawyers must be allowed to visit and interview or receive instructions from their prisoner-clients.

Rule 60 regulates the visits by lawyers. It provides as follows:

(1) A prisoner who after conviction has given notice of appeal shall be given reasonable facilities to see his or her advocate with reference to the appeal, in the sight, but not in the hearing of a prison officer.
(2) A prisoner who has been ordered to be repatriated out of Uganda shall be given all reasonable facilities to see his advocate and a representative of his state with reference to the order for repatriation, in the sight, but not in the hearing of a prison officer.
(3) Reasonable facilities shall be accorded to the advocate of a prisoner who is conducting any litigation, civil or criminal, in which the prisoner is a party, to see the prisoner with reference to such proceedings, in the sight, but not in the hearing of a prison officer.
(4) The advocate of a prisoner may, with the permission of the officer in charge, see a prisoner with reference to any other legal business but shall see him or her in the sight and hearing of a prison officer.
(5) The advocate of a prisoner may be accompanied by another person under his or her direct and immediate control for the purpose of interpretation or the making of a note.
(6) For the purpose of this rule, 'advocate of a prisoner' means either the prisoner's advocate himself or herself or the advocate's clerk.

894. It is noteworthy that the Rules permit a lawyer to see his prisoner-client 'in the sight but not in the hearing of a prison officer'. This is important, because lawyer-client communications made for the purpose of receiving legal advice are regarded by the law as confidential. The confidentiality enables a client to communicate with his lawyer as candidly and as fully as possible. The lawyer is in turn enabled to give appropriate advice based on full and candid information. It is unfortunate, though, that the confidentiality is limited to communications relating to civil or criminal litigation, and not to 'any other legal business' of a non-contentious nature. The justification for the restriction is probably security of the institution and

1187. Rules 63 and 92.
1188. Rules 54 and 58.

its staff. It is submitted however that if lawyers are trusted and allowed to see their prisoner-clients in confidence in connection with litigation they might as well see them under similar conditions in respect of *all* legal business they may be conducting on their behalf. Lawyers should be trusted that they will not abuse their privileged position whilst talking to their clients in prison. They should be trusted not to indulge in conduct that compromises the security of the institution. If they indulge in such conduct they would be violating their code of professional conduct. They would render themselves liable to disciplinary proceedings. They might even be prosecuted if their conduct amounted to crimes. The point to stress here, though, is that very few lawyers would sink that low, and if they did it will be seldom.

895. Rule 59 relating to letters from prisoners, is also flawed. In requiring prison officers to censor all letters to and from prisoners, it does not make an exception regarding letters to or from lawyers. It provides that:

(1) Every letter to or from a prisoner shall be read by the officer in charge or by a responsible officer deputed by him or her and it shall be within the discretion of the officer in charge or the deputed officer to stop any letter on the grounds that the contents are objectionable or that it is of inordinate length.
In the case of an outgoing letter, the prisoner shall be informed and given the opportunity to re-write the letter.
(2) No prisoner shall be permitted to write a letter or receive a letter from an ex-prisoner without the permission in writing of the officer in charge.

896. It is submitted that prisoners' letters to or from their lawyers should not be censored by prison officers. They are confidential if made for the purpose of receiving or imparting legal advice. As argued above, lawyers should be trusted that they will not indulge or encourage their clients to indulge in criminal conduct. This Rule, together with Rule 60, needs to be amended.

897. Regarding *discipline*, the Rules correctly provide that it must be maintained 'with fairness but firmness'. Doubtless, discipline is vital to a well-ordered community life in prison. It is also vital to the inculcation of the habit of obedience and law-abidingness. Nevertheless, if it is maintained without due regard to the principles of fairness and natural justice, it may defeat the whole purpose of imprisonment. Prisoners, on leaving prison, may start treating their fellow human beings in the outside world in exactly the same way that they have been treated by the prison authorities. This would be disastrous. To avoid such a situation, the Rules provide for fair procedures for dealing with infraction of prison discipline. In the first place, conduct that constitutes disciplinary offences is defined in the Rules. In all, the Rules list fifty 'minor offences' and fifteen 'aggravated offences'.[1189] In accordance with the principle of *audi altarem partem*, section 57 of the Prisons Act provides that:

1189. Rules 67 and 68.

No prisoner shall be punished for a prison offence until he has had an opportunity of hearing the charge against him and making his defence.

898. In this regard, Rule 69 provides as follows:

(1) Every prisoner charged with a prison offence shall be informed of the offence with which he is charged and shall be entitled to defend himself by -

(a) hearing and questioning any witness giving evidence against him;
(b) making a statement himself; and
(c) calling any witness whom he thinks necessary and whom the person trying the charge is satisfied will materially assist in determining whether or not the prisoner is guilty of the offence with which he is charged.
(2) Every charge against a prisoner shall be heard without delay.

899. Conviction for a prison offence may have far-reaching consequences for the prisoner. It may result in further deprivation of rights as attested by the kind of punishments that may be inflicted. For example: the guilty prisoner may be condemned to solitary confinement of not more than seven days; he or she may forfeit remission; he or she may be subjected to a reduced food ration; he or she may be subjected to corporal punishment not exceeding twelve strokes or in case of a person under the apparent age of 16 years, six strokes; and he or she may forfeit visits and letters from his or her relatives and reputable friends.[1190] The trial must therefore be as fair and transparent as possible. For this reason, it would be improper if the officer who witnessed the alleged offence acted as the prosecutor, or worse still, as judge. Neutral officers, not connected with the offence, should serve as prosecutors and as judges. This way, justice will not only be done but will also appear to be done.

900. The Rules make no specific provision for appeal against disciplinary decisions. Rule 66 provides for petition to the President and for 'complaints'. It provides that:

(1) Every prisoner may petition the President through the Commissioner and such petition shall be written in such form as the Commissioner shall direct.
(2) A prisoner may make complaints to a visiting justice, the Commissioner, the officer in charge, or to such other class or classes of prison officer as the Commissioner shall designate to hear complaints.
(3) Any request by a prisoner to see a person to whom he is entitled to make a complaint shall be recorded by the officer to whom the request is made and arrangements shall be made for the prisoner to see the person concerned at the first convenient opportunity.
(4) The officer in charge shall at a convenient hour on every day, other than Sundays and public holidays, see all prisoners who have requested to see him.

1190. Rules 70–79.

901. The Rule does not indicate what the scope of the petition or complaint should be. It will no doubt include the general prison conditions and treatment of prisoners either individually or as a group. It is in this respect that a prisoner who is aggrieved by a disciplinary decision may voice his grievance about such a decision. The unfortunate thing though is that by the time the prisoner gets the opportunity to complain, he may already have been punished. The other flaw in the complaints mechanism is that Rule 66 is not explicit about whether complaints must be voiced in the presence or absence of prison authorities.[1191] It is only when a visiting justice is on an inspection tour that the officer in charge and the next senior prison officer are, to a limited extent, forbidden to accompany the justice on the tour. Even then the officer in charge is the one who designates another officer to accompany the justice.[1192] These procedures no doubt inhibit the prisoner's ability to freely and fully voice his or her complaints before the powers that be and thus rob the complaints mechanism of transparency.

902. Though both the Act and the Rules are silent on judicial intervention, it is submitted that the courts have inherent jurisdiction under their own powers of review, to review decisions of prison authorities in exercise of their disciplinary powers. Those decisions will be invalidated at the instance of an aggrieved prisoner where they contravene the Act, the Rules, or principles of natural justice.

903. Mention must also be made of *work in prison*. Work is a human right.[1193] It is essential for the physical and mental health of every human person. It enables the person to earn an honest living, and to supply his or her needs and those of his or her dependents. By keeping the worker busy and occupied, work keeps him or her out of trouble and away from criminal activities. Prisoners, especially, need to work. Not only is it good for their physical and mental health, it also enables them to contribute to the cost of their upkeep whilst in prison. It trains them to be useful and responsible citizens and prepares them for reintegration into society. Work must therefore be provided to prisoners. To achieve this, however, work for prisoners must not be afflictive. It must be useful. It must be such as to increase their ability to earn an honest living after release.

904. According to the Prisons Act, every sentence of imprisonment must subject a prisoner during the term of the sentence to work at such labour as may be directed

1191. Rule 35 of the United Nations Standard Minimum Rules for the Treatment of Prisoners provides that:

> '(2) It shall be possible to make requests or complaints to the inspector of prison during his inspection. The prisoner shall have the opportunity to talk to the inspector or to any other inspecting officer without the director or other members of the staff being present.
>
> (3) Every prisoner shall be allowed to make a request or complaint, without censorship as to substance but in proper form, to the central prison administration, the judicial authority or other proper authorities through approved channels.'

1192. Rule 109.

1193. See Art. 23 of the Universal Declaration of Human Rights.

by the officer in charge with the approval of the Commissioner.[1194] Hard labour, afflictive as it is, however, is forbidden.[1195] Also forbidden is work as punishment for a disciplinary offence. Such punishment tends to diminish in the eyes of the prisoner the dignity of work. For prisoners serving long terms, emphasis is that on vocations such as carpentry, bricklaying, tailoring and metalwork.

905. Uganda's law regulating the prisons administration and the treatment of prisoners is generally sound. It is its implementation that has in the past been problematic. Like all other social institutions in the country, prisons have been adversely affected by the political turmoil, economic decay, and social and moral degeneration that have characterized the country's recent past. Prisons regulations have been deliberately ignored to suit the political ends of the rulers. Corruption within the prisons system has been rife and rampant. Physical facilities have been allowed to fall into disrepair for lack of funds. Prisons industries collapsed. Some prisoners have died because of poor diet, unsanitary living conditions, lack of adequate medical care or sheer callous indifference on the part of the prisons authorities. Political stability, a sound economy, and an unswerving commitment to the rule of law and to human rights are thus indispensable prerequisites to a sound and humane prisons system.

1194. Section 44.
1195. *Ibid.*, sec. 44(2).

Selected Bibliography

A. LEGISLATION

Anti-Corruption Act, Act No. 6 of 2009.
Children Act (Cap. 59).
Constitution of Uganda (Cap. 1).
Criminal Procedure Code Act (Cap. 116).
Customary Marriage Registration Act (Cap. 248).
Deportation Act (Cap. 308).
Diplomatic Privileges Act (Cap. 201).
Factories Act (Cap. 220).
Food and Drugs Act (Cap. 278).
Habitual Criminals (Preventive Detention) Act (Cap. 118).
Immigration (Control) Act (Cap. 60).
International Criminal Court Act, Act 11 of 2010.
Judicature Act (Cap. 13).
Local Government Act (Cap. 243).
Magistrates Courts Act (Cap. 16).
Mining Act (Cap. 248).
Official Secrets Act (Cap. 311).
Penal Code Act (Cap. 120).
Police Act (Cap. 303).
Prisons Act (Cap. 304).
Probation Act (Cap. 122).
Public Health Act (Cap. 281).
Shop Hours Act (Cap. 99).
Traffic and Road Safety Act (Cap. 361).
Trial on Indictments Act (Cap. 23).
Trout Protection Act (Cap. 229).
Uganda Peoples' Defence Forces Act (Cap. 307).
Weights and Measures Act (Cap. 103).

B. CASES

Abasi Kanyike v. Uganda S.Ct.Cr.App. No. 34 of 1989 (unreported).
Abdurasul G. Sabur v. R. [1958] E.A. 126.

Selected Bibliography

Abdulrehaman Husain Esmail v. Republic [1965] E.A. 1.
Abubakali & Anor. v. Uganda [1973] E.A. 230.
Adamu Mulira v. Reginam [1953] 20 E.A.C.A. 223.
Agustino Orete & Anor. v. Uganda [1966] E.A. 430.
Aikaeli s/o Alifayo v. R. [1954] 21 E.A.C.A. 371.
Akber Rashid Nathani v. Republic [1965] E.A. 777.
Alai bin Sururu v. Uganda [1967] E.A. 596.
Ali Fadhul v. State H.Ct.Misc.Appl. No. MMB 8 of 1992 (unreported).
Ali s/o Mzee v. R. [1960] E.A. 404.
Allekisi Mukasa v. Rex [1936–1951] 6 U.L.R. 162.
Amisi Kibazo v. Uganda [1965] E.A. 507.
Amisi Magala & Anor. v. Uganda [1971] U.L.R. 14.
Amratlal v. Uganda [1970] E.A. 401.
Andrea Obonyo & Anor. v. R. [1962] E.A. 542.
Andrews v. Director of Public Prosecutions [1937] A.C. 576.
Apulunari Butere v. Uganda H.Ct.Monthly Bulletin No. 19 of 1968.
Arafaeri Kirikarama & Anor. v. Uganda H.Ct.Monthly Bulletin No. 98 of 1964.
Aramanani Kampayani v. Uganda S.Ct.Cr.App. No. 5 of 1987 (unreported).
Athuman v. Republic [1967] E.A. 401.
Attorney General v. Gaburiel Ottii [1957] E.A. 341.
Attorney General v. Joseph Tumushabe Const. Appl. No 3 of 2008, [2008] UGSC 9 (9 July 2008).
Attorney General v. Susan Kigula and 417 Others, Const. App. No. 3 of 2006, [2009] UGSC 6, 21 August 2009.
Attorney Genera v. Uganda Law Society, Const. Appeal No. 1 of 2006 [2009] UGSC 2 (20 January 2009).
Attorney-General v. Leveller Magazine & Anor. [1979] A.C. 440.
Attorney-General v. Onyango s/o Oludhe & Anor. [1954] 21 E.A.C.A. 238.
Attorney-General for Nothern Ireland v. Gallagher [1961] 3 All E.R. 299.
Attorney-General for Nyasaland v. Jackson [1957] R. & N.L.R. 443.
Attorney-General for Nyasaland v. Lojasi [1962] Rhodesia & Nyasalanda Law Reports 185.
Attorney General of Israel v. Eichmann (1962) 36 International Law Reports 277.
Attorney-General of Tanganyika v. Jerome Silvester Chisanga [1962] E.A. 312.
Attorney-General of Tanganyika v. Shamba Ali Kajembe [1958] E.A. 505.
Arvind Patel v. Uganda, Cr. App. No. 36 of 2002, [2003] UGSC 35 (27 October 2003).
Avone v. Uganda [1969] E.A. 129.
Ayor v. Uganda E.A. 303.
Baigumamu v. Uganda [1973] E.A. 26.
Balaki Kirya & Anor. v. Uganda H.Ct.Cr.App. No. 75 of 1984 (unreported).
Basi v. Reginam [1956–1957] 8 U.L.R. 189.
Beckford v. R. [1987] 3 All E.R. 425.
Bennett & Newton (1913) 9 Cr.App.Rep. 146.
Bernard Nyeko Nyeko & Anor. v. Uganda H.Ct.Misc, Cr. Rev. No. 8 of 1992 (unreported).
Binuge & Anor. v. Uganda, Cr. App. No. 23 of 1989, [1991] 5 (31 May 1991).

Black-Clawson Int. Ltd. v. Papierwerke Waldhof-Aschaffenburg A.G. [1975] A.C. 591.
Boniface Mohindi v. R. [1957] E.A. 566.
Bradford Election Petition (No. 7) (1869) 19 L.T. 723.
Bratty v. Attorney-General for Nothern Ireland [1961] 3 All E.R. 523.
Brian Mubiru Guweddeko v. Uganda S.Ct.Cr.App. No. 28 of 1991 (unreported).
Brigadier Smith Opon Achak & Anor v. Uganda Cr. App. No. 18 of 1992, [1993] UGSC 10 (5 November 1993).
Bukenya & Anor. v. Uganda [1972] E.A. 549.
Bukenya Joseph v. Uganda, Cr. App. No. 222 of 2003, [2010] UGSC 32 (23 July 2010).
Bumbakali Lutwama & Anor. v. Uganda S.Ct.Cr.App. No. 38 of 1989 (unreported).
Bwambale Muchunguzi v. Uganda Cri. App. No. 96 of 2006, [2010] UGCA 44 (8 November 2010).
Byabagambi Gabriel v. Uganda, Cr. App. No. 16 of 2002, [2004] UGSC 5 (15 August 2004).
Capt. Mike Muwonge & Anor v. Uganda Cr. App. No. 6 of 1990 [UGSC 11 (19 July 1993).
Celestino Along & Anor. v. Uganda S.Ct.App. No. 2 of 1992 (unreported).
Chamba v. Republic [1970] E.A. 280.
Chan Wing-Siu & Anor. v. The Queen [1985] A.C. 168.
Chande & Anor. v. R. [1961] E.A. 587.
Chemingwa v. R. [1956] 23 E.A.C.A. 451.
Cheung Singh v. R. [1956] E.A.C.A. 459.
Choitram v. Reginam [1952] 26 K.L.R. 93.
Chokwe v. Republic [1969] E.A. 23.
Christie v. Lechinsky [1947] 1 All E.R. 567.
Christopher Kiwala v. Regina H.Ct.Monthly Bulletin No. 47 of 1962.
Christopher Kizito v. Uganda, Cr. App. No. 18 of 1993, [1995] UGSC 12 (28 June 1995).
Chung Chi Cheung v. The King [1939] A.C. 160.
Cpl Kasirye Hamuza & Anor. *v.* Uganda Cr. App. No. 44 of 2001, [2004] UGSC 36 (36 May 2004).
Commissioner of Customs & Excise v. Justo Otya H.Ct.Monthly Bulletin No. 4 of 1968.
Connelly v. Director of Public Prosecutions [1964] A.C. 1254.
Constante Mbuzehasi & Anor. v. Lukiiko H.Ct.Cr.App. No. 233 of 1964; H.Ct. Monthly Bulletin No. 4 of 1965.
Curley (1909) 2 Cr.App.Rep. 96, 109.
Dabholker v. King [1948] A.C. 221.
Dallison v. Caffery [1965] 1 Q.B. 348
David Kamundi Gatihi v. Republic [1973] E.A. 540.
Dharmasena v. The King [1951] 1 A.C. 1.
Dickson v. Del Solar [1929] All E.R. 140.
Dim Kifuko v. Rex [1936–1951] 6 U.L.R. 273.
Director of Public Prosecutions v. Beard [1920] All E.R. 21.

Selected Bibliography

Director of Public Prosecutions v. Edirisa Vasanye H.Ct.Monthly Bulletin No. 3 of 1965.

Director of Public Prosecutions v. Majewski [1976] 2 All E.R. 142.

Director of Public Prosecutions v. Nieser [1958] All E.R. 662.

Director of Public Prosecutions v. Sezi & Anor. [1974] E.A. 287.

Director of Public Prosecutions v. Withers [1975] A.C. 842.

Dr. Kizza Besigye & Others v. Attorney General Const. Petition No. 7 of 2007 [2010] UGCC 6 (12 October 2010). *Dr Kizza Besigye & Others v. Attorney General*

Dracaku s/o Afia & Anor. v. R. [1963] E.A. 363.

Ediyamu v. Mengo Lukiiko H.Ct.Monthly Bulletin No. 25 of 1958.

Edward s/o Michael v. Rex [1948] 1 T.L.R. 308.

Emilio Guma v. Uganda H.Ct.Cr.Revision No. 103 of 1991 (unreported).

Eryeza Munerya v. Uganda H.Ct.Monthly Bulletin No. 23 of 1966.

Esperito Wasswa *v. Uganda* [1977] E.A. 299.

Etyeku & Anor. v. Reginam [1956–1957] 8 U.L.R. 96.

Ezera Kyabanamizi & Anor. v. R. [1962] E.A. 309.

Festo Magembe v. R. [1959] E.A. 258.

Field & Anor. v. Receiver of Metropolitan Police [1907] 2 K.B. 853.

Francis Sebanenya & Anor. v. Uganda S.Ct.Cr.App. No. 17 of 1989 (unreported).

Funo & Anor. v. Uganda [1967] E.A. 632.

Galikuwa v. R. [1951] 18 E.A.C.A. 175.

Gaston [1981] 73 Cr.App.Rep. 164.

Gathuri Njuguna v. Republic [1965] E.A. 583.

George Buwanika & Anor. v. R. [1957] E.A. 279.

George Woodgate v. R. [1959] E.A. 525.

Gilbert v. Republic [1972] E.A. 51.

Girdher Dhanji Masrani v. Uganda [1960] E.A. 320.

Gouriet v. Union of Post Office Workers & Anor. [1978] A.C. 435.

Gulamhusein Merali v. Rex [1921–1952] 1 T.L.R. 358.

Gusambizi s/o Wesonga v. R. [1948] 15 E.A.C.A. 65.

Haining v. Republic [1970] E.A. 620.

Haji Moledina & Anor. v. R. [1960] E.A. 678.

Haji Muhamad Senyomo Birikadde v. Uganda [1986] H.Ct.Monthly Bulletin 6.

Harji Kureji Patel v. R. [1955] 22 E.A.C.A. 536.

Harry Isiko v. Uganda H.Ct.Cr.App. No. 7 of 1991 (unreported).

Hassam v. R. H.Ct.Monthly Bulletin No. 24 of 1959.

Hawkins v. R. [1959] E.A. 47.

Henry Kato v. R. [1960] E.A. 981.

Hitila v. Uganda [1969] E.A. 219.

Hoareau v. R. [1962] E.A. 809.

Hofni Topacho Ongiretho & Anor v. Uganda Cr. App. No. 1 of 1993, [1994] UGSC 9 (4 March 1994).

Hoyle v. Reginam [1956–1957] 8 U.L.R. 314.

Hunter v. Reginam [1956–1957] 8 U.L.R. 366.

Hyam v. Director of Public Prosecutions [1974] 2 All E.R. 41.

Ibingira & Anor. v. The Attorney General [1966] E.A. 306.

Ibrahim Bilal v. Uganda C.A.Cr.App. No. 5 of 1983 (unreported).
Idi s/o Waziri v. R. [1961] E.A. 624.
In re the Matter of an Application of Joyce Lwebuga wife of Eriabu Lwebuga an Unconvicted Prisoner at Njabule Prison, H.Ct.Misc. Cause No. 11 of 1963 (unreported).
In re Mlambo [1992] 4 SA 144.
In re Wright [1996] B.L.R. 689.
Innocent Manjesa v. State C.A.Cr.App. No. 30 of 1991 (unreported).
Isaya Bukumu v. Uganda C.A.Cr.App. No. 24 of 1989 (unreported).
Isaac Newton Ojok v. Uganda S.Ct.Cr.App. No. 33 of 1991 (unreported).
Ismael Bin Farah v. R. [1956] 29 K.L.R. 183.
Israel Kamukolse v. R [1956] 23 E.A.C.A 521.
Jackson v. R. [1962] R. & N.L.R. 157.
Jaffer v. Republic [1973] E.A. 39.
Jagat Singh v. Reginam [1953] 22 E.A.C.A. 283.
James Philip v. Rex [1952] 19 E.A.C.A. 231.
James Sawoabiri & Anor. v. Uganda S.Ct.Cr.App. No. 5 of 1990 (unreported).
Jayesh Thakker v. Uganda Cr. Session Case No. 84 of 2007 [2007] UGHC 36 (5 December 20070.
Jephlin Lubega & Anor. v. Uganda S.Ct.Cr.App. No. 35 of 1992 (unreported).
Jesani v. Republic [1969] E.A. 600.
John Katende v. R. H.Ct.Cr.App. No. 149 of 1960; H.Ct.Monthly Bulletin No. 33 of 1960.
John Mubiru v. Uganda [1971] U.L.R. 1.
John Reuben Asia v. R. H.Ct.Monthly Bulletin No. 722 of 1962.
Jones v. United States 363 U.S. 257 (1960).
Jongo s/o Kego v. R. [1960] E.A. 130.
Joseph s/o Odoro v. R. [1954] E.A.C.A. 311.
Joseph Bukenya v. Uganda [1971] U.L.R. 50.
Joseph Byaruhanga v. Uganda [1973] U.L.R. 4.
Justini Ngozebwa v. R. H.Ct.Cr.App. No. 215 of 1954 (unreported).
Kabwiso Issa v. Uganda Cr. App. No. 7 of 2002, [2003] UGSC 36 (27 October 2003).
Kalume wa Tuku v. R. [1954] 21 E.A.C.A. 201.
Kamadi Kaibale v. Uganda H.Ct.Cr.App. No. 488 of 1963; H.Ct.Monthly Bulletin No. 2 of 1964.
Kamau s/o Gikera & Anor. v. R. [1955] 22 E.A.C.A. 539.
Kantilal Jivraj & Anor. v. R. [1961] E.A. 6.
Karamagi & Anor. v. Uganda H.Ct.Cr.App. No. 338-9 of 1969 (unreported).
Karuhanga v. Attorney-General [2014] UGCA 14 (4 August 2014).
Karuma s/o Kaniu v. The Queen [1955] A.C. 197.
Karuna Bukenya v. R. [1952] 19 E.A.C.A. 234.
Kassim Mpanga v. Uganda, Cr. App. No. 30 of 1994, [1995] UGSC 14 (13 September 1995).
Kasto Budebo v. Uganda, Cr. App. No. 22 of 1993, [1994] UGSC 13 (7 October 1994).
Kasturilal Laroya v. Mityana Staple Cotton Co. Ltd. & Anor. [1958] E.A. 194.

Selected Bibliography

Katalagala & Anor. v. R. H.Ct.Cr.App. No. 6-7-30 of 1959; H.Ct.Monthly Bulletin No. 28 of 1959.
Kateba v. Republic [1967] E.A. 215.
Katengele v. Republic [1969] E.A. 603.
Katorogo v. Reginam [1956–1957] 8 U.L.R. 358.
Kayongo v. R. H.Ct.Monthly Bulletin No. 24 of 1960.
Kabegambire Wilber v. Uganda Cr. App. No. 56 of 2006, [2010] UGCA 43 (24 November 2010).
Kelly Omuge & Anor. v. Uganda Ct.A.Cr.App. No. 3 of 1986 (unreported).
Kekinyumu v. Uganda [1969] E.A. 333.
Kerementi Lyangombe & Anor. v. R. [1959] E.A. 678.
Keteta v. Republic [1972] E.A. 532.
Kigorogolo v. Rushereka [1969] E.A. 426.
Kimweri v. Republic [1968] E.A. 452.
Kityo v. Uganda [1967] E.A. 23.
Kiyongo George v. Uganda, Cr. App. No. 13 of 1998, [1998] UGSC 12 (8 November 1998).
Kiyengo Zaverio v. Uganda Cr. App. No 35 2003, [2005] UGSC 6 (13 April 2005).*Kongoro s/o Mrisho v. R.* [1956] 23 E.A.C.A. 532.
Kupuliano Okello & Anor. v. Uganda H.Ct.Monthly Bulletin No. 91 of 1967.
Kyagonga v. Uganda [1973] E.A. 486.
Kyamanywa Simon v. Uganda, Constitutional Reference No. 10 of 2000.
Kyazike v. Uganda Cr. Appeal No. 15 of 2009, [2010] UGSC 22 (25 January 2010).
Lai Wee Lian v. Singapore Bus Service (1978) Ltd. [1984] A.C. 729.
Laila Jhina Mawji v. The Queen [1956] 23 E.A.C.A. 609.
Law Advocacy for Women in Uganda v. Attorney General, Const. Petition Nos 13/05 & 05/06 [2007] UGCC 1 (5 April 2007).
Lawrence Oguda v. R. [1960] E.A. 745.
Lembeni Mwale v. Regina [1958] R. & N.L.R. 527.
Lerunyani v. Republic [1968] E.A. 107.
Letsholo & Anor v. State [1999] B.L.R. 278 (HC).
Lim Chin Aik v. R. [1963] E.A. 1 All E.R. 223.
Lugobo & Anor. v. Uganda [1967] E.A. 440.
Lukwago v. R. H.Ct.Monthly Bulletin No. 34 of 1958.
Lynch v. Director of Public Prosecutions for Northern Ireland [1975] 1 All E.R. 913.
M'liara s/o M'yeka v. R. [1951] 18 E.A.C.A. 169.
Mabonga v. R. H.Ct.Monthly Bulletin No. 55 of 1959.
Mafabi s/o Mafabi v. Regina [1956–1957] 8 U.L.R. 59.
Magezi Robert v. Uganda Cr. Case No. 71 of 2006, [2010] UGCA 46 (11 November 2010).
Mahuku v. Uganda [1970] E.A. 495.
Majawa v. Regina [1959] R. & N.L.R. 52.
Major John Kazorra v. Uganda H.Ct.Misc.Appl. No. 109 of 1991 (unreported).
Malungu s/o Kieti v. R. [1959] E.A. 322.
Manga Bhula v. Rex [1936–1951] 6 U.L.R. 240.
Manjesa v. State [1991] B.L.R. 391 (CA).

Manuel Kayongo & Anor. v. Regina H.Ct.Monthly Bulletin No. 3 of 1963.
Martin G. Luima & Anor. v. Rex [1949] 16 E.A. 128.
Marwa s/o Robi v. R. [1959] E.A. 660.
Masembe & Tabula v. Rex [1936–1951] 6 U.L.R. 195.
Mathias Kitimbo alias Matyansi Ngobi v. Busoga [1965] E.A. 162.
Matovu Musa Kassim v. Uganda, Cr. App. 27 of 2002, [2005] UGSC 17 (18 August 2005).
Mayanja v. R. H.Ct.Monthly Bulletin No. 26 of 1960 (unreported).
Mbande v. Republic [1971] E.A. 553.
Mbazira Siraj *v.* Uganda Cr. App. No. 7 of 2004, [2007] UGSC 2 (20 March 2007).
Mbeluke v. Republic [1971] E.A. 479.
Medadi Tindarwesire & Anor. v. Uganda S.Ct.Cr.App. No. 14 of 1992 (unreported).
Mehar Singh v. R. [1936–1951] 6 U.L.R. 265.
Merali v. R. [1953–1957] 2 T.L.R. 100.
Mfaume v. Republic [1973] E.A. 563.
Misaki Choda v. Regina [1957] E.A. 495; H.Ct.Monthly Bulletin No. 12 of 1957.
Moevao v. Department of Labour [1981] NZLR 464.
Mohamed Sirimenda v. R. H.Ct.Cr.App. No. 639 of 1962; H.Ct.Monthly Bulletin No. 48 of 1963.
Molelekedi v. State [1990] B.L.R. 630 (CA).
Mudangule v. State, [1986] B.L.R. 265.
Mugasa Joseph v. Uganda Cr. App. No. 241 of 2003, [2010] UGCA 15 (15 April 2010).
Muhwezi Alex & Anor. v. Uganda Cr. App. No. 21 of 2005, [2010] UGSC 12 (13 April 2010).
Muiruri v. Republic [1967] E.A. 808.
Mukasa v. A. Luzinda H.Ct.Monthly Bulletin No. 4 of 1960.
Mukwaya Manasse v. Uganda, Cr. App. No. 7 of 1994 [2009] UGSC 12 (21 December 2009).
Mukwaya & seven others v. Uganda H.Ct.Misc.Cr.Appl. No. 267-8 of 1971 (unreported).
Mulcahy v. R. (1868) L.R3 H.L. 396.
Mulji Lalji Kotecha v. Uganda H.Ct.Monthly Bulletin No. 1 of 1968.
Mureeba Janet & Anor v. Uganda Cr. App. No.13 of 2003 [2006] UGSC 7 (21 July 2006).
Murray v. Minister of Defence [1988] W.L.R. 692.
Musa & Anor. v. Republic [1970] E.A. 42.
Musa Kakade v. R. [1963] E.A. 36.
Musa s/o Saidi v. R. [1962] E.A. 455.
Musoke v. R. [1956–1957] 8 U.L.R. 108.
Musoke v. Uganda [1972] E.A. 137.
Mustafa Huseni v. Uganda H.Ct.Monthly Bulletin No. 182 of 1968.
Mutambo & Anor. v. The people [1965] Zambia Law Reported 147.
Muyimba v. Uganda [1969] E.A. 433.
Muzaya Thomas & Anor. v. Uganda Cri. App. No. 3 of 2006, [2007] UGSC 1, 30 May 2007.
Mwandikwa s/o Mutisya v. R. [1959] E.A. 18.

Mwangi Njoroge v. R. [1963] E.A. 624. *Mwenda & Anor v. Attorney General* Const. Petition Nos. 12 of 2005 and 3 of 2006 [2010] UGCC 5 (25 August 2010).
Nakafunga v. Reginam [1956–1957] 8 U.L.R. 151.
Nambale v. R H.Ct.Monthly Bulletin No. 53 of 1959.
Namuddu Christine v. Uganda, Cr. Appl. No. 3 of 1999, [2001] UGSC 2 (17 January 2001).
Nanyonjo & Anor v. Uganda Crim. App. No. 24 of 2004, [2007] UGSC 10 (5 July 2007).
National Coal Board v. Gamble [1959] 1 Q.B. 11.
Ndege v. Uganda [1979] H.Ct.Bulletin 162.
Nikolas Ogulu & Anor. v. Uganda H.Ct.Cr.App. No. 396-7 of 1968; H.Ct.Monthly Bulletin No. 181 of 1968.
Nkanabanemeheto s/o Masakura v. R. [1959] E.A. 598.
Norman Godinho v. Rex [1936–1951] 6 U.L.R. 143.
Nyakite s/o Oyugi v. R. [1959] E.A. 322.
Nyige s/o Suwatu v. R. [1959] E.A. 974.
Ochiti v. Uganda, Cr. App. No. 15 of 1998, [1998] UGSC 2 (4 December 1998).
Odeke s/o Taram v. R. [1958] E.A. 690.
Ogola v. Republic [1973] E.A. 277.
Ojok v. Uganda [1970] E.A. 575.
Okello s/o Kamuleti v. Uganda Ct.A.Cr.App. No. 2 of 1978 (unreported).
Okeny Kamu s/o Okok v. R. [1960] E.A. 178.
Okute s/o Kaliebi & Anor. v. R. [1941] 8 E.A.C.A. 78.
Omar v. State [1998] B.L.R. 237 (HC).
Ondimu s/o Ondimu v. Rex [1951] 19 E.A.C.A. 239.
Ongodia and Erima v. Uganda [1967] E.A. 137.
Opoya v. Uganda [1967] E.A. 752.
Otende Osejani v. Uganda [1963] E.A. 627.
Ouko v. Republic [1966] E.A. 286.
Ovuloo v. Regina H.Ct.Monthly Bulletin No. 119 of 1957.
Owoo s/o Okot v. Reginam [1956–1957] 8 U.L.R. 225.
Ozia v. Reginam [1956–1957] 8 U.L.R. 202.
Palmer v. Reginam [1971] 1 All E.R. 1077.
Paskazia d/o Kabaikye v. R. [1954] 21 E.A.C.A. 359.
Paulo Omale v. Uganda Cr. App. No 6 of 1977 (unreported).
Perera v. The King [1951] A.C. 421.
Pett v. Greyhound Racing Association (No. 1) [1968] 2 All E.R. 545.
Pimako Karemira v. R. [1957] E.A. 582.
Philip Muswi s/o Mosola v. R. (1956) 23 E.A.C.A. 622.
Phillips v. Eyre [1870–1871] 6 L.Q.B. 1.
Pool v. R. [1958] E.A. 688.
Pratt & Anor. v. Attorney General for Jamaica & Anor. [1993] 4 All E.R. 769, [1993] 3 W.L.R. 995.
Prince Kesi Kagoro v. R. H.Ct.Cr.App. No. 259 of 1953; H.Ct.Monthly Bulletin No. 64 of 1958.
Proprietary Articles Association v. Attorney General for Canada [1931] A.C. 318.

Prosecutor v. Anto Furundžija, Case No. IT-95-17/1, Judgement, 10 December 1998.
Prosecutor v. Jean-Paul Akayesu, Case No. ICTR-96-4T, Judgment, 2 September 1997.
Prosecutor v. Georges Ruggiu, Case No. ICTR-97-32-1, Judgment and Sentence, 1 Jun. 2000.
Prosecutor v. Zoran Kupreškić, Mirjan Kupreškić, Vlatko Kupreškić, Drago Josipović, and Dragan Papić, Case No. IT-95-16-T, Trial Chamber Judgement, 14 January 2000.
Queen v. Desire Munanyeza [2009] QCCS 2201 (Quebec Superior Court, 22 May 2009).
Queen v. Tripoli [1955] Supreme Court Report 438 (Canada).
Queen v. Latimer [1886] 17 Q.B.D. 359.
R. v. Absolom & Anor. [1957] E.A. 660.
R. v. Akbarali K. Jetha [1947] 14 E.A.C.A. 22.
R. v. Ali Sokhair [1932–1935] 5 U.L.R. 62.
R. v. Anwali H.Ct.Monthly Bulletin No. 41 of 1958.
R. v. Apili d/o Elok [1932–1935] 5 U.L.R. 64.
R. v. Baker [1895] 1 Q.B. 797.
R. v. Bateman (1845) 1 Cox C.C. 186.
R. v. Bateman (1925) 19 Cr.App.R. 8.
R. v. Beecham (1851) 5 Coc C.C. 181.
R v. Bentham [2005] UKHL 18.
R. v. Bigali s/o Kite [1943] 10 E.A.C.A. 42.
R. v. Blaue [1975] 3 All E.R. 446.
R. v. Bourne [1938] All E.R. 615; [1939] 1 K.B. 887.
R. v. Bourne [1952] 36 Cr.App.R. 125.
R. v. Brown (1890) 24 Q.B.D. 357.
R. v. Byrne [1960] 3 All E.R. 107.
R. v. Carr [1957] 1 W.L.R. 165.
R. v. Clemens & Anor. [1898] 1 Q.B.D. 556.
R. v. Clouden [1987] Crim. L.R. 56.
R. v. Cogan [1976] Q.B. 217.
R. v. Dalip Singh [1943] 10 E.A.C.A. 121.
R v. Dawson and *R v. Wenlock* [1960] 1 All E.R. 558.
R. v. Dishon Odinga [1959] E.A. 12.
R. v. Dominiko Omenyi s/o Obuka [1943] 10 E.A.C.A. 81.
R. v. Eagleton (1855) Dears C.C. 515.
R. v. Edward Stanley Ross [1936–1951] 6 U.L.R. 37.
R. v. Erunasani Sekoni s/o Eria & Anor. [1947] 14 E.A.C.A. 74.
R. v. Fabiano Kinene [1941] 8 E.A.C.A. 96.
R. v. Fitzpatrick [1977] N.I. 20.
R. v. Franklin (1883) 15 Cox C.C. 163.
R v. Fundakubi [1948] 3 S. Afr. 810, 818 (AD).
R v. G & Anor [2003] All E. R. 765.
R. v. Gokaldas Kanji Karia & Anor. [149] 16 E.A.C.A. 116.
R. v. Governor of Pentonville Prison, Ex Parte Chinoy [1992] 1 All E.R. 317.

Selected Bibliography

R. v. Gray [1900] 2 Q.B. 36.
R. v. Hill [1986] 1 Supreme Court Report 313 (Canada).
R v. Horseferry Magistrates' Court: Experte Bennett [1994] 1 A.C. 42.
R. v. Hussein Bin Habib [1960] E.A. 182.
R. v. Hyde [1990] 3 All E.R. 892.
R. v. Jack Jezelani [1946] 14 E.A.C.A. 70.
R. v. Jackson 198 E.R. 1037.
R. v. Johnson (1864) Lee & Ca. 489.
R. v. Kabande w/o Kihigwe [1948] 15 E.A.C.A. 135.
R. v. Kantilal C. Raval & Anor. [1951] 18 E.A.C.A. 203.
R. v. Katete s/o Muruli & Anor. [1936–1951] 6 U.L.R. 200.
R. v. Kemp [1956] 3 All E.R. 249.
R. v. Kibayi w/o Salim Cherwan [1951] E.A.C.A. 203.
R. v. Leonard Holmes [1946] All E.R. 524.
R. v. Lewis [1979] 2 All E.R. 665.
R. v. Luseru Wandera s/o Wandera [1948] 15 E.A.C.A. 105.
R. v. Lloyd [1966] 1 All E.R. 107.
R. v. Lujo s/o Mgomba [1946] 13 E.A.C.A. 156.
R. v. Mburugu [1947] 20 K.L.R. 62.
R. v. McDonnell [1966] 1 Q.B. 233.
R. v. McLean [1911] K.B. 332.
R. v. McNally [1954] 2 All E.R. 372.
R. v. Meja [1962] R. & N.L.R. 45.
R. v. Mikaeri Kyeyune & Anor. [1941] 8 E.A.C.A. 84.
R. v. Mohamed Ali [1947] 14 E.A.C.A. 126.
R. v. Mulji Jamnadas & Anor. [1946] 13 E.A.C.A. 147.
R. v. Muttra Prasad [1913] 2 U.L.R. 76.
R. v. Mwanga s/o Manaa [1939] 3 E.A.C.A. 28.
R. v. Ngereza s/o Masaga & Anor. [1962] E.A. 766.
R. v. Nyungido s/o Luhende [1948] 15 E.A.C.A. 132.
R. v. Nyansio Katunzi [1946] 13 E.A.C.A. 154.
R. v. Oddy [1974] 2 All E.R. 666.
R. v. Onyango s/o Nanzalo [1932–1935] 5 U.L.R. 69.
R. v. Pearson (1835) 2 Lew. C.c. 216.
R. v. Pembliton [1874–1880] AU E.R. 1163.
R. v. Petro Mangongo s/o Katwa [1944] 11 E.A.C.A. 100.
R. v. Pio Riri H.Ct.Monthly Bulletin No. 64 of 1959.
R. v. R – (rape: marital exemption) [1991] 4 All E.R. 481.
R. v. Ramazani Nswazalugudo [1932–1935] 5 U.L.R. 5.
R. *v. Ring* 17 Cox C.C. 497.
R. v. Robertson [1968] 3 A E.R. 557.
R. v. Rootes (Kenya) Ltd. & Anor. [1958] E.A. 13.
R. v. Rothwell (1871–1874) 12 Cox C.C. 145.
R. v. Rubarangero H.Ct.Cr.Session No. 89 of 1959; H.Ct.Monthly Bulletin No. 66 of 1959.
R. v. Quick & Anor. [1973] 3 All E.R. 347.
R. v. Sadiki Kyoyo & Anor. [1943] 10 E.A.C.A. 103.

R. v. Samson [1939] E.A.C.A. 154.
R. v. Sang [1980] A.C. 402.
R. v. Sawedi Mukasa s/o Abdulla Aligawesa [1946] 13 E.A.C.A. 97.
R. v. Sharmpal Singh s/o Pritman [1962] E.A. 13.
R. v. Silvesteri Eletu s/o Egaru [1936–1951] 6 U.L.R. 247.
R v. Smurthwaite [1994] 1 All E.R. 898.
R. v. Suke d/o Samwe & Anor. [1947] 14 E.A.C.A. 134.
R. v. Tabulayenka [1943] 10 E.A.C.A. 51.
R. v. Thomas [1950] 1 K.B. 26.
R. v. Wallace [1958] E.A. 582.
R. v. Warn [1936–1938] 26 Cr.App.R. 115.
R. v. Watton [1979] 68 Cr.App.Rep. 292.
R. v. Wedeza [1956–1957] 8 U.L.R. 241.
R. v. Williams (Roy) [1977] 1 All E.R. 874.
R. v. Yafesi Nabende [1948] 15 E.A.C.A. 71.
R. v. Yakobo Mbugeramula [1951] 18 E.A.C.A. 207.
R. v. Yozefu Muinda [1936–1951] 6 U.L.R. 163.
R. v. Zakayo Itima s/o Birigenda [1948] E.A.C.A. 15.
Raghib Singh Lamba v. R. [1958] E.A. 337.
Rahim Rajan v. R. [1958] E.A. 448.
Ramadhani v. Republic [1974] E.A. 81.
Ramakolwane Ditloi & Anor. v. State Botswana H.Ct.Cr.App. No. 90 of 1985 (unreported).
Ramenlal T. Bhatt v. R. [1957] E.A. 332.
Rasul & Anor. v. R. [1954] 21 E.A.C.A. 229.
Raymond v. Attorney General [1982] 1 Q.B. 839.
Re H.P.C. Productions Ltd. [1962] Ch. 466.
Re An Application by Ajit Singh [1959] E.A. 782.
Re Castioni [1886] All E.R. 640.
Re London and Globe Corporation Ltd. [1903] 1 Ch. 728.
Regina v. Bumbakali Kyewalabye [1956–1957] 8 U.L.R. 5.
Regina v. Candukmon s/o Oyaru [1956–1957] 8 U.L.R. 337.
Regina v. City of Sault Ste. Marie 85 D.L.R. (d) 161 (1978).
Regina v. Court [1989] A.C. 28; [1988] 2 All E.R. 221.
Regina v. Mageta s/o Kachehakana [1956–1957] 8 U.L.R. 294.
Regina v. Manley (1844) 1 Cox C.C. 104.
Regina v. Mohan [1976] Q.B. 1; [1975] 2 All E.R. 193.
Regina v. Mukasa & Anor. [1956–1957] 8 U.L.R. 321.
Regina v. Nasani Kibuka H.Ct.Monthly Bulletin No. 20 of 1963.
Regina v. Nyamitare s/o Kachumita [156–157] 8 U.L.R. 292.
Regina v. Ramzan Ahmad Jamal [1955] 22 E.A.C.A. 504.
Regina v. Sharp [1957] 2 W.L.R. 472.
Regina v. Sumba s/o Semafu & Anor. [1956–1957] 8 U.L.R. 28.
Regina v. Toro Tea Company Limited [1956–1957] 8 U.L.R. 343.
Regina v. Webb [1964] 1 Q.B. 357.
Regina v. Wedeza s/o Fungo [1956–1957] 8 U.L.R. 240
Regina v. Zindoga [1980] Zimbabwe Law Reports 86.

Selected Bibliography

Republic v. Arael [1967] E.A. 378.
Republic v. Mohamed [1973] E.A. 238.
Republic v. Sefu Said [1964] E.A. 178.
Richard Oneka v. Uganda H.Ct.Rev. Order No. 107 of 1991 (unreported).
Robert Austin Mullery v. R. [1958] E.A. 138.
Robert Sabiti v. Uganda S.Ct.Cr.App. 4 of 1989 (unreported).
Rwarinda & Anor. v. R. H.Ct.Monthly Bulletin No. 40 of 1959.
Rwamunda v. Uganda, Cr. App. No. 6 of 1993, [1994] UGSC 10 (2 June 1994)
S. v. Gabriel [1971] 1 South African Law Reports 646.
S. v. Manoko [1977–1979] Bophuthatswana Law Reports 152.
S. v. Mehlap [1963] 2 South Afr. Law Rep. 29.
S. v. Ndhlovu [1965] 4 South African Law Reports 692.
Sabani v. Uganda [1974] E.A. 460.
Sabane Bbale Anor. v. Uganda H.Ct.Cr.App. No. 576 of 1968; H.Ct.Monthly Bulletin No. 143 of 1968.
Said Kigozi v. R. [1958] E.A. 1.
Said Nsubuga v. R. [1941] 8 E.A.C.A. 81.
Saidere v. Republic [1973] E.A. 98.
Saja s/o Mabako v. Reginam [1956–1957] 8 U.L.R. 56.
Saleh Ahmed v. R. [1961] E.A. 669.
Sam Ekolu *v.* Uganda, Cr. App. No. 15 of 1994, [1995] UGSC 7 (5 May 1995). *Sapsford v. Sapsford & Furtado* [1954] 2 All E.R. 372.
Sarwano Mawanda v. R. [1962] E.A. 119.
Seidi v. Republic [1969] E.A. 280.
Sekitoleko v. Uganda [1967] E.A. 531.
Semayo Otika v. Acholi District Administration H.Ct.Civil Suit No. 106 of 1966 (unreported).
Semewa Kizza v. Regina H.Ct.Cr.App. No. 632 of 1962 (unreported).
Semi Longa v. Uganda [1964] E.A. 512.
Sewa Singh Mandia v. Republic [1966] E.A. 315.
Sewava v. Uganda [1966] E.A. 487.
Shaban Birumba & Anor. v. Uganda S.Ct.Cr.App. No. 32 of 1989 (unreported).
Sherman v. United States, 356 U.S. 369 (1958).
Sherras v. De Rutzen [1895] All E.R. 1167.
Silagi *Buroro Gordon v. Uganda* Cr. App. No. 122 of 2005, [2010] UGSC 42 (15 November 2010).
Simoni Musoke v. R [1958] E.A. 715.
Sisipata Opale s/o Idiawo v. R. [1962] E.A. 661.
Smith v. Hughes [1960] 2 All E.R. 859.
Solomon Hotema v. United States 186 U.S. 313 (1901).
Stanley Musinga & Anor. v. Rex [1951] 18 E.A.C.A. 211.
State v. Chibidu [1988] B.L.R. 467 (HC).
State v. Majeremane & Others [1997]B.L.R. 630(HC).
State v. Mokgosana [2001] 1 B.L.R. 291 (HC).
State v. Nkatswe [2002] 2 B.L.R. 441 (HC).
State v. Ntsima [1991] B.L.R. 251(HC).

State v. Sibanda [2002] 2 B.L.R. 386 (HC). *State v. Nkatswe* [2002] 2 B.L.R. 441 (HC).
S.S. Lotus Case (*France v. Turkey*) 1227 P.C.I.J. (ser.A) No. 10 (September 7).
SGT Canbera Dickson v. Uganda. Cr. App. No. 284 of 2003, [2010] UGCA 25 (6 June 2010).
Sweet v. Parsley [1969] 1 All E.R. 347.
Tadeo Oyee s/o Duru v. R. [1959] E.A. 407.
Teddy Sseezi Cheeye v. Uganda Cr. App. No. 105 of 105, [2010] UGCA 41 (20 October 2010).
Terrah Mukindia v. Republic [1966] E.A. 425.
Thomas Machola v. Regina [1964] B. L.R. 143.
Tigo Stephen v. Uganda SC Cr. App. No. 8 of 2009, [2009] UGSC 7, 10 May 2011.
Tindigwihura Mbahe v. Uganda S.Ct.Cr.App. No. 9 of 1992 (unreported).
Tororo Town Council v. P.M. Luande H.Ct.Monthly Bulletin No. 367 of 1971.
Treasury v. Harris [1957] 2 All E.R. 455.
Tuch & Sons v. Priester (1887) 19 Q.B.D. 629.
Tumuheirwe v. Uganda [1967] E.A. 328.
Twelve & Anor. v. R. [1957] R& N.L.R. 265.
Uganda v. Abdalla Mukasa H.Ct.Cr.Session No. 13 of 1990 (unreported).
Uganda v. Absolom Kagwisagye H.Ct.Monthyly Bulletin No. 6 of 1969.
Uganda v. Akua & Anor. [1973] E.A. 247.
Uganda v. Alozio Kibombo 9 H.Ct.Monthly Bulletin 153 (1978).
Uganda v. Amisi [1970] E.A. 291.
Uganda v. Arafairi Karyegeya [1972] U.L.R. 10.
Uganda v. Augustine Musana & Anor. H.Ct.Cr.Session No. 28 of 1984, H.Ct. Monthly Bulletin No. 20 of 1984.
Uganda v. Aventura Ovu [1972] U.L.R. 14.
Uganda v. Baguma [1970] E.A. 167.
Uganda v. Balaki Kirya & Anor. H.Ct.Cr.S.C. No. 75 of 1984.
Uganda v. Baziraneyiza s/o Kasiku H.Ct.Monthly Bulletin No. 191 of 1969.
Uganda v. Beatrice Nadunga H.Ct.Cr.Session No. 81 of 1990 (unreported).
Uganda v. Benedicto Karerengabo [1971] U.L.R. 6.
Uganda v. Benjamin Bwambale & Anor. H.Ct.Cr.Session No. 304 of 1991 (unreported).
Uganda v. Bonefasi Muvaga [1937] U.L.R. 30.
Uganda v. Bosco Obol H.Ct.Cr.Session No. 75 of 1990 (unreported).
Uganda v. Chemisto A. Mashandich & Anor Cr. Case No 2 of 2010, [2010] UGHC 50 (13 September 2010).
Uganda v. Commissioner of Prisons, Ex Parte Matovu [1966] E.A. 514.
Uganda v. Constantine Zake H.Ct.Cr.Session No. 20 of 1985; [1985] H.Ct. Bulletin 18.
Uganda v. Christopher Lugaya H.Ct.Monthly Bulletin No. 154 of 1971.
Uganda v. Dominiko Musoke H.Ct.Monthly Bulletin No. 148 of 1969 (unreported).
Uganda v. Elong Richard H.Ct.Cr.Session No. 301 of 1991 (unreported).
Uganda v. Firimigiyo Kakooza [1984] H.Ct.Bulletin 1.
Uganda v. Gabriel Habaasi H.Ct.Cr.Session No. 41 of 1992 (unreported).
Uganda v. Hadi Jamal [1964] E.A. 294.

Selected Bibliography

Uganda v. Hosia Rukagyaha & Anor. H.Ct.Cr.Session No. 43 of 1986 (unreported).
Uganda v. Ibrahim Seguya S.Ct.Cr.App. No. 3 of 1987 (unreported).
Uganda v. Joel Oluka H.Ct.Cr.Rev. No. 31 of 1991 (unreported).
Uganda v. John Kuka H.Ct.Cr.Session No. 75 of 1990 (unreported).
Uganda v. John Mukasa H.Ct.Cr.Rev. No. 714 of 1971 (unreported).
Uganda v. Joseph Jwarira [1972] U.L.R. 23.
Uganda v. Josephat Byebandwa H.Ct.Cr.Session No. 25 of 1988 (unreported).
Uganda v. L. Kakooza H.Ct.Cr.Session No. 6 of 1991 (unreported).
Uganda v. Karimalwa s/o Digarire H.Ct.Monthly Bulletin No. 189 of 1969.
Uganda v. Karasa [1974] E.A. 458.
Uganda v. Kayondo [1973] E.E. 269; [1972] U.L.R. 41.
Uganda v. Kwirima Bua & Anor. [1971] U.L.R. 24.
Uganda v. Leo Mubyazita [1972] U.L.R. 3.
Uganda v. Leo Nyendwoha H.Ct.Cr.Session No. 253 of 1991 (unreported).
Uganda v. Lochoro [1982] H.Ct.Bulletin 80.
Uganda v. Manuel Obbo H.Ct.Monthly Bulletin No. 32 of 1964.
Uganda v. Mayombwe [1973] E.A. 566.
Uganda v. Milenge & Anor. [1970] E.A. 269.
Uganda v. Mbazira [1973] E.A. 492.
Uganda v. Mohamed Juko & Anor. H.Ct.Cr.Session No. B12 of 1964; H.Ct. Monthly Bulletin No. 31 of 1964.
Uganda v. Muhanguzi & Anor. H.Ct.Cr.Session No. 290 of 1991 (unreported).
Uganda v. Muhoze H.Ct.Cr.Session No. 105 of 1991 (unreported).
Uganda v. Musana & Anor. H.Cr.Session No. 28 of 1984 (unreported).
Uganda v. Musese & Anor. H.Ct.Cr.Session No. 22 of 1982; [1982] H.Ct.Bulletin 72.
Uganda v. Mutagobya & Anor. H.Ct.Monthly Bulletin No. 120 of 1969.
Uganda v. Nambwegere s/o Rovumba [1972] U.L.R. 14.
Uganda v. Ndyanabo [1974] E.A. 552.
Uganda v. Ndyomugyenyi & Anor, Cr. Sc 003 of 2010, [2010] UGHC 49, 31 August 2010.
Uganda v. Nelson Kamugisha H.Cr.Session No. 27 of 1988 (unreported).
Uganda v. Nikolla & Anor. [1966] E.A. 345.
Uganda v. Obedi Asumani & Anor. H.Ct.Cr.Session No. 78 of 1990 (unreported).
Uganda v. Ojok & Anor. [1973] E.A. 489.
Uganda v. Okot [1974] E.A. 8.
Uganda v. Olum Tanga H.Ct.Monthly Bulletin No. 33 of 1971 (unreported).
Uganda v. Olungu [1973] E.A. 136.
Uganda v. Polasi Kasumba [1971] U.L.R. 34.
Uganda v. Polonali Kasangaki H.Ct.Cr.Session No. 111 of 1987 (unreported).
Uganda v. Rajab Kagolo Muwonge H.Ct.Misc.Cr.Appl. No. 123 of 1991 (unreported).
Uganda v. Rukwandura [1973] E.A. 574.
Uganda v. Segawa & Anor. H.Ct.Cr.Session No. 243 of 1991 (unreported).
Uganda v. Semeo Omulo H.Ct.Cr.Session No. 26 of 1986 (unreported).
Uganda v. Tigawalana Bakali Ikoba & Ors Cr. App. No. 21 of 2005, [2009] UGCA 51, 17 December 2009.

Uganda v. Tito Kasajagenda H.Ct.Cr.Session No. 263 of 1964; H.Ct.Monthly Bulletin No. 1 of 1965.
Uganda v. Walusekhe H.Ct.Monthly Bulletin No. 52 of 1964 (unreported).
Uganda v. Wodada & Anor. [1972] U.L.R. 25.
Uganda v. Yasin Amis H.Ct.Cr.Session No. 4 of 1992 (unreported).
Uganda v. Yonasani Kirya H.Ct.Monthly Bulletin No. 63 of 1969.
Uganda v. Yowasi Birungi [1973] U.L.R. 47.
Uganda v. Zaberi Bakenge [1971] U.L.R. 48.
Uganda v. Zubairi & Anor. [1973] E.A. 470.
Valezi Kashizha s/o Madagede v. R. [1954] 21 E.A.C.A. 371.
Verrier v. Director of Public prosecutions [1967] 2 A.C. 195
Vezeau v. R. [1977] 1 S.C.R. 277 (Canada).
Vithlani v. Reginam [1956–1957] 8 U.L.R. 155.
Wafula v. R. H.Ct.Cr.App. No. 272 of 1958; H.Ct.Monthly Bulletin No. 73 of 1958.
Walusimbi & Anor. v. Uganda, Cr. App. No. 28 of 1992, [1994] UGSC 6 (18 March 1994).
Wambalugu v. Reginam [1956–1957] 8 U.L.R. 346.
Wakigona v. Reginam [1956–1957] 8 U.L.R. 160.
Wanjiko w/o Mukiri v. Reginam [1954] 21 E.A.C.A. 386.
Wasaja v. Uganda [1975] E.A. 181.
Wasswa & Anor. v. R. H.Ct.Monthly Bulletin No. 20 of 1961.
Waugh v. R. [1950] A.C. 203 (P.C.).
West Rand Central Mining Gold Co. Ltd. v. Rex [1905] 2 K.B. 391.
William Sebugenyi v. R. [1959] E.A. 411.
Wilson v. Reginam [1955] 22 E.A.C.A. 372.
Wiltshire v. Barrett [1965] 2 All E.R. 271.
Yakobo Abuni v. R. H.Ct.Monthly Bulletin No. 55 of 1963.
Yakobo Uma & Anor. v. R. [1963] E.A. 542.
Yesaya v. Republic [1970] E.A. 667.
Yokana Mato v. Uganda H.Ct.Monthly Bulletin No. 60 of 1965.
Yokoyadi Lakora s/o Omeri v. R. [1960] E.A. 323.
Yolamu Arua v. R. [1960] E.A. 146.
Yonasani Balinda v. Uganda S.Ct.Cr.App. No. 5 of 1989 (unreported).
Yovan v. Uganda [1970] E.A. 405.
Yowana Sebuzukira v. Uganda [1965] E.A. 684.
Yowana Sserunkuma v. Uganda S.Ct.Cr.App. No. 8 of 1989 (unreported).
Yowanina Namayanja v. Reginum [1953] 20 E.A.C.A. 204.
Yoweri Damulira v. R. [1956] 23 E.A.C.A. 501.
Yuill v. Yuill [1945] P. 15.
Yunusu Musungu & Anor. v. Uganda H.Ct.Cr.App. No. MM 3 of 1989 (unreported).
Yusuf Omari v. Republic [1964] E.A. 162.
Yusuf Gitta v. R. [1959] E.A. 211.
Yusufu Ssebuguzi v. Uganda S.Ct.Cr.App. No. 6 of 1989 (unreported).
Zedekia Lukwago v. Reginam [1956] 23 E.A.C.A. 507.
Zus v. Uganda [1967] E.A. 420.

C. Journal Articles

Cantini, P. 'The Evolution of Blood-Money for Homicide in Somalia'. *Journal of African Law* 7 (1971): 15.

Choo, Andrew L.T. '*Ex Parte* Bennett: The Demise of the *Male Captus, Bene Detentus* Doctrine in England'. *Criminal Law Forum* 5 (1994): 165.

Cook, R.C. 'Blood-Money and the Law of Homicide in the Sudan'. *Sudan Law Journal* (1962): 178.

Friedland, Morton L. 'Codification in the Commonwealth: Earlier Efforts'. *Criminal Law Forum* 2 (1990): 45.

Heymann, Philip B. & Ian Heath Gershengorn. 'Pursuing Justice, Respecting the Law'. *Criminal Law Forum* 3 (1991): 1.

Katende, J.W. 'Why Were Punishments in Pre-Colonial Africa Mainly Compensatory Rather than Punitive?'. *Journal of the Denning Law Society* 2 (1967).

Morris, H.F. 'How Nigeria Got Its Criminal Code'. *Journal of African Law* 2, no. 37 (1970): 14.

Nsereko, D.D. Ntanda. 'The Police, Human Rights and the Constitution: An African Perspective'. *Human Rights Quarterly* 15 (1993): 465.

Nsereko, D.D. Ntanda. 'The Poisoned Tree: Responses to Involuntary Confessions in Criminal Proceedings in Botswana, Zambia, and Uganda'. *African Journal of International & Comparative Law* 5 (1993): 606.

Nsereko, D.D. Ntanda 'Extenuating Circumstances in Capital Offences in Botswana'. *Criminal Law Forum: An International Journal* 2 (1991): 235–268.

Nsereko, D.D. Ntanda. 'Minimum Sentences and Their Effect on Judicial Discretion'. *Crime, Law and Social Change: An International Journal* 31 (1999): 363–384.

Nsereko, D.D. Ntanda. 'The Abuse of Process Doctrine in the Administration of Criminal Justice before National Courts and International Tribunals'. UBLJ 7 (2008): 29.

Odoki, Benjamin J. 'Reducing Delay in the Administration of Justice: The Case of Uganda'. *Criminal Law Forum* 5 (1994): 57.

Read, S. James. 'Criminal Law in the Africa of Today and Tomorrow'. *Journal of African Law* 5 (1963): 7.

Read, S. James. 'Crime and Punishment in East Africa: The Twilight of Customary Law'. *Howard Law Journal* 10 (1964): 164.

Read, S. James. 'Some Aspects of Murder in East Africa'. *East African Law Journal* 1 (1965): 37.

Read, S. James. 'Some Aspects of Manslaughter in East Africa'. *East African Law Journal* 1 (1965): 260.

Read, S. James. 'How to Set a Trap and When Not To'. *Eastern Africa Law Review* 3 (1970): 103.

Read, S. James. 'The Advantage of Counsel'. *East African Law Journal* 7 (1971): 291.

Ssekandi, Francis M. 'Uganda and Kondos: The Capital Punishment Revisited'. *Eastern Africa Law Review* 3 (1970): 3.

Ssekandi, Francis M., Autochthony. 'The Development of Law in Uganda'. *New York Law School Journal of International and Comparative Law* 5 (1983): 1.
Smith, A.T.H. 'Judicial Law Making in the Criminal Law'. *The Law Quarterly Review* 46 (1984): 100.

D. Books and Books Chapters

Ayume, Francis J. *Criminal Procedure and Law in Uganda.* Nairobi: Longman Kenya Ltd., 1986.
Brown, Douglas. *Criminal Procedure in Uganda and Kenya.* London: Sweet and Maxwell, 1970.
Colvin, Eric. 'Criminal Law and the Rule of Law'. In *Crime, Justice & Codification*, edited by Fitzgerald, Patrick. Vancouver: Carswell, Toronto, Calgary, 1986.
Cross & Jones. *Introduction to Criminal Law*. 9th edn. edited by Richard Card. London: Butterworths, 1980.
Fitzgerald, Patrick (ed.). *Criminal Law, Justice & Codification*. Vancouver: Carswell, Calgary, 1986.
Fitzgerald, Patrick. 'Criminal Law, Rationality and Justice'. In *Criminal Law, Justice & Codification*, edited by Fitzgerald, Patrick. Vancouver: Carswell, Toronto, Calgary, 1986, 1–22.
Fitzgerald, P.J. *Criminal Law and Punishment.* Oxford: Oxford University Press, 1962.
Haydon, E.S. *Law and Justice in Buganda.* London: Butterworths, 1960.
Kenyatta, Jomo. *Facing Mount Kenya.* London: Secker & Warburg, 1938.
Milner, Alan (ed.). *African Penal Systems.* London: Routledge & Kegan Paul, 1969.
Mohr, J.W. 'Criminal Law: Is there a Legal or Social Logic for its Removal?'. In *Criminal Law, Justice & Codification*, edited by Fitzgerald, Patrick. Vancouver: Carswell, Toronto, Calgary, 1986, 31–50.
Morris, H.F. & Read, James S. *Uganda: The Development of Its Laws and Constitution.* London: Stevens & Sons, 1966.
Nsereko, D.D. Ntanda. 'Victims of Crime and Their Rights'. In *Criminology in Africa*, edited by Mushanga, Musa. Rome: United Nations International Crime and Justice Research Institute, 1992.
Okonkwo, Cyprian O. & Naish, Michael E. *Criminal Law in Nigeria: Excluding the North*. London: Sweet & Maxwell, 1964.
Pursley, Robert D. *Introduction to Criminal Justice.* 3rd edn. New York: Macmillan Publishing Company, 1984.
Read, James, S. 'Kenya, Tanzania and Uganda'. In *African Penal Systems*, edited by Milner, Alan. London: Routledge & Kegan Paul, 1969.
Roscoe, John. *The Baganda. Their Customs and Beliefs.* 2nd edn. Frank Cass & Co. Ltd., 1965.
Roscoe, John. *The Banyankore.* London:Cambridge University Press, 1924.
Smith, J.C. & Hogan, Brian. *Criminal Law.* 7th edn. London: Butterworths & Co. Publishers Ltd., 1992.

Selected Bibliography

Stuart, Don. *Canadian Criminal Law: A Treatise.* 2nd edn. Toronto: The Carswell Company Limited, 1987.

Tyter, Tom R. *Why People Obey the Law.* New Haven and London: Yale University Press, 1990.

Williams, Glanville. *Textbook of Criminal Law.* 2nd edn. London: Stevens & Sons, 1983.

Index

The numbers here refer to paragraph numbers.

Index

www.ingramcontent.com/pod-product-compliance
Lightning Source LLC
Chambersburg PA
CBHW071412230926
51846CB00001B/66